Hospital and Physician Law

HOSPITAL AND PHYSICIAN LAW

Marilyn E. Phelan, Kimberly P. Mayfield &
Ryan P. Phelan

Hospital and Physician Law

Marilyn E. Phelan, Kimberly P. Mayfield & Ryan P. Phelan

Published by:

Vandeplas Publishing, LLC – January 2022

801 International Parkway, 5th Floor
Lake Mary, FL. 32746
USA

www.vandeplaspublishing.com

ISBN 978-1-60042-540-0

PREFACE

This book provides a succinct coverage of important legal and tax issues hospitals and physicians may confront in the practice of medicine and in their involvement in the healthcare industry generally. The book addresses and summarizes complex legal issues in a clear and understandable format to furnish the reader not only with a recognition of crucial laws applicable to the health care industry but also assistance and guidance in solving some of the legal and tax problems associated with the provision of state and national health care.

The book is both general, in that the chapters summarize applicable legal and tax issues, and specific, as the chapters also particularize some of the laws affecting specialized areas of healthcare. Included in the nine chapters are discussions of legal issues relating to hospital medical staff; patients' rights; a hospital's potential liability for negligence in providing health care services, including that of its physicians; hospital medical records; telehealth services; the reorganizations of hospitals and affiliated entities; and other laws applicable to various specialized healthcare matters, such as blood transfusions, emergency treatment, consents for treatment, and a patient's right to refuse treatment. Legal issues and ethical concerns relating to specialized subjects, such as abortion and sterilization procedures and hospital and physician involvement in services that include artificial insemination, in vitro fertilization, and surrogate parenting, are addressed in some detail. The book further discusses governance issues to include a summary of the fiduciary duties of members of hospital governing boards and sets out governmental regulations that either influence or directly affect healthcare decisions. It also includes laws relating to employment issues, to include the concept of the power to hire and to fire and discrimination in employment laws. The book additionally provides information regarding tax laws relating to obtaining and maintaining tax-exempt status for the many nonprofit hospitals and includes a discussion of the involvement of otherwise tax-exempt hospitals in unrelated activities that will subject them to the unrelated business income tax.

We welcome your comments and questions.

Marilyn E. Phelan
Kimberly P. Mayfield
Ryan P. Phelan

Acronyms

ACO	Medicare Accountable Care Organization
ACA	Patient Protection and Affordable Care Act of 2010
ADA	Americans with Disabilities Act
ADEA	Age Discrimination in Employment Act
A.I.D.	Artificial insemination donor
AIDS	Acquired Immune Deficiency Syndrome
CAMH/98	Comprehensive Accreditation Manual for Hospitals
CHIP	Children's Health Insurance Program
CHS	Carolinas Healthcare System
CMS	Centers for Medicare and Medicaid Services
COBRA	Emergency Medical Treatment and Active Labor Act
CON	Certificate of Need
CSA	Controlled Substances Act
DEA	Drug and Enforcement Administration
D&E	Dilation and excavation (standard) abortion
DNR	Do Not Resuscitate
DRG	Diagnosis Related Group
D&X	Dilation and extraction (intact dilation and excavation) abortion
EEOC	Equal Employment Opportunity Commission
EPA	Equal Pay Act
HER	Electronic health record
FDA	Food and Drug Administration
FOIA	Freedom of Information Act
FTC	Federal Trade Commission
FTCA -	Federal Tort Claims Act
GINA	Genetic Information Nondiscrimination Act
HCFA	Health Care Financing Administration
HHS	U.S. Department of Health and Human Services
HIPAA	Health Insurance Portability and Accountability Act
HITECH	Health Information Technology for Economic and Clinical Health

HIV	Human Immunodeciency Virus
HMO	Health Maintenance Organization
HSA	Health Systems Agency
I.R.C.	Internal Revenue Code
IRS	Internal Revenue Service
IVF	In vitro fertilization
JCAHO	Joint Commission on Accreditation of Healthcare Organizations or Joint Commission
LLC	Limited liability company
MACPAC	Medicaid and CHIP Payment and Access Commission
MAO	Medicare Advantage Organization
MCCRB	Medicare Geographic Classification Review Board
MMA	Medical Malpractice Act
MOON	Medicate Outpatient Observation Notice
MSP	Medicare Secondary Payer
MSSP	Medicare Shared Savings Program
NIED	Negligent infliction of emotional distress
OCR	HHS Office of Civil Rights
OIG	Office of the Inspector General
OSHA	Occupational Safety and Health Administration
PHI	Protected health information
PPS	Prospective Payment System
PRO	Utilization and Quality Control Peer Review Organization
PVS	Persistent vegetative state
RPM	Remote patient monitoring
RFRA	Religious Freedom Restoration Act of 1993

TABLE OF CONTENTS

CHAPTER I.
ORGANIZATIONAL STRUCTURE OF HOSPITALS

The state carries out its governmental function to provide for the health of its citizens through the hospitals, which can be either public or private. The difference between public and private types of hospitals relates to ownership and thus control of hospital facilities. While services in the two types are basically the same, there can be variance in patient charges, facilities, and patient care. Public hospitals are owned and operated by the government. Private hospitals can be for-profit or nonprofit. The private hospitals generally will be incorporated and thus subject to state law applicable to corporations whether profit or nonprofit.

This chapter briefly discusses the organizational structure of a hospital and reviews legal issues relating to the organization and operation of a hospital's medical staff.

Public hospitals are governmentally owned and thus are subject to statutory law regarding establishment, funding, and operation.[1] The differing statutory laws, which provide legal constraints concerning funding, policies, and programs of public hospitals, will vary from state to state and per type of public hospital, whether a federal, state or local governmental institution. Additionally, management of the various types of public hospitals will differ.

A state may, and generally does, delegate to the cities or counties its governmental power to provide health care.[2] Public hospitals may be city or county hospitals or may be established by a hospital district created by a state or local government. For city hospitals, the governing body of the city is the ultimate authority; however, a city can delegate management authority to a Board of Managers. For county hospitals, the governing body of the county becomes the hospital's governing body, which generally appoints a board of managers to control daily activities of such a hospital. While hospital districts become separate political subdivisions of the state, they usually are governed by the body establishing them—either the city or the county. Some hospitals are federally owned and operated. Accordingly, it is imperative to consult state and federal statutes regarding the operation of public hospitals.

Because public hospitals are governmentally funded and controlled, they usually have reduced, or even free, patient rates.[3] Limited governmental funding

---

1 In National Medical Enterprises, Inc. v. Sandrock, 72 N.C. App. 245, 324 S.E.2d 268 (1985), a court ruled that because public hospitals are owned and operated by governmental entities, revenues from a public hospital inure to the governmental entity in control of the hospital.

2 See, e.g., Tex. Health & Safety Code §§ 122.004, 263.021, 265.001 to 265.012. For Louisiana, a "county" is a "parish" and, for Alaska, a "borough."

3 In Memorial Hospital v. Maricopa County, 415 U.S. 250 (1974), the Supreme Court considered an Arizona statute that required individual county governments to provide necessary hospital and medical care for their indigent sick; however, an indigent had to have been a resident of the county for the preceding twelve months to be eligible for free nonemergency medical care. A county refused to admit to its public hospital an indigent, who had not been a resident for twelve months. The Supreme Court decided a state may not protect the public fisc "by drawing an invidious distinction between classes of its citizens" and ruled the Arizona statute was unconstitutional. The Court noted that if a county does not provide needed treatment for newly arrived residents, the cost will be shifted to private nonprofit hospitals that were "already in precarious financial straits."

But see In re Bermudes, 141 Idaho 157, 106 P.3d 1123 (2005), in which the Supreme Court of Idaho ruled that Idaho Code § 31-3502(12), which provided for medical indigency benefits for residents of the state and excluded benefits for a person coming into the state for temporary purposes, was not unconstitutional. The Idaho Supreme Court distinguished the case from Memorial Hospital v. Maricopa County, 415 U.S. 250 (1974), stating that the U.S. Supreme Court had held Arizona's one-year residence requirement penalized

for a public hospital can cause facilities and access to physician care to be substantially lesser than that available in a private hospital.

B. PRIVATE HOSPITALS

Although management of private hospitals differs from the public hospitals, private hospitals, as health care entities, are likewise subject to considerable governmental regulation. A private hospital either can be privately owned and have for-profit status, or it can be established and operated as a nonprofit organization and, pursuant to § 501(c)(3) of the Internal Revenue Code (I.R.C.), be classified as a tax-exempt charitable organization for tax purposes.[4] Still, because the rendering of medical care is itself considered a charitable activity,[5] the activities of a for-profit hospital do not differ substantially from those of a nonprofit, tax-exempt hospital. The difference in the two types of health care entities is in the residual ownership of assets of the hospital or the right to share in the hospital's net earnings. For a nonprofit hospital, there is the additional requirement that the hospital must provide community benefits and follow the requirements of I.R.C. § 501(r) to obtain and maintain tax-exempt status.[6]

In an early discussion of the difference between nonprofit and for-profit hospitals, a distinguished law professor[7] theorized that consumers preferred nonprofit hospitals based on their belief that they would receive better care in a hospital whose management was concerned solely with the treatment of illness rather than with a concern of meeting shareholder demands for greater dividends. However, the professor concluded that the then currently available

---

indigents for exercising their right to travel to and settle in Arizona whereas the waiting period in Idaho was only thirty days. It noted that unlike the indigent in Memorial Hospital, who was utterly refused medical treatment, the plaintiff had received extensive medical treatment as emergency treatment. The Idaho Supreme Court decided that because counties in Idaho did not have unlimited funds with which to pay medical provers for services rendered to indigent patients, the payment of medical indigency benefits only to persons who were physically present in Idaho for at least thirty days and intended to remain, or not move elsewhere, was rationally related to the legitimate state interest of allocating limited funds.

4 Section 501(c)(3) status for hospitals is discussed in Chapter VII.

5 See early discussion in Sound Health Assoc. v. Comm., 71 T. C. 158 (1978) and further discussion in Chapter VII.

6 See detailed discussion in Chapter VII.

7 Robert C. Clark, Harvard Distinguished Service Professor, Emeritus, and Austin Wakeman Scott Professor Law, Emeritus.

evidence did not confirm this belief.[8] He contended that participation in federal subsidy programs or eligibility for reimbursement under Medicare and Medicaid should be conditioned upon compliance with certain federal minimum standards concerning the structure and governance of hospitals. He further suggested as guidelines that all chief officers of a hospital should be someone other than physicians who currently practice medicine, teach, or do research within the hospital;[9] that at least seventy percent of the directors or trustees should meet this test; that all directors except the chief executive officer should not be officers or employees of the hospital; and that at least a majority of the directors or trustees should be consumers.[10]

C. NONPROFIT HOSPITAL

While a for-profit corporate hospital is a privately shareholder owned corporation operated by a board of directors consisting of individuals or other private corporations, a nonprofit corporate hospital is subject to ownership and control by a citizen-controlled board of directors and a hospital medical staff, and it has no shareholders.[11] Any members a nonprofit hospital may have do not have a property interest in the assets or the equity of the nonprofit hospital. Also, any revenue received by a nonprofit hospital is used to improve hospital facilities and to enlarge the field and scope of the hospital's charitable activities in

8 Robert C. Clark. Does the Nonprofit Form Fit the Hospital Industry? 93 Harv. L. Rev. 1417 (1980). Professor Clark concluded that experiences with fraud and self-dealing in health care institutions suggested organizational form may play little role in the efficient management or delivery of quality health care. He contended that a hospital administrator may prefer the nonprofit hospital because the administrator's conduct is less tightly controlled by a charitable corporation's board of trustees than by a board of directors responsive to shareholder demands. He also decided that physicians preferred practicing in nonprofit hospitals because they could relate better to trustees who had no personal stake in the hospital's financial performance. Professor Clark pointed out that physicians did not need to contend with the monitoring and economizing present in for-profit hospitals and noted that physicians were more in control in a nonprofit hospital than in a for-profit hospital ran by non-physician managers and shareholders.

9 Professor Clark noted the efforts to counterbalance physician dominance of nonprofit hospitals by more consumer control of the governance structure of nonprofit hospitals.

10 Consider these recommendations in Internal Revenue Code (I.R.C.) § 501(r), the provisions of which are summarized in Chapter VII.

11 See discussion of medical staff in Section D in this Chapter. See discussion of a hospital's governing body, members, and employees in Chapter VI.

providing health care to the public. Further, except for reasonable salaries, earnings cannot be distributed to individuals or to private entities.

Nonprofit hospitals are managed by a governing body, which corresponds to a board of directors in for-profit corporate hospitals, an administrator that corresponds to a president of a for-profit corporation, and a medical staff. Members of the medical staff--physicians who provide medical services to the hospital--generally are independent of the hospital. They are neither employees nor agents of the hospital.[12] Yet members of the medical staff, even though organized as an independent entity, make numerous administrative decisions for the hospital.[13] Because important administrative decisions are made by an independent body, the administrative structure of a nonprofit hospital differs from other nonprofit organizations.

As noted above and discussed in Chapter VII, a nonprofit hospital will qualify for exemption from Federal income taxation under I.R.C § 501(c)(3). Additionally, pursuant to I.R.C. §§ 509(a)(1) and 170(b)(1)(A)(iii), a § 501(c)(3) nonprofit hospital is automatically classified as a "public charity" for tax purposes and thus will not have the "private foundation" status defined in I.R.C. § 509 that may classify some of its affiliated and related organizations. A hospital's affiliated and related organizations will qualify for tax-exempt status under § 501(c)(3) if they provide funding and services for the hospital and also can qualify for "public charity" status if they meet the requirements of I.R.C. §§ 509 (a)(1), (2), or (3).[14] Still, although hospitals, and any separate nonprofit entities established to fund a hospital or to provide hospital services, qualify for exemption from federal income taxes, qualification is not automatic. A hospital and its affiliated and related organizations must apply to the Internal Revenue Service

12 See discussion in Chapter IV of the liability for negligent patient care by a member of the hospital staff as opposed to the hospital in which the staff member provides medical services.

13 See 42 C.F.R. § 482.22 for the requirement that participating hospitals in the Medicare program have an organized medical staff. The medical staff is responsible for hospital policies.

14 See discussion of these Code sections in Chapter VIII. Pursuant to I.R.C. § 509, a § 501(c)(3) organization is classified for tax purposes as either a "public charity" or as a "private foundation." A taxpayer receives a less beneficial charitable contribution deduction for a donation to a "private foundation" than for a donation to a "public charity." A nonprofit, tax-exempt hospital will automatically qualify as a public charity while its affiliated and related organizations qualify for public charity status if they are funded by the general public and/or provide services to the general public. These organizations generally are private foundations for tax purposes if they have only a few donors. A discussion of public charity versus private foundation tax classification for hospitals and their affiliated and related organizations is set out in Chapter VIII.

for recognition of federal tax-exempt status and must satisfy requirements of § 501(c)(3) to obtain and to maintain that tax-exempt status.

The requirements for a tax-exempt hospital and any tax-exempt affiliated and related organizations, which are discussed in Chapters VII and VIII, provide requirements that are mandated by the tax law and that correspondingly determine much of the organizational structure of the nonprofit, tax-exempt hospitals. Formation and governance rules for hospitals generally are set out in detail in Chapter VI. The remaining discussion in this chapter sets out rules regarding the establishment and operation of a hospital's medical staff.

D. MEDICAL STAFF

A hospital must have a medical staff to treat its patients; a physician, in turn, must have medical staff privileges in various hospitals to have access to the hospital's equipment, services, and facilities to treat the physician's patients.[15] Members of the medical staff are not employees of the hospital. These physicians are generally considered to be independent contractors.[16] The governing board of the hospital determines who can be admitted to the medical staff. Only

15 In Walsky v. Pascack Valley Hospital, 145 N.J. Super. 393, 367 A.2d 1204 (Ch. Div. 1976), judgment aff'd, 156 N.J. Super. 13, 383 A.2d 154 (App. Div. 1978), the court noted a hospital's governing body and its medical staff are dependent upon each other. As the court commented, no hospital can be better than its medical staff, and no physician can practice medicine without having available to the physician the services and facilities of a hospital.

16 See Dattilo v. Tucson General Hospital, 23 Ariz. App. 392, 533 P.2d 700, (Ariz. Div. 2 1975).

See also Carter-Shields, M.D. v. Alton Health Institute, 777 N.E.2d 948 (Ill. 2002), where the Supreme Court of Illinois ruled an employment agreement between a physician and a non-licensed, general not-for-profit corporation, to provide services as a primary care physician was void as it violated the prohibition against the corporate practice of medicine. The court pointed out that the defendant corporation was not licensed to provide medical services to the public and, thus, was not subject to the state requirements assuring the protection of the public health and welfare. The court further noted the proscription against the corporate practice of medicine is animated by the public policy purpose of safeguarding the public health and welfare by protecting the physician-patient relationship from lay interference with the physician's professional judgment. The court commented that the exercise of control or influence over the medical decision-making of a physician by a lay, unlicensed corporation divides the physician's loyalty between the "often divergent interests of the corporation" and the patient. Although the court noted there was a narrow exception for an entity, such as a hospital, that must meet certain professional criteria established by the legislature to become a licensed health-care provider, the exemption would not apply to a charitable nonprofit health organization.

In Berlin v. Sarah Bush Lincoln Health Center, 688 N.E.106 (Ill. 1997), a physician wanted the court to declare unenforceable a restrictive covenant in a general surgery agreement with the hospital. The Illinois Supreme Court concluded a licensed hospital was exempt from the corporate practice of medicine and could employ licensed physicians to provide medical services.

those physicians who are admitted to the medical staff of a hospital and who are permitted by law to provide patient service independently in the hospital, can practice in that hospital.[17]

1. Organization and Operation of the Medical Staff

The hospital staff is organized and operates under bylaws approved by the governing body.[18] Because the medical staff is responsible for the quality of medical care provided to patients by the hospital, hospitals are under a duty to their patients to exercise reasonable care in granting staff privileges to physicians so that only competent physicians are given the privilege of using hospital facilities.[19]

The medical staff periodically conducts appraisals of its members and examines the credentials of candidates for medical staff membership.[20] The medical

---

17 Early discussion in Accreditation Manual for Hospitals (AMH/93), Joint Commission on Accreditation of Healthcare Organizations, 53, 54 (1992). The Joint Commission has authored several recent comprehensive accreditation manuals for hospitals and has registered them with the U.S. Copyright Office. There is a 2021 Comprehensive Accreditation Manual for Hospitals that is updatable in a three-ring binder.

The Joint Commission on Accreditation of Healthcare Organizations (JCAHO or Joint Commission) is discussed in Chapter II.

18 See 42 C.F.R. § 482.22. See also Medical Staff of Avera Marshall Regional Medical Center v. Avera Marshall, 857 N.W.2d 695 (Minn. 2014), where the Supreme Court of Minnesota ruled that hospital bylaws were an enforceable contract and that medical staff had the capacity to sue the hospital in which they worked. In the case, the governing board of a nonprofit hospital announced a plan to repeal the hospital's medical staff bylaws and replace them with revised bylaws. The hospital's medical staff then sued seeking a declaration that the medical staff had standing to sue the hospital and that the medical staff bylaws were an enforceable contract between the hospital and the medical staff. The hospital contended the medical staff was a department or agent of the hospital rather than a voluntary association existing separately from the hospital. The court noted that Minn. Stat. §540.151 grants an unincorporated association the right to sue and be sued. The statute states that people who associate under a common name "may sue in or be sued by such common name." The court decided the medical staff had the capacity to sue the hospital.

19 See Johnson v. Misericordia Community Hospital, 99 Wis. 2d 708, 301 N.W.2d 156 (1981).

See also Horowitz v. Plantation Gen. Hosp. Ltd. P'ship, 959 So.2d 176, (Fla. 2007), in which a statute required doctors to be financially able to pay malpractice claims. The Supreme Court of Florida ruled that hospitals did not have an affirmative duty to condition the granting of staff privileges on a doctor's proof of compliance with the financial responsibility statute.

Additionally, see McCord v. Laurens County Health Care System, 429 S.C. 286, 838 S.E.2d 220 (S.Car. 2020), in which the Supreme Court of South Carolina ruled that a hospital's failure to ensure that a doctor practicing at the hospital maintained malpractice insurance coverage did not breach patients' admission contracts and that the hospital's failure to ensure a doctor had medical malpractice insurance to cover patients' claims was not negligence.

20 42 C.F.R. § 482.22.

staff makes recommendations to the governing body on the appointment of the candidates.[21] Still, the final authority as to those doctors who are permitted to join a hospital's staff is the hospital's governing body.[22] While the hospital's governing body must rely on the medical staff, and in particular the credentials committee, to investigate and evaluate an applicant's qualifications for the requested privileges, the delegation of the responsibility to investigate and evaluate the professional competence of applicants for clinical privileges does not relieve the governing body of its duty to appoint only qualified physicians and surgeons to its medical staff.[23] Further, the governing body itself must periodically monitor and review the competency of the medical staff.[24] Failure to do so can cause the hospital and its governing body to be held liable for any injuries resulting from what is deemed to be the negligent supervision of members of the medical staff.[25] A hospital assumes responsibilities for the care of its patients and thus must meet the standards of responsibility commensurate with that trust.[26]

21 42 C.F.R. § 482.22.

22 See Ad Hoc Executive Committee of Medical Staff of Memorial Hosp. v. Runyan, 716 P.2d 465 (Colo. 1986), in which the court ruled a hearing committee of the medical staff lacked standing to sue the governing body of a hospital. The governing body had reversed a decision of the hearing committee to suspend staff privileges to a physician. The court stated that the committee was subordinate to the governing body.

23 See Comprehensive Accreditation Manual for Hospitals (CAMH/98), Joint Commission on Accreditation of Healthcare Organizations, 26, 56 (1999). See also Johnson v. Misericordia Community Hospital, 99 Wis. 2d 708, 301 N.W.2d 156 (1981), wherein the court stated the governing body should solicit information from an applicant and from the applicant's peers, including those not referenced in the application, who are knowledgeable about the applicant's education, training, experience, health, competence and ethical character. The hospital governing body should determine if the applicant is currently licensed to practice in the state and if the physician's licensure or registration has been or is currently being challenged. It should inquire whether the applicant has been involved in any adverse malpractice action and whether the physician has experienced a loss of medical organization membership or medical privileges or membership at any other hospitals. The investigating committee must also evaluate information obtained through its inquiries and must make a reasonable judgment as to the approval or denial of each application for staff privileges. The court in Misericordia determined that a hospital would be charged with obtaining and evaluating the knowledge concerning its medical staff applicants. The hospital's failure to exercise that degree of care, skill and judgment that is exercised by the average hospital in approving an applicant's request for privileges is negligence. Still, the court stated hospitals are not insurers of the competence of their medical staff; a hospital will not be negligent if it exercised the above noted standard of care in selecting its staff.

24 Blanton v. Moses H. Cone Memorial Hosp., Inc., 319 N.C. 372, 354 S.E.2d 455 (1987).

25 In Darling v. Charleston Community Memorial Hospital, 33 Ill. 2d 326, 211 N.E.2d 253 (1965), the court early suggested the governing body has the duty to establish a mechanism to evaluate the quality of patient care provided by the hospital and its medical staff.

26 See Purcell v. Zimbelman, 18 Ariz. App. 75, 500 P.2d 335 (Div. 2 1972).

The bylaws for the medical staff must describe the organization of the medical staff and the qualifications to be met by a candidate for membership.[27] The bylaws also must describe the duties and privileges of each category of the medical staff.[28] The bylaws should include provisions for an executive committee that is empowered to act for the medical staff between medical staff meetings. According to standards established by the Joint Commission on Healthcare Organizations, the bylaws cannot be amended without the mutual consent of the medical staff and the hospital.[29]

2. Admission to Hospital Staff and Membership

An application for medical staff membership and privileges contains the information requested by the medical staff bylaws.[30] The applicant is required to give credentials, current board certification and licensures, names and addresses of references, and any challenges to licensure, medical memberships or denial of staff privileges at other hospitals, as well as any involvement in medical malpractice suits.[31] The applicant should release the credentials committee from any liability for review of the applicant's credentials.[32] The application is reviewed

---

27 42 C.F.R. § 482.22(a).

28 42 C.F.R. § 482.22(a).

29 Discussion in Comprehensive Accreditation Manual for Hospitals (CAMH/98), Joint Commission on Accreditation of Hospitals 58 (1999). As noted previously, more recent accreditation manuals are copyrighted but also available in a 2021 comprehensive manual printed in an updatable three ring binder.

30 Discussion in Comprehensive Accreditation Manual for Hospitals (CAMH/98), Joint Commission on Healthcare Organizations 55 (1999).

31 Id.

Four core criteria were set out as being essential to establishing and maintaining a qualified medical staff: current licensure, relevant training and experience, current competence, and ability to perform the privileges requested.

32 In Westlake Community Hosp. v. Superior Court, 17 Cal. 3d 465, 131 Cal. Rptr. 90, 551 P.2d 410 (1976), the court ruled a hospital bylaw, which precluded judicial action by an aggrieved applicant for medical staff privileges, violated public policy and could not bar a plaintiff's access to the courts.

Still, in King v. Bartholomew County Hosp., 476 N.E.2d 877 (Ind. Ct. App. 1985), the court ruled a hospital acted within its proper discretion in requiring an applicant for medical staff privileges to execute a grant of immunity and a release from liability for members of the reviewing body.

See also Ariz. Rev. Stat. § 36-445.02, which provided immunity from civil damages for the actions of a committee established to evaluate applications for admission to a hospital's medical staff.

and, with the recommendations of the staff credentials committee, the governing body of the hospital makes the ultimate decision on whether to grant privileges.[33]

A physician does not have an absolute right to practice medicine in a hospital.[34] A staff member's privileges can be restricted by reasonable and non-discriminatory rules and regulations. Courts have stated it is important that a hospital retain only competent and highly compatible physicians on its medical staff.[35] Thus, a court will not substitute its judgment for that of a medical board with regard to denial of membership on a hospital's medical staff if the staff selection is administered with fairness and is geared by a rationale compatible with the hospital's responsibility, and, as one court enunciated, unencumbered with irrelevant considerations.[36] Courts have ruled persons with only a

33 Discussion in Comprehensive Accreditation Manual for Hospitals (CAMH/98), Joint Commission on Healthcare Organizations 26, 56 (1999).

34 In Barrows v. Northwestern Memorial Hosp., 123 Ill. 2d 49, 525 N.E.2d 50 (1988), the court would not review the decision of a private hospital's refusal to appoint a physician to its medical staff. The court noted that most courts have ruled the decision of hospital authorities in these matters is final.

35 Yashon v. Hunt, 825 F.2d 1016 (6th Cir. 1987). In Patrick v. Cleveland Scene Pub. LLC, 582 F. Supp. 2d 939 (N.D. Ohio 2008), aff'd, 360 Fed. Appx. 592 (6th Cir. 2009), the court ruled a physician who brought an action against a publisher of a magazine article that allegedly questioned the physician's medical training and qualifications, was required to prove actual malice because the court decided the article's imputations were matters of public concern. The court determined the physician failed to prove actual malice on the part of the publisher. The court stated that a "general-purpose public figure" is one who attains such pervasive fame or notoriety that the person becomes a public figure for all purpose and in all contexts and, thus, is required to prove the defendant published allegedly defamatory statements with actual malice. The court ruled that analyzing whether a plaintiff is a limited-purpose public figure proceeds in two stages: first, a public controversy must exist, and second, the nature and extent of the individual's involvement in the controversy must be ascertained. The court stated it must consider three factors: the extent to which participation in a controversy is voluntary; the extent to which there is access to channels of effective communication to counteract false statements; and the prominence of the role played in the public controversy.

36 See Sosa v. Board of Managers of Val Verde Memorial Hospital, 437 F.2d 173 (5th Cir. 1971). See also Garibaldi v. Applebaum, 742 N.E.2d 279 (Ill. 2000), in which the Supreme Court of Illinois commented that courts exercise only a limited form of review in cases involving medical staffing decisions. The plaintiff in Garibaldi, a surgeon whose clinical privileges were extinguished by a hospital's exclusive contract with a physicians' group, brought a complaint that hospital's bylaws were violated when his right to perform open-heart procedures at the hospital was revoked without affording him notice and a hearing. The case considered what procedural rights, if any, a physician has under hospital bylaws when a hospital enters into an exclusive contract with a competing group of physicians for the performance of the same work as the physician performs. The surgeon had clinical privileges at a hospital as a member of a group of physicians whose organization was dissolved. A new group was formed, but it did not include the surgeon. This group entered into an exclusive contract with the hospital, the effect of which was to revoke the surgeon's right to perform open-heart procedures at the hospital without affording him the benefit of notice and a hearing in violation of the hospital's then-current bylaws. The Illinois Supreme Court found that the surgeon

specialized training (such as podiatrists), those doctors who do not have medical malpractice insurance, and those individuals who cause frictions or who demonstrate anger and impatience toward other doctors and nurses, can be denied membership.[37] Still, courts have also ruled persons cannot be denied admission because they are not members of a county medical society or because they did not graduate from a school of medicine approved by the American Medical Association.[38] Some courts have ruled that membership on the medical staff can be denied when a hospital has an exclusive contract with another physician or group of physicians.[39] Courts have generally held that membership cannot be conditioned upon favorable recommendations by members of the hospital medical staff.[40] However, a hospital policy that places a moratorium on the number of physicians admitted to the medical staff generally will be upheld if the hospital has a legitimate reason for so limiting the number of its medical staff.[41]

Courts have drawn a distinction between private and public hospitals in determining whether a physician who is denied membership on a hospital's medical staff must be provided with due process safeguards.[42] Public hospitals are restricted by constitutional guarantees under the Fourteenth Amendment to

had not suffered a revocation, suspension, or reduction of his privileges and thus would not review the hospital's internal staffing. That court noted that internal staffing decisions of private hospitals were not subject to judicial review.

37 See Pollock v. Methodist Hospital, 392 F. Supp. 393 (E.D. La. 1975) and Shaw v. Hospital Authority of Cobb County, 614 F.2d 946 (5th Cir. 1980).

38 See Foster v. Mobile County Hospital Bd., 398 F.2d 227 (5th Cir. 1968), in which the Court of Appeals for the Fifth Circuit ruled a hospital may not delegate to others its power to determine what physician may use its facilities. The Fifth Circuit held that a requirement that the physician be a member of a county medical society amounted to a preference in favor of the society and was a discrimination against those physicians who are not members of the society.

In a 1958 decision in Duson v. Poage, 318 S.W.2d 89 (Tex. Civ. App. Houston 1958), writ refused n.r.e., a Texas court ruled it was an unlawful delegation of power of the hospital board to itself determine the qualifications of its staff members if it required that a staff member be a graduate of a school of medicine approved by the American Medical Association.

39 Jefferson Parish Hosp. Dist. No. 2 v. Hyde, 466 U.S. 2 (1984) (abrogated on other grounds by, Illinois Tool Works Inc. v. Independent Ink, Inc., 547 U.S. 28 (2006)).

40 See Foster v. Mobile County Hospital Bd., 398 F.2d 227 (5th Cir. 1968).

41 See Hackett v. Metropolitan General Hosp., 465 So. 2d 1246 (Fla. 2d DCA 1985).

However, see also Walsky v. Pascack Valley Hospital, 145 N.J. Super. 393, 367 A.2d 1204 (Ch. Div. 1976), judgment aff'd, 156 N.J. Super. 13, 383 A.2d 154 (App. Div. 1978), in which the court found that a moratorium on appointments to the medical staff was not related to the maintenance of quality patient care and, thus, was invidious discrimination against newly admitted members of the medical society.

42 See Bricker v. Sceva Speare Memorial Hospital, 111 N.H. 276, 281 A.2d 589 (1971).

the United States Constitution.[43] If a physician can demonstrate a property interest or a liberty interest in membership on the medical staff, the constitutional mandates of due process must be met.[44] On the other hand, courts have ruled a private institution is not subject to the due process safeguards applicable to a public hospital, that the exclusion of a physician from the medical staff rests within the discretion of the hospital governing body and is not subject to review by the courts.[45] Still, courts have stated certain powers of the governing board of a hospital are fiduciary powers and must be exercised reasonably and for the good of the public they serve.[46] In addition, courts have recognized that some measure of control is called for in the operation of private hospitals.[47] Thus, some courts have ruled exclusion from staff privileges must be in accordance with the bylaws of a private hospital and will be reviewed by a court if an exclusion from membership is arbitrary, capricious or unreasonable.[48] Some earlier courts determined that if a private hospital was the recipient of public funds or Hill-Burton funds, the constitutional mandates of due process had to be met.[49] Most courts,

---

43 In re Zaman, 285 S.C. 345, 329 S.E.2d 436 (1985).

44 See decisions in Board of Regents of State Colleges v. Roth, 408 U.S. 564 (1972) and Perry v. Sindermann, 408 U.S. 593 (1972).

45 Settler v. Hopedale Medical Foundation, 80 Ill. App. 3d 1074, 36 Ill. Dec. 157, 400 N.E.2d 577 (3d Dist. 1980).

46 Holmes v. Hoemako Hospital, 117 Ariz. 403, 573 P.2d 477, 7 A.L.R.4th 1231 (1977).

47 See Westlake Community Hosp. v. Superior Court, 17 Cal. 3d 465, 131 Cal. Rptr. 90, 551 P.2d 410 (1976), in which the court noted California decisions had established that before a public or a private hospital may deny a doctor the right to practice the doctor's profession at the hospital, either by the termination of existing staff privileges or by the denial of an initial application for such privileges, the hospital had to provide a fair procedure that afforded the doctor an opportunity to answer the charges upon which the exclusion rests.

48 In Christopher v. Stouder Memorial Hosp., 936 F.2d 870 (6th Cir. 1991), the Court of Appeals for the Sixth Circuit ruled that a Title VII claim could be brought against a hospital even though the hospital did not employ the claimant if the hospital interfered with the claimant's employment opportunities. In Stouder, a hospital denied a nurse work privileges to serve as a private duty scrub nurse for a medical partnership allegedly in retaliation of a sex discrimination action she had brought against another hospital. The Sixth Circuit ruled the nurse could bring a Title VII claim against the hospital even though it was not her employer. (Also, see discussion of Title VII in Chapter VI.)

In Rodriguez-Erdman v. Ravenswood Hosp. Medical Center, 163 Ill. App. 3d 464, 114 Ill. Dec. 576, 516 N.E.2d 731 (1st Dist. 1987), an Illinois court commented the weight of authority is that the scope of judicial review in cases in which a private hospital has denied staff membership or revoked or reduced a physician's staff privileges is limited to the issue of whether in doing so it complied with its bylaws.

49 See, e.g., Walsky v. Pascack Valley Hospital, 145 N.J. Super. 393, 367 A.2d 1204 (Ch. Div. 1976), judgment aff'd, 156 N.J. Super. 13, 383 A.2d 154 (App. Div. 1978). (Also see discussion of Hill-Burton funds in Chapter II.)

however, agree the acceptance of federal funds does not change the character of a private hospital to a public hospital.[50] Still, the appointment of a majority of the members of the hospital governing board by a governmental agency can constitute state action and, thus, cause a private hospital to be considered public.[51] Accordingly, because some courts have determined that the governing bodies of private hospitals must follow procedures set out in the bylaws regarding staff appointments, the bylaws may require that a private hospital provide a physician with procedural due process.[52]

A physician does not have a constitutional right to staff privileges in a public hospital merely because the physician is licensed to practice medicine.[53] The expectancy of reappointment to the medical staff has not been held to be a claim of entitlement amounting to a property interest.[54] However, the right to practice medicine has been deemed to be a liberty interest.[55] A public hospital cannot exclude a physician from practice by rules, regulations, or acts of the hospital's governing authorities if the rules, regulations, or acts are arbitrary, capricious, or discriminatory.[56] Further, if the physician complies with the rules of a public

---

50 Pariser v. Christian Health Care Systems, Inc., 816 F.2d 1248 (8th Cir. 1987); Martin Memorial Hosp. Ass'n, Inc. v. Noble, 496 So. 2d 222 (Fla. 4th DCA 1986).

51 Sosa v. Board of Managers of Val Verde Memorial Hospital, 437 F.2d 173 (5th Cir. 1971).

52 See discussion in Accreditation Manual for Hospitals (AMH/88), Joint Commission on Accreditation of Healthcare Organizations 114 (1987). The JCAHO required that medical staff bylaws provide for a fair hearing and for appellate review procedures. These procedures could differ for staff members holding clinical privileges and applicants for membership or privileges on the medical staff.

Further, in Pariser v. Christian Health Care Systems, Inc., 816 F.2d 1248 (8th Cir. 1987), the court ruled bylaws are an enforceable part of a contract between a hospital and a physician with privileges at the hospital. The court applied Illinois law in determining that a court would annul the suspension or revocation of staff privileges not accomplished in accordance with the bylaws.

53 See Sosa v. Board of Managers of Val Verde Memorial Hospital, 437 F.2d 173 (5th Cir. 1971). See also Ezekwo v. New York City Health & Hospitals Corp., 940 F.2d 775 (2d Cir. 1991), wherein the Court of Appeals for the Second Circuit ruled a third-year resident had a property interest in acquiring the position of Chief Resident. In this case, the hospital adopted a policy and practice of awarding the position of Chief Resident to all third-year residents on a rotating basis. The Second Circuit found that the hospital residency directors and doctors changing the method of selecting the Chief Resident before deciding to apply the new standard, denied the claimant the position. The hospital contended the decision to pass over the claimant was purely academic and, thus, the claimant was not denied due process. The court, on the other hand, decided the claimant should have been notified of the change in policy and should have been given an opportunity to address the residency directors' concerns before the directors utilized the policy against her.

54 Suckle v. Madison General Hospital, 499 F.2d 1364 (7th Cir. 1974).

55 Pollock v. Methodist Hospital, 392 F. Supp. 393 (E.D. La. 1975).

56 In re Zaman, 285 S.C. 345, 329 S.E.2d 436 (1985).

hospital, the physician is entitled to a hearing and an explanation of the reasons medical staff privileges were denied.[57]

For those hospitals subject to due process requirements, the fundamental requirement of due process applicable to an applicant for medical staff privileges is the opportunity to be heard at a meaningful time and in a meaningful manner.[58] However, the overall concept of due process of law is a flexible one; the type of procedural protections required in a particular situation depends largely upon the circumstances of the situation.[59] A physician is not guaranteed the right to prehearing discovery, to call witnesses, to the assistance of counsel, or to a written decision explaining the findings and rationale of the board in denying membership on the medical staff.[60] A court's review of the decision generally is limited to determining whether the procedures used violated any federal rights and whether the administrative body was presented with substantial evidence to support its ultimate action.[61] It is not the function of courts to review the merits of the charges brought against a physician. The decision of a hospital's

---

57 See Sosa v. Board of Managers of Val Verde Memorial Hospital, 437 F.2d 173 (5th Cir. 1971). See also Caine v. Hardy, 943 F.2d 1406 (5th Cir. 1991), in which the Court of Appeals for the Fifth Circuit ruled a public hospital could suspend an anesthesiologist's staff privileges prior to a formal hearing but after an investigation and conferences regarding the death of one of his patients. The Fifth Circuit noted the suspension fell within the public safety exception to the general procedural due process requirement that deprivation of property be preceded by notice and a hearing. That court also noted adequate post-deprivation remedies were available under hospital bylaws.

58 Yashon v. Hunt, 825 F.2d 1016 (6th Cir. 1987).

59 Id. In Yashon, the Court of Appeals for the Sixth Circuit stated that three factors should be considered in determining whether a particular procedure should be required: (1) whether a private interest will be affected by official action; (2) whether there is a risk of an erroneous deprivation of the interest through the procedures used and the probable value, if any, of additional or substitute procedural safeguards; and (3) the government's interest, including fiscal and administrative burdens, which additional or substitute procedural requirements would entail.

The Court of Appeals for the Eighth Circuit, in Pariser v. Christian Health Care Systems, Inc., 816 F.2d 1248 (8th Cir. 1987), ruled a physician who brought charges against another physician to the executive committee could not participate as a judge in making the decision to suspend staff privileges.

60 In Yashon v. Hunt, 825 F.2d 1016 (6th Cir. 1987), the Sixth Circuit ruled the lack of established standards did not render a decision of the board arbitrary. It stated notice to the physician in such an informal setting need only be specific enough to enable the physician to respond to any charges raised against the physician; it did not need to rise to the level of specificity required of a criminal indictment.

In re Zaman, 285 S.C. 345, 329 S.E.2d 436 (1985), the Supreme Court of South Carolina determined a physician's right to a fair and meaningful hearing under due process was violated when three of the physician's original accusers were members of the board that made the final decision to deny the physician membership on the medical staff.

61 Yashon v. Hunt, 825 F.2d 1016 (6th Cir. 1987).

governing body concerning the granting of hospital privileges is afforded great deference.[62] Moreover, proceedings and records of hospital staff committees are not subject to discovery, and no person in attendance at a meeting of a staff committee can be required to testify as to what transpired at the meeting.[63]

3. Professional Review Committees

Physicians who are denied medical staff privileges have sought damages for lost earnings, emotional distress, defamation of character, discrimination, and violation of antitrust laws.[64] To provide members of a hospital review committee

---

62 Id.

63 West Covina Hospital v. Superior Court, 226 Cal. Rptr. 132, 718 P.2d 119 (1986). However, in Pisel v. Stamford Hospital, 180 Conn. 314, 430 A.2d 1 (1980), the Supreme Court of Connecticut decided a staff committee member could testify voluntarily about proceedings of the committee. The Connecticut Supreme Court explained that state statutes precluding the introduction into evidence of records and opinions of medical review committees do not preclude a physician who attended a peer review meeting from testifying. The court ruled that in a medical malpractice action in which a physician was not asked to disclose what occurred at the meeting but was called as an expert witness for the limited purpose of answering a hypothetical question based upon evidence, the physician was not precluded from answering the question.

See also Rodriguez-Erdman v. Ravenswood Hosp. Medical Center, 163 Ill. App. 3d 464, 516 N.E.2d 731 (1st Dist. 1987), in which the court held that pursuant to 210 Ill. Comp. Stat. Ann. 85/10.2, a hospital and the individual physicians were immune from civil damages based upon actions taken by them in the peer-review process. The court decided the immunity statute promoted a legitimate state interest in improving the quality of health care.

64 See, e.g., Spencer v. Community Hospital of Evanston, 87 Ill. App. 3d 214, 408 N.E.2d 98 (1st Dist. 1980) (holding modified by, Barrows v. Northwestern Memorial Hosp., 153 Ill. App. 3d 83, 505 N.E.2d 1182 (1st Dist. 1987)), in which a physician sued members of a review committee when the physician was denied membership on the medical staff. The court ruled the report of the committee was conditionally privileged because of the strong interest a hospital has in ascertaining the quality of medical care rendered by admitting physicians. Because the report was conditionally privileged, the burden was on the physician to prove malice that would cause an abuse of the privilege. According to the court, abuse of the privilege occurs if the publisher has no grounds to believe in the truth of the defamatory matter.

See also Rodriguez-Erdman v. Ravenswood Hosp. Medical Center, 163 Ill. App. 3d 464, 516 N.E.2d 731 (1st Dist. 1987), wherein the court ruled that a hospital and the individual physicians were statutorily immune from civil damages based on actions taken by them in a peer-review process.

Statutes that provide immunity from liability for members of a peer-review committee generally do not include immunity from liability for discrimination. See 42 U.S.C. §111 and 29 U.S.C. § 1112(a).

In Colorado State Bd. of Medical Examiners v. Ogin, 56 P.3d 1233 (Colo. App. 2002), as modified, (2002), the court ruled the American with Disabilities Act (see discussion of the act in Chapter VI) does not prevent a professional licensing agency from imposing disciplinary sanctions against a "qualified individual with a disability." The court stated the Act does not protect an individual with a disability who, by virtue of disability, is a direct threat to the public's safety. There was evidence in the case that the anesthesiologist plaintiff's disorder caused him to fall asleep during surgery. The court ruled the sanction of license revocation against the anesthesiologist for professional misconduct was not manifestly excessive in relation to

protection from personal liability from these claims, provisions should be made that applicants for medical staff privileges release the review committee from any liability relating to the review process.[65] Federal statutes and some state statutes provide for immunity from liability from many of these claims.[66] Congress adopted the Hospital Care Quality Improvement Act in 1986 to encourage physicians to serve on professional peer-review committees by eliminating the fear of private money damage liability through a provision for some immunity from liability.[67] Some states have followed the lead of Congress in adopting state statutes providing immunity from liability for most claims against members of the review committee.[68]

---

the need to ensure public safety. It ruled the Board of Medical Examiners was afforded great discretion in determining appropriate sanctions for unprofessional conduct, and the Board's determination must be upheld on review unless it bore no relation to the conduct in question or was manifestly excessive in relation to the needs of the public. The court stated that a reviewing court cannot substitute its judgment for that of the board as to what constitutes appropriate sanctions.

Peer-review action is immunized from antitrust liability if the action was taken in the reasonable belief that it was in the furtherance of quality health care.

See Jefferson Parish Hosp. Dist. No. 2 v. Hyde, 466 U.S. 2 (1984) (abrogated on other grounds by, Illinois Tool Works Inc. v. Independent Ink, Inc., 547 U.S. 28 (2006)), in which the Supreme Court determined an exclusive contract with a group of physicians did not violate the Sherman Act; thus, there was no antitrust violation.

(See further discussion of antitrust laws in Chapter II.)

65 In King v. Bartholomew County Hosp., 476 N.E.2d 877 (Ind. Ct. App. 1985), the court ruled a hospital acted within its proper discretion in requiring an applicant for medical staff privileges to execute a grant of immunity and release from liability for members of the reviewing body.

In Kwoun v. Southeast Missouri Professional Standards Review Organization, 811 F.2d 401 (8th Cir. 1987), the Court of Appeals for the Eighth Circuit ruled members of the original peer-review group enjoyed absolute immunity from common-law and constitutional claims asserted against them in connection with their decision to recommend exclusion of a physician from Medicare and Medicaid reimbursement programs.

66 See, e. g., Hospital Care Quality Improvement Act Pub. L. No. 99-660, codified at 42 U.S.C. §§ 11101 et seq.

67 See 42 U.S.C. § 11101. Congress adopted the Hospital Care Quality Improvement Act of 1986 in response to congressional recognition of a national need to restrict the ability of incompetent physicians to practice in the nation's hospitals because of the increasing occurrence of medical malpractice and the need to improve the quality of medical care. Congress determined that while some of the problems could be remedied through effective professional peer review, the threat of private liability had, in the past, unreasonably discouraged physicians from participating in such peer review.

In accordance with delegations contained the Act, the Secretary of the Department of Health and Human Services promulgated regulations that established the National Practitioner Data Bank, 45 C.F.R. § 60.1. The Data Bank collects and releases information that the Act requires health care entities to report regarding the professional competence and conduct of physicians, dentists, and other health care practitioners.

68 See, e.g., Ariz. Rev. Stat. Ann. §36-445.02.

The Hospital Care Quality Improvement Act ("HCQIA") provides that a professional review body reviewing the qualifications of physicians, including any person acting as a member or staff to the body, any person under contract or other formal agreement with the body, and any person who participated with or assisted the body with respect to any action regarding physicians who are investigated, will not be liable in damages under any federal or state law with respect to the action.[69] The HCQIA specifically states that a person providing information to the professional review body regarding the competence or professional conduct of a physician will also not be held liable in damages under any federal or state laws because of having provided the information.[70]

---

69 42 U.S.C. § 11111. The HCQIA provided immunity under state laws. The section does not apply to damages relating to the civil rights of any person including rights under 42 U.S.C. §§ 2000e. The United States and any state are not precluded from bringing action under the Clayton Act, 15 U.S.C. § 15c, for antitrust violations.

To be immune from liability, the professional body must meet the standards set out at 42 U.S.C. § 11112(a). These standards require a physician be given due process. A professional review action must be taken in the reasonable belief the action was in the furtherance of quality health care and after a reasonable effort to obtain the facts of the matter. The involved physician must be given adequate notice and hearing procedures or other processes as are fair to the physician under the circumstances. The action must be taken in the reasonable belief that the action was warranted by the facts known after a reasonable effort to obtain the facts and after giving the physician adequate notice and hearing procedures. A physician must be given notice stating that a professional review action has been proposed to be taken against the physician, the reasons for the proposed action and that the physician has the right to request a hearing on the proposed action. The hearing must be given not less than thirty days after the date of the notice. The physician must be given a list of witnesses expected to testify at the hearing on behalf of the professional review body. The hearing must be held either before an arbitrator mutually acceptable to the physician and the health-care entity, before a hearing officer who is appointed by the entity and who is not in direct economic competition with the physician involved, or before a panel of individuals who are appointed by the entity and are not in direct economic competition with the physician involved. The right to the hearing may be forfeited if the physician fails, without cause, to appear. The physician has the right to representation by an attorney or other person of the physician's choice, to have a record made of the proceedings, to obtain copies of the proceedings upon payment of any reasonable charges for the preparation of such copies, to call and examine witnesses, and to present evidence determined by the hearing officer to be relevant. The physician also has the right to submit a written statement at the close of the hearing and to receive the written recommendation of the arbitrator, officer, or panel, including a statement of the basis for the recommendations. 42 U.S.C. § 11112. If the standards are not met, a physician may recover attorney's fees should the physician prevail in a lawsuit. 42 U.S.C. § 11113. The HCQIA does not apply to activities of professional review bodies regarding nurses, other licensed health-care practitioners, or other health professionals who are not physicians. 42 U.S.C. § 11115(c).

In Doe v. Rogers, 139 F. Supp. 3d 120 (D.C. D. C. 2015), the court ruled the HCQIA granting immunity from liability for those who participate in medical professional peer review action did not violate the due process clause; it stated a physician's allegations that an adverse action report impaired his ability to obtain clinical privileges and foreclosed his freedom to take advantage of other employment opportunities failed to support a reputation-plus due process claim. The court also ruled the adverse action report did not qualify as a stigma for purpose of the physician's stigma-plus due process claim.

70 42 U.S.C. § 11111(a)(2).

In Frelich v. Upper Chesapeake Health, Inc. 313 F.3d 205 (4th Cir. 2002), a physician, whose medical staff privileges were terminated after the hospital in which she practiced undertook an extensive review of

Pursuant to the HCQIA, each health care entity that takes a professional review action adversely affecting the clinical privileges of a physician for a period longer than thirty days, or that accepts the surrender of clinical privileges of a physician while the physician is under an investigation by the entity for possible incompetence or improper professional conduct, must report the action to the Board of Medical Examiners.[71] When a physician applies for membership on the medical staff or for clinical privileges at the hospital, the hospital must request from the Secretary of Health and Human Services, or a private or public agency designated by the secretary, information reported about that physician.[72] A hospital must also request information regularly regarding physicians on the medical staff.[73]

her application for reappointment, brought an action challenging the constitutionality of the HCQIA, 42 U.S.C. §§ 11101 et seq., that granted immunity to medical professional peer review participants. The Court of Appeals for the Fourth Circuit pointed out a "legitimacy" of Congress's purpose in enacting HCQIA in that prior to the act, there was an increasing occurrence of medical malpractice and a need to improve the quality of medical care. That court noted that Congress enacted the HCQIA to facilitate frank exchanges of information among professionals conducting peer review inquiries without reprisals in civil lawsuits. The Fourth Circuit stated that hospital authorities have both the discretion and the protection to discharge their assigned tasks and declined to interfere in hospital governance.

71 42 U.S.C. § 11133. Failure to do so can cause loss of immunity. 42 U.S.C. § 11111(c). Each entity (including an insurance company) that makes payment under a policy of insurance in settlement of, or in satisfaction of a judgment in a medical malpractice action or claim, must report the information to the state licensing board. 42 U.S.C. § 11131. The report must include the name of the physician, the amount of the payment, and the name of any hospital with which the physician is affiliated.

72 42 U.S.C. § 11133.

73 42 U.S.C. § 11134.

CHAPTER II.
GOVERNMENTAL REGULATION

Hospitals are subject to extensive governmental regulation. Hospitals must be licensed, and most are accredited. Various functions of a hospital in delivering health care to its patients are heavily regulated, e. g., the dispensing of drugs and participation in the Medicare and Medicaid programs. Financing and construction of hospital buildings have been subject to substantial federal and state regulation. Reimbursement for patient care by the federal government and even rates charged by hospitals are subject to regulation. Further, as noted in Chapters VII and VIII, the activities of a tax-exempt hospital are extensively regulated and must be carefully monitored to assure that tax-exempt status will not be lost.

A. NATIONAL HEALTH PLANNING

Congress attempted at various times to control the national problem of spiraling health care costs. It is useful to review some of the former attempts to address nationally the problems of providing adequate health care to the public. In considering these attempts, one must note the Hospital Survey and Construction Act,[1] commonly known as the Hill-Burton Act, which was enacted in 1946 as a very early effort to assist the states in carrying out programs for the construction and modernization of public and nonprofit community hospitals in order to furnish adequate hospital, clinic, or similar services to the public.[2] Although the act was superseded in 1974, and Hill-Burton funds were, as a consequence, no longer available for hospital construction and modernization, certain requirements of the act (one being that hospitals that received Hill-Burton funds had to provide some uncompensated care) can still be relevant.[3]

The Hill-Burton Act was intended to address postwar and post-depression problems with respect to the adequacy and distribution of health facilities by means of a program of grants-in-aid to the states.[4] The U. S. Surgeon General was directed to issue regulations prescribing that all state plans must provide for adequate hospitals and other facilities for persons residing in the state. Although regulations were issued, hospitals receiving aid through Hill-Burton funds were

1 42 U.S.C. § 291.

2 See 42 U.S.C. § 291.

3 See e.g., 42 C.F.R. § 124.501(b)(1).

4 See, discussion in American Hosp. Ass'n v. Schweiker, 721 F.2d 170 (7th Cir. 1983).

reluctant to provide the uncompensated charitable services required by the act.[5] As a result of several lawsuits brought by private citizens and public interest groups against federally assisted hospitals to enforce compliance with the Hill-Burton obligations, new regulations were issued in 1979.[6] These regulations provided that obligations under the Hill-Burton Act must continue for twenty years after the completion of construction or until the amount of a grant or loan from Hill-Burton funds had been repaid.[7]

The 1979 regulations relating to the Hill-Burton Act provided that a hospital constructed with Hill-Burton funds had to provide uncompensated care equal to the lesser of either three percent of the facility's operating cost for the last fiscal year or ten percent of all federal assistance received by the facility, adjusted to make allowance for inflation for each year after 1979.[8] The regulations also provided that amounts received as reimbursement from insurance programs, or under Medicare or Medicaid, could not be counted in computing the amount of uncompensated services rendered.[9] Hospitals that utilized Hill-Burton funds could not refuse to participate in Medicare or Medicaid programs or discriminate against individuals who were recipients of aid under those programs. Hospitals that received the funds could not adopt admission policies that had the effect of excluding individuals on impermissible grounds.[10] If a hospital that received Hill-Burton funds in the past failed to meet its annual compliance level in any year, it had to adopt and implement an affirmative action plan which included provisions that could reasonably be expected to enable the facility to meet its annual compliance level.[11]

---

5 American Hosp. Ass'n v. Scheweiker, 721 F.2d 170 (7th Cir. 1983).

6 42 C.F.R. Part 124.

7 42 C.F.R. § 124.501(b)(1).

In Metropolitan Medical Center and Extended Care Facility v. Harris, 693 F.2d 775 (8th Cir. 1982), the Court of Appeals for the Eighth Circuit ruled that indigents receiving Hill-Burton free care were not covered by Medicare; thus, a provider was precluded from receiving Medicare payments for its Hill-Burton costs.

8 42 C.F.R. § 124.503(a).

See, however, Gillis v. U.S. Dept. of Health and Human Services, 759 F.2d 565 (6th Cir. 1985), in which the Court of Appeals for the Sixth Circuit ruled that 42 U.S.C.A. § 300-6 did not provide a private right of action to force the government to investigate and ascertain on a periodic basis whether each entity that received financial assistance under the Hill-Burton Act was complying with its obligations.

9 42 C.F.R. § 124.509.

10 42 C.F.R. § 124.603(c).

11 42 C.F.R. § 124.504.

The Hill-Burton Act was followed in 1975 by a comprehensive national act, the National Health Planning and Resources Development Act,[12] which encouraged the establishment and integration of federal, state, and local health planning administration.[13] Cost of medical care was to be contained through federal and state agencies that would determine the appropriateness of various health care construction and equipment proposals to ensure that only needed additions were made.[14] Each state developed its detailed state health plan. Although state participation was not required, those states that did not participate faced significant losses in federal funding for health-related programs.[15] At the state level, the act created two separate bodies, a State Health Planning and Development Agency and a local Health Systems Agency (HSA) concerned with health planning in a particular metropolitan area.[16] Each proposal to extend health care in a particular area through the construction of a health facility or the acquisition of major medical equipment required a Certificate of Need (CON) prior to any construction or equipment acquisition.[17] The local HSA reviewed each application for a CON.

Problems soon developed in the implementation of the national health planning program. Actions by the state agencies in denying certificates of need were often deemed to be arbitrary and capricious.[18] Charges of conspiracy and violation of antitrust laws also were made.[19] There were difficulties in making short-term projections of medical costs to consumers to justify approvals or denials

---

See American Hosp. Ass'n v. Schweiker, 721 F.2d 170 (7th Cir. 1983), and Wyoming Hosp. Ass'n v. Harris, 727 F.2d 936 (10th Cir. 1984), in which the courts of appeal ruled the 1979 regulations to be valid.

12 Former 42 U.S.C. §§ 300k to 300n-6, repealed by Pub. L. No. 99-660 (1986).

13 Pub. L. No. 93-641, codified at 42 U.S.C. § 300k (repealed).

14 See discussion by the Supreme Court of West Virginia in Princeton Community Hosp. v. State Health Planning, 174 W. Va. 558, 328 S.E.2d 164 (1985).

15 Princeton Community Hosp. v. State Health Planning, 174 W.Va. 558, 328 S.E.2d 164 (1985).

16 See, discussion by the Supreme Court in National Gerimedical Hospital and Gerontology Center v. Blue Cross of Kansas City, 452 U.S. 378 (1981).

17 See former 42 U.S.C. § 300m-6.

18 National Gerimedical Hospital and Gerontology Center v. Blue Cross of Kansas City, 452 U.S. 378 (1981).

19 See discussion by the Supreme Court in National Gerimedical Hospital and Gerontology Center v. Blue Cross of Kansas City, 452 U.S. 378 (1981) and by the Court of Appeals of the Eleventh Circuit in St. Joseph's Hosp., Inc. v. Hospital Corp. of America, 795 F.2d 948 (11th Cir. 1986).

of applications for CONs.[20] A later reduction in federal financial services caused some states to abandon the program.[21] In 1986, Congress repealed the act.[22] Still, while some states repealed their individual CON laws, many states continue currently to have CON programs with some having enacted laws to modify or change their CON programs.[23]

National health care planning was enhanced and broadened through the creation of the Medicare and Medicaid programs discussed below.

B. LICENSURE

As clearly established in national health planning acts, there is a crucial public interest in the proper maintenance of hospitals; the state currently, vis-a-vis its power to promote public health, regulates hospitals through licensing requirements.[24] Licensure is used both to assure that hospitals meet minimum quality standards of health care and to control the rising costs of health care.[25]

20 See, discussion in Morton F. Plant Hosp. Ass'n, Inc. v. State, 491 So. 2d 586 (Fla. 1st DCA 1986).

21 See, e.g., Tex. Rev. Civ. Stat. Ann. art. 4418h.

Federal funding for the Texas Health Facilities Commission and the State Certificate of Need Program expired in 1981.

22 Pub. L. No. 99-660, 100 Stat. 3799, 1986 U.S. Code Cong. & Admin. News.

23 See, e.g., Miss. Code §§ 41-7-171 et. seq., which requires a CON for financing of a new health project.

In Miss. State Dept. Of Health v. Miss. Baptist Medical Center, 663 So2d 563 (Miss. 1995), the Supreme Court of Mississippi reviewed the CON procedure and stated that it was conceived as a basic component in an overall effort to control unnecessary capital expenditures that contribute greatly to a national health bill. The court noted that cost containment was the primary purpose of the CON procedure.

In Family Medical Imaging v. West Virginia Health Care, 218 W.Va. 146, 624 S. E.2d 493 (2005), the Supreme Court of West Virginia ruled that applicants for a CON to provide ultrasound diagnostic services in a six-county area failed to establish a significant number of pre-existing clients in two counties and, therefore, did not show a need for the proposed services.

24 See, e.g., Cal. Health & Safety Code § 1253; Ill. Hosp. Licensing, 210 Ill. Comp. Stat. Ann. §§ 85/1 to 85/16; N.Y. Pub. Health Law §§ 2801-a and 2805; Tex. Health & Safety Code Ann. § 241.021, W. Va. Code Ann. § 16-5B-1.

25 In American Hosp. Ass'n v. Hansbarger, 600 F. Supp. 465 (N.D. W. Va. 1984), aff'd, 783 F.2d 1184 (4th Cir. 1986), several nonprofit and governmental hospitals sued to challenge a state's regulating statute, W. Va. Code Ann. § 16-5B-6a, which required nonprofit hospitals to have consumer representatives on their boards of directors. The statute required at least forty percent of members of the board had to be representatives from small business, organized labor, elderly persons, and persons whose incomes are less than the national median income. Women, racial minorities, and disabled persons were given special consideration. The hospitals contended the statute was unconstitutional in that it caused unequal treatment of nonprofit hospitals. The court, however, determined there was no constitutional violation.

The state licensing power generally is held by a state agency; administrative bodies have substantial authority to grant, deny, or revoke a hospital's license.[26] A court normally will not substitute its judgment for that of an administrative body when the latter's determination to grant, deny or revoke a license is supported by substantial evidence; however, elementary rules of due process are applicable requiring that a hospital be given the right to be heard and to present evidence on its behalf.[27]

C. ACCREDITATION

Most hospitals have sought accreditation by the Joint Commission on Accreditation of Healthcare Organizations (JCAHO), generally referred to as Joint Commission. The Joint Commission is a nonprofit corporation that was formed in 1951 to create and maintain professional standards for evaluating hospital performance. The body was governed by a twenty-two-member Board of Commissioners, appointed by the American College of Physicians, the American College of Surgeons, the American Dental Association, the American Hospital Association, and the American Medical Association.[28]

The JCAHO standards are published in the Joint Commission's Accreditation Manual, which is updated regularly.[29] Hospitals have been inspected by a team

26 See, e.g., Cal. Health & Safety Code § 1254; N.Y. Pub. Health Law §§ 2801a, 2805; W. Va. Code Ann. § 16-5B-3.

27 See, Woodwiss v. Jacobs, 27 Misc. 2d 602, 211 N.Y.S.2d 217 (Sup 1961), where a New York court ruled a hospital, whose license was revoked, was entitled to a hearing and an opportunity to refute charges against the institution. The court stated the hospital was entitled to a decision based on findings of fact that could be judicially reviewed.

28 See early discussion in "Joint Commission on Accreditation of Hospitals," 146 J.A.M.A. 263, 834 (1951) and 147 J.A.M.A. 761, 1242 (1951), and in "A History of the Joint Commission on Accreditation of Hospitals," 258 J.A.M.A. 936, 938 (1987).

The Joint Commission provides accreditation and certification services for more than 20,000 health care organizations and programs in the United States. It accredits over eighty percent of U.S. hospitals. The purpose of accreditation is to enhance the quality of care and patient safety by meeting accreditation standards.

29 The Joint Commission authored and copyrighted updated comprehensive manuals for hospitals in 2009 and 2011. The Joint Commission has licensed the 2009 and 2011 copyrighted manuals to third parties who pay licensing fees to exercise some or all the rights it owns, including reproduction, distribution, public performance and display of the works, and preparation of derivative works. The Joint Commission has granted the Joint Commission Resources, Inc., which it controls, the right to carry out the Joint Commission's education, publication, and accreditation preparation functions and to copy, sell, distribute, and publish materials owned by the Joint Commission.

of surveyors designated by JCAHO to conduct on-site visits of a hospital to evaluate the quality of the facility's environment and to review its administrative records to determine whether they conform to applicable standards.[30] Any individual or group, including patients interested in the accreditation of a facility, can request an interview with the surveyors to present information or recommendations bearing on the facility's fitness for accreditation. Notice of the opportunity to request interviews is posted by the facility in a public place several weeks in advance of the survey.[31] From information collected during the survey, the Accreditation Committee will make a preliminary decision to accredit or not to accredit.[32] A hospital is entitled to a review before an Appeals Hearing Board if the decision is adverse and can have a final review by the JCAHO Board of Commissioners.[33]

Both federal and state governments have relied upon standards of the Joint Commission as a guarantee of high quality of medical care.[34] Hospitals accredited by JCAHO generally will meet the conditions of participation required for a hospital to qualify as a provider in the Medicare and Medicaid programs.[35]

A 2021 Comprehensive Manual for Hospitals is available in a three-ring updatable binder.

30 See early rules set out in Comprehensive Accreditation Manual for Hospitals (CAMH/98), Joint Commission on Accreditation of Healthcare Organizations (1999). To be accredited a hospital must have a governing body, an organized medical staff and nursing service, and the primary functions of diagnosis treatment and rehabilitation. It must have all current licenses required by governmental authorities having jurisdiction.

31 Discussion refers to procedures set out in an earlier accreditation manual, the Comprehensive Accreditation Manual for Hospitals (CAMH/98), Joint Commission on Accreditation of Healthcare Organization (1999).

32 See Comprehensive Accreditation Manual for Hospitals (CAMH/98), Joint Commission on Accreditation of Healthcare Organizations (1999). Earlier, there were seven possible accreditation decisions: (1) Accreditation with Commendation; (2) Accreditation; (3) Accreditation with Type I Recommendations; (4) Provisional Accreditation; (5) Conditional Accreditation; (6) Preliminary Nonaccreditation; and (7) Not Accredited.

33 Discussion in Comprehensive Accreditation Manual for Hospitals (CAMH/98, Joint Commission on Accreditation of Healthcare Organizations (1999).

34 See discussion in "A History of the Joint Commission on Accreditation of Hospitals, "258 J.A.M.A. 936, 939 (1987). Many states have incorporated JCAHO standards into their hospital licensure systems.

35 42 U.S.C. §§ 1395aa(c), 1395bb, and 1395x(e).

Two federally subsidized health insurance programs, commonly known as the Medicare and Medicaid programs, provide insurance for the cost of hospital and related posthospital services for specified individuals, to include the elderly, disabled, and low-income persons.[36] The Medicare and Medicaid programs are governed by very complex statutes.[37] As one court commented, interpretation and application of provisions relating to these programs is "no simple feat."[38] A comprehensive review of all the provisions related to the Medicare and Medicaid programs is beyond the scope of this book, but a brief summary follows to describe the programs and inform the reader of the major provisions.

Medicare is a social insurance program administered by the federal government that covers the elderly and persons with disabilities while Medicaid is a public welfare program administered separately by each state and covers low-income persons who cannot afford the cost of medical care. The programs authorize the Secretary of the U.S. Department of Health and Human Services (HHS) to determine what claims are covered in accordance with regulations prescribed by the Secretary.[39] Providers participating in the program receive

---

36 Both programs were promulgated under the Social Security Amendments of 1965, Title XVIII of the Social Security Act, 42 U.S.C.A. § 1395, which amended the Social Security Act of 1935. Medicare taxes, which is a part of Social Security taxes, fund the Medicare program. Payments are made from the Federal Hospital Insurance Trust Fund. 42 U.S.C. § 1395g.

37 See 42 U.S.C. §1395 et seq. Both Medicare and Medicaid programs are promulgated under the Social Security Amendment of 1965.

38 See comment in Collins v. Wellcare Healthcare Plans, Inc., 73 F. Supp. 3d 653, 660 (E.D. La. 2018).

39 42 U.S.C.A. § 1395(a).

In Thomas Jefferson University v. Shalala, 512 U.S. 504 (1994), the Supreme Court ruled a hospital was not entitled to reimbursement of its cost of a residency program. The hospital trained interns and residents by having them provide patient care. The Secretary of HHS pointed out the Medicare program was forbidden by regulation from "participating in increased costs resulting from redistribution of costs from educational institutions to patient care institutions." The Court agreed with the Secretary that a hospital's increased costs from educational activities in the clinical training of residents and interns was a shifting of educational costs to the hospital. It also agreed with the Secretary that Medicare providers may not be reimbursed for such educational costs.

The HHS issued final rules on Medicare Accountable Care Organizations (ACOs), which support options for health providers to coordinate care for patients. The rules established a voluntary Medicare Shared Savings Program and a complementary program to help test an Advance Payment model that would provide additional support to physician-owned and rural providers in participating in the Medicare Shared Savings Program (MSSP). The MSSP, which provides incentives for health care providers who agree to work together and become accountable for coordinating care for patients, was created pursuant to § 1899 of the Social Security Act, 42 U.S.C. § 1395jj, added by §3022 of the Affordable Care Act, Pub. L. No. 111-148 (2010). The program is intended to encourage providers of services and suppliers (hospitals and physicians) to create a new type of health care entity, the ACO, which agrees to be held accountable for improving the health

payments either covering the costs of certain services they have rendered or based on a fixed rate for each "Diagnosis Related Group" (DRG).[40]

A hospital must meet certain conditions to participate in the Medicare and Medicaid programs.[41] A hospital must be licensed pursuant to state law and must

---

and experience of care for individuals and improving the health of populations while reducing the rate of growth in health care spending. The goal of the ACO is to deliver high quality care for Medicare beneficiaries instead of the fragmented care that has been part of fee-for-service health care. The ACO would be a patient-centered organization where the patient and providers are partners in care decisions and Medicare would pay with lump sum payments no matter how many services were delivered. See Notice 2011-20 for guidance regarding the participation of tax-exempt organizations in non-MSSP activities through ACOs.

40 42 U.S.C. § 1395g(a). Medicare reimbursement changed in 1983 from a retrospective reimbursement to a prospective payment system (PPS). See Social Security Amendments of 1983, Pub. L. No. 98-21, 98th Cong., 1st Sess. Under PPS, hospitals were paid on a predetermined amount for each inpatient case. Rates differed for urban and rural hospitals. The rates were the product of two numbers: the weight assigned by the Secretary of HHS to a DRG and a national average cost of treating a Medicare patient. 42 U.S.C. § 1395ww(d)(e). A DRG is a grouping of comparable types of patients and illnesses whose cost of treatment is expected to be similar. The weight assigned to each DRG was multiplied by the national average rate to determine a hospital's payment for treating a patient falling within that DRG. The PPS system completely changed the method of reimbursing a hospital's Medicare costs. Prior to 1983, hospitals were reimbursed for the "reasonable costs" of providing patient care. (Hospitals still are reimbursed for most outpatient expenses based on reasonable costs.) To recover these costs, hospitals entered into agreements with the Secretary of HHS to provide Medicare beneficiaries with medical services. Payments to the hospitals were determined by "fiscal intermediaries," usually private insurance companies, which acted as agents for the Secretary. Payments were made on a "reasonable cost" analysis that allowed for provisional payments to a hospital during a given year based on estimates of the hospital's costs. After the end of each fiscal year, the hospital submitted a cost report to the intermediary that audited the report to determine reimbursable costs. This determination was set forth in a Notice of Program Reimbursement (NPR). If the hospital disagreed with an intermediary's decision, it could request a hearing before the Provider Reimbursement Review Board (PRRB) when the amount in controversy was $10,000 or more. 42 U.S.C. § 1395oo(a). The PRRB is a body within the HHS. The provider had to file a request for a hearing within 180 days after notice of the intermediary's final determination. 42 U.S.C. § 1395oo(a). The Secretary of HHS may review the decision of the PRRB. 42 U.S.C. § 1395oo(f). Under the amended prospective payment system, a hospital may obtain administrative review before the PRRB after the Secretary has made a "final determination" as to the amount of payment under 42 U.S.C.A. § 1395ww(b) or (d). 42 U.S.C. § 1395oo(a)(1)(A)(ii). If the final administrative decision is adverse to the provider, the provider may obtain judicial review in the appropriate district court. The district court's review is in accordance with the Administrative Procedure Act and is based on the administrative record. See 5 U.S.C. § 706.

41 Conditions of participation at 42 C.F.R. § 482.1.

In Blue Valley Hospital, Inc. v. Azar, 919 F.3d 1278 (10th Cir. 2019), an acute care hospital that provided a range of medical services brought an action seeking injunctive relief to prevent the HHS and the Centers for Medicare and Medicaid Services (CMS) from terminating its Medicare certification and provider contracts pending review by an administrative appeals board and subsequent judicial review and to enjoin HHS and CMS from publishing, disseminating, or communicating to third parties or the public any notice or communication suggesting that the hospital's Medicare participation right had been or would be decertified or terminated. The Court of Appeals for the Tenth Circuit ruled the hospital had to exhaust its administrative appeals before a federal court would have jurisdiction. For a treatment facility to retain hospital classification under the Medicare and Medicaid program the facility must be "primarily engaged" in providing care to "inpatients." After CMS had conducted an unannounced onsite survey of the hospital,

be in conformity with laws relating to fire and safety.[42] It also must have an effective governing body legally responsible for the conduct of the hospital that has adopted bylaws for its governance.[43] In addition, a hospital must have a chief executive officer and a medical staff all of whom are licensed or registered in accordance with applicable laws.[44] Every patient must be under the care of a physician.[45] The buildings of the hospital must be constructed, arranged, and maintained to insure the safety of the patient and to provide facilities for diagnosis and treatment and for special hospital services appropriate to the needs of the community.[46] Standards were established for hospital buildings.[47] A hospital must have an organized nursing department, medical record department, pharmacy or drug storage area, diagnostic radiologic services, laboratory services, food and dietetic services, and a utilization review plan.[48] A hospital that loses its accreditation generally also will lose its right to participate in the Medicare program.[49]

1. Medicare Program

Congress enacted the Medicare Act in 1965 by adding a new Title, Title XVIII, to the Social Security Act.[50] The Medicare Act is administered by the federal government and covers the disabled and elderly persons who have paid into

---

it sent the hospital a noncompliance notice detailing deficiencies the onsite survey uncovered. Specifically, CMS determined that the facility did not meet either the two-patient average daily census requirement or the two-night average length of stay requirement. The court ruled the Medicare Act's administration channeling requirement precluded the court's jurisdiction, that the exhaustion requirements were not excused, and that due process did not require the hospital be given a pre-termination hearing.

42 42 C.F.R. § 482.11.

43 42 C.F.R. § 482.12.

44 42 C.F.R. §§ 482.11 to 482.12.

45 42 C.F.R. § 482.12(c).

46 42 C.F.R. § 482.41.

47 42 C.F.R. § 482.41(a).

48 42 C.F.R. §§ 482.23 to 482.30.

49 Accreditation must be distinguished from certification by the Secretary of HHS for eligibility in federal assistance programs. While accreditation may be a component of certification, the two are not necessarily coextensive. An institution may either be accredited by JCAHO or may meet requirements equivalent to such accreditation requirements. Thus, an institution could bypass JCAHO accreditation and seek certification directly from the secretary. See 42 U.S.C.A. § 395x(e).

50 Discussion in Collins v. Wellcare Healthcare Plans, Inc., 73 F. Supp. 3d 653 (E.D. La. 2018).

the Medicare system through the years by payroll or self-employment taxes.[51] The traditional Medicare program consists of five parts–Part A, B, C, D, and E. Parts A and B are mutually exclusive parts that create, describe, and regulate traditional fee-for-service, government-administered medicare.[52] Part C outlines the Medicare Advantage program, described below. Part D provides for prescription drug coverage for Medicate beneficiaries. Part E contains definitions and exclusions;[53] its definitions define posthospital extended care services to include skilled nursing facilities consisting of nursing care and bed and board.[54]

Parts A and B contain provisions that entitle eligible persons to have the Centers for Medicare and Medicaid Services (CMS)[55] directly pay medical providers for eligible persons' hospital and outpatient care.[56] Part A provides insurance for hospital and hospital-related services,[57] and its costs are categorized into DRGs that are calculated separately for urban and rural hospitals.[58] The separate rural and urban prospective payment rates has caused rural hospitals to

51 Discussion in Thomas Jefferson Univ. v. Shalala, 512 U.S. 504 (1994).

52 See U.S.C. §§ 1395c to 1395i-5; 1395-j to 1395-w. See also In re Avandia Mktg. Sales Practices Products Liability Litigation, 685 F.3d 353 (3rd Cir. 2012).

Part B separately pays clinicians for E-visits, which are non-face-to-face patient-initiated communications through an online patient portal. Medicare beneficiaries can receive a specific set of services through telehealth, discussed below.

53 42 U.S.C. § 1395y(b). An inclusion is the Medicare Secondary Payer Act (MSP), discussed below.

54 42 U.S.C. § 1395x.

55 The Center for Medicare and Medicaid Services (CMS) is a federal agency within the Department of Health and Human Services (HHS) to administer the Medicare and Medicaid programs. The CMS and the Joint Commission ensure compliance with federal regulatory standards for hospitals to ensure quality care and patient safety.

56 Discussion by the Court of Appeals of the Eleventh Circuit in Humana Medical Plan, Inc. v. Western Heritage Insurance Co., 832 F.3d 1229 (11th Cir. 2019).

57 5742 U.S.C. § 1395g(a). If a hospital admits a patient as an inpatient based on a physician's order, Part A generally will cover inpatient services. If a patient needs a skilled nursing facility (SNF) after the patient leaves the hospital, Part A would pay for the SNF only if the patient had a prior qualifying inpatient stay.

58 5842 U.S.C. § 1395g(a). The Health Care Financing Administration (HCFA) developed prospective rating formulas to calculate the reimbursement in each case. The concept behind the DRG was that the costs incurred in treating patients with a particular diagnosis should be the same. The DRG formula covered all hospital services. Hospitals had to contain costs to meet the HCFA fixed reimbursement. (Determination of payments under the system at 42 C.F.R. Part 412.)

Medicare payment for inpatient stays begins after a patient satisfies the Part A inpatient hospital deductible. The amount of the Medicare payments is based on a DRG reflecting the severity of the patient's condition.

receive less reimbursement than urban hospitals.[59] Under Part B, reimbursement for services is based on reasonable charges, or for hospitals, on reasonable costs, and generally are greater than Part A payments.[60] There are often questions whether costs for hospital-based physicians, such as pathologists, radiologists, and anesthesiologists, are Part A or Part B payments.[61] Part A payments include

59 42 U.S.C. §§ 1395g(a) and 1395ww. See also 42 C.F.R. § 412.63.

60 42 U.S.C. §§ 1395j to 1395uu. Thus, while under the Prospective Payment System (PPS), discussed in note 40, inpatient care was based on a preestablished rate for each DRG, hospitals were reimbursed for most outpatient expenses based on reasonable costs. Reasonable costs are those costs that are appropriate and helpful in developing and maintaining the operation of patient care facilities and activities. 42 C.F.R. § 413.9. Providers of service are paid the lesser of reasonable cost of services or the customary charges made by the provider for the same service. 42 C.F.R. § 413.13. For outpatient stays, Medicare Part B (rather than part A) pays eighty percent (80%) of the amount billed, with the patient being responsible for twenty percent (20%) (frequently covered by medigap insurance, which is a Medicare supplement insurance policy). However, some people have Part A coverage but not Part B coverage; these people are responsible for the full cost of outpatient treatment.

In 2014, the CMS adopted a "two-midnight" policy under which Medicare generally treats a hospital stay as outpatient unless the doctor expects the beneficiary to remain in a hospital for a time covering at least two midnights.

CMS had concluded short inpatient stays should be treated as outpatient care if the patient remained in the hospital for less than two midnights. Because of the differences in the payment for inpatient and outpatient hospital care, patients had to pay more for long outpatient stays than they would have paid if they had been admitted as inpatients. Hospitals now are required to give patients who are in observation status for a period lasting more than twenty-four hours notice that the patient is considered an outpatient and must explain the differences in the hospital bill. (Pub. L. No. 114-41, 129 Stat. 443, 42 U.S.C. § 1305.) A hospital must give a patient notice within thirty-six hours to inform the patient of treatment as an outpatient and explain the implications for the hospital bill. In 2016, CMS published a proposal--the Medicate Outpatient Observation Notice (MOON), to provide notice to patients pursuant to the requirement. Hospitals had to begin providing MOON by March 2017. The MOON requires a hospital to explain why a stay is not an inpatient admission, the hospital's charges, how post-hospital care is covered, and information for Medicare participants who are covered by Medicaid. 42 U.S.C. § 1305.

61 42 C.F.R. §§ 405.550(b), 405.552 to 405.556 set out the requirements for these type services to qualify as Part B payments.

See 42 U.S.C. § 1395. Beginning in 1984, doctors could elect to become "participating physicians" if they agreed to accept Medicare's approved charge as full payment on all claims, less any deductible. 42 U.S.C. § 1395u(h)(1). Nonparticipating physicians could decide whether to accept Medicare's approved charge on a case-by-case basis and, therefore, could charge patients more than the approved charge reimbursable from Medicare. However, Congress also added subsection (j) to 42 U.S.C. § 1395u to provide that a nonparticipating physician could not charge a Medicare patient more than the physician's actual charges. Each physician's actual charges had to be monitored to determine whether to apply sanctions against those physicians who knowingly and willfully charged a Medicare patient an amount more than their actual charges. The incentives offered to induce doctors to become "participating physicians" were the direct payment from Medicare, the dissemination of participating physicians' names through directories and toll-free telephone information lines, and rates potentially higher than for most nonparticipating doctors after the freeze period. 42 U.S.C. § 1395u(h). Physicians who treat Medicare patients had to elect annually whether to become participating physicians. 42 U.S.C. § 1395u(h). An election is irrevocable for one calendar year. Medicare claims were handled and paid by carriers designated by the Secretary of HHS for geographic locations, i.e., the states.

In Multnomah County Medical Soc. v. Scott, 825 F.2d 1410 (9th Cir. 1987), the Court of Appeals for the Ninth Circuit decided the 1984 amendments to the Medicare law were in the public interest to provide incentives

payments for post-hospital extended care services and home health services.[62] Utilization review committees are established by each state to review the extent of care needed by each patient. These committees consist of at least two physicians and may include other professional personnel such as registered nurses or medical social workers.[63] Post hospital extended care services Medicare benefits are reviewed by a utilization review committee to determine if the services are medically necessary.[64]

---

for physicians to become "participating physicians" and to accept assignment for all Medicare claims. The Ninth Circuit ruled a nonprofit medical professional organization was not entitled to the names and addresses of Medicare beneficiaries under the Freedom of Information Act. The medical organization wanted to send the beneficiaries a copy of its newsletter explaining the changes in the Medicare law along with a list of both participating and nonparticipating physicians. The court ruled the organization had a commercial interest in the list of beneficiaries and that the interest did not warrant disclosure under the FOIA. The beneficiaries had a right not to have their age and disability status made public in the absence of more compelling public and private interests favoring disclosure.

62 42 U.S.C. § 1395d(a). Hospice care was covered under Medicare if conditions set out in the Regulations, 42 C.F.R. part 418, are met. A "hospice" is a public agency or a private organization or a subdivision of either of these, which is primarily engaged in providing care to terminally ill individuals in the form of providing physicians' services, nursing care, medical social services, and counselling services both to the terminally ill individual and to the family members or other persons caring for the individual at home. See 42 C.F.R. §§ 418.3 and 418.50. Short-term inpatient care is provided in participating hospice inpatient units or in participating hospitals. Inpatient care may also be furnished as a means of providing respite for the individual's family or other persons caring for the individual at home. See 42 C.F.R. § 418.98. A freestanding hospice that provides inpatient care directly must comply with standards set out at 42 C.F.R. § 418.100. It must provide 24-hour nursing services, sufficient to meet total nursing needs, which are in accordance with the patient plan of care. Each patient must receive treatments, medications, and diet as prescribed and must be kept comfortable, clean, well-groomed, and protected from accident, injury, and infection. The hospice must meet safety, health, cleanliness, and fire protection standards as set out at 42 C.F.R. § 418.100. Medicare reimbursement is provided for routine home care, inpatient respite care, and physicians' services. See 42 C.F.R. §418.302. For services to be covered by Medicare, certification must be obtained that the individual is terminally ill; and the individual must elect to receive care with a hospice. See 42 C.F.R. §§ 418.22 and 418.24.

63 42 U.S.C. § 1395x(k).

64 42 U.S.C. § 1395f(a)(6). See also 42 C.F.R. § 405.1137. The attending physician must be given an opportunity to consult with the committee before the committee can find that further services are not necessary. See 42 U.S.C. § 1395x(k)(4). If a patient is eligible for extended care, Medicare will cover the services up to 100 days during any spell of illness. See 42 U.S.C.A. § 1395d(a)(2)(A).

In Lawrence Memorial Hosp. v. Burwell, 812 F.3d 257 (2d Cir. 2016), an acute care hospital geographically located in an urban area had sought reclassification as a "rural hospital" in order to participate in a favorable drug pricing program. The Court of Appeals for the Second Circuit pointed out that hospitals initially are classified to urban or rural areas based on their geographical location. Hospitals' reimbursements are calculated based on rates prospectively determined for a fiscal year, not on the hospitals' actual costs, and to calculate these rates, the Secretary of HHS establishes a nationwide standardized rate for hospitals located in urban or rural areas. Congress amended the Medicare Act to create the Medicare Geographic Classification Review Board (MCCRB) to consider hospitals' applications to change the hospital's geographic classification for purposes of determining the hospital's average standardized reimbursement amount or wage index. See 42 U.S.C. § 1395ww(d)(10)(C)(i). The Medicare statute permits a hospital to be classified

Part C of the Medicare program is the Medicare Advantage program under which Medicare persons may elect to receive their benefits through original Medicare or a private organization, known as a Medicare Advantage Organization (MAO). Part C permits beneficiaries to have access to a wide array of private health plan choices in addition to traditional fee-for-service Medicare; it enables the Medicare program to utilize innovations that have helped the private market contain costs and expand healthcare delivery options.[65] A court[66] set out the process as follows: the CMS pays a MAO a fixed amount for each enrollee to deliver their benefits.[67] The MAO then delivers Medicare benefits to the enrollee, and the MAO assumes the risks related to insuring those beneficiaries.[68] The MAO is required to provide the benefits covered under Parts A and B to enrollees, but it may also provide additional benefits to its enrollees.

Part E includes the Secondary Payer Act,[69] which applies to Parts A, B, C, and D. Before 1980, Medicare paid for all medical treatment within its scope and private insurers merely picked up whatever expenses remained.[70] However, in an effort to curb the rising costs of Medicare Congress enacted the Medicare Secondary Payer (MSP) provisions[71] in 1980 to make private insurers covering

---

as urban for some purposes and rural for others. Pursuant to 42 U.S.C. § 1395ww(d)(10), a MGCRB can redesignate hospitals to a different area from that to which they have been otherwise designated in order to receive a different wage reimbursement rate. However, in 2000, the Secretary of HHS issued a regulation, known as the "reclassification rule," 42 C.F.R. § 412.230(a)(5)(iii), which provided that a hospital, reclassified from urban to rural under subsection (d)(10), could not thereafter receive an additional reclassification by the MGCRB for reclassification as urban. The hospital sued for injunctive relief to prevent the Secretary from applying the reclassification rule to an application the hospital had filed with the MCCRB for redesignation as an "urban hospital" to receive the more favorable wage reimbursement rate under the Medicare statute. The court ruled the regulation contravenes the plain language of the statute and, thus, exceeded the Secretary's authority. The court ruled the regulation was invalid. The court added that there could be several situations in which hospitals could be treated as rural for some purposes and urban for others.

65 Collins v. Wellcare Healthcare Plans, Inc., 73 F. Supp. 3d 653 (E.D. La. 2018).

66 Id.

67 42 U.S.C. §§ 1395w-21, 1395w-23.

68 42 U.S.C. § 1495w-22(a)(1)-(3). See In re Avandia Mktg. Sales Practices Products Liability Litigation, 685 F.3d 353 (3rd Cir. 2012).

The MAO administers the provision of Medicare benefits pursuant to a contract with CMS.

69 42 U.S.C. § 1395y.

70 See discussion by the Court of Appeals for the Eleventh Circuit in Humana Medical Plan, Inc. v. Western Heritage Insurance Co., 832F.3d 1229 (11 Cir. 2016).

71 Omnibus Reconciliation Act of 1980, Pub. L. No 90-499, 94 Stat. 2599, codified at 42 U.S.C. § 1395y. The statute provides that Medicare cannot pay medical expenses when payment has been made or can reasonably be expected to be made under a workman's compensation law plan of the United States or a State or under an automobile or liability insurance policy or plan (including a self-

the same treatment as the 'primary' payers and Medicare the 'secondary' payer.[72] The MSP designates Medicare as the secondary payer with respect to nearly all insurers and nearly all categories of Medicare eligibility.[73] The MSP forbids payment by Medicare when another insurer has paid or is expected to pay.[74] Additionally, the MSP requires all payments by Medicare to be conditioned on reimbursement whenever Medicare discovers that another insurer has paid or should have paid.[75]

To ensure efficiency and quality in the Medicare program, hospitals receiving Medicare funds had to maintain agreements with Utilization and Quality Control Peer Review Organizations (PROs).[76] A PRO is a group of physicians, with at least one individual representative of consumers, which reviews the professional activities of local physicians and hospitals that receive Medicare funds to determine: (1) whether the services are reasonable and medically necessary, (2) whether the quality of the services meets professionally recognized standards of health care, and (3) whether services and items proposed to be provided by a hospital on an inpatient basis could be effectively provided more economically, consistent with the provisions of appropriate medical care, on an outpatient basis or in an inpatient health care facility of a different type.[77]

---

insured plan) or no-fault insurance. 42 U.S. C. § 1935y(b)(2)(A)(ii). If a primary plan has not made or cannot reasonably be expected to make payment, Medicare can make a conditional payment and because Medicare remains the secondary payer, the primary plan must reimburse Medicare for the conditional payment. 42 U.S.C. §§ 1395y(b)(2)(B)(i) and (ii).

72 Discussion by the Court of Appeals for the Fifth Circuit in Caldera v. Insurance Co. of the State of PA, 716 F.3d 861 (5th Cir. 2013) and by the Court of Appeals for the Eleventh Circuit in Humana Medical Plan, Inc. v. Western Heritage Insurance Co., 832F.3d 1229 (11 Cir. 2016). See also Collins v. Wellcare Healthcare Plans, Inc. 73 F. Supp. 3d 653 (E.D. La 2018). Medicare serves as a back-up insurance plan to cover what is not paid for by a primary insurance plan. As the Eleventh Circuit noted in Humana Medical Plan, Medicare benefits became an entitlement of last resort, available only if no private insurer was liable. Because Medicare is a "secondary payer" of medical benefits, it is precluded from providing benefits when a "primary plan" could be expected to pay. See discussion by the Court of Appeals for the Third Circuit in Taransky v. Sec'y of HHS, 760 F.3d 307 (3rd Cir. 2014).

Congress also created a private right of action. 42 U.S.C. § 1395(b)(3)(A). However, it is not explicit as to who may bring suit or against whom, or under what conditions suit may be brought.

73 Discussion by the Court of Appeals for the Ninth Circuit in DeVita Inc. v. Virginia Mason Memorial Hospital, 981 F.3d 679 (9th Cir. 2020). See also the Ninth Circuit's discussion in California Insurance Guarantee Assoc. v. Azar, 940 F.3d 1061 (9th Cir. 2019).

74 42 U.S.C. § 1395(b)(2)(A).

75 42 U.S.C. § 1395(b)(2)(B).

76 42 U.S.C. § 1320c. PROs superseded Professional Standards Review organizations (PSROs).

77 42 U.S.C. § 1320c-1, 1320c-13(1)(A) to (C). Failure of a Medicare provider to deliver services econom-

The primary goal of Congress in enacting the Peer Review Improvement Act[78] is to provide a review system that will end excessive reimbursements to hospitals for treatment of Medicare patients.[79]

2. Medicaid Program

Title XIX of the Social Security Act,[80] commonly known as "Medicaid," makes federal grants-in-aid available to states to enable a state to furnish medical assistance on behalf of families with dependent children. The act also provides assistance for the aged, blind, or disabled individuals whose income and resources are insufficient to meet the costs of necessary medical services and provides aid to help families and individuals attain or retain capability for independence or self-care.[81] Through the use of federal funds, the Medicaid Act operates to

---

ically and only when medically necessary, that meet professionally recognized standards, and that are supported by evidence of necessity and quality could result in sanctions, including temporary or permanent exclusion from the Medicare program. See 42 U.S.C. § 1320c-5. Any provider who is dissatisfied with a determination of a PRO is entitled to a reconsideration of the determination by a reviewing organization. Pursuant to 42 U.S.C. § 405(g), review is with the Secretary of HHS. The PRO recommendation is submitted to the Office of the Inspector General (OIG). The OIG determination can be heard before an Administrative Law Judge and reviewed by an Appeals Council. After a final decision on the merits of the sanctions, the provider can seek judicial review. See 42 C.F.R. part 1004 for the procedures for review of a decision of a PRO.

In Lavapies v. Bowen, 687 F. Supp. 1193 (S.D. Ohio 1988), decision aff'd, 883 F.2d 465 (6th Cir. 1989), a physician was notified she would be excluded from participation in the Medicare program for a period of one year after a PRO determined she had failed to provide medical services that met professionally recognized standards. The court decided suspension of provider status under the Medicare program implicated a property interest protected under the Fifth Amendment in that suspension from the program would have an impact on the ability of the physician to admit patients to local hospitals and to participate in HMOs. In addition, the physician will not be permitted to continue as the medical director of an alcohol treatment program administered by the health district. The court also noted that because the government would publish a notice of the physician's suspension, there would be potential impact on the physician's ability to practice; thus, the publication could rise to the implication of a liberty interest. The court determined that because the PRO failed to inform the physician of the evidence against her prior to her pre-suspension hearing, she was denied due process.

78 42 U.S.C. § 1320c.

79 See American Hosp. Ass'n v. Bowen, 834 F.2d 1037 (D.C. Cir. 1987), for an excellent and thorough discussion of the PRO program by the Court of Appeals for the District of Columbia Circuit.

80 42 U.S.C. § 1396. The act established the Medicaid and CHIP Payment and Access Commission (MACPAC) to review policies of the Medicaid program and State Children's Health Insurance Program (CHIP). The committee reviews payment policies to determine the degree to which federal and state policies provide health care coverage to the needy population.

81 42 U.S.C. § 1396. See, the Supreme Court's view as to the construction and application of the Medicaid Act at 85 L Ed 2d 935 (1985).

In Wilder v. Virginia Hosp. Ass'n, 496 U.S. 498 (1990), the Supreme Court ruled a health care provider may

enable participating states to provide medical services to welfare recipients (the "categorically needy") and if the state chooses, to other needy individuals (the "medically needy").[82] A state participation in Medicaid is voluntary; however, if a state does choose to participate, it must comply with the requirements set out in the act.[83] To participate, a state must submit a medical assistance plan that meets with the approval of the Secretary of HHS.[84]

---

bring an action under 42 U.S.C. § 1983 to challenge the method by which a state reimburses health care providers under the Medicaid Act. The Court decided the Boren Amendment to the Medicaid Act created a right, enforceable in a private cause of action pursuant to 42 U.S.C. § 1983, to have a state adopt rates that are reasonable and adequate to meet the costs of an efficient and economical health care provider.

82 Beal v. Doe, 432 U.S. 438 (1977). See also 42 U.S.C. § 396a(a)(10)(A), (C).

83 Harris v. McRae, 448 U.S. 297 (1980).

In National Federation of Independent Business v. Sebelius, 567 U.S. 519 (2012), the Supreme Court referred to a key provision of the Patient Protection and Affordable Act, 42 U.S.C. § 1396d(a), which expanded the scope of the Medicaid program and increased the number of individuals that states must cover. The act increased federal funding to cover the states' costs in expanding Medicaid to provide coverage by 2014 to adults with incomes up to 133 percent of the federal poverty level. The Court ruled the Patient Protection and Affordable Care Act of 2010 (ACA), Publ. L.No.111-148, 124 Stat. 119 (2010), is constitutional and upheld the Medicaid expansion. The Court, however ruled unconstitutional the part of the act that threatened states with loss of their existing Medicaid funding if they declined to comply with the expansion.

In Burwell v. Hobby Lobby Stores, Inc., 573 U.S. 682 (2014), the Supreme Court ruled HHS regulations in the ACA that require employers' group health plans to provide coverage for twenty contraceptive methods approved by the Food and Drug Administration (FDA), including four that are abortifacients, violated the Religious Freedom Restoration Act of 1993 (RFRA), 42 U.S.C. § 2000bb et seq., as they apply to those closely held for-profit corporations wherein the shareholders have sincere Christian beliefs that life begins at conception. The owners of two businesses who had religious objections to abortion contended that if they complied with the HHS mandates, they would be facilitating abortions, and if they did not comply, they would pay as much as $1.3 million per day in penalties, or about $475 million per year in the case of one of the companies. The Supreme Court determined that Congress designed the RFRA to provide very broad protection for religious liberty and did not intend to put merchants to such a choice. It noted that RFRA's definition of "persons" included corporations and stated that the purpose of extending rights to corporations was to protect the rights of persons associated with a corporation, including shareholders, officers, and employees. The Court commented that protecting the free-exercise rights of closely held corporations "protects the religious liberty of the humans who own and control them." The Court referred to the prohibition in RFRA for the federal government to take any action that substantially burdens the exercise of religion unless that action constitutes the least restrictive means of serving a compelling government interest. It ruled that the HHS regulations, which imposed the obligation for closely held corporations to provide methods of contraception that violate the sincerely held religious beliefs of the companies' owners, violated RFRA because, as the Court decided, there were other ways in which Congress or HHS could equally ensure that every woman had cost-free access to the contraceptives at issue in the case. (Discussion of abortions in Chapter V.)

In Armstrong v. Exceptional Child Center, Inc., 575 U.S. 320 (2015), providers of residential habilitation services to Medicaid-eligible individuals brought action against the Director and Deputy Director of a state's Department of Health and Welfare, challenging that department's failure to amend existing Medicaid reimbursement rates and seeking injunctive relief. The Supreme Court ruled that the ability to sue to enjoin unconstitutional actions by state officers does not rest upon an implied right of action in the Supremacy Clause and that the Medicaid Act did not authorize providers' private action for injunctive relief to enforce the act's reimbursement-rate standard against a state.

84 42 U.S.C. §§ 1396 to 1396a.

Participating states must provide the categorically needy with financial assistance in five categories of medical treatment.[85] Although a participating state need not provide funding for all medical treatment within the five categories, the act does require that a state Medicaid plan establish reasonable standards for determining the extent of medical assistance under the plan that is consistent with the objectives of the federal act.[86]

---

85 42 U.S.C. § 396d(a) and 42 C.F.R. §§ 440.10 to 440.50, 440.210. These are: inpatient hospital services; outpatient hospital services; other laboratory and X-ray services; skilled nursing facility services; and physician's services. The act also specifies that other types of remedial care, such as chiropractor's services; home health services; private duty nursing services; clinic services; dental services; physical therapy and related services; prescribed drugs; dentures and prosthetic devices and eyeglasses; and other diagnostic, screening, preventive, and rehabilitative services can be provided. See 42 U.S.C. § 1396d(a).

86 42 U.S.C. § 1396a(a)(17) and 42 C.F.R. §§ 440.210 to 440.270. Since 1976, Congress has prohibited the use of any federal funds to reimburse the states for the cost of abortions. See, e.g., Pub. L. No. 95-205, 91 Stat. 1460; Pub. L. No. 95-480, 92 Stat. 1586; Pub. L. No. 96-123, 93 Stat. 926; Pub. L. No. 98-619, 98 Stat. 3321. The funding restriction is commonly known as the Hyde Amendment.

In Maher v. Roe, 432 U.S. 464 (1977), the Court ruled Connecticut's exclusion of funding for nontherapeutic abortions did not violate the equal protection clause of the Fourteenth Amendment. See also Williams v. Zbaraz, 448 U.S. 358 (1980). The Court ruled in Beal v. Doe, 432 U.S. 438 (1977), that the Social Security Act, Title XIX, does not require the funding of nontherapeutic abortions as a condition to participation in the joint federal-state Medicaid program. In Maher v. Doe, the Court determined that a participating state need not pay for nontherapeutic abortions when it pays for childbirth.

In Harris v. McRae, 448 U.S. 297 (1980), the Supreme Court ruled that regardless of whether the freedom of a woman to choose to terminate her pregnancy for health reasons lies at the core of the due process liberty recognized in Roe v. Wade, 410 U.S. 113 (1973) (holding modified by, Planned Parenthood v. Casey, 505 U.S. 833 (1992)), a woman's freedom of choice does not carry with it a constitutional entitlement to the financial resources to avail herself of that choice. The Court also determined that the Medicaid Act does not obligate a participating state to pay for any abortion for which Congress has withheld federal funding even if the abortion was medically necessary.

In State of Ga. by Dept. of Medical Assistance v. Heckler, 768 F.2d 1293 (11th Cir. 1985), the Court of Appeals for the Eleventh Circuit determined the federal government was not required to reimburse the state for amounts paid for abortions performed prior to the Hyde Amendments.

In State of Ill. by Illinois Dept. of Public Aid v. U.S. Dept. of Health and Human Services, 772 F.2d 329 (7th Cir. 1985), the Court of Appeals for the Seventh Circuit ruled the federal government could not be required to reimburse the state for monies expended by the state in providing medically necessary abortions even though the state had been required to pay for such abortions by court order. However, in Com. of Pennsylvania v. Department of Health and Human Services, 723 F.2d 1114 (3d Cir. 1983), the Court of Appeals for the Third Circuit ruled the federal government was obligated to continue paying its share of Medicaid benefits for abortions performed during a reasonable time needed to provide public welfare recipients with notice of the reduction of benefits following adoption of the Hyde Amendments. (Further discussion of legal issues relating to abortions and federal funding for abortions is in Chapter V.)

In Bethesda Lutheran Homes and Services, Inc. v. Leean, 122 F.3d 443 (7th Cir. 1997), the Court of Appeals for the Seventh Circuit ruled a nonprofit organization that offered long term care to severely intellectually and developmentally disabled individuals could not refuse admission at its facility to nonresidents of the state. Nonresidents of the state were ineligible for Medicaid benefits at the facility. Nonetheless the Court ruled the nonprofit organization could not give preference to residents of the state.

The Medicaid program is based upon financial contributions by both the federal government and the participating state. Federal financial assistance is provided for all legitimate state expenditures under an approved Medicaid plan.[87]

Each state must identify a single state agency to operate the program.[88] The state health agency, or other appropriate state medical agency, must be responsible for establishing and maintaining health standards for private and public institutions that are recipients of medical assistance under the plan. Reimbursement to health providers differs in the state—some base reimbursement on costs and others employ some form of prospective payment or DRG. All individuals who wish to make application for medical assistance under the state plan must have an opportunity to do so.[89]

3. Fraud Provisions under Medicare and Medicaid Programs

Medicare fraud, roughly estimated at ten percent of Medicare's costs every year, has long plagued the healthcare system.[90] Hospitals and physicians are subject to civil and criminal penalties for violating the Medicare or Medicaid provisions.[91] The filing of false statements and the making of false representations regarding any Medicare or Medicaid benefits are felony offenses.[92] Accepting

---

87 See H.R. Rep. No. 213, 89th Cong., 1st Sess. 72-74, reprinted in 1965 U.S. Code Cong. & Admin. News 1943.

88 U.S.C. § 396a(a)(5) and 45 C.F.R. § 201.5.

89 42 U.S.C. § 1396a(a)(8). See 45 C.F.R. § 206.10 for application procedures. See 42 C.F.R. §§ 435.100 to 435.852 for requirements for coverage by Medicaid.

In Tekkno Laboratories, Inc. v. Perales, 933 F.2d 1093 (2d Cir. 1991), the Court of Appeals for the Second Circuit ruled the Eleventh Amendment was applicable to claims against the states by Medicaid providers. The Second Circuit noted that suit on these claims in federal court was barred because the claim involved a suit by a private party that would be paid from public funds in the state's treasury.

In Cruz v. Commissioner of Public Welfare, 395 Mass 107, 478 N.E.2d 1262 (1985), the Supreme Court of Massachusetts ruled any undocumented person residing in the United States under color of law within the meaning of federal regulations could receive Medicaid benefits even if that person was not eligible under state regulations. See 42 C.F.R. § 435.402. That court ruled a state program must meet the requirements of the federal act and its implementing regulations.

90 Discussion by the Court of Appeals for the Sixth Circuit in United States v. Daneshvar, 925 F.3d 766 (6th Cir. 2019).

91 42 U.S.C. § 1320a-7b. See also 42 C.F.R. §§ 455.1 to 455.106. A Medicaid agency must have methods for investigating suspected fraud cases.

92 42 U.S.C. §1320a-7b.

In U.S. v. Brown, 763 F.2d 984 (8th Cir. 1985), a pharmacy and one of its pharmacists were convicted of filing false claims for payment under the Medicaid program. The submission of a claim for reimbursement for

any remuneration directly or indirectly, whether in cash or in kind, in return for referring an individual to a person or entity for the furnishing of medical services, subject to reimbursement under either the Medicare or the Medicaid program, is a felony offense.[93]

Physicians must not be given benefits for admitting patients to hospitals.[94] Any payments or benefits received for the referral of Medicaid or Medicare patients are deemed to be "kickbacks" and are illegal under Medicare and Medicaid provisions.[95] Physicians and hospitals that are participating physicians or suppliers under the Medicare program and that accept assignments, may not knowingly and willfully violate the provisions of the assignments or agreements.[96] Physicians and hospitals may not charge Medicaid recipients more than the amount of reimbursement by the state.[97]

---

brand name drugs, when generic or over-the-counter drugs had been dispensed, was held to be a misrepresentation of a material fact within the meaning of the Medicaid fraud statute.

In U.S. v. Greber, 760 F.2[d] 68 (3[d] Cir. 1985), Medicare fraud was established when payments were made to a physician in return for referrals by that physician of Medicare patients to use the payer's laboratory services. The Court of Appeals for the Third Circuit ruled that if the payments were intended to induce the physician to use the organization's services, the statute was violated even if the payments were also intended to compensate the physician for professional services.

In Mayers v. U.S. Dept. of Health and Human Services, 806 F.2d 995 (11th Cir. 1986), the Court of Appeals for the Eleventh Circuit ruled the Civil Monetary Penalties and Assessment Act, 42 U.S.C. § 1320a-7a, providing for civil penalties for filing false Medicare claims for reimbursement, was constitutional. The Eleventh Circuit further determined that a penalty assessed against a chiropractor of $1,791,100, based upon the receipt of $24,697.73 from the Medicare program for filing false claims, was warranted by the aggravating circumstances in the case.

93 42 U.S.C. § 1320a-7b(b). Any type of payment or benefit in return for purchasing, leasing, or ordering any goods, facility, service, or item for which payment may be made under either the Medicare or the Medicaid program is also an illegal remuneration. Punishment has been a fine of not more than $25,000 or imprisonment for not more than five years, or both.

In U.S. v. Lipkis, 770 F.2d 1447 (9th Cir. 1985), a medical organization agreed to refer laboratory work to a medical laboratory organization for a kickback payment of twenty percent of the laboratory's revenue from the referrals. The FBI determined that the medical laboratory was paying illegal kickbacks as an inducement for the referral of Medicare business.

94 42 U.S.C. § 1320a-7b(b).

95 U.S. v. Lipkis, 770 F.2d 1447 (9th Cir. 1985); U.S. v. Greber, 760 F.2d 6 (3[d] Cir. 1985).

96 42 U.S.C. § 1320a-7(b)(7).

97 42 U.S.C. § 1320a-7b(d).

In Glengariff Corp. v. Snook, 122 Misc. 2d 784, 471 N.Y.S.2d 973 (1984), a patient was given a private room in a nursing home, rather than a semiprivate room, upon request of the patient's son. The patient became a Medicaid recipient after she entered the nursing home. The son had agreed to pay the nursing home a higher amount than the reimbursement by the state. The court ruled that the nursing home could not charge more than the amount provided by the state under the Medicaid program. The court noted that the knowing and willful charging of money to others as a requirement for a Medicaid patient's continued stay in a nursing home was a felony; thus, the court stated that if the nursing home operator required monetary

Physician home visits, which cost Medicare more than treatment in a doctor's office, can constitute fraud. To qualify for a home visit, a patient must be homebound, which occurs if the patient has a condition because of an illness or injury that restricts the patient's ability to leave the patient's place of residence without the aid of a supportive devise, such as a cane or wheelchair. Additionally, the patient must need a physician's services. However, these visits have occurred even when a patient was not homebound and did not need healthcare services.[98]

E. CONTROLLED SUBSTANCES ACT

Hospitals must have pharmaceutical services. This requirement carries with it additional governmental regulations, for the production, distribution, and use

supplements from non-financially responsible relatives of patients, it could be found guilty under the Medicaid fraud statute.

98 In United States v. Daneshvar, 925 F.3d 766 (6th Cir. 2019), a non-medical professional person opened an organization called Mobile Doctors, which was headquartered in Chicago but eventually expanded into seven states. This service offered physician services to homebound Medicare beneficiaries and hired doctors who agreed to assign their Medicare billing rights to the company. After a home visit, each doctor would fill out a routing slip describing the patient's diagnoses using Medicare codes and certifying that a qualified home visit had occurred. The original or the routing slip stayed with the patient file, while the carbon copy went to Mobile Doctors, which sought payment from Medicare. Upon receipt of payment, Mobile Doctors would then pay the physician-employee a percentage of what the company received from billing Medicare. The problem was that a large portion of Mobile Doctors' patients did not qualify as being homebound. For many patients, Mobile Doctors exaggerated the services they needed. Mobile Doctors also engaged in upcoding, a fraudulent practice in which a healthcare provider submitted a Medicare code for a more serious and more expensive diagnosis or procedure than the provider diagnosed or performed. Regardless of how healthy a patient was, the doctor usually selected only the two most expensive Medicare reimbursement codes for home healthcare. These codes are supposed to be rare but Mobile Doctors utilized them for almost every doctor's visit, even short visits that involved no tests or other assessments. To justify higher-reimbursement codes, Mobile Doctors instructed their physicians to list at least three diagnoses in the patient file; if the doctors did not list enough, a staff member added more to meet the three-diagnoses minimum. Typical diagnoses used to pad the claims were conditions common to persons over fifty years of age: degenerative joint diseases, degenerative disk disease, high blood pressure, chronic pain, arthritis, and vitamin D deficiency. Mobile Doctors only paid their physicians if they checked at least one of the top two billing codes on their routing slips. If the doctor billed for the higher of the top two codes, the doctor was paid more. The defendant began conducting home visits; in return for submitting his routing slips, he received payment from Mobile Doctors. According to one medical assistant, as many as half of the defendant's patients were not homebound. The defendant conducted the most home visits of any doctor employed by Mobile Doctors. He saw almost twenty patients per day. The defendant's conviction for conspiracy to commit health care fraud and his sentence of twenty-four months imprisonment and restitution $900,000 was affirmed by the appellate court.

of drugs or controlled substances are the most regulated of hospital services.[99] Some states regulate hospital pharmaceutical services through the licensing of the hospital; others require a separate license for a hospital pharmacy.

The distribution of drugs, as well as research in and treatment of drug abuse and rehabilitation programs, is covered by the Controlled Substances Act (CSA).[100] Enacted in 1970 with the main objectives of combatting drug abuse and controlling the legitimate and illegitimate traffic in controlled substances, the CSA creates a comprehensive, closed regulatory regime criminalizing the unauthorized manufacture, distribution, dispensing, and possession of substances classified in the Act's five schedules.[101] Controlled substances are classified into five schedules, I through V.[102] Substances listed in Schedule I, which includes marijuana, are the most restricted in terms of access and use, while those in Schedule V are the least restricted.[103] Although substances on Schedules II through V may be dispensed and prescribed for medical use, Schedule I drugs cannot be dispensed under a prescription.[104]

---

99 Both the states and the federal government regulate the production, distribution, and use of controlled substances or drugs. See Controlled Substance Act, 21 U.S.C.A. § 801 for the federal act. Each of the states adopted either the Uniform Controlled Substance Act or the Uniform Narcotic Drug Act.

100 Pub. L. No. 91-513, 21 U.S.C.A. § 801, 951. Congress enacted the CSA three years after the United States ratified the Single Convention on Narcotic Drugs in 1967, which is a codification of a single convention on international narcotics control. In 2017, a Memoranda of President, 82 F.R. 50305, set out the policy of the United States "to use all lawful means to combat the drug demand opioid crisis currently afflicting our country." The memoranda described the crisis as a public health emergency, and heads of executive departments and agencies were directed, consistent with law, to exercise all appropriate emergency authorities to reduce the number of deaths and minimize the devastation the drug demand and opioid crisis has inflicted upon American communities.

101 See, Marin Alliance for Medical Marijuana v. Holder, 866 F. Supp. 2d 1142 (N.D. Calif. 2011). See also Gonzales v. Oregon, 546 U.S. 243 (2006).

102 21 U.S.C.A. §§ 801(6), 812. See 21 U.S.C.A. § 812 and 21 C.F.R. §§ 1308.11 to 1308.15 for a list of the controlled substances in each schedule.

103 Discussion in Marin Alliance for Medical Marijuana v. Holder, 866 F. Supp. 2d 1142 (N.D. Calif. 2011).

104 United States v. Oakland Cannabis Buyers' Co-op, 532 U.S. 483 (2001). The inclusion of marijuana on Schedule I reflects the federal government's determination that it has no currently accepted medical use at all. As such, the federal CSA makes it illegal to manufacture, distribute, or possess marijuana. See 21 U.S.C. § 841. Further, it is illegal under the CSA to open, use, lease or maintain any place for the purpose of manufacturing, distributing, or using any controlled substances. 21 U.S.C. § 856(a)(1).

Several states have legalized the medical use of marijuana; however, federal law does not protect the use of the drug and it can prosecute a person protected under state law. As an example, California enacted the Compassionate Use Act in 1996, Cal. Health & Safety Code § 11362.5, to permit seriously ill patients to obtain medical marijuana upon written or oral recommendation of a physician. In Gonzales v. Raich, 545

Every person who manufactures, distributes, or dispenses any controlled substance must annually obtain a Certificate of Registration with the Drug Enforcement Administration (DEA).[105] All applicants and registrants must provide effective controls and procedures to guard against theft and diversion of controlled substances.[106] Registrants must maintain records and inventories of

U.S. 1 (2005), the Supreme Court ruled that the legislature's authority under the Commerce Clause includes the power to prohibit local cultivation and use of marijuana. It reasoned that the CSA was within Congress' Commerce Clause power because production of marijuana, even if limited to home consumption, has a substantial effect on the supply and demand in the national market for marijuana. The Court stated that exemptions permitting marijuana use under the Compassionate Use Act would have a significant impact on both the supply and demand sides of the market marijuana because they would provide physicians with an economic incentive to grant their patients permission to use the drug which, in turn, could only increase the supply of marijuana in the California market. On remand to the Ninth Circuit Court of Appeals, Raich v. Gonzales, 500 F.3d 850 (9th Cir. 2007), the Ninth Circuit concluded Raich failed to meet her burden of establishing a likelihood of success on her claims based on fundamental rights protected by the Fifth and Ninth Amendments and rights reserved to the states under the Tenth Amendment. Later, in United States v. Marin Alliance for Medical Marijuana, 139 F. Supp. 3d 1039 (N.D. Calif. 2015), the court ruled the Department of Justice was precluded from enforcing a permanent injunction prohibiting a medical marijuana dispensary from distributing marijuana to the extent the dispensary complied with California law.

In United States v. Blomquist, 362 F. Supp. 3d 744 (W.D. Mich. 2019), the court ruled the CSA criminalizing the local manufacturing and personal consumption of marijuana did not exceed Congress' authority under the Commerce Clause and that classification of marijuana as a Schedule I controlled substance was not arbitrary or a violation of due process. The court further held that a defendant bears the burden of proving complete compliance with the state medical marijuana laws and determined that the defendant in the case failed to meet requirements of an immunity provision under Michigan's Medical Marijuana Act, MMMA § 333.26421 et seq. The Michigan law permits persons to grow and use marijuana for personal medical reasons. The defendant, who held a valid, state-issued medical marijuana card but was charged with violations of federal law for cultivating over 100 marijuana plants and possessing over thirty-seven pounds of marijuana, contended the federal government could not prosecute him until after a state court had determined he violated state law. The court referred to the decision of the Michigan Supreme Court in People v. Hartwick, 498 Mich. 192, 870 N.W.2d 37 (2015), wherein that court held there must be the existence of a bona fide physician-patient relationship in which the physician completes a full assessment of the patient's medical history and current medical condition and from which results a professional opinion that the patient has a debilitating medical condition and would benefit from the use of marijuana to treat the condition. The court stated that possessing a registry identification card would establish the second and third elements, but not the first. The court denied the defendant's motion to dismiss the indictment and enjoin his prosecution.

105 21 C.F.R. §§ 1301.21, 1301.32. (The DEA is an agency within the Department of Justice.) DEA Form 224 is used for authorization to conduct instructional activities with controlled substances listed in Schedule II through V; DEA Form 225 is used to apply for registration to manufacture or distribute controlled substances, to conduct research with controlled substances listed in Schedules I through V, and to conduct chemical analysis with any controlled substance; DEA Forms 226 or 227 are used by persons applying for reregistration. DEA Form 363 is used to apply for registration to conduct a narcotic treatment program.

106 21 C.F.R. § 1301.71. To determine whether a registrant has provided effective controls against diversion, the administrator uses the security requirements set forth in 21 C.F.R. §§ 1301.72 to 1301.76 as standards for the physical security controls and operating procedures necessary to prevent diversion. Controlled substances must be stored in secure storage areas as described in 21 C.F.R. § 1301.72. Controls over employees are required. A comprehensive employee screening program must be conducted providing for inquiry into any conviction of crimes or unauthorized use of controlled substances by any employees or applicants for employment. See 21 C.F.R. §§1301.76, 1301.90 to

all drugs for at least two years for inspection and copying by authorized employees of the DEA.[107] Each inventory must contain a complete and accurate record of all controlled substances on hand on the date the inventory is taken.[108] A new inventory must be taken every two years.[109]

A prescription for a controlled substance listed in any of the schedules may be issued only by: (1) an individual practitioner who is a physician, dentist, veterinarian and licensed or otherwise authorized to prescribe controlled substances by the jurisdiction in which the practitioner is licensed to practice the practitioner's profession, (2) an institutional practitioner, which is a hospital licensed or registered to dispense controlled substances in the course of professional practice, (3) a pharmacist licensed by a state to dispense controlled substances, or (4) a long-term care facility, which is a nursing home, retirement care, mental care or other institution that provides extended health care to resident patients.[110]

A prescription for a controlled substance must be issued only for a legitimate medical purpose.[111] The responsibility for the proper prescribing and dispensing of controlled substances is upon the prescribing practitioner but a corresponding responsibility rests with the pharmacist who fills the prescription.[112] An order purporting to be a prescription issued not in the usual course of professional treatment or in legitimate and authorized research is not a prescription and the person knowingly filling a purported prescription, as well as the person issuing it, shall be subject to penalties provided for violations of the provisions of law relating to controlled substances.[113] A prescription may not be issued in order for an individual practitioner to obtain controlled substances that will supply the individual practitioner with drugs for general dispensing to patients.[114] Prescriptions must be dated, signed, and bear the full name and address of the patient and the practitioner as well as the registration number of

1301.93.

107 21 C.F.R. §§ 1304.03, 1304.04. An inventory must be taken the first day of engaging in dispensing controlled substances. See 21 C.F.R. § 1304.13.

108 21 C.F.R. § 1304.11.

109 21 C.F.R. § 1304.13.

110 21 C.F.R. §§ 1306.2 to 1306.03, 1306.06, 1306.21.

111 21 U.S.C.A. § 829 and 21 C.F.R. § 1306.04.

112 21 C.F.R. § 1306.04(a).

113 21 C.F.R. § 1306.04(a).

114 21 C.F.R. § 1306.04(b).

the practitioner.[115] Controlled substances listed in Schedule II cannot be refilled.[116] Schedule III or IV controlled substances may be refilled up to five times within six months of initial issuance if authorized by the attending physician and by state law.[117]

One of the conditions of participation in the Medicare program is that a hospital either must have a pharmacy directed by a registered pharmacist or must have a drug storage area under competent supervision.[118] The pharmacist must be responsible for developing, supervising, and coordinating all the activities of the pharmacy services. The pharmaceutical service must have an adequate number of personnel to ensure quality pharmaceutical services, including emergency services.[119] Current and accurate records must be kept of the receipt and disposition of all scheduled drugs.[120] All compounding, packaging, and dispensing of drugs and biologicals must be under the supervision of a pharmacist and performed consistent with state and federal laws.[121] Drugs and biologicals must be kept in a locked storage area; outdated, mislabeled, or otherwise unusable drugs and biologicals must not be available for patient use.[122] Drugs and biologicals not specifically prescribed as to time or number of doses must automatically be stopped after a reasonable time that is predetermined by the medical staff.[123] Drug administration errors, adverse drug reactions, and incompatibilities must be immediately reported to the attending physician and, if appropriate, to the hospital-wide quality assurance program. Abuses and losses of controlled substances must be reported.[124]

115 21 C.F.R. § 1306.05(a).

116 21 C.F.R. § 1306.12.

117 21 C.F.R. § 1306.22.

118 42 C.F.R. § 482.25(a)(1).

119 42 C.F.R. § 482.25(a)(2).

120 42 C.F.R. § 482.25(a)(3).

121 42 C.F.R. § 482.25(b)(1).

122 42 C.F.R. § 482.25(b)(2), (3).

123 42 C.F.R. § 482.25(b)(5).

124 42 C.F.R. § 482.25(b)(6), (7).

F. ALCOHOL AND DRUG ABUSE TREATMENT

Alcohol and drug abusers, who are suffering from medical conditions, cannot be discriminated against in admission or treatment solely because of their alcohol or drug problem by any private or public general hospital or by any outpatient facility that receives support in any form from any program supported in whole or in part by federal funds.[125] Records of the identity, diagnosis, prognosis, or treatment of any patient that are maintained in connection with the performance of any program or activity relating to alcohol or drug abuse that was assisted, directly or indirectly, by any department or agency of the federal government, are confidential and can be disclosed only for certain designated purposes.[126]

---

125 42 U.S.C.A. §§ 290dd to 2.

126 42 U.S.C.A. §§ 290dd-3, 290ee-3. The contents of the record could be disclosed in accordance with the prior written consent of the patient but only in connection with regulations prescribed by the Secretary of HHS. Records could be released without the written consent of the patient as follows: to medical personnel to the extent necessary to meet a bona fide medical emergency; to qualified personnel for the purpose of conducting scientific research, management audits, financial audits, or program evaluation, but personnel may not identify any individual patient in any report; or if authorized by an appropriate order of a court granted after application showing good cause therefore. Before authorizing a release of the records, a court had to weigh the public interest and the need for disclosure against the injury to the patient and to the physician-patient relationship. If a court granted an order permitting disclosure of all or any part of the record, the court had to impose appropriate safeguards against unauthorized disclosure. Except as authorized by a court order, no record could be used to initiate or substantiate any criminal charges against a patient or to conduct any investigation of a patient. A violation of the statute prohibiting disclosure of records subjected the violator to a fine.

Although records could be released upon the written consent of the patient, regulations, 42 C.F.R. § 2.31, required that the consent contain the following: (1) name of program that was to make the disclosure; (2) name or title of person or organization to which disclosure was to be made; (3) name of patient; (4) purpose or need for the disclosure; (5) extent or nature of information to be disclosed; (6) statement that consent was subject to revocation at any time except to the extent that action had been taken in reliance thereon and a specification of the date, event, or condition upon which it would expire without express revocation; (7) date on which consent was signed; and (8) signature of patient. The consent could not have a duration longer than reasonably necessary to effectuate the purpose for which it was given. If the patient was a minor and state law required consent of a parent or guardian, the signature of the minor and the minor's parent, guardian, or other person authorized under state law to act in the minor's behalf, was required. 42 C.F.R. § 2.14(c). If a minor could act alone under state law, any disclosure had to be consented to only by the patient. 42 C.F.R. § 2.14(b). For a patient who had been adjudicated as lacking the capacity (for any reason other than insufficient age) to manage the patient's own affairs, consent had to be given by the guardian or other person authorized under state law to act in the patient's behalf. For deceased patients, consent had to be given by the executor, administrator, or other personal representative. If no appointment of personal representative had been made, the consent had to be given by the patient's spouse, or if none, by any responsible member of the patient's family. 42 C.F.R. § 2.15.

Patient identifying information had to be disclosed to medical personnel who had a need for information about a patient to treat a condition that posed an immediate threat to the health of any individual and that required immediate medical intervention. 42 C.F.R. § 2.51. The patient identifying information had to be

A court could order the disclosure of the identity, diagnosis, prognosis, or treatment of a drug or alcoholic patient in instances where the records would otherwise be prohibited; however, the statute permitting relief from the duty not to disclose was not an affirmative grant of jurisdiction to authorize or compel disclosures.[127] In the absence of a court order, a request or a subpoena had no effect; the person maintaining the records had to refuse the request unless and until a court order was issued.[128]

An order compelling disclosure could authorize disclosure of confidential communications made by a patient to a program in the course of diagnosis, treatment, or referral for treatment only if: (1) the disclosure was necessary to protect against an existing threat to life or of serious bodily injury, including circumstances that constituted suspected child abuse and neglect and verbal threats against third parties, (2) the disclosure was necessary in connection with investigation or prosecution of an extremely serious crime, such as one that directly threatens loss of life or serious bodily injury, including homicide, rape, kidnaping, armed robbery, assault with a deadly weapon, or child abuse and neglect, or (3) the disclosure was in connection with litigation or an administrative proceeding in which the patient offered testimony or other evidence pertaining to the content of the confidential communications.[129] An order

disclosed to medical personnel of the FDA who asserted a reason to believe that the health of any individual could be threatened by an error in the manufacture, labeling, or sale of a product under FDA jurisdiction and that the information would be used for the exclusive purpose of notifying patients or their physicians of potential dangers. Patient identifying information could also be disclosed to conduct scientific research under certain circumstances set out on 42 C.F.R. § 2.52.

127 42 U.S.C.A. §§ 290dd-3, 290ee-3.

128 42 C.F.R. § 2.61.

129 42 C.F.R. §2.63.

In Matter of Baby X, 97 Mich. App. 111, 293 N.W.2d 736 (1980), a court ruled the confidentiality of the records of a drug abuser must give way to the best interests of a child who was born to the drug abuser and who began exhibiting symptoms of drug withdrawal within hours of birth. The mother had asserted the confidentiality of the records relating to her treatment as a drug abuser; however, state law mandated disclosure of child abuse and neglect. The court ruled that a district court may authorize disclosure where treatment records are found to be necessary and material.

In State v. Andring, 342 N.W.2d 128 (Minn. 1984), a defendant who had been treated was charged with criminal sexual conduct involving sexual contact with a stepdaughter and niece. The court ruled that the records could be used in child abuse proceedings, but that defendant's statements made during group therapy could not be disclosed.

See, however, more recent regulations at 42 C.F.R. § 2.63.

See also Matter of Doe Children, 93 Misc. 2d 479, 402 N.Y.S.2d 958 (Fam. Ct. 1978), in which the court ruled a court can require a patient's counselor at a treatment center to give testimony in child protection proceedings.

authorizing the disclosure of patient records for purposes other than criminal investigation or prosecution could be applied for by any person having a legally recognized interest in the disclosure which was sought.[130] The application had to be filed separately or as part of a pending civil action in which it appeared that the patient records were needed to provide evidence. An application had to use a fictitious name, such as John Doe, to refer to any patient and could not contain or otherwise disclose any patient identifying information unless the patient was the applicant or had given a written consent to disclosure or the court had ordered the record of the proceeding sealed from public scrutiny.[131]

An order authorizing the disclosure or use of patient records to investigate criminally or to prosecute a patient could be applied for by the person holding the records or by any person conducting investigative or prosecutorial activities with respect to the enforcement of criminal laws.[132] The application had to be filed separately as part of an application for a subpoena or other compulsory process, or in a pending criminal action. The application had to use a fictitious name unless the court had ordered the record of the proceeding sealed from public scrutiny.[133]

G. MEDICAL RECORDS

A hospital has a duty to prepare and maintain timely and accurate medical records for everyone who is evaluated or treated as an inpatient or an outpatient, for ambulatory care or emergency treatment, or who receives patient-care services in a hospital-administered home-care program. The JCAHO had established standards for the maintenance of medical records. Many states have statutory provisions relating to medical records.[134] Hospitals that participate in

130 42 C.F.R. § 2.64. The patient and the person holding the records had to be given adequate notice and an opportunity to file a response.

131 42 C.F.R. § 2.64.

132 42 C.F.R. § 2.65.

133 42 C.F.R. § 2.65. Unless the program or the person holding the records are being investigated, 42 C.F.R. § 2.66, the person holding the records had to be given adequate notice and an opportunity to appear and be heard. 42 C.F.R. § 2.65(b).

134 Discussion in Comprehensive Accreditation Manual for Hospitals (CAMH/98), Joint Commission on Accreditation of Healthcare Organizations 47–8 (1992).

the Medicare program must meet standards set out in federal regulations for maintenance of medical records.[135]

Medical records serve as a basis for planning patient care and for providing continuity in the evaluation of the patient's condition and treatment; they furnish documentary evidence of the course of the patient's medical evaluation, treatment, and change in condition during the hospital stay and while being in a hospital-administered home-care program. The records document the communication between the practitioner responsible for the patient and assist in protecting the legal interests of the patient, hospital, and practitioner.[136] The records provide data for use in continuing education and in research. As required by the Joint Commission, the records must be sufficiently detailed to enable a consultant to render an opinion after an examination of a patient and for another practitioner to assume care of the patient.

All entries made in a medical record must be entered only by those persons who are given that right in the hospital and staff policies.[137] All entries must be dated and authenticated according to a method established to identify the author of the entries.[138] Each entry must be legible and complete.[139]

---

135 42 C.F.R. § 482.24.

136 See discussion in Comprehensive Accreditation Manual for Hospitals (CAMH/98), Joint Commission on Accreditation of Healthcare Organizations 47 (1999).

As an example, a determination of death should be placed in a patient's record indicating what tests and procedures were selected to declare a patient brain-dead prior to withdrawal of life-sustaining support. (Discussion for a patient's right to refuse treatment and the patient's right to die is in Chapter III.)

In re Severns, 425 A.2d 156 (Del. Ch. 1980) involved a guardian's request for authorization to discontinue all medical supportive measures for the guardian's comatose ward. A Delaware court stated a no-code blue order should be posted on the comatose patient's chart.

In Public Health Trust of Dade County v. Valcin, 507 So. 2d 596 (Fla. 1987), the Supreme Court of Florida ruled that a hospital may be held liable for the significant omission of its employee doctors to prepare operative notes for its medical records. The court stated every hospital would do well to ensure that a patient's medical records contain a sufficient operative note. However, if the physician is found to be an independent contractor, the hospital may not necessarily be found liable for any negligence on the part of the physician. The court adopted, with some modification, the shifting of the burden of producing evidence when essential medical records are found to be either missing or inadequate through the physician's negligence.

137 See Comprehensive Accreditation Manual for Hospitals (CAMH/98), Joint Commission on Accreditation of Healthcare Organizations (1999).

138 See 42 C.F.R. § 482.24(c)(1), which provided that the author of each entry had to be identified, and the author had to authenticate each entry. The authentication could include signatures, written initials, or computer entry.

139 42 C.F.R. § 482.24(c)(1).

Medical records must be retained and preserved for a period following the discharge of a patient.[140] A hospital must have adequate personnel to ensure prompt completion, filing and retrieval of its records.[141] Further, the hospital must have a system of coding and indexing its medical records that permits timely retrieval by diagnosis and procedure to support medical care evaluation studies.[142]

Medical records are property of the hospital and maintained for benefit of the patient, the medical staff, and the hospital.[143] Still, although the records are the property of the hospital, a hospital should provide a patient with reasonable access to the medical information contained in the record.[144]

Medical records are confidential and generally can be removed from the hospital's jurisdiction and safeguarding only in accordance with a court order,

140 42 C.F.R. § 482.24(b)(1) required medical records to be retained in their original or legally reproduced form for a period of at least five years.

Tenn. Code Ann. § 68-11-305 requires a hospital to retain and preserve records that related directly to the care and treatment of a patient for a period of ten years following the discharge of the patient or the patient's death. For patients under mental disability or minority, complete hospital records must be retained for the period of minority or known mental disability, plus one year, or ten years following the discharge of the patient, whichever is longer. An x-ray film can be retired four years after the date of exposure, provided the signed written finding of interpretations of a radiologist, who has read the film, is retained for the same period as other hospital records.

141 42 C.F.R. § 482.24(a).

142 42 C.F.R. § 482.24(b)(2).

143 Tenn. Code Ann. § 68-11-304 provides that hospital records are and shall remain the property of the various hospitals, subject to court order to produce the records.

144 In Bondu v. Gurvich, 473 So. 2d 1307 (Fla. 3d DCA 1984) (disapproved of by, Martino v. Wal-Mart Stores, Inc., 908 So. 2d 342 (Fla. 2005)), the majority created a tort action arising when a hospital failed to provide required hospital records, resulting in a patient losing an underlying malpractice action. The majority noted courts have recognized the existence of causes of action for negligent failure to preserve evidence for civil litigation and for intentional interference with prospective civil action by the spoliation of evidence. The court stated a hospital's duty to make and maintain medical records, and to furnish the records to a patient or a patient's personal representative upon request, is provided for statutorily.

In Rabens v. Jackson Park Hospital Foundation, 40 Ill. App. 3d 113, 351 N.E.2d 276 (1st Dist. 1976), the court ruled there is a common-law duty of a hospital to disclose upon request, medical data to a patient or the patient's agent. The patient has a cause of action for breach of the hospital's duty to furnish hospital records when the patient is told he would be charged for a copy of his hospital bill.

In Cannell v. Medical and Surgical Clinic, S.C., 21 Ill. App. 3d 383, 315 N.E.2d 278 (3d Dist. 1974), the court decided the physician-patient relationship requires the disclosure of medical data to a patient or the patient's agent on request. The court stated the patient should not be forced to engage in legal proceedings to obtain medical information. However, the court further stated that although medical information must be given the patient, the physician's records themselves need not be turned over to the patient.

subpoena, or statute.[145] The written consent of the patient is required for the release of any medical information to persons not otherwise authorized to receive the information.[146] Records of the identity, diagnosis, prognosis, or treatment of any patient that are maintained in connection with the performance of any alcohol or drug abuse prevention function, conducted or regulated either directly or indirectly by any federal agency or department, may be disclosed only for special purposes as set out in federal regulations.[147] These records may not be released in response to a subpoena; an authorizing court order is required to release the records.[148]

Although a medical record is hearsay,[149] hospital records nonetheless generally are admissible into evidence upon the same basis as other regularly kept

---

145 Federal regulations require a hospital to have a procedure for ensuring the confidentiality of patient records. Information from or copies of records may be released only to authorized individuals, and the hospital must ensure that unauthorized individuals cannot gain access to or alter patient records. Original records may be released by the hospital only in accordance with federal or state laws, court orders, or subpoenas. See 42 C.F.R. § 482.24(b)(3).

Iowa Code § 147.135 provided that peer-review records are privileged and confidential and are not subject to discovery, subpoena, or other means of legal compulsion for release to a person other than an effected licensee or a peer-review committee and are not admissible into evidence in a judicial or administrative proceeding other than a proceeding involving licensee discipline or a proceeding brought by a licensee subject to peer-review board and whose competence is at issue.

In Jaffee v. Redmond, 518 U.S. 1 (1996), the Supreme Court ruled that conversations between a patient and her therapist and the notes taken during their counseling sessions are protected from compelled disclosure. The counselor was a licensed clinical social worker. The Court ruled the privilege for treatment by psychiatrists and psychologists applies with equal force to clinical social workers.

In re Roger B, 84 Ill. 2d 323, 418 N.E.2d 751 (1981), the court ruled as to the confidentiality of adoption records, that there is no constitutional right in an adoptee to determine the adoptee's genealogical origin, noting the state concern in promoting the confidentiality of the records to protect the integrity of the adoption process. The court stated only three states, Alabama, Florida, and Kansas, grant the adoptee access to original birth records; forty-two states provide for sealed birth records. A state must protect the interests of the adoptee as well as the rights of the natural and the adopting parents. The interests of all three are balanced. Still a court may, for good cause, order records to be opened.

In Application of Maples, 563 S.W.2d 760 (Mo. 1978), an adopted child brought an action to require a court to order the opening of the records of his adoption. The Supreme Court of Missouri ruled a refusal to open the records did not violate the First Amendment; it stated the closing of the records manifested a legislative intent that opening, or disclosure, be with caution. The Missouri Supreme Court did recognize it could, for cause, release the portion of the adoption proceeding it deemed necessary to satisfy the needs of the applicant, measuring that need against the rights of the natural parents, the adoptive parents, and the societal need to protect and maintain a viable system for adoptions.

146 Early discussion in Comprehensive Accreditation Manual for Hospitals (CAMH/98), Joint Commission on Accreditation of Healthcare Organizations (1999).

147 42 C.F.R. pt. 2.

148 42 C.F.R. § 2.61.

149 Hearsay is an out-of-court statement that is offered to prove the truth of the matter asserted. The problem with admitting hearsay is that its evidentiary value depends upon the credibility of the

records.[150] Some states have specific statutory authorization for the admission of hospital records.[151] In like manner as for commercial records, a foundation for hospital records must be established indicating that it is the practice to make the medical record routinely, promptly and accurately in the course of hospital operations.[152] Because most of the states have enacted a physician-patient privilege, the custodian of the records may be required to refuse to provide the records in response to a subpoena.[153]

---

declarant without the assurances of oath, presence, or cross-examination.

150 A business record is a document that is made in the regular course of business at or within a reasonable time after the event recorded occurred and under circumstances that can be assumed to reflect the actual event.

151 See, e.g., Tenn. Code Ann. §§ 68-11-402 to 68-11-405. The records must be filed with the court within five days after the custodian is served with a subpoena. The custodian of the medical record states by affidavit that the custodian is the duly authorized custodian of the record, that a copy of the record attached to the affidavit is a true copy of all records described in the subpoena, and that the records are prepared by the personnel of the hospital in the ordinary course of hospital business at or near the time of the act, condition or event reported in the record. See Tenn. Code Ann. § 68-11-405.

152 In Parkson v. Central DuPage Hosp., 105 Ill. App. 3d 850, 61 Ill. Dec. 651, 435 N.E.2d 140 (1st Dist. 1982), the plaintiff sought the medical records of patients who had been treated for the same disease as the plaintiff. The court ruled the hospital could assert a physician-patient privilege to protect the records of its patients. The limited exception relating to the confidentiality of medical records is applicable to disclosure of the records of the patient who is bringing the malpractice action. The court held that a broadening of communication involving patients who are not parties to the litigation would not serve the public interest nor the private interests of those nonparty patients. The court opined that even though a trial court could order that the names and identifying numbers of the patients be excluded from the records, a patient's identity nonetheless might not remain confidential. The court decided certain histories of a patient's prior and present medical conditions are cumulative and can make the possibility of recognition very high.

In State ex rel. Lester E. Cox Medical Center v. Keet, 678 S.W.2d 813 (Mo. 1984), a court determined there is no peer-review privilege to protect from discovery factual information presented to a peer-review committee. Information contained in records of other patients are relevant or can lead to discovery of evidence relevant to the plaintiff's claim. The court did recognize, however, that patients are entitled to protection from humiliation or embarrassment and ruled that the plaintiff would be limited to an in-camera examination of the records sought.

In Mt. Diablo Hospital Dist. v. Superior Court, 183 Cal. App. 3d 30, 227 Cal. Rptr. 790 (1st Dist. 1986), a court ruled minutes of a medical staff committee responsible for evaluation and improvement of quality of care rendered in a hospital are protected as records of a proceeding not subject to discovery under the evidence code.

153 Ziegler v. Superior Court In and For Pima County, 134 Ariz. 390, 656 P.2d 1251 (Ct. App. Div. 2 1982). A patient, who had brought an action for medical malpractice based upon an alleged unnecessary implantation of a heart pacemaker, sought the records of other hospital patients who had undergone similar surgery. The court decided a blanket prohibition against the examination and use of the medical records of other patients based upon a physician-patient privilege would result in an injustice. According to the court, hospitals assume responsibilities for the care of patients and must meet standards of responsibility commensurate with that trust. The court stated the confidentiality of patient records can be amply protected by concealing the identity of the patients.

A patient's medical records generally are available to medical staff committees for study and evaluation for the purposes of research and are available to obtain statistics and information relating to the prevention and treatment of diseases, illnesses, and injuries.[154] Records remain confidential; consequently, the names and identity of the patients must be protected.[155]

1. Health Insurance Portability and Accountability Act (HIPAA)

In 1996, Congress passed the Health Insurance Portability and Accountability Act (HIPAA)[156] to encourage the development of a health information system. Its purposes includes making improvements to the portability and continuity of health-insurance coverage, combatting healthcare fraud and healthcare abuse, and simplifying the administration of health insurance.[157] The HIPAA provided for the establishment of national standards for the electronic transmission of certain health information, such as standards for certain health care transactions conducted electronically and code sets and unique identifiers for health care providers and employers. It also requires the formation of national standards to

---

In Rudnick v. Superior Court, 11 Cal. 3d 924, 114 Cal. Rptr. 603, 523 P.2d 643 (1974), the court commented that the purpose of the physician-patient privilege is to preclude humiliation of a patient that might follow from the disclosure of ailments. Thus, if disclosure reveals nothing of any communication concerning the patient's ailments, disclosure of a patient's name does not violate the privilege. However, if the disclosure of the patient's name inevitably, in the context of the disclosure, reveals confidential information, namely ailments, then the disclosure violates the privilege. Conversely, if the disclosure reveals ailments but not the patient's identity, then, according to the court, the disclosure will appear not to violate the privilege.

In Community Hospital Ass'n v. District Court In and For Boulder County, 194 Colo. 98, 570 P.2d 243 (1977), a court ruled the physician-patient privilege statute was not violated by the production of records of patients when the identity, and the surgeries performed upon the patients, were adequately protected. The court ruled a prohibition against production of the records could result in an injustice. The order requiring the hospital to reproduce copies of the records stated that all reference on the records to name, address, marital status, and occupation of the patients was to be removed and that the records would be filed with the court and sealed by the court to be opened only upon order of the court.

In Shelton v. Morehead Memorial Hosp., 318 N.C. 76, 347 S.E.2d 824 (1986), the court ruled that records of a hospital's medical review committee relating to an investigation of alleged medical malpractice are protected by statute. Records of the hospital's board of trustees, however, are not protected because the court determined the board is not the peer-review committee.

154 See, e.g., Mont. Code § 50-16-202.

155 Mont. Code § 50-16-204. Discussion of a patient's privacy rights in Chapter III.

156 Pub. L. 104-191, title II, §§ 261 et seq., 110 Stat. 1936, 2021, 2033 (1996). 42 U.S.C. §§ 1320d-1320d-8.

157 Discussion in Menorah Pak Center for Senior Living v. Rolston, 2020 Ohio 6658, 173 N.E.3d 432 (Ohio 2020) (citing Tovino, "A Timely Right to Privacy," 104 Iowa L. Rev. 1361, 1367 (2019)).

protect the privacy and security of personal protected health information (PHI). Additionally, it established patient-privacy protection.[158]

The HIPAA Privacy Rule,[159] discussed in Chapter III, applies only to protected health information in electronic form and requires covered entities, defined below, to implement certain administrative, physical, and technical safeguards to protect this electronic information.[160] The HIPAA Enforcement Rule[161] establishes rules governing the compliance responsibilities of covered entities with respect to the enforcement process, including rules governing investigations, rules governing the process and grounds for establishing the amount of a civil penalty where a violation of a HIPAA Rule has been found, and rules governing the procedures for hearings and appeals where a covered entity challenges a violation determination.[162] Health plans, health care clearing houses, and certain health care providers are "covered entities" under HIPAA regulations.[163]

The HIPAA regulations generally prohibit covered entities from using or disclosing personal PHI.[164] The regulations do permit covered entities to disclose PHI through the judicial process or if an individual expressly authorizes release of the individual's medical information in a valid authorization form.[165] A valid

158 Discussed in Chapter III.

159 45 C.F.R. pt. 160 and subpts A and E of pt. 164.

160 45 C.F.R. pt. 160 and subpts A and C of pt. 164.

161 45 C.F.R. pt. 160, subpts C-E.

162 The Health Information Technology for Economic and Clinical Health (HITECH) Act, 41 U.S.C. §§ 13101 et seq., discussed below, was enacted in 2009 to require modification of some of the HIPAA Rules to strengthen HIPAA privacy, security, and enforcement.

163 45 C.F.R. § 164.102(a).

164 45 C.F.R. §§ 164.508(a)(1); 164.502(a). HIPAA, 42 U.S.C. § 1320d-6, provides that a person who knowingly uses or causes to be used a unique health identifier, obtains individually identifiable health information relating to an individual, or discloses individually identifiable health information to another person is subject to a fine of not more than $50,000, imprisonment for not more than one year, or both. If the offense is committed under false pretenses, the fine can be increased to $100,00, imprisonment increased to five years, or both.

165 45 C.F. R. §§ 164.512(e); 501(a)(1)(iv). A covered entity may not use or disclose PHI without an authorization that is valid. See Tex. Civ. Prac. & Rem. Code §74.052, which sets out an authorization form for release of PHI. Section 74.052(c) states the prescribed form set out therein is in accordance with the "Standards for Privacy of Individually Identifiable Health Information (HIPAA Privacy Rule, 45 C.F.R. Parts 10 and 164. Section 74.052 provides that notice of a health care claim under § 74.051 (discussed in Chapter IV) must be accompanied by a medical authorization in the form prescribed in the section. The statute states that if the authorization required by this section is modified or revoked, the physician or health care provider to whom the authorization has been given shall have the option to abate all further proceedings until sixty days following receipt of a replacement

authorization must contain a description of the information to be used or disclosed that identifies the information in a specific and meaningful fashion, the name or other specific identification of the person or class of persons authorized to make the requested use or disclosure, the name or other specific identification of the person or class of persons to whom the covered entity may make the requested use or disclosure, a description of each purpose of the requested use or disclosure, an expiration date or an expiration event that relates to the individual or the purpose of the use or disclosure, and the signature of the individual and date.[166] Additionally, the authorization must contain statements adequate to place the individual on notice of (1) the individual's right to revoke, the exceptions to the right to revoke and a description of how the individual may revoke, (2) that a covered entity may not condition treatment, payment, enrollment or eligibility for benefits on whether the individual signs the authorization, and (3) the potential for information disclosed pursuant to the authorization to be subject to redisclosure by the recipient and no longer protected by HIPAA.[167] The HIPAA regulations set forth circumstances when a written authorization is invalid and prohibit only the conditioning of medical treatment or health care benefits on the execution of a HIPAA authorization.[168]

The HHS was tasked with providing Congress recommendations on standards with respect to individuals' PHI.[169] A court pointed out that to ensure patient access to PHI is not thwarted by excessive fees, HHS adopted rules that limited what companies can charge for delivering PHI.[170] These restrictions are known as "Patient Rate." As that court noted, for years, the medical records industry understood that limitations imposed by the Patient Rate applied only to requests for PHI made by the patient for use by the patient. For other types of requests, the records industry understood that the allowable fee was not restricted by the Patient Rate. However, that understanding changed in 2016 when HHS issued a guidance document that stated the Patient Rate applies even

---

authorization that must comply with the form specified in this section.

166 45 C.F.R. § 164.508(c)(1)(i)-(vi).

167 45 C.F.R. § 164.508(c)(2), (b)(4).

168 45 C.F.R. §§ 164.508(b)(2), (b)(3), (b)(4).

169 Discussion in Ciox Health, LLC v. Azar, 435 F. Supp. 3d 30 (D.C. 2020).

170 Ciox Health, LLC v. Azar, 435 F. Supp. 3d 30 (D.C. 2020).

to requests to deliver PHI to third parties. According to the court, that change caused medical records companies to lose millions of dollars in revenue.[171]

The HHS issued a "Final Rule," known as the "Privacy Rule" in 2000, which established an individual's right to access PHI and the permissible fee that can be charged for such production.[172] For requests brought by an individual seeking that individual's own PHI–known as a "personal use request"—the Privacy Rule permitted a covered entity to charge a reasonable, cost-based fee. The Privacy Rule made clear that the purpose of the Patient Rate is to ensure individuals will be deterred from seeking PHI due to its cost. The HHS, however, did not require charging the Patient Rate when cost of obtaining and transmitting PHI is to be borne by someone other than the patient. As one court noted, the Final Rule made an express distinction between patient-requested PHI and non-patient-requested PHI.[173]

The Privacy Rule includes the prohibition of a covered entity from releasing PHI stored in any format to a third party without a "valid authorization."[174] Because this authorization was burdensome, Congress enacted the Health Information Technology Act (HITECH) to create a "third-party directive," which is a simplified process for requesting delivery of certain PHI to third persons.

2. Health Information Technology (HITECH)

The HITECH Act[175] was enacted in 2009 in response to the growth of distinct digital-record formats and storage systems. The Act was designed to encourage the adoption of sophisticated electronic health record (EHR) technology by

171 Ciox Health, LLC v. Azar, 435 F. Supp. 3d 30 (D.C. 2020). Ciox challenged the 2016 expansion of the Patient Rate as a violation of the procedural and substantive protections of the Administrative Procedure Act.

172 See 45 C.F.R. § 164.524. Discussion of Privacy Rule in Chapter III.

In Association of American Physicians & Surgeons, Inc., 224 F. Supp. 2d 1115 (S.D. Tex. 2002), the plaintiffs unsuccessfully contended the Privacy Rule, as established by the HHS pursuant to HIPAA, violated the Fourth Amendment's prohibition against unreasonable government searches and seizures, complaining the Privacy Rule gave the government "virtually unrestricted access" to medical records without a warrant.

173 Ciox Health, LLC v. Azar, 435 F. Supp. 3d 30 (D.C. 2020). The Patient Rate applies to the former but not the latter.

174 45 C.F.R. §164.502(a)(1)(iv).

175 42 U.S. C. § 13101. Discussion in Ciox Health, LLC v. Azar, 435 F. Supp. 3d 30 (D.C. 2020).

health care providers.[176] Congress' goal in enacting the Act was for health care providers to use EHRs for all patients by 2014.

The HITECH Act created incentive payments for eligible health care providers–individual hospitals and health care professionals–that demonstrated "meaningful use" of certified EHR technology.[177] Additionally, the HITECH Act entitles patients to obtain for themselves PHI contained in an EHR or to direct the information to a third party without need for a "valid authorization" under the HIPAA Privacy Rule. In 2013, HHS amended the Privacy Rule and broadened the third-party directive created by the HITECH Act to reach requests for PHI contained in any format, not just in an EHR. The HITECH Act requires providers to comply with security and privacy standards established under the HIPAA.[178]

The HITECH Act also sets a statutory cap on the fee a covered entity may charge a patient for delivering EHRs,[179] and the Patient Rate applies when an individual directs a covered entity to send the PHI to a third party.[180]

3. Reporting Requirements

Although medical records are confidential, there is some medical information that must be reported to various governmental agencies or departments. Births

176 Discussion in United States v. Kettering Health Network, 816 F.3d 399 (6th Cir. 2016). An EHR is an electronic record of health-related information on an individual that is created, gathered, managed, and consulted by authorized health care clinicians and staff. Discussion in Ciox Health, LLC v. Azar, 435 F. Supp. 3d 30 (D.C. 2020).

177 42 C.F.R. § 495.2. Incentive payments are calculated using a formula that takes account of each individual provider's volume of patients. See 42 C.F.R. §§ 495.102(a)(1) (eligible professionals) and 495.104(c)(2) (hospitals).

178 45 C.F.R. §§ 164.312(a)(2)(iv) and 164.306(d)(3). See 42 C.F.R. §§ 495.6(j)(16)(ii), (l)(15)(ii).

179 See 45 U.S.C. § 16835(e)(3) and 45 C.F.R. § 164.524(c)(4). A copy of information in electronic form cannot be greater than the entity's labor costs in responding to the request for the copy, but that cost includes skilled technical staff time spent to create and copy the electronic file, such as compiling, extracting scanning and burning PHI to media, and distributing the media. However, actual labor costs associated with the retrieval of electronic information would not be recoverable under the Patient Rate. Nor would fees associated with maintaining systems and recouping capital for data access, storage and infrastructure be considered reasonable, cost-based fees.

180 45 C.F.R. § 164.524. This limitation applies regardless of whether the individual requested that the copy of PHI be sent to the individual or directed that the covered entity send the copy directly to a third party designated by the individual. Only request for PHI made directly by a third party with HIPAA authorization, or another permissible disclosure provision in the Privacy Rule, would not be subject to the Patient Rate cap.

and deaths must be reported.[181] Communicable diseases often must be reported.[182] Some states require that wounds be reported.[183] Some also require that severe burn injuries be reported.[184] A physician who diagnoses or treats a sexually transmitted disease generally must make a record and report the case to the state department of health.[185] Some states require health facilities keep on file all information relating to the performance of an abortion.[186] In some states, all medical and personal information relevant to a person's treatment for tumors must be reported.[187] States require suspected instances of child abuse or neglect be reported.[188] Some also require abuse of disabled and elderly persons to be reported.[189] Courts in some states have determined that a physician or hospital must warn those third parties identified by a mentally ill patient as the object of the patient's hostilities.

a. Child Abuse

States have a strong interest in the prevention of child abuse.[190] Accordingly, states have statutes requiring those persons in a position where child abuse is most likely to be detected, to report promptly all suspected and known instances of child abuse to the authorities for follow-up investigations.[191] The law in the states imposes an affirmative duty upon certain specified professionals, including medical practitioners, to report these cases or suspected cases.[192] Courts have

181 See, e.g., Mont. Code Ann. §§ 50-15-201, 50-15-401; Tenn. Code Ann. §§ 68-3-301, 68-3-502.

182 See, e.g., Tenn. Code Ann. § 68-5-101; N.Y. Pub. Health Law §§ 2101, 2102.

183 N.Y. Penal Law § 265.25.

184 N.Y. Penal Law § 265.26.

185 See, e.g., Mont. Code Ann. § 50-18-106; Tenn. Code Ann. §§ 68-10-101, 68-10-102.

186 See, e.g., Mont. Code Ann. § 50-20-110.

187 Mont. Code Ann. § 50-15-703.

188 See, e.g., Fla. Stat. § 415.504.

189 See, e.g., Fla. Stat. § 415.103.

190 Discussion in Storch v. Silverman, 186 Cal. App. 3d 671, 231 Cal. Rptr. 27 (2d Dist. 1986).

191 See, e.g., Cal. Penal Code § 11165; Tex. Fam. Code Ann. § 34.01.

192 Gross v. Haight, 496 So. 2d 1225 (La. Ct. App. 5th Cir. 1986).

Cal. Penal Code § 11166 required a health practitioner, with knowledge of or observance of a patient reasonably suspected to have been a victim of child abuse, to report the abuse to a child protective agency immediately or, as soon as practically possible, by telephone.

stated that the duty to report known or suspected child abuse takes precedence over any physician-patient privilege.[193] In some states, a medical practitioner who fails to so report is statutorily liable in civil damages for any subsequent injury to the child.[194]

Parents of children suspected of child abuse have brought suits for damages against those persons reporting the parents' suspected abuse of their children.[195] The parents have contended that they have a fundamental interest in the care, custody, companionship, and management of their child. As a matter of familial privacy, families should be able to remain together free from undue outside interference. Thus, where a state moves to terminate the relationship between a parent and child, it must provide the parents with fundamentally fair procedures.[196] However, parental autonomy is not absolute.[197] While parents enjoy an inherent right to the care and custody of their own children, courts have deemed the state, in its recognized role as parens patriae, to be the ultimate protector of the rights of minors.

Although the parens patriae interest in promoting the welfare of the child favors preservation, not severance, of natural family bonds, the countervailing state interest in curtailing child abuse is also great; thus, courts have determined that in cases of suspected abuse or neglect, the state has a clear interest in protecting the child, and may, if necessary, go as far as to separate neglectful parents from their children. Because the parents' needs or rights have been considered secondary to the state's strong interest in protecting children where the potential for abuse or neglect exists, most states provide immunity from liability for those persons required to report instances of suspected child abuse.[198]

---

193 Storch v. Silverman, 186 Cal. App. 3d 671, 231 Cal. Rptr. 27 (2d Dist. 1986).

194 Storch v. Silverman, 231 Cal. Rptr. 27 (2d Dist. 1986) (person who failed to report suspected child abuse as required by statute was also guilty of a misdemeanor).

195 Discussion in Lehman v. Stephens, 148 Ill. App. 3d 538, 499 N.E.2d 103 (4th Dist. 1986). While parents enjoy an inherent right to the care and custody of their own children, courts have deemed the state, in its recognized role as parents patriae, to be the ultimate protector of the rights of minors.

196 Lehman v. Stephens, 499 N.W.2d 103 (4th Dist. 1986).

197 Id.

198 Id.

b. Reportable Diseases

Communicable diseases generally must be reported by a physician or hospital.[199] Courts have ruled that under some circumstances exposing third parties to a communicable disease may violate their constitutional rights.[200] However, the stigma imposed by a person identified as having contacted a certain calamitous disease, AIDS being an early and prime example, may implicate constitutional privacy rights of the victim of the disease.[201]

---

199 See, e.g., Cal. Health & Safety Code §§ 3123, 3125; Tenn. Code Ann. § 68-5-101.

Minn. Stat. § 144.4175 provides for voluntary reporting by any licensed health professional or other human services professional regulated by the state as to any person who is a health threat to others. If these persons have knowledge or reasonable cause to believe that a person is a health threat to others, they can report the information to the commissioner of health. A licensed health professional or other human services professional regulated by the state, who makes such a report in good faith, is not subject to liability for reporting in any civil, administrative, disciplinary, or criminal action. Minn. Stat. § 144.4175(2).

Tenn. Code Ann. § 68-5-102 requires a practitioner of medicine, who had examined any person infected with any communicable disease, to notify immediately the health authorities of the town or county where the diseased person is found. In the event of death, the practitioner had to notify the person to whom the body is delivered of the known or suspected communicable, contagious, or infectious disease, including Acquired Immune Deficiency Syndrome (AIDS), so that necessary and proper precautions can be taken in the handling preparation for disposition and disposition of the body.

200 Jarrett v. Faulkner, 662 F. Supp. 928 (S.D. Ind. 1987).

201 See Local 1812, American Federation of Government Employees v. U.S. Dept. of State, 662 F. Supp. 50 (D.D.C. 1987), in which the court ruled Department of State's employee medical fitness program that included mandatory testing of blood for the presence of the HIV was rational and closely related to fitness for duty. The court stated the Department of State had demonstrated a serious ground for concern about additional risk the disease would develop from the placement of HIV carriers in many foreign posts and medical care at the posts would be inadequate to diagnose and treat the medical problems that could develop in any infected person. The court held that an HIV-infected person was not "otherwise qualified" for worldwide foreign service duty and, thus, was not discriminated against under the Rehabilitation Act, 29 U.S.C.A. §§ 791 et seq.

See Thomas v. Atascadero Unified School Dist., 662 F. Supp. 376 (C.D. Cal. 1986), in which the parents of a child infected with the AIDS virus brought an action against the school district and school officials to require the school district to permit the child to attend regular kindergarten classes. The court ruled the child was disabled for purposes of the Rehabilitation Act and was otherwise qualified to attend regular kindergarten classes for purposes of the act in the absence of evidence that the child posed a significant risk of harm to his kindergarten classmates or teachers. The child had acquired AIDS virus as an infant as the result of contaminated blood transfusions when he was treated in a hospital for complications arising from his premature birth. The court noted the virus was transmitted from one person to another only by infected blood, semen, or vaginal fluids (and possibly, by mother's milk).

In Rasmussen v. South Florida Blood Service, Inc., 500 So. 2d 533 (Fla. 1987), the Supreme Court of Florida discussed the right of privacy that was first recognized by the Supreme Court in Griswold v. Connecticut, 381 U.S. 479 (1965). The court commented that the essential zone of privacy is the right to prevent disclosure of identity in a damaging context, and that the federal right of privacy extended protection in some circumstances against disclosure of personal matters. The court noted the Florida state constitution was amended in 1980 to include an express right of privacy and concluded the Florida amendment was intended to protect the right to determine whether sensitive information about oneself will be disclosed to others. The Florida Supreme Court opined that the suspicion of AIDS could lead to discrimination in

Some states enacted legislation to address the problems relating to persons who are a health threat to others, particularly, as an example, much earlier, for those who were carriers of the AIDS virus.[202] These statutes varied in their attempts to protect members of society; some were directed towards protecting the AIDS victim while others were more concerned with the protection of third parties.[203]

H. TELEHEALTH SERVICES

Innovations in technology, as well as COVID-19 having spread through communities, has continuously led to accepted health care services through virtual

---

employment, education, housing, and even medical treatment. Thus, that court decided a victim of AIDS supposedly through blood transfusions, could not obtain a list of the blood donors to compare against a list of known AIDS victims.

In Doe v. Shady Grove Adventist Hosp., 89 Md. App. 351, 598 A.2d 507 (1991), the court ruled an individual seeking damages for disclosure of information relating to the individual's AIDS diagnosis was entitled to an order sealing the record to the extent necessary to protect the confidentiality of the individual's identity.

202 See, e.g., Cal. Health & Safety Code § 199.20; Minn. Stat. § 144.4171.

In Estate of Mauro By and Through Mauro v. Borgess Medical Center, 137 F.3d 398 (6th Cir. 1998), the Court of Appeals for the Sixth Circuit ruled a hospital employee, a surgical technician, who was terminated because he was infected with HIV, was not an "otherwise qualified" person under the Americans with Disabilities Act (ADA). (Discussion of ADA in Chapter VI.) The court noted a person is not qualified if the person poses a direct threat to the health and safety of others and the threat cannot be eliminated by a reasonable accommodation. The Sixth Circuit commented that a surgical technician must place the technician's hands upon and into a surgical incision to provide room and visibility for a surgeon and the technician risked a needle stick or a minor laceration. A wound causing an HIV infected surgical technician to bleed could have catastrophic results in a body cavity. Thus, the Sixth Circuit determined the surgical technician posed a direct threat to the health and safety of others.

203 Minn. Stat. § 144.4173 authorized the commissioner of health, or a local board of health with express delegated authority from the commissioner, to commence a legal action against a carrier who was a health threat to others and engaged in noncompliant behavior. To protect the public health in an emergency, the court could order a health officer or peace officer to take a person into custody and could transport the person to an appropriate emergency care or treatment facility for observation, examination, testing, diagnosis, care, treatment, and if necessary, temporary detention. Minn. Stat. § 144.4182.

Compare with Cal. Health & Safety Code § 199.20, which provided that to protect the privacy of individuals who were the subject of blood testing for antibodies to the probable causative agent of AIDS, no person could be compelled to identify or provide identifying characteristics that would identify any individual who was the subject of such a blood test.

See Tarrant County Hosp. Dist. v. Hughes, 734 S.W.2d 675 (Tex. App. Fort Worth 1987), in which the court ruled the mother of a girl who died from AIDS, after being given a blood transfusion by the hospital, could recover the blood donors' identities. The court applied a balancing test comparing the interest served by the state action regarding discovery with the donors' interest in privacy. The court determined the plaintiff's interest in the identity of the blood donors was legitimate and that the blood donors did not possess a need of anonymity greater than the plaintiff's need.

patient-physician visits that permit individuals to access their care at locations of their choice. The delivery of health services from a distance to an accepted healthcare system called "telehealth" permits health care providers to connect with patients at any time or place and reduces costs for medical services.[204]

Telehealth, sometimes used interchangeably with "telemedicine,"[205] is defined as the delivery of health care services by a licensed health professional, acting within the scope of the health professional's license, certification, or entitlement to a patient, at a different location than the health profession, using synchronous or asynchronous telecommunication technology.[206] Synchronous telemedicine is a two-way audiovisual link between a patient and a care provider that permits real-time interaction to take place. Asynchronous telemedicine is a store-and-forward videoconferencing that transmits a recorded health history to a health practitioner, who is usually a specialist. It involves acquiring medical data and then transmitting that data to a physician or medical specialist at a convenient time for assessment offline.[207]

204 Additionally, the CMS has broadened telehealth access to Medicare patients. CMS will pay for these services at the same rate as an in-person visit. See 42 U.S.C. § 1395m and 42 C.F.R. § 410.78.

Medicare Part B pays for E-visits or patient-initiated online evaluation and management conduct when there is an established relationship with a patient.

Medicare patients may use telecommunication technology for office, hospital visits and other services that generally have occurred in-person. Practitioners who can receive payment for covered telehealth services can in some states include nurse practitioners, physician assistants, nurse midwives, certified nurse anesthetists, clinical psychologists, clinical social workers, registered dietitians, and nutrition professionals.

The Texas Administrative Code § 174.5(c) requires that a prescription can only be issued if there is a patient-practitioner relationship as defined in the Texas Occupation Code § 111.005. Section 111.05(c) provides that patient-practitioner relationship is not present if a practitioner prescribes an abortifacient or any other drug or device that terminates a pregnancy.

205 Telemedicine centers on the practice of medicine via a remote means whereas telehealth is a more comprehensive provision of health care services. Telehealth covers all aspects of healthcare services, including health information and patient education, through videoconferencing, remote patient monitoring, and storage and transmission technologies. Remote patient monitoring (RPM) includes reporting, collecting, transmitting, and evaluating patient health information using electronic devices–a patient can track and record their vitals through an electronic device.

206 See e.g., Tex. Occupations Code, tit. 3, subtitle. A, § 111.001(3), Fla. Stat. § 456.47, Ind. Code 25-1-9.5-6, and Md. Health Occupations Code § 1-1001(E).

207 See definition of asynchronous store and forward technologies in 42 C.F.R. § 410.78 The transmission generally does not occur simultaneously. The data is temporarily stored for transfer at a later time, either via a secure web server, encrypted e-mail, specially designed store-and-forward software, or electronic health records. The consulting provider reviews the stored data and makes a diagnosis, treatment, and planning recommendation that are electronically transferred or faxed back to the referring provider.

Communication is HIPAA compliant;[208] one state defined telehealth as the delivery of health care services using interactive electronic communications and information technology, in compliance with HIPAA, including: (1) secure video conferencing, (2) store and forward technology, or (3) remote patient monitoring technology between a provider in one location and a patient in another location.[209] Physicians providing telehealth services are required to keep and maintain an adequate medical record just as they are if their services are provided in person.[210] One state included in its statute a requirement that the telehealth provider document in the patient's medical record the health care services rendered using telehealth accounting to the same standard as used for in-person service.[211]

An issue that telehealth providers must consider is the standard of care that applies in telehealth communication with a patient. Because a plaintiff in a medical malpractice lawsuit must prove that a health care provider breached the standard of care, determining the standard of care that applies for a telehealth provider is crucial. The standard can be a local or national standard, but a patient must consent to receive virtual services. States that have adopted telehealth statutes generally provide that the standard of care for telehealth services is subject to the standard of care that would apply to the provision of the same health care service or procedure in an in-person setting,[212] but a state may require verbal consent from a patient prior to a telehealth consultation.

There is an issue when the patient and the provider are in different locations. Medical professionals are generally licensed on a state-by-state basis; thus, a physician licensed in one state cannot practice in another without a license from

208 The HHS Office of Civil Rights (OCR) did not penalize physicians for noncompliance with HIPAA when they served patients in good faith through common communication technologies such as FaceTime or Skype during the COVID-19 public health emergency.

209 Indiana IC 25-1-9.5-6. RPM permits providers to record and monitor a patient's health data remotely. It uses technological devices to obtain vital signs needed to monitor a patient's condition. It is generally recommended for patients with chronic diseases, such as diabetes, asthma, and cardiovascular illnesses.

210 See, e. g., Fla. Stat. § 456.47(3), Md. Health Occupations Code §§ 1-1003 and 1-1006, Ind. IC §25-1-9.5-6, and Texas Occupations Code, title 3, subtitle A, §111.07.

211 Florida statutes § 456.47. It provides that medical records, including video, audio, electronic, or other records generated because of providing such services are confidential. See §§ 395.3025(4) and 456.057.

212 See e. g., Texas Occupations Code, tit. 3, subtitle. A, § 111.007. A Texas statute, Tex. Insurance Code § 1455.004, requires a health benefit plan to provide coverage for a health care service or procedure as a telemedicine medical service or a telehealth service on the same basis and to the same extent the plan provides coverage for the service or procedure in an in-person setting.

that state. Interstate agreements can provide for health care providers to practice in the different states.[213]

A physician who provides telehealth services should obtain the informed consent of the patient, or another appropriate individual authorized to make health care treatment decisions for the patient,[214] and must ensure the confidentiality of the patient's medical information is maintained.[215]

I. APPLICATION OF ANTITRUST LAWS TO NONPROFIT HOSPITALS

1. Introduction

Nonprofit organizations are not exempt from the provisions of the Sherman Act.[216] While nonprofit enterprises have often escaped liability under the antitrust laws, there is no language in the Sherman Act that would prevent its application to the nonprofit organization.[217] The Supreme Court has stated that it is "beyond debate that nonprofit organizations can be liable under the antitrust laws."[218] However, because the Sherman Act regulates "commerce" that affects

213 Most, though not all, of the states have a telehealth statute but provisions of the various state acts vary; thus prior to providing telehealth services, a hospital and/or physician should consult the state statute and a healthcare attorney in the state.

214 See e.g., Texas Occupations Code tit. 3, subtitle. A, § 111.002.

215 See e.g., Texas Occupations Code tit. 3, subtitle. A, § 111.003.

216 15 U.S.C. §§ 1 et seq.

217 See 15 U.S.C. §§ 7, 15.

There is no distinction in the statutes between business and nonprofit organizations and no other language in the statute that would limit jurisdiction to corporations. Section 13c of the Sherman Act, 15 U.S.C. § 13c, provides that the price discrimination provisions of the act, 15 U.S.C. §§ 13 to 13b, 21a, will not apply to purchases of supplies for their own use by schools, colleges, universities, public libraries, churches, hospitals, and charitable institutions not operated for profit. However, this provision has limited application.

218 See American Soc. of Mechanical Engineers, Inc. v. Hydrolevel Corp., 456 U.S. 556 (1982).

In Federal Trade Commission v. Penn State Hershey Medical Center, 838 F.3d 327 (3rd Cir. 2016), the Court of Appeals for the Third Circuit ruled that merging hospitals failed to rebut the presumption of anticompetitive effects from a merger of two hospitals. The court affirmed that once the government established a prima facie case that the merger may substantially lessen competition, the burden shifted to the hospitals to rebut the government's prima facie case. The court rejected the hospitals' two efficiencies-based defenses. The court noted that it had never formally adopted the efficiencies defense. It stated that the language of the Clayton Act, 15 U.S.C. § 18, must be the linchpin of any efficiencies defense and that, because the Clayton Act speaks in terms of "competition," a successful efficiencies defense requires proof that a merger is not anticompetitive.

trade among the several states,[219] the courts have examined practices of non-profit organizations to determine whether a particular activity is commercial in nature.[220] Still, the increased importance of private associations in the affairs of individuals and organizations has led to substantial expansion of judicial control over the internal affairs of associations not for profit and, in that context, a broader application of the antitrust laws to nonprofit organizations.[221]

There is an exemption from the antitrust laws for state action, thus public hospitals may have immunity from liability. In a very early Supreme Court case,[222] the Supreme Court ruled that the Sherman Act does not reach state action or official action directed by a state but later stated that sovereign compulsion was a prerequisite for "state-action" immunity.[223] Then in 1984, Congress enacted the Local Government Antitrust Act[224] to broaden the scope of antitrust immunity applicable to local governments after Congress decided a surge in the filing of antitrust lawsuits threatened to undermine local government's ability to govern in the public interest. However, in 1991, the Court of Appeals for the Tenth Circuit[225] ruled that an Oklahoma public trust hospital was not a special function governmental unit for purpose of antitrust immunity under the Local Government Antitrust Act of 1984. Still, recently the Court of Appeals for the Fourth Circuit[226] ruled a hospital authority in North Carolina qualified as a

---

219 15 U.S.C. §§ 1, 2.

220 Arizona v. Maricopa County Medical Soc., 457 U.S. 332 (1982).

221 In U.S. v. Rockford Memorial Corp., 898 F.2d 1278 (7th Cir. 1990), the court held that a proposed merger of the two largest hospitals in a city of 140,000 persons would violate § 7 of the Clayton Act and § 1 of the Sherman Act. The court noted that hospital prices should be higher in markets with fewer hospitals.

In Schacht v. Northshore University Health System, 2017 IL App 2d 160969-U (Ill. App. Ct. 2d Dist. 2017), the court ruled physician plaintiffs failed to plead an antitrust injury from the merger of two hospitals and practice groups. The plaintiffs contended the defendants had attempted monopolization of outpatient physician service groups by acquiring outpatient primary care and specialist physician groups contracting with the dominant insurer and instituting a referral policy created through its bundling agreement with the insurer that encouraged referrals to the defendant physician groups and facilities to the virtual exclusion of the plaintiffs and others in that class. The plaintiffs contended the defendants acquired monopoly power in the relevant geographic market. The court, however, ruled that the plaintiffs had to establish the defendants engaged in prohibited anticompetitive conduct and that the conduct resulted in an antitrust injury. The court affirmed the trial court's dismissal of the plaintiff's antitrust complaint.

222 Parker v. Brown, 317 U.S. 341 (1943).

223 Cantor v. Detroit Edison Co., 428 U.S. 579 (1976).

224 15 U.S.C. §§ 34 et seq.

225 Tarabishi v. McAlester Regional Hosp., 951 F.2d 1558 (10th Cir. 1991).

226 Benitez v. Charlotte-Mecklenburg Hospital Authority, 992 F. 3d 229 (4th Cir. 2021).

local government and thus was subject to antitrust immunity under that Act. The Fourth Circuit decided the hospital authority was covered by the Act as it fell into the final category of the Act–a "special function governmental unit established by State law in one or more states."[227] The Fourth Circuit rejected plaintiff's contention that the hospital authority could not be regarded as a local government because it received more than fifty percent of all inpatient revenue in the Charlotte area, stating that if limitations should be imposed on when an entity could no longer qualify as "local government," Congress should do that, not the courts.

2. Rule of Reason Standard

Activities of a nonprofit enterprise that are not commercial in nature have been evaluated under the antitrust laws using a "rule of reason" standard.[228] Those activities that are premised on public service or public welfare have been evaluated using this standard.[229] However, certain conduct, such as price fixing, is

227 See 15 U.S.C. § 34(1)(B).

228 The rule of reason is a standard, based upon common-law tradition, used to analyze transactions that provide restraints upon trade. The facts peculiar to the business, the history of the restraint, and the reasons why it was imposed are analyzed to determine the competitive effects of an agreement. If the restraint is found to be unreasonable in terms of its impact on competitive conditions, the agreement is in violation of the Sherman Act.

In Wilk v. American Medical Ass'n, 895 F.2d 352 (7th Cir. 1990), the Court of Appeals for the Seventh Circuit ruled that the American Medical Association violated the Sherman Act by conducting an illegal boycott in restraint of trade. Conduct of the American Medical Association was evaluated under the rule of reason. The court found that the association's actions in preventing medical physicians from referring patients to chiropractors and from accepting patients from chiropractors prevented chiropractors from obtaining access to hospital diagnostic services and membership on hospital medical staffs.

In Tarabishi v. McAlester Regional Hosp, 951 F.2d 1558 (10th Cir. 1991), the Court of Appeals for the Tenth Circuit ruled a physician failed to prove claims of conspiracy to monopolize and conspiracy in restraint of trade regarding a hospital that had terminated his staff privileges and that revoked his surgical and emergency room privileges, which meant he could no longer treat his patient in the hospital's emergency room nor perform surgery at the hospital. The hospital eventually revoked all the physician's staff privileges with the result that he could no longer use hospital facilities for any purpose. The Tenth Circuit determined the physician had failed to prove the hospital had evidenced monopoly power in its pricing and that this failure was fatal to the physician's monopolization claims against the hospital. After the hospital terminated the physician's staff privileges, the physician opened his own medical practice consisting of some surgery. He later explored the possibility of establishing an outpatient surgical clinic and prepared a Certificate of Need application. The hospital had informed the physician that it had no interest in his medical practice, but it later decided to open its own outpatient surgical department and then opposed the physician's Certificate of Need application on the ground that the proposed facility would duplicate its surgical services. (Discussion of Certificate of Need above and discussion of a hospital's medical staff in Chapter I.)

229 Boddicker v. Arizona State Dental Ass'n, 549 F.2d 626 (9th Cir. 1977); Feminist Women's Health Center, Inc. v. Mohammad, 415 F. Supp. 1258 (N.D. Fla. 1976). In the Feminist Women's Health Center

deemed to be a per se violation of the Sherman Act regardless of the fact that a nonprofit organization is involved.[230] Likewise, courts have refused to tolerate anticompetitive conduct even though the health care industry was involved.[231] Although Congress has stated that the health care industry does not respond

---

case, the court stated the defendant had the burden of proving that it had a good faith motive to protect the public health and welfare.

230 Arizona v. Maricopa County Medical Soc., 457 U.S. 332 (1982); U. S. Dental Institute v. American Ass'n of Orthodontists, 396 F. Supp. 565 (N.D. Ill. 1975). If the challenged conduct is inconsistent with the public welfare, the per se rules will cause the practices to fall under the prohibitions of the Sherman Act. The Supreme Court ruled in Maricopa County Medical Society that price fixing agreements not premised on public service or ethical norms are per se violations of the Sherman Act.

231 National Gerimedical Hospital and Gerontology Center v. Blue Cross of Kansas City, 452 U.S. 378 (1981); Jefferson Parish Hosp. Dist. No. 2 v. Hyde, 466 U.S. 2 (1984) (abrogated on other grounds by, Illinois Tool Works Inc. v. Independent Ink, Inc., 547 U.S. 28 (2006)).

In Federal Trade Commission v. Penn State Hershey Medical Center, 838 F.3d 327 (3rd Cir. 2016), the Court of Appeals for the Third Circuit ruled merging hospitals failed to rebut the presumption of anticompetitive effects from a merger of two hospitals. The court affirmed that once the government established a prima facie case the merger may substantially lessen competition, the burden shifted to the hospitals to rebut the government's prima facie case. The court rejected the hospitals' two efficiencies-based defenses. The court noted it had never formally adopted the efficiencies defense. It stated that the language of the Clayton Act, 15 U.S.C.A. § 18, must be the linchpin of any efficiencies defense and that, because the Clayton Act speaks in terms of "competition," a successful efficiencies defense requires proof that a merger is not anticompetitive. The court held that equities favored a preliminary injunction against the proposed merger and reversed the ruling of the district court.

In Federal Trade Commission v. Advocate Health Care Network, 841 F.3d 460 (7th Cir. 2016), the Court of Appeals for the Seventh Circuit ruled the district court below erred in denying the Federal Trade Commission (FTC) a preliminary injunction to enjoin a proposed merger of hospitals pending the FTC's administrative trial on the merits of an antitrust claim. The court noted a horizontal merger case under the Clayton Act, 15 U.S.C.A. § 18, which forbids asset acquisitions that may lessen competition in any "section of the country," depends on the proper definition of geographic markets for hospitals. The FTC relied on a method called the hypothetical monopolist test, which asks what would happen if a single firm became the sole seller in a proposed region. The appellate court disagreed with the district court's finding that the FTC had not shown a relevant geographic market. The appellate court ruled that if the firm could profitably raise prices above competitive levels, that region is a relevant geographic market. The court pointed out that most hospital care is brought in two stages. In the first, insurers and hospitals negotiate to determine whether the hospitals will be in the insurers' networks and how much the insurers will pay them. In the second stage, hospitals compete to attract patients based primarily on non-price factors like convenience and reputation for qualify. The court stated that concerns about potential misuse of market power resulting from a merger must consider this two-stage process. The court decided markets for hospital services have three notable features. First, because most patients prefer to go to nearby hospitals, there are often only a few hospitals in a geographic market. Second, patients vary in their hospital preferences. Finally, consumers do not directly pay the full cost of hospital case. Instead, insurance companies cover most hospital costs. Insurance thus splits hospital competition into two stages: one in which hospitals compete to be included in insurers' networks, and a second in which hospitals compete to attract patients. The court decided that the geographic market question is therefore most directly about the "likely response of insurers," not patients, to a price increase. The court decided the geographic market question asks how many hospitals insurers can convince most customers to drive past to save a few percent of their health insurance premiums and decided that number probably was very small.

to classic marketplace forces,[232] the Supreme Court nonetheless has refused to exempt health care organizations from antitrust provisions.[233]

The Supreme Court used the rule of reason standard to evaluate a contract between a public hospital and a firm of anesthesiologists requiring that all anesthesiologic services for the hospital's patients be performed by that firm. The Court refused to rule that the contract was a tying arrangement and found no violation of antitrust provisions.[234]

---

232 See S. Rep. No. 1285, 93rd Cong., 2d Sess. 39.

233 National Gerimedical Hospital and Gerontology Center v. Blue Cross of Kansas City, 452 U.S. 378 (1981); Arizona v. Maricopa County Medical Soc., 457 U.S. 332 (1982).

In St. Joseph's Hosp., Inc. v. Hospital Corp. of America, 795 F.2d 948 (11th Cir. 1986), a hospital challenged the action of a competitor that delayed the hospital's hearing on its application for a certificate of need to expand its cardiac care services, as being a violation of the Sherman Act. However, the Court of Appeals for the Eleventh Circuit ruled that delaying tactics did not violate the antitrust act. The Eleventh Circuit stated joint efforts of the competitor to influence public officials did not violate the antitrust provisions despite the fact that the actions were intended to eliminate competition. However, that court determined the alleged misrepresentations made to the governmental body by the competitor did not enjoy immunity from antitrust liability.

In United States v. Anthem, 855 F.3d 345 (D.C. Cir. 2017), the Court of Appeals for the District of Columbia affirmed a lower court's issuance of a permanent injunction against the merger of the second and third largest national health insurance carriers on the ground that the merger was likely to lessen competition substantially in at least two markets. The court ruled the district court had acted within its discretion in enjoining permanently the merger. It decided the health insurance carriers failed to show extraordinary efficiencies needed to offset the anticompetitive effect of the merger in the market for the sale of insurance to national accounts in states where carriers competed prominently. They also failed to show extraordinary efficiencies to offset the anticompetitive effect of the merger in the market for the sale of health insurance to large group employers in the state.

234 Jefferson Parish Hosp. Dist. No. 2 v. Hyde, 466 U.S. 2 (1984) (abrogated on other grounds by, Illinois Tool Works Inc. v. Independent Ink, Inc., 547 U.S. 28 (2006)). The Supreme Court noted an inquiry into the validity of a tying arrangement must focus on the market or markets in which the two products are sold because that is where the anticompetitive forcing has its impact. The Court stated an analysis of the tying issue must focus on the hospital's sale of services to its patients rather than its contractual arrangements with the providers of anaesthesiologic services. The Court concluded that whether principles concerning tying arrangements should be applied to the contract between the hospital and the anaesthesiologists turned not on the functional relation between them but rather on the character of the demand for the two items. The Court stated an inquiry of whether the contract violated the Sherman Act necessarily involved an inquiry into the actual effect of the exclusive contract on competition among anaesthesiologists. However, that competition took place in a market the court determined had not been defined. The Court found that the market was not necessarily the same as the market in which hospitals compete in offering services to patients. The Court decided a market may encompass competition among anaesthesiologists for exclusive contracts and may be state-wide or merely local.

In Mitchell v. Frank R. Howard Memorial Hosp., 853 F.2d 762 (9th Cir. 1988), a hospital entered into an exclusive contract for hospital-based radiology services with a particular radiologist. The Court of Appeals for the Ninth Circuit held that the hospital was not sufficiently involved in interstate commerce to provide Sherman Act jurisdiction with respect to a challenge by another radiologist that the exclusive arrangement violated the antitrust provisions.

Certain medical peer-review activities are insulated from antitrust liability by the Health Care Quality Improvement Act of 1986.[235] Peer-review action is immunized from liability if the action was taken in the reasonable belief that it was in the furtherance of quality health care.[236]

3. Tiered networks

Antitrust issues have surfaced regarding health insurance in networks. Health insurance has added complexity to healthcare through factors such as co-pays, deductibles, in-network providers, and out-of-network providers. A network consists of a group of physicians and hospitals that accept a certain health insurance plan; the insured patient must choose a doctor in that plan's network to have coverage. In a tiered network, insurers place healthcare providers that offer better value in lower costs and higher quality health care services in top tiers. Insureds who use providers in the top tiers pay lower out-of-pocket costs for medical care. In a narrow network, the insured is offered less in-network providers from which to choose in exchange for lower premiums and lower out-of-pocket costs. Healthcare providers want insurers to steer insureds towards them because of the increased patient volume steering generates.[237]

Tiered provider networks are becoming increasingly popular to manage spiraling health care costs. "Tiered networks" can give consumers lower

235 42 U.S.C. §§ 11101 to 11152.

In Summit Health, Ltd. v. Pinhas, 500 U.S. 322 (1991), an ophthalmologist sued a hospital alleging that he was excluded from the ophthalmological services market in his area when he refused to follow an allegedly unnecessarily costly surgical procedure used at the hospital. The suit alleged that the hospital, its staff, and others had entered a conspiracy in violation of the Sherman Act to drive the ophthalmologist out of business. According to the physician, when he refused to follow a procedure that caused increased patient costs, the defendants initiated an adverse peer review report about the ophthalmologist and planned to disseminate it. Dissemination of the report would allegedly have prevented the physician from continued competition in the marketplace. The defendants contended that there was no factual nexus between the restraint on the surgeon's practice and interstate commerce. The district court dismissed the physician's complaint, but the Supreme Court ruled that a conspiracy to eliminate the ophthalmological department of a hospital would affect interstate commerce. Four justices dissented. Justice Scalia, in his dissenting opinion, decided that the physician might be the victim of a business tort but that he did not have a legitimate grievance under the Sherman Act.

236 642 U.S.C. § 11112(a). The act states that it does not change other immunities under the law. See 42 U.S.C. § 11115(a) including the state action immunity. Thus, states can immunize peer-review actions that do not meet the federal standard. Discussion of peer review immunity in Chapter I.

Discussion of charitable and governmental immunity generally in Chapter IV.

237 Discussion in United States v. Charlotte-Mecklenburg Hospital Authority, 248 F. Supp. 3d 720 (W.D. N. Car. 2017).

coinsurance payments or better-quality healthcare services depending on the tier the patient chooses. Health insurance plans group providers into tiers based on the cost or efficiency of care they deliver. They can then steer patients to choose providers in lower cost tiers through lower premiums or reduced cost sharing from deductibles or co-pays.[238]

4. Steering

The steering of patients away from a hospital is one of the greatest threats to a hospital's revenues. Steering is a method by which insurers offer insureds options to reduce healthcare expenses. Typically, steering occurs when an insurer offers its insureds a financial incentive to use a lower-cost provider or lower-cost provider network. Insurers want to steer insureds towards lower-cost providers and offer innovation steering insurance plans. Steering is an example of competitive behavior in tiered or narrow networks; consumers will have lower premiums and copays in exchange for choosing from a smaller list of healthcare providers.[239]

A hospital authority's steering restrictions can have adverse effects on competition. There have been questions whether the relationship between a hospital system and an insurance company will operate as an unreasonable restraint on trade, specifically whether a hospital authority's contract with insurance companies include "steering" restrictions that limit insurance companies' ability to inform their customers about, or incentivize them to use, other health-service providers that may be able to provide better or more affordable service.[240]

---

238 Tiered networks supposedly help constrain health plan costs by steering patients to lower-cost providers, while encouraging hospitals and physicians to improve their efficiency or accept discounted payment rates in exchange for preferred-tier placement.

239 See discussion in United States v. Charlotte-Mecklenburg Hospital Authority, 248 F. Supp. 3d 720 (W.D. N. Car. 2017).

240 In United States v. Charlotte-Mecklenburg Hospital Authority, 248 F. Supp. 3d 720 (W.D. N. Car. 2017), the United States and the State of North Carolina brought an action against a hospital authority, alleging the hospital authority, Carolinas Healthcare System (CHS), violated the Sherman Act in connection with its mandatory steering restrictions in agreements with insurers. CHS contracted with insurance companies that prohibited certain competitive behavior. One of these competitive behaviors was steering. Plaintiffs also alleged that CHS used its contracts with insurance companies to restrict the flow of information to consumers, specifically, that it limited the ability of insurance companies to share comparative cost and quality information with consumers. CHS maintained and enforced steering restrictions in its contracts with several insurance companies that collectively insured more than eighty-five percent of the commercially insured residents in a city area. The steering restrictions with each insurer varied but ranged from an outright prohibition to granting CHS

A hospital can impose restrictions in its contracts with insurers that prevent insurers from steering insureds toward the hospital's competitors. Some hospitals have imposed anti-steering provisions in its contracts with insurers to protect itself from steering that would induce price competition and potentially the hospital to lower its high prices. When a hospital negotiates with insurers, a hospital generally negotiates prices and terms of network participation for inpatient hospital services and other healthcare services at the same time. Anti-steering provisions then apply to hospital services and other negotiated services. These provisions generally prevent insurers from offering tiered networks that feature a hospital's competitors in the top tiers and narrow networks that only include a hospital's competitors. Anti-steering provisions generally create disincentives that deter insurers from providing to their enrollees truthful information about their healthcare options and the benefits of price and quality competition among healthcare providers that the insurers could offer if they could steer.[241]

A hospital's conditioned access to inpatient services can be challenged as being a tying arrangement. A tying arrangement occurs when a "seller with market power in one product market extends its market power to a distinct product market.[242] As one court opined, to accomplish this objective, the seller conditions the sale of one product (the tying product) on the buyer's purchase of a second product (the tied product).[243] That court deemed the essential

the right to terminate the contract if the insurer steered patients. The government contended the restrictions consistently created disincentives and deterred insurers from providing patients with full information about healthcare options, including price and cost comparisons across healthcare providers. As an example, an insurance company could be restricted from telling one of its enrollees that he or she could receive certain treatment for less money or from a better healthcare provider. The insurance companies felt compelled to agree to the restrictions to maintain their relationships with CHS because of its market power as the dominant hospital authority system in the area. The court ruled the government carried an initial burden of alleging a facially plausible claim that CHS violated the Sherman act and denied CHS's motion for judgment on the pleadings.

As noted previously, in Benitez v. Charlotte-Mecklenburg Hospital Authority, 992 F. 3d 229 (4th Cir. 2021), the Court of Appeals for the Fourth Circuit ruled the hospital authority qualified as a local government and thus was subject to antitrust immunity under the Local Government Antitrust Act of 1984, 15 U.S.C. § 34 et seq. The Fourth Circuit rejected plaintiff's contention that the hospital authority could not be regarded as a local government because it received more than fifty percent of all inpatient revenue in the Charlotte area, stating that if limitations should be imposed on when an entity could no longer qualify as "local government," Congress should do that, not the courts.

241 Discussion in United States v. Charlotte-Mecklenburg Hospital Authority, 248 F. Supp. 3d 720 (W.D. N. Car. 2017).

242 Cascade Health Sols. v. PeaceHealth, 515 F.3d 883 (9th Cir. 2008).

243 515 F.3d at 912.

characteristic of an invalid tying arrangement to be the "seller's exploitation of its control over the tying product to force the buyer into the purchase of a tied product that the buyer either did not want at all, or might have preferred to purchase elsewhere on different terms."[244] Hospital contracts that are system wide and require health plans to include a hospital's inpatient service in tied markets can force insurers to include in their networks inpatient services at a hospital as a condition to access to patient services and reduce consumers' incentives to obtain acute inpatient hospital services from core cost-effective providers. This can deprive insurers and their enrollees of the benefits of a competitive market for their purchase of inpatient hospital services.

244 515 F.3d at 913-14.

CHAPTER III. PATIENT RIGHTS

A. INTRODUCTION

The Joint Commission (JACHO) early set out certain rights and responsibilities of patients in a former accreditation manual.[1] Patient rights that are mandated

1 Discussion in Comprehensive Accreditation Manual for Hospitals (CAMH/98), Joint Commission on Accreditation of Healthcare Organizations (1999).

in the manual include: considerate care that safeguards the patient's personal dignity and respects the patient's cultural, psychosocial, and spiritual values; impartial access to treatment and accommodations regardless of the individual's psychosocial, spiritual and cultural variables that influence the perceptions of illness;[2] a patient's right to privacy; and the confidentiality of personal records. Those not directly involved in the treatment of the patient are to disclose affirmatively their purposes and obtain permission of the patient to be present. Additionally, the manual provides that the patient has the right to communicate with those responsible for the patient's care and to receive from them adequate information concerning the nature and extent of the patient's medical problem, the planned course of treatment, and the prognosis. The manual also states a patient has the right to refuse treatment to the extent permitted by law and to be informed of the medical consequences of any action.[3] The patient should be informed if the hospital proposes to engage in or perform human experimentation or other research educational projects affecting care or treatment; the patient has the right to refuse any such activity. Some of the most significant and also the most controversial of these patient rights are discussed in this chapter.

B. PRIVACY RIGHTS

One of Congress's objectives in enacting HIPAA[4] was to address concerns about the confidentiality of patients' individually identifiable health information. Accordingly, Congress authorized the Secretary of HHS to promulgate privacy regulations addressing patients' rights to their individually identifiable health information, procedures for exercising these rights, and the uses and disclosures

---

See Md. Code Ann. § 19-342, which provided that the administrator of a hospital was responsible for making available to each hospital patient a copy of the patient's bill of rights adopted by the hospital under the guidelines of the Joint Commission. Discussion of the Joint Commission (JACHO) in Chapter II.

2 The Md. Code Ann. § 19-343 provides that it is the right of any resident of a health-care facility to be treated with consideration, respect, and full recognition of human dignity and individuality. Md. Code Ann. § 19-355 states that a hospital or related institution cannot discriminate in providing personal care because of an individual's race, color, or national origin.

3 Md. Code Ann. § 19-350 provided a hospital could not demand or accept final payment unless the hospital had given the patient an itemized statement that described briefly but clearly each item and the amount charged for it.

4 Pub. L. 104-191, title II, §§ 261 et seq., 110 Stat. 1936, 2021, 2033 (1996). 42 U.S.C. §§ 1320d-1-1320d-8. Discussed also in Chapter II.

of the information. The Secretary then issues lengthy and comprehensive privacy and disclosure regulations.[5] The HIPAA Privacy Rule[6] requires covered entities, described below, to have safeguards in place to ensure the privacy of protected health information (PHI). It further sets out circumstances under which covered entities may use or disclose an individual's PHI and gives individuals rights with respect to their PHI, including rights to examine and obtain a copy of their health records and to request corrections.

The HHS issued its "Final Rule," known as the "Privacy Rule," in 2000. This Rule established an individual's right to access PHI and the permissible fee that can be charged for its production.[7] For requests brought by an individual seeking that individual's own PHI–known as a "personal use request"—the Privacy Rule permits a covered entity to charge a reasonable, cost-based fee. The Privacy Rule makes clear that the purpose of the Patient Rate is to ensure individuals will not be deterred from seeking PHI due to its cost, but that HHS did not require charging the Patient Rate when cost of obtaining and transmitting PHI is to be borne by someone other than the patient. As one court noted, the Final Rule makes an express distinction between patient-requested PHI and non-patient-requested PHI.[8]

The use and disclosure requirements in the Privacy Rule regulations apply to "covered entities," which include health plans, healthcare clearinghouses and health care providers who transmit any health information in electronic form in connection with standard transactions. The requirements also apply to "business

5 See 45 C.F.R. pts. 160 and 164. See Tex. Civ. Prac. & Rem. Code §74.052, which sets out an authorization form for release of PHI. Section 74.052(c) states the prescribed form, which is set out in the statute, is in accordance with HIPAA, 45 C.F.R. Parts 160 and 164. Section 74.052 provides that notice of a health care claim under § 74.051 (discussed in Chapter IV) *must* be accompanied by a medical authorization in the form prescribed in the section. The statute states that if the authorization required by the section is modified or revoked, the physician or health care provider to whom the authorization has been given has the option to abate all further proceedings until sixty days following receipt of a replacement authorization that must comply with the form specified in the section.

6 45 C.F.R. pt. 160 and subpts A and E of pt. 146.

7 See 45 C.F.R. § 164.524.

In Association of American Physicians & Surgeons, Inc., 224 F. Supp. 2d 1115 (S.D. Tex. 2002), the plaintiffs unsuccessfully contended the Privacy Rule, as established by the HHS pursuant to HIPAA, violated the Fourth Amendment's prohibition against unreasonable government searches and seizures, complaining the Privacy Rule gave the government "virtually unrestricted access" to medical records without a warrant.

8 Ciox Health, LLC v. Azar, 435 F. Supp. 3d 30 (D.C. 2020). The Patient Rate applies to the former but not the latter.

associates" of the covered entities.[9] Authorization required to disclose or use a patient's PHI depends on the nature of the use. For purposes such as including a patient in a directory of individuals in a facility, the covered entity must inform the patient in advance and give the patient the opportunity to agree to or prohibit or restrict that disclosure.[10] In other instances, such as for treatment, payment, or health care operations, the HIPAA Privacy Rule permits covered entities to use and disclose PHI without obtaining authorization from the patient.[11]

The Privacy Rule includes the prohibition of a covered entity from releasing PHI stored in any format to a third party without a "valid authorization."[12] Because this authorization is burdensome, Congress enacted the HITECH in 2009 to create a "third-party directive," which is a simplified process for requesting delivery of certain PHI to third persons.[13] Still, HITECH includes provisions designed to strengthen privacy and security protections for health information established by HIPAA. The HITECH requires HIPAA covered entities and business associates to provide for notification of breaches of unsecured PHI. HITECH also establishes new limitations on the use and disclosure of PHI for marketing and fundraising purposes, prohibits the sale of PHI, expands individuals' rights to access the PHI, and provides for restrictions on certain disclosures of PHI to health plans.[14]

---

9 42 U.S.C. § 17934. The regulations provide that business associates are associates outside the workforce of the covered entity that provide legal, actuarial, consulting, and other services to the covered entity. 45 C.F.R. § 160.103.

10 45 C.F.R. § 164.510. In some instances, a signed authorization is required. See 45 C.F.R. § 164.508.

11 45 C.F.R. § 164.502(a)(1)(ii). Still, the Privacy Rule limits the use or disclosure of the information to the minimum amount necessary to achieve the purpose of the use. 45 C.F.R. § 164.502(b)(1).

In Kuligoski v. Brattleboro Retreat, 203 Vt. 328, 156 A.3d 436 (Vt. 2016), the Supreme Court of Vermont noted two exceptions relevant to the disclosure obligation. One is a dangerous patient exception to the confidentiality requirement that is intended to "avert a serious threat to health or safety." 45 C.F.R. § 164.512(j). This exception permits disclosure when it is necessary to prevent or lessen a serious and imminent threat to the health of safety of a person or the public. The second useful exception to which the Vermont Supreme Court referred was one that provided for standard uses and disclosure for involvement in an individual's care, citing to the provision for emergency circumstances. 45 C.F.R. § 164.510(b)(3).

12 45 C.F.R. §164.502(a)(1)(iv).

13 Discussion of HITECH in Chapter II.

14 In Cross v. Formative Health Management, 439 F. Supp. 3d 646 (E.D. N.C. 2020), patients brought a class action against medical record providers for overcharging them for their medical records in alleged violation of HIPAA and HITECH and their implementing regulations governing fees for provision of medical records, and for unjust enrichment. The court ruled that the issue of the amount of charges permitted under HITECH and the Privacy Rule, where an attorney requests

Remedies for patients who believe their privacy and security rights have been violated are limited. No private of action exists for patients and insured whose rights are violated under HIPAA rules.[15] However, patients who believe their privacy and security rights have been violated may file a complaint with the covered entity itself; and the covered entity can impose sanctions on members of its workforce.[16]

The Genetic Information Nondiscrimination Act (GINA)[17] was enacted in 2008 to prohibit discrimination based on an individual's genetic information in both health coverage and employment contexts.[18] Additionally, GINA contains

---

medical records on behalf of a client for a personal injury matter, as in this case, was properly an issue to be determined by HHS and subject to resolution as a matter of federal law. The court decided the plaintiffs had not demonstrated that justice and equity under North Carolina law required an equitable remedy of unjust enrichment and dismissed their unjust enrichment claim.

15 In Acara v. Banks, 470 F.3d 569, 571 (5th Cir. 2006), the Court of Appeals for the Fifth Circuit noted every district court that had considered this issue agreed the statute does not support a private right of action.

In Byrne v. Avery Center for Obstetrics and Gynecology, 314 Conn. 433, 102 A3d 32 (Conn. 2014), the Supreme Court of Connecticut noted that there is no private right of action, express or implied, under HIPAA, which the court stated enforces its provisions through administrative imposition of fines and imprisonment.

In Lawson v Halpern-Reiss and Central Vermont Medical Center, 210 Vt. 224, 212 A.3d 1213 (Vt. 2018), a patient brought action against a hospital for damages resulting from disclosure to a third party of information obtained by medical personnel during treatment. An emergency room nurse supplied otherwise confidential medical information to a police officer based on her good-faith belief that providing the information was necessary to prevent a patient from driving drunk from the hospital and thus endangering the patient and the public. The Supreme Court of Vermont concluded from other case law that HIPAA and its implementing regulations can be utilized to inform the standard of care applicable to claims arising from allegations of negligence in the disclosure of patients' medical records pursuant to a subpoena.

In Shepherd v. Costco Wholesale Corporation, 482 P.3d 390 (Ariz. 2021), a customer brought statutory, tort, and fraud claims against a pharmacy for disclosing his prescription for erectile dysfunction medication to his ex-wife. The Supreme Court of Arizona, in a matter of first impression, ruled that HIPAA could inform the standard of care in a negligence claim for disclosure of medical information. While the Arizona Supreme Court recognized that HIPAA does not provide for a private right of action, it stated that HIPAA does not preclude state law tort claims, such as a negligent disclosure of medical information claim.

16 45 C.F.R. § 164.530(d)(1) and (e)(1). Additionally, a patient can file a complaint with the Secretary of HHS. 45 C.F.R. § 306(a).

17 Pub. L. 110-233 122 Stat. 881, 42 U.S.C. § 2000ff.

18 In North Coast Women's Care Medical Group, Inc. v. Superior Court, 44 Cal. 4th 1145, 81 Cal. Rptr. 3d 708, 189 P.3d 959 (2008), a lesbian patient sued a medical group and two of its physicians for their refusal to perform intrauterine insemination on her, contending their refusal violated the Unruh Civil Rights Act, Civ. Code § 51, requirement to provide "full and equal accommodations, advantages, facilities, privileges, or services" to all persons notwithstanding their sexual orientation. An amendment to the Unruh Civil Rights Act added sexual orientation to its antidiscrimination prohibitions. The California Supreme Court ruled the First Amendment, or a religious exemption, did not guarantee the physicians a right to deny fertility treatment to lesbian patients. The court stated a religious objector has no federal free exercise right to an exemption from a neutral and valid law

privacy protections for genetics that required HHS to revise the Privacy Rule to clarify that genetic information is health information and to prohibit health plans, health insurance issuers and issuers of Medicare supplemental policies from using or disclosing genetic information for underwriting purposes.

C. DUTY TO TREAT

Generally, unless emergency treatment is required, no one has the right to demand admission to a hospital.[19] Courts have stated the governing board determines the right of admission to the benefits of the hospital, and the courts will not review a board's discretion.[20] Although a private hospital is under no obligation in the absence of an emergency to admit any patient and can reject a patient for whatever reason or for no reason at all, once a hospital has initiated the care and treatment of a patient, it cannot act unreasonably in removing the patient from the hospital.[21] If more steps are taken than are necessary to determine whether to admit a patient, the patient may be deemed to have been admitted. In this instance, the patient must be kept in the hospital and the patient's treatment

---

of general applicability because compliance with the law was contrary to the objector's religious beliefs. The court decided the law need not be justified by a compelling governmental interest even if the law had the incidental effect of burdening a religious practice.

19 See, e. g. the Arizona Supreme Court decision in Guerrero v. Copper Queen Hospital, 112 Ariz. 104, 537 P.2d 1329 (1975) and the Kentucky Supreme Court decision in Hill v. Ohio County, 468 S.W.2d 306 (Ky. 1970).

In Jackson v. Mercy Health Center, Inc., 1993 OK 155, 864 P 2d 839 (Okla. 1993), the Supreme Court of Oklahoma ruled that a hospital was not liable for failing to treat a visitor who became dizzy while he was holding his wife's hand during the time she was being anesthetized for surgery. The Oklahoma Supreme Court stated that the medical provider need not have waited before rendering aid to see if the visitor would suffer total collapse. It ruled the hospital was within the protection of the Good Samaritan Act when its personnel escorted the visitor out of the surgery area, seated him on the bed in the hallway, and then redirected their attention to the wife.

Discussion of emergency treatment and the Good Samaritan Act below.

20 See, Supreme Court of Kentucky decision in Hill v. Ohio County, 468 S.W.2d 306 (Ky. 1970).

21 See, Le Juene Road Hospital, Inc. v. Watson, 171 So. 2d 202 (Fla. 3d DCA 1965).

See also, Davis v. Johns Hopkins Hospital, 622 A.2d 128 (Ct. App. Md. 1993), wherein the court ruled a hospital had no duty to admit a child to its intensive care unit on an emergency basis because the unit was full and there were no facilities available to treat the child properly. The court also ruled that the hospital's referral to another hospital did not constitute abandonment of the patient.

Discussion of discharge of patients below.

continued if it is foreseeable that the patient's condition will be aggravated, or the danger increased by removal of the patient.[22]

A patient's rights with respect to treatment by a physician is based upon and is a part of the patient/physician relationship. A physician is under no obligation to enter into a general contract for the treatment of a patient.[23] Further, a physician may limit an obligation by undertaking to treat a patient only for a certain ailment or injury and at a certain place and at a specified time.[24] When the professional services of a physician are accepted by another person for medical or surgical treatment, the relationship of physician and patient is created. The relationship is a consensual one wherein the patient knowingly seeks the assistance of a physician, and the physician knowingly accepts the individual as a patient.[25] Once a physician undertakes to examine or treat a patient, the physician cannot abandon the patient.[26]

D. EMERGENCIES

Many states require that a licensed hospital make its emergency services available to all persons.[27] Courts have ruled a hospital may not deny its emergency

22 See, Le Juene Road Hospital, Inc. v. Watson, 171 So. 2d 202 (Fla. 3d DCA 1965).)

23 See, Giallanza v. Sands, 316 So. 2d 77 (Fla. 4th DCA 1975), in which the court stated that when professional services of a physician are accepted by another person for medical or surgical treatment, the relationship of physician and patient is created. However, a physician is not bound to render professional services to everyone who applies. By notice or special agreement, a physician can limit the extent and scope of employment.

24 In Vidrine v. Mayes, 127 So. 2d 809 (La. Ct. App. 3d Cir. 1961), the court stated that a physician is not required to accept professional employment on terms conditioned by the patient. At that time, physicians ended undertaking childbirth in a patient's home because facilities of modern medicine were then available to afford the safest possible delivery.

25 See, Giallanza v. Sands, 316 So. 2d 77 (Fla. 4th DCA 1975).

26 In McGulpin v. Bessmer, 241 Iowa 1119, 43 N.W.2d 121 (1950), the Iowa Supreme Court stated that when a physician takes charge of a case, employment continues until it is ended by natural consent, by the physician's dismissal, or when the physician's services are no longer needed. The court ruled that a physician who leaves a patient in a critical stage of a disease without reason or sufficient notice to enable the patient to procure another physician, is culpable for dereliction of duty.

In Methodist Hospital v. Ball, 50 Tenn. App. 460, 362 S.W.2d 475 (1961), the court ruled that a person brought to a hospital on a stretcher was a patient even though he was never given a room in the hospital and stayed in the emergency room only about forty-five minutes. The court ruled the hospital would be liable for the negligence of the intern, who was found to be a hospital employee.

27 See e.g., 210 Ill. Comp. Stat. Ann. § 80/1; N.Y. Pub. Health Law § 2805-b.

care to any patient without cause.[28] The duty a hospital owes a patient in need of emergency care generally is determined by state statutes and regulations.[29] Ordinarily a hospital may not transfer emergency patients until all medically

See, also however, Harper v. Baptist Medical Center-Princeton, 341 So. 2d 133 (Ala. 1976), in which the Alabama Supreme Court ruled a private hospital had no duty to provide care to an emergency patient.

In Thompson v. Sun City Community Hosp., Inc., 141 Ariz. 597, 688 P.2d 605 (1984) (rejected by, Matsuyama v. Birnbaum, 452 Mass. 1, 890 N.E.2d 819 (2008)), the Supreme Court of Arizona determined it is the public policy of the state that a general hospital may not deny emergency care to any patient without cause.

In Moran v. Prime Healthcare Management, Inc. 3 Cal. App. 5th 1131 (Ct. App. Cal. 2016), a California appellate court granted standing to a "self-pay patient" who contended he was charged more for emergency care than were persons with insurance. The plaintiff cited the Hospital Fair Pricing Act, Health & Safety Code § 12400 et seq., which requires licensed hospitals to maintain and administer "an understandable written policy regarding discount payments for financially qualified patients as well as an understandable written charity care policy" and details mandatory requirements for the policy. The court ruled the patient did not have a reasonable expectation that a person receiving medical treatment at a hospital's emergency room who pays for it out of pocket can be charged substantially more for that care than one who is covered by either a government-sponsored program or private insurance. However, the court also ruled the patient stated a claim that the financial liability provision of the hospital's contract was unconscionable.

In Marks v. Mandel, 477 So. 2d 1036 (Fla. 3d DCA 1985), the court ruled a hospital's emergency room policy and procedure manual could be admitted as evidence when the manual showed a general industry custom, or standard, or showed the hospital violated its own policy or an industry standard.

In Hastings v. Baton Rouge General Hosp., 498 So. 2d 713 (La. 1986), the Supreme Court of Louisiana ruled that a hospital is responsible for the failure of the physicians on duty to furnish the care and attention reasonably required by an emergency patient's condition.

28 See Thompson v. Sun City Community Hosp., Inc., 141 Ariz. 597, 688 P.2d 605 (1984) (but rejected by, Matsuyama v. Birnbaum, 452 Mass. 1, 890 N.E.2d 819 (2008)).

In Stanturf v. Sipes, 447 S.W.2d 558 (Mo. 1969), the Supreme Court of Missouri commented that although a hospital owes the public no duty to accept any patient and need not assign any reason for its refusal to accept a patient for hospital services, the maintenance of a ward to render first aid to injured persons has become a well-established adjunct to the business of a hospital.

29 In Abercrombie v. Osteopathic Hosp. Founders Ass'n, 950 F.2d 676 (10th Cir. 1991), the Court of Appeals for the Tenth Circuit noted a strict liability standard, rather than a negligence standard, applies under the Emergency Medical Treatment and Active Labor Act (COBRA), 42 U.S.C. §v1395dd. COBRA, which applies to any hospital that receives Medicare payments and has an emergency department, was enacted to prevent the practice of inappropriately transferring or "dumping" patients. One requirement of the act is for a hospital to provide a medical screening examination to determine whether an emergency medical condition exists when an individual presents himself/herself at a hospital and requests an examination and treatment for the medical condition. Another requirement is that a patient who has an emergency medical condition which has not been stabilized may not be transferred out of the hospital.

In Thompson v. Sun City Community Hosp., Inc., 141 Ariz. 597, 688 P.2d 605 (1984) (rejected by, Matsuyama v. Birnbaum, 452 Mass. 1, 890 N.E.2d 819 (2008)), the Supreme Court of Arizona ruled that hospitals are required to have on call one or more physicians licensed to practice medicine and surgery, or a resident physician, or an intern physician. The imposition of a duty to render emergency care to indigents charges private hospitals with the same duty as public hospitals under a statutory plan that permits reimbursements from public funds for some emergency care charges incurred at the private hospital. The duty of care owed by a physician to a patient is determined by common-law principles that require deference to that which is usually done by members of the profession. It is distinct from the hospital duty.

indicated emergency care has been completed.[30] A hospital also may not transfer a patient without due consideration for the patient's condition and the facilities existing for the patient's care.[31] Courts have ruled that when a hospital holds itself out to the public as providing a given service, such as emergency services, and a patient engages the services of the hospital without regard to the identity of a particular physician, but rather the patient is relying upon the hospital to deliver the desired health care and treatment, the doctrine of respondeat superior applies. The hospital then is vicariously liable for damages proximately resulting from the neglect of the physicians even though the hospital had an independent contractual relationship with the physicians.[32] A full-service hospital may be estopped to deny that physicians and other personnel on duty in its emergency

30 See 42 U.S.C. § 1395dd which requires hospitals that are part of the Medicare program to provide for an appropriate medical screening examination for patients requesting treatment at the emergency department to determine whether an emergency exists. If the patient is in labor, the hospital must stabilize the medical condition or provide for treatment or transfer the patient to another medical facility. A hospital may not transfer the patient if the medical condition has not been stabilized or if the patient is in active labor unless the patient, or the legally responsible party acting for the patient, requests the transfer, or a physician determines that benefits of transfer outweigh the risks to the patient. A violation of the provisions relating to transfers can result in civil penalties.

The emergency services section of the hospital manual published by the Joint Commission provides that no patient should arbitrarily be transferred if the hospital where the patient is initially seen had the means for adequate care of the patient's problems.

In Thompson v. Sun City Community Hosp., Inc., 141 Ariz. 597, 688 P.2d 605 (1984) (rejected by, Matsuyama v. Birnbaum, 452 Mass. 1, 890 N.E.2d 819 (2008)), the Supreme Court of Arizona ruled a hospital director was mandated to use the standards of the Joint Commission as a guideline for minimum requirements.

31 In Hastings v. Baton Rouge General Hosp., 498 So. 2d 713 (La. 1986), the Supreme Court of Louisiana ruled a hospital responsible for derelictions by emergency room physicians. The court recognized that a hospital must act through its medical staff. The court further stated the fact that a patient had less than a fifty percent chance of survival did not relieve the hospital from liability. If a hospital destroys any substantial possibility of a patient's survival by refusing to render emergency care, the court held that the conduct of the hospital becomes the proximate cause of the patient's death.

32 In Hardy v. Brantley, 471 So. 2d 358 (Miss. 1985), the Supreme Court of Mississippi applied this general principle to suits against hospitals because the court recognized hospitals are not merely physical facilities where physicians practice their professions. The court noted that hospitals hold themselves out to the public as offering and rendering quality health-care services, stating that patients often seek emergency care and treatment from a hospital rather than from a physician. The court noted that a patient entering a hospital emergency room seldom knows the name of the physician who will treat the patient.

In New Biloxi Hospital, Inc. v. Frazier, 245 Miss. 185, 146 So. 2d 882 (1962), the Supreme Court of Mississippi earlier found a hospital liable for the negligent failure of its nurse to stop a man from bleeding to death. In this case, the court stated a hospital rendering emergency treatment has a duty to exercise due care to see that all which is immediately and reasonably necessary to the preservation of life and limb is done before the patient is discharged.

In Brownsville Medical Center v. Gracia, 704 S.W.2d 68 (Tex. App. Corpus Christi 1985), writ refused n.r.e., (1986), the court ruled a physician hired to perform emergency services was the ostensible agent of the medical center; accordingly, the medical center was vicariously liable for the physician's negligence.

room are employees of the hospital regardless of the nature of the employment contract between the hospital and the emergency room staff.[33] Courts have held hospitals liable for the negligent acts of emergency room physicians under the doctrine of "ostensible" or "apparent" agency or agency by estoppel.[34]

All fifty states and the District of Columbia have enacted some form of Good Samaritan legislation in "varying degrees of immunity to different classes of rescuers under a multitude of settings.[35] The Supreme Court of Oklahoma has

---

33 In Berlin v. Sarah Bush Lincoln Health Center, 279 Ill. App. 3d 447, 664 N.E.2d 337 (4th Dist. 1996), rev'd, 179 Ill. 2d 1, 688 N.E.2d 106 (1997), the court ruled the Illinois Licensing Act, 210 Ill. Comp. Stat. Ann. ch. 85 par. 1, prohibited hospitals from employing physicians. Pursuant to the act, corporations could not obtain licenses to practice medicine; thus, the court decided a hospital could grant staff privileges to a physician but could not employ a physician. In reversing the appellate court, the Supreme Court of Illinois, 688 N.E.2d 106 (Ill. 1997), concluded that a licensed hospital was exempt from the prohibition of corporate practice of medicine and could employ licensed physicians to provide medical services.

In Smith v. Baptist Memorial Hosp. System, 720 S.W.2d 618 (Tex. App. San Antonio 1986), writ refused n.r.e., (1987), disapproved of by St. Luke's Episcopal Hosp. v. Agbor, 952 S.W.2d 503 (Tex. 1997)) and Nills v. Angel, 995 S.W.2d 262 (Tex. App. Texarkana 1999)), the court stated sound public policy demands that a "full-service hospital," which has an emergency room as part of its facilities, make a statement to the public when it opens its emergency room to provide emergency care for the public. The court ruled an agency by estoppel is established by creating the appearance that the hospital's agents, not independent contractors, will provide medical care to those who enter the hospital. The court stated the appearance is what the patient observes and what the patient relies upon when entering a full-service hospital. However, in Nicholson v. Memorial Hosp. System, 722 S.W.2d 746 (Tex. App. Houston 14th Dist. 1986), writ refused n.r.e., (1987), the court found no ostensible agency when a patient asked the hospital to recommend a physician. The court decided the recommended physician treated the patient as an independent physician.

34 The "ostensible" or "apparent" agency theory was based on the Restatement Second, Torts § 429. Section 429 provided that one who employs an independent contractor to perform services for another, which are accepted in the reasonable belief that the employer or its agents are rendering the services, is subject to liability for physical harm caused by the negligence of the contractor in supplying the services to the same extent as though the employer were personally, or by its servants, supplying the services.

In Popovich v. Allina Health System, 946 N.W. 2d 885 (Minn. 2020), the Supreme Court of Minnesota ruled that, as a matter of first impression, a plaintiff could assert a claim against a hospital to hold it vicariously liable for the professional negligence of an independent contractor based on a theory of apparent authority. The court held, as a matter of first impression, that a plaintiff states such a claim where a hospital holds itself out as a provider of emergency medical care, and a plaintiff relied on the hospital to select the personnel to provide services.

35 See, Tex. Civ. Prac. & Rem. Code § 74.151, which provides that a person who in good faith administers emergency care is not liable in civil damages for an act performed during the emergency unless the act is willfully or wantonly negligent, including a person who administers emergency using an automated external defibrillator or administers emergency care as a volunteer and is a first responder as defined in Tex. Gov. Code § 421.095. The section states it does not apply to care administered for or in expectation of remuneration or by a person who was at the scene of the emergency because that person or someone who represented that person as an agent was soliciting business or seeking to perform a service for remuneration. It also does not apply to a person whose negligent act or omission was a producing cause of the emergency for which care was being administered.

In Velazquez v. Jiminez, M.D, St. Peter's Medical Center, Maak, R.N., Healy, R.N., and Does, M.D, 172 N.J.

posited that a Good Samaritan Act "abrogates the common-law rescue doctrine for medical providers in an effort to *encourage* them to risk helping strangers in need of succor, *even when they have no duty to render aid.*[36] The court stated that the Act's immunity does not apply in the context of a hospital/patient relationship, i. e, a hospital is never a Good Samaritan vis-a-vis its own patient.[37]

E. BLOOD TRANSFUSIONS

Patients who have contracted a disease, such as hepatitis and, in earlier cases, AIDS, as a consequence of a blood transfusion,[38] have sought recovery from the

240, 798 A2d 51 (N.J. 2002), the Supreme Court of New Jersey concluded the New Jersey Good Samaritan Act could not be invoked to immunize a physician who responded in a hospital setting to an emergency call by another physician to assist the latter physician's patient in crisis. The court stated: "Good Samaritan legislation has at its core, the goal of encouraging the rendering of medical care to those who need it but otherwise might not receive it (ordinarily roadside accident victims), by persons who come upon victims by chance, without the accoutrements provided in a medical facility, including expertise, assistance, sanitation or equipment." The court summarized the varying state Good Samaritan statutes. It noted that eleven jurisdictions exclude from statutory immunity emergency care rendered to patients within a hospital or other health care facility whereas Good Samaritan statutes in seven jurisdictions immunize emergency care provided in a hospital setting. It stated some state statutes, such as that in New Jersey, do not explicitly address whether in-hospital care can be shielded from liability under a Good Samaritan statute. Some state statutes immunize "emergency medical or professional assistance to a person in need thereof," some "emergency care or assistance in an emergency," or, in some states, "aid or assistance necessary or helpful in the circumstances to other persons who have been injured or are ill as the result of an accident or illness or...trauma." One state extends coverage to emergency care given "wherever required." 172 N.J. at 252 3.

In Chamley v. Khokha, M.D. and Mercy Medical Center, 730 N.W. 2d 864 (N.D. 2007), the Supreme Court of North Dakota ruled that a general surgeon, as a salaried hospital employee who received remuneration for assisting a patient's urologist with emergency surgery to remove the patient's kidney, was precluded from claiming immunity under the state's Good Samaritan Act. The court precluded coverage under that act for the hospital physician because the hospital physician had expectation of remuneration.

36 Jackson v. Mercy Health Center, Inc., 864 P.2d 839, 843 (Ok. 1993).

37 The Oklahoma Supreme Court stated in Jackson v. Mercy Health Center, Inc, 864 P.2d 839 (1993), that Good Samaritan immunity rests on three elements: (1) the absence of a prior contractual relationship between the rescuer and the injured person, (2) the characterization of the rescuer's act as having been done in good faith, voluntarily and without compensation and (3) the injured person's apparent need of emergency medical aid. It noted that gross negligence or willful or wanton acts are excluded from statutory protection.

38 The possibility of contracting AIDS through a blood transfusion is now very low and can presently be prevented. Screening of the body for human immunodeficiency virus (HIV) antibody was initiated in 1985 and has substantially lessened the possibility of contracting AIDS through a blood transfusion.

In Estate of Amos v. Vanderbilt University, 62 S.W.3d 133 (Tenn. 2001), the Supreme Court of Tennessee ruled a hospital owed a duty to warn of a patient's potential exposure to HIV from a blood transfusion during a surgery, which occurred before the hospital had a policy requiring patients to be notified when they received blood during surgery. A patient, who had died of AIDS prior to the court's decision, had

blood supplier upon the theory that supplying blood by transfusion constitutes a sale with an implied warranty that the blood is reasonably fit for the purpose of its intended use.[39] Although some courts have ruled that a blood transfusion is an incidental and secondary adjunct to the provision of hospital services, and thus, is not within the provisions of sales law,[40] other courts extended the scope for warranty and strict liability in blood transfusion cases and have held hospitals, as well as blood banks, liable when the blood contained harmful impurities.[41] These decisions prompted states to provide varying degrees of statutory

---

surgery in 1984 before blood banks tested blood for HIV. In 1985, the hospital began screening for HIV in blood to be used in transfusions. In 1987, it began offering free HIV testing to all patients who had received blood transfusions at its facility. It also established a procedure for notifying a patient when it learned the patient had received blood from a donor who had tested positive for HIV. The hospital did not undertake to identify and warn all prior patients who had received blood transfusions that they could be exposed to the HIV virus. Thus, the patient was not warned of any potential danger from her surgery in 1984. In 1989, the patient gave birth to a daughter who became infected with HIV in utero and died three months after birth. The patient then was tested for HIV. Before the test, she was unaware that she had HIV. She and her husband sued the hospital for wrongful birth, negligence, and negligent infliction of emotional distress. The court ruled the hospital had a duty to warn the patient so that she could avoid spreading the deadly disease to her husband and her child.

39 See U.C.C. §§ 2-314, 2-315 relating to the implied warranty of merchantability, which requires fitness for ordinary uses, and the implied warranty of fitness for particular purposes. If injury or death resulted from blood that was contaminated with serum hepatitis or the AIDS virus, a contention can be made that the hospital breached an implied warranty under the Uniform Commercial Code or a sales act because the blood was impure and unfit for its intended use.

See discussion below of a patient's right to refuse a blood transfusion.

40 In Williamson v. Memorial Hospital of Bay County, 307 So. 2d 199 (Fla. 1st DCA 1975), the court ruled that while a blood bank could be held for breach of implied warranty, a hospital could not. The court concluded that the use of whole blood is a service, not a sale.

In Perlmutter v. Beth David Hospital, 308 N.Y. 100, 123 N.E.2d 792 (1954), the New York Court concluded the furnishing of blood for a transfusion at a stated sum of money as part of a medical treatment was not a purchase and sale of a quantity of blood. The court ruled a patient subjected to a blood transfusion containing harmful impurities could not recover on the theory of implied warranty.

In Goelz v. J. K. & Susie L. Wadley Research Institute and Blood Bank, 350 S.W.2d 573 (Tex. Civ. App. Dallas 1961), writ refused n.r.e., (1962), the court found the provision of blood was a service rather than a sale of a product in a transfusion case involving a blood bank rather than a hospital.

41 See, e.g., DeBattista v. Argonaut-Southwest Ins. Co., 403 So. 2d 26 (La. 1981), wherein the Supreme Court of Louisiana determined a state statute, providing that warranties of merchantability and fitness were applicable to contracts for sale of blood, did not preclude strict liability. That court stated it was not necessary to establish an implied warranty to impose strict liability on the preparer and distributor of blood.

In Kozup v. Georgetown University, 851 F.2d 437, (D.C. Cir. 1988), the Court of Appeals for the District of Columbia ruled a hospital was not entitled to a summary judgment regarding a claim filed by parents of a child who died from a blood transfusion contaminated with the virus now known to transmit AIDS. The university hospital gave the infant the blood transfusion without obtaining a consent from the parents. The hospital contended the transfusion was necessary to save the life of the infant.

immunity for blood and blood products.[42] Thus, statutory law in most states created a shield for blood and blood products barring strict liability claims.[43]

Even though blood shield statutes may immunize a provider of defective blood from strict liability, hospitals can be liable for faulty or improperly administered blood transfusions on a negligence theory.[44] To prevail on a negligence theory, a plaintiff must show that a hospital violated a standard of care established by looking to the conduct of the medical profession in similar circumstances as of a particular date.[45]

---

42 See, e.g., Md. Code Ann., Health-Gen. § 18-402, Tenn. Code Ann. § 472-316(5).

43 See Zichichi v. Middlesex Memorial Hosp., 204 Conn. 399, 528 A.2d 805 (1987), in which the Supreme Court of Connecticut noted that almost every state has a statute regulating the transfer of blood and its derivatives and that these statutes attempt to limit liability. It commented that while the wording of the various "blood shield" statutes varies, courts construing the statutes have uniformly ruled that they constitute a complete bar to any action based on strict liability. The Connecticut Supreme Court noted that in some jurisdictions, even without the benefit of a statute, courts recognized the inherent policy concerns and ruled that a blood transfusion is a "service" rather than a "sale."

In Coffee v. Cutter Biological, 809 F.2d 191 (2d Cir. 1987), the Court of Appeals of the Second Circuit analyzed the Kentucky blood shield statute. The court noted Kentucky's blood shield statute was intended to preclude the assertion of product liability claims arising out of the sale of blood components. The statute sets out that the supplying of blood or blood derivatives is to be considered a service and not a sale.

In Roberts v. Suburban Hosp. Ass'n, Inc., 73 Md. App. 1, 532 A.2d 1081 (1987), the court ruled a blood transfusion constituted the provision of a service rather than the sale of a product. The court stated some states specifically declare a transfusion to be a service; others simply exclude liability except for negligence; others limit liability only if the defect cannot be detected.

44 See, e.g., early decision in Kozup v. Georgetown University, 663 F. Supp. 1048 (D.D.C. 1987), judgment aff'd in part, vacated in part on other grounds, 851 F.2d 437 (D.C.Cir. 1988).

45 See Kozup v. Georgetown University, 663 F. Supp. 1048 (D.D.C. 1987), judgment aff'd in part, vacated in part on other grounds, 851 F.2d 437 (D.C. Cir. 1988) and McKee v. Miles Laboratories, Inc., 675 F. Supp. 1060 (E.D. Ky. 1987), judgment aff'd, 866 F.2d 219 (6th Cir. 1989). The court in both cases pointed out that the medical community did not reach a consensus as to the proposition that AIDS was transmittable by blood until 1984. In reviewing the history related to discovering a method for screening for HIV prior to blood transfusions, these courts noted that in 1984, scientists identified the virus HTLV-III as the cause of AIDS and that by 1985, an enzyme-linked immunosorbent assay (ELISA) test was made available to screen for the antibodies sensitive to HTLV-III. One court pointed out that once it was available, the Centers for Disease Control issued guidelines for implementing the ELISA test and noted the laboratory test proved 98.6 percent effective in detecting exposure to AIDS. It also commented that, when coupled with a second test, the Western Blot Analysis, the rate of detection for exposure to AIDS rises to a 100 percent. The courts rejected the plaintiffs' claims that the suppliers of blood contaminated with the AIDS virus were negligent in not testing the blood for the AIDS virus. Although the patients who were recipients of the blood through transfusions died from AIDS, the court in both cases pointed out that at the time of the transfusions, no pharmaceutical company, blood bank, hospital or federal health care regulator in the United States took special AIDS-related measures in connection with transfusions. The courts determined the blood suppliers did not violate a standard of care because the standard of care as of the date of the transfusions in the two cases did not require the supplier to screen or perform alternative testing to eliminate the risk of AIDS contamination. Consequently, no negligence occurred, and the blood suppliers met the standard of care as then existed within the industry.

The presence of hepatitis or the AIDS virus in blood can be discovered by application of certain tests. Courts have ruled that failure to use the known methods of discovery and testing can constitute negligence.[46]

Transfusions of blood collected from paid rather than voluntary donors increase the incidence of hepatitis dramatically. As one court pointed out, the ratio of hepatitis cases resulting from transfusions of commercial blood to those resulting from transfusions of volunteer blood has been estimated to be at least ten to one.[47] Several courts have indicated that the source of transfused blood is relevant to a plaintiff's prima facie case of negligence against a blood supplier.[48]

In United Blood Services, a Div. of Blood Systems, Inc. v. Quintana, 827 P.2d 509 (Colo. 1992), the Colorado Supreme Court ruled a court could not prevent testimony from experts sufficiently familiar with the applicable standard of care for a blood bank's conduct in 1983 regarding the possibility of AIDS transmission by blood transfusions and donor screening. The experts would have testified that the standard was deficient in guarding against the transmission of AIDS. The Colorado Supreme Court decided that excluding this testimony was tantamount to permitting the blood banking community to establish its own standard of legal liability.

In Snyder v. Mekhjian, 125 N.J. 328, 593 A.2d 318 (1991), the Supreme Court of New Jersey ruled that plaintiffs in an AIDS case had a right to question a blood donor concerning the defendant blood bank's screening procedures. The court decided a patient is entitled to learn whether the blood bank conducted a physical examination of the donor and whether it made a reasonable effort to learn if the donor was in a high-risk category.

46 See McDaniel v. Baptist Memorial Hospital, 469 F.2d 230(6th Cir. 1972) and Klaus v. Alameda-Contra Costa Medical Assn. Blood Bank, Inc., 62 Cal. App. 3d 417, 133 Cal. Rptr. 92 (1st Dist. 1976). In Klause, a California court ruled that failure to screen blood donors effectively can also constitute negligence.

47 See Belle Bonfils Memorial Blood Bank v. Hansen, 665 P.2d 118 (Colo. 1983).

See also 21 C.F.R. § 606.121(c)(5), which required that every container of donated blood be prominently labeled "paid donor" or "volunteer donor."

48 See Supreme Court of Colorado decision in Belle Bonfils Memorial Blood Bank v. Hansen, 665 P.2d 118 (Colo. 1983).

In Rasmussen v. South Florida Blood Service, Inc., 500 So. 2d 533 (Fla. 1987), the Supreme Court of Florida refused to grant discovery of the names of blood donors to a victim of AIDS. The court determined that disclosure of the identity of the blood donors could be extremely disruptive and even devastating to the individual donors. The court decided the probative value of the discovery sought by the plaintiff was "dubious at best." It determined that if the requested information was released, and the plaintiff queried the donors' friends and fellow employees, it would be functionally impossible to prevent occasional reference to AIDS. The court further stated that because AIDS was the modern-day equivalent of leprosy, the suspicion of AIDS could lead to discrimination in employment, education, housing, and even medical treatment for donors. It concluded the disclosure implicated a constitutionally protected privacy interest because, by the very nature of the case, disclosure of donor identities was disclosure in a damaging context.

But see Tarrant County Hosp. Dist. v. Hughes, 734 S.W.2d 675 (Tex. App. Fort Worth 1987), in which the Texas court disagreed with the decision of the Supreme Court of Florida in Rasmussen v. South Florida Blood Service, Inc., 500 So. 2d 533 (Fla. 1987). The Texas court ruled the requirement that a hospital disclose the identity of donors of blood given in a transfusion to a patient of the hospital who contracted AIDS, did not violate the donors' rights to privacy. The court determined that without the information the plaintiff would not be able to prosecute her cause of action for wrongful death against the hospital. The Texas court noted the discovery order contained safeguards for the privacy interests of the donors.

Additionally, evidence of the source of transfused blood and of the availability of other, less risky alternative sources bears upon the reasonableness of the risk.[49] Some states have enacted statutes establishing criteria for the acceptability of blood donors and requiring that blood be tested for the potential presence of causative agents of certain diseases.[50]

F. TREATMENT OF MENTALLY ILL

The mentally ill often are treated as a distinct group. Courts earlier ruled this classification and special treatment is rational and completely within the constitutional restraints imposed by the equal protection clause.[51] This special treatment includes mentally ill persons being confined for treatment in a state institution for an indefinite period.[52] Still, the nature and duration of commit-

---

In Weaver v. Myers, M.D., 229 So.3d 1118 (Fla. 2017), the Supreme Court of Florida reiterated that a patient's medical records enjoy a confidential status, stating in this case that confidentiality is by virtue of the right to privacy contained in the Florida Constitution. The court ruled that a husband maintained his constitutional right to privacy after his death and that his wife had standing to raise his right to privacy. The court stated that the wife did not waive her husband's right to privacy to overall health information by filing a medical malpractice claim and that the husband's right to privacy was violated by statutory provisions requiring secret, ex parte interviews.

49 Discussion in Belle Bonfils Memorial Blood Bank v. Hansen, 665 P.2d 118 (Colo. 1983).

50 See, e.g., Tenn. Code Ann. § 68-32-101, which provided that any person seventeen through sixty-five years of age was acceptable as a blood donor on a voluntary basis only. If a person knew he/she had received a confirmed positive result from the Human T Lymphotropic Virus type III antibody test (HTLV-III), or if a person knew he was suffering from a confirmed case of AIDS, then it was unlawful for the person to be, or attempt to be, a blood donor, except when deemed necessary for medical research. Tenn. Code Ann. § 68-32-104. A patient in Tennessee who was treated by a health professional or health facility had the option of designating donors to provide blood or blood products necessary for medical treatment except in emergency situations where the physician determined that failure to transfuse would be life threatening to the patient. Tenn. Code Ann. § 68-32-103. All facilities in Tennessee collecting fresh human blood or plasma directly from an individual donor had to have the blood or plasma tested for the potential presence of the causative agent for AIDS. See Tenn. Code Ann. § 68-32-102(a). See also Tenn. Code Ann. § 68-32-102(c), which provided that any person who contracted AIDS from contaminated blood or blood product had a cause of action for damages, including all medical expenses, against a facility supplying untested blood, if that person could establish he/she received any untested blood, or blood product from the supplier, except in emergency situations where the attending physician determined that failure to transfuse would be life threatening to the patient.

51 Cospito v. Heckler, 742 F.2d 72 (3d Cir. 1984).

52 In re Ballay, 482 F.2d 648 (D.C. Cir. 1973).

All states have statutes providing for involuntary civil commitment to mental institutions. See, e.g., Ariz. Rev. Stat. Ann. § 6-501; Ga. Code Ann. § 88-501-507.1; 405 Ill. Comp. Stat. Ann. 5/3-100; N.J. Rev. Stat. 30.4 et seq.; Pa. Cons. Stat. Ann. tit. 50, §§ 4401 et seq.; Tex. Health & Safety Code §§ 574.001 to 574.070.

ment must bear some reasonable relation to the purpose for which the individual is committed.[53]

After making a finding that individuals with mental illness are vulnerable to abuse and serious injury Congress has provided for the protection and treatment for the mentally disabled by enacting the Protection and Advocacy for Mentally Ill Individuals' Act.[54] The purpose of the act is to ensure the rights of individuals with mental illness are protected and to assist states to establish and operate a protection and advocacy system for individuals with mental illness that would protect and advocate the rights of these individuals. The act provides that persons with developmental disabilities have a right to appropriate treatment, services, ongoing participation in a manner appropriate to the person's capabilities in the planning of mental health services, reasonable explanation of objectives of treatment and the nature and significant possible adverse effects of recommended treatment, freedom from restraint or seclusion other than in special circumstances set out in the act, and confidentiality of the person's records.[55] Thus, although as a general rule a state is under no constitutional duty to provide services for persons within its borders,[56] a state must provide certain services and care to persons who have been institutionalized and are, as a result, wholly dependent on the state.[57]

A mental health facility includes those parts of a hospital that provide diagnosis, treatment, and care for the mentally ill.[58] Patients generally may be admitted and detained for treatment in a mental health facility on a voluntary basis, upon court-ordered temporary and extended mental health treatment, and upon

---

In Karsjens v. Lourey, 988 F.3d 1047 (8th Cir. 2021), the Court of Appeals for the Seventh Circuit ruled, as a matter of first impression, that conditions of confinement for a civilly committed individual violate substantive due process if they amount to the individual's punishment.

53 See Jackson v. Indiana, 406 U.S. 715 (1972) in which the Supreme court stated due process requires, at the least, that the nature and duration of commitment bear some reasonable relation to the purpose for which the individual is committed. Still, the Supreme Court had not established a constitutional standard for evaluating the conditions of a civilly committed individual's confinement.

54 42 U.S.C. §§ 10801 et. seq.

55 See 42 U.S.C.A. § 10841. Each state must review and revise its laws to ensure mentally ill persons receive the protection and services they require. 42 U.S.C. §§ 10801.

In Brooks v. Johnson and Johnson, Inc., 685 F. Supp. 107 (E.D. Pa. 1988), the court decided that the Mental Health Patient's "Bill of Rights," 42 U.S.C. § 10846, did not provide a private right of action.

56 Harris v. McRae, 448 U.S. 297 (1980); Maher v. Roe, 432 U.S. 464 (1977).

57 Youngberg v. Romeo, 457 U.S. 307 (1982).

58 See, e.g., Tex. Health & Safety Code § 571.003(13).

emergency detention or protective custody.[59] Hospitals treating the mentally ill must maintain the confidentiality of records relating to the personal life of the patient.[60]

Courts have denied a state authority to administer psychotropic drugs forcibly to involuntarily committed persons.[61] As one court stated, neither mental illness nor institutionalization per se can justify overriding an individuals' fundamental right to refuse antipsychotic medication.[62]

Treatment of the mentally ill who have been confined for treatment in a state institution has involved the use of forced psychiatric treatment imposed upon these patients without their consent and often against their will. Courts have recognized persons properly committed to a mental institution may be legally competent.[63] As one court stated, the state may not act in a parens patriae relationship to a mental hospital patient unless the patient also has been adjudicated

59 See, e.g., Tex. Health & Safety Code §§ 572.001 to 575.003.

60 See, e.g., Ariz. Rev. Stat. Ann. § 36-509.

61 See, e.g., Riese v. St. Mary's Hosp. and Medical Center, 259 Cal. Rptr. 669, 774 P.2d 698 (Cal. 1989), in which the court ruled that absent a judicial determination of incompetency, an involuntary mental health patient's informed consent would be required before treatment with antipsychotic drugs.

In State ex rel. Jones v. Gerhardstein, 141 Wis. 2d 710, 416 N.W.2d 883 (1987), a Wisconsin court stated that while dangerousness may justify legitimately the state's authority to commit an individual involuntarily, it did not justify the abrogation of the individual's right of informed consent with respect to psychotropic drugs.

62 Rivers v. Katz, 67 N.Y.2d 485, 504 N.Y.S.2d 74, 495 N.E.2d 337 (1986).

The Wisconsin Supreme Court ruled in In re Melanie L., 349 Wis.2d 148, 833 NW.2d 607 (Wis. 2013), that a county had failed to establish by clear and convincing evidence a patient was substantially incapable of applying an understanding of the advantages and disadvantages of a particular medication to her own mental illness. The court noted that a person has the right to refuse medication unless a court determines the person is incompetent to make such a decision.

63 See In re Milton, 29 Ohio St. 3d 20, 505 N.E.2d 255 (1987) (holding modified by, Steele v. Hamilton Cty. Community Mental Health Bd., 90 Ohio St. 3d 176 736 N.E.2d 10 (2000)).

incompetent.[64] If the patient has not been adjudicated incompetent, courts have more recognized the patient's right to refuse treatment.[65]

64 In re Milton, 29 Ohio St. 3d 20, 505 N.E.2d 255 (1987) (holding modified by Steele v. Hamilton Cty. Community Mental Health Bd., 90 Ohio St. 3d 176, 736 N.E.2d 10 (2000)).

In Matter of Peter by Johanning, 108 N.J. 365, 529 A.2d 419 (1987), the New Jersey Supreme Court ruled an ombudsman can approve a surrogate decision to decline life-sustaining treatment on behalf of an elderly, incompetent nursing home resident only when one of the three following tests are satisfied: (1) The subjective test--it is clear the patient would have refused the treatment under the circumstances involved. (2) The limited-objective test--there is some trustworthy evidence the patient would have refused the treatment, and the burdens (the pain and suffering) of the patient's continued life with the treatment markedly outweigh the benefits (any physical pleasure, emotional enjoyment, or intellectual satisfaction) that the patient may still be able to derive from life. (3) The purely objective test--the pain and suffering of the patient's life with the treatment clearly and markedly outweigh the benefits the patient derives from life, and the patient is suffering from so much pain that prolonging the patient's life would be inhumane.

In Matter of Jobes, 108 N.J. 394, 529 A.2d 434 (1987), the Supreme Court of New Jersey set out guidelines and procedures under which life-sustaining medical treatment could be withdrawn from a nonelderly nursing home patient in a persistent vegetative state who, prior to her incompetency, failed to express adequately her attitude toward the treatment. The court stated the "substituted judgment" approach best accomplishes the goal of having the patient make her own decision.

65 In United States v. Charters, 839 F.2d 479 (4th Cir 1987), the Court of Appeals for the Fourth Circuit decided a mentally ill pretrial detainee has a constitutionally protected interest in deciding for himself whether to accept or forego medical treatment. The Fourth Circuit commented that when a detainee is competent to consent to or refuse medical care, the detainee's constitutional interest in deciding outweighs the government's interest in medicating the detainee against her will. The court also stated a patient is entitled to be presumed competent until adjudicated incompetent. If found incompetent, the custodian of the patient must apply for a court order permitting forcible medication.

In Rogers v. Commissioner of Dept. of Mental Health, 390 Mass. 489, 458 N.E.2d 308 (1983), the Supreme Court of Massachusetts early ruled an involuntarily committed mental patient has the right to make treatment decisions and does not lose that right until the patient has been adjudicated incompetent by a judge through incompetency proceedings. The court also ruled a patient must be found incompetent before a judge may make a substituted judgment decision. If the patient is found incompetent, the judge should make a determination of an appropriate treatment plan. A guardian should be appointed to monitor the treatment process to ensure the substituted judgment treatment plan is followed. The court noted a substituted judgment decision is distinct from a decision by doctors as to what is medically in the "best interests" of the patient. According to the court in the Rogers case, the substituted judgment decision should be that which would be made by the incompetent person, if that person were competent, but considering the present and future incompetency of the individual as one of the factors that would necessarily enter into the decision-making process of a competent person and giving the fullest possible expression to the character and circumstances of that individual. The court noted the decision is not simply a question whether treatment is to be rendered, but also may entail a choice between alternative treatments. The court rejected the suggestion by the American Psychiatric Association that if a substituted judgment is required, the decision as to substituted judgment should be made by a qualified physician and not a judge. The court affirmed that medical advice and opinion outline should be used in making the substituted judgment for the incompetent but that the doctrines of informed consent and right of privacy, which underlie the substituted judgment determination, have as their foundations the right to bodily integrity and control of one's own fate. According to the court, those rights are superior to institutional considerations. The court concluded only if a patient poses an imminent threat of harm to the patient or to others and only if there is no less intrusive alternative to antipsychotic drugs may the state invoke its police powers without prior court approval to treat the patient by forcible injection of antipsychotic drugs over the patient's objection.

G. INCOMPETENTS

The right of an individual to make decisions regarding his/her body, deemed to be a right of privacy, extends to an incompetent person who is unable to exercise the right in his/her own behalf.[66] As one court stated, the right to make a medical decision for one's self is not lost because of one's mental illness.[67] If a patient is incompetent to make that decision, a representative for the incompetent must give or withhold consent.[68] Some courts have determined that a health-care provider can rely on the consent of the patient's prescribed relative; however, if none of the prescribed relatives are available to give consent, then the provider must obtain judicial approval of the medical procedure or a guardian must be appointed to make the decision.[69] Some courts have required that

66 Corbett v. D'Alessandro, 487 So. 2d 368 (Fla. 2d DCA 1986).

67 See Barclay v. Campbell, 704 S.W.2d 8 (Tex. 1986).

As a matter of first impression, the Supreme Court of New Hampshire, in In re Guardianship of L.N., 173 N.H. 77, 237A3d 222 (N.H. 2020), ruled that a guardian's general statutory authority to give consent to enable a ward to receive medical treatment includes authority to terminate life support. The court also ruled, as a matter of first impression, that end-of-life decisions are included in a guardian's power.

68 In Matter of Guardianship of Ingram, 102 Wash. 2d 827, 689 P.2d 1363 (1984), the Supreme Court of Washington stated that the finding of incompetency merely means that the ward's rights will be exercised by the guardian on the ward's behalf.

69 In Winters v. Miller, 446 F.2d 65 (2d Cir. 1971), the Court of Appeals for the Second Circuit ruled the state may not act in parens patriae for a mental hospital patient unless the patient has been adjudicated as being incompetent.

In Ritz v. Florida Patient's Compensation Fund, 436 So. 2d 987 (Fla. 5th DCA 1983), parents of an intellectually and developmentally disabled adult who were not appointed as guardians of their adult child gave consent to surgery. The court ruled the consent was not invalid because the parents were not appointed guardians. The court stated that when an adult child is incompetent and has no legally appointed guardian, the right to consent to medical or surgical treatment resides in the parent who has legal responsibility to maintain and support the child.

In Matter of Quinlan, 70 N.J. 10, 355 A.2d 647 (1976), the parent of an adult child sought to be appointed guardian of the child to authorize the parent to consent to the removal of procedures sustaining his adult child's vital processes. The Supreme Court of New Jersey reversed the decision of the trial court that had denied the request. The court noted the right of privacy includes a patient's decision to decline treatment under certain circumstances even if the decision might lead to death.

In Anderson v. Wiener, 100 A.D.2d 919, 474 N.Y.S.2d 801 (2d Dep't 1984), the court ruled that when an appropriate relative is available to grant or deny consent, the sole role of the judiciary is to resolve any dispute that may arise concerning the patient's ability to grant consent. Once the incapacity of the patient to consent has been established, the health-care provider may rely on the consent of the patient's prescribed relative. The court stated that where the patient's inability to consent is beyond legal question, and the spouse, parent or adult child of the patient consents to the proposed medical procedure, it is unnecessary for the provider to obtain judicial approval. However, if none of these prescribed relatives is available to give consent, then the facility must obtain judicial approval of the medical procedure. The court decided it is only in this instance the court exercises its power as parens patriae to determine whether the interests of the patient warrant the performance of the proposed procedure.

the parent or appointed guardian must nonetheless seek judicial approval for an extraordinary, irreversible procedure that would seriously affect a person's bodily integrity.[70]

When a person is incompetent to give consent, the guardian of the ward must do what the ward would do if competent to make the decision.[71] The guardian

---

See In re Estate of Dorone, 349 Pa. Super. 59, 502 A.2d 1271 (1985), order aff'd, 517 Pa. 3, 534 A.2d 452 (1987), in which a hospital administrator was appointed to give consent to a blood transfusion for a person who was unconscious because of an accident. The patient was a Jehovah's Witness and carried a card stating that, for religious reasons, no blood transfusions should be given the cardholder. The surgeon had determined the person would die without surgery and that at least one blood transfusion would be necessary during surgery. The patient's parents would not authorize a blood transfusion and later challenged the order of the court appointing the hospital administrator as the guardian to their adult child. The court ruled the court had discretion in appointing a guardian and it should not have appointed the parents because they had an interest adverse to the incompetent.

70 In Cruzan by Cruzan v. Director, Missouri Dept. of Health, 497 U.S. 261 (1990), the Supreme Court ruled a state may require that evidence of an incompetent's wishes as to withdrawal of life-sustaining treatment be proved by clear and convincing evidence. The Court noted that although a competent person would have a constitutionally protected right to refuse lifesaving hydration and nutrition, an incompetent person may not possess the same right because the incompetent person is unable to make an informed and voluntary choice to exercise that hypothetical right or any other right. The Supreme Court stated that a state need not accept the "substituted judgment" of close family members in the absence of substantial proof that their views reflect those of the patient's. The Court further stated its decision in Michael H. v. Gerald D., 492 U.S. 937 (1989), upholding a state's favored treatment of traditional family relationships, may not be turned into a constitutional requirement that a state must recognize the primacy of these relationships in all situations. As the Court stated, a decision upholding a state's right to permit family decision making may not be turned into a constitutional requirement that the state recognize the decision making.

In Matter of Guardianship of Ingram, 102 Wash. 2d 827, 689 P.2d 1363 (1984), the court ruled a guardian may not consent to some cases. A proposed laryngectomy to be performed on the patient was invasive surgery that would have resulted in loss of speech. The court determined this consequence was more severe than a loss of a limb and that judicial approval was required before the guardian could consent to the surgery.

The Supreme Court of New Hampshire, In re Guardianship of L.N, 173 N.H. 77, 237 A.2d 222 (N.H. 2020), stated that it was not alone in rejecting the proposition that a guardian must in all cases seek court approval before authorizing the withdrawal life support from a ward. Still, that court also stated that it did not intend to imply that court involvement is never necessary or appropriate. The court concluded that the general power to give or withhold consent to medical treatment for a ward includes the power to withdraw life-sustaining treatment in appropriate circumstances without prior court approval. That court did state that judicial intervention would be warranted if a disagreement arose among the patient, family, guardian, or doctors, or if there was evidence of improper motives or malpractice.

71 In Rasmussen by Mitchell v. Fleming, 154 Ariz. 207, 741 P.2d 674 (1987), the Supreme Court of Arizona noted that courts have developed two standards to guide surrogate decision making: "substituted judgment" and "best interests." Under the substituted judgment standard, the guardian attempts to reach the decision that the incapacitated person would make if that person were able to choose. This standard, the court decided, best guides a guardian's decision making when a patient has manifested the patient's intent while competent. However, if there is no reliable evidence of a patient's intent, then the court stated the substituted judgment standard should be abandoned in favor of the "best interests" standard. Under this standard, the surrogate decision maker assesses what medical treatment would be in the patient's best interests as determined by objective criteria as relief from suffering, preservation or restoration of functioning, and quality and extent of sustained life.

makes a decision based upon the doctrine of substituted judgment or in some cases, the best interest of the patient.[72] As one court stated, the goal is not to do what most persons would do or what is believed to be the wise thing to do but rather what the particular individual would do if the individual were competent and understood all the circumstances, including present and future competency.[73] If court approval is sought in making a decision to give or withhold consent, the court also makes a "substituted judgment" for the ward.[74] The courts should consider all relevant facts that would influence the person's decisions regarding medical treatment.[75]

In Riese v. St. Mary's Hosp. and Medical Center, 259 Cal. Rptr. 669, 774 P.2d 698 (Cal. 1989), the California Supreme Court ruled an involuntarily committed patient who was receiving medications as a result of the patient's mental illness must be given, as soon as possible after detention, written and oral information about probable effects and possible side effects of medications, including why medication is being given or recommended; the likelihood of improvement without medication; reasonable alternative treatments available; and information concerning name, dosage and frequency of medication. The court ruled that in the absence of judicial determination of incompetency, the involuntary mental health patient's informed consent would be required before treatment with antipsychotic drugs.

72 In Brophy v. New England Sinai Hosp., Inc., 398 Mass. 417, 497 N.E.2d 626 (1986), the Massachusetts Supreme Court ruled that substituted judgment to discontinue artificial maintenance of life would be honored.

See also, In re Estate of Dorone, 349 Pa. Super. 59, 502 A.2d 1271 (1985), order aff'd, 517 Pa. 3, 534 A.2d 452 (1987), in which the court determined a guardian could give consent for a blood transfusion for a Jehovah's Witness, who was unconscious because of an accident, even though the individual carried a card stating that for religious reasons that person did not want a blood transfusion. The court decided a medical alert card is nonevidence of what a patient would do if competent. It would not support application of a substituted judgment. To determine the validity of the card as to the incompetent's decision, the court stated that circumstances regarding the signing of the card would need to be considered. For example, the individual may have signed the card at a religious meeting at which the patient felt some pressure to do so.

73 In In re Guardianship of D.E., 173 N.Y. 550, 243 A.3d 908 ((2020), the Supreme Court of New Hampshire, ruled, as a matter of apparent first impression, that the best interest standard governs a guardian's health care decision for a ward, including a decision to withhold life-sustaining treatment from the ward. The court had held a hearing in which only the ward's adult children were present. The ward's children testified that when their father was in the intensive care unit, they executed a "Do Not Resuscitate (DNR)" order for him. The ward had no previous DNR order. When the ward's condition improved and he was transferred to a medical ward, he specifically told his children that he wanted the DNR order removed. The court ruled that a trial court's review of a guardian's decision to withhold life-sustaining treatment from a ward is deferential and should the trial court decline to remove a limitation on a guardian's authority, then the relevant provision in statutes governing written directives for medical decision making for adults without capacity to make health care decisions apply. The court also ruled that because the ward had not executed an advance directive, he did not have an "agent," and no "surrogate" had been appointed for him.

74 See the Supreme Court of Washington's decision in Matter of Guardianship of Ingram, 102 Wash. 2d 827, 689 P.2d 1363 (1984).

75 Pursuant to In Matter of Guardianship of Ingram, 102 Wash. 2d 827, 689 P.2d 1363 (1984), courts should consider the following: the ward's prognosis if the ward chose no treatment; the prognosis if the ward chose one treatment over another; the risk of adverse side effects from the proposed treatments; the ability of the ward to cooperate and assist with post treatment therapy; the ward's

As a general rule, a hospital need not seek a court order in decisions involving the withdrawing or the withholding of medical treatment by artificial means for the terminally ill patient.[76] Courts have ruled that physicians, hospitals, or their administrators only need act in good faith with respect to the proper treatment of the patient in honoring their respective professional oaths and duties to render proper care in the light of the patient's rights to refuse treatment.[77] A

---

religious or moral views regarding medical care of the dying process; and the wishes of family and friends, if those wishes would influence the ward's decision. Courts also may consider what most people would do in similar circumstances, but this should not be regarded as controlling. Additionally, courts should, if possible, interview the patient and observe the patient's physical and mental condition to ascertain the patient's wishes.

76 In Matter of Spring, 380 Mass. 629, 405 N.E.2d 115 (1980), the Supreme Court of Massachusetts suggested a variety of circumstances to be considered in deciding whether there should be an application for a prior court order for medical treatment of an incompetent patient. The court listed the following: the extent of impairment of the patient's mental faculties; whether the patient is in the custody of a state institution; the prognosis without the proposed treatment; the complexity, risk, and novelty of the proposed treatment and its possible side effects; the patient's level of understanding and probable reaction; the urgency of decision; the consent of the patient, spouse, or guardian; the good faith of those who participate in the decision; the clarity of professional opinion as to what is good medical practice; the interests of third persons; and the administrative requirements of any institution involved. The court noted that action taken without judicial approval might be the subject of either criminal or civil liability but commented that no prosecutor has proceeded to trial when a physician chose to terminate life-preserving treatment or omit emergency treatment in a hopeless case. The court also noted there is responsible opinion that a duly appointed guardian of an incompetent patient may give effective consent for a ward to undergo whatever medical treatment the guardian believes will be in the ward's best interest. The court commented that under the "substituted judgment" doctrine, the guardian, like the court, must seek to identify and effectuate the ward's actual values and preferences. The court stated that court approval may serve the useful purpose of resolving a doubtful or disputed question of law or fact but does not eliminate all risk of liability. The court decided private medical decisions must be made responsibly, subject to judicial scrutiny if good faith or due care is brought in question in subsequent litigation. The concurrence of qualified consultants may be highly persuasive on issues of good faith and good medical practice.

See In re Guardianship of Grant, 109 Wash. 2d 545, 747 P.2d 445 (1987), opinion amended, 757 P.2d 534 (Wash. 1988), wherein the court listed circumstances where prior court authorization would not be required to withhold life-sustaining treatment.

77 See, e.g., John F. Kennedy Memorial Hosp., Inc. v. Bludworth, 452 So. 2d 921 (Fla. 1984). The Supreme Court of Florida stated that to be relieved of potential civil and criminal liability, guardians, consenting family members, physicians, hospitals, or their administrators only need act in good faith. To be held civilly or criminally liable, there must be a showing their actions were not in good faith but were intended to harm the patient. The court noted that prior court approval generally is not required, but if there is disagreement among the physicians or family members, or evidence of wrongful motives or malpractice, judicial intervention may be required.

In Matter of Farrell, 108 N.J. 335, 529 A.2d 404 (1987), and Matter of Jobes, 108 N.J. 394, 529 A.2d 434 (1987), the Supreme Court of New Jersey ruled that if the guidelines relating to the withdrawal of life-sustaining procedures are followed in good faith, no criminal or civil liability will attach to anyone involved in the

physician or hospital will not be either civilly or criminally liable unless there is a showing their actions were not in good faith, but rather were intended to harm the patient.[78]

1. Right to Refuse Treatment

Most courts have determined that a patient has the right to refuse treatment in appropriate circumstances.[79] This right has been premised on the right of

---

implementation of a surrogate decision to decline medical treatment.

In re Fiori, 543 Pa. 592, 673 A.2d 905 (1996), the Supreme Court of Pennsylvania recognized the right of an individual to refuse medical treatment, ruling that the right to self-determination does not cease upon the incapacitation of the individual and that a patient's right to self-determination outweighs any interests a state may have in maintaining life sustaining treatment for a patient. For a patient in a persistent vegetative state (PVS) who had not created advance written directives prior to incapacitation, the court ruled the "substituted judgment standard" is the proper approach. Under this standard, a substitute decision maker can determine what measures the PVS patient would have desired considering the patient's prognosis. The court considered and rejected the standard adopted by a minority of the states that requires a "clear and convincing" evidence of a patient's intent to withdraw life support. The court also ruled a close family member is well-suited to the role of substitute decision maker because close family members are "usually the most knowledgeable about the patient's preferences, goals, and values." The court decided "concomitant with the substitute decision maker's exercise of the PVS patient's right to refuse treatment, the surrogate must also obtain written statements of two doctors qualified to evaluate the patient's condition." The court further decided the statements must certify the patient had been diagnosed as being in a permanent vegetative state. The court also commented that when physicians and a close family member agree and when there is no dispute between "interested parties," there is no need for court involvement. As the court stated, when all affected parties concur in the proposed plan of medical treatment, court approval of the plan is "neither necessary nor required." The court disagreed with the Attorney General that approval of a decision to terminate life-support is a "uniquely judicial function." It also did not agree with the Attorney General that it would be abandoning its role as a court by refusing to be involved in such decisions. The court commented that the philosophy only courts can provide the necessary safeguards to assure protection of life is a "narrow and unhealthy view" that violates the "essential and tradition respect for family."

78 Some states legislatively have recognized the right of adult individuals to have life-sustaining procedures withheld or withdrawn in instances of a terminal condition. See N.M. Stat. § 24-7-1, called the "Right to Die Act." The act provides that any physician or hospital that withheld maintenance medical treatment from a terminally ill patient or individual in an irreversible coma by relying on a document executed under the "Right to Die Act" is presumed to be acting in good faith. There will be no civil or criminal liability unless it is proven that the physician or hospital violated the standards of reasonable care. The death of the terminally ill patient is deemed not to be a suicide. N.M. Stat. § 24-7-8.

79 In Thor v. Superior Court, 5 Cal. 4th 725, 21 Cal. Rptr. 2d 357, 855 P.2d 375 (1993), the court ruled a physician has no duty to treat an individual who declines medical intervention after reasonable disclosure of available choices with respect to proposed therapy, including nontreatment, and of dangers inherently involved in each. The court concluded a competent adult patient's informed refusal discharges the obligation to render further treatment. A prisoner serving a life sentence jumped from a wall and suffered injuries that rendered him a quadriplegic. His condition was irreversible. The prisoner refused to be fed and refused to consent to forced feeding procedures. The court recognized the patient's right of control over the patient's body and decided prison medical personnel would not incur liability for failing to treat the patient.

privacy or on a common-law right to be free from invasion of one's bodily integrity.[80] As one court stated, an individual has the right to seek treatment from a physician or a hospital and to specify the conditions of that treatment--whether the patient wishes a local anesthetic as distinguished from a general anesthetic, whether or not the patient wants medication, and whether the patient agrees to a blood transfusion.[81]

The right of a patient to refuse treatment can be limited because the state has an interest in protecting the sanctity of the lives of its citizens.[82] The state interest has been identified with the preservation of life,[83] the protection of interests

---

In Brophy v. New England Sinai Hosp., Inc., 398 Mass. 417, 497 N.E.2d 626 (1986), the Supreme Court of Massachusetts commented that the law protects a person's right to accept or reject treatment whether the decision is wise or unwise. The court noted there has been a shift from a paternalistic view of what is best for the patient to the question of what decision will comport with the will of the person involved, whether that person is competent or incompetent.

80 See, In re Brown, 478 So. 2d 1033 (Miss. 1985), wherein the Supreme Court of Mississippi likened the right to refuse treatment to the doctrine of informed consent, stating the right to refuse treatment, manifested in the doctrine of informed consent, implies a right to refuse treatment.

81 In In re Brown, 478 So. 2d 1033 (Miss. 1985), the Supreme Court of Mississippi commented that a hospital presented with these conditions has the right to decline treatment if the conditions are unreasonable or unacceptable.

82 See, In Matter of Requena, 213 N.J. Super. 443, 517 A.2d 869 (App. Div. 1986), wherein the court ruled a patient has a right to make an informed decision exercising the patient's right to die even though there is a hospital resolution that the hospital will not participate in the withholding or withdrawing of artificial feeding or fluids.

In Washington v. Glucksberg, 521 U.S. 702 (1997), the Supreme Court ruled that there is no liberty interest in an asserted right to assistance in committing suicide and that Washington's ban on assisted suicide was related rationally to a legitimate governmental interest.

In Vacco v. Quill, 521 U.S. 793 (1997), the Supreme Court ruled a state statute prohibiting assisted suicide does not violate the equal protection clause. The Supreme Court stated that neither an assisted-suicide ban nor a law permitting patients to refuse medical treatment treats anyone differently from anyone else or draws any distinctions between persons. The Supreme Court decided that ending or refusing lifesaving medical treatment is not the same as assisted suicide. It concluded the "distinction between letting a patient die and making that patient die is important, logical, rational, and well established."

Oregon's Death with Dignity Act, Or. Rev. Stat. § 127.805, legalizes physician aid in dying. To be eligible for aid in dying, a patient must be an adult, be suffering from a terminal disease, be an in-state resident, and have voluntarily expressed a wish to die.

83 In Jehovah's Witnesses in State of Wash. v. King County Hospital Unit No. 1, 278 F. Supp. 488 (W.D. Wash. 1967), judgment aff'd, 390 U.S. 598 (1968), the court ruled a parent may not deprive a child of lifesaving treatment, however well-intentioned.

In John F. Kennedy Memorial Hosp., Inc. v. Bludworth, 452 So. 2d 921 (Fla. 1984), the Supreme Court of Florida noted that although the state does have an interest in preserving life, there is a substantial distinction in the state's insistence that human life be saved where the affliction is curable, as opposed to the state interest where the issue is not whether, but when, for how long, and at what cost to the individual his/her life may be briefly extended.

In Public Health Trust of Dade County v. Wons, 541 So. 2d 96 (Fla. 1989), the Florida Supreme Court ruled that any hospital wishing to contest a patient's refusal of treatment must commence court proceedings

of innocent third parties, the prevention of suicide,[84] and the maintenance of the ethical integrity of the medical profession. Still, a patient's right to refuse medical treatment has almost been ruled absolute even in a life-threatening situation.[85]

---

and sustain its heavy burden of proof that the state's interest outweighs the patient's constitutional right of privacy and right of religion. The lower court had ruled the physician could order a blood transfusion for a Jehovah's Witness who had two minor children and who had refused a blood transfusion necessary to save her life. The Florida Supreme Court did decide the fact the patient had two minor children did not override her right of privacy and religion.

In Iafelice by Iafelice v. Luchs, 206 N.J. Super. 103, 501 A.2d 1040 (1985), judgment aff'd, 221 N.J. Super. 278, 534 A.2d 417 (App. Div. 1987), the court ruled when a case involves the protection of actual or potential life that cannot protect itself, the interest of the state in sustaining that life is given effect. Parents cannot deny a child treatment for a condition that threatened the child's life.

In People v. Collins, 60 N.Y.2d 214, 469 N.Y.S.2d 65, 456 N.E.2d 1188 (1983), the parents of an infant born with spina bifida, had elected a conservative course of medical treatment for the infant. A resident of the State of Vermont intervened and contested the treatment. The court ruled the Family Court Act § 1032 provided for a child protective agency to initiate proceedings on behalf of a child, but a person who had no relationship with either the child, its parents, or family had no right to intervene. See also Matter of Storar, 52 N.Y.2d 363, 438 N.Y.S.2d 266, 420 N.E.2d 64 (1981), in which the court likened to an infant an adult who was never competent and ruled it was unrealistic to determine a patient's decision regarding medical treatment.

84 In Baxter v. State of Montana, 354 Mont. 234, 224 P.2d 1211 (Mont. 2009), the Supreme Court of Montana ruled that nothing in Montana Supreme Court precedent or Montana statutes indicated that physician aid in dying is against public policy. The plaintiff who was terminally ill with lymphocytic leukemia and with diffuse lymphadenopathy was being treated with multiple rounds of chemotherapy that typically became less effective over time. The plaintiff wanted the option of ingesting a lethal dose of medication prescribed by his physician and self-administered at the time of the plaintiff's own choosing. The court affirmed a lower court decision that a patient could use the assistance of a physician to obtain a prescription for a lethal dose of medication.

In Morris v. Brandenburg, 376 P.3d 836 (N.M. 2016), the Supreme Court of New Mexico ruled a physician aid in dying is not a fundamental or important right under the inherent rights clause of the state constitution. While the court noted that it is unlawful in the state to assist someone in committing suicide, N.M. Stat. § 30-2-4, it referred to exceptions that narrowed the statute's application if physicians comply with rigorous requirements of each act. The court referred to statutes, N.M. Stat. §§ 24-7A-1 to 24-7A-18, that provide that a physician who withdraws life-sustaining treatment from a patient, at the patient's direction and in compliance with the statute, is immune from criminal liability for such actions. Additionally, the court ruled that a physician who administers pain medication to a patient in compliance with other statutes, N.M. Stat. §§ 24-1D-1 to 24-1D-6, is immune from criminal liability even if administering the medication hastens the patient's death.

In Myers v. Schneiderman, 30 N.Y.3d 1, 85 N.E.3d 57 (Ct. App. N.Y. 2017), the New York Court of Appeals ruled that the state's legislature has a rational basis for criminalizing assisted suicide and that terminally ill patients have no constitutional right to "aid-in-dying," defined as the right of a mentally competent and terminally ill person to obtain a physician's prescription for a lethal dosage of drugs to be taken at some point to cause death.

85 See Supreme Court of Florida decision in Satz v. Perlmutter, 379 So. 2d 359 (Fla. 1980).

See also In re Guardianship of Barry, 445 So. 2d 365 (Fla. 2d DCA 1984), wherein the court ruled interests of a terminally ill incompetent infant outweighed those of the state and that the child's parents could validly assert privacy interest on the child's behalf.

In Matter of Farrell, 108 N.J. 335, 529 A.2d 404 (1987), the Supreme Court of New Jersey stated that when a party declines life-sustaining medical treatment, the patient's common-law and constitutional rights are

The right to refuse treatment has been a part of the right of freedom of religion.[86] For example, an individual's decision to forego traditional medical care and to rely on faith healing is encompassed within the freedom of religion.[87] Courts have decided members of the Jehovah's Witness faith may refuse to consent for religious reasons to the administration of blood transfusions.[88] However, courts have ruled parents may not deprive a minor child of treatment based upon religious beliefs.[89]

---

balanced against the state interests.

86 Discussion in In re Milton, 29 Ohio St. 3d 20, 505 N.E.2d 255 (1987) (holding modified by Steele v. Hamilton Cty. Community Mental Health Bd., 90 Ohio St. 3d 176, 736 N.E.2d 10 (2000)).

87 See, however, Application of President and Directors of Georgetown College, Inc., 331 F.2d 1000 (D.C. Cir. 1964), wherein the Court of Appeals for the District of Columbia Circuit ruled a mother with a seven-month-old child living at home could not refuse a blood transfusion based upon her religious beliefs as a Jehovah's Witness. The court decided the state had a responsibility to prevent possible abandonment of the child.

Still, in another early decision, In re Brooks' Estate, 32 Ill. 2d 361, 205 N.E.2d 435 (1965), an Illinois court stated that even though a patient's beliefs may be unwise, foolish, or ridiculous, in the absence of an overriding danger to society, the court would not permit interference for the sole purpose of compelling the patient to accept medical treatment forbidden by the patient's religious principles.

88 See discussion by the Mississippi Supreme Court in In re Brown, 478 So. 2d 1033 (Miss. 1985).

In Fosmire v. Nicoleau, 75 N.Y.2d 218, 551 N.Y.S.2d 876, 551 N.E.2d 77 (1990), the court ruled a patient has the right to refuse to consent to a blood transfusion even if the patient's life is in danger and the patient has minor children. An adult Jehovah's Witness refused to consent to a blood transfusion prior to delivery of her baby and persisted in her refusal after losing a substantial amount of blood following Cesarean birth of the child. The appellate court ruled the trial court should not have ordered the transfusion, deciding that there is no exception to the right of a competent adult to determine the course of the adult's medical treatment. Although the court recognized the right of the state to protect the welfare of children, the court ruled that the right to decide one's course of treatment is not conditioned on the patient being without minor children. The court commented that the state cannot go so far as to intervene in every personal decision a parent makes which may jeopardize the family unit or the parental relationship.

In In re Milton, 29 Ohio St. 3d 20, 505 N.E.2d 255 (1987) (holding modified by Steele v. Hamilton Cty. Community Mental Health Bd., 90 Ohio St. 3d 176, 736 N.E.2d 10 (2000)), the court ruled a patient could refuse medical treatment based on her religious beliefs even though the patient was under the delusion she was the wife of a faith healer and evangelist. The court decided the state may not act in parens patriae relationship to a mental hospital patient unless the patient has been adjudicated as being incompetent. The court stated an involuntary mental patient remains free to refuse treatment when the treatment would violate the religious beliefs of the patient in the absence of a finding of incompetence.

In Shorter v. Drury, 103 Wash. 2d 645, 695 P.2d 116 (1985), after a husband and wife both refused a blood transfusion, the wife did not survive surgery. The court ruled the husband and wife assumed the risk of death based upon the consequences of refusal to permit a blood transfusion, but they did not assume the risk of negligence of the physician in performing the surgery.

89 See decision of the Supreme Court of New Jersey in Matter of Grady, 85 N.J. 235, 426 A.2d 467 (1981).

See also In re Estate of Dorone, 349 Pa. Super. 59, 502 A.2d 1271 (1985), order aff'd, 517 Pa. 3, 534 A.2d 452 (1987), in which the court denied the right of parents of an adult male to serve as guardian of their adult child. The parents would have refused to permit a blood transfusion because they and the patient were Jehovah's Witnesses. The court appointed a guardian, other than the patient's parents, to determine the wishes of the patient.

2. Physician Directives

A patient may have expressed an intent not to have life-sustaining medical intervention.[90] This intent might be embodied in a written document, referred to as a "living will" or "directive to physicians," that states the person's desire not to have certain types of life-sustaining treatments administered under certain circumstances, or it may be evidenced in an oral directive to a family member, friend, or health-care provider.[91] Courts have stated these documents may be appropriate to determine what course of treatment a patient, who currently is unable to express the patient's wishes would have wished to pursue.[92] Courts

90 See Supreme Court of New Jersey discussion in Matter of Conroy, 98 N.J. 321, 486 A.2d 1209 (1985).

In Anderson v. St. Francis-St. George Hosp., Inc., 77 Ohio St. 3d 82, 671 N.E.2d 225 (1996), the court ruled a medical provider who administered a life-prolonging treatment or procedure to a patient against the patient's instructions, was not liable in damages to the patient. The court stated that when a patient clearly delimits the medical measures the patient is willing to undergo and a health care provider disregards the instructions, the health care provider would be liable only for damages arising from a battery inflicted on the patient. The court decided the patient suffered no damages due directly to the battery.

91 See Matter of Conroy, 98 N.J. 321, 486 A.2d 1209 (1985).

In Saunders v. State, 129 Misc. 2d 45, 492 N.Y.S.2d 510 (Sup 1985), the court decided that only the legislature has authority to enact a statute recognizing the validity of living wills, or "directive to physicians," that prescribe the means of execution of these documents and the general guidelines that may be applicable to a broad range of situations. The court stated a "living will" could be a patient's informed medical consent authorizing the refusal or discontinuance of further medical treatment by artificial means or devices when or if the patient is terminally ill with death imminent.

The Texas Natural Death Act, Tex. Health & Safety Code Ann. § 672.001 sets out a written directive form that can be used. The form must be signed by the declarant in the presence of two witnesses who are not related to the declarant and who would not be entitled to any of the estate of the declarant.

Nevada provides for a healthcare power of attorney, Nev. Rev. Stat § 162A.860, and a physician's directive in its Rights of the Terminally Ill, Nev. Rev. Stat §§ 449.535 to 449.690.

See, Wash. Rev. Code Ann. § 70.122.010, which recognizes the right of an adult person to make a written directive instructing the person's physician to withhold or withdraw life-sustaining procedures in the event of a terminal condition. The act prescribes a form to be used as a written directive to a physician to withhold or withdraw life-sustaining procedures. The act provides that no physician or health facility acting in good faith in accordance with the statute, will be criminally or civilly liable for withholding or withdrawing life-sustaining procedures or for failing to effectuate the directive of the qualified patient pursuant to the Act. Wash. Rev. Code Ann. §§70.122.050, 70.122.060. The withholding or withdrawal of life-sustaining procedures from a qualified patient pursuant to the act is deemed not to constitute a suicide. No policy of life insurance is legally impaired or invalidated by the withholding or withdrawal of life-sustaining procedures from an insured qualified patient notwithstanding any term of the policy to the contrary. Wash. Rev. Code Ann. §70.122.070.

92 In DeGrella By and Through Parent v. Elston, 858 S.W.2d 698 (Ky. 1993), the Supreme Court of Kentucky ruled an incompetent person can exercise the right to withdrawal of medical treatment when that person is in a persistent vegetative state through the process of surrogate decision-making if the wishes of the patient are known. The court decided a patient's statements of choice made before the patient became incompetent is competent evidence upon which a surrogate decision-maker could exercise substitute judgment.

have recognized that the rights of terminally ill competent patients to refuse or to discontinue extraordinary medical treatment is not lost when and if they suffer irreversible brain damage, become comatose, and are no longer able to express personally their wishes.[93] Thus, although a "living will" or "directive to physicians" that states a patient's intention under these circumstances, is not necessarily legally binding, courts nonetheless have given effect to the documents as evidence of the patient's intent.[94]

In re Guardianship of Tschumy, 853 N.W.2d 728 (Minn. 2014), the Supreme Court of Minnesota ruled a guardian's statutory medical consent power included the power to consent to the removal of the guardian's ward from life support systems when all interested parties agree removal was in the ward's best interests. The court decided court approval is not required before a guardian has the power to consent to necessary medical treatment for a ward. It referred to a statute, Minn. Stat. § 524.5-313(c)(4)(I), that gives a guardian authority to authorize removal of a ward's life-sustaining treatment without court approval when all interested parties agree removal is in the ward's best interest.

The New Hampshire Supreme Court, In re Guardianshp of L.N., 173 H.H. 77, 237 A.3d 222 (N.H 2020), ruled that a guardian's general statutory authority to give consent to enable a ward to receive medical treatment includes the authority to terminate life support. The court ruled, as a matter of first impression, that end-of-life decisions are included in a guardian's power. The court also rejected the proposition that a guardian must in all cases seek court approval before authorizing the withdrawal of life support from a ward.

The Supreme Court of New Hampshire, In re Guardianship of D.E., 173 N.H. 550, 243 A.3d 908 (N.H. 2020), also ruled that a ward who had not executed an advance directive did not have an "agent" and no surrogate had been appointed for him pursuant to state statutes. The ward's children testified that when their father was in intensive care, they executed a "Do Not Resuscitate" (DNR) order for him. The ward did not have a previous DNR order. When the ward's condition improved and he was transferred to a medical ward, he specifically told his children that he wanted the DNR order removed.

93 Saunders v. State, 129 Misc. 2d 45, 492 N.Y.S.2d 510 (Sup 1985).

94 In Matter of Conroy, 98 N.J. 321, 486 A.2d 1209 (N.J. 1985), the New Jersey Supreme Court commented that although a court or surrogate decision makers should consider all evidence tending to demonstrate a person's intent with respect to medical treatment, the probative value of the evidence may vary depending on the remoteness, consistency, and thoughtfulness of the person's prior statements or actions and maturity at the time of the statements or acts. The court determined that life-sustaining treatment may be withheld or withdrawn if either of two tests—a limited-objective or a purely-objective test—is satisfied. Under the limited-objective test, life-sustaining treatment may be withheld or withdrawn if there was some trustworthy evidence the patient would have refused the treatment, and the decision maker is satisfied burdens of the patient's continued life with the treatment outweigh the benefits of life for the patient. There must be some trustworthy evidence the patient would have wanted the treatment terminated. Under the purely-objective test, the net burdens of the patient's life with the treatment should clearly and markedly outweigh the benefits the patient derives from life. Further, the recurring, unavoidable, and severe pain of the patient's life with the treatment should be such that the effect of administering life-sustaining treatment would be inhumane.

Although a hospital generally need not admit a patient in the absence of an emergency, once a hospital has initiated the care and treatment of a patient, it cannot act unreasonably in removing the patient from the hospital.[95] The duty to treat is breached when a patient is wrongfully discharged from a hospital before the patient is cured.[96] A hospital's duty to treat embraces a duty not to discharge a patient prematurely and abandon the case.[97] Abandonment is the termination of the professional relationship between the physician and/or hospital and the patient at an unreasonable time or without affording the patient the opportunity to procure an equally qualified replacement.[98] If the patient is not in need of immediate medical attention, furnishing the patient a list of substitute physicians to replace the attending physician is a reasonable means of severing the professional relationship.[99]

When a patient is no longer in need of treatment, courts have ruled the patient can be forced to leave the hospital.[100] Because a hospital has a moral duty to reserve its accommodations for persons who need medical and hospital care, it has the right to remove a patient no longer in need of treatment who insists on remaining in the hospital.[101]

---

95 Morrison v. Washington County, Ala., 700 F.2d 678 (11th Cir. 1983) (holding modified on other grounds by, Helicopter Support Systems, Inc. v. Hughes Helicopter, Inc., 818 F.2d 1530 (11th Cir. 1987)).

In Swaw v. Klompien, 168 Ill. App. 3d 705 522 N.E.2d 1267 (1st Dist. 1988), a surgeon was required to continue to care for a patient until the threat of postoperative complications was past.

96 Modla v. Parker, 17 Ariz. App. 54, 495 P.2d 494 (Div 1 1972).

97 Miller v. Greater Southeast Community Hosp., 508 A.2d 927 (D.C. 1986).

In Brownsville Medical Center v. Gracia, 704 S.W.2d 68 (Tex. App. Corpus Christi 1985), writ refused n.r.e., (1986), the court held a hospital liable for the death of a child who was transferred to a public hospital when the parents were unable to pay for the hospital's treatment. The child was prepared for surgery but then transferred to another hospital. The court decided evidence was sufficient to show the hospital was negligent in stopping the medical care and treatment of an admitted child.

98 In Payton v. Weaver, 131 Cal. App. 3d 38, 182 Cal. Rptr. 225 (1st Dist. 1982), the court stated the rule to be that a physician generally may abandon a patient only after due notice and ample opportunity is afforded the patient to secure the presence of other medical attendance.

99 Miller v. Greater Southeast Community Hosp., 508 A.2d 927 (D.C. 1986).

100 Jersey City Medical Center v. Halstead, 169 N.J. Super. 22, 404 A.2d 44 (Ch. Div. 1979).

101 Lucy Webb Hayes Nat. Training School for Deaconesses and Missionaries, 281 F. Supp. 116 (D. D.C. 1967).

In Wyckoff Heights Medical Center v. Rodriguez, 191 Misc. 2d 207,741 N.Y.S. 2d 400 (2002), a New York

Hospitals have been held liable to third parties for prematurely discharging mentally ill or dangerous patients.[102] Most courts have ruled that a hospital has a duty to warn third parties of any violence directed against a third party by a dangerous, mentally ill patient.[103]

---

court granted a hospital an injunction to enforce a discharge issued against a patient. The court found no state cases that squarely addressed whether a mandatory injunction could be used to require a patient to leave a hospital following a discharge notice and referred to Jersey City Medical Center v. Halstead, 169 N.J. Super 22, 404 A.2d 44 (Sup. Ct. 1979), wherein a New Jersey court recognized an injunctive right to eject a hospital patient who refused to leave following a discharge. It also referred to the decision in Lucy Webb Hayes Nat. Training School for Deaconesses and Missionaries, 281 F. Supp. 116 (D.D.C. 1967).

102 In Semler v. Psychiatric Institute of Washington, D.C., 538 F.2d 121 (4th Cir. 1976), the Court of Appeals for the Fourth Circuit ruled that a psychiatric institute had a duty to protect the public by retaining custody over a dangerous, mentally ill patient until the patient was released by court order and ruled the institute was negligent in transferring the patient to outpatient status. The patient had killed a girl while transferred to outpatient status.

In Burroughs v. Board of Trustees of Alachua General Hospital, 328 So. 2d 538 (Fla. 1st DCA 1976), a patient who suffered from depression associated with alcoholism was given a day pass from the hospital. The court ruled the hospital was not immune from liability for an automobile accident caused by the patient while he was on day pass.

In Durflinger v. Artiles, 234 Kan. 484, 673 P.2d 86 (1983) (disapproved of by Boulanger v. Pol, 258 Kan. 289, 900 P.2d 823 (1995)), the Supreme Court of Kansas ruled a hospital has a duty to the patient and to the public to use reasonable and ordinary care and discretion in discharging a committed patient. The court stated that a hospital should discharge such a patient when the patient is no longer in need of care and treatment, i.e., when the patient is no longer dangerous to the patient or others.

But see Hennepin County v. Levine, 345 N.W.2d 217 (Minn. 1984), in which the Supreme Court of Minnesota determined that issuance of passes to persons committed to treatment facilities as mentally ill and dangerous was a method of treatment and not a form of discharge or provisional discharge subject under statute to approval by a special review board. The court ruled passes could be issued by the head of treatment facility without the prior approval of the board.

103 In Jablonski by Pahls v. U.S., 712 F.2d 391 (9th Cir. 1983), the Court of Appeals for the Ninth Circuit ruled a district court finding, that the proximate cause of a patient's girl-friend's death was a psychiatrist's failure to warn the girlfriend the patient's violence was likely to be directed against her, was not clearly erroneous. The psychiatrist did not record and transmit information to the police even though the psychiatrist had diagnosed the patient as being dangerous. The hospital contended the patient was an outpatient, and it had no duty to warn the deceased.

In Peck v. Counseling Service of Addison County, Inc., 146 Vt. 61, 499 A.2d 422 (1985), the Supreme Court of Vermont stated that although there generally is no duty to control the conduct of another to protect a third person from harm, there is an exception where the special relationship between the two persons gives one a definite control over the actions of the other. There is also an exception where a special relationship exists that imposes a duty upon one to control the actions of another. The court concluded that the relationship between a community mental health agency and a voluntary outpatient created a duty to exercise reasonable care to protect potential victims of another's conduct.

In Kuligoski v. Battleboro Retreat and Northeast Kingdom Human Services, 203 Vt. 328, 156 A.2d 436 (Vt. 2016), the Supreme Court of Vermont ruled that while defendants had no duty enforceable by a third party to treat a patient, to seek involuntary commitment of the patient, or to adopt a particular discharge plan, there is a duty to provide reasonable information to notify a patient's caregiver of the risks, and of steps he or she can take to mitigate risks, when the patient is discharged from a hospital after being diagnosed with a psychotic disorder. The facts in the case centered around an unprovoked, spontaneous act of violence directed against a stranger by an individual suffering from a serious mental illness A dissent in the case, 156 A.3d at 475, 476, stated the act could not have been prevented short of anticipatory confinement in a hospital; the dissent characterized the majority opinion as "a preposterous, reckless decision" that delivered a cautionary statement involving the threat of tort liability to a hospital for releasing a mentally ill person to people not sufficiently warned/trained to provide care and control. The dissent referred to what it designated as the majority's "rather cavalier" disposal of HIPAA's Privacy Rule regarding the confidentiality of patient's records. The dissent thought that decisions to create and impose new legal duties on other learned professions would have "profound consequences," stating it was "presumptuous" to impose a "novel legal duty on mental health care professionals without extensive discussion of the professional knowledge, skills, and practice standard–if any–that may apply and the policy consequences that may result." The dissent thought the majority opinion to be "the essence of judicial arrogance."

See Minn. Stat. § 148.975 and 976 relating to a health practitioner's duty to warn of serious, specific threats to a potential victim. The act provides that the duty to predict, warn of, or take reasonable precautions to provide protection from violent behavior arises only under limited circumstances, those being instances in which the patient or other person has communicated to the practitioner a specific, serious threat of physical violence against a specific, clearly identified, or identifiable potential victim. The act also provides there is no cause of action against a practitioner for disclosing confidences to third parties in a good-faith effort to discharge a duty to those parties even though a duty is not statutorily present.

CHAPTER IV.
HOSPITAL AND PHYSICIAN LIABILITY

A. GENERAL LIABILITY PRINCIPLES

1. Standard of Care

The duty of a hospital to use care in the treatment of its patients is an obligation created by law. A breach of that duty is a failure to observe a reasonable standard of due care under the circumstances and gives rise to a tort action.[1]

1 See, Berry v. Druid City Hospital Bd., 333 So. 2d 796 (Ala. 1976).

See also, McNulty v. City of New York, 100 N.Y.2d 227, 762 N.Y.S.2d 12, 792 N.E.2d 162 (2003), where a New

Some courts have ruled hospitals liable under a contract theory, determining it is a breach of contract when a procedure is not performed in a manner specified in an express or an implied contract.[2] Consider, for example, a case in which a patient was admitted to a hospital's maternity ward and was injured when her child was delivered by an unqualified hospital employee because a doctor was unavailable when the patient was ready for delivery. The patient could allege the existence of an implied contract that the hospital would have a physician available at the crucial time[3] and could also have an action in tort.[4]

The general principles that ordinarily govern in negligence cases also apply in medical malpractice claims. However, the standard applied in medical malpractice cases, in evaluating the conduct of the average layperson in terms of the hypothetical conduct of a reasonably prudent person acting under the same

---

York court ruled a doctor who treated a patient with infectious meningitis owed no duty of care to warn the patient's friend, who accompanied the patient to the emergency room and spent time at her bedside, that she had been exposed to an infectious illness and should seek treatment. The friend later became ill with the same type of meningitis and suffered significant hearing loss in one ear as well as tinnitus. The court noted the duty of care is based on a doctor-patient relationship and the friend's injury did not arise from treatment of the patient.

In Tex. Civ. Prac. & Rem. Code § 74.155, the Texas Legislature set out the standard of care for a physician, health care provider, and first responder relating to or impacted by a pandemic disease, which is defined in the statute as an infectious disease that spreads to a significant portion of the population of the United States and that poses a substantial risk of a significant number of human fatalities, illnesses, or permanent long-term disabilities, or a disaster declaration related to a pandemic disease. The statute provides that except in the case of reckless conduct or intentional, willful, or wanton misconduct, a physician, health care provider, and first responder are not liable for an injury or death arising from care, treatment, or failure to provide care or treatment relating to or impacted by a pandemic disease or a disaster declaration related to a pandemic disease if they prove by a preponderance of the evidence that the disease or disaster declaration was a producing cause of the care, treatment, or failure to provide care or treatment that allegedly caused the injury or death; or the individual who suffered injury or death was diagnosed or reasonably suspected to be infected with a pandemic disease at the time of the care, treatment, or failure to provide care or treatment. The statute sets out the care, treatment, or failure to provide care or treatment relating to or impacted by a pandemic disease.

2 Paul v. Escambia County Hospital Bd., 283 Ala. 488, 218 So. 2d 817 (1969).

In Newton v. Kaiser Foundation Hospitals, 184 Cal. App. 3d 386, 228 Cal. Rptr. 890 (3d Dist. 1986), the court also ruled a duty of care can arise from a contract. The court found a contract between the hospital and a pregnant woman requiring that the hospital provide care for the patient and her child during the birth process. The court ruled the mother had a contract with the hospital that she would be delivered of a healthy fetus.

3 Paul v. Escambia County Hosp. Bd., 283 Ala. 488, 218 So. 2d 817 (1969).

4 See Berry v. Druid City Hospital Bd., 333 So. 2d 796 (Ala. 1976), in which a plaintiff could not have brought an action in tort against a public hospital because it would have been barred by governmental immunity. Nonetheless, the Supreme Court of Alabama permitted the plaintiff to bring an action for breach of an implied agreement between the plaintiff and the hospital that, when the plaintiff was accepted for treatment in the emergency room of the hospital, the plaintiff would be given the required treatment. The governmental immunity defense is inapplicable to the action for breach of an implied contract. (Discussion of governmental immunity defense below.)

or similar circumstances, also must take into account the specialized knowledge or skill of the defendant.[5] Thus, hospitals and physicians are required to use the degree of care, skill, and learning ordinarily possessed and exercised by other hospitals and physicians in similar circumstances, which constitutes the care and skill that is expected of a reasonably competent hospital and/or physician in the same or similar circumstances.[6] Advances in the profession, availability of special facilities, and specialists are considered.[7] Hospitals also may be liable for damages to unborn children at the time of an alleged negligence of the hospital.[8]

Many states require a prospective plaintiff to be given notice of an intent to initiate litigation for medical negligence. These state statutes often include substantial additional requirements for filing a medical negligence lawsuit.[9] The

---

5 Shilkret v. Annapolis Emergency Hospital Ass'n, 276 Md. 187, 349 A.2d 245 (1975).

Texas Civ. Prac. & Rem. Code § 74.401 states that a person may qualify as an expert witness on whether a physician departed from accepted standards of medical care only if the person is a physician who is practicing medicine at the time testimony is given or was practicing medicine at the time the claim arose; has knowledge of accepted standards of medical care for the diagnosis, care, or treatment of the illness, injury, or condition involved in the claim; and is qualified on the basis of training or experience to offer an expert opinion regarding the accepted standards of medical care.

6 In Lauro v. Travelers Ins. Co., 261 So. 2d 261 (La. Ct. App. 4th Cir. 1972), writ denied, 262 La. 188, 262 So. 2d 787 (1972), the court stated the measure of duty of a hospital is to exercise that degree of care, skill, and diligence used by hospitals generally in that community.

In Estate of Hagedorn v. Peterson, 690 N.W.2d 84, 89 (Iowa 2004), the Supreme Court of Iowa ruled the locality rule was the law in Iowa. It defined the locality rule in its original form as the requirement that a "physician is bound to use that degree of knowledge, skill, care and attention ordinarily exercised by physicians under like circumstances and *in like localities*." The court noted the rule was formulated over 100 years ago "to protect rural practitioners presumed to be less adequately informed than their colleagues in the city." The court also noted that in a medical malpractice case, a jury can consider the facilities, equipment, and resources available to the physician at the time of the physician's diagnosis and treatment. Thus, a jury can decide whether a physician used the degree of skill, care, and learning ordinarily possessed and exercised by other physicians in *similar circumstances*. 690 N.W.2d at 92.

7 Shilkret v. Annapolis Emergency Hospital Ass'n, 276 Md. 187, 349 A.2d 245, 99 A.L.R.3d 1119 (1975).

8 See discussion of rights of minors below.

9 See, e.g., Fla. Stat. § 766.106(2)(a)-3(a), which statute provides that no suit may be filed for ninety days after notice is mailed. Additionally, along with the pre-suit notice, a plaintiff must provide a verified written opinion from a medical expert to corroborate the plaintiff's "reasonable grounds" to initiate a medical negligence lawsuit. The presuit notice must include a list, if available, of all known health care providers the plaintiff has seen for the injuries complained of subsequent to the alleged act of negligence; a list, if available, of all known health care providers who treated or evaluated the plaintiff during the two-year period prior to the alleged act of negligence; copies of all medical records the plaintiff's experts relied on in forming their opinions; and an executed authorization form permitting the release of medical information.

The Florida statute also provides for many additional prerequisites to filing a medical negligence lawsuit.

There are several prerequisites to filing a health care claim in Texas. Tex. Civ. Prac. & Rem. Code § 74.051 requires a person asserting a health care liability claim to give written notice of the claim by certified mail, return receipt requested, to each physician or health care provider against whom the claim is being made

Court of Appeals for the Eleventh Circuit[10] has ruled that a state required medical negligence pre-suit authorization form did meet requirements of the HIPAA[11] and its regulations[12] regarding valid and written authorization requirements for disclosure of protected health information. The Eleventh Circuit additionally ruled the state statute was not preempted by HIPAA.[13]

In the past, nonprofit hospitals were seldom subject to claims for damages based upon negligence because nonprofit hospitals generally were immune from

---

at least sixty days before filing a suit in any court in the state based upon a health care liability claim. The notice must be accompanied by the authorization form for release of protected health information (PHI) that is required under § 74.052 (discussion of form in Chapters II and III.) The party to the claim must state that it has fully complied with §§ 74.051 and 74.052 and must provide evidence the court may require to determine if the provisions of Chapter 74 of the Civ. Prac. & Rem. Code have been met. This notice tolls the statute of limitations, for all parties and potential parties, to and including a period of seventy-five days following the giving of the notice. (Section 74.251 sets the statute of limitations to be two years from the occurrence of the breach or tort or from the date the medical or health care treatment that is subject of the claim or the hospitalization for which the claim is made is completed provided that minors under the age of twelve years have until their fourteenth birthday in which to file a claim or have a claim filed on their behalf. Still, the statute also provides that all health care liability claims must be brought not later than ten years after the date of the act or omission that gave rise to the claim; thus, all claims must be brought within ten years, or they are time barred.) Section 74.351 of the Civ. Prac. & Rem. Code requires a claimant in a health care liability claim, not later than the 120th day after the date the defendant's original answer is filed, to serve on that party or the party's attorney one or more expert reports, with a curriculum vitae of each expert listed in the report for each physician or health care provider against whom a liability claim is asserted. Each defendant physician or health care provider whose conduct is implicated in a report must then file and serve any objections to the sufficiency of the report not later than the later of the twenty-first day after the date the report is served or the twenty-first day after the date the defendant's answer is filed, or all objections are waived. If the expert report has not been served within the period specified above, the court, on motion of the affected physician or health care provider, must enter an order dismissing the claim and awarding the physician or health care provider reasonable attorney's fees as well as court costs incurred by the physician or health care provider. Discovery procedures are set out in Tex. Civ. Prac. & Rem. Code § 74.352.

10 Murphy v. Daley, 768 F.3d 1360 (11th Cir. 2014).

11 42 U.S.C. §§ 1320d et seq.

12 45 C.F.R. § 164.508.

13 In Murphy v. Dulay, 768 F.3d 1360 (11th Cir. 2014), the Court of Appeals for the Eleventh Circuit ruled that HIPAA and its regulations contain express preemption provisions that "shall supersede any contrary provision of State law." See 42 U.S.C. § 1320d-7(a)(1). (Discussion of HIPAA privacy rules in Chapter III.)

Tex. Civ. Prac. & Rem. Code § 74.051(d) states that all parties to a health care liability claim shall be entitled to obtain complete and unaltered copies of the patient's medical records from any other party within forty-five days from the date of receipt of a written request for the records but that the receipt of a medical authorization in the form required by § 74.052 executed by the claimant *shall* be considered compliance by the claimant. Additionally, a request for the medical records of a deceased person or a person who is incompetent is deemed to be valid if accompanied by an authorization in the form required by § 74.052 signed by a parent, spouse, or adult child of the deceased or incompetent person. (Further discussion of authorization form in Chapters II and III.)

liability under the doctrine of charitable immunity.[14] However, most states have abrogated the doctrine of charitable immunity.[15] As a result, nonprofit hospitals can be subject to liability for the negligent acts of their employees, including nurses, residents, and interns.[16]

---

14 Discussion of charitable immunity below.

In Kostera v. Bacharach Institute for Rehabilitation, 2015 WL 4643642 (N.J. Super. Ct. App. Div. 2015), the plaintiff slipped and fell on a patch of ice on a walkway owned and maintained by the defendant, a non-profit corporation organized exclusively for hospital purposes. The defendant contended any damages award should be limited to $250,000 pursuant to the state's Charitable Immunity Act, N.J. Stat. Ann. 2A:53A-7 to 2A:53A-13. The court explained that the question of whether a nonprofit organization is entitled to a limitation on damages afforded to those institutions organized exclusively for hospital purposes, turns on the purpose of the institution, not the use to which the facility is put on any given day. The court noted the state's Charitable Immunity Act extended to the buildings and other facilities used for the purposes of the qualifying organization, such as a hospital. It recognized that the established test for determining whether a party is a beneficiary of the works of a charity has two prongs. The first is that the institution pleading the immunity, at the time in question, was engaged in the performance of the charitable objectives it was organized to advance. The second is that the injured party must have been a direct recipient of those good works. The court concluded the plaintiff was not a direct beneficiary of the defendant's benefactions for purposes of the Charitable Immunity Act.

15 See, however, N.J. Rev. Stat. 2A:53A-7, which retains some charitable immunity for hospitals.

See also Tex. Civ. Prac. & Rem. Code § 84.006, which limits the liability of charitable organizations to $500,000 for each person and $1,000,000 for each single occurrence of bodily injury or death and $100,000 for each single occurrence for injury or destruction of property. There is no limitation on liability caused by intentional or willful negligence or conscious or reckless disregard for the safety of others.

In Miller v Johnson, 295 Kan. 636, 289 P.3d 1098 (Kan. 2012), the Kansas Supreme Court ruled that a noneconomic damages cap of $250,000 in malpractice actions was reasonably necessary in the public interest to promote the public welfare, as would support a finding that the cap did not unconstitutionally infringe on a right to a jury trial or a right to remedy. The court found that the Kansas legislature had substituted an adequate statutory remedy for noneconomic damages cap's modification of the right to a jury trial and the right to a remedy.

In Siebert v. Okun, 485 P.3d 1265 (N. Mex. 2021), the Supreme Court of New Mexico ruled that a nonmedical, nonpunitive damages cap under the Medical Malpractice Act (MMA), N.M.S. §§ 41-5-1 to -29, did not violate the right to a trial by jury. Defendants in the case had moved to reduce a jury award of $2,600,000 to conform with the $600,000 cap on all nonmedical and nonpunitive damages in MMA actions.

16 In Krane v. Saint Anthony Hosp. Systems, 738 P.2d 75 (Colo. App. 1987), the court recognized the "captain of the ship" doctrine as being applicable to preclude liability against a hospital for the negligence of a surgical nurse even though the nurse was the hospital's employee. The court determined that once the operating surgeon assumed control in the operating room, the surgeon was liable for the negligence of all those persons working under the surgeon's supervision. The court stated that both the operating surgeon and the hospital could not be liable for the same act of negligence. The question in the case was whether the operating surgeon had assumed control. Because the negligent act of the surgical nurse took place over two hours into the surgery, the court determined the surgeon's responsibility superseded that of the hospital.

In Sparger v. Worley Hospital, Inc., 547 S.W.2d 582 (Tex. 1977), the Texas Supreme Court ruled a hospital liable for injuries resulting from the failure to remove a sponge from the plaintiff's abdominal cavity after an operation. The jury found the surgical nurses were negligent with respect to the sponge but refused to find the surgeon was negligent in failing to look for the sponge before closing the incision in the plaintiff's abdomen. On appeal, the court of appeals had held the surgeon liable as a matter of law for negligence of the nurses under the so-called captain of the ship doctrine. The hospital contended the physician should bear the sole liability because the captain of the ship doctrine made the nurses the physician's exclusive

2. Vicarious Liability

A hospital can be liable for the negligent acts of members of the medical staff under the doctrine of vicarious liability, or respondeat superior.[17] To establish liability under this theory, two elements must exist. Generally, there must be a master-servant relationship and the activity of the agent must be within the scope of the employment.[18] Some courts have ruled a decision to treat a patient

---

employees. However, the Texas Supreme Court decided the captain of the ship doctrine was a false issue. Notwithstanding, the court did comment that a general employee of one employer may become the borrowed servant of another. Under the borrowed servant doctrine, the Texas Supreme Court stated the essential inquiry would be whether the surgeon had the right to control the assisting nurses in the details of the specific act raising the question of liability. It noted the principle of borrowed servant cuts across the entire law of principal and agent and employer and employee. In discussing the captain of the ship doctrine, the court noted that it was an adaptation of the borrowed servant principle and that it had been used as a basis for a surgeon's liability in addition to the surgeon's responsibility under the borrowed servant doctrine. The court then stated that it disapproved of the captain of the ship doctrine and held that it was a false special rule of agency. The court ruled that operating surgeons and hospitals should be subject to the same principles of agency law applicable to others. According to the Texas Supreme Court, the facts of a case cause a person to become a surgeon's employee or borrowed servant as a matter of law. Accordingly, the court ruled the nurses were borrowed servants of the physician as the physician had had no control over their selection and did not instruct them and found that only the hospital was liable in damages to the plaintiff.

In St. Joseph Hospital v. Wolff, 999 S.W.2d 57 (Ct. App. Tex. 1999), the court ruled that any error in failing to give a jury borrowed-servant doctrine instruction was harmless.

17 In Braden v. Saint Francis Hosp., 714 P.2d 505 (Colo. App. 1985), the court stated a hospital has a duty to supervise the competence of its staff.

In Blanton v. Moses H. Cone Memorial Hosp., Inc., 319 N.C. 372, 354 S.E.2d 455 (1987), the Supreme Court of North Carolina determined a hospital can be liable for the negligence of a doctor on its medical staff if it breached a duty owed to a patient. The court ruled a hospital is under a duty to use reasonable care in the selection of its agents and held that a hospital owes a duty to its patients to ascertain whether a physician is qualified to perform an operation before granting the physician the privilege to do so.

In G.L. v. Kaiser Foundation Hospitals, Inc., 306 Or. 54, 757 P.2d 1347 (1988), the Supreme Court of Oregon ruled a hospital was not liable when a patient was assaulted by a hospital employee. The court stated a master generally is not liable for intentional or willful wrongdoing of an employee. The court determined the attack was outside the scope of employment of the employee. According to the court, an employer should be liable for intentional torts of an employee only if the act was undertaken with the intent of furthering the master's business, however misguided that intent might seem.

In Park North General Hosp. v. Hickman, 703 S.W.2d 262 (Tex. App. San Antonio 1985), writ refused n.r.e., (1986) and (disapproved of by St. Luke's Episcopal Hosp. v. Agbor, 952 S.W.2d 503 (Tex. 1997)), a Texas appellate court stated a hospital owes a duty to its patients to exercise reasonable care in the selection of its medical staff and in granting specialized privileges. The court ruled a hospital must screen physicians seeking admittance to the staff and stated a hospital also has a duty to monitor and review the competency of the medical staff periodically. (Discussion of medical staff in Chapter I.)

18 Discussion of the doctrine of vicarious liability of a hospital in Classen, "Hospital Liability for Independent Contractors, Where Do We Go From Here?," 40 Ark. L. Rev. 469 (1987). The author noted that an exception to the doctrine of vicarious liability involves the use of independent contractors. Hospitals may escape liability for the negligent acts of independent staff physicians who work for the hospital on a contractual basis. The author commented that courts have examined the existence of a contract and the hospital's right to control the time, manner and method of the physician's

in a particular manner is entirely within the discretion of the treating physician, and the negligence of the treating physician in the treatment of the patient cannot be imputed to the hospital unless the physician is an agent of the hospital.[19] Still, when a patient goes to a full-service hospital for care and treatment, the patient generally does so in reliance on the reputation of the institution and the skill and expertise of its personnel.[20] Thus, other courts have ruled patients who are unaware of the independent status of the treating physicians should not be bound by limitations contained in a private contract between a hospital and

---

actions in determining the "employment status" of the physician. The author pointed out instances where hospitals nonetheless have been held liable for the actions of physicians deemed to be independent contractors. This can occur when the patient looks to the hospital to provide medical services rather than to a particular physician. However, when the patient does look to a physician to provide treatment, the hospital will not be liable for the physician's malpractice, but it may share in the liability if hospital employees are also negligent. The author recommended that hospitals should take measures to ensure that patients will not assume physicians are employees of the hospital. As an example, the physician should bill for the physician's services and not the hospital. The physicians should staff the emergency rooms. Notices may be posted that physicians are not employees of the hospital.

19 In Smith v. St. Francis Hosp., Inc., 676 P.2d 279 (Ct. App. Div. 1 1983), the court noted the general rule that the extent of the duty of a hospital with respect to actual medical care of a professional nature, such as is furnished by a physician, is to use reasonable care in selecting medical doctors.

In Hohenleitner v. Quorum Health Resources, Inc., 435 Mass. 424, 758 N.E.2d 616 (2001), the Supreme Court of Massachusetts recognized what it termed "the guiding principle" used to decide cases involving an assertion of vicarious liability-the right to control the physical conduct of the other in the performance of the service. It determined that, although the manager of the defendant hospital had the right to exercise considerable direction and supervision over the nursing staff's activities, it left patient care issues to the medical staff and members of the board who acted for the city; thus, the hospital could not be liable for the negligence of a nurse who was employed by the city.

20 Sztorc v. Northwest Hosp., 496 N.E.2d 1200 (Ill. App. 1st Dist. 1986).

a doctor.[21] Consequently, a hospital may be vicariously liable under the doctrine either of "ostensible" or "apparent" agency or "agency by estoppel."[22]

A hospital may be liable for invasion of a patient's privacy.[23] It also can be liable in damages if it does not take reasonable care in making its premises safe

---

21 In Gilbert v. Sycamore Mun. Hosp., 156 Ill. 2d 511, 622 N.E.2d 788 (1993), the court ruled that, under the doctrine of apparent authority, a hospital could be vicariously liable for the negligent acts of a physician providing care at the hospital, regardless of whether the physician was an independent contractor unless the patient knew or should have known the physician was an independent contractor. The court ruled that if a hospital holds itself out as a provider of emergency room care without informing a patient that care is provided by an independent contractor, and if a patient relies upon the hospital to provide complete emergency room care, rather than relying upon a specific physician, the hospital can be liable for the negligent acts of the physician.

In Steinberg v. Dunseth, 259 Ill. App. 3d 533, 197 Ill. Dec. 587, 631 N.E.2d 809 (4th Dist. 1994), the court ruled a physician who employed another physician was not vicariously liable for the covering physician's negligent acts. The court stated a physician may be held liable if the physician negligently selects a covering physician who the referring physician should have known was inadequate. The court noted the general rule that a referring physician will not be liable for the other physician's negligence unless there is some control of the course of treatment of one by the other, or agency, or negligence in the referral. The court recognized physicians who employ other physicians are sometimes held vicariously liable for the negligence acts of the other physicians committed while acting in the scope of employment despite the argument that the other physicians are independent contractors. The court referred to physicians who are employed together, who diagnose and treat the case together, without withdrawal by or discharge of either. Both physicians were responsible if the treatment was negligent.

In Kashishian v. Port, 167 Wis. 2d 24, 481 N.W.2d 277 (1992), the Supreme Court of Wisconsin ruled a patient who is unaware that a physician providing treatment was not the employee or agent of the hospital should have a right to look to the hospital in seeking compensation for any negligence in providing emergency room care. The court decided the fact that the physician was an independent contractor, unbeknownst to the patient, should not prohibit a patient from seeking compensation from the hospital offering emergency room care.

22 In Bain v. Colbert County Northwest Alabama Health Care Authority, 233 So.3d 945, (Ala. 2017), a patient's estate brought a medical malpractice action against a hospital and nurses after the patient died when an ascending aortic aneurysm dissected. The Supreme Court of Alabama ruled that evidence a hospital operated an emergency room that was "open for business" was insufficient to establish the hospital's apparent authority over the emergency room physician and thus did not support the imposition of vicarious liability on the hospital for the alleged negligence of the physician. The court stated a Board of Health regulation requiring a hospital's governing authority to ensure services performed under a contract were provided in a safe and effective manner did not impose a nondelegable duty on the hospital to provide emergency medical physician services that fell within the applicable standard of care.

In Popovich v. Allina Health System, 946 N.W.2d 885 (Minn. 2020), the Supreme Court of Minnesota ruled that a plaintiff may assert a claim against a hospital to hold the hospital vicariously liable for the professional negligence of an independent contractor based on a theory of apparent authority. The court further ruled that a plaintiff states such a claim where a hospital held itself out as a provider of emergency medical care and the plaintiff relied on the hospital to select the personnel to provide the services.

23 See Vassiliades v. Garfinckel's, Brooks Bros., 492 A.2d 580 (D.C. 1985), in which the court ruled it is an invasion of a patient's privacy to use before and after photos of cosmetic surgery. The court stated there is a strong public policy in favor of the confidentiality of the physician/patient's treatment except in cases involving gun wounds and child neglect.

In Smith v. Long Island Jewish-Hillside Medical Center, 118 A.D.2d 553, 499 N.Y.S.2d 167 (2d Dep't 1986),

for its patients and other hospital invitees.[24] A hospital has a duty to make a reasonable inspection of its equipment and to remedy any discoverable defects.[25]

Because the number of health care liability claims has increased inordinately in the past few years and the filing of these claims is a contributing factor affecting the medical professional liability rates, as well as the availability and affordability of adequate professional liability insurance, some states have enacted statutes limiting the amount of liability of health-care providers.[26] While some

---

the court held that the right to privacy is personal. The court ruled that parents of a deceased child could not bring an action for violation of the right of privacy of the child when the hospital displayed photos of a child who had died of leukemia in the hospital.

24 In Hitchings v. Albemarle Hospital, 220 F.2d 716 (4th Cir. 1955), the Court of Appeals of the Fourth Circuit noted that a hospital is not an insurer of the safety of its patients; however, the court ruled a hospital has a duty to exercise reasonable care to maintain in reasonably safe condition that part of the hospital designed for patients' use.

In Emmons v. Baptist Hosp., 478 So. 2d 440 (Fla. 1st DCA 1985), a Florida court ruled a hospital must clean its floors more often than most business establishments. The court stated it must give its patients and other invitees warning of concealed perils.

In Roettger v. United Hospitals of St. Paul, Inc., 380 N.W.2d 856 (Minn. Ct. App. 1986), a Minnesota court ruled a private hospital is not an insurer of the safety of its patients but stated it nonetheless must exercise reasonable care for the protection and well-being of its patients. The court asserted the known physical and mental condition of the patient dictates the extent of care that must be exercised, and that reasonable care required to be exercised must be in proportion to the patient's inability to look after the patient's own safety.

In Burns v. Forsyth County Hosp. Authority, Inc., 81 N.C. App. 556, 344 S.E.2d 839 (1986), a North Carolina court ruled a hospital has a duty to provide for a patient's safety while the patient is on hospital premises.

25 In Hector v. Cedars-Sinai Medical Center, 180 Cal. App. 3d 493, 225 Cal. Rptr. 595 (2d Dist. 1986), the court ruled a hospital was not liable to a patient for a defective pacemaker. The court stated the hospital was not liable as it was not the seller of the pacemaker but rather was the provider of medical services.

In Blanton v. Moses H. Cone Memorial Hosp., Inc., 319 N.C. 372, 354 S.E.2d 455 (1987), the Supreme Court of North Carolina ruled a hospital is negligent if it does not follow standards of the JCAHO. (Discussion of the Joint Commission in Chapter II.)

26 See, e.g., Cal. Civ. Code § 3333.2; Neb. Rev. Stat. §§ 44-2801 to 442855; Ohio Rev. Code Ann. § 2307.43; Tex. Civ. Prac. & Rem. Code §§ 74.001 et seq.

Section 74.301 of the Tex. Prac. & Rem. Code limits the civil liability for noneconomic damages of a physician or heath care provider other than a health care institution, inclusive of all persons and entities for which vicarious liability theories may apply, to an amount not to exceed $250,000 for each claimant, regardless of the number of defendant physicians or health care providers other than a health care institution. The limit of civil liability for noneconomic damages for all health care institutions is limited to an amount not to exceed $500,000 for each claimant.

courts have ruled these statutes unconstitutional,[27] others have upheld statutory limitations on damage recoveries.[28]

B. CONSENTS FOR TREATMENT

It is well established that a physician must obtain a patient's consent before commencing surgery or other course of treatment.[29] Treatment not authorized by a patient may amount to a common-law battery, and, thus, give rise to liability to a patient even if the medical treatment is needed and is properly performed.[30] The consent doctrine is grounded in a nonconsensual touching of the body akin to

---

27 See Wright v. Central Du Page Hospital Ass'n, 63 Ill. 2d 313, 347 N.E.2d 736, 80 A.L.R.3d 566 (1976) (but rejected by Gourley ex rel. Gourley v. Nebraska Methodist Health System, Inc., 265 Neb. 918, 663 N.W.2d 43 (2003)).

In Kansas Malpractice Victims Coalition v. Bell, 243 Kan. 333, 757 P.2d 251 (1988) (but disapproved of by Bair v. Peck, 248 Kan. 824, 811 P.2d 1176 (1991)), the Supreme Court of Kansas court ruled a cap of $1,000,000 on noneconomic loss and medical expenses and the requirement of an annuity for payment of future economic loss in all medical malpractice cases was unconstitutional under the Kansas Bill of Rights.

In Lucas v. U.S., 757 S.W.2d 687 (Tex. 1988) (rejected by Adams By and Through Adams v. Children's Mercy Hosp., 832 S.W.2d 898 (Mo. 1992)), the Supreme Court of Texas ruled statutory damages limitations are unconstitutional when applied to damages in common law medical malpractice actions. The court ruled Tex. Rev. Civ. Stat. Ann. art. 4590i, §§ 11.02 and 11.03 (now Tex. Civ. Prac. & Rem. Code § 74.001) were inconsistent with the Texas Constitution. However, in Rose v. Doctors Hosp., 801 S.W.2d 841 (Tex. 1990), the Texas Supreme Court ruled its decision in Lucas did not extend to wrongful death actions and ruled that the legislature could constitutionally curtail damages in wrongful death actions.

28 In English v. New England Medical Center, Inc., 405 Mass. 423, 541 N.E.2d 329 (1989), the Supreme Court of Massachusetts stated that there is a rational relationship between a state statute's cap on damages and the statute's legitimate objective of preserving assets of a charity.

See decision of the Supreme Court of Virginia in Robinson v. Charleston Area Medical Center, Inc., 186 W. Va. 720, 414 S.E.2d 877 (1991).

29 Canterbury v. Spence, 464 F.2d 772 (D.C. Cir. 1972) (but rejected by Cheung v. Cunningham, 214 N.J. Super. 649, 520 A.2d 832 (App. Div. 1987), which was reversed by the New Jersey Supreme Court, 111 N.J. 573, 546 A.2d 501 (N.J. 1988)). In Laureano-Quinones v. Carrion, 982 F.3d 846 (1st Cir. 2020), the Court of Appeals for the First Circuit referred to the Canterbury case and pointed out that it concerned the law of the District of Columbia not Puerto Rico. The First Circuit further noted the Supreme Court of Puerto Rico had expressly rejected Canterbury's approach and evaluated medical malpractice allegations based on lack of informed consent from the perspective of the physician rather than the patient.

30 Cathemer v. Hunter, 27 Ariz. App. 780, 558 P.2d 975 (Div. 1 1976).

See Tex. Civ. Prac. & Rem. Code § 74.106 which sets out the effect of a health care liability claim based on the alleged negligent failure of a physician or health care provider to disclose or adequately disclose the risks and hazards involved in the medical care or surgical procedure rendered by the physician or health care provider. See also Section 74.101, which sets out the theory of recovery.

assault and battery.[31] The right of a person to make decisions regarding body and life also has been elevated to a right of privacy; thus, a failure to obtain consent to treatment can violate a patient's right of privacy.[32]

Although responsibility for obtaining consent for treatment rests with the physician and not the hospital, the hospital can be liable if hospital personnel are aware there is no authorization for treatment or in cases where the physician is deemed to be the agent for the hospital.[33] Medical treatment that will otherwise be a battery in the absence of a proper consent can sometimes be justified in an emergency.[34] However, even in this context, consent is not necessary if the patient is either unconscious or without legal capacity to give consent

31 Sangiuolo v. Leventhal, 132 Misc. 2d 680, 505 N.Y.S.2d 507 (Sup 1986).

In Cardwell v. Bechtol, 724 S.W.2d 739 (Tenn. 1987), the Supreme Court of Tennessee commented that if a battery exists, malpractice may not necessarily be reached. The court noted that a malpractice claim based upon negligence in the care and treatment of a patient is not concerned with the consent of the patient but stated consent does not free a hospital of negligence. The court ruled that when treatment is performed without consent and without the protection of an emergency, a hospital is liable for injuries regardless of negligence.

32 Price v. Sheppard, 307 Minn. 250, 239 N.W.2d 905 (1976).

In Duncan v. Scottsdale Medical Imaging, 205 Ariz. 306, 70 P.3d 435 (Ariz. 2003), the Supreme Court of Arizona ruled that when a patient gives limited or conditional consent, a health care provider has committed a battery if the evidence shows the provider acted with willful disregard of the consent given. Additionally, the Arizona Supreme Court stated that if a patient's consent is obtained by a provider's fraud or misrepresentation, a cause of action for battery is appropriate.

33 See Krane v. Saint Anthony Hosp. Systems, 738 P.2d 75 (Colo. App. 1987), in which the court decided a hospital generally does not have a duty to advise the patient prior to surgery as to the surgical procedure to be employed and the risks involved. The hospital also has no duty to obtain an informed consent similar to that which the surgeon is obligated to obtain. The court stated that the surgeon, not the hospital, has the technical knowledge and training necessary to advise each patient of the risks of the surgery prior to the patient giving his consent. Further, the hospital does not know the patient's medical history or the details of the surgery to be performed.

In Pauscher v. Iowa Methodist Medical Center, 408 N.W.2d 355 (Iowa 1987), the Supreme Court of Iowa ruled a hospital does not have a duty to inform a patient of matters that lie at the heart of the doctor-patient relationship.

In Sangiuolo v. Leventhal, 132 Misc. 2d 680, 505 N.Y.S.2d 507 (Sup 1986), the court noted that generally only the person touching or directing the touching should be liable. The court stated the physician, as an independent provider of medical care, had the obligation to inform the patient of the risks, benefits, and alternatives to the treatment the physician was going to administer.

In Alexander v. Gonser, 42 Wash. App. 234, 711 P.2d 347 (Div. 3 1985), the court ruled a hospital was not under a duty to obtain consent to treatment. The court stated any duty to inform the patient of test results would have been that of the patient's privately retained physician and not the hospital or its personnel. The court stated that to hold a hospital or its employees with a duty to intervene in the independent physician/patient relationship would be more disruptive than beneficial to a patient. However, the court did recognize a hospital may be liable because of vicarious liability for the failure of an employee physician to obtain consent. The court further commented that a hospital has a duty to intervene in the treatment of its patients if there is obvious negligence.

34 Discussion of emergencies is in Chapter III.

and a guardian or agent for the patient is unavailable in an instance when time is of the essence.

Consent for treatment should be in written form signed by the patient or by the person authorized to give consent for the patient.[35] Consent for one type of treatment does not constitute consent for another type or additional treatment.[36]

Persons must give written consent to be the subjects of research.[37] Persons who are subjects of research must be informed of the consequences to them of the research.[38]

1. Informed Consent

It generally is impossible to obtain valid consent to treatment unless the patient understands the nature of the treatment and the risk of undesirable consequences from the treatment.[39] Thus, in order for the patient's consent to be effective, the consent must have been an "informed" consent, one that is given after the patient has received a fair and reasonable explanation of the contemplated

---

35 See, e.g., Tex. Proc. & Rem. Code § 74.105 which states that consent to medical care is effective if it is given in writing, signed by the patient or a person authorized to give the consent and by a competent witness, and if the written consent specifically states the risks and hazards that are involved in the medical care or surgical provided in the form and to the degree required by a disclosure panel as set out in Section 74.103.

See Wash. Rev. Code § 7.70.060, which provided that a consent signed by a legally competent patient is prima facie evidence the patient gave informed consent to the treatment administered. The patient has the burden of rebutting this by a preponderance of the evidence.

See also Iowa Code § 147.137.

36 In Pauscher v. Iowa Methodist Medical Center, 408 N.W.2d 355 (Iowa 1987), the Supreme Court of Iowa recognized an action for battery may lie when a patient consents to one type of treatment and the physician intentionally deviates from the consent and performs a substantially different treatment. See also Moser v. Stallings, 387 N.W.2d 599 (Iowa 1986).

37 45 C.F.R. §§ 46.116, 46.117. The general requirements for informed consent regarding subjects of research are set out in 45 C.F.R. § 46.116.

38 45 C.F.R. § 46.117. A short form can be used indicating that the elements of informed consent required by 45 C.F.R. § 46.116 have been presented orally to the subject or the subject's legally authorized representative. The short form requires a witness to the oral presentation.

39 Canterbury v. Spence, 464 F.2d 772 (D.C. Cir. 1972) (but rejected by Cheung v. Cunningham, 214 N.J. Super. 649, 520 A.2d 832 (App. Div. 1987), which was reversed by the New Jersey Supreme Court, 111 N.J. 573, 546 A.2d 501 (N.J. 1988)).

In Arato v. Avedon, 23 Cal. Rptr. 2d 131, 132, 858 P.2d 598, 600 (Cal. 1993), the Supreme Court of California stated that a physician's duty to disclose to a patient information material to a decision whether to undergo treatment is the central constituent of the legal doctrine known as "informed consent."

treatment or procedures.[40] A physician then, has a duty to make adequate disclosure to the patient.[41] The Court of Appeals for the District of Columbia has ruled that this duty entails more than a duty to answer the patient's questions; it is a duty to provide the information the patient needs to make an intelligent decision.[42]

---

40 See Sard v. Hardy, 281 Md. 432, 379 A.2d 1014 (1977).

In Pauscher v. Iowa Methodist Medical Center, 408 N.W.2d 355 (Iowa 1987), the Supreme Court of Iowa recognized an issue of "informed" consent is not an action for battery but rather is an action in negligence, imposing upon the doctor a duty reasonably to disclose information material to the patient's decision.

In re Gardner, 534 A.2d 947 (Me. 1987), the Supreme Court of Maine stated the doctrine of informed consent is an actionable species of medical negligence.

In Binur v. Jacobo, 135 S.W.3d 646 (Tex. 2004), the Supreme Court of Texas ruled an erroneous prognosis that is the basis for recommending surgery cannot be the basis of a cause of action for lack of informed consent. The plaintiff contended a surgeon failed to obtain her informed consent to the surgical removal of both her breasts. She alleged the physician told her that she would definitely develop breast cancer and that this was the reason she consented to a prophylactic bilateral mastectomy. The court held that the evidence supported a finding that the surgeon properly obtained the patient's informed consent prior to performing the mastectomy. It stated that the plaintiff might have pursued a claim against the surgeon for negligence in reaching his prognosis, but she had no basis for a claim of lack of informed consent.

In Schaub v. Sanchez, 229 S.W.2d 322 (Tex. 2007), the Supreme Court of Texas defined informed consent as failing to disclose the risks or hazards that could have influenced a reasonable person in deciding to give or withhold consent. The court stated that a physician who provides treatment without consent commits a battery. The court then reiterated that mistreatment may constitute negligence, but it does not give rise to a claim for lack of informed consent. The plaintiff sued two physicians for allegedly failing to obtain her informed consent to perform a stellate ganglion block, which is a spinal injection that anesthetizes a collection of nerves in the patient's neck. The court noted the plaintiff did not complain that she was unaware of the risks or hazards of the block, finding that she had twice undergone the procedure.

41 Still, as the court noted in Johns Hopkins Bayview Medical Center, Inc. v. Byrom, 2021 WL 321745 (Md. Ct. Spec. App. 2021), while a fully informed patient has the right to make decisions about the patient's own healthcare, a necessary corollary of the right is that absent negligence by the healthcare professional, the patient is responsible for the consequences of the choices the patient makes. The patient, fully informed of the choices and the risks attendant to each of those choices, chose an induced vaginal delivery over a cesarean section. Precisely as her doctors predicted, the consequences of that choice were disastrous.

Tex. Civ. Prac. & Rem. Code § 74.104 requires a physician or health care provider to disclose to the patient, or the person authorized to consent for the patient, the risks and hazards involved in the kind of care for any medical care or surgical procedure that appears on a disclosure panel's list. If the requirements of Section 74.105, discussed above regarding disclosure, are met, the physician or health care provider is considered to have complied with Section 74.104.

42 See Canterbury v. Spence, 464 F.2d 772 (D.C. Cir. 1972) (rejected by, Cheung v. Cunningham, 214 N.J. Super. 649, 520 A.2d 832 (App. Div. 1987), which was reversed by the New Jersey Supreme Court, 111 N.J. 573, 546 A.2d 501 (N.J. 1988)). Still, as noted previously, in Laureano-Quinones v. Carrion, 982 F.3d 846 (1st Cir. 2020), the Court of Appeals for the First Circuit referred to the Canterbury case and pointed out that it concerned the law of the District of Columbia, not Puerto Rico. (See note 29, supra.)

In Otwell v. Bryant, 497 So. 2d 111 (Ala. 1986), the Supreme Court of Alabama commented a physician is not required to inform the patient of every risk involved in a procedure, rather the physician must inform of the significant perils. The court ruled the question of whether there was "informed" consent is a question of fact for the jury.

The basis of the doctrine of informed consent is the patient's right to exercise control over the patient's body by the patient deciding whether to submit to the particular therapy.[43] The doctrine requires the physician to explain to the patient, before the patient is subjected to medical treatment, the procedures involved as well as the material risks or dangers inherent in or collateral to the therapy so that the patient can make an intelligent and informed choice about whether to undergo the treatment.[44] This duty to disclose requires a physician to reveal to the patient the nature of the ailment, the nature of the proposed treatment, the probability of success of the contemplated therapy and its alternatives, and the risk of unfortunate consequences associated with the treatment.[45] The

---

In Arato v. Avedon, 23 Cal. Rptr. 2d 131, 858 P.2d 598 (1993), the court declined to endorse a physician's mandatory disclosure of life expectancy probabilities to a patient who must make an informed decision regarding medical treatment. The court ruled that it is a question of fact whether a physician has disclosed to a patient all material information that the physician knew or should know would be regarded as significant by a reasonable person in the patient's position. The court decided statistical life expectancy data is information that lies outside the significant risks associated with a given treatment. The court ruled the question of whether a physician should disclose this information turns on the standard of practice within the medical community. Because it is a fact question whether a physician should disclose this information, a trial court can permit expert testimony on the issue.

In Parris v. Sands, 25 Cal. Rptr. 2d 800 (2d Dist. 1993), the court noted appellate courts have rejected a general duty of disclosure concerning a treatment or procedure a physician does not recommend. Thus, a physician need not inform a patient of a "school of thought" based on views of other health care providers.

In Cardwell v. Bechtol, 724 S.W.2d 739 (Tenn. 1987), the Supreme Court of Tennessee stated that whether a patient was given adequate information depends on the nature of the treatment, the extent of the risks involved, and the standard of care of the treating physician.

In Quimby v. Fine, 45 Wash. App. 175, 724 P.2d 403 (Div. 1 1986), the court commented that an action based on lack of informed consent is different from that of medical negligence. Lack of informed consent is not limited to breach of professional standards of care. It can be based on a dishonest and unfair practice used to promote the entrepreneurial aspects of a doctor's practice.

43 Canterbury v. Spence, 464 F.2d 772 (D.C. Cir. 1972) (rejected by Cheung v. Cunningham, 214 N.J. Super. 649, 520 A.2d 832 (App. Div. 1987), and reversed by the New Jersey Supreme Court, 111 N.J. 573, 546 A.2d 501 (N.J. 1988)).

44 Sard v. Hardy, 281 Md. 432, 379 A.2d 1014 (1977).

In Laureano-Quinones v. Carrion, 982 F.3d 846 (1st Cir. 2020), the Court of Appeals for the First Circuit ruled a doctor was not liable for medical malpractice regarding an informed claim filed following a patient's abdominoplasty surgery. The patient signed a consent form that alerted her to, among other things, the risk of scarring. The surgery left the patient with a scar she alleged looked like a second belly button. The doctor contended that he had agreed to perform a cosmetic scar revision and repositioning procedure, but the procedure did not occur after the patient refused to sign a form the doctor required her to sign in advance. The patient contended that if the doctor had advised she could obtain bad results from the surgery, she would not have agreed to the surgery. The First Circuit referred to Canterbury v Spence and stated that under Puerto Rico law, courts determine the scope of a physician's duty of disclosure by looking to the prevailing medical practice and assessing causation between the negligent omission and the harm by questioning what a physician could foresee as a normal consequence of the physician's omission.

45 In Arato v. Avedon, 858 P.2d 598 (Cal. 1992), the widow and children of a patient who died of pancreatic cancer brought an action against the treating physicians, contending that the physicians failed to obtain the informed consent for a particular course of treatment by failing to disclose information

law does not permit a physician to substitute the physician's judgment for that of the patient in the matter of consent to treatment.[46]

Once circumstances give rise to a duty on the part of a physician to inform a patient, the next inquiry is the scope of the disclosure the physician is legally required to make.[47] Some states have ruled that a physician has a duty to disclose the risks and alternatives a reasonable prudent physician would disclose under the same or similar circumstances.[48] This standard for determining the adequacy of disclosure would require the testimony of expert witnesses.[49] Other states require that a physician disclose that information a reasonably prudent person in the patient's position would require to be suitably informed and, thus, to make a decision regarding treatment.[50] In a suit based on the failure to provide

---

regarding the life expectancy of pancreatic cancer patients. The Supreme Court of California ruled a physician's duty to disclose to a patient all material information needed to make an informed decision regarding a proposed treatment does not include a duty to disclose life expectancy data. The court ruled that as a matter of law the physicians did not have a duty to disclose statistical life expectancy data.

46 Sard v. Hardy, 281 Md. 432, 379 A.2d 1014 (1977).

47 Canterbury v. Spence, 464 F.2d 772 (D.C. Cir. 1972) (rejected by Cheung v. Cunningham, 214 N.J. Super. 649, 520 A.2d 832 (App. Div. 1987), which was reversed by the New Jersey Supreme Court, 111 N.J. 573, 546 A.2d 501 (N.J. 1988)).

48 See, e.g., Cooper v. Roberts, 220 Pa. Super. 260, 286 A.2d 647 (1971).

49 In Bly v. Rhoads, 216 Va. 645, 222 S.E.2d 783 (1976), the Supreme Court of Virginia stated matters involved in the disclosure syndrome cannot be left to lay witnesses.

50 In Canterbury v. Spence, 464 F.2d 772 (D.C. Cir. 1972) (rejected by Cheung v. Cunningham, 214 N.J. Super. 649, 520 A.2d 832 (App. Div. 1987), which was reversed by the New Jersey Supreme Court, 111 N.J. 573, 546 A.2d 501 (N.J. 1988), the Court of Appeals for the District of Columbia Circuit determined the scope of the physician's communication to the patient must be measured by the patient's need; that need is the need for information material to the decision. The District of Columbia Circuit stated that all risk potentially affecting the decision must be unmasked to the patient. This court recognized a physician might not know with complete exactitude what the patient would consider important to the physician's decision but stated that based on the physician's medical training and experience the physician can sense how the average, reasonable patient expectably would react. When nondisclosure of risk information is open to debate by reasonable-minded persons, the District of Columbia Circuit determined the issue is for the finder of facts. The court stated the question for the jury is what a prudent person in the patient's position would have decided if suitably informed of all perils bearing significance.

In Pauscher v. Iowa Methodist Medical Center, 408 N.W.2d 355 (Iowa 1987), the Supreme Court of Iowa concluded the patient rule is applicable in all informed consent cases, in both elective and non-elective medical procedures. The court stated that while most aspects of the physician-patient relationship must be dominated by the superior skill and knowledge of the physician, the decision to consent to a medical procedure is not a medical decision. The court decided it is a personal "and often difficult decision to be made by the patient with the physician's advice and consultation." To make an informed decision, the patient must have the information reasonably necessary to the process. Thus, the patient rule makes full disclosure the rule; however, it permits numerous exceptions that the physician, who has access to the medical knowledge involved, can assert.

informed consent, a patient must show that the patient would not have agreed to the proposed treatment had risk disclosure been adequate.[51] An objective standard, adopted by some courts, of demonstrating what a reasonably prudent person in the patient's position would have done if adequately informed of the risk or alternative, has the effect of shielding the physician from the hindsight of a particular patient.[52] Because courts have failed to adopt uniform standards defining the adequacy of the divulgence, some states have adopted statutes to define the limits of the doctrine of informed consent.[53]

---

51 Canterbury v. Spence, 464 F.2d 772 (D.C. Cir. 1972) (rejected by Cheung v. Cunningham, 214 N.J. Super. 649, 520 A.2d 832 (App. Div. 1987)), which was reversed by the New Jersey Supreme Court, 111 N.J. 573, 546 A.2d 501 (N.J. 1988).

52 See discussion in Canterbury v. Spence, 464 F.2d 772 (D.C. Cir. 1972) (rejected by Cheung v. Cunningham, 214 N.J. Super. 649, 520 A.2d 832 (App. Div. 1987), which was reversed by the New Jersey Supreme Court, 111 N.J. 573, 546 A.2d 501 (N.J. 1988)). A more subjective approach of requiring the patient to prove that the patient would have refused to consent if informed of the hazards involved also provides protection for the physician who discloses the major risks.

In Pauscher v. Iowa Methodist Medical Center, 408 N.W.2d 355 (Iowa 1987), the Supreme Court of Iowa commented that the patient will ordinarily be required to present expert testimony relating to the nature of the risk and the likelihood of its occurrence for the jury to determine, from the standpoint of the reasonable patient, whether the risk is in fact a material one. A physician can establish several situations that would be a defense to an informed consent action. These include: situations in which complete and candid disclosure would have a detrimental effect on the physical or psychological well-being of the patient; situations in which a patient is incapable of giving consent by reason of mental disability or situations in which an emergency made it impractical to obtain consent; situations in which the risk is either known to the patient or is so obvious as to justify a presumption on the part of the physician that the patient has knowledge of the risk; situations in which the procedure itself is simple and the danger remote or commonly appreciated to be remote; and situations in which the physician does not know of an otherwise material risk and should not have been aware of it in the exercise of ordinary care.

53 See, e.g., Neb. Rev. Stat. § 44-2816, which defined informed consent to mean consent to a procedure based on information that ordinarily would be provided to the patient under like circumstances by health-care providers engaged in a similar practice in the locality or in similar localities. Failure to obtain informed consent included failure to obtain any express or implied consent for any operation, treatment, or procedures in a case in which a reasonably prudent health-care provider in the community or similar communities would have obtained an express or implied consent for the operation, treatment, or procedures under similar circumstances.

See Tex. Civ. Prac. & Rem. Code §§ 74.001 et seq., which provides that the only theory on which recovery may be obtained in a suit against a physician or health-care provider based on the failure of the physician or health-care provider to disclose or adequately to disclose the risks and hazards involved in the medical treatment rendered by the physician or health-care provider, is that of negligence in failing to disclose the risks or hazards that could have influenced a reasonable person in making a decision to give or withhold consent. The Texas Medical Disclosure Panel was created to determine which risks and hazards related to medical care and surgical procedures must be disclosed by health-care providers or physicians to patients or persons authorized to consent for their patients and to establish the general form and substance of the disclosure. Consent to medical care is considered effective if it is given in writing, signed by a patient or person authorized to give the consent and by a competent witness, and if the written consent specifically states risks and hazards involved in the medical care or surgical procedure in the form and to the degree required by the panel. The Texas Medical Disclosure Panel provided a disclosure and consent form that could be used by physicians.

2. Minor's Consent

A parent generally has the right to consent to medical treatment on behalf of a minor child.[54] Because a child is not legally competent to give a binding consent to any medical services rendered to the child, the parent gives effective consent.[55] When parents refuse to consent to treatment, a physician or health-care provider can seek a court order if the physician deems the treatment to be necessary.[56] In some extraordinary circumstances, the consent of the parents to

---

See Wash. Rev. Code § 7.70.050, which codified the duty to disclose. A patient must prove that a health-care provider failed to inform the patient of a material fact relating to treatment, that the patient consented to treatment without being aware of that fact, and that a reasonably prudent patient under similar circumstances would not have consented, given that information. The patient also must demonstrate the treatment in question proximately caused injury to the patient.

See 45 C.F.R. § 46.116, which requires informed consent by a person who will be a subject of research. The regulation sets out the requirements for an informed consent in this context.

54 In Matter of Grady, 85 N.J. 235, 426 A.2d 467 (1981), the Supreme Court of New Jersey nonetheless noted a parent may not deprive a child of a lifesaving treatment however well-intentioned. The court emphasized the right of the state to deny to parents the power of life or death over their children. The court stated that even where a decision to withhold a lifesaving treatment is based on constitutional grounds, such as religious beliefs, it must yield to a state's interest as parens patriae, in protecting the health and welfare of the child. When the case involved the protection of an actual or potential life that cannot protect themself, then the interest of the state in sustaining life is given effect over the right of the parent to consent or to withhold consent.

55 In Bowen v. American Hosp. Ass'n, 476 U.S. 610 (1986), the Supreme Court stated a hospital's withholding treatment from a handicapped infant when no parent consent was given does not violate Section 504 of the Rehabilitation Act of 1973, 29 U.S.C. § 794, for, according to the court, without the parents' consent, the infant was neither otherwise qualified for treatment nor denied care solely because of the infant's disability.

In Hughson v. St. Francis Hosp. of Port Jervis, 92 A.D.2d 131, 459 N.Y.S.2d 814 (2d Dep't 1983), the court stated an expectant mother's consent cannot be for herself alone. According to the court, a physician must disclose to an expectant mother the available alternatives to treatment and the reasonably foreseeable risks and benefits involved. The consent of the mother must then be made with knowledge of the risks to her unborn child. The physician owes an independent duty of disclosure, via the mother, to the unborn child.

See Tex. Fam. Code Ann. § 35.02, which required a consent to contain the name of the minor; name of one or both parents, if known; name of the guardian, if any had been appointed; name of the person giving consent and that person's relation to the minor child; a statement of the nature of the medical treatment to be given; and the date on which the treatment was to begin.

56 In the case, In Interest of Ivey, 319 So. 2d 53 (Fla. 1st DCA 1975), a Florida court ruled that the state of Florida, as parens patriae, has a wide range of power for limiting parental freedom and authority in matters affecting a child's welfare. According to the court, the natural rights of parents to the custody and control of their child are subject to the power of the state and may be restricted and regulated by appropriate legislative or judicial action. The court decided the state, as parens patriae, may step in and protect the rights of a child threatened with death when the child's natural parents will not consent to medical treatment and/or blood transfusions because of religious beliefs or otherwise.

In People ex rel. Wallace v. Labrenz, 411 Ill. 618, 104 N.E.2d 769 (1952), the Supreme Court of Illinois affirmed the appointment of a guardian to consent to a blood transfusion for a child when the parents,

medical treatment for their child may require independent and objective investigation of the motivation and reasoning of the parents.[57]

The statute of limitations on personal injury suits may be tolled for minors.[58] In most states a person under eighteen years of age is under a legal disability regardless of whether the person is married.[59] This period of disability is not

---

Jehovah's Witnesses, refused on religious grounds. The court stated the right to practice religion does not include the liberty to expose a child to ill health or to death.

57 See Hart v. Brown, 29 Conn. Supp. 368, 289 A.2d 386 (Super. Ct. 1972), in which the court reviewed the consent of the parents of identical twins to the transplantation of a kidney from one twin to the other. The court pointed out one of the legal problems required a balancing of the rights of the minor children—more directly the rights of the donor child. The court determined the natural parents could substitute their consent for that of their minor children after a close, independent, and objective investigation for their motivation and reasoning. That consent was accomplished by the participation of a clergyman, the physicians, an attorney-guardian-ad-litem for the donor and for the donee, and by a court.

58 In Strahler v. St. Luke's Hosp., 706 S.W.2d 7 (Mo. 1986), the court ruled it is not realistic to rely upon parents to bring malpractice actions within the time provided.

In Sax v. Votteler, 648 S.W.2d 661 (Tex. 1983), the Texas Supreme Court ruled a state medical malpractice limitations statute was unconstitutional as applied to minors.

In Nelson v. Krusen, 678 S.W.2d 918 (Tex. 1984), the Texas Supreme Court ruled the two-year statute of limitations arising out of medical malpractice violated the open courts provision of the state constitution by eliminating a cause of action before the party knows the party is injured.

See also Morrison v. Chan, 699 S.W.2d 205 (Tex. 1985), in which the Texas Supreme Court clarified when the two-year statute of limitations under Tex. Rev. Civ. Stat. Ann. Art. 4590i §10.01 (now Tex. Civ. Prac. & Rem. Code §§ 74.001 et seq.) would violate the open courts provision of the Texas Constitution. The court stated that if the plaintiff could have discovered the injury, the two-year statute of limitations applies. However, if the parties could not discover the injury within the two-year period, the statute does not bar the action.

In Moore ex rel. Moore v. Memorial Hosp. of Gulfport, 825 So. 2d 658 (Miss. 2002), the Supreme Court of Mississippi ruled that plaintiffs in a medical malpractice suit, who brought an action against a physician, a community hospital, and a pharmacy, were entitled to have the statute of limitations lengthened against the hospital. It noted the statute of limitations would be tolled until a plaintiff can reasonably be held to have knowledge of an injury, the cause of the injury, and the causative relationship between the injury and the conduct of a physician and a hospital. The plaintiffs alleged a physician 's prescription of drugs to the plaintiff mother while she was pregnant caused her child's kidney failure. The plaintiffs also contended the pharmacy was negligent in selling a drug contra-indicated for pregnant women. The court held that the plaintiffs did not have a cause of action against the pharmacists who dispensed the drug because, under the learned intermediary doctrine, a pharmacist has no legal duty to warn a pregnant woman of the hazards of taking a certain medication during pregnancy. Under the learned intermediary doctrine, a pharmaceutical company is required only to warn a prescribing physician of the dangers inherent in its products. The Supreme Court of Mississippi extended the intermediary doctrine to pharmacists and pharmacies. It ruled that pharmacists and pharmacies owe no legal duty to warn in the context of prescription medication. This court noted there is an exception if a person informed a pharmacists of the person's health problems that contra-indicated the use of a drug and in instances where a pharmacist filled a prescription in a quantity inconsistent with the recommended dosage guidelines. The court stated a physician has a duty to be fully aware of the characteristics of drugs the physician is prescribing, the amount that can be administered safely, and the different medication a patient is taking. The physician has the duty to warn of danger or side effects associated with a drug.

59 See, e.g., Tex. Civ. Prac. & Rem. Code § 16.001. Section 74.251 of the Tex. Civ. Prac. & Rem. Code states that minors under the age of twelve years shall have until their fourteenth birthday in which

included in the limitations period; thus, the statute of limitations generally does not begin to run until a child reaches majority even though the child's parents or guardian could bring an action before that date.[60]

In instances in which the parents of a minor child cannot be located to give consent to medical treatment, some states give named relatives power to consent to treatment for the child.[61] When minors are deemed to be "mature," they generally may give consent on their own behalf.[62]

---

to file a claim, or have a claim filed on their behalf; however, all claims must be brought within ten years or, as provided by Section 74.151(b), they are time barred.

60 In Shack v. Holland, 389 N.Y.S.2d 988 (N.Y. Sup. 1976), the court ruled an unborn child can maintain an action for prenatal injuries. The statute of limitations was tolled for the unborn child but not for the mother's claim for loss of services and medical expenses.

61 See Bonner v. Moran, 126 F.2d 121 (D.C. Cir. 1941).

See also Moss v. Rishworth, 222 S.W. 225 (Tex. Comm'n App. 1920), in which a court even earlier ruled that sisters who were temporary custodians of a child had no authority to give consent to perform an operation on the child in the absence of an emergency. The court stated that the parent was the only one who could legally give consent to perform the operation.

But see Tex. Fam. Code Ann. § 35.01, which provided that certain listed persons could consent to medical treatment of a minor when the person having the power to consent could not be contacted and actual notice to the contrary had not been given by that person. The persons listed are (1) a grandparent, (2) an adult brother or sister, (3) an adult aunt or uncle, (4) an educational institution in which the minor is enrolled that has received written authorization to consent from the person having the power to consent, (5) any adult who has care and control of the minor and who has written authorization to consent from the persons having the power to consent, (6) any court having jurisdiction of the child, or (7) any adult responsible for the care and control of the minor under the jurisdiction of a juvenile court.

62 In Bonner v. Moran, 126 F.2d 121 (D. C. Cir. 1941), the court noted a child who is close to maturity may give consent.

In Cardwell v. Bechtol, 724 S.W.2d 739 (Tenn. 1987), the Supreme Court of Tennessee ruled that although parental consent is generally required to treat a minor, there is a mature minor exception. The court ruled that treatment could be provided a mature minor who was seventeen years of age without consent of the parents.

See Tex. Fam. Code Ann. § 35.03, which provides that a minor can consent to medical and surgical treatment and dental care in the following instances: (1) if the minor is on active duty with the armed services of the United States; (2) if the minor is sixteen years of age or older and resides separate and apart from the minor's parents or guardian and is managing her own financial affairs; (3) if the minor consents to the diagnosis and treatment of any infectious, contagious, or communicable disease that is required by law to be reported to a physician, dentist or local health officer, including all sexually transmitted diseases; (4) if the minor is unmarried and pregnant and consents to treatment, other than abortion, related to her pregnancy; (5) if the minor is eighteen years of age or older and consents to the donation of blood; or (6) if the minor consents to examination and treatment for chemical addiction, chemical dependency, or any other condition directly related to chemical use. A physician, dentist, or medical facility can rely on the written statement of the minor containing the grounds on which the minor has capacity to consent to the minor's own medical treatment.

Discussion of a minor's consent to an abortion is in Chapter V.

Legal consequences follow from a determination of whether death has occurred. Some examples include: the proximate cause and time of death in homicide cases, the termination of life support efforts, and the liability for death claims under an insurance contract.[63] Courts have stated that death is both a legal and a medical question.[64] In the past, the definition of death was both medically and legally a relatively simple matter. When the heart stopped beating and the lungs stopped breathing, the individual was dead according to physicians and according to the law.[65] In the past, no mechanical means were available to maintain heart and lung action. Because respiration, heart action, and brain function are so closely related, without artificial support, the cessation of any one of them will bring the others to a halt. Later, with the advancement of medical science, the traditional common-law heart and lungs definition is no longer adequate.[66] Courts and legislatures in many states have reconsidered the definition of death because of several factors, including, modern medicine's technological ability to sustain life in the absence of spontaneous heartbeat or respiration; the advent of successful organ transplantation capabilities that creates a demand for viable organs from recently deceased donors; the enormous expenditure of resources involved if persons who are in fact dead are treated as being medically alive; and the need for a precise time of death so that persons who have died may be treated appropriately.[67] In some states, brain death is deemed to be death so that

63 In re Welfare of Bowman, 94 Wash. 2d 407, 617 P.2d 731 (1980).

64 Id.

65 In State v. Fierro, 124 Ariz. 182, 603 P.2d 74 (1979), the Supreme Court of Arizona early referred to the common-law definition of death as the cessation of life, the total stoppage of the circulation of blood and the cessation of the animal and vital functions consequent thereon, i.e., respiration, and pulsation. Under the common law definition, even if the brain is not functioning, the individual is not dead if the individual is breathing, and blood is flowing through the veins.

66 In re Welfare of Bowman, 94 Wash. 2d 407, 617 P.2d 731 (1980).

67 See, e.g., Kan. Stat. Ann. § 77-205, Md. Code Ann., Health-Gen § 5-202, and Mont. Code Ann. § 50-22-101.

life supports may be terminated at that point.[68] Brain stem death draws a clear line between brain death and the persistent vegetative state.[69]

Under the Uniform Determination of Death Act, an individual who has sustained either irreversible cessation of circulatory and respiratory functions, or irreversible cessation of all functions of the entire brain, including the brain stem, is dead.[70] A determination of death must be made in accordance with accepted medical standards.[71] Under the Uniform Brain Death Act, which was superseded by the Uniform Determination of Death Act, death occurred when an individual has sustained irreversible cessation of all functioning of the brain, including the brain stem.[72] The Uniform Determination of Death Act codified both the common-law basis for determining death, i.e., the total failure of the cardiorespiratory system, and the extension of the common law to include new procedures for determination of death based upon irreversible loss of all brain functions. Although cases may continue to be determined under the common-law definition, when artificial means of support preclude a determination of

68 See, e.g., Tex. Health & Safety Code § 671.001. The statute provides that a person will be considered dead if, based on ordinary standards of medical practice, there is irreversible cessation of spontaneous respiratory and circulatory functions. If artificial means of support preclude a determination that spontaneous respiratory and circulatory functions have ceased, a person is considered legally dead if in the announced opinion of a physician, based on ordinary standards of medical practice, there is the irreversible cessation of all spontaneous brain function. Death is to be pronounced before artificial means of supporting respiratory and circulatory functions are terminated.

69 In the case of In re Welfare of Bowman, 94 Wash. 2d 407, 617 P.2d 731 (1980), a physician testified that a child, who had been admitted to a hospital after suffering massive physical injuries was brain-dead under the Harvard criteria developed in 1968 which constituted the basis for determination of brain death. The physician testified the child showed no brain activity; thus, the physician wanted to remove the child from a ventilator, a recommendation to which the child's mother consented. (Discussion of "Right to Die" in Chapter III.)

70 Unif. Determination of Death Act § 1 (1980).

In Strachan v. John F. Kennedy Memorial Hosp., 109 N.J. 523, 538 A.2d 346 (1988), the Supreme Court of New Jersey noted the Uniform Determination of Death Act had then been adopted by at least thirteen states and the District of Columbia. The court approved the standards to determine death as set out in the act and ruled that a hospital was negligent when it failed to remove an individual from a respirator until three days after the emergency room physician pronounced the victim was brain-dead. The court ruled the hospital negligently withheld the body of the victim from his parents.

The Unif. Determination of Death Act was adopted by at least forty-three states and the District of Columbia as of 2021.

71 Unif. Determination of Death Act § 1 (1980).

72 Unif. Brain Death Act §1 (1978).

death under that definition, the act recognizes that death can be determined by the alternative procedures.[73]

The Uniform Determination of Death Act[74] sets out the additional following facts relating to the determination of death. The concept of "entire brain" distinguishes determination of death under "neocortical death" or "persistent vegetative state." The act does not deem these to be valid medical or legal bases for determining death. The act sets the general legal standard for determining death, but not the medical criteria for doing so. The medical profession remains free to formulate acceptable medical practices and to utilize new diagnostic tests, and new biomedical knowledge. Presumably, no person authorized by law to determine death, who makes a determination in accordance with the act, should be liable for damages in any civil action or be subject to prosecution in any criminal proceedings. The act does not address time of death; time of death should be determined by expert testimony before the appropriate court.

When an individual is legally and medically dead, a hospital may not withhold the dead body.[75] Although a dead body is not considered as property, the law does recognize a right arising out of the duty of the nearest relatives of the deceased to bury their dead.[76] The right authorizes and requires the nearest relative to take possession and control of the dead body for the purpose of giving it a decent burial.[77] This qualified right in the dead body, called a quasi-property

---

73 Unif. Determination of Death Act Pref. Note (1980).

74 Id.

75 In Strachan v. John F. Kennedy Memorial Hosp., 209 N.J. Super. 300, 507 A.2d 718 (N.J. App. Div. 1986), judgment aff'd in part, rev'd in part, 109 N.J. 523, 538 A.2d 346 (1988), a New Jersey court noted that early common law refused to recognize the concept of a property right in the body of a deceased person. However, the prevailing view in New Jersey then evolved that the right to bury the dead and preserve the remains is a quasi-right in property, the infringement of which may be redressed by an action in damages. The theory of an alleged wrongful withholding of a dead body is based upon an unjustified interference with a quasi-property right. On appeal, the court ruled that the duty of a hospital to the parents of a suicide victim was not to have in place procedures for removal of their child from life support systems or to release to the parents their child's dead body, but rather to act reasonably honoring the parents' legitimate request to turn over the child's dead body. The court decided that the evidence supported a jury's conclusion that the hospital had negligently withheld the suicide victim's body from his parents and that the parents were not required to prove physical injury to recover emotional distress damages.

76 See, e.g., Ariz. Rev. Stat. Ann. § 36-831, which provided the duty to bury rested with the surviving spouse, or the parent for a minor child, or the adult children if there is no surviving spouse. If none are financially able, a charitable organization or the county can assume responsibility.

77 See Cal. Health & Safety Code § 7100, which provides the right to control disposition of the remains of a deceased person rests first with the surviving spouse, then the surviving child or children, next the surviving parent or parents, then with the next of kin, and finally with a public administrator

right, is not a property right in a commercial sense but rather is a right of possession for the purpose of burial.[78] Some courts have ruled there arises from the relationship an emotional interest that should be protected and that others have a duty not to injure intentionally or negligently.[79] Thus, upon the death of a patient, the hospital is responsible both for informing the proper members of the family, in an acceptable manner, of the death, and for properly releasing the body to the appropriate family members.[80]

Any interference with the right of possession of the body of a deceased by mutilation, or by otherwise disturbing the body without the consent of the persons who have the right of possession of the body, is an actionable wrong for which a claim for damages may be maintained.[81]

---

if the decedent had sufficient assets. Liability for burial rests jointly and severally on the kin of the decedent.

In Parker v. Quinn-McGowen Co., 262 N.C. 560, 138 S.E.2d 214 (1964), the Supreme Court of North Carolina early commented that the rights of one legally entitled to the custody of a body are violated if another unlawfully withholds the dead body from that person. The survivor has the legal right to bury the body in the condition it was in when life became extinct.

78 In Prosser and Keeton on Torts §63 (5th ed. 1984), Dean William Lloyd Prosser commented that the "quasi-property right" concept evolved "out of thin air" to protect the personal feelings of the survivors. Prosser commented that in the earlier days of common law, as Blackstone averred, no property right existed relative to a dead body; instead matters concerning corpses were left to the ecclesiastical courts.

In Holland v. Metalious, 105 N.H. 290, 198 A.2d 654 (1964), the Supreme Court of New Hampshire noted that the surviving spouse and next of kin, in that order, are accorded proprietary rights to determine matters relating to burial, at least in the absence of testamentary or other direction by the decedent. The court stated the wishes of the decedent would be carried out as far as possible but that rights in the matter of burial and disinterment are not absolute and would be governed by rules of propriety and reasonableness determinable by a court of equity upon due application. The decedent's will had donated his body to scientific use; however, the donee rejected the body. The court held that in this instance the wishes of the surviving spouse and children take precedence over the decedent's directive.

79 In Gratton v. Baldwinsville Academy and Central School, 49 Misc. 2d 329, 267 N.Y.S.2d 552 (Sup. 1966), the court recognized a cause of action for emotional disturbance in New York. The court stated that surviving next of kin has a right to immediate possession of a decedent's body for preservation and burial, and damages can be awarded against a person who unlawfully interferes with the right.

In Dumouchelle v. Duke University, 69 N.C. App. 471, 317 S.E.2d 100 (1984), a North Carolina court stated a person may recover damages for mental suffering caused by negligent or unintentional mishandling or mutilation of a body. However, in Parker v. Quinn-McGowen Co., 262 N.C. 560, 138 S.E.2d 214 (1964), the North Carolina Supreme Court earlier held that the unauthorized embalming of a body received for burial did not constitute mutilation. The Parker court stated the mere fact of unauthorized embalming, without more, does not constitute such a mishandling or mutilation of a body as to support a cause of action by the next of kin for mental anguish.

80 Strachan v. John F. Kennedy Memorial Hosp., 209 N.J. Super. 300, 507 A.2d 718 (App. Div. 1986), judgment aff'd in part, rev'd in part, 109 N.J. 523, 538 A.2d 346 (1988)

81 Terrill v. Harbin, 376 S.W.2d 945 (Tex. Civ. App. Eastland 1964).

An autopsy is the inspection and partial dissection of a dead body to learn the cause of death.[82] The next of kin of a deceased has the right to grant or deny authority for a private or unofficial autopsy.[83] Further, the state has the right under the police power to perform an official autopsy of the body of a person who dies under suspicious circumstances.[84] Any unauthorized autopsy is a mutilation of the body of the deceased and provides the next of kin a cause of action.

---

82 Lashbrook v. Barnes, 437 S.W.2d 502 (Ky. 1969).

83 Leno v. St. Joseph Hospital, 55 Ill. 2d 114, 302 N.E.2d 58 (1973).

In Scarpaci v. Milwaukee County, 96 Wis. 2d 663, 292 N.W.2d 816 (Wis. 1980), the Supreme Court of Wisconsin ruled that a statute granting immunity from suit did not bar the parents' claim for an alleged unauthorized performance of an autopsy on the body of their deceased child. The complaint in this case alleged that a medical examiner ordered an autopsy either without any subjective determination as to whether there was any reason to believe death was due to any of the statutory circumstances authorizing an autopsy or despite his subjective determination that there was no reason to believe death was due to any of the statutory circumstances.

84 Leno v. St. Joseph Hospital, 55 Ill. 2d 114, 302 N.E.2d 58 (1973).

for damages.[85] Many states have enacted statutes that provide for nonofficial autopsies to be performed upon authorization of the next of kin.8866

A hospital has a duty to obtain consent before removing organs for donation or otherwise.[87] The Uniform Anatomical Gift Act, which has been adopted

---

85 In Leno v. St. Joseph Hospital, 55 Ill. 2d 114, 302 N.E.2d 58 (1973), an Illinois court ruled there is no requirement of unanimity on the part of those who are of equal status concerning the place or mode of burial. The court stated anyone can consent to an autopsy and there is no requirement that other next of kin be notified of the autopsy.

In Lashbrook v. Barnes, 437 S.W.2d 502 (Ky. 1969), the mother of the deceased gave consent to an autopsy but later sued the physician claiming that the physician had mutilated the body of the deceased. The brain was removed from the body, and it was difficult and impracticable to place it back in the body. Although the mother did not know what an autopsy entailed, the Kentucky Supreme Court ruled that the physician had permission for an autopsy from a person legally authorized to give permission and that the mother was estopped from claiming otherwise.

In French v. Ochsner Clinic, 200 So. 2d 371 (La. Ct. App. 4th Cir. 1967), writ refused, 251 La. 34, 202 So. 2d 652 (1967), an autopsy was performed without consent; however, the autopsy did not mutilate the body or interfere with the burial. The court nonetheless ruled dissection is mutilation. The court stated the widow did not receive the body of her husband in the same condition as at the time of his death. The court decided the primary consideration is not the extent of the mutilation per se but rather it is the effect of the mutilation on the feelings and emotions of those who have the duty of burial.

See Burse v. Wayne County Medical Examiner, 151 Mich. App. 761, 391 N.W.2d 479 (1986), in which a nonconsensual autopsy was performed on a person who died in a car accident. The court ruled the county medical examiner was authorized by law to perform autopsies. Because the performance of an autopsy was a governmental function, the medical examiner was immune from liability. The court noted that if a decedent's death was violent or unexpected, a medical examiner has the authority to investigate the cause of death even if another physician has already certified as to the death.

In Torres v. State, 34 Misc. 2d 488, 228 N.Y.S.2d 1005 (Ct. Cl. 1962), an unauthorized autopsy and burial of a body by a hospital caused the hospital to be liable in damages to the next of kin. The hospital officials attempted to notify the next of kin of the death of a patient but at the wrong address. The body was buried when there was no response from the next of kin.

In Dean v. Chapman, 1976 OK 153, 556 P.2d 257 (Okla. 1976), a daughter sued for mental suffering when an autopsy was performed on her father in an open and public site in which observation was allowed. The Oklahoma Supreme Court ruled there was no willful wrong of such a character that mental suffering was recognized.

In Terrill v. Harbin, 376 S.W.2d 945 (Tex. Civ. App. Eastland 1964), writ dismissed, 1964, the court ruled an invasion of another's rights, such as an autopsy, that exceeds spousal permission is a trespass.

In Norton v. Scotland Memorial Hospital, 793 S.E.2d 703 (N.C. App. 2016), the court ruled that a negligent infliction of emotional distress (NIED) claim against a hospital at which an autopsy of a patient is allegedly performed does not involve medical malpractice and thus a medical expert's certification is not required in the pleadings. Additionally, the court determined that because the wife and children failed to allege extreme and outrageous conduct, they failed to state a NIED claim against the hospital.

86 See, e.g., Okla. Stat. tit. 21 § 1154, which provides that autopsies may be performed when death occurs under circumstances in which a medical examiner is authorized by law to conduct an autopsy. The statute also provides that a spouse or next of kin charged by law with the responsibility for burial may authorize an autopsy to determine the cause of death.

87 Strachan v. John F. Kennedy Memorial Hosp., 209 N.J. Super. 300, 507 A.2d 718 (N.J. App. Div. 1986), judgment aff'd in part, rev'd in part, 109 N.J. 523, 538 A.2d 346 (1988).

Tex. Health & Safety Code § 692.013 provides that a hospital must establish a protocol for identifying potential organ and tissue donors when death occurs in the hospital.

by most of the states, authorizes individuals to make anatomical gifts of their bodies or parts. It also permits certain persons, other than donors, to make an anatomical gift on behalf of a donor during the donor's lifetime.[88] The act designates the persons who may execute an anatomical gift and the persons or organizations who may become donees.[89] The act recognizes that some states and many private organizations have created donor registries for the purpose of making anatomical gifts. The act also permits gifts to be made on state-issued identification cards and under limited circumstances, to be made orally. Except for oral gifts, there is no witnessing requirement to make an anatomical gift.[90] The act permits anatomical gifts to be amended or revoked by the execution of a later-executed record, by destruction of a document of gift, and, under limited circumstances, by oral revocations. An individual can sign a refusal that bars all other persons from making an anatomical gift of the individual's body or parts by a signed record, a will, or, under limited circumstances, orally.[91] The act provides that parties cannot make or revoke anatomical gifts in contravention of a donor's wishes.[92]

88 Unif. Anatom. Gift Act § 4 (2006). In 2021, the Act had been adopted by at least forty-seven states and the District of Columbia.

89 Unif. Anatom. Gift Act §§ 4 (2006).

Ariz. Rev. Stat. Ann. § 36-842 provides that the persons who may donate all or a part of a decedent's body include the decedent's spouse, an adult child, a parent, an adult sister or brother, and the decedent's guardian. Ariz. Rev. Stat. Ann. § 6-843 provides that qualified donees of a dead body include a hospital, a physician, and a medical or dental school.

90 Unif. Anatom. Gift Act § 5 (2006).

91 Unif. Anatom. Gift Act §§ 6,7 (2006).

In Georgia Lions Eye Bank, Inc. v. Lavant, 255 Ga. 60, 335 S.E.2d 127 (1985), the Supreme Court of Georgia court ruled an eye bank was not liable for damages for the alleged wrongful removal of corneal tissue of an infant following death. The court pointed out that there is no constitutionally protected right in a decedent's body and that the concept of a quasi-property right evolved in recognition of the interests of the surviving relatives in possession and control of the decedent's body. The court stated the common-law concept is not of constitutional dimension and a common-law right of action may be abrogated by the legislature. The court stated that health regulation is of the utmost consequence to the general welfare, and thus, individuals must submit to reasonable, impartial legislation, not against the general policy of the state, for the good of the public irrespective of pecuniary loss.

92 Unif. Anatom. Gift Act § 8 (2006).

D. CHARITABLE AND GOVERNMENTAL IMMUNITY

The concept of vicarious liability of an employer for the torts of its employees is based on the concept that losses should be borne by the entity, as a cost of business, rather than by the injured party. Theoretically this concept should not apply to an organization that is not operating a business for profit; thus, immunity from tort liability evolved for certain governmental and charitable organizations. These organizations historically had been given special protection, at the expense of an injured party, in the form of an immunity from liability. An immunity admits that a wrong has been committed but provides a complete defense for the protected class. In a few states, charitable organizations, including hospitals, may have some immunity from liability. Additionally, for public hospitals, governmental immunity may apply to avoid tort liability.

The charitable immunity doctrine has diminished considerably in importance in most states.[93] The current approach to possible charitable immunity is that if there is a danger of dissipation of a charity's assets, insurance is available to guard against it, and prudent management should provide the protection. Although the doctrine of charitable immunity has been abrogated in many states, some states also provide for a qualified immunity.[94]

The concept of governmental immunity can provide public hospitals immunity from liability. If a hospital is either an agency of the federal government or of a state government, it may have governmental immunity for the torts of its employees or officials. Additionally, for suits in federal courts, the Eleventh Amendment to the U.S Constitution grants immunity to a state from suit by a private citizen in a federal court. Still, the federal government waives immunity

93 Although many states abrogated charitable immunity, the concept has been reinstated in some states through the enactment of statutes that place a cap on the amount of damages that can be awarded against a charity.

94 In Kuchera v. Jersey Shore Family Health Center, 221 N.J. 239, 111 A.3d 84 (2015), an individual who attended free eye screening offered by the State Commission for the Blind and Visually Impaired at an outpatient health care facility, which was owned and operated by a nonprofit hospital, brought a premises liability action against the facility after she slipped and fell on a wet spot on the facility's floor. The Supreme Court of New Jersey determined that the facility was a nonprofit institution organized exclusively for hospital purposes rather than for religious, charitable, or educational purposes; thus, the facility was subject to limited liability rather than absolute immunity under the state's Charitable Immunity Act, N.J. Stat. Ann. 2A:53A-7 and 8. The court thought the concerns, that premises liability actions could sap nonprofit hospital resources, were ameliorated by the organization's opportunity to obtain indemnification from the entities with which the hospital contracted to maintain its facilities.

in limited cases pursuant to the Federal Tort Claims Act (FTCA),95 and many states have tort claims acts that waive immunity from liability for some torts.96 The extent of waiver of immunity from state to state.97

95 9528 U.S.C. §§ 1346, 1402, 1504, 2110, 2402, 2671-2680.

In Estate of Booker v. Greater Philadelphia Health Action, Inc., 10 F. Supp. 3d 656 (E.D. Pa. 2014), the court ruled an employee of a federally funded community health center was the health center's patient with respect to services rendered to the employee. This entitled the health center and its physicians to coverage pursuant to the Federally Supported Health Centers Assistance Act, 42 U.S.C. §§ 233 and 254b. The court noted that because of the health center's status as a federally funded community health center, the health center and its employees were entitled to medical malpractice liability coverage under the FTCA, 28 U.S.C. §§ 1346, 2671 to 2680. The court ruled the federally funded community health center was entitled to immunization from personal liability for malpractice claims if the allegedly negligent parties were acting within the scope of their employment and providing services within the scope of the center's federally funded activities. Because the court found FTCA coverage applied, the court ruled that plaintiff's exclusive remedy was against the United States. The Public Health Service Act, 42 U.S.C. § 254b, makes a suit against the United States the exclusive remedy for medical negligence claims against public or private nonprofit health entities receiving federal funds under the act as well as its employees. Qualified health centers are those that serve medically underserved populations or special medically underserved populations comprised of migratory and seasonal agricultural workers, the homeless, and residents of public housing. These federally funded community health centers and their employees are entitled to FTCA coverage for malpractice claims against them if they are deemed to be employees of the Public Health Service for purposes of 42 U.S.C. § 233 (and, thus, federal employees) with respect to actions or omissions that are the subject of the underlying malpractice claims. The FTCA grants absolute immunity to certain federally funded community health centers and their employees to enable the centers to redirect funds spent on malpractice insurance premiums toward patient care. FTCA coverage is provided at no cost. The Secretary of Health and Human Services (HHM) can deem non-profit private entities receiving federal funds pursuant to 42 U.S.C. § 254b to be employees of the Public Health Service for purposes of § 233a. To obtain the deemed Public Health Service status for itself and its employees, an entity must submit an application to the HHM verifying that it and its employees meet certain requirements. In Estate of Booker, the health center employed the physician the plaintiff claimed was negligent. The physician was a pediatrician who provided services to an employee of the entity. HHM decided the patient, who was an employee of the hospital, was not a patient of the entity under 42 U.S.C. §33(g)(1)(B). However, the court found she was a patient under the act and that the entity and its physicians were entitled to FTCA coverage with respect to act and omissions giving rise to the plaintiff's malpractice claims. Accordingly, the court ordered the United States to be substituted for the health care center and its physicians as the defendant in the action.

96 See Marilyn E. Phelan, Kimberly Mayfield, and Jay M. Phelan, "Sovereign Immunity Law," Vandeplas Publishing, 2019, for a discussion of the concept and extent of governmental immunity.

97 See Tex. Civ. Prac. & Rem. Code § 74.003 which states that sovereign immunity from suit or from liability regarding any medical liability is not waived.

CHAPTER V.
SPECIALIZED LEGAL ISSUES

The specialized ethical and legal issues discussed in this chapter address the difficult, conflicting, and often changing statutory and judicial laws on certain medical procedures that can bring into question the integrity and reputation of the medical profession. Issues relating to abortions, sterilization, right to procreate, artificial insemination, in vitro fertilization, and surrogate parenting present far-reaching and varying ethical and legal concerns for patients, their doctors, and for the public.

A. ABORTIONS

1. Introduction

One of the most controversial medical procedures, the abortion procedure, ends a pregnancy by the removal or expulsion of a fetus either in an in-clinic abortion, the surgical abortion, or by a drug induced abortion, the medication abortion. Differing statutory and judicial laws address difficult and controversial issues for both types of abortion procedures as legislatures and courts attempt to balance protection for unborn children and the health of the mother with a woman's right to have an abortion. Conflicting issues include late term abortions, state required parental notification for pregnant minors, state mandated disclosure of abortion risks to include imposed waiting periods, a natural father's rights to prevent an abortion, the rights of a fetus, First Amendment rights of abortion protestors, federal funding for abortions, and rights of hospitals to refuse to perform abortions. A history of abortion jurisprudence and the abortion procedure follows.

2. Fourteenth Amendment Liberty Prohibition

The Fourteenth Amendment prohibits a state from depriving "any person of life liberty, or property, without due process of law." In Griswold v. Connecticut,[1] the Supreme Court decided the Fourteenth Amendment identifies implied rights, one being a right of privacy. Later, in Roe v. Wade,[2] the Court concluded that a right to privacy interest under the Fourteenth Amendment's concept of personal liberty was broad enough to cover an abortion decision.[3] The Court commented,

1 381 U.S. 479 (1965).

2 410 U.S. 113 (1973).

3 The Supreme Court decided in Roe v Wade that a fetus would be guaranteed the Fourteenth Amendment right to life only if a fetus is a "person" and decided "person" does not include the unborn. In a concurring opinion in the Supreme Court decision in Ohio v. Akron Center for Reproductive Health, 497 US. 502, 520 (1990), Justice Scalia stated: "The Constitution contains no right to abortion.

however, that recognizing a right of privacy acknowledges as appropriate some state regulation in areas protected by that right. The Court concluded that while the right of personal privacy includes an abortion decision, the right is not unqualified and must be considered against important state interests in regulation. The extent of the Supreme Court identified right of a woman to abort her unborn child and state interests in regulation of that right to protect the unborn continually plague the courts, state legislatures, and Congress.

a. Supreme Court's Determination of Woman's Right to Abortion

In 1973, in Roe v. Wade,[4] the Supreme Court ruled state criminal abortion legislation to be unconstitutional.[5] The Supreme Court stated in Roe v. Wade that a state criminal abortion statute, which excepted from criminality only a life-saving procedure on behalf of a pregnant woman without regard to pregnancy stage and without recognition of other interests involved, violated the due process clause of the Fourteenth Amendment. The Court in Roe adopted a trimester-based framework when deciding the point during a pregnancy at which a state's interest in regulating abortion was significant enough to impose restrictions on the procedure. The Court decided that abortions in the first trimester were safe. During the first trimester then, the state was deemed not to have a compelling interest and could not restrict abortion. During the second

It is not to be found in the longstanding traditions of our society, nor can it be logically deduced from the text of the Constitution–not, that is, without volunteering a judicial answer to the nonjusticiable question of when human life begins." In a dissenting opinion in June Medical Services v. Russo, 140 S. Ct. 2103, 2150 (2020), Justice Thomas stated, "Roe is grievously wrong for many reasons, but the most fundamental is that its core holding—that the Constitution protects a woman's right to abort her unborn child–finds no support in the text of the Fourteenth Amendment."

4 Roe v. Wade, 410 U.S. 113 (1973) (holding modified by, Planned Parenthood of Southeastern Pennsylvania v. Casey, 505 U.S. 833 (1992)). The Supreme Court considered a constitutional challenge to Texas statutes prohibiting abortions except for the purpose of saving a pregnant mother's life.

5 In Roe v. Wade, 410 U.S. 113 (1973), the Supreme Court pointed out that a large majority of the states banned abortions unless performed to save or preserve the life of a pregnant woman. Although the American Medical Association then shared the antiabortion mood prevalent in the United States, a trend toward liberalization of abortion statutes had resulted in the 1970s in about one-third of the states adopting less stringent laws. The Court noted state laws were often designed to protect the woman rather than prenatal life.

In Doe v. Bolton, 410 U.S. 179 (1973), the Supreme Court ruled some provisions of a Georgia statute were unconstitutional. The Court ruled unconstitutional, as a violation of the Fourteenth Amendment, provisions of the statute requiring: 1. that abortions be performed in a hospital accredited by the Joint Commission on Accreditation of Hospitals; 2. that the procedure be approved by the hospital staff abortion committee; and 3. that the performing physician's judgment be confirmed by the independent examinations of the patient by two other licensed physicians.

trimester, a state could restrict abortion to ensure a woman's safety.[6] During the third trimester–when science then considered a fetus viable–the Court determined a state's interest was compelling enough to prohibit the procedure completely unless the woman's life or health was in danger.

Since Roe, courts have continually addressed laws that impede or obstruct a woman's ability to obtain an abortion. The Supreme Court ruled in 1983 that states could not, under the guise of protecting maternal health or potential life, intimidate women into continuing pregnancies.[7] In 1986, in Thornburgh v. American College of Obstetricians and Gynecologists,[8] the Supreme Court ruled that in giving a woman information so that she could give a voluntary and informed consent to an abortion, the state could not require her physician to give her information designed to influence her informed choice between abortion or childbirth.[9]

---

6 Additionally, in 1983, the Supreme Court, in Simopoulos v. Virginia, 462 U.S. 506 (1983), upheld a Virginia statute requiring abortions performed during the second trimester to be performed in licensed clinics.

7 City of Akron v. Akron Center for Reproductive Health, Inc., 462 U.S. 416 (1983).

8 476 U.S. 747 (1986).

9 In Thornburgh, the Court noted that since the Roe v. Wade decision, states and municipalities have adopted several measures seemingly designed to prevent a woman, with the advice of her physician, from exercising what the court deemed to be her freedom of choice. In the 5-4 decision in Thornburgh, the Supreme Court held unconstitutional the Pennsylvania Abortion Control Act, which required a woman to be informed of the name of the physician who would perform the abortion, the medical risks of the abortion procedure to be used and of carrying her child to term, and the fact that there may be detrimental physical and psychological effects of the abortion. The act also required a woman to be told that medical benefits could be available for prenatal care, childbirth, and neonatal care, that the father was liable to assist in the child's support, and that printed materials were available from the state describing the fetus and listing agencies offering alternatives to abortion. The act additionally required the printed material to include a statement that there were agencies willing to help the mother carry her child to term and to assist her after the child is born. The statement also had to provide a description of the probable anatomical and physiological characteristics of an unborn child at two-week gestational increments. After the first trimester, physicians were required to report the basis for a determination that a fetus was not viable. Additionally, steps were required to be taken during a post viability abortion to preserve the life and health of any unborn child intended to be born.

The Supreme Court overruled parts of its decisions in Akron and Thornburgh in Planned Parenthood of Southeastern Pennsylvania v. Casey, 505 U.S. 833 (1992). Although the Court, in Casey, rejected the rigid trimester framework of Roe v. Wade, discussed below, the Casey Court also ruled that to the extent Akron and Thornburgh found a constitutional violation when the government required the giving of truthful, non-misleading information about the nature of the abortion procedure, the attendant health risks and those of childbirth, and the probable gestational age of the fetus, the decisions were inconsistent with Roe. In Casey, the Court ruled that its former decision in Akron, in which it invalidated a twenty-four-hour waiting period, was wrong. The Court in Casey concluded that important decisions will be more informed and deliberate if they follow some period of reflection, deciding a waiting period was a reasonable measure to implement a state's interest in protecting the life of an unborn. The Court also concluded that regula-

After Roe, disagreements also surfaced as to the determinations in Roe regarding when the abortion decision could be made.[10] In 1992, in Planned Parenthood of Southeastern Pennsylvania v. Casey,[11] the Supreme Court rejected the rigid trimester framework of Roe v. Wade. The plurality opinion in Casey deemed the trimester framework from Roe to be a rigid prohibition on all previability regulation, all aimed at the protection of fetal life. The Casey Court noted that medical advances had made it safe for women to have abortions later in pregnancy but the Court also advanced viability to an earlier time in the pregnancy. After reaffirming Roe's conclusions on a woman's right to choose an abortion, the three authoring justices in Casey realigned the "other side of the equation"–the state's interest in protection of potential life.[12] Rather than the traditional strict scrutiny standard, the three justices adopted an undue burden standard for a state to meet. The Casey Court decided that to protect the central right recognized in Roe, while at the same time accommodating the state's interest in potential life, an undue burden standard should be employed to determine whether a statute is valid. The Casey Court concluded an undue burden would exist if the purpose or effect of a statutory provision placed substantial obstacles in the path of a woman seeking an abortion before the fetus attained viability.[13]

Under the undue burden standard, the three justices divided pregnancy into two stages with different rules applying to each stage. Before viability of the fetus,

---

tions that do no more than create a structural mechanism by which a state, or the parent or guardian of a minor, may express profound respect for the life of the unborn, are permitted if they are not a substantial obstacle to the woman's exercise of the right to choose. As the Supreme Court noted in Gonzales v. Carhart, 550 U.S. 124 (2007), discussed below, "Casey, in short, struck a balance."

10 In Roe v. Wade, the Supreme Court posited that a woman's fundamental right to terminate her pregnancy may be restricted only in the service of two compelling state interests: the interest in maternal health (which becomes compelling at the stage in pregnancy at which an abortion becomes more hazardous than carrying the pregnancy to term) and the interest in protecting the life of the fetus (which becomes compelling only at the point of viability).

11 505 U.S. 833 (1992).

12 Id. at 871.

Discussion by the Supreme Court of Kansas in Hodes & Nauser, Mds, P.A. v Schmidt, 309 Kan 610, 440 P.3d 461 (Kan. 2019).

13 Generally, under the undue burden test set out in Casey, for a state regulation to place an undue burden on a woman's right to terminate a pregnancy as set out in Roe v. Wade, the state regulation must have the purpose or effect of placing a substantial obstacle in the path of a woman seeking an abortion of a nonviable fetus. In adopting this test, the Supreme Court recognized that even though the Court had determined in Roe v. Wade that a woman has a liberty interest in deciding whether to terminate a pregnancy, the right to do so is limited. The Court stated that the limitation is the state's "important and legitimate interests in preserving and in protecting the health of the pregnant woman "and "in protecting the potentiality of human life," quoting Roe v. Wade, 410 U.S. at 162.

states could adopt measures designed to ensure a woman's choice is informed but those measures designed to advance this interest should not be invalidated if their purpose is to persuade a woman to choose childbirth over abortion.[14] Thus, the Court in Casey also decided a state provision requiring that a woman be informed of the availability of information relating to the consequences to the fetus did not interfere with a constitutional right to privacy between a pregnant woman and her doctor. The Casey Court additionally decided a one-parent consent requirement that provided for a judicial bypass procedure, a twenty–four hour waiting period, and various reporting and recordkeeping requirements of a Pennsylvania statute were constitutional.[15] Still, the Casey Court also decided the measures must not be an undue burden on the right of a woman to terminate a pregnancy.[16]

---

14 Planned Parenthood v. Casey, 505 U.S. 833, 878 (1992).

15 In Barnes v. Moore, 970 F.2d 12 (5th Cir. 1992), the Court of Appeals for the Fifth Circuit ruled a Mississippi statute, Miss. Code Ann. § 41-41-33, was constitutional based upon the Supreme Court's decision in Planned Parenthood of Southeastern Pennsylvania v. Casey, 505 U.S. 833 (1992). The act required a physician to inform a patient of the medical risks of an abortion and required a twenty-four-hour waiting period between disclosure of the information and performance of an abortion except for a medical emergency.

16 In Edwards v. Beck, 946 F. Supp. 2d 843 (E.D. Ark. 2013), a district court granted a preliminary injunction against members of the state's medical board for physicians who provided abortion services and who challenged the constitutionality of an Arkansas statute prohibiting abortions if a heartbeat is detected and the gestational period is twelve weeks or more. The Arkansas law prohibited the abortion of a viable fetus unless necessary to preserve the life or health of the pregnant woman or the pregnancy was the result of rape or incest. The court noted state statistics showed that twenty percent of abortions in Arkansas occurred at or after twelve weeks. The court decided physicians had carried their burden to show they were likely to prevail with their claim the state statute's prohibition of abortions at twelve-week gestation, when a fetal heartbeat is detected, impermissibly infringed a woman's right to choose to terminate a pregnancy before viability.

In Planned Parenthood Southeast, Inc. v. Strange, 33 F. Supp. 3d 1330 (M.D. Ala. 2014), opinion supplemented, 33 F. Supp. 3d 1381 (M.D. Ala. 2014) and as corrected, and order amended, 2014 WL 5426891 (M.D. Ala. 2014), the court ruled unconstitutional a state statute that required all doctors providing abortions to have staff privileges at a local hospital to perform designated procedures. The court decided the statute violated the substantive due process rights of women seeking abortions. The court found the evidence demonstrated the requirement would have the result of closing three of the state's five abortion clinics—clinics the court determined performed only early abortions, before viability.

In Whole Woman's Health v. Lakey, 769 F.3d 285 (5th Cir. 2014), vacated in part, 135 S. Ct. 399, 190 L. Ed. 2d 247 (2014), the court granted in part a stay of a district court's granting of injunctive relief with respect to the enforcement of two provisions of a Texas abortion law. The Court of Appeals for the Fifth Circuit decided the state had a substantial likelihood of success of its claim that the provisions were not unconstitutional. In 2013, the Texas Legislature passed HB 2 that requires (1) any physician performing an abortion must have active admitting privileges at a hospital within thirty miles of the location where the abortion is performed and (2) all abortion clinics existing on or after September 1, 2014, must comply with the same minimum standards required of ambulatory surgical centers. The Fifth Circuit ruled the requirements to be facially constitutional in Planned Parenthood of Greater Texas Surgical Health Services v. Abbott, 748 F.3d 583 (5th Cir. 2014). (In 2016, the Supreme Court struck down the Texas Act. See discussion below of the 5-3

Before 2000, most first-trimester abortions were surgical, performed by a procedure commonly known as vacuum aspiration or suction curettage.[17] In 2000, the FDA approved the distribution and use of the drug mifepristone, which is used in medication abortions. Mifepristone is a prescription drug that terminates a pregnancy by detaching the gestational sac from the uterine wall. In the clinical trials, the woman returned two to four days later and took a second medication, misoprostol, which induced contractions to complete the medication abortion. The use of mifepristone and misoprostol to cause a medication abortion is a two-part regimen. First, the patient takes mifepristone. This drug blocks the body's receptors for the hormone necessary to sustain pregnancy, which then causes the pregnancy tissue and lining of the uterus to break down and separate from the uterine wall. Then twenty-four to forty-eight hours after taking mifepristone, the patient takes misoprostol, another oral medication.

Supreme Court decision in Whole Woman's Health v. Hellerstedt, 136 S. Ct. 2292 (2016).)

In Jackson Women's Health Organization v Dobbs, 951 F.3d 246 (5th Cir. 2020), the Court of Appeals for the Fifth Circuit ruled a Mississippi statute that prohibited abortions, with limited exceptions, after fifteen weeks' gestational age, violated a women's right to choose abortion. See also Jackson Women's Health Organization v. Dobbs, 945 F.3d 265 (5th Cir. 2019), cert. gr. 209 L. Ed. 2d 748 (2021).

In Planned Parenthood of Greater Texas Surgical Health Services v. City of Lubbock, 2021 WL 2385110 (N.D. Tex. 2021), a city adopted an ordinance declaring it to be a "sanctuary city for the unborn." The ordinance included a private-enforcement section permitting certain family members and citizens to sue abortion providers or those who aid or abet abortions. Instead of waiting to be sued and challenging the ordinance, plaintiffs sued the city to enjoin it from maintaining in force and enforcing the ordinance and to declare it invalid. The court ruled the plaintiffs failed to show they had Article III standing to sue the city and dismissed the case for lack of jurisdiction.

In Whole Woman's Health v. Jackson, 141 S. Ct. 2494 (2021), in a 5-4 decision, the Supreme Court denied injunctive relief in a challenge of the constitutionality of a Texas abortion restriction legislation that would be enforced by private individuals rather than by governmental officials. The statute authorizes private civil actions against persons who abort an unborn child with a detectable fetal heartbeat. The majority ruled that while the statute raised serious constitutional questions, "it presented complex and novel antecedent procedural questions" that warranted denial of the plaintiffs' application for injunctive relief. The majority noted that while federal courts "enjoy the power to enjoin individuals tasked with enforcing laws," courts do not have the power to enjoin the laws. The majority decided it is unclear whether the Court could issue an injunction against state judges asked to decide a lawsuit under Texas law. The Court also noted that the sole private-citizen respondent in the case had filed an affidavit stating that he had no present intention to enforce the law.

In an interlocutory appeal from a federal district court denying a motion to dismiss a § 1983 action against members of state agencies, judiciary authorized to enforce state abortion laws, and a pro-life activist seeking injunctive relief to prevent the Texas abortion restriction bill from taking effect, the Court of Appeals for the Fifth Circuit ruled in Whole Woman's Health v. Jackson, 13 F. 4th 434 (5th Cir. 2021), that the state agency officials, judges, and court clerks acting under direction of judges were not amenable to suit and that the pro-life activist was entitled to a stay of the district court proceedings pending appeal.

17 Discussion by the Supreme Court of North Dakota in MKB Management Corp. v. Burdick 855 N.W.2d 31 (N. Dak. 2014). In this procedure, a surgical abortion is performed by inserting a speculum into a pregnant woman's vagina, dilating the cervix, and then inserting a tube into her uterus to empty the contents by suction.

Misoprostol causes uterine contractions that expel the contents of the uterus. The patient will then experience cramping and bleeding that signals pregnancy is being expelled.[18]

Laws that regulate the method of abortion differ for abortion procedures. For example, a physician may perform one type of abortion but can be prohibited from performing another type. As an example, the partial birth abortion, or dilation and excavation (D&E) abortion, has been banned by some states and by the federal government while approved in other states.[19] Additionally, the Supreme

18 Discussion in American College of Obstetricians and Gynecologists v. U.S. Food and Drug Administration, 472 F. Supp. 3d 183 (D. Md. 2020), order granting a preliminary injunction stayed pending disposition of appeal for Court of Appeals for the Fourth Circuit, 141 S. Ct. 578 (2021). The court pointed out that under current FDA requirements, certified healthcare providers generally prescribe and dispense the drugs for a medication abortion as follows: the healthcare provider must assess a patient's eligibility for a medication abortion, which includes determining the patient has been pregnant for less than the maximum ten weeks to be eligible for a medication abortion and that the patient does not have an ectopic pregnancy, one in which the fertilized egg is growing outside the uterus. The initial assessment may take place in person and may require an ultrasound or blood work to establish the existence of a pregnancy. In telemedicine, the healthcare provider would make the necessary determinations based on the patient's reported medical history, last menstrual period, result of over-the-counter pregnancy tests, and symptoms. If eligible for a medication abortion, the patient is counselled on the risks and alternatives and the healthcare provider reviews with the patient other required information. After obtaining the patient's informed consent, the prescriptions of mifepristone and misoprostol are issued. The healthcare provider gives the patient specific instructions for use of the drugs and follow-up care, including information about potentially serious complications and how to address them if they arise. If not already at the healthcare provider's hospital, clinic, or medical office, the patient visits that facility to pick up the prescribed mifepristone. The patient signs a Patient Agreement Form containing information about mifepristone and its risks. Once obtaining the drug, she can take it orally at any location of her choosing, including at home. Then, twenty-four to forty-eight hours later, she orally takes misoprostol, which can also be taken at a location of the patient's choosing. Her healthcare provider will have discussed with her the necessity of arranging to be in a comfortable location shortly after taking misoprostol when cramping and bleeding will begin. Patients are advised to follow up with the healthcare provider seven to fourteen days later to ensure the abortion was successful. When the FDA approved mifepristone, it recognized the drug carried serious risks, such as an incomplete abortion or serious bleeding. To mitigate potential complications, the FDA placed several restrictions on dispensing and distributing the drug, including that it be prescribed only by a qualified physician and that it be administered in a hospital, clinic, or medical office only by or under the supervision of the physician.

There is a question whether a state law that permits telemedicine abortions can be challenged as permitting a dangerous abortion procedure. Permitting the dispensing of mifepristone and misoprostol by technological devices, when a physician does not visit with the patient before or after the drugs have induced an abortion, can be very dangerous for the pregnant woman and will, of course, destroy the unborn child. Telemedicine precludes an in-person examination and an in-person counseling requirement prior to an abortion as well as post abortion treatment relating to possible hemorrhaging or blood clotting from post abortion severe bleeding.

19 A partial birth abortion, a dismemberment abortion known as Dilation and Evacuation (D&E), is used in the second trimester because at that stage of fetal development, the fetus is larger, particularly the head, and the bones are more rigid, requiring dismemberment.

Court has declared unconstitutional a state statute prohibiting the procedure. Conversely the intact partial birth abortion procedure, or dilation and extraction (D&X) abortion, is criminal based on a federal statute, the Partial-Birth Abortion Act of 2003,[20] which the Supreme Court has declared to be constitutional. Discussion of these procedures and the Supreme Court decisions follows.

In 2000, in Stenberg v. Carhart[21] the Supreme Court ruled unconstitutional Nebraska's law that made it a criminal offense to perform a partial birth abortion, the dilation and excavation (D&E) abortion, unless the procedure was necessary to save the life of the mother. The Court decided in Stenberg that the Nebraska statute was in violation of the Constitution as interpreted in Roe v. Wade and Planned Parenthood of Southeastern Pennsylvania v. Casey. The Stenberg Court declared the statute unconstitutional because it lacked a requisite exception "for preservation of the health of the mother" and because the Court decided it imposed an undue burden on a woman's right to make an abortion decision.[22]

Subsequently, in 2007, in Gonzales v. Carhart,[23] the Supreme Court considered the validity of a federal statute that was enacted after the Stenberg deci-

20 18 U.S.C § 1531.

21 530 U.S. 914 (2000).

22 In Hodes Nauser, MDs, P.A. v. Schmidt, 309 Kan. 610, 440 P.3d 461 (Kan. 2019), the Kansas Supreme Court ruled that abortion providers who brought action seeking to enjoin enforcement of the Kansas Unborn Child Protection from Dismemberment Abortion Act, which would ban, with limited exceptions, the D&E abortion procedure, were likely to show the act violated the Fourteenth Amendment and granted an injunction.

In EMW Women's Surgical Center v. Friedlander, 960 F.3d 785 (6th Cir. 2020), the Court of Appeals of the Sixth Circuit ruled that the burdens imposed by Kentucky H.B. 454, which criminalized a physician's performance of a standard D&E abortion unless fetal demise occurred before the fetus was removed from the uterus, dramatically outweighed any benefit it provided and, thus, it violated the Fourteenth Amendment. The dissent in the case pointed out that plaintiffs in the case were two abortion providers and an abortion clinic. The dissent discussed their lack of any rights to abortions, noting that abortion providers do not have a Fourteenth Amendment right to perform abortions.

In EMW Women's Surgical Center v. Friedlander, 831 Fed. Appx. 748 (6th Cir. 2020), the Sixth Circuit additionally ruled that the Attorney General of Kentucky could not intervene in the case. The Acting Secretary of Kentucky would not file a petition for certiorari in the case, and the Sixth Circuit denied the Attorney General a right to continue the appeal in defense of the state law. The dissent pointed out that with no one "in court to defend H.B. 454," the plaintiffs' challenge to that law would succeed.

In Hopkins v. Jegley, 510 F. Supp. 3d 638 (E.D. Ark. 2021), the court ruled a physician who sought declaratory and injunctive relief challenging the constitutionality of an Arkansas statute, specifically one that imposed civil liability and criminal penalties on physicians performing dismemberment abortions (D&E abortion) unless necessary to prevent serious health risk to a pregnant woman, had standing to bring the action. The court ruled the plaintiffs, which included a healthcare provider, were entitled to a preliminary injunction enjoining enforcement of the statute. The court's denial of a stay of the preliminary injunction, 2021 WL 259651, is on appeal.

23 550 U.S. 124 (2007).

sion to regulate intact Dilation and Extraction (D&X) abortion procedures in the second and third trimester of a pregnancy--the Partial-Birth Abortion Act of 2003.[24] The D&X, or intact D&E, differs from the non-intact D&E abortion in that it removes an intact fetus from the uterus, pulling the fetus out intact.[25] In Gonzales, the Supreme Court upheld the act against a facial attack, ruling the act is not void for vagueness and does not impose an undue burden on a woman's right to an abortion despite its lack of a health exception.[26]

The Partial-Birth Abortion Ban Act of 2003, which, as noted above, was enacted after the Supreme Court ruled in Stenberg[27] that Nebraska's partial birth abortion statute violated the Constitution, prohibits a dilation and extraction (D&X) abortion that is not necessary to save the life of a mother.[28] The act defines "partial-birth abortion" as a procedure in which the doctor (1) deliberately and intentionally vaginally delivers a living fetus until the entire fetal head is out the mother's body or, in the case of breech presentation, any part of the fetal trunk past the navel is outside the mother's body, for the purpose of performing an overt act that the person knows will kill the partially delivered living fetus and (2) performs the overt act, other than completion of delivery, that kills the fetus.[29] The Court in Gonzales decided the act is more specific concerning

24 Pub. L. 108-115, 117 Stat. 1201, 18 U.S.C. § 1531. The act bans intact D&E, or D&X, abortions, that it describes as being a gruesome and inhumane procedure. Because the act only applies to viable fetuses and particularly in later term abortions, abortion providers may induce death of the fetus before the procedure is performed either by injecting potassium chloride into the fetus's heart or by injecting digoxin intra-amniotically twenty-four hours before the procedure to cause cardiac arrest.

25 In Gonzales, 550 U. S. 124, 150-54 (2007), the Court contrasted a permissible law prohibiting dilation and extraction (D&X) abortions that are characterized in the Partial Birth Abortion Act of 2003 as being inhumane procedures and are never medically necessary, with the standard D&E abortions that were considered in Stenberg.

26 The Court also approved a state statute requiring the presence of a second physician during an abortion performed after viability.

In an earlier Supreme Court decision, in Planned Parenthood Ass'n of Kansas City, Mo., Inc. v. Ashcroft, 462 U.S. 476 (1983), the Court concluded that a second physician's presence provided assurance the State's compelling interest in protecting the life of a viable fetus was protected more fully than with only one physician in attendance. However, in Thornburgh v. American College of Obstetricians and Gynecologists, 476 U.S. 747 (1986) (overruled in part by Planned Parenthood of Southeastern Pennsylvania v. Casey, 505 U.S. 833 (1992)), the Court ruled provisions of a Pennsylvania statute that contained such a provision, were unconstitutional because there was no exception for the existence of a medical emergency requiring an immediate abortion to save the life of the pregnant woman.

27 Stenberg v. Carhart, 530 U.S. 914 (2000), discussed above.

28 The federal law banned one method of partial-birth abortion, intact D&E, while permitting alternative, standard D&E, or pre-abortion fetal demise.

29 As discussed in a dissenting opinion in Whole Woman's Health v. Paxton, 978 F.3d 895, 913 (5th Cir.

the instances to which it applies and, thus, is more precise in its coverage than the Nebraska statute and ruled that on its face the partial birth regulation did not have the purpose or effect of placing a substantial obstacle in the path of a woman seeking an abortion before viability. This Court explained that the purpose of regulating the procedure for abortions by intact dilation and evacuation in which the fetus is removed in parts, expresses respect for the legitimate governmental interests in the dignity of human life and recognition of a state's interest in regulating the medical profession as well as potential life. The Court referred to Supreme Court precedent that provides a state may not prohibit a woman from making the ultimate decision to terminate a pregnancy before viability and that the undue burden standard governs the analysis of abortion regulations under federal law. The Court then explained that where a state has a rational basis to act and does not impose an undue burden on a woman's right to an abortion before viability, a state may use its regulatory powers to bar certain procedures and substitute others in the furtherance of legitimate interests in regulating the medical profession to promote respect for human life, including the life of the unborn.[30]

2020), a physician extracts from the womb an unborn child, using forceps, scissors, or a similar instrument that "slices, crushes, or grasps" fetal body parts one at a time, piece by piece, arm by arm, leg by leg. The physician places each body part on a tray to keep inventory and ensure that nothing is left behind. Sometimes the heart is still beating on the tray. The fetus dies by bleeding to death as his or her body is torn apart. Justice Willett stated in the dissenting opinion that the majority "takes the view that a woman's right to have an abortion has no end while the State's interest in recognizing fetal humanity has no beginning."

In West Alabama Women's Center v. Williamson, 900 F.3d 1310 (11th Cir. 2018), the Court of Appeals for the Eleventh Circuit described the procedure as a particularly gruesome type of abortion wherein the unborn child dies the way anyone else would if dismembered alive. The Court stated the unborn child bleeds to death as it is torn limb from limb, but it can survive for a time white its limbs are being torn off.

In Magers v. Alabama Women's Center Reproductive Alternatives, LLC, 325 So.3d 788 (Ala. 2020), the Alabama Supreme Court expressed concern that "states remain severely constrained in their ability to account for the unborn by enacting and enforcing laws that protect them in the womb, even in the face of a procedure as horrific as dismemberment abortion."

30 A partial birth abortion can cross the line from an abortion to infanticide. As many have contended, pulling a fetus further down the birth canal transforms a fetus into a living person who clearly should have rights and who is deserving of protection.

In West Alabama Women's Center v. Williamson, 900 F.3d 1310 (11th Cir. 2018), in a constitutional challenge brought against an Alabama law regulating abortions by intact dilation and evacuation, two of the three justices thought they were duty-bound to follow Roe and Casey and strike down the law even though they considered D&E abortions as being brutal.

In Magers v. Alabama Women's Center Reproductive Alternatives, LLC, 325 So.3d 788 (Ala. 2020), the Alabama Supreme Court referred to Alabama law that provides an unborn child is a legal person and the estate of a child who is killed by abortion in utero can sue the abortion providers for wrongful death.

In Casey, Stenberg, and Gonzales, the Supreme Court considered the balance between the state's interest in unborn life and a woman's right to an abortion. Then, in 2016, in Whole Woman's Health v. Hellerstedt,[31] the Supreme Court considered the balance between the state's interest in protecting women's health and a woman's right to an abortion. In a 5-3 decision, the Supreme Court ruled unconstitutional under Roe v. Wade and Casey, a Texas statute that regulated admitting privileges for a physician performing or inducing an abortion and that required abortion facilities to meet "minimum standards" for ambulatory surgical centers. The Supreme Court referred to evidence in the case that showed the number of facilities providing abortions in Texas dropped in half as the admitting-privileges requirement began to be enforced. The Court decided that, with the surgical-center requirement, the Texas statute had imposed an undue burden on the right of women in Texas to seek pre-viability abortions. The Court concluded that a finding of an undue burden was "shorthand for the conclusion that a state regulation has the purpose or effect of placing a substantial obstacle in the path of a woman seeking an abortion of a nonviable fetus."[32] The Court determined the provisions together created an "impermissible obstacle as applied to all women seeking a pre-viability abortion" and particularly created an obstacle for poor, rural, or disadvantaged women.

The Supreme Court issued its most recent ruling explaining and applying the undue burden in terms of balancing the state's interest in protecting women's health and a woman's right to an abortion in 2020 in June Medical Services v. Russo.[33] In a 5-4 decision, the Supreme Court ruled unconstitutional Louisiana's statute that was almost identical to the Texas "admitting privileges" law that the Court declared unconstitutional in Whole Woman's Health v. Hellerstedt.[34]

31 136 S. Ct. 2292 (2016).

32 Hellerstedt, quoting Casey, 505 U.S. 833, 877 (1992). Some have argued that Hellerstedt did not equate the undue burden test to the rational basis test and that Hellerstedt requires courts to apply "close scrutiny." Justice Thomas, in a dissent in Hellerstedt, 136 S. Ct. at 2324, considered whether the majority transformed "the undue-burden test to something more akin to strict scrutiny."

33 140 S. Ct. 2103 (2020). Some justices, including Chief Justice Roberts in Russo, have rejected the balancing test. The Supreme Court of Kansas, Hodes & Nauser, Mds, P.A. v. Schmidt, 440 P.3d 461, 664 (Kan. 2019), noted that it has never adopted the undue burden standard, stating that "the undue burden standard has proven difficult to understand and apply."

34 In 2021, in Bristol Regional Women's Center v. Slatery, 988 F.3d 319 (6th Cir. 2021) the Court of Appeals for the Sixth Circuit denied a stay pending the appeal of a district court imposing a permanent injunction regarding enforcement of a Tennessee statute that imposed a waiting period for a woman seeking an abortion. The Tennessee statute prohibited a physician from performing an abortion unless the woman had been informed, orally and in person by the attending physician, of the prob-

A plurality of four Justices decided that "enforcing the admitting-privileges requirement would drastically reduce the number and geographic distribution of abortion providers, making it impossible for many women to obtain a safe, legal abortion in the state and imposing substantial obstacles on those who could."[35]

Although the Supreme Court has not addressed a state's separate interest in eliminating discrimination as a reason for an abortion, the Court of Appeals for the Sixth Circuit did consider this issue in 2021 in a case[36] involving a doctor and four medical service providers who challenged and sought an injunction regarding a state "Antidiscrimination Law." The statute[37] prohibited a doctor from performing an abortion with knowledge that the woman's reason for aborting her pregnancy was that her fetus had Down syndrome and she did not want a child with Down syndrome.[38] The state pointed out that the statute sends a message to

---

able gestational age of the fetus, that the fetus could be viable if enough time had elapsed since the woman's last menstrual cycle or the time of conception, of the numerous public and private agencies and services that are available to assist a woman during her pregnancy and after the birth of her child if she chooses not to have the abortion, and of the normal and reasonably foreseeable medical benefits, risks, or both of undergoing an abortion or continuing the pregnancy to term. The physician was required to provide a description of the method of abortion to be used and the medical instruction to be followed after the abortion. There was a forty-hour waiting period that began when the woman received the mandated information; that time would be reduced to twenty-four hours in the event of a court order temporarily, preliminarily, or permanently enjoining enforcement of the waiting period. The woman had to sign a consent form acknowledging that she had received the requisite information. The majority of the court thought it likely the district court's factual findings would compel a conclusion that the waiting period unduly burdened women's abortion rights. The dissent pointed out that no federal appellate court has successfully struck down an abortion waiting period, noting that the Supreme Court ruled waiting periods constitutional in Planned Parenthood v Casey, 505 U.S. 833, 881-87 (1992). The dissent stated that the majority has decided "to chart its own course," and in doing so, has called into question waiting-period laws in fourteen states.

35 The four Justice plurality, Justice Breyer, Justice Ginsburg, Justice Sotomayor, and Justice Kagan, applied the balancing approach set out in Whole Woman's Health v. Hellerstedt, weighing the statute's asserted benefits against its burdens. In a solo opinion concurring in the judgment, Justice Roberts rejected the undue burden test and rejected an argument that Casey mandated a balancing test or that either Casey or Hellerstedt conducted such a balancing test in reaching the respective constitutional conclusions. The Chief Justice opined that the only question should be whether a statute places a "substantial obstacle in the path of a woman seeking an abortion of a nonviable fetus." However, the opinion in Russo did not refer to "viability" at all in its discussion of the legal standards.

36 Preterm-Cleveland v. McCloud, 994 F. 3d 512 (6th Cir. 2021).

37 H.B. 214, O.R.C. § 2919.10(B).

38 As the Sixth Circuit pointed out in Preterm-Cleveland v. McCloud, 994 F.3d 512, 517 (6th Cir. 2021), a violation of the statute has severe consequences in that a violation is a fourth-degree felony punishable by up to eighteen months in prison. O.R.C. §§ 2919.10(C) & 2919.14(A(4). The State Medical Board is required to revoke the doctor's license and a doctor is subject to civil liability for compensatory and exemplary damages. Sections 2919.10(D) and (E).

citizens in the state that Down syndrome children, whether born or unborn, are "equal in dignity and value." Additionally, the majority agreed with the state that the statute did not create a substantial obstacle to a woman's ability to choose or obtain an abortion.[39]

b. Minors' Rights to Abortions

Counts have consistently and continually addressed state restrictions on the right of a minor to obtain an abortion without parental consent. In 1979, in Bellotti v. Baird,[40] the Supreme Court created a narrow legal path for an unemancipated minor to obtain an abortion without parental consent by permitting a minor to obtain a state court order finding either that the abortion would be in her best interest or that she was sufficiently mature to make her own decision. In 1983, in City of Akron v. Akron Center for Reproductive Health, Inc.,[41] the Court ruled that although there was sufficient state interest in the protection of immature minors to require parental consent for a minor to obtain an abortion, a state had to provide an alternative procedure whereby a pregnant minor could demonstrate that she was sufficiently mature to make the abortion decision herself or that, despite her immaturity, an abortion would be in her best interest. Later, in 1990, in Hodgson v. Minnesota,[42] the Supreme Court ruled constitutional a state statute providing that no abortion could be performed on a minor until at least forty-eight hours after both her parents had been notified. It also ruled as constitutional the statutory requirement that the minor either notify both parents or obtain a judicial bypass. Still, the Court ruled unconstitutional a provision in the statute requiring that both parents be notified regardless of whether

39 Preterm-Cleveland, 994 F.3d 512, 521-3 (6th Cir. 2021). The court pointed out that the statute does not prohibit a woman from aborting an unborn child with Down syndrome; it prohibits a doctor from aborting a pregnancy when the doctor knows the woman's particular reason is that she knows or has reason to know the forthcoming child will have Down syndrome and because of that, she does not want it.

See, however, Reproductive Health Services of Planned Parenthood of the St. Louis Region, Inc. v. Parson, 1 F.4th 552 (8th Cir. 2021), pet. for cert. docketed, wherein the Court of Appeals for the Eighth Circuit ruled that abortion providers, who challenged a Missouri statute prohibiting abortions where the pregnant woman's reason to abort was solely based on a fetus's sex, race, or prospective down Syndrome, were likely to prevail in challenging the constitutionality of that statute. The Eighth Circuit affirmed a district court's granting of a preliminary injunction to bar enforcement of the statute.

40 443 U.S. 622 (1979).

41 462 U.S. 416 (1983).

42 497 U.S. 417 (1990).

both wished notification or had assumed responsibility for the upbringing of the minor, stating that this requirement did not reasonably further any legitimate state interest. In 1990, in Ohio v. Akron Center for Reproductive Health,[43] the Court ruled constitutional a state statute that made it a crime for a physician or other person to perform an abortion on an unmarried, unemancipated, minor woman unless the physician provided timely notice to one of the minor's parents or a juvenile court issued an order authorizing the minor to consent. The statute required that to obtain a judicial bypass of the notice requirement, the minor had to present clear and convincing proof that she had sufficient maturity and information to make the abortion decision herself, that one of her parents was engaged in a pattern of physical, emotional, or sexual abuse against her, or that notice was not in her best interests. The Court decided that, by requiring the juvenile court to authorize her consent upon determining the abortion was in her best interest and in cases where she had shown a pattern of abuse, the statute satisfied the requirement that she be permitted to show that, even if she could not make the decision by herself, the abortion would be in her best interests. In 1992, in Planned Parenthood of Southeastern Pennsylvania v. Casey,[44] the Court affirmed that a state may require consent of a parent or guardian before a minor can obtain an abortion provided there is an adequate judicial bypass procedure and ruled constitutional a state statute providing for a one-parent consent requirement with a judicial bypass procedure.[45]

Despite Supreme Court rulings that a state can require parental consent for a minor to obtain an abortion if there is a judicial bypass procedure that will permit a minor to show an abortion would be in her best interests, state restrictions on minors' access to abortions continue to be constitutionally challenged.[46]

---

43 497 U.S. 502 (1990).

44 505 U.S. 833 (1992),

45 In 2019, in Planned Parenthood of Indiana and Kentucky v. Box, 937 F.3d 973 and 949 F.3d 997 (7th Cir. 2019), rehearing en banc denied and vacated by Box v. Planned Parenthood, 141 S. Ct. 184 (2020), an abortion provider brought an action alleging that an amendment to Indiana's parental consent and judicial bypass statutes requiring that parents be notified before pregnant, unemancipated minors could obtain abortions without parental consent unless notice was not in the minor's best interests, unconstitutionally burdened minors' rights to abortions. Although judgment was vacated by the Supreme Court in Box, wherein the case was remanded in light of the 5-4 decision in June Medical Services v. Russo, 140 S. Ct. 2103 (2020), discussed above, the Court of Appeals for the Seventh Circuit, in Planned Parenthood of Indiana and Kentucky, Inc., 991 F.3d 740 (7th Cir. 2021), would not vacate its earlier ruling, 937 F.3d 973 (7th Cir. 2019), after assessing the precedential force of Supreme Court decisions issued without a majority opinion.

46 Following the Supreme Court remanding June Medical Services v. Russo, 140 S. Ct. 2103 (2019), in

c. Rights of Natural Fathers

The right of a husband or an unmarried father of an unborn child to challenge a woman's right to an abort the natural father's unborn child has been an issue with the courts. A state court ruled in 1984 that a husband or natural father was constitutionally prohibited from enjoining his wife's abortion.[47] Later, in 1988 and in 1992, the Supreme Court declared invalid a husband or unmarried father notification provision.[48] A husband made a more recent challenge to a wife's right to abort his unborn child in Magers v. Alabama Women's Center Reproductive Alternatives.[49] In Magers, a father brought a unsuccessful wrongful-death action against an abortion provider after his wife took an abortifacient pill she had procured from the abortion provider.[50]

2021, in Planned Parenthood of Indiana and Kentucky, Inc., 991 F.3d 740 (7th Cir. 2021), pet. cert. docketed, the Court of Appeals for the Seventh Circuit considered vacating its earlier ruling, 937 F.3d 975 (7th Cir. 2019), wherein it had affirmed a district court's grant of a preliminary injunction against enforcement of a new Indiana statutory restriction on minors' access to abortions. The Seventh Circuit applied the rule in Marks v. United States, 430 U.S. 188 (1977), for assessing the precedential force of Supreme Court decisions issued without a majority opinion. The court reasoned that Marks does not permit dicta in a non-majority opinion to overrule an otherwise binding precedent. It then stated that it had applied the binding standards from Hellerstedt, 136 S. Ct. 2292 (2016), and because Hellerstedt has not been overruled by a majority decision of the Supreme Court, it again affirmed the district court's preliminary injunction barring enforcement of the challenged law pending full review in the district court. The Seventh Circuit held that the Supreme Court's fragmented decision in Russo did not require a reconsideration of its prior holding.

47 In Coleman v. Coleman, 57 Md. App. 755, 471 A.2d 1115 (1984), a court had ruled a husband is constitutionally prohibited from enjoining his wife's abortion and that, during the first trimester, it is a woman's prerogative to have an abortion—a right the court stated is based on her constitutional right of privacy. The court declared that the right is not subject to veto by her husband, the natural father, or the state.

48 Doe v. Smith, 486 U.S. 1308 (1988) and Planned Parenthood of Southeastern Pennsylvania v. Casey, 505 U.S. 833 (1992). In Doe v. Smith, the Supreme Court denied an application for a writ of injunction brought by the natural unmarried father of an unborn child to prevent the mother from obtaining an abortion. In Doe v. Smith, the Supreme Court noted the circumstances of the case, i.e., that the father was sporadically employed at low-paying jobs, that he had two children from his first wife, and that the mother of the unborn child was not physically, emotionally, or economically willing to bear the child. The Court determined the interest of the father in the fetus would not outweigh the constitutionally protected right of the mother to abort her child.

49 325 So.3d 788 (Ala. 2020).

50 Under Alabama, an unborn child is a legal person and the estate of a child who was killed by abortion in utero can sue the abortion providers for wrongful death. Still, the Alabama Supreme Court affirmed dismissal of the action based on the father's appellate brief failing to comply with a briefing rule.

d. Rights of a Fetus

Issues that include the status of a fetus and the question of whether the estate of a child killed by an abortion in utero can sue an abortion provider as well as whether ad litem can stand in support of the rights of an unborn child, continually plague the courts.[51] In Roe v. Wade,[52] the Supreme Court held that because the word "person," as used in the Fourteenth Amendment, does not include the unborn and because a state does not have an interest in defending the life of a non-person, a state cannot ban an early abortion. Still, the Supreme Court in Roe also stated that, with respect to a state's important and legitimate interest in potential life, the compelling point with respect to a fetus is the fetus's "viability." The Court noted that at viability, the fetus "then presumably has the capability of meaningful life outside the mother's womb" and that a state may then "go so far as to proscribe abortion during that period, except when it was necessary to preserve the life or health of the mother."[53] Later, in 1989, in Webster v. Reproduction Health Services,[54] the Supreme Court noted that viability is the point at which a state's interest in potential human life must be safeguarded.[55]

In 2019, in Box v. Planned Parenthood of Indiana,[56] the Supreme Court acknowledged that a state has a legitimate interest in the proper disposal of fetal

51 Refer to Magers v. Alabama Women's Center Reproductive Alternatives, LLC, 325 So.3d 788 (Ala. 2020), cited above, wherein the Alabama Supreme court referred to Alabama law that provides an unborn child is a legal person and the estate of a child killed by abortion in utero can sue the abortion providers for wrongful death.

In State v. Green, 474 P.3d 886 (Ct. Crim. App. Okla. 2020), the Oklahoma Court of Criminal Appeals held that a viable unborn fetus constitutes a child under eighteen within the protection of the criminal child neglect statute, 10A O.S. Supp. 201, § 1-1-105-(47). The defendant in the case was subjected to criminal liability for child neglect by her use of illegal drugs while thirty-three weeks pregnant. The court ruled that the statute did not violate her right of privacy as defined in Planned Parenthood v. Casey, 505 U.S. 833 (1992) or in Carey v. Population Servs. Int'l, 431 U.S. 678 (1977), regarding the sale of contraceptives. The court stated that the case was not about a woman's right to an abortion or any person's right to secure contraceptives.

52 410 U.S. 133, 158 (1973) and discussed in detail above.

53 Id. at 163-4.

54 492 U.S. 490 (1989).

55 In 1994, in Doe v. Shalala, 862 F. Supp. 1421 (D. Md. 1994), a district court decided that an interest in protecting the life of the fetus becomes an issue only at the point of viability. The court referred to the Supreme Court decision in Roe v. Wade that embryos are not persons with legally protected interests. Thus, the court refused to appoint a guardian-ad-litem for what it termed an ex-utero embryo--a preborn child in being as a human embryo—and ruled that the embryo did not have standing to challenge the NIH Human Embryo Research Panel holding meetings or making recommendations to the National Institutes of Health (NIH) on the issue of human fetal research.

56 139 S. Ct 1780 (2019).

remains[57] and ruled constitutional a state statute that regulated the disposition of fetal remains. The statute prohibited abortion providers from treating the bodies of aborted children as "infectious waste" and incinerating them alongside used needles, laboratory-animal carcasses, and surgical byproducts.[58]

In Planned Parenthood of Indiana and Kentucky, Inc. v. Commissioner of Indiana State Department of Health,[59] plaintiffs sought declaratory and injunctive relief from a law that sought to protect unborn children from being aborted solely because of their race, sex, or disability. The court ruled the law violated Supreme Court precedent that a woman may terminate her pregnancy prior to viability and that a state may not prohibit a woman from exercising that right for any reason. The court also invalidated the part of the law requiring abortion clinics to bury or cremate fetal remains.

As noted previously, in Preterm-Cleveland v. McCloud,[60] the Court of Appeals for the Sixth Circuit considered the constitutionality of a law in Ohio that prohibited a doctor from performing an abortion if the doctor knew the woman's reason for having an abortion was that she did not want a child with Down syndrome. The state in that case asserted the statute protected the Down syndrome community–both born and unborn–from what the state perceived as discriminatory abortions. The state "produced evidence that, in the United States and abroad, fetuses with Down syndrome are disproportionally targeted for abortions."[61]

---

57 The Court referred to its earlier decision in Akron v. Akron Center for Reproductive Health, Inc., 461 U.S. 416 (1983).

58 See an earlier Supreme Court decision in Planned Parenthood Ass'n of Kansas City, Mo., Inc. v. Ashcroft, 462 U.S. 476, (1983), in which the Court concluded the state has a compelling interest in protecting the life of a viable fetus and that the requirement of a second physician's presence during an abortion provided assurance the state's interest was protected more fully than with only one physician in attendance. However, in Thornburgh v. American College of Obstetricians and Gynecologists, 476 U.S. 747 (1986) (overruled in part by Planned Parenthood of Southeastern Pennsylvania v. Casey, 505 U.S. 833 (1992)), the Court ruled a Pennsylvania statute unconstitutional that had such a provision because there was no exception for the existence of a medical emergency requiring an immediate abortion to save the life of the pregnant woman.

59 888 F.3d 300 (7th Cir. 2018), reh'g en banc granted, judgment vacated, 727 Fed. Appx. 208 (7th Cir. 2018), order vacated, 917 F.3d 532 (7th Cir. 2018), petition for certiorari filed and opinion reinstated, 917 F.3d 532 (7th Cir. 2018).

60 994 F.3d 512 (6th Cir. 2021).

61 Id. at 517. One Sixth Court justice, id. at 545, referred to a state's "compelling interest in preventing abortion from becoming a tool of modern-day eugenics" and stated that this interest is "especially important in light of this country's ignoble history with eugenics, "referring to the Supreme Court's infamous decision in Buck v. Bell, 274 U.S. 200 (1927). (Discussion below of the Supreme Court

3. First Amendment Issues

First Amendment concerns relating to abortion issues include the extent demonstrations that will interfere with a woman's right to an abortion are permitted near an abortion clinic,[62] state law restrictions on abortion counselling, state required notices for clinics that serve pregnant women, and the question of whether operation of a federal program, Title X of the Public Health Service Act, discussed below, is compatible with free speech.

In 1994, in Madsen v. Women's Health Center, Inc.,[63] the Supreme Court ruled a state court's establishment of a thirty-six-foot buffer zone around entries to an abortion clinic and to the clinic driveway did not violate the free speech provision of the First Amendment. The state court had established a buffer zone that prohibited anti-abortion protestors from "congregating, picketing, patrolling, demonstrating, or entering" any portion of a public right-of-way or private property within thirty-six feet of the property line of the abortion clinic. Still, the Court also ruled the state court could not establish the thirty-six-foot buffer zone on the north and west of the clinic, noting that the protestors' activities in this area did not obstruct clinic access or vehicular traffic and did not interfere with clinic operations. The Court further ruled that a 300-foot buffer around clinic staff residences did violate the First Amendment.[64]

---

decision regarding sterilization in Buck v. Bell.) In a concurring opinion, another justice wrote separately "to emphasize Ohio's compelling state interest in prohibiting its physicians from knowingly engaging in the practice of eugenics." Id. at 538-9. This Justice stated: "Many think that eugenics ended with the horrors of the Holocaust. Unfortunately, it did not. The philosophy and the pure evil that motivated Hitler and Nazi Germany to murder millions of innocent lives continues today. Eugenics was the root of the Holocaust and is a motivation for many of the selective abortions that occur today." He referred to the founder of Planned Parenthood, Margaret Sanger, being sympathetic to some aspect of the eugenics movement, which included supporting the Supreme Court's decision in Buck v. Bell.

62 In New York State Organization for New York State Nat. Organization for Women v. Terry, 886 F.2d 1339 (2nd Cir. 1989), the Court of Appeals for the Second Circuit ruled plaintiffs who filed suit to enjoin protestors from converging each day to close a facility at which abortions were performed, had standing to pursue the action. The court noted the plaintiffs were facing a realistic and immediate danger of suffering an injury caused by the protestors.

63 512 U.S. 1277 (1994).

64 In Pro-Choice Network v. Schenck, 34 F.3d 130 (2d Cir. 1994), republished at 67 F.3d 359, the Court of Appeals for the Second Circuit approved in part and disapproved in part an injunction prohibiting abortion opponents from engaging in certain activities near an abortion clinic. The court ruled the portion of the injunction establishing a "bubble zone" around the clinic to prohibit all demonstration within fifteen feet of the facility's doorways, doorway entrances, driveways, driveway entrances, and parking lot entrances, was unconstitutional. The court ruled the bubble zone provi-

In 1997, in Schenck v. Pro-Choice Network of Western New York,[65] the Supreme Court upheld provisions imposing a "fixed bubble" or "fixed buffer zone" limitations on access to abortion clinics but held that provisions imposing "floating bubble" or "floating buffer zone" limitations violated the First Amendment. The fixed buffer zone prevented physical obstruction of access to abortion clinics and excluded crowds of protesters from a fifteen-foot zone around clinic entrances. The floating buffer zones prevented pro-life protestors, except for two sidewalk counselors, from communicating a message from a normal conversational distance or from handing leaflets to people who were entering or leaving the clinics and who were walking on the public sidewalks. The Court ruled the fixed buffer zones around the doorways, driveways and driveway entrances were necessary to ensure that people and vehicles trying to enter or exit the clinic property or clinic parking lots could do so. However, the Court determined the floating buffer zones around people entering and leaving the clinics burdened more speech than was necessary to serve relevant governmental interests. The Court stated leafletting and commenting on matters of public concern were classic forms of speech that lie at the heart of the First Amendment. It noted that speech in public areas is at its most protected on public sidewalks. Under the floating buffer zones, protestors on the public sidewalks who wished to communicate their message to incoming or outgoing patients or clinic employees had to move as the individual moved and had to maintain fifteen feet of separation.[66]

---

sion burdened the abortion opponents' constitutionally protected expression. The court also ruled a provision of the injunction requiring abortion opponents' to "cease and desist" from counselling persons who did not want the counselling, was invalid. See also Pro-Choice Network v. Schenck, 67 F.3d 359 (2d Cir. 1994), vacated in part on reh'g en banc, 67 F.3d 377 (2d Cir. 1995), aff'd in part, rev'd in part, 519 U.S. 357 (1997).

In American Life League, Inc. v. Reno, 47 F.3d 642 (4th Cir. 1995), the Court of Appeals for the Fourth Circuit ruled the Freedom of Access to Clinic Entrances Act (FACE), 18 U.S.C. § 248, which Congress enacted in response to violence and access obstruction at facilities providing abortions, did not violate the free exercise clause. The Fourth Circuit noted that those opposed to abortions retained their freedom to express their "deeply held moral or religious views in a peaceful non-obstructive way."

65 519 U.S. 357 (1997).

66 In U.S. v. Scott, 187 F.3d 282 (2d Cir. 1999), in a civil contempt action that was brought against an abortion protestor, the Court of Appeals for the Second Circuit enjoined the protestor from demonstrating within fourteen feet of an abortion clinic and from positioning himself within five feet of persons or vehicles near the clinic once the individual indicated she did not wish to talk with or receive literature from the protestor. The court ruled the injunction did not violate the protestor's First Amendment rights given his records of harassing and abusive conduct.

In Tatton v. City of Cuyahoga Falls, 116 F. Supp. 2d 928 (N.D. Ohio 2000), the court ruled a city did not violate an anti-abortion protestor's free speech in preventing him from displaying at a civic parade a

In 2000, in Hill v. Colorado,[67] the Supreme Court ruled constitutional a Colorado statute that made it unlawful to approach within eight feet of another person, to pass leaflets to that person, and to attempt to counsel the person without the person's consent if the person is within a hundred feet of any health care facilities. The Court agreed the statute regulated speech but ruled that any violation of a speaker's First Amendment rights was abridged by the protection the statute provided for unwilling listeners.[68]

In 2014, in McCullen v. Coakley,[69] the Supreme court reversed the Court of Appeals for the First Circuit, wherein it had affirmed the district court in ruling constitutional a Massachusetts statute that made it a crime to stand knowingly on a public way or sidewalk within thirty-five feet of an entrance or driveway to any place, other than a hospital, where abortions were performed.[70] Petitioners were individuals who attempted to engage women approaching Massachusetts abortion clinics in "sidewalk counselling," which involved offering information about alternatives to abortion and helped women pursue these options. The petitioners contended the thirty-foot buffer zones displaced them from their previous positions outside the clinics and hampered them considerably in their counseling efforts. The Supreme Court ruled the Massachusetts statute was unconstitutional as a violation of the First Amendment. While the Court agreed that the buffer zones served the state's legitimate interests in maintaining public

---

photograph of an aborted fetus.

67 530 U.S. 703 (2000).

68 In New York ex rel. Spitzer v. Operation Rescue National, 273 F.3d 184 (2d Cir. 2001), the Court of Appeals for the Second Circuit ruled unconstitutional an injunction against pro-life activists that expanded the buffer zones at two clinics beyond fifteen feet and included the elimination of the "sidewalk counsellor" exception. The "sidewalk counsellor" exception permitted protestors to enter the buffer zones and approach patients entering or leaving the facilities for "sidewalk" counselling consisting of conversation of a nonthreatening nature. The court also vacated a provision that banned a pro-life activist from using sound amplification equipment at protests near covered health facilities. The lower court had found the activists violated the Freedom of Access to Clinic Entrances Act, 18 U.S.C. §§ 248 et seq. The Second Circuit was concerned that the lower court had overstated the protestors' activities and often had characterized as criminal behavior what the appellate court termed "legitimate First Amendment activity."

In State v. Logsdon, 160 Ohio App. 3d 517, 2005-Ohio-1875, 827 N.E.2d 869 (1st Dist. Hamilton County 2005), the court ruled an abortion protester could not be convicted of criminal trespass for entering an abortion clinic to retrieve an antiabortion sign taken from him by the clinic's president and executive director.

69 573 U.S. 464 (2014).

70 Massachusetts amended its Reproductive Health Care Facilities Act, Mass. Gen. Laws ch. 266, §§ 120E1/2(a), (b), to address clashes between abortion opponents and advocates of abortion rights outside clinics where abortions were performed.

safety on streets and sidewalks and in preserving access to adjacent reproductive healthcare facilities, it determined that the zones imposed "serious burdens on petitioners' speech, depriving them of their two primary methods of communicating with arriving patients: close, personal conversations and distribution literature." The Court decided the buffer zones burdened substantially more speech than necessary to achieve the state's asserted interests. It pointed out the state had not shown it had seriously undertaken to address the problems with the less intrusive tools readily available to it. It noted that the state had not identified "a single prosecution or injunction against individuals outside abortion clinics since the 1990s." In affirming that "the prime objective of the First Amendment is not efficiency," the Court stated that to meet the requirement of narrow tailoring to satisfy the First Amendment, "the government must demonstrate that alternative measures that burden substantially less speech would fail to achieve the government's interests, not simply that the chosen route is easier." [71]

In 2018, in National Institute of Family and Life Advocates v. Becerra,[72] the Supreme Court ruled unconstitutional, as a content-based regulation of speech, a state requirement that licensed clinics primarily serving pregnant women have a notice of the existence of publicly funded family planning services. The purpose of the notice was to make certain state residents knew their rights and what health care services were available to them. The notice also required unlicensed pregnancy-related clinics to disseminate notice that they were not licensed. Some of the petitioners were pro-life centers that offered pregnancy-related services. The Court noted that one of the state-sponsored services the licensed notice required the petitioners to advertise was abortion—the very practice the petitioners were devoted to opposing. The Court stated that speech is not unprotected merely because it is uttered by professionals and decided that even assuming the state's interest in providing low-income women with information about state-sponsored service was substantial, the licensed notice was not sufficiently drawn to promote it. The Court pointed to the fact that the

71 In Bruni v. City of Pittsburgh, 824 F.3d 353 (3d Cir. 2016), the court ruled a city ordinance that prohibited certain speech within fifteen feet of health care facilities possibly violated the plaintiffs' First Amendment rights. Plaintiffs had engaged in what they called "sidewalk counselling" on a public sidewalk outside of a Planned Parenthood facility in an effort, through close conversation, to persuade women to forego abortion services. The court decided the Supreme Court decision in McCullen v. Coakley, 573 U.S. 464 (2014), which struck down a similar state law, provided the plaintiffs the right to obtain an appropriate development of a factual record for the court to consider the issue.

72 138 S. Ct. 2361 (2018).

notice requirement applied only to clinics that have a "primary purpose" of providing family planning or pregnancy-related services while excluding several other types of clinics that also served low-income women. The Court reasoned that the State could inform women of its services without burdening the clinics with unwanted speech, most obviously through a public-information campaign.

Courts have also addressed a question of whether the operation of a federal program, Title X of the Public Health Service Act,[73] is compatible with free speech. The statute requires nondirective pregnancy counselling in Title X programs. The HHS Department promulgated a final rule that permitted physicians and providers to counsel patients on abortion, but that abortion could not be the only option presented even if the patient did not want to receive counseling about other options. The Final Rule required the patient's options to be presented in a factual, objective, and unbiased manner, and for any option presented, the provider was required to discuss the risks and side effects to both the mother and her unborn child. Additionally, physicians and providers could not refer the patient for an abortion even if that was her desire during nondirective counseling.[74]

4. Funding for Abortions

Although the Supreme Court has determined a woman has a constitutionally protected liberty interest to decide whether to terminate a pregnancy, it has ruled that the government need not subsidize abortions. The Supreme Court has stated a woman's freedom of choice does not carry with it a constitutional entitlement to the financial resources to avail herself of the full range of protected choices.[75]

---

73 42 U.S.C. § 300(a)-6. Title X promotes public health and welfare by expanding, improving and better coordinating family planning services and population research activities of the federal government. It restricts the use of federal funds by family planning clinics where abortion is a method of family planning.

74 HHS interpreted the phrase "pregnancy counseling" as distinct from the term "referrals."

In California by and through Becerra v. Azar, 950 F.3d 1067 (9th Cir. 2020), cert granted, the Court of Appeals for the Ninth Circuit ruled the HHS acted reasonably in implementing the final rule that prohibits physicians and other providers in Title X programs from referring patients for an abortion even if that is the patient's wish. In Mayor and City council of Baltimore v. Azar, 973 F.3d 258 (4th Cir. 2021), cert. granted, the Court of Appeals for the Fourth Circuit ruled that HHS acted arbitrarily and capriciously in promulgating the final rule. Both cases are on appeal to the Supreme Court.

75 Harris v. McRae, 448 U.S. 297 (1980).

See 42 C.F.R. §§ 50.304, 50.306. Federal financial assistance is available for an abortion if the life of the

In 1977, in Maher v. Roe,[76] the Court rejected claims that refusing Medicaid funds for nontherapeutic abortions, while defraying the medical costs of childbirth, infringed the fundamental right to choose to terminate a pregnancy by abortion. The Court in Maher ruled the government need not fund elective abortions because withholding such funds rationally furthered the state's legitimate interest in normal childbirth. In 1989, in Webster v. Reproductive Health Services,[77] the Supreme Court ruled that a statutory ban on the use of public employees and facilities for performance or assistance of nontherapeutic abortions, was not unconstitutional. In 1991, in Rust v. Sullivan,[78] the Supreme Court ruled regulations implementing Title X of the Public Health Service Act,[79] which restrict the use of federal funds by family planning clinics where abortion is a method of family planning, do not violate the First and Fifth Amendments. The Court noted the government may choose not to subsidize speech.[80] In 1996, in Dalton v. Little Rock Family Planning Services,[81] the Supreme Court validated a state constitutional amendment that prohibited any public funds being used to pay for any abortion except to save the mother's life.[82]

---

mother is endangered and in certain cases of victims of rape or incest.

76 432 U.S. 464 (1977).

77 492 U.S. 490 (1989).

78 500 U.S. 173 (1991).

79 Pub. L. No. 91 572, 84 Stat. 1504 (1970), 42 U.S.C. § 300a-4(c).

80 Chief Justice Rehnquist ruled that the government had not discriminated based on viewpoint but rather had chosen to fund one activity to the exclusion of another. Four justices dissented; Justice Blackmun contended that by refusing to fund those family-planning projects that advocate abortion, because they advocate abortion, the government "plainly has targeted a particular viewpoint."

In Coe v. Melahn, 958 F.2d 223 (8th Cir. 1992), the Court of Appeals for the Eighth Circuit ruled constitutional a state statute providing that no health insurance policy could cover elective abortions unless the coverage was via an optional rider and separate premiums. The court stated the plaintiff failed to demonstrate the statute placed an absolute obstacle or severe limitation on an abortion decision.

In Mayor of Baltimore v. Azar, 973 F.3d 258 (4th Cir. 2020), cert. granted, the court ruled that the HHS acted arbitrarily and capriciously in promulgating a rule requiring entities receiving Title X funds, but offering abortion-related services pursuant to another source of funds, to separate physically their abortion-related services from Title X services. Pursuant to Title X, 42 U.S.C. § 300(a), the HHS Secretary is authorized to make grants to, and to enter into contracts with public or nonprofit private entities, to assist in the establishment and operation of voluntary family planning projects that must offer a broad range of acceptable and effective family planning methods and services. Grants and contracts made under this subchapter are made in accordance with regulations as the Secretary promulgates. HHS has never allowed grantees to use Title X funds to "provide" abortions as a method of family planning. See 42 C.F.R. § 59.5(a)(5).

81 516 U.S. 474 (1996).

82 In Planned Parenthood Affiliates of Michigan v. Engler, 73 F.3d 634 (6th Cir. 1996), the Court of Appeals for the Sixth Circuit ruled that a state participating in Medicaid must fund abortions of preg-

5. Rights of Hospitals to Refuse to Perform Abortions

Courts have disagreed on whether a hospital can refuse to permit its facilities to be used for abortions.[83] In 1977, in Poelker v. Doe,[84] the Supreme Court ruled a city need not provide publicly financed hospital services for nontherapeutic abortions even though it did provide these services for childbirth. Still other courts have interpreted the Supreme Court's decision to be limited to the governmental funding for abortions and have determined that the refusal to permit access to the facilities of a public hospital for abortions creates a governmental obstacle to the access to an abortion.[85] In 1989, in Webster v. Reproductive Health Services,[86] the Supreme Court decided Roe v. Wade does not limit the authority of a state to refuse to permit public employees to perform abortions in public hospitals.[87]

---

nancies resulting from rape or incest as well as abortions necessary to save the life of the mother. The court noted that in 1994 Congress expanded the Hyde Amendment to allow federal funding for abortions of pregnancies resulting from rape or incest as well as abortions necessary to save the life of the mother. The court determined the Hyde Amendment is not simply a federal appropriations bill; rather, according to the Sixth Circuit, it "defines medically necessary abortions that must be funded by the federal government and by participating states."

83 In Doe v. Bellin Memorial Hospital, 479 F.2d 756 (7th Cir. 1973), the court found no constitutional objection to a private hospital refusing to permit its facilities be used for abortions. The Supreme Court of New Jersey, in Doe v. Bridgeton Hospital Ass'n, Inc., 71 N.J. 478, 366 A.2d 641 (1976), determined a New Jersey statute to that effect, N.J. Rev. Stat. 2A:65A-1, was not applicable to nonsectarian nonprofit hospitals.

84 432 U.S. 519 (1977). The Supreme Court reversed a decision of the Court of Appeals for the Eighth Circuit, Doe v. Poelker, 515 F.2d 541 (8th Cir. 1975), wherein the Eighth Circuit had ruled the provision of publicly financed hospital services for childbirth, but not for elective abortions, was invidious discrimination.

85 In Nyberg v. City of Virginia, 667 F.2d 754 (8th Cir. 1982), the Court of Appeals for the Eighth Circuit determined that the Supreme Court decision in Poelker v. Doe, 432 U.S. 519 (1977), was limited to the "spending" of public funds to hire doctors who would perform abortions or otherwise to "provide" publicly financed hospital services for indigent women. The Eighth Circuit commented there is a fundamental difference between providing direct funding to affect an abortion decision and allowing staff physicians to perform abortions at an existing publicly owned hospital.

86 492 U.S. 490 (1989).

87 In Greenville Women's Clinic v. Bryant, 222 F.3d 157 (4th Cir. 2000), the Court of Appeals for the Fourth Circuit ruled South Carolina's regulation establishing standards for licensing abortion clinics did not violate the due process and equal protection clauses of the Fourteenth Amendment. Officials of two abortion clinics contended the regulation placed an undue burden on women's decisions to seek abortions and distinguished between clinics that performed a specified number of abortions and those that did not.

B. STERILIZATION

Courts have determined the constitutional right of personal privacy includes the right to be sterilized[88] and that the right is free from interference by the state or by a spouse.[89] Problems that have plagued physicians, hospitals, and courts relate to the sterilization of individuals who are not competent to exercise their constitutional rights.[90] The right to procreate has been designated as being a right fundamental to the very existence and survival of the race[91] and because the right is a basic liberty of which an individual is deprived forever through unwanted sterilization,[92] courts have decided that they must take particular care to protect the rights of the mentally impaired when considering the prospect of sterilization.[93]

In 1927, in Buck v. Bell,[94] the Supreme Court permitted state sterilization of persons believed to suffer from hereditary conditions after the Court decided welfare of the patient and society would benefit from such sterilization.[95]

---

88 In an early decision in Hathaway v. Worcester City Hospital, 475 F.2d 701 (1st Cir. 1973), the Court of Appeals for the First Circuit recognized the existence of a right to be sterilized.

In Matter of Grady, 85 N.J. 235, 426 A.2d 467 (1981), the court commented that the Supreme Court decisions in Roe v. Wade, 410 U.S. 113 (1973) and Doe v. Bolton, 410 U.S. 179 (1973), invalidating restrictions on abortion, expanded the right to control one's body. The court decided the thrust of these cases was unmistakable when considering whether the constitutional right of privacy includes the right to be sterilized.

89 See, Ruby v. Massey, 452 F. Supp. 361 (D. Conn. 1978) and Ponter v. Ponter, 135 N.J. Super. 50, 342 A.2d 574 (Ch. Div. 1975). In Ponter, a New Jersey court ruled a woman has a constitutional right to obtain a sterilization operation without consent of her husband.

90 See, e.g., Matter of Guardianship of Eberhardy, 102 Wis. 2d 539, 307 N.W.2d 881 (1981).

91 Discussion of right to procreate is below.

92 In Skinner v. State of Okla. ex rel. Williamson, 316 U.S. 535 (1942), the Supreme Court prohibited the sterilization of a thrice-convicted robber, commenting that the power to sterilize, if exercised, may have subtle, far-reaching and devastating effects. The Court decided that in evil or reckless hands it can cause races or types that are inimical to the dominant group to wither and disappear.

In Beck v. Lovell, 361 So. 2d 245 (La. Ct. App. 1st Cir. 1978), writ denied, 362 So. 2d 802 (La. 1978), a court ruled that, in the absence of an emergency, the relationship of husband and wife does not confer authority on a spouse to grant permission for surgery on his spouse. The court stated consent to sterilization must be given by the person involved, and without that consent, a physician is liable for an otherwise skillful performance of the surgery. The physician had obtained the consent of the husband to ligate his wife's tubes but did not have her consent.

93 In Vaughn v. Ruoff, 253 F.3d 1124 (8th Cir. 2001), the Court of Appeals for the Eighth Circuit ruled a wife, who had been diagnosed as mildly intellectually disable, possessed a protected liberty interest under the Fourteenth Amendment in a decision as to whether to have a tubal ligation.

94 274 U.S. 200 (1927).

95 In the infamous decision in Buck v. Bell, 274 U.S. 200 (1927), Justice Holmes commented that many

However, a rising tide of criticism of compulsory sterilization[96] and changed attitudes toward the mentally and dintellectually disabled called into question the constitutionality of mandatory sterilization without due process procedures and the consent of the person to be sterilized.[97]

Issues relating to sterilization of mentally incompetent persons include questions of who may give consent to sterilization.[98] Some courts have stated that courts may not authorize the sterilization of mentally defective persons in the absence of specific statutory authority,[99] recognizing that it is the state that, under certain circumstances, can prevent procreation.[100] The Supreme Court has

persons in institutions could be discharged with safety and could become self-supporting with benefit to themselves and to society if they were incapable of procreating. He also stated it is better for the world, if instead of waiting to execute degenerate offspring for crimes, or to let them starve for their imbecility, society can prevent those who are manifestly unfit from continuing their kind. According to Justice Holmes, "the principle that sustains compulsory vaccination is broad enough to cover cutting the Fallopian tubes." In Buck v. Bell, the Supreme Court permitted the sterilization of a mentally defective person whose mother was feeble-minded and who was the mother of an illegitimate feeble-minded child. Justice Holmes stated that "three generations of imbeciles are enough."

96 See, e.g., Conservatorship of Valerie N., 40 Cal. 3d 143, 219 Cal. Rptr. 387, 707 P.2d 760 (1985).

97 In Matter of Truesdell, 313 N.C. 421, 329 S.E.2d 630 (1985), the Supreme Court of North Carolina ruled the party requesting a sterilization order must prove by clear, strong, and convincing evidence that there is substantial likelihood the intellectually disabled person will voluntarily or otherwise engage in sexual activity likely to cause impregnation and would be unable to care for a child or children, or the child or children would have a tendency to serious physical, mental, or nervous disease or deficiency. The petitioner should demonstrate it is for the public good or the best interest of the patient that the patient be sterilized.

98 In Ruby v. Massey, 452 F. Supp. 361 (D. Conn. 1978), the court ruled that the sterilization decision for a child who is mentally incapable of deciding cannot be made by the child's parents, stating that parents could neither veto nor give valid consent to the sterilization of their children. The court noted that because no one may subject children to a sterilization operation without their consent, resort to state courts is the only avenue to obtain a valid consent for such operations.

In Matter of A. W., 637 P.2d 366 (Colo. 1981), the Supreme Court of Colorado noted the inconvenience of caring for an incompetent child, accompanied with fears of sexual promiscuity or exploitation, may lead parents to seek solutions that infringe upon their offspring's fundamental procreative rights.

99 In Guardianship of Tulley, 83 Cal. App. 3d 698, 146 Cal. Rptr. 266 (1st Dist. 1978), a parent, the guardian of an incompetent who could not comprehend her personal needs and could not cope with the menstrual cycle, wanted to surgically sterilize the ward. The court ruled that in the absence of specific statutory authority, courts may not authorize the sterilization of mentally defective persons. The court stated the awesome power to deprive a person of that person's fundamental right to bear or beget offspring must be founded on an explicit authorization of the legislature rather than from a mere inference deduced from the general principles of the common-law canons of equity jurisprudence.

100 In re Moore's Sterilization, 289 N.C. 95, 221 S.E.2d 307 (1976), the Supreme Court of North Carolina stated the right to procreate is not absolute but rather is vulnerable to a certain degree of state regulation. The court ruled that when there is overwhelming evidence that a potential parent will be unable to provide a proper environment for a child because of the potential parent's mental ill-

determined that a judge who entered an order for sterilization was immune from damages.[101] Since that date, courts have been less reluctant to authorize a guardian of an incompetent person to give consent to sterilization.[102] The trend has been away from compulsory sterilization toward sterilization based on substituted consent.[103]

---

ness or intellectual disability, the state may have a sufficient interest in preventing the procreation of children who will become a burden on the state and, thus, the court can order sterilization.

101 In Stump v. Sparkman, 435 U.S. 349 (1978), the judge had ordered, upon a mother's petition, that the mother's minor daughter be sterilized. The daughter and her husband later sued the judge, the mother, and the mother's attorney for damages because the daughter was unable to have children. In Sparkman v. McFarlin, 601 F.2d 261 (7th Cir. 1979), the Court of Appeals for the Seventh Circuit court ruled that other defendants in the suit, i.e., the mother and the mother's attorney, were also not liable in damages to the daughter and her husband because there was no evidence of a conspiracy.

102 See P.S. by Harbin v. W.S., 452 N.E.2d 969 (Ind. 1983), wherein the Supreme Court of Indiana ruled a trial court had jurisdiction to authorize sterilization when it had before it clear and convincing evidence such a medical procedure was in the best interests of child.

In Matter of Grady, 85 N.J. 235, 426 A.2d 467 (1981), the Supreme Court of New Jersey decided it has inherent power under its parens patriae jurisdiction to decide whether to authorize sterilization for incompetent persons and set out procedures to be followed in an application for sterilization of an incompetent. In every proceeding, the court should appoint an independent guardian ad litem who must have a full opportunity to meet with the incompetent person, to present proofs, to cross-examine witnesses at the hearing, and in general to represent zealously the interests of the ward. A trial court should receive independent medical and psychological evaluations by qualified professionals. Although the incompetent need not be present at the hearing, if the court determines his/her presence would not be useful, the trial judge should personally meet with the individual to obtain the judge's own impression of competency. The judge must find the individual lacks capacity to decide about sterilization and that the incapacity is not likely to change in the foreseeable future. The court must be persuaded by clear and convincing proof that sterilization is in the incompetent person's best interests. The court should consider facts such as whether a female incompetent can become pregnant; the possibility that the incompetent will experience trauma or psychological damage if she becomes pregnant and, conversely, the possibility of trauma or psychological damage from a sterilization operation; the likelihood that the individual will voluntarily engage in sexual activity or be exposed to situations where sexual intercourse may be imposed upon her; the inability of the incompetent to understand reproduction or contraception; and the ability of the incompetent to care for a child.

103 In Conservatorship of Valerie N., 40 Cal. 3d 143, 219 Cal. Rptr. 387, 707 P.2d 760 (1985), a California court determined there is a constitutional right to substituted consent to sterilization, ruling a state statute prohibiting sterilization of a person under conservatorship deprived developmentally disabled persons of privacy and liberty interests.

In Matter of Grady, 85 N.J. 235, 426 A.2d 467 (1981), the New Jersey Supreme Court granted a trial court the right to give substituted consent to a female incompetent, stressing that it was not permitting compulsory sterilization but that the exercise of parens patriae power of the court to authorize sterilization was intended to compensate for the incompetent person's inability to exercise her own constitutional rights. The court pointed out that in determining whether to authorize sterilization, a court should consider only the best interests of the incompetent person and not the interests or convenience of society in having the incompetent person sterilized.

See, however, Matter of Guardianship of Eberhardy, 102 Wis. 2d 539, 307 N.W.2d 881 (1981), in which the Supreme Court of Wisconsin upheld the trial court's judgment declining to permit the guardian of an incompetent to give consent to the ward's sterilization. The Wisconsin Supreme Court determined that because there are complex problems of public policy involved, it would be better to defer to the legislature

Courts have ruled private hospitals, at least religious, nonprofit hospitals, may refuse to perform sterilization procedures.[104] However, once a state hospital has undertaken to provide general hospital care, courts have ruled a state hospital may not constitutionally draw the line at medically indistinguishable surgical procedures.[105]

Federal Medicaid funds are available for sterilizations only if performed on individuals who are at least twenty-one years of age, are not mentally incompetent, and have given informed consent consistent with requirements prescribed by federal regulations.[106] At least thirty days must have elapsed between the date of the informed consent and the date of the sterilization, except in the case of premature delivery or emergency abdominal surgery. Federal Medicaid funds are not available for the sterilization of a mentally incompetent or institutionalized individual.[107]

---

to provide answers to the problem. The court stated the legislature should conduct appropriate hearings and undertake fact-finding that could lead to the declaration of a public policy and legislative guidelines for the exercise of the court's plenary jurisdiction.

104 See, e.g., Taylor v. St. Vincent's Hospital, 523 F.2d 75 (9th Cir. 1975), wherein the Court of Appeals for the Ninth Circuit stated that if a private hospital's refusal to perform sterilization infringes upon any constitutionally cognizable right to privacy, the infringement is outweighed by the need to protect the freedom of religion of a denominational hospital with religious or moral scruples against sterilizations and abortions. The court ruled the receipt of federal funds by the hospital did not mean it acted under color of state law. Further, the fact the hospital had the only maternity department in the city did not bring it under color of state law as providing an essential public service.

In Swanson v. St. John's Lutheran Hospital, 189 Mont. 259, 615 P.2d 883 (1980), the Supreme Court of Montana awarded damages to a nurse whose employment was terminated when she refused, under state's "conscience law," to participate in tubal ligation.

105 In Hathaway v. Worcester City Hospital, 475 F.2d 701 (1st Cir. 1973), the Court of Appeals for the First Circuit stated a decision to terminate the possibility of any future pregnancy would seem to embrace all the factors deemed important in Roe v. Wade, 410 U.S. 113 (1973) (holding modified by, Planned Parenthood of Southeastern Pennsylvania v. Casey, 505 U.S. 833 (1992)). The court decided a complete ban on surgical procedures relating to a fundamental interest in pregnancy decisions is far too broad when other comparable surgical procedures are performed.

In Walker v. Pierce, 560 F.2d 609 (4th Cir. 1977), the Court of Appeals for the Fourth Circuit concluded a physician could pursue the policy of having patients who were unable to support themselves financially to submit to sterilization or to seek another physician. The court noted the physician did not force his views on a patient on Medicaid who refused sterilization after she was delivered of her third child.

106 See 42 C.F.R. §§ 50.203, 50.204. Requirements for informed consent at 42 C.F.R. § 50.205. The Medicaid agency must obtain documentation showing that the requirements of the regulations were met before making payment. See 42 C.F.R. §§ 50.208, 50.209.

107 42 C.F.R. § 50.206.

C. RIGHT TO PROCREATE

Courts have ruled that the right to prevent conception complements a fundamental right to procreate. In 1942, the Supreme Court stated that individuals have a fundamental decisional right to procreate[108] and later ruled, in 1965 in Griswold v. Connecticut,[109] that the right to procreate or not to procreate is a fundamental right of marital privacy.[110] Then, in 1972, in Eisenstadt v. Baird,[111] the Supreme Court stated this right is not restricted to married couples.[112] In 1977, in Carey v. Population Services, Intern.,[113] the Supreme Court ruled that limiting the distribution of nonprescription contraceptives to licensed pharmacists imposed a significant burden on the right of individuals to use contraceptives.

Because courts have determined the right to prevent conception includes a right of access to contraceptives, courts have ruled restrictions on the distribution of contraceptives burden the freedom to make individual decisions in matters of procreation.[114] Further, because a state may not impose a blanket prohibition, or even a blanket requirement of parental consent, on the choice of a minor to terminate her pregnancy, the Supreme Court also has ruled that the blanket prohibition of the distribution of contraceptives to minors is

---

108 See 1942 Supreme Court decision in Skinner v. State of Okla. ex rel. Williamson, 316 U.S. 535 (1942).

109 381 U.S. 479 (1965).

110 In Griswold, the Supreme Court sought to preserve the right of privacy in marriage against governmental intrusion in the form of a law forbidding the use of contraceptives. The Supreme Court determined a state's birth control law unconstitutionally intruded upon the right of marital privacy. The state anticontraceptive statute had forbade all married persons the right to use birth-control devices.

111 405 U.S. 438 (1972).

112 In Eisenstadt v. Baird, the Court stated that if under Griswold v. Connecticut, the distribution of contraceptives to married persons cannot be prohibited, a ban on distribution to unmarried persons would be equally impermissible.

113 431 U.S. 678 (1977).

114 See, e.g., Carey v. Population Services, Intern., 431 U.S. 678 (1977).

unconstitutional.[115] Additionally, the Supreme Court has stated prohibition of any advertisement or display of contraceptives is unconstitutional.[116]

Courts have ruled that publicly operated family planning clinics have no constitutional obligation to notify the parents of an unmarried minor child that their child is seeking family planning services, including contraceptives.[117] Courts also have ruled invalid state statutes that require parental notification when federal funds are used to fund family planning programs or to reimburse a clinic or a physician.[118] Presumably, a state can impose parental consent requirements when only state funds are involved.[119] Additionally, in 1988, in Bowen v. Kendrick,[120] the Supreme Court ruled the Adolescent Family Life Act,[121] which provides grants to public or nonprofit private organizations or agencies for ser-

---

115 Id.

In State v. Green, 474 P.3d 886 (Ct. Crim. App. Okla. 2020), the defendant in the case was subjected to criminal liability for child neglect by her use of illegal drugs while thirty-three weeks pregnant. The Oklahoma Court of Criminal Appeals held that a viable unborn fetus constitutes a child under eighteen within the protection of the criminal child neglect statute, 10A O.S. Supp. 201, § 1-1-105-(47) and ruled that the statute did not violate the mother's right of privacy as set out in Carey v. Population Servs. Int'l, 431 U.S. 678 (1977), regarding the sale of contraceptives. The court in State v. Green stated that the case was not about a person's right to secure contraceptives.

116 Carey v. Population Services, Intern., 431 U.S. 678 (1977).

117 See., e. g., Doe v. Irwin, 615 F.2d 1162 (6th Cir. 1980), wherein the Court of Appeals for the Sixth Circuit decided that, although parents have a right to the care, custody and nurturing of their children and that a child is not a mere creature of the state, the court is not required to decide whether parental rights "outweigh" the privacy rights of minor children. There is no constitutional obligation on the part of a center to notify the parents prior to distributing contraceptives to their minor children.

In Planned Parenthood Ass'n of Utah v. Matheson, 582 F. Supp. 1001 (D. Utah 1983), the court commented that the right of privacy extends to a minor and stated that decisions of whether to accomplish or to prevent conception are among the most private and sensitive. The court ruled a state statute infringes upon a minor's right to privacy in requiring that a minor's parents be notified before the minor can obtain contraceptives. The court ruled there must be a procedure whereby a mature minor or a minor who can demonstrate the minor's best interest is contrary to parental notification, can obtain contraceptives confidentially.

118 See, e.g., Jane Does 1 through 4 v. State of Utah Dept. of Health, 776 F.2d 253 (10th Cir. 1985).

In Planned Parenthood Ass'n of Utah v. Dandoy, 810 F.2d 984 (10th Cir. 1987), the Court of Appeals for the Tenth Circuit ruled the state could not refuse to reimburse a provider for giving family planning advice to a Medicaid bona fide person including an unmarried minor who did not provide evidence of parental consent. The court decided if the state participates in the Medicaid program, it accepts the limitation on state statutes or regulations that conflict with federal statutes.

119 In Jane Does 1 through 4 v. State of Utah Dept. of Health, 776 F.2d 253 (10th Cir. 1985), the Court of Appeals for the Tenth Circuit held that a state can require an unmarried minor to have prior written parental consent in seeking family planning services if only state funds are involved.

120 487 U.S. 589 (1988).

121 Pub. L. 97-35, 95 Stat. 578, 42 U.S.C. § 300z et. seq. The 1981 Adolescent Family Life Act (AFLA) provides federal funding to public and nonprofit organizations to counsel members to abstain from sex until marriage. Federal funding is provided through AFLA.

vices and research in the area of premarital adolescent sexual relations and pregnancy, was constitutional despite the fact federal funds had been made available to many organizations with institutional ties to religious organizations. The act stated federally provided services in the area covered by the act, i.e., care to pregnant adolescents and adolescent parents and prevention services for the prevention of adolescent sexual relations, should promote the involvement of parents and should emphasize the provision of support by other family members, religious and charitable organizations, voluntary associations, and other groups. The Court determined the act had a valid secular purpose in that it was motivated primarily, if not entirely, by the legitimate purpose of eliminating or reducing social and economic problems caused by teenage sexuality, pregnancy, and parenthood. Although the act increased the role of religious organizations in programs sponsored by the act, the Court decided the challenged provisions of the act were also motivated by other, entirely legitimate secular concerns, such as attempting to enlist the aid of other groups in the private sector to increase broad-based community involvement.

D. ARTIFICIAL INSEMINATION, IN VITRO FERTILIZATION, AND SURROGATE PARENTING

The advances of biomedical science have produced a new era of genetics permitting childless couples to have children biologically related to them when they cannot do that otherwise. Still, the various procedures that tamper with nature in the interest of assisting childless couples to conceive present numerous legal and ethical problems. Legislation is often inadequate to provide answers to the complicated moral and ethical concerns.

1. Artificial Insemination

A New York court initially ruled that a child conceived by artificial insemination using semen contributed by a sperm donor, with or without the husband's consent, is not the legitimate child of the husband.[122] However, later decisions

122 In Gursky v. Gursky, 39 Misc. 2d 1083, 242 N.Y.S.2d 406 (Sup. 1963), a New York court ruled artificial insemination through use of donor semen was adultery on the part of the mother. The court held that the child was not a child born in wedlock and, as a result, was illegitimate, deciding the husband of the mother was not required to support the child. See, however, In re Adoption of

have recognized the strong presumption of legitimacy of children born during marriage, and courts generally now rule that a child born of consensual artificial insemination, from an artificial insemination donor (A.I.D.), is the legitimate child of the married couple.[123] Some states have enacted statutes governing the status and rights of A.I.D. children.[124] These statutes generally provide that any

---

Anonymous, 74 Misc. 2d 99, 345 N.Y.S.2d 430 (Sur. Ct. 1973), in which a New York court later held that a child born as a result of artificial insemination through use of donor semen was the legitimate child of the husband when the husband's consent was given to the procedure. The court noted Gursky had been criticized and stated that unless there was absolute medical proof of the husband's sterility, the husband was presumed to be the child's father. The court noted the moral and religious objections to A.I.D. but commented that there are stronger objections to adulterous relationships. In addition, the court noted there is a liberal policy for the protection of children. As there is no purpose in stigmatizing the child by compelling the parents to adopt the child formally, the court determined a child born of consensual A.I.D. during a valid marriage is a legitimate child.

In Claudia B. v. Darrin M., 128 NYS.3d 10 (S. Ct. 1st Dept. N.Y. 2020), a biological mother filed a paternity petition against a sperm donor seeking to have him declared the father of her child. After a relationship between the mother and the respondent ended, the mother asked the respondent to donate his sperm so that she could conceive a child. Although the respondent agreed, there was a nonfinal draft agreement that provided respondent would have no parental rights or responsibility as to the child and that respondent would not be named as the father on the birth certificate. Respondent contended he only intended to be a donor, not a parent. After submitting to DNA testing that revealed respondent was the father of the child, the court entered an order of filiation declaring the sperm donor to be the child's biological father. The court rejected respondent's claim that an unsigned, nonfinal, preconception agreement could be used to equitably estop the mother from asserting paternity as to the known sperm donor.

123 In People v. Sorensen, 68 Cal. 2d 280, 66 Cal. Rptr. 7, 437 P.2d 495 (1968), the court decided the public policy of the state favored legitimation and that no valid public purpose was served by stigmatizing as illegitimate an artificially conceived child. The court noted legitimacy is a legal status that may exist even though a husband is not the natural father of a child.

See also In re Baby Doe, 291 S.C. 389, 353 S.E.2d 877 (1987), in which the Supreme Court of South Carolina ruled a husband who consents to A.I.D. is the legal father of a child born of A.I.D. and will be charged with the legal responsibilities of paternity, including support. The court also ruled consent need not be in writing. The court stated it may be implied from conduct that evidences knowledge of the procedure and a failure to object.

In Shin v. Kong, 80 Cal. App. 4th 498, 95 Cal. Rptr. 2d 304 (1st Dist. 2000), the court ruled a person who learned he was not the biological father of a child born during his marriage did not have a cause of action against the physician who had artificially inseminated his wife.

124 See, e.g., Ark. Stat. Ann. § 28-9-209(c), which provides that any child conceived following artificial insemination of a married woman with the consent of the husband is their child. Consent is presumed unless the contrary is shown by clear and convincing evidence.

See also Cal. Civ. Code § 7005, which provides that if artificial insemination is under the supervision of a licensed physician and the husband gives consent, the husband is treated as the natural father. The husband's consent must be in writing and signed by him and his wife. The statute provides that the donor of the semen is not treated as the child's natural father.

See Or. Rev. Stat. §§ 677.360 and 365, which provide that only licensed physicians can select artificial insemination donors or perform artificial insemination. The written consent of the woman and, if married, of the husband, is required. Section 677.370 prevents from being a donor a person who has a disease or defect transmissible by genes or who has a venereal disease. See also Or. Rev. Stat. §109.239, which provides that the donor of semen has no right to the child if the donor is not the husband. As set out in Or. Rev. Stat. § 109.243, the child is deemed to have been legitimately conceived by the husband.

child conceived following artificial insemination with donor semen with the written consent of the husband, is the child of the married couple.[125] In addition, some state statutes specifically provide the donor of the semen is treated as not being the natural father of the child.[126]

Concerns and legal issues are enhanced when children are conceived through artificial insemination in same sex marriages. In 2016, a New York court[127] ruled a same sex former partner of a child's mother has standing to seek joint custody and visitation with the child. Later, in 2018, a New York court[128] ruled that the presumption of legitimacy afforded to a child born to a marriage applied to a child born to a lesbian married couple and precluded a sperm donor from

---

125 See, e.g., Tex. Fam. Code Ann. § 12.03, which provides that if a husband consents in writing and the consent is acknowledged, the child is the legitimate child of both the husband and the wife. The child is not the child of the donor unless the donor is the husband.

A Uniform Parentage Age § 703, provides that an individual who consents to assisted reproduction by a woman with the intent to be a parent of a child conceived by the assisted reproduction is a parent of the child.

See decision in Claudia B. v. Darrin M., 128 NYS.3d 10 (S. Ct. 1st Dept. N.Y. 2020), discussed above, wherein the court ruled a sperm donor is a child's biological father when there is no final written agreement between the parties as to the status of the sperm donor.

The Supreme Court of Kansas, in the Matter of the Parentage of M.F. by and through K.L, 312 Kan 322, 475 P.3d 642 (Kan. 2020), ruled that a former same-sex partner of a biological mother who conceived a child through artificial insemination, could establish a legal fiction of biological parentage by asserting the Kansas Parentage Act, K.S.A. 23-2208(a)(4). The court stated that she need not show the existence of a written or oral co-parenting agreement with the birth mother.

126 In Jhordan C. v. Mary K., 179 Cal. App. 3d 386, 224 Cal. Rptr. 530 (1st Dist. 1986), a donor who provided semen directly to the child's mother brought action to establish his paternity rights to the child. Although the California statute, Cal. Civ. Code § 7005(b), stated the donor of semen provided to a physician is not the natural father of the child conceived through artificial insemination, the court ruled in Jhordan C. that the statute was not applicable because the semen was not provided to a physician but rather was given directly to the mother. The court decided the donor could establish paternity of the child.

In C. M. v. C. C., 152 N.J. Super. 160, 377 A.2d 821 (Juv. & Dom. Rel. Ct. 1977), the donor of semen, used by an unmarried woman to artificially inseminate herself, brought an action to obtain visitation rights with respect to the child born because of the artificial insemination. The court ruled the donor was the natural father and was entitled to visitation rights with respect to his illegitimate child. As there was no husband and because the donor was known, the donor could establish himself as the natural father. The court stated that when a donor donates his semen anonymously, the donor impliedly gives it without taking on the responsibilities of fatherhood. Further, when the mother is married and the husband consents to the procedure, the husband takes upon himself the responsibilities of fatherhood. However, the court decided it would not take a position as to the propriety of the use of artificial insemination between unmarried persons but rather would be concerned with the best interest of the child in granting custody or visitation rights. The court decided it is in the child's best interest to have two parents whenever possible and noted that the donor was capable and interested in caring for the child.

127 Brooke S.B. v. Elizabeth A.C.C., 28 N.Y.3d 1, 61 N.E.3d 488 (Ct. App. N.Y. 2016).

128 In the Matter of Christopher YY v. Jessica ZZ, 159 A.D.3d 18, 69 N.Y.S. 3d 887 (2018).

asserting paternity.[129] The Supreme Court of Hawaii[130] has ruled that in divorce proceedings, the "wife" of a child's biological mother was the child's legal parent and that a spouse could not rebut the statutory marital presumption of parentage by demonstrating by clear and convincing evidence a lack of consent to the other spouse's artificial insemination procedure.[131]

Written consent of both spouses should be obtained before a physician or hospital performs artificial insemination.

2. In Vitro Fertilization

In vitro fertilization is the process whereby an egg is removed from a woman, is then fertilized in a receptacle by sperm of the woman's husband, and thereafter is implanted in the woman's womb. Although the legality of in vitro fertilization (IVF) has been questioned,[132] the statutes of some states provide for the procedure.[133] The principal legal issues that have occurred have involved disposition of cryopreserved IVF pre-embryos.

In a case decided in 2001 that involved a divorced couple who had undertook IVF during their marriage and who disagreed after their marriage was dissolved on the disposition of their pre-embryos, the Supreme Court of New Jersey[134]

129 The parties had entered into a written agreement wherein the sperm donor expressly waived any claims to paternity to a child conceived from his donated sperm and further waived any right to custody or visitation.

130 LC and MG, 143 Hawaii 302, 430 P.3d 400 (Haw. 2018).

131 In LC and MG, 430 P.3d 400 (Haw. 2018), the Supreme Court of Hawaii stated that recognition of a common law rule permitting a spouse to rebut the marital presumption of parentage based on a lack of consent to artificial insemination does not consider the best interest of the child conceived through artificial insemination. The court decided that, in addition to the financial implications, permitting a spouse to rebut parentage of a child conceived through artificial insemination during an intact marriage could have consequences well beyond the financial aspects of the child's best interests, such as the child's sense of belonging and acceptance.

132 See, e.g., Smith v. Hartigan, 556 F. Supp. 157 (N.D. Ill. 1983) in which the court considered the Illinois Abortion Law which contained a provision that could be interpreted as prohibiting in vitro fertilization. See 720 Ill. Comp. Stat. Ann. § 510/1 (formerly Ill. Rev. Stat. 38, par. 81–21).) A physician sued to have the statute declared unconstitutional. The physician had refused to perform in vitro fertilization because of the fear of possible state prosecution. The court ruled the physician had no standing to sue because the state attorney general had stated he would not prosecute. The state's attorney general interpreted the statute as not prohibiting the procedure.

133 See., e. g., Ky. Rev. Stat. Ann. §199.590. See also discussion in Surrogate Parenting Associates, Inc. v. Com. ex rel. Armstrong, 704 S.W.2d 209 (Ky. 1986).

134 J.B. v. M.B., 170 N.J. 9, 783 A.2d 707 (2001).

ruled that an agreement regarding disposition of the pre-embryos is enforceable but subject to the right of either party to change his or her mind about disposition up to the point of use or destruction of any stored preembryos.[135] Later, in 2003, the Supreme Court of Iowa[136] ruled a statute governing child custody does not apply to frozen human embryos and that it would violate public policy to enforce a prior agreement regarding use or disposition of embryos when a party has changed his or her mind.[137] The Supreme Court of Arizona[138] validated a prior agreement between a divorced couple regarding the disposition of the couples' cryopreserved embryos.[139]

Written consent of both spouses should be obtained before a physician or hospital performs in vitro fertilization.

3. Surrogate Parenting

State statutes were intended to solve legal problems associated with husbands who were infertile. Surrogate parenting, where the problem is the wife's infertility, was not contemplated. The surrogate process involves an agreement between a couple and a third party whereby the third party becomes a surrogate mother for the couple through the process of artificial insemination of the

---

135 In J.B. v. M.B., 170 N.J. 9, 783 A.2d 707 (2001), the New Jersey Supreme Court ruled that, in a divorce proceeding, disposition of cryopreserved pre-embryos, which were created in connection with an in vitro fertilization procedure, should be determined by the party wishing to avoid procreation. The wife, who wanted the pre-embryos destroyed, contended that if the pre-embryos were successfully implanted, she would be forced to become a biological parent. Her husband, on the other hand, could have other children; thus, his right to procreate was not lost if he was denied the opportunity to use or donate the pre-embryos. Noting the parties had not entered into a contract regarding disposition of the cryopreserved pre-embryos, the court granted the wife the right to prevent implantation of the pre-embryos and ordered them destroyed.

136 In re Marriage of Witten, 672 N.W.2d 768 (Iowa 2003).

137 The Iowa Supreme Court held that agreements entered at the time in vitro fertilization is commenced are enforceable and binding, subject to the right of either party to change his or her mind regarding disposition of embryos. The court ruled that if the donors cannot reach a mutual decision on disposition, then no transfer, release, disposition, or use of the embryos can occur. The court stated that neither party may use or dispose of embryos without the consent of the other party.

138 Terrell v. Torres, 248 Ariz. 47, 456 P.3d 13 (Ariz. 2020).

139 In Terrell v. Torres, the couple had agreed that in the event they separated, divorced, died, or became incapacitated, the embryos would be discarded, be donated to another couple, or one of the partners could use the embryos with the contemporaneous permission of the other. Torres wanted the embryos for future implantation and Terrell, who did not wish to father any future children with Torres, asked that the embryos be donated to another couple. The court concluded the parties' agreement directed donation of the embryos to another couple.

third party with the husband's semen.[140] The surrogate mother and her husband, if she is married, consent to surrender custody upon birth of the child and to terminate their parental rights. The surrogate's husband may file an affidavit of non-consent to the artificial insemination so that he, the surrogate's husband, will not be deemed to be the father of the child.[141] Then when the child is born to the surrogate mother, the donor of the semen files a petition seeking an order of affiliation to have his name on the birth certificate as the natural and legal father of the child.[142] The wife of the natural father then adopts the child.[143]

Surrogate parenting poses many difficult legal questions that states have dealt with in different ways. Some courts earlier held these contractual arrangements to be voidable.[144] However, the Supreme Court of Iowa[145] later ruled that gestational surrogacy agreements are not prohibited by statute and are not unenforceable as against public policy.[146] The Supreme Court of Tennessee[147] has

---

140 See discussion in Syrkowski v. Appleyard, 420 Mich. 367, 362 N.W.2d 211 (1985).

141 See decision of the Michigan Supreme Court in Syrkowski v. Appleyard, 420 Mich. 367, 362 N.W.2d 211 (1985).

142 In Syrkowski v. Appleyard, 420 Mich. 367, 362 N.W.2d 211 (1985), the Supreme Court of Michigan noted that a state statute provided for the father of a child born out of wedlock to seek an order of affiliation. The court ruled the child born to a surrogate mother was born out of wedlock, even though the surrogate mother was married, because the husband of the surrogate mother filed a non-consent to artificial insemination. The court decided a circuit court had jurisdiction over the biological father's request for an order of affiliation declaring his paternity of the child.

143 See, e.g., Matter of Baby M., 217 N.J. Super. 313, 525 A.2d 1128 (Ch. Div. 1987), judgment aff'd in part, rev'd in part, 109 N.J. 396, 537 A.2d 1227 (1988).

144 See, e.g., Surrogate Parenting Associates, Inc. v. Com. ex rel. Armstrong, 704 S.W.2d 209 (Ky. 1986), in which the Supreme Court of Kentucky decided a surrogate mother's consent to surrender parental rights to the child is no more legally binding than the decision of an unwed mother during her pregnancy that she will put her baby up for adoption. Under the Kentucky adoption statutes, there was a five-days' consent feature in the termination of parental rights. See Ky. Rev. Stat. Ann. § 199.500(5). The policy of voluntary termination is to preserve to the mother her right of choice regardless of decisions made before the birth of the child. The court ruled this same policy should apply to a surrogate mother to give her the opportunity to reconsider her decision to fulfill the role as surrogate mother. Should the surrogate mother reconsider, the court stated she will forfeit her rights to whatever fees are provided for in the contract. Both the mother and the biological father will then have the statutory rights and obligations that exist in the absence of the contract.

145 P.M. and C.M. v. T.B. and D.B., 907 N.W.2d 522 (Iowa 2018).

146 In P.M. and C.M. v. T.B. and D.B., the Iowa Supreme Court ruled a surrogate mother is not the "biological" mother of a child and that the surrogate mother's rights to due process and equal protection are not violated when a court terminates the presumptive parental rights of her and her husband, establishes paternity in the biological father, and awards him permanent legal and physical custody of the child the surrogate mother delivered.

147 In re Baby, 447 S.W.2d 807 (Tenn. 2014).

also ruled that public policy does not prohibit the enforcement of traditional surrogacy contracts. However, that court also ruled that public policy of the state does impose certain restrictions.[148] One court ruled a clause in a surrogate parenting contract that prohibited the surrogate from having an abortion is unenforceable.[149]

The biological father will have difficulty in some states in establishing paternity of the child should the surrogate breach the contract. In most states, there will be a strong or conclusive presumption of paternity of the surrogate's husband. Further, several states have statutes providing that any child conceived following artificial insemination with donor semen is the child of the married couple. With respect to a surrogate's husband, while an affidavit of non-consent to the artificial insemination filed by the surrogate's husband can cause the surrogate's husband to be deemed not to be the father of the child, some states also have provisions specifically stating that the donor of the semen is treated as not being the natural father of the child.[150] The Supreme Court of Kentucky has ruled that specific performance to compel proposed conception, gestation and

148 The Tennessee Supreme Court ruled that public policy requires compliance with statutory procedures for termination of parental rights and stated that it will not permit parties to terminate parental rights of a traditional surrogate through judicial ratification of a surrogacy contract prior to birth of the child. The court held that the surrogate retains parental rights unless and until such rights are terminated in a future proceeding. The court also stated that compensation contingent upon the surrender of the child, or that is contingent upon termination of the surrogate's parental rights, or that exceeds the reasonable costs of services, expenses, or injuries related to the pregnancy, the birth of the child, or other matters inherent to the surrogacy process, are prohibited. It voided contractual terms that would circumvent the established procedures for determining a person's status as a legal parent or that terminates parental rights. It also ruled as prohibited the termination of parental rights in an involuntary proceeding absent a finding that the parent is unfit or that substantial harm to the child will result if parental rights are not terminated.

149 See, e.g, Matter of Baby M., 217 N.J. Super. 313, 525 A.2d 1128 (Ch. Div. 1987), judgment aff'd in part, rev'd in part, 109 N.J. 396, 537 A.2d 1227 (1988), wherein the court ruled that after conception, only the surrogate has the right, to the exclusion of the sperm donor, to decide whether to abort the fetus. The court stated the surrogate's decision to abort must comply with Roe v. Wade, 410 U.S. 113 (1973) (holding modified by, Planned Parenthood of Southeastern Pennsylvania v. Casey, 505 U.S. 833 (1992)). In Matter of Baby M, 109 N.J. 396, 537 A.2d 1227 (1988), the New Jersey Supreme Court invalidated the surrogate contract.

The Uniform Parentage Act, § 804, states that the intended parent, or if there are two intended parents, will assume responsibility for the financial support of the child immediately on birth, but it also states that the act does not enlarge or diminish the surrogate's right to terminate her pregnancy.

150 See, e.g., Cal. Civ. Code § 7005(b) and Tex. Fam. Code § 12.03.

The Uniform Parentage Act, § 805, provides that unless a surrogacy agreement expressly provides otherwise, the marriage of a surrogate after the agreement is signed by all parties does not affect the validity of the agreement and her spouse's consent to the agreement is not required. Her spouse is not a presumed parent of a child conceived by assisted reproduction under the agreement.

birth generally is not available to the male donor.[151] If the biological father has been both acknowledged contractually and can be confirmed scientifically, the question of custody of the child born of a surrogate becomes a difficult question should the surrogate refuse to terminate parental rights.[152] Courts generally will consider the welfare of the child over the rights of the parents and will determine custody by virtue of its responsibility as parens patriae.[153]

The payment to the surrogate mother for bearing the child presents additional concerns. Many states prohibit the payment of compensation for a consent for adoption. Additionally, some states have imposed criminal sanctions for what is termed the buying and selling of babies.[154] Still courts generally have approved the payment of compensation in surrogate parenting, holding the surrogate contract to be a valid agreement and not compensation for a consent for adoption.[155]

---

151 Surrogate Parenting Associates, Inc. v. Com. ex rel. Armstrong, 704 S.W.2d 209 (Ky. 1986).

152 See, e.g., discussion by the Supreme Court of New Jersey in Matter of Baby M, 109 N.J. 396, 537 A.2d 1227 (1988).

See In Matter of Adoption of Baby Girl L.J., 132 Misc. 2d 972, 505 N.Y.S.2d 813 (Sur. Ct. 1986), wherein a New York court found a child conceived by a surrogate mother should be raised as the child of his biological father and the latter's spouse because, by court investigation, it was found it would be in the best interest of the child to approve the adoption. The court found there was no other alternative, such as denying the adoption to discourage the procedures, because the child needed a home.

153 Matter of Baby M, 109 N.J. 396, 537 A.2d 1227 (1988).

154 See, e.g., Ky. Rev. Stat. Ann. §199.590(2) and Cal. Penal Code §73(a).

In Matter of Adoption of Baby Girl L.J., 132 Misc. 2d 972, 505 N.Y.S.2d 813 (Sur. Ct. 1986), the court noted all fifty states have enacted legislation to regulate adoptions and because of the great demand for "desirable children," many of the states have imposed criminal sanctions for compensation paid in connection with an adoption. The court commented these criminal sanctions are the legislatures' responses to a growing "baby black market" where children are often auctioned to the highest bidder. The court noted that in New York, it is a misdemeanor for any person to violate willfully the provisions of its adoption statutes.

In Matter of Adoption of Paul, 146 Misc. 2d 379, 550 N.Y.S.2d 815 (Fam. Ct. 1990), the court ruled it could not accept the surrender and termination of parental rights of a surrogate mother unless the surrogate could swear under oath that she had not and would not request, accept, or receive a payment in exchange for surrender of the child. The court stated remuneration to a mother, in exchange for her surrender of a child for adoption, violated the state's well-established policy against trafficking in children. The court rejected the argument that "surrogate motherhood" is analogous to sperm donation in that it provides to infertile couples a means to achieve parenthood and should therefore be approved as a matter of equal protection. The court stated there is a very significant difference between the two methods of procreation. A sperm is merely a gamete, potentially capable, if successfully joined with an egg, of creating an embryo, which must then survive gestation to birth. The surrogate mother, on the other hand, is supplying a life-in-being, having provided not only the egg, but also protection and nourishment during gestation, as well as the delivery of a human child capable of independent survival. According to the court, it is this difference that renders surrogate mothering for financial gain illegal baby selling.

155 In Surrogate Parenting Associates, Inc. v. Com. ex rel. Armstrong, 704 S.W.2d 209 (Ky. 1986), the Supreme Court of Kentucky concluded the surrogate parenting procedure does not involve the buy-

A few courts have approved the concept of surrogate parenting as an extension of an individual's right to privacy.[156] Additionally, some courts have ruled the surrogate who voluntarily chooses to enter a contract would be deprived of her constitutionally protected right to perform services if the contract is denied.[157]

ing and selling of babies. The court decided there are fundamental differences between the two. A Kentucky statute, Ky. Rev. Stat. Ann. § 199.590(1), prohibited the sale, purchase, or procurement for sale or purchase of any child for the purpose of adoption. The court ruled the statute was intended to keep baby brokers from overwhelming an expectant mother, or the parents of a child with financial inducements, to part with the child. The central fact in the surrogate parenting procedure is that the agreement to bear the child is entered into before conception. The essential considerations for the surrogate mother are not avoiding the consequences of an unwanted pregnancy or the fear of the financial burden of child rearing. On the contrary, according to the court, the essential consideration is to assist a person or couple, who desperately want a child but are unable to conceive one in the customary manner, to achieve a biologically related offspring. Still, the dissenting opinion commented that the primary purpose of a surrogate group was "to locate women who will readily, for a price, allow themselves to be used as human incubators and who are willing to sell, for a price, all of their parental rights in a child thus born."

The New Jersey Supreme Court invalidated a surrogacy contract in Matter of Baby M, 109 N.J. 396, 537 A.2d 1227 (1988), ruling a surrogacy contract conflicts with (1) laws prohibiting the use of money in connection with adoptions, (2) laws requiring proof of parental unfitness or abandonment before termination of parental rights is ordered or an adoption is granted, and (3) laws that make surrender of custody and consent to adoption revocable in private placement adoptions. The court determined that although the arrangement to pay the surrogate mother is a payment for her services and not for the adoption, it nonetheless is clear that the money is paid and accepted in connection with an adoption. The court noted a termination of parental rights is obtained not by proving the statutory prerequisites but by claiming the benefit of contractual provisions. The court further ruled a contractual agreement to abandon one's parental rights, or not to contest a termination action, will not be enforced. The court stated the contract's basic premise, that the natural parents can decide in advance of birth which one is to have custody of the child, bears no relationship to the settled law that the child's best interests determine custody. The court decided a surrogacy contract is a sale of a child, or at the very least, the sale of a mother's right to her child, with the only mitigating factor being that one of the purchasers is the father. The court declared the contract to be void.

The Tennessee Supreme Court has ruled, In re Baby, 447 S.W.3d 807 (Tenn. 2014), that compensation in a surrogacy contract that is contingent upon the surrender of the child, is contingent upon termination of the surrogate's parental rights, or that exceeds the reasonable costs of services, expenses, or injuries related to the pregnancy, the birth of the child, or other matters inherent to the surrogacy process, is prohibited.

156 See, however, Doe v. Kelley, 106 Mich. App. 169, 307 N.W.2d 438 (1981), in which the court stated that while the decision to bear or beget a child has been found to be a fundamental interest protected by the right of privacy, there is no prohibition on the state's interference with a surrogate parenting agreement. The court decided such a prohibition does not directly prohibit a couple from having a child; rather it acts to preclude the couple from paying consideration with their use of adoption procedures in the state. The court determined the right of privacy does not give a surrogate mother the right to bear a child for pay nor to use the adoption laws to transfer the child to the contracting couple. Still, the court noted that although it had strong reservations about surrogate parenting arrangements, both on moral and ethical grounds, it opined that current legislation in the state did not expressly foreclose the use of surrogate mothers or the paying of compensation to them. The court determined that as with any contractual arrangement, it would continue to review the agreement for fairness, fraud, undue influence, or excessive payment.

157 The New Jersey Supreme Court ruled a surrogate contract was void, in Matter of Baby M, 109 N.J.

There have been issues relating to a former spouse implanting cryopreserved pre-embryos, discussed above, in a surrogate mother.[158] Some courts have ruled that a former spouse, who implants pre-embryos from a prior marriage in a surrogate mother, violates the procreate, or not to procreate, right of the other prior spouse.[159]

E. WRONGFUL PREGNANCY, WRONGFUL BIRTH, AND WRONGFUL LIFE

Wrongful pregnancy, wrongful birth, and wrongful life are three distinct causes of action, but all involve the unwanted birth of a child.[160] Wrongful pregnancy and wrongful birth actions are brought on behalf of the parents of an unwanted

---

396, 537 A.2d 1227 (1988), but decided best interest of the child justified awarding custody of the child to the father and his wife. It ruled the surrogate mother was entitled to visitation rights.

158 In J.B. v. M.B, 170 N.J. 9, 783 A.2d 707 (2001), the former wife's right not to become a parent conflicted with the former husband's right to procreate. The New Jersey Supreme Court ruled that the former husband and former wife never entered into a separate binding contract providing for disposition of pre-embryos and further ruled that the former wife's fundament right not to procreate would be irrevocably extinguished if a surrogate mother bore the former wife's child through use of the pre-embryos. The court noted that the right of the former husband to procreate using the former wife's egg would be terminated if the pre-embryos were destroyed, but that he retained the capacity to father children. The court decided it would not force the former wife to become a biological parent against her will. It noted that her right not to procreate could be lost through attempted use or through donation of the pre-embryos and that implantation, if successful, would result in the birth of her biological child. The court was concerned that this could have life-long emotional and psychological repercussions.

159 In Litowitz v. Litowitz, 102 Wash. App. 934, 10 P.3d 1086 (Div. 2 2000), judgment rev'd, 146 Wash. 2d 514, 48 P.3d 261 (2002), opinion amended, 53 P.3d 516 (Wash. 2002), in a divorce action involving a dispute over custody of pre-embryos, the court ruled the progenitor had the right to control the destiny of the pre-embryos. While married, the parties had contracted with an egg donor and an in vitro fertilization clinic to produce a child or children. The husband's sperm fertilized five donated eggs that began cell division. Three of the five pre-embryos were implanted in a surrogate mother while the other two were cryopreserved. The surrogate bore the couple a child, but the couple had separated by the time the child was born. In the divorce proceedings, the wife wanted the pre-embryos awarded to her for implanting in a surrogate. The husband wanted the pre-embryos awarded to him. The court noted the husband contributed the DNA and recognized if any one of the pre-embryos became a child in a setting where the husband had contact with the child, he would be thrust into a life-time parenting role. The court decided that if he had the right to control whether the pre-embryos continued to life, he also could exercise this right for the purpose of avoiding parenthood. The court held the contracts the couple had signed did not require the husband to continue with the parties' family planning prior to the divorce and ruled the husband's right not to procreate compelled an award to him of the pre-embryos.

160 Bruggeman By and Through Bruggeman v. Schimke, 239 Kan. 245, 718 P.2d 635 (1986).

child whereas a wrongful life action is brought on behalf of an impaired child who seeks damages for the alleged negligence of a hospital or physician in causing the child's impairment.[161] A wrongful pregnancy, or wrongful conception, action involves the parents of a healthy but unwanted child bringing a claim for damages suffered as a result of giving birth to the unwanted child, often after an unsuccessful sterilization procedure. A wrongful birth claim is brought by parents of a child born with a birth defect who claim that they would have avoided conception or terminated the pregnancy had they been properly advised of the risks of birth defects to the potential child.[162] While the wrongful pregnancy action typically involves a healthy, but unwanted child, the wrongful birth action usually involves a planned child who is born deformed.[163] A wrongful life action is brought on behalf of an impaired child who will allege that but for the negligent advice to the child's parents from a defendant physician or health-care provider, the child would not have been born.[164]

There have been three views relating to the wrongful pregnancy action. Some courts have denied the parents any recovery for rearing a healthy, although unwanted child, the theory being that a parent cannot have been damaged by the birth of a normal, healthy child.[165] Under this view, the parents of a child born to a mother upon whom an unsuccessful sterilization procedure has been performed, may only recover damages occurring because of the pregnancy and

161 Jackson v. Bumgardner, 318 N.C. 172, 347 S.E.2d 743 (1986), involved an action for medical malpractice following an unplanned pregnancy. The physician improperly failed to replace an intrauterine device resulting in the plaintiff's wife's pregnancy and the subsequent birth of a healthy child. The court noted the distinction between wrongful pregnancy cases and the wrongful birth or wrongful life cases. The court stated a majority of courts have viewed wrongful pregnancy, or wrongful conception, cases as being indistinguishable from an ordinary medical malpractice action.

162 Ellis v. Sherman, 512 Pa. 14, 515 A.2d 1327 (1986).

163 Bruggeman By and Through Bruggeman v. Schimke, 239 Kan. 245, 718 P.2d 635 (1986).

164 Jackson v. Bumgardner, 318 N.C. 172, 347 S.E.2d 743 (1986).

In Wood v. University of Utah Medical Center, 2002 UT 134, 67 P.3d 436 (Utah 2002), the Supreme Court of Utah ruled constitutional the Utah Wrongful Life Act. The parents of a Down Syndrome child brought an action against a hospital and others alleging the hospital was negligent in that it misread genetic tests and failed to inform the parents of the test results, specifically, of the likelihood that their child would have Down Syndrome.

165 Discussion in Byrd v. Wesley Medical Center, 237 Kan. 215, 699 P.2d 459 (1985).

In Smith v. Gore, 728 S.W.2d 738 (Tenn. 1987), the Supreme Court of Tennessee ruled that birth of a normal child is not a cognizable legal injury and limited damages to those immediately related to pregnancy and birth of the child.

birth. The parents may not recover costs of rearing the child.[166] The second view, called the full-damage rule, a rule that has been adopted by a minority of courts, would permit the parents to recover all damages and expenses including the costs of rearing the child.[167] The third view, called the ordinary tort-benefit rule, permits the parents the recovery of all damages but requires that the damage award be reduced by the value of benefits the parents will receive because of having a normal, healthy child.[168]

---

166 In Boone v. Mullendore, 416 So. 2d 718 (Ala. 1982), the Alabama Supreme Court stated that the cornerstone of the denial of the costs of rearing a child is the idea that a normal, healthy life should not be the basis for a compensable wrong. The court opined that to permit the parents to keep their child and to shift the entire costs of the child's upbringing to the negligent health-care provider would result in a penalty wholly out of proportion to the culpability involved.

In Macomber v. Dillman, 505 A.2d 810 (Me. 1986), a physician performed a tubal ligation on the plaintiff for permanent sterilization. She, however, conceived and gave birth to a healthy child. The Supreme Court of Maine permitted the plaintiff to recover as damages the hospital and medical expenses incurred for the sterilization procedure and the pregnancy, pain and suffering connected with the pregnancy, loss of earnings by the mother during that time, and the husband's proven damages for loss of consortium of his wife. Still, in deciding public policy refuted a parent's being damaged or injured by the birth and rearing of a healthy, normal child, the court would not award damages for the cost of rearing the child.

In Miller v. Johnson, 231 Va. 177, 343 S.E.2d 301 (1986), the Supreme Court of Virginia limited the damage recovery in a wrongful pregnancy action, but stated the mother was entitled to recover damages, if proven, for emotional distress causally resulting from the tortiously caused physical injury.

In Szekeres by Szekeres v. Robinson, 102 Nev. 93, 715 P.2d 1076 (1986), the parents of a healthy child brought an action against the physicians and the hospital that performed failed surgical sterilization procedures. The Supreme Court of Nevada ruled the birth of a healthy, although unwanted child, did not result in legally compensable damages in tort; however, the court decided the physicians and the hospital could be sued on a contract theory for at least the costs of medical, surgical, and hospital care associated with the failed surgery.

In Jackson v. Bumgardner, 318 N.C. 172, 347 S.E.2d 743 (1986), the Supreme Court of North Carolina limited recovery for wrongful conception to hospital costs and medical expenses of pregnancy, pain and suffering connected with the pregnancy, lost wages, and where claimed by the husband, loss of consortium. This court refused to award damages for the cost of rearing the child.

167 In Byrd v. Wesley Medical Center, 237 Kan. 215, 699 P.2d 459 (1985), the Supreme Court of Kansas stated the full recovery rule has little support. The court determined that as a matter of public policy, the birth of a normal and healthy child does not constitute a legal harm for which damages are recoverable. The court commented that while it would recognize a wrongful death action because of the great value it placed on human life, it could not recognize an action for wrongful conception of a normal, healthy child even though the birth was one of the consequences of a negligently performed sterilization.

In Fulton-DeKalb Hosp. Authority v. Graves, 252 Ga. 441, 314 S.E.2d 653 (1984), the Supreme Court of Georgia ruled that the recovery of expenses for an unsuccessful medical procedure that led to conception included costs of delivery, lost wages, damages for pain and suffering and medical complications, and loss of consortium.

In James G. v. Caserta, 175 W. Va. 406, 332 S.E.2d 872 (1985), the Supreme Court of West Virginia recognized a cause of action for wrongful pregnancy and ruled that damages, including the costs of the initial unsuccessful sterilization operation, prenatal care, childbirth, postnatal care and a second sterilization operation, if obtained, pain and suffering by the mother, and loss of consortium and wages, are recoverable.

168 Sherlock v. Stillwater Clinic, 260 N.W.2d 169 (Minn. 1977), but rejected by Szekeres by Szekeres v.

The wrongful birth action is based on the claim that the negligent advice or treatment by a physician or health-care provider deprives the parents of a deformed child the choice of avoiding conception or of terminating the pregnancy.[169] The theory is that the physician or other health-care provider failed to discover the birth defect and to advise the parents so that they could decide intelligently whether to forebear having the child, or after the mother has become pregnant, to consider the termination of the pregnancy.[170] Some courts[171] have ruled that a state statute that prohibits a cause of action for wrongful birth or wrongful life does not interfere with a woman's right to an abortion.[172]

Robinson, 102 Nev. 93, 715 P.2d 1076 (1986).

169 In Tillman v. Goodpasture, 424 P.3d 540 (Kan. App. 2018), parents filed suit against a physician for wrongful birth, based on allegations that the physician failed to diagnose severe structural abnormalities and defects in their child's brain in utero. The court ruled constitutional a state statute, Kan Stat. § 60-1906, that eliminated a cause of action for wrongful birth.

170 In James G. v. Caserta, 175 W. Va. 406, 332 S.E.2d 872 (1985), the Supreme Court of West Virginia stated that with the increased knowledge in the field of genetic counseling, there is the "concomitant recognition that the ordinary standard of care may require appropriate tests and counseling with parents who are more likely to bear children with birth defects."

Then, in Ellis v. Sherman, 512 Pa. 14, 515 A.2d 1327 (1986), the Supreme Court of Pennsylvania commented that if the parents of a child born with a hereditary disease can establish their claim against the physician, that the physician failed to inform them that their child might be born with a hereditary disease transmitted by the father, they could recover not only for their mental anguish but also for expenses related to the birth and care of the child.

171 See, e. g., decision of the Minnesota Supreme Court in Hickman v. Group Health Plan, Inc., 396 N.W.2d 10 (Minn. 1986).

172 In Hickman, the plaintiff, who had a child born with Down syndrome, challenged a Minnesota statute, Minn. Stat. § 145.424(2), that prohibited a cause of action for wrongful birth or wrongful life. The plaintiff contended the statute was unconstitutional under Roe v. Wade, 410 U.S. 113 (1973). The Minnesota Supreme Court stated that the statute must be a significant burden on a woman's right to an abortion to be unconstitutional under Roe v. Wade.

In Campbell v. U.S., 962 F.2d 1579 (11th Cir. 1992), the Court of Appeals for the Eleventh Circuit dismissed an action for wrongful birth, noting that Georgia has not recognized a wrongful birth cause of action. The court ruled that the state's refusal to recognize the cause of action did not place a significant burden on a woman's right to terminate a pregnancy.

In Norman v. Xytex Corp., 310 Ga. 127, 848 S.E.2d 835 (Ga. 2020), parents brought action against a sperm bank, alleging that it had sold them human sperm under false pretenses about the characteristics of the sperm donor and that the child conceived with that sperm suffered from impairments inherited from the sperm donor. The Supreme Court of Georgia ruled the claim that the parents would not have purchased sperm from a particular donor had the sperm bank revealed true facts about the donor was a wrongful birth claim and thus barred under state law. The court held that the parents could not recover costs of pregnancy and raising the child. Still, the Georgia Supreme Court ruled the parents' negligent misrepresentation claim, asserting that the sperm bank incorrectly represented it had screened the medical and mental health history of its donors, was not a wrongful birth claim and thus was not barred.

In adopting the concept stated by one court[173] that "basic to our culture is the precept that life is precious," some courts and states have not recognized a wrongful life action brought by a deformed child.[174] The theory is that to recognize wrongful life as a tort does violence, and is completely contradictory, to the precept and belief that life is precious. The difficulty with the wrongful life action, and in some states also with the wrongful birth action, is that many courts are unwilling to recognize as a legal injury the existence of life, even with severe defects.[175] The essence of an action brought by an injured child is that the child's very life is wrongful.[176] The philosophical problem of finding that a defective life is worth less than no life at all has perplexed most courts.[177] Still, some courts have decided the award of damages to a severely intellectually disabled or suffering child does not disavow value of life.[178]

---

173 Berman v. Allan, 80 N.J. 421, 404 A.2d 8 (1979).

174 In Bruggeman By and Through Bruggeman v. Schimke, 239 Kan. 245, 718 P.2d 635 (1986), the Supreme Court of Kansas decided an action for wrongful life should not be recognized judicially in Kansas, noting that in a wrongful life claim, the child does not allege that the physician's negligence caused the child's deformity, but rather that the physician's negligence in failing to inform the child's parents adequately of the risk of the birth of a deformed child caused the child to experience the pain and suffering attributable to the deformity. The court stated, however, that a legal right not to be born, i.e., to be dead, rather than to be alive with deformities, is a theory completely contradictory to the law in Kansas.

In James G. v. Caserta, 175 W. Va. 406, 332 S.E.2d 872 (1985), the Supreme Court of West Virginia determined that a duty to inform does not extend to an unborn child, that it is the parents' decision to risk conception or to terminate a pregnancy.

175 See, e. g., early decisions of the Supreme Court of North Carolina Azzolino v. Dingfelder, 315 N.C. 103, 337 S.E.2d 528 (1985); Jackson v. Bumgardner, 318 N.C. 172, 347 S.E.2d 743 (1986).

In Nelson v. Krusen, 678 S.W.2d 918 (Tex. 1984), the Supreme Court of Texas found no cause of action in Texas for wrongful life.

176 In Procanik by Procanik v. Cillo, 97 N.J. 339, 478 A.2d 755 (1984), rejected by, Smith v. Cote, 128 N.H. 231, 513 A.2d 341 (1986), a physician negligently failed to diagnose the mother had contracted German measles in the first trimester of her pregnancy. Her child was born with a congenital rubella syndrome. The child sued alleging that the doctors negligently deprived his parents of the choice of terminating her pregnancy.

177 See, e.g., decision of the New Jersey Supreme Court in Procanik by Procanik v. Cillo, 97 N.J. 339, 478 A.2d 755 (1984), that was rejected by the Supreme Court in New Hampshire in Smith v. Cote, 128 N.H. 231, 513 A.2d 341 (1986).

178 In Turpin v. Sortini, 31 Cal. 3d 220, 182 Cal. Rptr. 337, 643 P.2d 954 (1982), rejected by Smith v. Cote, 128 N.H. 231, 513 A.2d 341 (1986)), a California court permitted damages for the extraordinary expense for specialized teaching, training, and hearing equipment for a suffering child but denied damages for pain, suffering, or other general damages.

In Procanik by Procanik v. Cillo, 97 N.J. 339, 478 A.2d 755 (1984), rejected by, Smith v. Cote, 128 N.H. 231, 513 A.2d 341 (1986), the Supreme Court of New Jersey commented that when a child requires extraordinary medical care, the financial impact is felt not just by the parents, but also by the injured child. The court determined that recovery of the cost of extraordinary medical expenses by either the parents or the infant, but not both, is consistent with the principle that the doctor's negligence vitally affects the entire family. The court did not, however, award the child damages for emotional distress attendant on birth defects because the court decided that claim was based on the contention the infant would be better off not being born.

CHAPTER VI.
GOVERNING BOARD, MEMBERS, AND EMPLOYEES

A. INTRODUCTION

This chapter summarizes rules relating to hospital governance, including powers of hospital boards and employment laws. A private hospital generally is incorporated and thus must function in accordance with the corporate statutes of the state where the corporation is created and operates. Accordingly, this chapter also sets out the general rules applicable to corporations and, more specifically, those relating to the nonprofit corporation as most hospitals are nonprofit entities.

A corporation must have consent from the state to be formed and to operate in the state; thus, a corporation cannot exist until a charter from the state, or a state's general law, grants it that authority. State statutes, which prescribe procedures by which corporations are created and operate, set out as the first step in the incorporation process the filing with the secretary of state of Articles of Incorporation, called a Certificate of Formation in a few states. The articles of incorporation, or certificate of formation, will state the name and address of the corporation, its purpose and duration, the names and addresses of members of its board of directors and provide for a designated agent to be registered with the state for service of process.[1] After approval of the articles or certificate of formation and the state issuing a charter to a newly formed corporation, the corporation adopts adopt bylaws. Bylaws of a corporation determine the internal governance of a corporation and management of its affairs.[2]

Corporate hospitals generally are organized differently from other corporations, and their governance rules may not fit precisely within a state's corporate statutes. For example, hospitals typically will have a governing body, rather than

1 If the corporation is for-profit; the articles or certificate of formation would also set out the amount and type of shares of stock authorized to be issued. In most states, nonprofit corporations cannot issue shares of stock.

Amendments to the articles or certificate of formation must be made through articles of amendment filed with the secretary of state.

2 A bylaw is an agreement or contract to conduct corporate affairs as between the corporation and its directors, as well as its members, although nonprofit corporations often do not have members. Corporate bylaws include all regulations of a corporation. Until repealed, generally by a majority vote of its board, bylaws are continuing rules for governance of the corporation. The power to alter, amend or repeal bylaws or to adopt new bylaws is vested in the corporate board of directors unless otherwise provided in the articles of incorporation or in the bylaws.

See Medical Staff of Avera Marshall Regional Medical Center v. Avera Marshall, 857 N.W.2d 695 (Minn. 2014), in which the Supreme Court of Minnesota ruled that hospital bylaws are an enforceable contract. The court also ruled that members of the medical staff have the capacity to sue the hospital in which they worked.

a board of directors, and will have an administrator and hospital staff, rather that corporate officers. Nonetheless hospital corporations are subject to the state's corporate statutes, and members of a hospital board must be aware of the relevant provisions of those statutes that are summarized in this chapter.[3]

B. GOVERNING BOARD

The governing board of a corporate hospital generally functions in the same manner as a board of directors of a for-profit corporation; thus, members of a hospital governing board will be referred to as directors in this chapter.[4] Except for the first board of directors, which is established by the articles of incorporation or certificate of formation,[5] corporate bylaws determine the number of directors and how they are elected or appointed.[6] A change in the number of directors is made by amending the bylaws unless the articles of incorporation provide that a change must be made by amending the articles.[7] Some states do not require that directors be residents of the state of incorporation unless the

3 Most states have separate corporate statutes for nonprofit corporations. Still, corporate statutes for nonprofit corporations do not differ substantially from those for the for-profit corporations. The principal difference is the inability of nonprofit corporations to distribute their profits to private individuals or other private corporations. The rules that are summarized in this chapter, which address principally the nonprofit corporation, then will also be applicable for the most part to hospitals that are privately owned and have shareholders.

4 Laws relating to a corporation's board of directors are set out in the state's corporate statutes, thus, to determine laws governing corporate directors, hospital board members and advisors must consult the state's corporate statutes, either its regular corporate statutes if the hospital is a private, for-profit entity, or the separate statutes for nonprofit corporations for a nonprofit hospital.

The Texas Nonprofit Corporation Act, Tex. Bus. Orgs. Code § 22.233, has a provision stating that churches are not required to have officers, that duties and responsibilities of corporate officers may be vested in the corporation's board of directors or other designated body in any manner provided for by the certificate of formation or bylaws of the corporation.

5 As noted previously, in some states, such as Texas, the articles of incorporation are referred to as the certificate of formation. See Tex. Bus. Orgs. Code ch. 22.

6 See Mod. Nonprofit Corp. Act § 18 (1964).

7 See Model Nonprofit Corporation Act § 18 (1964. Requirements for nonprofit corporations in most states are derived either from the Model Nonprofit Corporation Act (1964) or the Revised Model Nonprofit Corporation Act (1987), and this chapter will reference provisions in either or both of these acts to set out general laws relating to nonprofit corporations.

articles of incorporation or the bylaws provide otherwise.[8] Many state statutes require there be at least three directors of a nonprofit corporation.[9]

The term of office of a director should be set out in the corporate bylaws.[10] The first board of directors, named in the articles of incorporation, holds office until the first annual election of directors or for the time as prescribed in the articles of incorporation or the bylaws. Thereafter, directors are elected or appointed in the manner stated in the articles or in the bylaws.[11] Terms of office of directors need not be uniform.[12] Each director holds office until the director's successor is elected or appointed.[13]

A majority of the number of directors fixed by the bylaws or by the articles of incorporation generally constitutes a quorum for the transaction of business.[14] The Model Nonprofit Corporation Act provides that the articles of incorporation or the bylaws can provide otherwise but in no event can a quorum be less than one-third of the number of directors.[15] An act of the majority of the directors present at a meeting at which a quorum is present constitutes an act of the board of directors unless the articles or bylaws provide for a greater number.[16]

---

8 Mod. Nonprofit Corp. Act § 17 (1964).

9 Mod. Nonprofit Corp. Act § 18 (1964) and Revised Model Nonprofit Corporation Act §8.03 (1987).

See Tex. Bus. Orgs. Code § 22.204(a), N.Y. Not-for-Profit Corp. Law § 702(a), and Wa. St. § 2404. The Washington nonprofit statute, Section 2404(2), provides that a nonprofit corporation must have three directors if the corporation is a public charity for tax purposes. See discussion and requirements for public charities in Chapter VIII.

California statutes provide that the bylaws establish the number of directors. See Cal. Corp. Code §§ 5151, 7151.

10 If there is no provision in the bylaws, the Model Nonprofit Corporation Act § 18, states the term is for one year. Revised Model Nonprofit Corporation Act § 8.05(a), states that the corporate articles or bylaws must specify the terms of directors and, except for designated or appointed directors, the term for each director may not exceed five years. It also states that if the articles or bylaws do not specify a term, the term for each director will be one year.

11 See e. g., the Mod. Nonprofit Corp. Act § 18 (1964) and the Rev. Mod. Nonprofit Corp. Act § 8.04.

12 Mod. Nonprofit Corp. Act § 18 (1964).

13 See Mod. Nonprofit Corp. Act § 18 (1964) and Rev. Mod. Nonprofit Corp. Act § 8.05(c) and (d).

14 Mod. Nonprofit Corp. Act § 20 (1964) and Rev. Mod. Nonprofit Corp. Act §8.24(b) (1987).

15 Mod. Nonprofit Corp. Act § 20 (1964).

16 Mod. Nonprofit Corp. Act § 20 (1964) and Rev. Mod. Nonprofit Corp. Act § 8.24(b) (1987).

1. Selection of the Governing Board

Members of a nonprofit corporation's governing board are elected or appointed in the manner and for the terms provided in the articles of incorporation or in the bylaws.[17] A vacancy occurring in the board is generally filled by vote of a majority of the remaining board members (directors), unless the articles or bylaws provide for some other method.[18] A director elected or appointed to fill a vacancy is elected or appointed for the unexpired term of that director's predecessor.[19]

Generally, any directorship to be filled because of an increase in the number of directors is filled by vote of a majority of the remaining directors.[20] However, statutes in some states provide instead that a directorship must be filled by election at either an annual meeting or a special meeting of members of the corporation.[21] If a corporation does not have members, or members do not have a right to vote, the directorship is then filled as provided for in the articles of incorporation or in the bylaws.[22]

2. Meetings of a Governing Board

Meetings of the governing board, whether regular or special meetings, may be held within or without the state of incorporation.[23] Attendance of a director at any meeting constitutes a waiver of notice of the meeting except when a director

17 Mod. Nonprofit Corp. Act § 18 (1964) and Rev. Mod. Nonprofit Corp. Act § 8.05 (1987).

18 See e.g., Mod. Nonprofit Corp. Act § 19 (1964).

19 Mod. Nonprofit Corp. Act § 19 (1964).

20 See, Mod. Nonprofit Corp. Act § 19 (1964)

See N.Y. Not-for-Profit Corp. Law § 705(a); Ariz. Rev. Stat. Ann. § 10-71(D).

21 California statutes provide that once members have been admitted, a bylaw changing a fixed number of directors or changing from a fixed to a variable board, or vice versa, can only be adopted by approval of the members. Cal. Corp. Code §§ 5151, 7151.

22 See. e.g., Tex. Bus. Orgs. Code § 22.206, which provides that directors other than the initial directors are elected or appointed in the manner provided by the certificate of formation or bylaws. If there is no provision in the certificate of formation or bylaws for the election of directors, directors other than the initial directors are elected by the board of directors.

23 Mod. Nonprofit Corp. Act § 22 (1964) and Rev. Mod. Nonprofit Corp. Act § 8.20(b) (1987).

See Tex. Bus. Orgs. Code § 22.217, which states that regular meetings of the board of directors may be held with or without notice as prescribed by the bylaws. See also Cal. Corp. Code §§ 5211(a)(5), 7211(a)(5) and N.Y. Not-for-Profit Corp. Law § 710.

attends a meeting for the express purpose of objecting to the transaction of any business at that meeting because the meeting was not lawfully called or convened.[24] Some states provide that regular board meetings may be held without notice.[25] Special meetings are held upon notice prescribed in the bylaws.[26]

3. Management of A Nonprofit Hospital Corporation

The activities and affairs of a nonprofit corporation are conducted, and all corporate powers are exercised, under direction of the governing board.[27] Courts have stated that bylaw provisions that vest in the governing board of a nonprofit corporation the right to manage the corporation affairs and even to control the election of successors to the board, do not infringe upon any property or other enforceable right of the members, if any.[28] Courts have ruled that it is

---

24 See Mod. Nonprofit Corp. Act § 22 (1964). The Rev. Mod. Nonprofit Corp. Act § 8.23(b) (1987) provides that a director's attendance at or participation in a meeting waives any required notice of the meeting unless the director objects to lack of notice and does not thereafter vote for or assent to the objected to action.

25 See Tex. Bus. Orgs. Code § 22.217(a); Cal. Corp. Code §§ 5211(a)(2), 7211(a)(2); N.Y. Not-for-Profit Corp. Law § 711(a).

26 See, e.g., Tex. Bus. Orgs. Code § 22.217(b).

27 See Mod. Nonprofit Corp. Act § 17 (1964). See also Cal. Corp. Code §§ 5210, 7210; N.Y. Not-for-Profit Corp. Law § 701; and Tex. Bus. Orgs. Code § 22.201.

The Rev. Mod. Nonprofit Corp. Act § 8.01(c) (1987) and the New York statute provide that the articles may authorize a person or persons to exercise some or all of the powers that would otherwise be exercised by a board. These acts provide that this person or persons shall then have the duties and responsibilities of the directors. The Revised Model Act provides that the directors will be relieved from duties and responsibilities to the extent thus delegated.

28 In New Orleans Opera Ass'n, Inc. v. Southern Regional Opera Endowment Fund, 993 So. 2d 791 (La. Ct. App. 4th Cir. 2008), writ denied, 996 So. 2d 1114 (La. 2008), the court ruled that while an endowment fund's board of directors had the power to amend its articles of incorporation for internal governance, the board did not have a right to amend its articles to alter the exclusive third-party beneficiary status of its founder. The court noted decisions in which Louisiana courts had ruled that a corporate charter, or articles of incorporation, is a contract between the corporation and its shareholders (for profit corporations) and that it forms a contractual relationship between the shareholders themselves, which sets forth rights, obligations, and liabilities. The court stated Louisiana has always viewed a corporate charter as contractual in nature. The court ruled the purpose of the corporation must be ascertained from the collective will of the natural persons who created it.

See also Bailey v. American Soc. for Prevention of Cruelty to Animals, 282 A.D. 502, 125 N.Y.S.2d 18 (1st Dept. 1953), judgment aff'd, 307 N.Y. 679, 120 N.E.2d 853 (1954), and Brown v. Giuffre, 548 S.W.2d 102 (Tex. Civ. App. Houston 1st Dist. 1977).

not unlawful, arbitrary or unreasonable for the governing board of a nonprofit corporation to be granted these powers.[29]

As a general rule, the governing board may delegate management of activities of a corporation to committees, but all activities and affairs of the corporation must be managed, and all corporate power exercised, under the ultimate direction of the board.[30] The board may designate and appoint committees if the articles or the bylaws so provide and if the board appoints the committees by resolution adopted by a majority of the board members (directors).[31] Still, these committees may not exercise extraordinary powers, such as appointing or removing members, altering bylaws, amending or restating the articles of incorporation, selling, purchasing, leasing or mortgaging property, or adopting a plan of merger, consolidation or of corporate dissolution.[32]

For those states that do not have provisions authorizing the governing board to delegate its management powers, or for those that do not have a similar provision providing for delegation of board authority, there is some question about the authority of a board of a nonprofit organization to delegate its duties. If a governing board is subject to the more restrictive delegation rules applicable to trusts, a board's delegation of its duties is limited.[33]

4. Action of the Governing Board

All corporate action to be taken by the governing board generally requires action at a meeting of the board. The vote of a majority of directors present at the time of the vote, if a quorum is present at that time, is the act of the board.[34] Directors acting separately and not collectively as a board cannot bind the corporation.[35]

---

29 See discussion in In re Mt. Sinai Hospital, 250 N.Y. 103, 164 N.E. 871 (1928) and Brown v. Giuffre, 548 S.W.2d 102 (Tex. Civ. App. Houston 1st Dist. 1977).

30 See e. g., Cal. Corp. Code §§ 5210, 7210.

31 See Mod. Nonprofit Corp. Act § 21 (1964) and Rev. Mod. Nonprofit Corp. Act § 8.25 (1987).

32 Mod. Nonprofit Corp. Act § 21 (1964).

33 The Uniform Prudent Management of Institutional Funds Act, which has been adopted by all but one of the states, provides in its Section 5 that boards of nonprofit organizations can delegate to committees, officers, or employees, or to outside agents, including investment counsel, the authority to act in place of the board in investment and reinvestment of institutional funds.

34 See, e. g., N.Y. Not-for-Profit Corp. Law § 708; Cal. Corp. Code §§ 5211(a)(8), 7211(a)(8); and Tex. Bus. Orgs. Code § 22.214.

35 See, e.g., discussion in Bayer v. Beran, 49 N.Y.S.2d 2 (Sup 1944).

The articles or bylaws may provide that participation in a meeting of the board may be by means of a conference telephone or similar communications equipment that permits all persons participating in the meeting to hear each other at the same time. If the condition is met, participation by these means constitutes presence in person at a meeting.[36]

5. Removal of Directors of the Governing Board

A board member generally may be removed from office pursuant to any procedure provided for in the articles of incorporation,[37] but normally only if the number of votes cast to remove the director would be sufficient to elect the director.[38] Most states require that a special meeting must be called for these purposes and require notice of the meeting to state the purpose(s).[39] A governing board generally may remove a director without cause if the director was elected by a vote of the directors then in office.[40] If the court finds that the director engaged in fraudulent conduct or grossly abused the director's authority or discretion, states that have adopted the Revised Model Nonprofit Corporation Act permit a director to be removed by a court in a proceeding commenced either by the corporation, its members holding at least ten percent of the voting power, or the attorney general in the case of a public benefit corporation.[41] New York statutes have provided that any or all of the directors can be removed for cause by vote of the members or by vote of the directors provided there is a quorum of not less than a majority present at the meeting of directors at which the action is taken.[42] Further, if the certificate of incorporation or the bylaws provide, a director can be removed without cause by vote of the members.[43] Pennsylvania

36 See e. g., Cal. Corp. Code §§ 5211(a)(6) and N.Y. Not-for-Profit Corp. Law § 708(c).

37 See Mod. Nonprofit Corp. Act § 18 (1964).

38 See requirement set out in Rev. Mod. Nonprofit Corp. Act § 8.08(c).

39 Rev. Mod. Nonprofit Corp. Act § 8.08(e).

40 Rev. Mod. Nonprofit Corp. Act § 8.08(h).

41 Rev. Mod. Nonprofit Corp. Act § 8.10.

42 N.Y. Not-for-Profit Corp. Law § 706. Section 706 provides that an action to procure a judgment removing a director for cause can be brought by the attorney general or by ten percent of the members whether or not entitled to vote. The court can bar from reelection any director so removed for a period fixed by the court.

43 N.Y. Not-for-Profit Corp. Law § 706(b).

statutes have provided that, unless the articles or bylaws provide otherwise, the entire board of directors or any individual director can be removed from office, without assigning any cause, by a majority vote of the qualified voting members.[44] New directors could be elected at the same meeting.[45] California statutes provide that directors can be removed without cause if members approved the action or, in a corporation without members, if it is approved by a majority of the directors then in office.[46] Arizona statutes provide that a member can bring charges against a director by fling the charges in writing with the secretary together with a petition for removal signed by ten percent of the members.[47] Removal must be voted upon at the next regular meeting or at a special meeting. For a nonprofit corporation that has members, the members can remove a director at the special meeting by a majority vote. The director must be informed in writing of the charges prior to the meeting and the director is entitled to be heard in person or by counsel. The director can also call witnesses.[48]

The general rule is that a corporation possesses the inherent power to remove a director for cause, regardless of the presence of a provision in the charter or bylaws.[49] However, in the absence of some provision in the charter or in the state statutes, a director generally cannot be removed or suspended from office without cause until the end of the director's term.[50]

44 See Pa. Stat. Ann. tit.15, § 5726, which states that unless provided otherwise in the bylaws, the governing board can declare vacant an office of a director if the director has been declared of unsound mind by order of the court or has been convicted of a felony, or for any other proper cause specified in the bylaws, or if, within sixty days after notice of selection, the director does not accept the office either in writing or by attending a meeting of the directors. A court can remove a director in case of fraudulent or dishonest acts, or gross abuse of authority or discretion with reference to the corporation, or for any other proper cause upon petition of any member or director. The corporation is made a party to the action.

45 Pa. Stat. Ann. tit. 15, § 5726(a).

46 Cal. Corp. Code §§ 5222, 7222.

47 Ariz. Rev. Stat. Ann. § 10-713.

48 Ariz. Rev. Stat. Ann. § 10-713.

49 See, e.g., decision in Grace v. Grace Institute, 19 N.Y.2d 307, 279 N.Y.S.2d 721, 226 N.E.2d 531 (1967).

50 In Kirby v. Oatts, 151 N.E. 3d 1083 (Ohio 2020), an original board of trustees of a home association had brought an action after a board election against a dissident board for declaratory relief declaring the election valid and to prevent the dissident board from acting as trustees. The Supreme Court of Ohio determined that the original board request for declaratory relief was in the nature of a quo warranto action and thus the Court of Common Pleas lacked subject-matter jurisdiction to consider the request. The Ohio Supreme Court stated that a quo warranto action was the proper and exclusive remedy for determining the legal right of an officer of an incorporated nonprofit association to hold office. The court noted that in a quo warranto action against a person for usurping a corporate

6. General Duties of Directors of a Governing Board

Directors of corporations are fiduciaries and, as such, are subject to a duty of care and a duty of loyalty. Still, the duties of directors are less strict than those required of trustees.[51] Lesser standards have been applied to the corporate director based upon the theory that corporate directors have many areas of responsibility.[52] Trustees, on the other hand, generally are charged only with management of trust funds and can devote more time and expertise to the task.[53] Although corporate directors are held to lesser standards than are trustees, directors, as fiduciaries, have a status similar to that of trustees.[54] A director must act for the benefit of members of the corporation, and, in the case of a nonprofit corporation, for the benefit of the public.[55]

---

office, a court would render judgment on the rights of the claimants to that office and would oust and exclude a usurper from the office. The court pointed out that jurisdiction for quo warranto actions is exclusively vested in the courts of appeals and in the Supreme Court.

In Collins v. Beinecke, 67 N.Y.2d 479, 504 N.Y.S.2d 72, 495 N.E.2d 335 (1986), the officers of a foundation were the officers and directors of the foundation's creator corporation from which the foundation received its sole financial support. A substantial portion of the foundation's grants benefitted the corporation's employees and many of its charitable programs were continuations of programs established and conducted by the corporation. Another corporation purchased all the stock of the creator corporation, including all the stock of the defendants in the case. The directors refused to resign as directors of the foundation. The court ruled that although it had been the practice that officers and directors of the creator corporation would serve as directors of the foundation, customs and practices of the past are not enough to impose a fiduciary duty upon the defendants to resign. In the absence of evidence that the defendants had misused foundation assets or a showing that their acts were "unfair, oppressive or manifestly detrimental to the foundation's interests," the court decided there is no basis for an invocation of the court's equitable power to annul the defendants' acts nor to interfere in the legal relationship that the parties had structured for themselves.

51 Stern v. Lucy Webb Hayes Nat. Training School for Deaconesses and Missionaries, 381 F. Supp. 1003 (D.D.C. 1974).

52 Id.

53 Id.

54 See Supreme Court opinion in Pepper v. Litton, 308 U.S. 295 (1939).

55 See, e.g., Christiansen v. National Sav. and Trust Co., 683 F.2d 520 (D.C. Cir. 1982), wherein the Court of Appeals for the District of Columbia ruled that the fiduciary duties of a corporate director run to the corporation, and not directly to its members or to the public.

In Carlson v. Rabkin, 152 Ohio App. 3d 672, 789 N.E.2d 1122 (1st Dist. Hamilton County 2003), the court ruled that members of Save the Animals Foundation stated a prima facie case against directors of the corporation in the members' request to examine the foundation's books and records. The board of directors denied their requests, contending the members did not have "reasonable and proper purposes" for making the requests. The court noted the distinction between a member's direct action and a derivative action, commenting that when members bring a derivative cause of action against a nonprofit corporation, they are enforcing a corporate right just as shareholders may do in a for-profit corporation. The court set out the requirements for maintaining a derivative action. A court must look at the nature of the alleged wrong rather than the designation used by the plaintiffs to determine whether the claim is a direct claim, one

a. Duty of Care

The duty of care requires that directors exercise reasonable skills in the exercise of their responsibilities. A director should exercise the same care and skill that an ordinarily prudent person would exercise under similar circumstances in the director's personal affairs. While this duty is like a trustee's duty of care, a corporate director has broader discretion than does a trustee.[56] A director may delegate to officers or to committees the operation of the corporation. Further, while directors are liable for negligence in the performance of their duties, a "business judgment rule" affirms that directors are not insurers and are not liable for errors of judgment or for mistakes if they act with reasonable skill and prudence.[57]

---

that affects the plaintiff members individually, or is a derivative action, one that states an injury which indirectly affects the members. The court affirmed that claims for breach of fiduciary duties on the part of corporate directors or officers are brought in derivative suits because the damage that results from the fraudulent or negligent management of the corporation primarily is damage to the corporation and to the corporate assets. The derivation action affects members only indirectly and all of them alike. A member's statutory right to inspect the books and records of a nonprofit corporation, upon written demand stating a reasonable and proper purpose, is a direct claim, not a derivative one. The rights of members to demand an accounting, to call a special membership meeting, or to be compensated for a wrongful exclusion from the organization implicate individual rights of the members. The court decided that plaintiffs who were current members of the organization successfully stated claims against the directors to inspect the organization's books and records and to receive an accounting of the organization's transactions; the court denied claims of former members.

See Tex. Bus. Orgs. Code § 22.353, which provides that financial information of a nonprofit corporation is available for public inspection; however, a nonprofit corporation's books and records are not available to the public if the corporation solicits funds only from members of the corporation.

56 Discussion of the duties of directors of nonprofit corporations in Stern v. Lucy Webb Hayes Nat. Training School for Deaconesses and Missionaries, 381 F. Supp. 1003 (D.D.C. 1974).

57 The standard of care and loyalty prescribed for directors of nonprofit corporations under the Rev. Mod. Nonprofit Corp. Act § 8.30 adopts a form of the business judgment rule for directors and officers of nonprofit corporations.

The business judgment rule evolved from a determination that to make a corporation function effectively, those having management responsibility must have the freedom to make in good faith the many necessary decisions quickly and finally without the impairment of having to be liable for an honest error in judgment. Courts generally have held that in actions contesting directors' actions covered by the business judgment rule, a plaintiff has the burden of showing the director or officer failed to act in good faith, failed to act in a manner the director reasonably believed to be in the best interest of the corporation, or failed to exercise such care as an ordinarily prudent person in a like position would use in similar circumstances. See discussion by Court of Appeals of the Tenth Circuit in Financial Industrial Fund, Inc. v. McDonnell Douglas Corp., 474 F.2d 514 (10th Cir. 1973). The business judgment rule provides that directors or officers of a corporation will not be held liable for errors or mistakes in judgment, pertaining to law or fact, when they have acted on a matter calling for the exercise of their judgment or discretion if they have used their best judgment and have acted in good faith.

In Evans v. Armour & Co., 241 F. Supp. 705 (E.D. Pa. 1965), a court decided the business judgment rule does not conflict with the concept of negligence. When a court refuses to interfere in matters of business judgment, the court presupposed that in exercising that judgment, the director or officer exercised diligence.

The liability of corporate directors for damages caused by negligent or unauthorized acts rests upon the common law rule that renders every agent liable who violates the agent's authority or neglects a duty to the damage of his principal.[58] By accepting the office, directors implicitly undertake to give their best judgment to the enterprise.[59] Courts have ruled that acceptance of the office of director implies a knowledge of the duties assumed and that directors will not be excused because of their lack of experience or ability.[60] However, courts have also ruled that directors are not responsible for mere errors of judgment or want of care short of clear and gross negligence.[61] Directors have some protection for their negligent acts when they act under advice of counsel.[62]

b. Duty of loyalty

The duty of loyalty for a corporate director requires that a director not exploit corporate opportunities or misuse inside information. Only reasonable salaries may be paid board members, and often directors serve without compensation. A board member must account to the corporation for any profits received because of the directorship. A director may not obtain a private or secret profit because

---

In Oberbillig v. West Grand Towers Condominium Ass'n, 807 N.W.2d 143 (Iowa 2011), the Supreme Court of Iowa ruled the business judgment rule requires judicial deference to an association's exercise of its interpretive authority over an ambiguous bylaw. The court ruled that the "heart of the business judgment rule" is "judicial deference to business decisions by corporate directors."

58 See Robinson v. Linfield College, 42 F. Supp. 147 (E.D. Wash. 1941), judgment aff'd, 136 F.2d 805 (9th Cir. 1943).

59 In Pheasant Hills Eldridge Condominium Owners and Facilities Ass'n v. Ray, 886 N.W.2d 616 (Iowa Ct. App. 2016), the court ruled the business judgment rule required the court to defer to a homeowners' association's interpretation of its bylaws. The court stated the business judgment rule, absent a showing of self-dealing or conflict of interest, severely limits the second guessing of business decisions made by those whom a corporation has chosen to make these interpretations.

60 See, e. g., Minton v. Cavaney, 15 Cal. Rptr. 641, 364 P.2d 473 (1961) and Neese v. Brown, 218 Tenn. 686, 405 S.W.2d 577 (1964).

61 Bennett v. Propp, 41 Del. Ch. 14, 187 A.2d 405 (1962) and Hornstein v. Paramount Pictures, 292 N.Y. 468, 55 N.E.2d 740 (1944).

62 See e.g., opinion by the Court of Appeals for the Second Circuit in Spirt v. Bechtel, 232 F.2d 241 (2d Cir. 1956).

See also Rev. Mod. Nonprofit Corp. Act § 8.30(b) (1987).

The New Jersey Nonprofit Corporation Act, N.J. Rev. Stat. § 15A:6-14, provides that a trustee of a nonprofit corporation will not be liable if the trustee, in good faith, relies on the advice of counsel for the corporation, upon written reports setting forth the financial data concerning the corporation and prepared by independent certified public accountants, or upon financial statements presented to them as being correct by officers of the corporation.

of the director's official position.[63] The corporation must have the benefit of any advantage the director has acquired.[64]

A conflict-of-interest transaction is one in which a director of a corporation has a direct or indirect interest. An indirect interest as one in which another entity, in which the director has a material interest or in which the director is a general partner or a director, officer or trustee, is a party to the transaction.[65] For public benefit corporations, a conflict-of-interest transaction is generally not voidable or the basis for imposing liability on the director if the transaction was fair at the time it was entered into or if it was approved (a) in advance by the vote of the board of directors or a committee of the board when all material facts of the transaction and the director's interest were either disclosed or were known by the board or committee of the board and the director approving the transaction reasonably believed the transaction was fair to the corporation or (b) before or after it was consummated by obtaining approval of the attorney general or a court in which the attorney general was joined as a party.[66]

Although the corporate standard does not impose liability upon a director of a nonprofit corporation for a conflict-of-interest transaction if the transaction is fair to the corporation and the board was aware of all material facts relating to the transaction, those charitable organizations that are private foundations for tax purposes are nonetheless subject to substantial tax penalties for engaging in any form of conflict-of-interest transaction.[67]

The purchase or lease of corporate property by an officer or director is voidable,[68] and courts have ruled that a director may assert a fairness defense to a charge of self-dealing.[69] Nonetheless, courts have upheld conflict of interest transactions only if they are indeed fair and are for a sufficient consideration.[70]

---

63 See general standards of conduct requirements in Rev. Mod. Nonprofit Corp. Act §§ 8.30 to 8:33.

64 See Flynn v. Zimmerman, 23 Ill. App. 2d 467, 163 N.E.2d 568 (2d Dist. 1960) and Knox Glass Bottle Co. v. Underwood, 228 Miss. 699, 89 So. 2d 799 (1956).

65 See Rev. Mod. Nonprofit Corp. Act § 8.31(d).

66 This is the rule in states that have adopted the Revised Model Nonprofit Corporation Act. See Rev. Mod. Nonprofit Corp. Act § 8.31(b).

67 See self-dealing concept as applied to private foundations in Chapter VIII.

68 Oberhelman v. Barnes Inv. Corp., 236 Kan. 335, 690 P.2d 1343 (1984).

69 Johnston v. Greene, 35 Del. Ch. 479, 121 A.2d 919 (1956) and Wiberg v. Gulf Coast Land & Development Co., 360 S.W.2d 563 (Tex. Civ. App. Beaumont 1962), writ refused n.r.e., (1963).

70 See, e.g., the opinion of the Supreme Court of Wyoming in Voss Oil Co. v. Voss, 367 P.2d 977 (Wyo. 1962).

The presumption is against validity, and courts apply a more stringent test to determine fairness.[71]

Some courts have ruled that a corporate director cannot not cast a vote upon a matter in which the director had an adverse interest;[72] however, there has been some support that a vote of an interested director, while not necessarily valid, can be counted in favor of a transaction between the director and the corporation if the transaction appears to be fair and is characterized in good faith.[73]

A corporate director is under a fiduciary obligation not to divert a corporate business opportunity for the director's own personal gain.[74] This "corporate opportunity doctrine" is a species of the duty of a fiduciary to act with undivided loyalty to the corporation. Some courts have explained that the doctrine charges any interest acquired by a director with a trust for the benefit of the corporation.[75] The theory is that an insider should not use an inside position to benefit the insider by seizing an investment opportunity available to and suitable for the corporation. The doctrine operates because the corporation is not given the opportunity to engage in a potentially beneficial transaction.[76]

---

71 See Geominerals Corp. v. Grace, 232 Ark. 524, 338 S.W.2d 935 (1960), and Alcott v. Hyman, 42 Del. Ch. 233, 208 A.2d 501 (1965).

72 See Weiss Medical Complex, Ltd. v. Kim, 87 Ill. App. 3d 111, 408 N.E.2d 959 (1st Dist. 1980) and Davis v. Heath Development Co., 558 P.2d 594 (Utah 1976).

73 See discussion in Sterling v. Mayflower Hotel Corp., 33 Del. Ch. 293, 93 A.2d 107 (1952) and Application of Burkin,154 N.Y.S.2d 898, 136 N.E.2d 862 (1956).

74 In Northeast Harbor Golf Club, Inc. v. Harris, 1999 ME 38, 725 A.2d 1018 (Me. 1999), the Supreme Court of Maine discussed "corporate opportunity" in the context of a nonprofit corporation, deciding that even if an officer or director does not learn of an opportunity to engage in a business activity through the involvement of the officer or director in business of the corporation, an opportunity still may be considered a corporate opportunity if the officer or director knows the opportunity is closely related to a business in which the corporation is engaged or expects to engage. In stating that there is a strict requirement of full disclosure prior to taking advantage of any corporate opportunity, the court commented that full disclosure is important to prevent individual directors and officers from using their own "unfettered judgment" to determine whether a business opportunity is related to the corporation's business and, thus, would be in the corporate interest to take advantage of the opportunity.

75 In Matter of Safety Intern., Inc., 775 F.2d 660 (5th Cir. 1985), the Court of Appeals for the Fifth Circuit ruled the doctrine is applied in Texas if a corporation has a legitimate interest or expectancy in, and financial resources to take advantage of, a business opportunity. If a director diverts a business opportunity to the director, it is a breach of the duty of loyalty.

76 The Uniform Trust Code § 802(e) provided that there is a conflict between personal and fiduciary interests if a trustee engages in a transaction not concerning trust property that concerns an opportunity properly belonging to the trust.

If a corporate director obtains a business opportunity in the director's individual capacity, rather than the director's official capacity, and the opportunity is one that is not essential to the corporation nor one in which the corporation has no interest or expectancy, the director is entitled to treat the opportunity as the director's individual business opportunity.[77] The test in determining whether a corporate officer has appropriated a corporate opportunity is whether there was a specific duty on the part of the director to act or contract as a representative of the corporation.[78]

The law relating to a corporate director's duty regarding use of inside information is not well defined. Some courts consider inside information to be a corporate asset, and under some state law and under federal law, a director's duty relating to the use of insider information is a higher duty, resembling the stricter duty applicable to trustees.[79] Federal statutes provide that directors and shareholders of for-profit corporations, who have at least ten percent ownership in the corporation, must return to the corporation all profits derived from sales and purchases or purchases and sales of equity securities of the corporation occurring within a six-month period.[80] Liability attaches regardless of the intention of the insider.[81] Although this rule generally is not a part of state law, some states have adopted the concept.[82]

---

77 See, Equity Corp. v. Milton, 42 Del. Ch. 425, 213 A.2d 439 (1965), aff'd, 43 Del. Ch. 160, 221 A.2d 494 (1966); Tower Recreation, Inc. v. Beard, 141 Ind. App. 649, 231 N.E.2d 154 (1967); Miller v. Miller, 301 Minn. 207, 222 N.W.2d 71 (1974); and Klinicki v. Lundgren, 298 Or. 662, 695 P.2d 906 (1985).

78 See, Northwestern Terra Cotta Corp. v. Wilson, 74 Ill. App. 2d 38, 219 N.E.2d 860 (1st Dist. 1966); and Peterson Welding Supply Co., Inc. v. Cryogas Products, Inc., 126 Ill. App. 3d 759, 467 N.E.2d 1068 (1st Dist. 1984). According to the Illinois courts, a corporate opportunity exists when a proposed activity is reasonably incident to the corporation's present or prospective business and is one in which the corporation has the capacity to engage. An opportunity must have been in the line of the corporation's business and of a practical advantage to it.

79 See Securities Exchange Act, § 16(b); 15 U.S.C.A. §§ 8j(b), 78p.

80 Securities Exchange Act § 16(b); 15 U.S.C.A. §78p.

81 See discussion by the Court of Appeals for the Ninth Circuit in National Medical Enterprises, Inc. v. Small, 680 F.2d 83 (9th Cir. 1982).

82 In Diamond v. Oreamuno, 301 N.Y.S.2d 78, 248 N.E.2d 910 (1969) (rejected by Frankel v. Slotkin, 795 F. Supp. 76 (E.D. N.Y. 1992)), a New York court ruled that inside information of a corporate officer or director is an asset of the corporation, acquired by the insider as a fiduciary of the company. The court held that a misappropriation of insider information is a violation of that trust, quoting the well-established rule that a person, who acquires special knowledge or information because of the person's fiduciary relationship with another, is not free to exploit that knowledge or information for his/her own personal benefit but must account to the person's principal for any profits derived from use of the information. The court then likened a corporate director to a trustee in this regard and stated that "just as a trustee has no right to retain for himself the profits yielded by property placed

The requirements to obtain and maintain federal tax-exempt status for nonprofit organizations, set out in Chapters VII and VIII, present a type of federal standard of care for those nonprofit corporations that are tax exempt.

Members of a governing board (directors) who serve voluntarily on a hospital board may have immunity from liability. Congress enacted the Volunteer Protection Act,[83] following a determination that volunteers were discouraged from offering their services because of potential liability actions against them. The Volunteer Protection Act provides that no volunteer of a nonprofit organization or governmental entity will be liable for harm caused by an act or omission of the volunteer on behalf of the organization or entity if: (1) the volunteer was acting within the scope of his or her responsibilities in the nonprofit organization at time of the act or omission; (2) the volunteer was properly licensed, certified, or authorized (if appropriate or required) by the appropriate authorities for activities or practice in the state in which the harm occurred; (3) the harm was not caused by willful or criminal misconduct, gross negligence, reckless misconduct, or conscious, flagrant indifference to the rights or safety of the individual harmed by the volunteer; and (4) the harm was not caused by the volunteer operating a motor vehicle, vessel, aircraft, or other vehicle for which the state requires an operator's license or insurance. If the volunteer is found liable for harm caused an individual, the volunteer will be liable only for the amount of noneconomic loss allocated to the volunteer in direct proportion to the percentage of responsibility of the volunteer. There generally is no liability for punitive damages. The federal act preempts laws of any state to the extent

---

in his possession but must account to his beneficiaries, a corporate fiduciary, who is entrusted with potentially valuable information, may not appropriate that asset for his use even though, in so doing, he causes no injury to the corporation."

In Schein v. Chasen, 313 So. 2d 739 (Fla. 1975), the Supreme Court of Florida refused to extend what it termed the "innovative ruling" of the New York court in Diamond v. Oreamuno to someone who gave a tip of insider information. The court stated that the Diamond doctrine applied only to corporate fiduciaries who profit by insider information and should not cover inside aiders, abettors, or conspirators. The Florida Supreme Court commented that the Diamond rule was a significant alteration of common-law principles applicable to directors.

In Freeman v. Decio, 584 F.2d 186 (7th Cir. 1978), the Court of Appeals for the Seventh Circuit, applying Indiana law, refused to permit a suit by shareholders against corporate officers and directors for alleged illegal trading of corporate stock because of material insider information. The court opined that it would be better to determine whether there is any potential loss to the corporation from the use of insider information before deciding to characterize insider information as an asset with respect to which the insider owes the corporation a duty of loyalty. The court stated that courts should look first as to whether there was a possibility of a loss to the corporation before holding a director accountable to the corporation.

83 42 U.S.C. § 14501.

that such laws are inconsistent, but the act does not preempt any state law that provides additional protection from liability for volunteers.

Despite having immunity for their actions, members of a hospital governing body should nonetheless be familiar with the general provisions of applicable state statutes, such as the following requirements and prohibitions, to discharge properly their duties to the hospital. State statutes generally prohibit loans to directors and officers and prohibit distribution of income to members, directors, or officers except for payment of reasonable compensation. Should directors dissolve a nonprofit corporation, directors must consult state provisions regarding disposition of assets so that they do not wrongfully distribute organization resources. If the hospital is a tax-exempt organization, assets must be distributed to another § 501(c)(3) organization upon dissolution.[84] For a § 501(c)(3) organization that is also a private foundation for tax purposes, directors must follow requirements of Internal Revenue Code (I.R.C.) § 507 prior to dissolution.[85] Directors should acquire a basic level of understanding of financial reports and should require the organization to maintain accurate books and records. Directors should attend meetings and review minutes and other documents. Should a director object to a decision of a majority of the board, the director should note the objection in writing.

Directors should avoid any form of self-dealing.[86] If a director has an interest in a transaction with the nonprofit organization, the director should note that interest. The transaction must be fair and reasonable, and the interested director should not attempt to influence other members of the board. If the organization is a private foundation for tax purposes, the director must avoid having any transactions with the foundation. For hospitals that are § 501(c)(3) public charity, transactions with persons who are in a position to exercise substantial influence over the affairs of the hospital should be carefully monitored to assure these persons have no "excess benefits" from the transactions. Documentation as to the reasonableness of each compensation package for highly paid employees should be obtained.[87]

84 Discussion of 501(c)(3) organizations is in Chapter VII.

85 See discussion of private foundations, including the procedures to dissolve a private foundation that are set out in I.R.C. § 507, in Chapter VIII. As noted in Chapter VIII, failure to meet Code requirements relating to private foundations can subject a foundation and/or its managers and donors to substantial penalty taxes.

86 Discussion of self-dealing is in Chapter VIII.

87 Discussion of excess benefit transactions is in Chapter VIII.

Directors must make certain all tax returns are timely filed. Directors should also review the hospital's commercial activities to determine whether the hospital has unrelated business income, discussed in Chapter IX, that would subject the organization to income tax liability. Directors should make certain all social security and income taxes are properly withheld from salaries to employees and that quarterly returns are properly filed with payments timely made to the IRS.[88] Directors should be familiar with provisions relating to tax-exempt status and should carefully monitor the hospital's activities so that the hospital can maintain that status. Directors should establish and monitor fair and nondiscriminatory personnel policies and should obtain opinions of legal counsel and accountants where needed.[89]

C. MEMBERS OF A HOSPITAL NONPROFIT CORPORATION

A nonprofit corporation may have one or more classes of members or no members.[90] If the corporation has members, the designation of the class of membership, the manner of election or appointment, and the qualifications and rights of the members of each class must be set out in the articles of incorporation or in

88 In Jefferson v. U.S., 546 F.3d 477 (7th Cir. 2008), the Seventh Circuit Court of Appeals ruled that the president of the board of directors of a day care center would be liable for the center's federal employment and withholding back taxes even though the president served as a voluntary and uncompensated board president. The court found that the president had significant involvement in the center's financial affairs, including writing checks for the organization. The president had also directed payment of the taxes in the past. The president was assessed a penalty tax of $41,432 for taxes the day care center failed to pay.

The Internal Revenue Service (IRS) ruled in Rev. Rul. 84-83, 1984-1 CB 264, that directors of nonprofit organizations can be personally liable for unpaid employment taxes. However, pursuant to the Taxpayer Bill of Rights 2, Congress amended Section 6672 of the Internal Revenue Code (I.R.C.) to provide that volunteer board members of tax-exempt organization will be exempt from the penalty for failure to collect and pay over employment taxes if the volunteer is: (a) serving solely in an honorary capacity, (b) does not participate in the day-to-day financial operations of the organization, and (c) does not have actual knowledge of the failure on which the penalty was imposed. The exemption does not apply, however, if it results in no person being liable for the penalty tax. See I.R.C. § 6672(e).

89 Discussion of personnel employment issues below. Discussion of the tax-exempt status of a hospital and its related or affiliated organizations in Chapters VII and VIII.

90 See, Mod. Nonprofit Corp. Act § 11 (1964) and Rev. Mod. Nonprofit Corp. Act §§ 6.03 and 6.10 (1987).

the bylaws.[91] If the corporation has no members, that fact must also be stated in the articles or the bylaws.[92]

Courts have ruled that, although a nonprofit membership corporation is a corporate entity, members in nonprofit corporations are treated much the same as members in unincorporated associations and have applied the same rules concerning members to these two structural forms.[93] A member of a nonprofit corporation generally does not acquire a severable right to any of the property or funds of the corporation, but rather merely a right to the joint use and enjoyment of the corporate property and only so long as the person continues to be a member.[94] If a member withdraws from or abandons the nonprofit corporation, the membership can generally be terminated, and should a member have a right to share in the corporation's property, upon dissolution, that right will

91 Mod. Nonprofit Corp. Act §11 (1964) and Rev. Mod. Nonprofit Corp. Act §6.10 (1987).

The Rev. Mod. Nonprofit Corp. Act § 6.21 (1987) provides that a member may not be expelled or suspended except pursuant to a fair and reasonable procedure carried out in good faith.

Arizona statutes provide that members have the same rights unless the articles or bylaws establish classes of members with differing rights and obligations. See Ariz. Rev. Stat. Ann. §10-3610.

New York's Not-for-Profit Corp. Law § 601(e) provides for termination of membership upon death, resignation, expulsion, expiration of a term of membership or dissolution or liquidation.

92 Mod. Nonprofit Corp. Act § 11 (1964).

93 See, e.g., Order of St. Benedict of New Jersey v. Steinhauser, 234 U.S. 640 (1914). See also Raulston v. Everett, 561 S.W.2d 635 (Tex. Civ. App. Texarkana 1978).

The unincorporated association is not a legal entity; thus, the rights and obligations of the association are the cumulative rights and obligations of its members. Courts have ruled that associations may enact provisions governing admission of members and may prescribe the necessary qualifications of its members. See, e.g., Martin v. Curran, 303 N.Y. 276, 101 N.E.2d 683 (1951), and Evans v. Southside Place Park Ass'n, 154 S.W.2d 914 (Tex. Civ. App. Galveston 1941), writ refused. Uniform laws on unincorporated associations that have been adopted by some states, provide rights similar to those for corporations for unincorporated associations and/or their members. For states that have not adopted laws providing the somewhat corporate status for unincorporated associations, members of an association may be held personally liable for contracts of the association and may be held personally liable for torts committed by an individual acting in the individual's capacity as an association member.

The nature of a trust precludes members. A trust is established to benefit its beneficiaries which, for a charitable trust, would be specifically named charities or the public.

94 See, e.g., decision by the Supreme Court of Minnesota in Liggett v. Koivunen, 227 Minn. 114, 34 N.W.2d 345 (1948).

In Dueck v. Clifton Club Company, 95 N.E.3d 1032 (Ohio Ct. App. 8th Dist. 2017), appeal not allowed, 152 Ohio St. 3d 1409, 92 N.E.3d 879 (2018), the court stated a membership nonprofit corporation is similar to an unincorporated association even though it is incorporated. The court decided a member of the corporation does not acquire a severable right to any of the corporation's property or funds, but rather merely a right to the joint use and enjoyment so long as the person remained a member. The court stated members are do not have any title to any of the corporation property. It ruled that members have a right to use the property, but that access is by permission and regulation of the trustees.

terminate. Those members remaining who succeed the withdrawing member become entitled to the withdrawing member's interest, if any.[95]

Some states permit corporations to become members of nonprofit corporations;[96] consequently, control through holding companies can occur. While most states prohibit nonprofit corporations from issuing shares of stock, a few states do permit nonprofit corporations stock ownership.[97]

The right of members to vote may be limited, enlarged or denied to the extent provided for in the articles of incorporation or in the bylaws.[98] However, unless limited, each member, regardless of class, is entitled to one vote on each matter submitted to a vote of the members.[99] If the corporation provides that no members may vote, the directors have the sole voting power.[100] While courts have ruled that the right to vote is a property right for a shareholder of a business corporation,[101] the right to vote generally is not a vested right for a member of a nonprofit corporation.[102] Courts have ruled that the right of a member of a nonprofit corporation to vote is not constitutionally protected because a member of a nonprofit corporation does not have an interest in property of a nonprofit corporation.[103]

---

95 See Flanagan v. Benvie, 58 N.M. 525, 273 P.2d 381 (1954) and Raulston v. Everett, 561 S.W.2d 635 (Tex. Civ. App. Texarkana 1978).

A North Carolina statute, NC Gen. Stat. § 55A-29, protects members from denial of property rights to which they are entitled if they are expelled from membership.

California statutes provide that all rights of membership cease upon a member's death or dissolution unless the articles or bylaws provide otherwise. See Cal. Corp. Code §§ 5320, 7320.

96 See N.Y. Not-for-Profit Corp. Law § 601 and N.J. Rev. Stat. 15A:5-13. The New Jersey statute provides that if memberships are controlled by a corporate member, any memberships held by that corporation cannot be voted at any meeting.

97 See e.g., Pa. Stat. Ann. tit. 15, § 5752.

98 Mod. Nonprofit Corp. Act § 15 (1964).

99 Mod. Nonprofit Corp. Act § 15 (1964) and Rev. Mod. Nonprofit Corp. Act §7.21 (1987).

See Cal. Corp. Code §§ 5610, 7610.

100 Mod. Nonprofit Corp. Act § 15 (1964).

101 See, e.g., McLain v. Lanova Corp., 28 Del. Ch. 176, 39 A.2d 209 (1944), Drob v. National Memorial Park, 28 Del. Ch. 254, 41 A.2d 589 (1945), Reimer v. Smith, 105 Fla. 671, 142 So. 603 (1932), and Lord v. Equitable Life Assur. Society of U. S., 194 N.Y. 212, 87 N.E. 443 (1909).

102 See, e. g., Mackey v. Moss, 278 Ala. 55, 175 So. 2d 749 (1965), American Aberdeen-Angus Breeders' Ass'n v. Fullerton, 325 Ill. 323, 156 N.E. 314 (1927), and In re Mt. Sinai Hospital, 250 N.Y. 103, 164 N.E. 871 (1928).

See also N.Y. Not-for-Profit Corp. Law § 612.

103 See Westlake Hospital Ass'n v. Blix, 13 Ill. 2d 183, 148 N.E.2d 471 (1958); Harris v. Board of Directors

Members of a nonprofit corporation generally have the right to inspect the books and records of the corporation.[104] Most state statutes provide that books and records of a nonprofit corporation may be inspected by a corporate member or the member's agent or attorney, for any proper purpose at any reasonable time.[105] New York statutes provide that a person who has been a member of record for at least six months immediately preceding the member's demand, or any person holding at least five percent of any class of outstanding capital certificates, can examine the minutes in person or by agent or attorney during usual business hours upon at least five days written notice.[106] California statutes provide that the right of a member to inspect the books and records of a nonprofit corporation cannot be limited by contract or by the articles of incorporation or bylaws.[107] In addition, records must be made available in written form at the expense of the corporation.[108]

Some states provide members of a nonprofit corporation with a right to bring a member's derivative action.[109] A member's derivative suit permits a

---

of Community Hospital of Evanston, 55 Ill. App. 3d 392, 370 N.E.2d 1121 (1st Dist. 1977).

104 See Mod. Nonprofit Corp. Act § 25 (1964) and Rev. Mod. Nonprofit Corp. Act § 16.02(a) (1987).

See Cal. Corp. Code §§ 6333; N.Y. Not-for-Profit Corp. Law § 621; and Tex. Bus. Org. Code §§ 351-355.

In Save Columbia CU Committee v. Columbia Community Credit Union, 134 Wash. App. 175, 139 P.3d 386 (Div. 2 2006), the court ruled that members of a nonprofit corporation composed of credit union members did not have standing to bring a fiduciary duty claim against a credit union's board of directors. It further ruled that the members had no right to inspect the credit union's records. The members had alleged that some directors were serving illegally on the credit union's board of directors and that the directors had breached their fiduciary duties to the members. Save CU was a nonprofit corporation composed of Columbia Community Credit Union members who opposed the credit union's proposed conversion into a mutual savings bank. The court noted that Washington statutes do not expressly grant credit union members the right to assert a direct claim against a director for breaching a fiduciary duty. It noted courts had held that directors of a nonprofit corporation could not bring derivative actions against the corporation. The court commented that while the common law establishes that a credit union's directors owe its members fiduciary duties, none of the cases addressed whether a credit union director owes a fiduciary duty to an individual member. The court concluded that Save CU lacked standing to bring a fiduciary duty claim. The court also decided that the state's extensive regulatory oversight of the credit union, coupled with the fundamental differences between shareholders of a corporation and members in a credit union, "compel the conclusion that Columbia's members do not have the right to inspect the organization's books and records."

105 Mod. Nonprofit Corp. Act § 25 (1964).

106 N.Y. Not-for-Profit Corp. Law § 621(b).

107 Cal. Corp. Code §§ 6313, 8313.

108 Cal. Corp. Code §§ 6310, 8310.

109 See e. g., N.Y. Not-for-Profit Corp. Law § 623 and Cal. Corp. Code §§ 5710, 7710.

The Revised Nonprofit Corporation Act provides for the right in any member having five percent or more of the voting power or by fifty members, whichever is less, or by any director. See Rev. Mod. Nonprofit

member of a nonprofit corporation to institute a lawsuit for the corporation to secure a judgment in favor of the corporation for restoration of corporate property or for compensation to the corporation for losses suffered because of director actions.[110] In California, a member must demonstrate that the member has informed the corporation or the board in writing of the ultimate facts of each cause of action or has delivered a copy of the complaint to the corporation. A member must allege the member's efforts to cause the board to bring the action.[111] The member also must have been a member of the corporation at the time the particular complained of transaction occurred.[112] The member's derivative action can be brought to secure damages for an improper distribution of property of the corporation,[113] for a self-dealing transaction between the corporation and

---

Corp. Act § 6.30 (1987).

Pennsylvania statutes assume members have this right by providing for indemnification for a person who is party to an action to procure a judgment in favor of the corporation. See Pa. Stat. Ann. tit. 15, § 5742.

In Moore v. Christ's Christian Fellowship Church, Inc., 172 Ohio App. 3d 398, 875 N.E.2d 121 (5th Dist. Fairfield County 2007), some church members filed a derivative action against the directors and trustees of the church corporation in which they contended (1) that the directors and trustees committed financial misconduct, (2) that the directors and trustees refused to provide an accounting, (3) that the directors and trustees improperly converted corporate property, and (4) that the directors and trustees interfered with the church's ability to function as a religious entity. The court noted that members of the corporation were not defined nor were any requirements set forth for membership. It ruled that absent any specific definition of membership qualifications, the trustees were the sole members of the church corporation because they were named in the church's articles of incorporation as the corporation's sole members. The court stated that a right to file a derivative claim is a right conferred solely on corporate members or shareholders.

In Hicks v. Garrett, 2020 WL 4360835 (Tex. App. 2020), the court pointed out that while the Attorney General is the appropriate party to vindicate the public's rights in connection with public charities, a private party is not precluded from bringing an action on behalf of a nonprofit organization so long as that party has standing. The plaintiff had been the chair of the Board of Directors of a Christian foundation that was founded by her father to help churches in a particular county with evangelism and benevolence. The plaintiff asserted a cause of action for breach of fiduciary duty, seeking to correct what she believed were financial irregularities committed by the foundation's chief executive officer. The case presented the question of whether special standing could be bestowed on a person who is more than a mere member of the public when the Office of the Attorney General has declined to investigate. The court decided that the plaintiff had failed to identify any greater interest in the outcome of the case than the general public, pointing out that she was no longer the board chair nor a board member or a beneficiary of the foundation. The court apparently would not approve a derivative action. It concluded that because the plaintiff was suing only on behalf of the foundation, the trial court did not err in determining she had no standing to pursue the lawsuit.

110 See discussion in Fontheim v. Walker, 282 A.D. 373, 122 N.Y.S.2d 642 (1st Dep't 1953), judgment aff'd, 306 N.Y. 926, 119 N.E.2d 605 (1954).

111 Cal. Corp. Code §§ 5710(b)(2), 7710(b)(2).

112 Cal. Corp. Code §§ 5710(b)(1), 7710(b)(1). An officer of the corporation or a member of the board can file a motion for a hearing to require the complaining member to file a bond for reasonable expenses including attorneys' fees that might be incurred by the member and the corporation in the action. See Cal. Corp. Code §§ 5710(c), 7710(c).

113 See Cal. Corp. Code § 5420.

one or more of its directors,[114] and for breach of a charitable trust.[115] New York statutes provide that a member's derivative action can be brought by five percent or more of any class of members, capital certificate holders, or owners of a beneficial interest in the capital certificates of the corporation.[116] If the action is successful, the court can award the complaining members reasonable expenses, including reasonable attorneys' fees.[117]

D. HOSPITAL EMPLOYEES

1. Power to Hire and Power to Fire

The power to appoint and discharge employees for a nonprofit corporation is normally vested by the bylaws in a corporate officer or in the governing board directors. The law does not require that employment be rational, wise, or well-considered.[118] Generally, in the absence of a contract to the contrary, an employer has sole discretion in hiring and has the authority to discharge an employee

114 Cal. Corp. Code §§ 5233, 7236.

115 Cal. Corp. Code §§ 5142, 7142.

116 N.Y. Not-for-Profit Corp. Law § 623.

117 N.Y. Not-for-Profit Corp. Law § 623(e).

118 See, discussion by Court of Appeals of the Fifth Circuit in Phillips v. Goodyear Tire & Rubber Co., 651 F.2d 1051 (5th Cir. 1981).

See also Boyle v. Vista Eyewear, Inc., 700 S.W.2d 859 (Mo. Ct. App. W.D. 1985) (rejected by, Komm v. McFliker, 662 F. Supp. 924 (W.D. Mo. 1987)), in which the court cited the history of a public policy exception to the employment at-will doctrine. The court noted that although employers generally are free to discharge employees at will with or without cause, they are not free to require employees, on penalty of losing their jobs, to commit unlawful acts or acts in violation of a clear mandate of public policy expressed in the constitution, statutes and regulations promulgated pursuant to statute. The court noted that the at-will employment doctrine seemed to be falling most heavily and harshly upon professional and upper and middle level employees. These employees have the most to lose, frequently being the long-term employees who have greatest responsibility, and substantial investment in, and highest expectations from their careers. They often are at an age when replacement of their life and medical insurance programs and their retirement plans are difficult or impossible. At-will employment doctrine does not include nor contemplate a privilege in the employer to subject employees to risks of civil and criminal liability. A public policy exception is narrow enough in scope and application to be no threat to employers who operate within the mandates of the law and clearly established public policy as set out in duly adopted laws.

with or without cause.[119] Still, this general rule has been limited by nondiscrimination provisions of both state and federal statutes.[120]

---

119 See Wagner v. City of Globe, 150 Ariz. 82, 722 P.2d 250 (1986), in which the Supreme Court of Arizona listed three exceptions to the at-will employment doctrine. One is the implied contract exception wherein there is an implied promise of continued employment. Another is the public policy exception wherein an employer has undermined an important public policy. The third exception is the good faith and fair dealing exception that protects employees from termination for bad cause. Arizona recognizes all three exceptions. The court noted that an at-will employment contract can be modified by personnel manuals, guides, or rules by the employer. The court decided that the public policy exception protects an employee who refuses to participate in illegal behavior. It cited whistle-blowing activity as one that serves a public purpose and should be protected.

In Sabine Pilot Service, Inc. v. Hauck, 687 S.W.2d 733 (Tex. 1985), the Supreme Court of Texas carved out a narrow exception to the employment at-will doctrine. The exception covers the discharge of an employee for refusing to perform an illegal act, i.e., an act that carries a criminal penalty for performance. However, the court noted that numerous commentators have advocated exceptions to the at-will doctrine based upon a public policy exception, and the concurring opinion in the case stated that the decision does not preclude the court from broadening the exception when it may be warranted.

In Ramos v. Henry C. Beck Co., 711 S.W.2d 331 (Tex. App. Dallas 1986), the court ruled an employee, who can prove employment at will is subject to an oral or written agreement that the employee will not be terminated except for good cause, can recover for wrongful discharge.

See Bowman v. State Bank of Keysville, 229 Va. 534, 331 S.E.2d 797 (1985), in which the Supreme Court of Virginia ruled that while Virginia has not deviated from the common-law doctrine of employment-at-will, the rule is not absolute. The court applied a narrow exception to the doctrine when shareholder-employees are discharged for exercising their protected rights as shareholders in questioning the manner in which proxies are obtained for a proposed merger.

In Johnson v. McDonnell Douglas Corp., 745 S.W.2d 661 (Mo. 1988), the Missouri Supreme Court ruled there is no handbook exception to the at-will employment doctrine. The court stated that the unilateral act of publishing a handbook is not a contractual offer to employees. The handbook is merely an informational statement of self-imposed policies, providing a nonexclusive list of acts for which an employee might be subject to discipline. The court noted that several rules are couched in general terms and are open to broad discretion and interpretation. In addition, the rules are subject to change at any time. Thus, the court concluded that the handbook is not an offer to modify the at-will status of the employees. The court held that absent a valid contract of employment, the employee can be discharged with or without cause.

In Sargent v. Central Nat. Bank & Trust Co. of Enid, Okla., 1991 OK 23, 809 P.2d 1298 (Okla. 1991), the Supreme Court of Oklahoma noted an actionable tort claim arises when an employee is discharged either for refusing to violate a well-defined public policy or for performing an act in compliance with a clear and compelling public policy. It ruled a federal act permitting bank directors to dismiss officers "at pleasure" does not preempt Oklahoma's public policy exception to the at-will employment rule.

120 State statutes on employment discrimination vary. Some states have established Civil Rights Commissions to receive, investigate, and conduct hearings regarding charges of discrimination in hiring and firing.

See, e.g., Colo. Rev. Stat. §§ 24-34-301 et seq. and Ohio Rev. Code Ann. §§ 4112.01 et seq. Ohio Rev. Code Ann. § 4112.02, states it is an unlawful discrimination practice for any employer to discharge without just cause or to refuse to hire or otherwise to discriminate because of race, color, religion, sex, national origin, handicap, age, or ancestry.

Colo. Rev. Stat. § 24-34-402, states it is an unfair employment practice to refuse to hire, promote or demote, or discharge based on race, creed, color, sex, national origin, or ancestry.

In Texas, a Commission on Human Rights was established to execute the policies embodied in Title VII of the federal Civil Rights Act, 42 U.S.C. § 2000e discussed below. The Texas statute provided that it was an unlawful employment practice for an employer, employment agency, or labor union, to refuse to hire or to otherwise discriminate against an individual because of race, color, disability, religion, sex, national origin,

2. Occupational Safety and Health Act

The Occupational Safety and Health Act[121] was adopted to secure "so far as possible" safe and healthful working conditions for "every working man and woman in the Nation."[122] Labor, nonprofit and charitable organizations are covered by the act.[123] Congress delegated broad authority in the act to the Secretary of Labor to promulgate standards to ensure safe and healthful working conditions for workers.[124] The act authorizes the Occupational Safety and Health Administration (OSHA) to promulgate "start-up" standards on an expedited basis without public hearing or comment, based on "national consensus" or "established federal standards" that improve employee safety or health.[125] The act provides for mechanisms to update the standards.[126] There must be a finding that workplaces in question are not safe.[127] The OSHA is not entitled to regulate any risk, only those that present a significant risk of material health impairment.[128]

---

or age. See Tex. Labor Code § 21.051. The Commission would receive, investigate, and pass on complaints alleging violations of the statute.

In Hilton v. Southwestern Bell Telephone Co., 936 F.2d 823 (5th Cir. 1991), the Court of Appeals for the Fifth Circuit ruled AIDS and its related conditions were not considered handicaps under the Texas Commission on Human Rights Act and stated the only health conditions not listed in the statute that constitute protected handicaps are physiological impairments requiring special equipment for mitigation.

121 29 U.S.C. §§ 651 to 671.

122 29 U.S.C. § 651(b).

123 See 29 C.F.R. § 1975.4.

124 29 U.S.C. § 655.

125 29 U.S.C. § 655(a).

126 See 29 U.S.C.A. § 655), which sets out procedural and substantive criteria that standards must meet. In promulgating standards, OSHA must provide notice of proposed rulemaking, give interested parties an opportunity to comment, and hold a public hearing if requested. OSHA may also issue emergency temporary standards when it determines that employees are exposed to "grave danger from exposure" to toxic substances. Once OSHA has published an emergency standard, proceedings must commence for issuance of a regular standard.

127 In Industrial Union Dept., AFL-CIO v. American Petroleum Institute, 448 U.S. 607 (1980), the Supreme Court limited the otherwise extensive powers of the Secretary of Labor to promulgate voluminous standards. The Court concluded that "safe" is not the equivalent of "risk-free" and decided a workplace "can hardly be considered 'unsafe' unless it threatens the workers with a significant risk of harm." Thus, the Supreme Court ruled that before the Secretary can promulgate any permanent health or safety standard, the Secretary must make a threshold finding that the place of employment is unsafe in that significant risks are present that can be eliminated or lessened by a change in practices.

128 In American Federation of Labor and Congress of Indus. Organizations v. Occupational Safety and Health Admin., U.S. Dept. of Labor, 965 F.2d 962 (11th Cir. 1992), the Court of Appeals for the Elev-

To enforce provisions of the act, the Secretary of Labor is empowered to inspect any place of employment covered by the act at reasonable times.[129] Although a search warrant is not required under the act, the Supreme Court has held that a search warrant or its equivalent is constitutionally necessary for nonconsensual workplace inspections.[130] Nonconsensual administrative searches must comply with the probable cause requirement of the Fourth Amendment.[131] An employer who has received a citation for a serious violation of the requirements of the act or of any standard, rule, or order of the act or the regulations, is subject to a civil penalty for each violation.[132]

3. Workers' Compensation

Most state workers' compensations statutes do not exclude nonprofit organizations; thus, nonprofit organizations generally must also comply with state

---

enth Circuit ruled that OSHA must determine what health impairments are material and what constitute a significant risk of such impairment. The court stated that OSHA ultimately bears the burden of proving by substantial evidence a risk exists and that the proposed standard is necessary.

129 29 U.S.C. § 657. Section 657(f) states an inspection may be made pursuant to an employee complaint.

130 In Marshall v. Barlow's, Inc., 436 U.S. 307 (1978), the Supreme Court ruled that inspection without a warrant of a commercial enterprise violates the Fourth Amendment to the U.S. Constitution. The Court stated the Fourth Amendment protects commercial buildings as well as private homes from unwarranted searches by government officials, commenting that the owner of a business has not, by the necessary utilization of employees in his operation, thrown open areas where employees alone are permitted to the "warrantless scrutiny of government agents." The Supreme Court decided the fact that an employee is free to report, and the government is free to use, any evidence of noncompliance with the act that an employee observes, furnishes no justification for federal agents to enter a place of business from which the public is restricted "to conduct their own warrantless search."

131 Matter of Midwest Instruments Co., 900 F.2d 1150 (7th Cir. 1990). However, probable cause in the usual, criminal sense is not required of administrative warrants. Probable cause will support an OSHA warrant if the warrant application supports a "reasonable belief" or leads to a "reasonable suspicion" that the act or its regulations have been violated. The Court of Appeals for the Seventh Circuit ruled an OSHA warrant application must at least inform a magistrate of the substance of the employee complaints to enable the magistrate to exercise independent judgment as to whether an inspection is justified. The court decided a complaint that described the employees who are being injured, where they are being injured, the type of injuries, the number of injuries, and the believed cause of the injuries, is sufficient to support a reasonable belief OSHA is implicated and an inspection is warranted.

In Martin v. International Matex Tank Terminals-Bayonne, 928 F.2d 614 (3d Cir. 1991), the Court of Appeals for the Third Circuit ruled that because a magistrate has "ample specific evidence, including the first-hand observations of the compliance officer, to show a 'plausible basis for believing that violations are likely to be found, a wall-to-wall warrant is supported by administrative probable cause to inspect" and is not overly broad.

132 13229 U.S.C. § 666. An employer who willfully or repeatedly violates the act, or any standard, rule or order, is subject to an additional substantial penalty for each violation.

workers' compensation statutes. Workers' compensation is a form of strict liability. The employer is liable for injuries to workers arising during employment regardless of the employer's negligence. The common-law defenses of contributory negligence, assumption of risk, and the fellow servant rule, are abolished as defenses. The theory underlying the workers' compensation law is that the burden of accidents occurring during employment should fall upon the employer because the employer is in a better position, through insurance, to bear the cost.[133] An employee is entitled automatically to limited compensation if the employee suffers an injury by accident arising out of and in the course of employment.[134] Benefits to the employee include cash-wage benefits, a percentage of weekly wage, and hospital and medical expenses.[135] In exchange for modest but assured benefit, employees relinquish their common-law right to sue their employer.[136]

All states require a covered organization to carry workers' compensation insurance.[137] Some state acts are compulsory for all employers, and some are compulsory for employers employing more than a stated number of employees and elective for those employing fewer. Some states permit self-insurance, private insurance, and others, provide for insurance through state funds.[138]

E. DISCRIMINATION IN HOSPITAL EMPLOYMENT

1. Title VII

Nonprofit organizations that are engaged in activities affecting commerce and that have fifteen or more employees on each working day in each of twenty

133 Discussion in Lex. K. Larson, Workmen's Compensation Law.

134 Id. at § 1.10.

135 Id. a § 1.10. The remedy is in the nature of a compromise by which the employee accepts the limited compensation in return for an extended liability of the employer and an assurance that the employee will be paid. The employee files a claim with an administrative agency that determines the award.

136 Id.

137 Id. at § 92.10.

138 Id. at § 92.11. If an employer is required to carry worker's compensation but fails to do so, the employer will be liable for full damages and will not have defenses.

or more calendar weeks in the current or preceding year are subject to the Civil Rights Act of 1964, which is referred to as Title VII.[139] Title VII makes it an unlawful employment practice for any employer to fail or refuse to hire or to discharge any individual, or otherwise to discriminate against any individual with respect to compensation, terms, conditions, or privileges of employment, because of an individual's race, color, religion, sex, or national origin.[140] The act also prohibits an employer from limiting, segregating, or classifying employees or applicants for employment in any way that would deprive, or tend to

139 42 U.S.C. § 2000e(b).

In Scharon v. St. Luke's Episcopal Presbyterian Hospitals, 929 F.2d 360 (8th Cir. 1991), the Court of Appeals for the Eighth Circuit ruled that to apply Title VII and the Age Discrimination in Employment Act (discussed below) to the discharge of a chaplain at a church-affiliated hospital would be excessive governmental entanglement with religion.

In Walters v. Metropolitan Educational Enterprises, Inc., 519 U.S. 202 (1997), the Supreme Court addressed the issue of what persons are considered "employees" in determining whether an employer has fifteen or more employees for each working day in each of twenty or more calendar weeks in the current or preceding calendar year, to make an employer subject to Title VII. The Court ruled the "ultimate touchstone" under Section 2000e(b) in determining the existence of an employment relationship is whether an individual is on the employer's payroll.

In Robinson v. Shell Oil Co., 519 U.S. 337 (1997), the Supreme Court ruled that former employees are included within coverage of the act. It decided that the term "employees," as used in Title VII, is ambiguous on this issue but concluded that it is more consistent with the broader context of Title VII to include former employees.

In Oncale v. Sundowner Offshore Services, Inc., 523 U.S. 75 (1998), the Supreme Court ruled workplace harassment, when the harasser and the harassed employee are of the same sex, violates Title VII's prohibition against discrimination. The Supreme Court stated that Title VII protects men as well as women. In applying Title VII to same sex harassment cases, the Court commented that the severity of the harassment should be judged from the perspective of a reasonable person considering all the circumstances. In a same sex harassment case, the inquiry will require a careful consideration of the social context in which the behavior occurs and how it is experienced by the target victim.

In Doe v. Mercy Catholic Medical Center, 850 F.3d 545 (3d Cir. 2017), the Court of Appeals for the Third Circuit ruled a participant in a hospital's residency program is a hospital employee for purposes of Title VII.

140 42 U.S.C. § 2000e-2. It is a violation of Title VII for a job advertisement to indicate preference, limitation, specification, or discrimination based on sex or race, though specification based on sex is permitted if sex is a bona fide occupational qualification for a particular job. A bona fide occupational qualification exception as to sex is interpreted narrowly. Refusal to hire a person because of sex cannot be based on stereotyped characterizations of the sexes, nor may the preferences of coworkers, the employer, clients, or customers be considered. Benefits provided employees must be the same for male and female. See 29 C.F.R. § 1604.

In Ansonia Ansonia Bd. of Educ. v. Philbrook, 479 U.S. 60 (1986), the Supreme Court ruled the statute is satisfied if the employer reasonably accommodates an employee's religious needs.

In Christopher v. Stouder Memorial Hosp., 936 F.2d 870 (6th Cir. 1991), the Court of Appeals for the Sixth Circuit ruled a Title VII claim can be brought against an independent contractor if the independent contractor interferes with the claimant's employment opportunities. In Stouder, a hospital denied a nurse work privileges to serve as a private duty scrub nurse for a medical partnership allegedly in retaliation of a sex discrimination action she had brought against another hospital. The Sixth Circuit ruled she could bring a Title VII claim against the hospital even though it was not her employer.

deprive, any individual of employment opportunities or would otherwise affect the employee's status as an employee, because of the individual's race, color, religion, sex, or national origin.[141]

The act is enforced by the Equal Employment Opportunity Commission (EEOC).[142]

---

141 42 U.S.C § 2000e-2. Employer toleration of a racially discriminatory work atmosphere violates Title VII.

In Harris v. Forklift Systems, Inc., 510 U.S. 17 (1993), the Supreme Court ruled sexual harassment is actionable if it is "sufficiently severe or pervasive to alter the conditions of employment and create an abusive work environment." The challenged conduct must be severe or pervasive enough "to create an objectively hostile or abusive work environment—an environment that a reasonable person would find hostile or abusive." A court must look at all circumstances to determine whether an environment is "hostile" or "abusive." These may include the frequency of the discriminatory conduct; its severity; whether it is physically threatening or humiliating, or a mere offensive utterance; and whether it unreasonably interferes with an employee's work performance. No single factor is required.

In Burns v. McGregor Electronic Industries, Inc., 989 F.2d 959 (8th Cir. 1993), the Court of Appeals for the Eighth Circuit agreed that in hostile environment litigation, the appropriate standard is that of a "reasonable woman" under similar circumstances, rather than the "reasonable person" standard. See also Ellison v. Brady, 924 F.2d 872 (9th Cir. 1991).

In Faragher v. City of Boca Raton, 524 U.S. 775 (1998), the Supreme Court ruled an employer is vicariously liable for a supervisory employee's sexual harassment of a subordinate, but the employer is subject to an affirmative defense considering the reasonableness of the employer's conduct as well as that of a plaintiff victim. The Court decided that because hostile environment sexual harassment by supervisors and co-employees is "a persistent problem in the workplace," an employer reasonably should anticipate the possibility of such conduct occurring in its workplace. The Supreme Court referred to the failure of the employer to disseminate its policy against sexual harassment among its employees and noted that its officials made no attempt to keep track of conduct of supervisors.

In Pennsylvania State Police v. Suders, 542 U.S. 129 (2004), the Supreme Court noted that to establish a hostile work environment, plaintiffs must show harassing behavior "sufficiently severe or pervasive to alter the conditions of their employment." The Supreme Court ruled that to establish "constructive discharge," a plaintiff must make a further showing that the abusive working environment became so intolerable that her resignation qualified as a fitting response. An employer may defend against such a claim by showing both (1) that it had installed a readily accessible and effective policy for reporting and resolving complaints of sexual harassment, and (2) that the plaintiff unreasonably failed to avail herself of that employer-provided preventive or remedial apparatus. This affirmative defense will not be available to the employer, however, if the plaintiff quits in reasonable response to an employer-sanctioned adverse action officially changing her employment status or situation, for example, a humiliating demotion, extreme cut in pay, or transfer to a position in which the plaintiff would face unbearable working conditions. The Court noted it was following the path marked by its 1998 decisions in Burlington Industries, Inc. v. Ellerth, 524 U.S. 742 (1998), and Faragher v. City of Boca Raton, 524 U.S. 775 (1998). The Court's starting point is the Ellerth/Faragher framework.

142 42 U.S.C. § 2000e-5.

In Mach Mining, LLC v. E.E.O.C., 135 S. Ct. 1645 (2015), the Supreme Court stated that courts have authority to review whether the EEOC has fulfilled its Title VII duty to attempt conciliation with an employer as a prerequisite to a Title VII action. The EEOC had brought action against an employer, alleging that the employer had violated Title VII by engaging in sex discrimination in hiring. The employer contended the EEOC had not attempted to conciliate in good faith, and the EEOC countered that its conciliation efforts were not subject to judicial review but that nonetheless the two letters it had sent the employer provided adequate proof that it had fulfilled its statutory duty. The Supreme Court noted that Congress, by its choice of language, has imposed a mandatory duty on the EEOC to attempt conciliation and has made that duty a

The appropriate starting point for evaluation of a personal claim of employment discrimination under Title VII is the case of McDonnell Douglas Corp. v. Green.[143] In that case the Supreme Court stated that a complainant in a Title VII trial must carry the initial burden of establishing a prima facie case of racial or sex discrimination.[144] A complainant may establish a prima facie case of racial

---

precondition to filing a lawsuit. The Supreme Court stated compulsory prerequisites are routinely enforced by courts in Title VII litigation. The Court further stated that, to comply with the Title VII conciliation provision, the EEOC must inform the employer about the specific discrimination allegation. The notice must describe what the employer had done, and which employees (or class of employees) have suffered. In addition, the EEOC must try to engage the employer in a discussion to give the employer a chance to remedy the allegedly discriminatory practice. The Court ruled an affidavit from the EEOC stating it had performed these obligations should suffice to show the EEOC had met the conciliation requirement. If an employer presents concrete evidence that the EEOC did not provide the requisite information about the charge or attempts to engage in a discussion about conciliating the claim, a court must conduct the fact finding necessary to resolve that limited dispute. If the court finds for the employer, the appropriate remedy is to order the EEOC to undertake the mandated conciliation efforts. The Supreme Court found that the letters the EEOC had sent to the employer were insufficient to show the EEOC had satisfied its obligation.

143 McDonnell Douglas Corp. v. Green, 411 U.S. 792 (1973) (holding modified by Hazen Paper Co. v. Biggins, 507 U.S. 604 (1993)).

In Fort Bend County v. Davis, 139 S. Ct. 1843 (2019), the Supreme Court noted the requirement that before commencing a Title VII action in court, a complainant must file a charge with the EEOC. See 42 U.S.C. § 2000e-5(e)(1), (f)(1). On receipt of a charge, the EEOC notifies the employer and investigates the allegations. The Supreme Court noted that the EEOC may endeavor to eliminate the alleged unlawful employment practice by informal methods of conciliation and that it has the first option to bring a civil action against the employer in court. However, as the Court pointed out, the EEOC has no authority itself to adjudicate discrimination complaints. If the EEOC chooses not to sue, and whether or not the EEOC otherwise acts on the charge, a complainant is entitled to a "right-to-sue" notice 180 days after the charge is filed. See 29 C.F.R. 1601.28. On receipt of the right-to-sue notice, the complainant may commence a civil action against her employer. In Fort Bend County, the plaintiff filed a charge against her employer, Fort Bend County, for alleged sexual harassment and retaliation for reporting the harassment. While her EEOC charge was pending, Fort Bend fired her because she failed to appear for work on a Sunday and went to a church event instead. The plaintiff attempted to supplement her EEOC charge by handwriting "religion" on a form called an "intake questionnaire," but she did not amend the formal charge document. Upon receiving a right to sue letter, the plaintiff commenced suit in a federal district court, alleging discrimination based on religion and retaliation for reporting sexual harassment. After years of litigation, only the religion-based discrimination claim remained in the case. Fort Bend then asserted for the first time that the district court lacked jurisdiction to adjudicate her claim because her EEOC charge did not state a religion-based discrimination claim. The Supreme Court ruled that Title VII's charge-filing requirement is not jurisdictional. The Court noted that a claim-processing rule requiring parties to take certain procedural steps in, or prior to, litigation, may be mandatory in the sense that a court must enforce the rule if timely raised but stated that a mandatory rule of that sort, unlike a prescription limiting the kinds of cases a court may adjudicate, is ordinarily forfeited if not timely asserted. It ruled that Title VII's charge-filing requirement is a nonjurisdictional claim-processing rule.

144 In Meritor Sav. Bank, FSB v. Vinson, 477 U.S. 57 (1986), the Supreme Court ruled a claim of a hostile environment in the form of sexual harassment is sex discrimination that is actionable under Title VII. The Court stated the language of Title VII is not limited to economic or tangible discrimination. A former employee of a bank brought action against the bank and her former supervisor claiming that during her employment at the bank she had been subjected to sexual harassment by her supervisor. The Supreme Court held that the Court of Appeals in that case had erred in concluding that employers are always automatically liable for sexual harassment by their supervisors. However, the Court stated absence of notice to the employer does not necessarily insulate the employer from

or sex discrimination by showing that the complainant is a member of a minority, that the complainant applied and was qualified for a position for which the institution was seeking applicants, that despite proper qualifications the applicant was rejected and that, after the rejection, the position remained open and the institution continued to seek applicants from persons with the complainant's qualifications.[145] The burden then shifts to the institution to articulate some legitimate, nondiscriminatory reason for the applicant's rejection.[146]

---

liability. The bank's grievance procedure required an employee to complain first to her supervisor regarding such problems. The Supreme Court stated that because the supervisor was the guilty party, failure to invoke the procedure and report the grievance to him did not insulate the employer from liability.

In Scott v. Sears, Roebuck & Co., 798 F.2d 210 (7th Cir. 1986), the Court of Appeals for the Seventh Circuit did not find liability on the part of the plaintiff's employer when the plaintiff failed to show the sexual harassment was sufficiently severe or pervasive to alter her conditions of employment and to create an abusive working environment. The court stated the question of whether an employer is liable for sexual harassment by fellow employees becomes: did demeaning conduct and sexual stereotyping cause such anxiety and debilitation to the plaintiff that working conditions for her were poisoned?

In Thompson v. North American Stainless, LP, 562 U.S. 170 (2011), the Supreme Court ruled that a third-party retaliation claim is permitted under Title VII. After a woman had filed a retaliation Title VII suit against her employer, her employer terminated her fiancée. The fiancée then filed his own suit for retaliation under Title VII. The Sixth Circuit affirmed the district court ruling that Title VII does not permit third party retaliation claims. The Supreme Court reversed and stated that if facts alleged in the case were proven to be true, there was unlawful retaliation.

In Village of Tequesta v. Luscavich, 240 So. 3d 733 (Fla. 4th DCA 2018), the court ruled an employee's rejection of a one-event sexual advance by a supervisor at a non-work sponsored party can meet necessary elements of a claim for retaliation under the Florida Civil Rights Act.

145 McDonnell Douglas Corp. v. Green, 411 U.S. 792(1973) (holding modified by Hazen Paper Co. v. Biggins, 507 U.S. 604 (1993)).

In Holly D. v. California Institute of Technology, 339 F.3d 1158 (9th Cir. 2003), the Court of Appeals for the Ninth Circuit held that an employer was not vicariously liable for a supervisor's conduct for purposes of an employee's Title VII sexual harassment action against the supervisor. Although the supervisor made inappropriate sexual comments and engaged in a sexual relationship with the claimant, the Ninth Circuit decided that a reasonable woman in a state university employee's position will not have had cause to believe she will be fired or will suffer any other tangible employment action if she declines to have sex with her supervisor. The court was of the opinion the employee knew the supervisor would stop when she made it clear she wanted him to end the conduct. Further, the employee did not present any evidence connecting any discussion of her job duties or her continued employment with the supervisor's requests for sexual favors.

146 McDonnell Douglas Corp. v. Green, 411 U.S. 792 (1973) (holding modified by Hazen Paper Co. v. Biggins, 507 U.S. 604 (1993)).

In Crawford v. Metropolitan Government of Nashville and Davidson County, Tenn., 555 U.S. 271 (2009), the Supreme Court ruled Title VII's antiretaliation provision's protection extends to an employee who speaks out about discrimination not on her own initiative but in answering questions during an employer's internal investigation. In response to questions from an official of a local government during an internal investigation into rumors of sexual harassment by a school district employee relations director, the petitioner reported that the director had sexually harassed her. The school district soon fired the petitioner. She contended the school district was retaliating for her report of the director's behavior.

In Vance v. Ball State University, 570 U.S. 421 (2013), an African American state university employee

To dispel an adverse inference from a prima facie showing of employment discrimination, the employer need only articulate some legitimate, nondiscriminatory reason for the applicant's rejection.[147] Statistical proof that the work force is racially or sexually imbalanced or contains a disproportionately higher percentage of minority employees can be considered in determining motivation; however, courts will not require different business practices for an employer

---

brought a Title VII action for a hostile work environment and retaliation for the employee's complaints about racial harassment claims. The Supreme Court ruled an employer's liability for workplace harassment may depend on the status of the harasser. If the harassing employee is the victim's co-worker, the employer is liable only if it is negligent in controlling working conditions. If the harasser is a "supervisor," different rules apply. If a supervisor's harassment culminates in a tangible employment action, which is a significant change in employment status, such as hiring, firing, failing to promote, reassignment with significantly different responsibilities, or a decision causing a significant change in benefits, the employer is strictly liable. However, if no tangible employment action is taken, the employer may escape liability by establishing as an affirmative defense (1) that the employer exercised reasonable care to prevent and correct any harassing behavior and (2) that the plaintiff unreasonably failed to take advantage of the preventive or corrective opportunities the employer provided.

In Velazquez-Perez v. Developers Diversified Realty Corp., 753 F.3d 265 (1st Cir. 2014), the Court of Appeals for the First Circuit ruled an employer can be liable under Title VII for negligently permitting a female coworker's discriminatory efforts to cause a male employee's termination. The question before the court was: under what circumstances, if any, can an employer be held liable for sex discrimination under Title VII when it terminates a worker whose job performance has been maligned by a jilted co-worker's intent on revenge. The court recognized that, in applying Vance v. Ball State University, 570 U.S. 421 (2013), it had to consider that the Vance decision involved claims of hostile environment sexual harassment, not claims of quid pro quo harassment.

147 Furnco Const. Corp. v. Waters, 438 U.S. 567 (1978).

In University of Texas Southwestern Medical Center v. Nassar, 570 U.S. 338 (2013), a physician of Middle Eastern descent brought a Title VII action against a state university, alleging he was constructively discharged from a university faculty position because of racially and religiously motivated harassment by a superior and that the university retaliated against him for complaining harassment. The Supreme Court ruled that Title VII retaliation claims must be proved according to traditional principles of but for causation and not a lessened causation test that requires only a showing that retaliation is a motivating factor for the adverse employment action.

In Wholf v. Tremco, Inc., 26 N.E.3d 902 (Ohio Ct. App. 8th Dist.2015), the court ruled an employee was not required to prove conclusively the causation element in his prima facie case of retaliation. The employee contended the trial court erroneously applied the "but-for" causation standard articulated in University of Texas Southwestern Medical Center v. Nassar, 570 U.S. 338 (2013) to his retaliation claim. He contended the court should have applied the less stringent "motivating factor" causation standard that the courts applied prior to Nassar, which is set out in 42 U.S.C.A. § 2000e-3(a). The court found that the employee had brought a retaliation claim pursuant to state law that was almost identical to 2003e-3(a); consequently, it held that federal case law interpreting that section, including the "but-for" causation standard defined in Nassar was applicable to the employee's retaliation claim. The court ruled that the employee established his prima facie case of retaliation by producing evidence of his protected activity and of the adverse employment actions taken against him because of those activities. The court held that the trial court erroneously imposed the burden on the employee to prove conclusively the causation element in his prima facie case, when his initial burden only required production of some evidence as to each element of the prima facie case. The court decided the trial court misapplied the "but-for" standard of causation and, as a result, erroneously concluded that the employee failed to establish his prima facie case of retaliation in the first stage of the McDonnell Douglas analysis.

until a violation of the Civil Rights Act has been proven.[148] If there is that showing, the burden that shifts to the employer is proving that its employment decision was based on a legitimate consideration and not an illegitimate one such as race or sex.[149] There is no requirement that an employer hire a minority or female applicant whenever that person's objective qualifications are equal to those of a white male applicant.[150]

---

148 Furnco Const. Corp. v. Waters, 438 U.S. 567 (1978).

Still, in Griffin v. Carlin, 755 F.2d 1516 (11th Cir. 1985), the Court of Appeals for the Eleventh Circuit held that a prima facie case of disparate treatment may be established by statistics alone if they are sufficiently compelling.

Additionally, in Coates v. Johnson & Johnson, 756 F.2d 524 (7th Cir. 1985), the Court of Appeals for the Seventh Circuit ruled that strong statistical evidence may form a prima facie case in some cases.

149 Furnco Const. Corp. v. Waters, 438 U.S. 567 (1978).

In Evans v. Georgia Regional Hospital, 850 F.3d 1248, cert. denied, 138 S. Ct. 557 (2017), a lesbian former employee sued her former employer, alleging discrimination based on sexual orientation and gender nonconformity and retaliation in violation of Title VII. The Court of Appeals for the Eleventh Circuit ruled discrimination based on sexual orientation is not actionable under Title VII.

But see Hively v. Ivy Tech Community College of Indiana, 853 F.3d 339 (7th Cir. 2017), wherein the Court of Appeals for the Seventh Circuit ruled a person who alleges she experienced employment discrimination based on her sexual orientation has a claim of sex discrimination for Title VII purposes. The Seventh Circuit stated sexual-orientation discrimination is sex discrimination and thus is actionable under Title VII.

Further, in Zarda v. Altitude Express, Inc., 883 F.3d 100(2d Cir. 2018), cert. granted, 139 S.Ct. 1599 (2019), aff'd, 140 S. Ct. 1731, the Court of Appeals for the Second Circuit ruled that an employee is entitled to a bring a Title VII claim for discrimination based on sexual orientation. The court agreed that sexual orientation discrimination did not concern Congress when Congress enacted Title VII but decided that, in the context of Title VII, the statutory prohibition should extend to all discrimination because of sex. The Second Circuit has agreed with the Seventh Circuit that sexual orientation discrimination is motivated, at least in part, by sex and is thus a subset of sex discrimination. (Contrary: First, Third, Fourth, Fifth, Sixth, Eighth, Ninth, Tenth, and Eleventh Circuits.)

In Wittmer v. Phillips 67 Company, 915 F.3d 328 (5th Cir. 2019), a transgender woman brought a Title VII sex discrimination action against her employer. The Fifth Circuit noted its decision in Blum v. Gulf Oil Corp., 597 F.2d 936 (5th Cir. 1979), wherein it expressly held that Title VII does not prohibit discrimination based on sexual orientation. Still, apart from its holding in Blum, the court decided the plaintiff failed to establish a prima facie case of discrimination, stating that she did not present evidence that any non-transgender applicants were treated better than she. Additionally, the court found that the defendant corporation identified a legitimate non-discriminatory reason for rescinding its employment offer to her. The court agreed the plaintiff had made misrepresentations to the defendant corporation and that she failed to present a genuine issue of material fact that the non-discriminatory reason offered by the defendant for not hiring her was pretextual.

Presumably the Supreme Court settled this issue by its ruling in Bostock v. Clayton County, Georgia v Zarda v. Altitude Express, Inc., 140 S. Ct. 1731, (2020), that an employer violates Title VII by firing an individual for being homosexual or being a transgender person. The Supreme Court noted in that case that discrimination based on homosexuality or transgender treats individual employees differently because of their sex; thus, an employer who intentionally penalizes an employee for being homosexual or transgender also violates Title VII. The Court stated that when Congress chooses not to include any exceptions to a broad rule, the Court applies the broad rule.

150 Texas Dept. of Community Affairs v. Burdine, 450 U.S. 248 (1981).

In Flanagan v. Aaron E. Henry Community Health Services Center, 876 F.2d 1231 (5th Cir. 1989), a white

If the institution is able to sustain its burden, the burden shifts back to the complainant to demonstrate that the institution's stated reason for the complainant's rejection was in fact pretext.[151]

A claimant may prove a prima facie case of employment discrimination under a theory of disparate impact or disparate treatment.[152] Discriminatory motive is critical in demonstrating disparate treatment,[153] but, motive may

---

female physician, the only white employee at the community health center, was terminated from her position as a staff physician and was replaced by a black physician. The Court of Appeals for the Fifth Circuit upheld a jury verdict finding racial discrimination violative of Title VII, 42 U.S.C. §§ 1981, 2000e-2.

In International Union, United Auto., Aerospace and Agri. Implement Workers of America, UAW v. Johnson Controls, Inc., 499 U.S. 187 (1991), the Supreme Court ruled an employer may not exclude a female employee from certain jobs because of its concern for the health of a fetus the woman might conceive. The employer's fetal-protection policy excluded women with childbearing capacity from lead-exposed jobs. The Supreme Court ruled such a policy could only be defended as a "bona fide occupational qualification."

151 McDonnell Douglas Corp. v. Green, 411 U.S. 792 (1973) (holding modified by Hazen Paper Co. v. Biggins, 507 U.S. 604 (1993)).

In O'Loughlin v. Procon, Inc., 627 F. Supp. 675 (5th Cir. 1986), the Court of Appeals for the Fifth Circuit ruled an employer's stated reason for termination of an employee is pretextual only if the reason camouflages a discriminatory decision.

152 Griggs v. Duke Power Co., 401 U.S. 424 (1971). The Supreme Court ruled that Title VII prohibits an employer's actions if those actions are shown to have a disparate impact on African Americans.

In Lewis v. N.L.R.B., 750 F.2d 1266 (5th Cir. 1985), the Court of Appeals for the Fifth Circuit ruled a challenge to an employer's promotion practices is subject to disparate treatment rather than disparate impact. Under this analysis, the court held the employer must have had a discriminatory intent. Nonetheless the court stated that racial discrimination may be inferred if gross statistical disparities are shown in an analysis of the relevant statistics. In determining intent, the court noted that the trial court may examine "history of the employer's practices, anecdotal evidence of class members, and the degree of opportunity to treat employees unfairly in the appraisal process."

In Garcia v. Spun Steak Co., 998 F.2d 1480 (9th Cir. 1993), the Court of Appeals for the Ninth Circuit ruled an English-only rule at the workplace does not establish a prima facie case of employment discrimination. The EEOC had concluded that the mere existence of an English-only policy established a prima facie case of an abusive environment. However, the court found nothing in the legislative history of Title VII to indicate an English-only policy is presumed to be discriminatory.

In Texas Dept. of Housing and Community Affairs v. Inclusive Communities Project, Inc., 135 S. Ct. 2507 (2015), the Supreme Court explained that Griggs v. Duke Power Co., 401 U.S. 424 (1971), has placed important limits on Title VII disparate impact liability and stated that even in a disparate-impact case, hiring criteria can be considered.

153 Bryant v. International Schools Services, Inc., 675 F.2d 562 (3d Cir. 1982).

In E.E.O.C. v. Abercrombie & Fitch Stores, Inc., 135 S. Ct. 2028 (2015), the EEOC brought a Title VII action on behalf of a Muslim job applicant against a clothing retailer for religious discrimination because of the retailer's failure to accommodate the applicant's religious practice of wearing a headscarf. The retailer refused to hire the job applicant because the headscarf she wore pursuant to her religious obligations conflicted with the employer's employee dress policy. The Supreme Court ruled a job applicant seeking to prove a Title VII disparate treatment claim need only show that the need for a religious accommodation is a motivating factor in the prospective employer's adverse decision and need not show that the employer knows the applicant's practice is a religious practice that requires an accommodation. The Court stated that the rule for disparate-treatment claims based on a failure to accommodate a religious practice is straightforward and ruled an employer may not make an applicant's religious practice, confirmed or

be inferred from the mere fact of differences in treatment. Disparate impact is used to attack employment practices that are facially neutral but that fall more harshly on a protected class of employees.[154] The disparate impact model requires proof of a causal connection between a challenged employment practice and the composition of the work force. A claimant may show aptitude tests, height and weight requirements, and similar selection criteria that affect one class of employees more harshly than another.[155] However, absent proof that the disparate impact is caused by one or more of the challenged employment practices, a court will not require an employer to justify the legitimacy of any, or all, of its employment practices.[156] Additionally, while disproportionate impact

---

otherwise, a factor in employment decisions.

154 Pouncy v. Prudential Ins. Co. of America, 668 F.2d 795 (5th Cir. 1982).

In Young v. United Parcel Service, Inc., 135 S. Ct. 1338 (2015), the Supreme Court referred to the Pregnancy Discrimination Act (PDA), 42 U.S.C. § 2000e(k), which specifies that Title VII's prohibition against sex discrimination applies to discrimination "because of or on the basis of pregnancy, childbirth or related medical conditions." The Supreme Court noted that the act requires employers to treat women affected by pregnancy the same for all employment-related purposes as other persons not affected but similar in their ability or inability to work. The Court ruled an employee alleging disparate treatment in violation of the PDA may do so through application of the McDonnell Douglas framework. The Court referred to Texas Dept. of Community Affairs v. Burdine, 450 U.S. 248 (1981), wherein the Court had ruled that disparate-treatment law normally permits an employer to implement policies that are not intended to harm members of a protected class, even if their implementation sometimes harms those members, as long as the employer had a legitimate, nondiscriminatory, nonpretextual reason for doing so. The Court stated that an individual pregnant worker who seeks to show disparate treatment may make out a prima facie case under the McDonnell Douglas framework by showing that she belongs to the protected class, that she sought accommodation, that the employer did not accommodate her, and that the employer did accommodate others "similar in their ability or inability to work." The employer then may seek to justify its refusal to accommodate the plaintiff by relying on "legitimate, nondiscriminatory" reasons for denying accommodation. As the Court stated, that reason normally cannot consist simply of a claim that it is more expensive or less convenient to add pregnant women to the category of those whom the employer accommodates. If the employer offers a "legitimate, nondiscriminatory" reason, the plaintiff may show that it is in fact pretextual. The Court stated a plaintiff can create a genuine issue of material fact as to whether a significant burden exists by providing evidence the employer accommodated a large percentage of non-pregnant workers while failing to accommodate a large percentage of pregnant workers. The Court found the plaintiff created a genuine dispute as to whether her employer provided more favorable treatment to at least some employees whose situation could not reasonably be distinguished from hers.

155 Pouncy v. Prudential Ins. Co. of America, 668 F.2d 795 (5th Cir. 1982); Griggs v. Duke Power Co., 401 U.S. 424 (1971).

In Frazier v. Garrison I.S.D., 980 F.2d 1514 (5th Cir. 1993), the Court of Appeals for the Fifth Circuit ruled an employment teacher competency test having a 7.1 percentage point differential between black and white test takers did not, as a matter of law, state a prima facie case of disparate impact. It decided there was no significant statistical discrepancy between minority and nonminority pass rates.

156 Pouncy v. Prudential Ins. Co. of America, 668 F.2d 795 (5th Cir. 1982).

Still, in Connecticut v. Teal, 457 U.S. 440 (1982), the Supreme Court suggested applicants for hire can show a prima facie case of discrimination by showing facially neutral standards in question select applicants for hire in a significantly discriminatory pattern.

In Watson v. Fort Worth Bank and Trust, 487 U.S. 977 (1988), the Supreme Court determined disparate

might cause further inquiry, an inference of discrimination may nonetheless be negated by an employer's affirmative efforts to recruit minorities.[157]

The purpose of Title VII is to achieve equality of employment opportunities and to remove barriers that have operated in the past to favor an identifiable group of white employees over other employees.[158] However, discriminatory preference for any group, minority or majority is precisely and only what Congress has proscribed. Employers have faced loss of substantial federal contracts and liability to minorities for refusing to initiate affirmative action as a remedy for past discrimination; however, they have also faced liability to whites

---

impact analysis can be applied to cases in which subjective criteria are used to make employment decisions, that disparate impact analysis is not limited to cases in which employment decisions are based on tests, verbal skills, or height and weight requirements. The Court stated that if disparate impact analysis is limited to "objective" criteria, an employer can refrain from making standardized criteria absolutely determinative by simply including brief interviews with the candidates. In Watson, a female black employee was denied a promotion. She was told at one point that a teller position was a big responsibility with "a lot of money ... for blacks to count." The Court commented that although the remarks may not prove discriminatory intent, they do suggest a lingering form of the problem that Title VII was enacted to combat. The Court decided the inevitable focus on statistics in disparate impact cases cannot put undue pressure on employers to adopt inappropriate prophylactic measures. The Court prescribed a test for determining whether discrimination has occurred using the disparate impact analysis. The plaintiff has the burden of establishing a prima facie case of discrimination that goes beyond the need to show that there are statistical disparities in the employer's work force. The plaintiff must begin by identifying the specific employment practice that is challenged. Once the employment practice at issue has been identified, causation must be proved, i.e., the plaintiff must offer statistical evidence of a kind and degree sufficient to show that the practice in question caused the exclusion of applicants for jobs or promotions because of their membership in a protected group. Statistical disparities must be sufficiently substantial that they raise such an inference of causation. The employer then can present countervailing evidence to show that there are fallacies or deficiencies in the statistical data offered by the plaintiff. The employer may endeavor to impeach the reliability of the statistical evidence, or they may offer rebutting evidence demonstrating the probative weight the plaintiff's evidence should be accorded.

157 Washington v. Davis, 426 U.S. 229 (1976).

In Wards Cove Packing Co., Inc. v. Atonio, 490 U.S. 642 (1989), the Supreme Court reversed a court of appeal's ruling that a comparison between the percentage of workers who are nonwhite in unskilled positions with the percentage of skilled workers who are nonwhite can make out a prima facie case of disparate impact.

In Green v. USX Corp., 896 F.2d 801 (3d Cir. 1990), the Court of Appeals for the Third Circuit ruled that disparate impact of an employer's challenged action is relevant in considering the evaluation of a disparate treatment claim. The court concluded that use of applicant flow data is an appropriate means of demonstrating the disparate impact of a hiring practice. The plaintiff presented evidence regarding allegedly discriminatory interviews and showed the employer hired significantly less blacks.

158 In Rene v. MGM Grand Hotel, Inc., 305 F.3d 1061 (9th Cir. 2002), the Court of Appeals for the Ninth Circuit ruled a homosexual male former employee had a viable claim of discrimination under Title VII for sexual harassment by his former male supervisors and co-workers even though the employee also alleged that the motivation for discrimination was his sexual orientation. The court stated that sexual orientation is irrelevant for purposes of Title VII. It held that sexual orientation neither provides nor precludes a cause of action for sexual harassment. According to the court, it is enough that a harasser has engaged in severe or pervasive unwelcome physical conduct of a sexual nature.

for any voluntary preferences accorded minorities.[159] Because of the dilemma facing employers, courts have been reluctant to discourage implementation of bona fide affirmative action plans.[160] Consequently, a plaintiff in a reverse discrimination case must present evidence that would show some reason other than a remedial reason motivated an employer in implementing an affirmative action plan or that the plan adopted unreasonably exceeded its remedial purpose.[161]

It is not an unlawful employment practice to apply different standards of compensation, or different terms, conditions, or privileges of employment

---

159 Setser v. Novack Inv. Co., 657 F.2d 962 (8th Cir. 1981).

In Billish v. City of Chicago, 989 F.2d 890 (7th Cir. 1993), the Court of Appeals for the Seventh Circuit commented that the "Constitution is truly colorblind." The court noted that the equal protection clause forbids states to give preference to persons because of their race or ethnicity, but it recognized there is an exception in cases in which discrimination against whites is necessary to rectify previous discrimination in their favor committed by a state agency seeking to practice remedial discrimination. It ruled that the fact the percentage of blacks and Hispanics is far lower than their percentage in the relevant labor market does not establish a violation of "disparate impact."

160 Setser v. Novack Inv. Co., 657 F.2d 962 (8th Cir. 1981).

In Johnson v. Transportation Agency, Santa Clara County, Cal., 480 U.S. 616 (1987), the Supreme Court ruled that consideration of the sex of a female employee as one factor in promoting her over male employees under a voluntary affirmative action plan does not violate Title VII. The dissent opined that the decision would permit racial or sexual discrimination under Title VII when it was intended to overcome the effect, not of the employer's own discrimination, but of societal attitudes that have limited the entry of certain races, or of a particular sex, into certain jobs. The dissent commented that the Johnson decision contradicts the Supreme Court's earlier decision in Wygant v. Jackson Bd. of Educ., 476 U.S. 267 (1986), wherein the Supreme Court had ruled that a school board's policy of extending preferential protection against layoffs to some employees because of their race, violated the Fourteenth Amendment. The majority of the Court approved the hiring because the agency involved sought to take a moderate, gradual approach to eliminating an imbalance in its work force.

In Taxman v. Board of Educ. of Tp. of Piscataway, 91 F.3d 1547 (3d Cir. 1996), the Court of Appeals for the Third Circuit ruled Title VII does not permit an employer with a racially balanced work force to grant nonremedial racial preferences in order to promote "racial diversity." The court held that an employer cannot make an employment decision based upon an employee's race. The court decided that a nonremedial affirmative action plan is unconstitutional.

161 Setser v. Novack Inv. Co., 657 F.2d 962 (8th Cir. 1981). An employer's plan is a bona fide one if it is reasonably related to its remedial purpose. The Court of Appeals for the Eighth Circuit in Setser stated that once an employer has produced evidence that its treatment of a person is a direct consequence of its implementation of a bona fide affirmative action plan, the employer is entitled to a judgment as a matter of law unless the person shows that the purpose of the employer's affirmative action program is not remedial.

In Ricci v. DeStefano, 557 U.S. 557 (2009), a city used objective exams to identify firefighters best qualified for promotion. When results of an examination to fill vacant lieutenant and captain positions showed white candidates outperformed minority candidates, the city threw out the results based on statistical racial disparity. The white and Hispanic firefighters then sued the city. The Supreme Court ruled the city's action in disregarding the tests violated Title VII. The Court stated an employer must have strong basis in evidence to believe it will be subject to disparate-impact liability if it fails to make race-conscious discriminatory action.

pursuant to a bona fide seniority system if the differences are not the result of an intention to discriminate because of race, color, religion, sex, or national origin.[162]

2. Equal Pay Act

An employer engaged in commerce or in the production of goods for commerce may not pay different wages to employees of opposite sexes for equal work on jobs the performance of which requires equal skill, effort, and responsibility and that are performed under similar working conditions unless the payment is made pursuant to (1) a seniority system, (2) a merit system, (3) a system which measures earnings by quantity or quality of production, or (4) a differential

162 42 U.S.C. § 2000e-2(h).

See Firefighters Local Union No. 1784 v. Stotts, 467 U.S. 561 (1984), in which the Supreme Court pointed out individual members of a plaintiff class who can demonstrate that they have been actual victims of a discriminatory practice, may be awarded competitive seniority and given their rightful place in the seniority roster.

In U.S. v. Paradise, 480 U.S. 149 (1987), the Supreme Court validated a court ordered affirmative action plan establishing a one-for-one racial quota for promotions because of the employer's long history of excluding blacks from employment.

In Engquist v. Oregon Dept. of Agri., 553 U.S. 591 (2008), the plaintiff contended she had been discriminated against based on her race, sex, and national origin, but she also brought a so-called "class-of-one" claim, alleging that she was fired not because she was a member of an identified class, unlike her race, sex, and national origin claims, but simply for arbitrary, vindictive, and malicious reasons. The jury rejected the class-membership equal protection claims but found for the plaintiff on her class-of-one claim. The Supreme Court ruled a class-of-one theory of equal protection does not apply in the public employment context. The Supreme Court reiterated that it recognizes the government has significantly greater leeway in its dealings with citizen employees than in bringing its sovereign power to bear on citizens at large. It stated that government employees' rights must be balanced against the realities of the government context. The Court decided that if a class-of-one claim is recognized in the employment context, any personnel action in which a wronged employee can conjure up a claim of differential treatment suddenly will become the basis for a federal constitutional claim. The Court decided the Equal Protection Clause does not require "this displacement of managerial discretion by judicial supervision."

based on any factor other than sex.[163] The Equal Pay Act (EPA) is administered by the EEOC.[164]

A person alleging unequal pay need not show discriminatory intent. The EPA creates a type of strict liability; no intent to discriminate need be shown.[165] A person establishes a prima facie case by a showing of payment of different wages to employees of opposite sexes for equal work on the job.[166] Although job titles are entitled to some weight in the assessment of comparative responsibility, the controlling factor under the EPA is job content—the actual duties the respective employees are called upon to perform.[167]

---

163 29 U.S.C. § 206(d). Activities of nonprofit organizations are included under the act. See 29 U.S.C. § 203(r), which provides that activities performed for a business purpose are treated as ordinary commercial activities. As originally enacted, the EPA was inapplicable to state and local governments. However, coverage was extended to employees of state and local hospitals, institutions, schools, and public transit systems and later was extended to virtually all public employees, except public office holders and their staffs.

In Rizo v. Yovino, 887 F.3d 453 (9th Cir. 2018), judgment vacated and remanded, 139 S. Ct. 706 (2019), the Ninth Court of Appeals had ruled that an employee's prior salary cannot justify payment of a lower wage to her, that the catchall exception "any factor other than sex" is not applicable as a defense to an employee's prior salary. A math consultant's male colleagues were subsequently hired as math consultants at higher salary steps. In ruling that prior salary did not fit within the catchall exception, the court reasoned that this exception relates to legitimate factors other than sex, such as training, education, ability, or experience. On remand, Rizo v. Yovino, 950 F.3d 1217 (9th Cir. 2020), cert. denied, 141 S. Ct. 189 (U.S. 2020), the Ninth Circuit ruled that a county's standard procedure for setting an employee's starting salary that started with the employee's prior wages, is not a "factor other than sex" that can defeat a prima facie case of an equal pay violation.

164 Executive Order 12144 (1979).

165 Strecker v. Grand Forks County Social Service Board, 640 F.2d 96 (8th Cir. 1980) (overruled on other grounds by Robino v. Norton, 682 F.2d 192 (8th Cir. 1982)).

166 See Futran v. Ring Radio Co., 501 F. Supp. 734 (N.D. Ga. 1980); Brobst v. Columbus Services Intern., 761 F.2d 148 (3d Cir. 1985); E.E.O.C. v. Maricopa County Community College Dist., 736 F.2d 510 (9th Cir. 1984).

In Grigoletti v. Ortho Pharmaceutical Corp., 118 N.J. 89 (1990), the Supreme Court of New Jersey ruled that to establish a prima facie case under the Equal Pay Act, a plaintiff must show that her employer paid her a lower salary than that paid to employees of the opposite sex for equal work on jobs the performance of which required equal skill, effort, and responsibility and that were performed under similar working conditions. The court noted an equal-work comparison should focus on whether the jobs have a "common core" of tasks. Factors to be considered include quantity and quality of production, education, relevant prior work experience, conduct, and skill. If in the aggregate, the jobs require substantially similar skills, efforts, and responsibilities, the work should be adjudged equal despite minor variations. The court stated that the requirement that an employer rebut a prima facie case of compensation discrimination with a preponderance of the evidence differs substantially from the evidentiary burden a defendant must shoulder in a Title VII case. The court stated that if the evidence demonstrates a lesser degree of job similarity that will nonetheless satisfy the less-exacting standards of a prima facie case under Title VII, the burden that shifts to the defendant should be only the burden of production of an explanation. Thus, if a complainant can show only that the work is "similar," the defendant will be required to articulate a legitimate nondiscriminatory reason for the treatment of the plaintiff, and the ultimate burden of persuasion will remain on the plaintiff.

167 In Odomes v. Nucare, Inc., 653 F.2d 246 (6th Cir. 1981), the Court of Appeals for the Sixth Circuit

Once a prima facie case of unequal pay has been established, the defendant has four affirmative defenses.[168] The defendant must prove that any wage disparity was the result of a seniority system, a merit system, a system which measures earnings by quantity or quality of production, or that the differential was based on any other factor than sex.[169] A violation of the EPA is also a violation of Title VII.[170] The only justifiable pay differentials under Title VII are those attributable to the four affirmative defenses.[171]

ruled that positions of female nurse's aides and male orderlies were essentially the same. The court stated only substantial equality of skill, effort, responsibility, and working conditions is required. The issue of whether the jobs are substantially the same is resolved by an overall comparison of the work, not its individual segments.

In E.E.O.C. v. First Citizens Bank of Billings, 758 F.2d 397 (9th Cir. 1985), the Court of Appeals for the Ninth Circuit ruled that the Equal Pay Act does not require that jobs being compared be performed simultaneously. The court stated that the act applies to situations where an employee of one sex is hired for a particular job to replace an employee of the opposite sex. If a male is hired to replace a female, for example, violations of the act may be proved by comparing the female's salary to that of her male successor. Back pay may be awarded for the period prior to the male's hiring.

168 Strecker v. Grand Forks County Social Service Board, 640 F.2d 96 (8th Cir. 1980) (overruled on other grounds by Robino v. Norton, 682 F.2d 192 (8th Cir. 1982)).

In Gordon v. United States, 903 F.3d 1248 (Fed. Cir. 2018), female physicians alleged they were victims of gender discrimination when they did not receive raises at the same time a male doctor who was hired about the same time received an annual raise and they did not receive raises commensurate with those obtained by male doctors in the same department. The Court of Appeals for the Federal Circuit ruled that to establish a prima facie case of a violation of the EPA, a female physician had to establish that a pay differential between similarly situated employees was historically or presently based on sex. The court ruled that plaintiffs bear the burden of showing that a complained-of pay differential is based on sex and that evidence of clear pay disparities between plaintiffs and similarly situated male doctors does not permit a fact finder to draw an inference that discrimination based on sex exists or existed.

169 Strecker v. Grand Forks County Social Service Board, 640 F.2d 96 (8th Cir. 1980) (overruled on other grounds by Robino v. Norton, 682 F.2d 192 (8th Cir. 1982)).

In U.S. Equal Employment Opportunity Commission v. Maryland Insurance Administration, 879 F.3d 114 (4th Cir. 2018), the Court of Appeals for the Fourth Circuit ruled that showing each claimant earned less than at least one male comparator performing substantially equal work under similar working conditions was sufficient to establish a prima facie case of wage discrimination. The court stated that while an employer may be entitled to summary judgment on an EPA claim if the employer establishes an affirmative defense as a matter of law, "the burden on the employer necessarily is a heavy one."

170 In Washington County v. Gunther, 452 U.S. 161 (1981), the Supreme Court ruled that claims for sex-based wage discrimination can also be brought under Title VII provided the claim is not exempt because the wage differential is attributed to seniority, merit, quantity or quality of production, or any other factor other than sex.

171 Discussion in Schulte v. Wilson Industries, Inc., 547 F. Supp. 324 (S.D. Tex. 1982) and Futran v. Ring Radio Co., 501 F. Supp. 734 (N.D. Ga. 1980). A plaintiff who shows a violation of the EPA is entitled under Title VII to the difference between what the plaintiff would have earned and what the plaintiff did earn.

3. Age Discrimination in Employment Act

The Age Discrimination in Employment Act (ADEA) provides that an employer engaged in an industry affecting commerce with twenty or more employees for each working day in each of twenty or more calendar weeks in the current or preceding calendar year may not fail or refuse to hire or to discharge any individual or otherwise discriminate against any individual because of the individual's age.[172]

The ADEA is limited to persons who are at least forty years of age,[173] with its purpose being to promote employment of older persons based on their ability rather than on age, to prohibit arbitrary age discrimination in employment, and to help employers and workers find ways of meeting problems arising from the impact of age on employment.[174] While Title VII standards are applied to charges

---

172 29 U.S.C. §§ 621 et seq. See specifically Sections 623, 630(b).

In Blum v. Witco Chemical Corp., 829 F.2d 367 (3d Cir. 1987), the Court of Appeals for the Third Circuit stated it is sufficient to prove more favorable treatment to a "sufficiently younger" person, rather than to a person outside the protected class.

In Gilmer v. Interstate/Johnson Lane Corp., 500 U.S. 20 (1991), the Supreme Court ruled an age discrimination claim is subjected to compulsory arbitration. The Court stated a claimant is bound by an agreement to arbitrate and decided that there is no inconsistency between the important social policies furthered by the ADEA and the enforcement of agreements to arbitrate age discrimination claims.

In Fichman v. Media Center, 512 F.3d 1157 (9th Cir. 2008), in an age discrimination action brought by the former executive director of an organization operated by a nonprofit organization, the Court of Appeals for the Ninth Circuit ruled that members of the board of directors of the organization and independent producers were not "employees" under the ADEA.

The question of sovereign immunity, and others, can arise when the state or a political subdivision is the employer.

In Kimel v. Florida Bd. of Regents, 528 U.S. 62 (2000) three sets of plaintiffs filed suit under the ADEA seeking money damages for their state employers' alleged discrimination because of age. The Supreme Court noted that the ADEA contains a clear statement of Congress' intent to abrogate the States' sovereign immunity but dismissed the suit, ruling that the abrogation exceeded Congress' authority under Section 5 of the Fourteenth Amendment.

In Mount Lemmon Fire Dist. v. Guido, 139 S. Ct. 22 (2018), the Supreme Court ruled that the twenty-employee minimum does not apply to political subdivisions, citing 29 U.S.C. § 630(b), which defines the term "employer" to include a state or political subdivision of a state and any agency or instrumentality of a state or a political subdivision of a state. The Court also referred to its decision in EEOC v. Wyoming, 460 U.S. 226 (1983), to state that "applying the ADEA to state and local governments does not encroach on States' sovereignty or Tenth Amendment immunity." This statement in Guido appears to negate the Supreme Court's decision in Kimel that Congress cannot abrogate Eleventh Amendment immunity under the ADEA. Still, the Court's decision in Guido can be interpreted as the Supreme Court's validation of Eleventh Amendment immunity in the ADEA.

173 29 U.S.C.A. § 631. Persons over sixty-five who for two years prior to retirement were employed in executive or high policy-making positions are not subject to the act if those persons are entitled to an immediate annual nonforfeitable retirement benefit equivalent, originally, to $44,000 or more.

174 Schwager v. Sun Oil Co. of Pennsylvania, 591 F.2d 587 (10th Cir. 1979).

of age discrimination as purposes and structure of the acts are similar,[175] Title VII standards are not applied automatically in age discrimination cases.[176] An employer can establish a bona fide occupational qualification as a defense to a

---

See Monroe v. United Air Lines, Inc., 736 F.2d 394 (7th Cir. 1984), for a comprehensible discussion by the Court of Appeals of the Seventh Circuit of requirements under the act.

In Frazer v. KFC Nat. Management Co., 491 F. Supp. 1099 (M.D. Ga. 1980), aff'd, 636 F.2d 313 (5th Cir. 1981), the court stated the act is not intended to give employees the right to walk off their jobs and sue their employer because they dislike their changed job responsibilities. If employees walk out, the court ruled they can complain of discharge only if the offered or altered working conditions will have been so difficult or unpleasant that a reasonable person in the employee's shoes will have felt compelled to resign.

175 Schwager v. Sun Oil Co. of Pennsylvania, 591 F.2d 58 (10th Cir. 1979); Tuohy v. Ford Motor Co., 675 F.2d 842 (6th Cir. 1982).

In Verbraeken v. Westinghouse Elec. Corp., 881 F.2d 1041 (11th Cir. 1989), the Court of Appeals for the Eleventh Circuit provided three methods by which a plaintiff may establish a prima facie case of age discrimination: by direct evidence of discriminatory intent, by meeting the test originally set out for Title VII cases in McDonnell Douglas Corp. v. Green, 411 U.S. 792 (1973), or by statistical proof of a pattern of discrimination. Utilizing a modified McDonnell Douglas test, a prima facie case may be established with circumstantial evidence by proving that the plaintiff (1) was a member of the protected group of persons, (2) was subject to adverse employment action, (3) was replaced with a person outside the protected group, and (4) was qualified to do the job. The Eleventh Circuit noted that in reduction-in-force cases, the McDonnell Douglas test has been modified by eliminating the replacement requirement.

In O'Connor v. Consolidated Coin Caterers Corp., 517 U.S. 308 (1996), the Supreme Court ruled a plaintiff alleging he was discharged in violation of the ADEA need not show he was replaced by someone outside the age group protected by the ADEA to make out a prima facie case under the framework established by McDonnell Douglas Corp. v. Green, 411 U.S. 792 (1973). A worker, age fifty-six, was replaced by a forty-year-old worker. The Supreme Court ruled that the fact an ADEA plaintiff was replaced by some outside the protected class is not a proper element of the McDonnell Douglas prima facie case. The Court stated the fact a replacement is substantially younger than an ADEA plaintiff is a more reliable indicator of age discrimination than is the fact the plaintiff is replaced by someone outside the protected class.

In Smith v. City of Jackson, Miss., 544 U.S. 228 (2005), the Supreme Court ruled that disparate impact theory of liability is available to plaintiffs suing for age discrimination under the ADEA. Plaintiffs raised both disparate treatment and disparate impact theories of liability. Regarding their disparate treatment claim, the plaintiffs alleged that the defendants were motivated by age to implement a plan that discriminated against them intentionally. In a disparate treatment case, liability depends on whether the protected trait, age, actually motivated the employer's decision. A disparate treatment claim cannot succeed unless the employees' protected trait actually played a role in that process and had a determinative influence on the outcome. Proof of discriminatory motive, thus, is critical to the success of a plaintiff's discriminatory treatment claim. In contrast, in a disparate impact case, liability may result without a demonstration of discriminatory motive. Disparate impact claims arise from employment practices that are facially neutral in their treatment of groups but that, in fact, fall more harshly on one group than another and that cannot be justified by business necessity.

In Gomez-Perez v. Potter, 553 U.S. 474 (2008), the Supreme Court ruled the federal-sector provision of the ADEA, 29 U.S.C.A. § 633a(a), prohibits retaliation against a federal employee who complains of age discrimination.

176 Tuohy v. Ford Motor Co., 675 F.2d 842 (6th Cir. 1982).

charge of age discrimination.[177] A business necessity test, not a business convenience test, is used.[178]

4. Americans with Disabilities Act

The Americans with Disabilities Act (ADA)[179] was hailed as representing a "long-delayed but very necessary step to welcome individuals with disabilities fully

177 Id. See also Hodgson v. Greyhound Lines, Inc., 499 F.2d 859 (7th Cir. 1974).

In Trans World Airlines, Inc. v. Thurston, 469 U.S. 111 (1985), the Supreme Court ruled the policy of Trans World Airlines of transferring its captains who were sixty years of age to flight engineers only on a bid basis when other captains were transferred automatically, violated the ADEA. Age was not a bona fide occupational qualification for flight engineers.

In Western Air Lines, Inc. v. Criswell, 472 U.S. 400 (1985), the Supreme Court ruled the bona fide occupational qualification defense is an extremely narrow exception. The defense is available only if the job qualification is reasonably necessary to the overriding interest in public safety and if the employer is compelled to rely on age as a proxy for a safety related job qualification.

In E.E.O.C. v. Tennessee Wildlife Resources Agency, 859 F.2d 24 (6th Cir. 1988), the Court of Appeals for the Sixth Circuit referred to a two-prong test set out by the Supreme Court in Western Air Lines, Inc. v. Criswell, 472 U.S. 400 (1985). The Sixth Circuit ruled that Tennessee's mandatory retirement age of fifty-five for wildlife officers violated the ADEA because it violated the first prong of the Criswell test, i.e., it was not shown that physical and coronary fitness was reasonably necessary to the job of serving as a wildlife officer. There was no evidence that persons over fifty-five who had been permitted to continue to work had proved to be unsatisfactory.

In Meacham v. Knolls Atomic Power Laboratory, 554 U.S. 84 (2008), the Supreme Court ruled an employer defending a disparate-impact claim under the ADEA bears both the burden of production and the burden of persuasion for the "reasonable factors other than age" affirmative defense under 29 U.S.C. § 623(f)(1), which is listed alongside the bona fide occupational qualification exemption. When the government ordered its contractor to reduce its work force, the contractor had its managers score their subordinates on "performance," "flexibility," and "critical skills." These scores, along with points for years of service, were used to determine the employees who would be dismissed. Of the thirty-one employees who were laid off, thirty were at least forty years old.

178 In Hodgson v. Greyhound Lines, Inc., 499 F.2d 859 (7th Cir. 1974), the employer successfully demonstrated its maximum hiring age policy was founded upon a good faith judgment concerning the safety needs of its passengers and others and that its hiring policy was not the result of an arbitrary belief lacking in objective reason or rationale.

The exception to the ADEA is analyzed in terms of vocations within a general business rather than by duties performed.

The court ruled Mahoney v. Trabucco, 738 F.2d 35 (1st Cir. 1984), that the state could establish mandatory retirement age of fifty for state police officers even though, in that case, the plaintiff engaged primarily in administrative duties with no strenuous physical activity.

In Gross v. FBL Financial Services, Inc., 557 U.S. 16 (2009), the Supreme Court ruled a plaintiff bringing an age discrimination disparate treatment claim must prove that age is the "but for" cause of the challenged adverse employment action. The Supreme Court held that the burden of persuasion does not shift to the employer to show that it would have taken the action regardless of age, even when a plaintiff produces some evidence that age is one motivating factor in the decision. The Court affirmed it has never applied Title VII's burden-shifting framework to ADEA claims because, according to the Court, Title VII is materially different with respect to the relevant burden of persuasion.

179 42 U.S.C. §§ 12101 et seq.

into the mainstream of American society."[180] The purpose of the act was stated to be: (1) to provide a clear and comprehensive national mandate for elimination of discrimination against individuals with disabilities; (2) to provide clear, strong, consistent, enforceable standards addressing discrimination against individuals with disabilities; (3) to ensure that the federal government will play a central role in enforcing standards established on behalf of individuals with disabilities; and (4) to invoke congressional authority, including power to enforce the Fourteenth Amendment and to regulate commerce, to address major areas of discrimination faced daily by persons with disabilities.[181]

The ADA prohibits a covered entity[182] from discriminating against a "qualified individual with a disability"[183] because of the individual's disability with regard to job application procedures, hiring, advancement, or discharge of

---

180 Americans With Disabilities Act of 1990, Pub. L. No. 101-336, 104 Stat. 327, 4 U.S. Cong. & Admin. News 268 (1990).

181 42 U.S.C. § 12101(b).

182 A "covered entity" is an employer engaged in an industry affecting commerce that has fifteen or more employees for each working day of twenty or more calendar weeks in the current or preceding calendar year and any agent of such employer. 42 U.S.C. § 12111(5).

A covered entity must post notices in an accessible format to applicants, employees, and other persons describing provisions of the ADA. 42 U.S.C. § 12115.

183 The term "qualified individual with a disability" means an individual with a disability, who, with or without reasonable accommodation, can perform the essential functions of an employment position such individual holds or desires. See 42 U.S.C. § 12111(8).

Consideration is given to the employer's judgment as to what functions of a job are essential, and if an employer has prepared a written description before advertising or interviewing applicants for the job, the description is considered evidence of the essential functions of the job.

The term "disability" means, with respect to an individual, a physical or mental impairment that substantially limits one or more of the major life activities of the individual; a record of such an impairment; or being regarded as having an impairment. 42 U.S.C. § 12102(2). A "qualified individual with a disability" does not include any employee or applicant who is currently engaging in the illegal use of drugs, when a covered entity acts because of the drug usage. See 42 U.S.C. § 12114. An individual who has successfully completed a supervised drug rehabilitation program and is no longer engaging in the illegal use of drugs is not excluded as a qualified individual with a disability. The term "disability" does not include transvestism, transsexualism, pedophilia, exhibitionism, voyeurism, gender identity disorders not resulting from physical impairments or other sexual behavior disorders; compulsive gambling, kleptomania, or pyromania; or psychoactive substance use disorders resulting from current illegal use of drugs.

In Estate of Mauro By and Through Mauro v. Borgess Medical Center, 137 F.3d 398 (6th Cir. 1998), the Court of Appeals for the Sixth ruled that because a hospital employee, a surgical technician, who was terminated because he was infected with HIV, was not an "otherwise qualified" person under the ADA, his termination was not in violation of the ADA. The court noted a person is not qualified if the person poses a direct threat to the health and safety of others and the threat cannot be eliminated by reasonable accommodation.

In Murphy v. United Parcel Service, Inc., 527 U.S. 516 (1999), the Supreme Court ruled a person who was terminated because of high blood pressure, which exceeded the DOT's requirements for commercial vehicle drivers, did not have a cause of action under the ADA.

employees, employee compensation, job training, and other terms, conditions, and privileges of employment.[184] A covered entity is deemed to have discriminated against a qualified individual with a disability if the employer does not make reasonable accommodations to the known physical or mental limitations of an otherwise qualified individual with a disability who is an applicant or employee unless the covered entity can demonstrate the accommodation would impose an undue hardship on the entity's business.[185] No qualified individual

---

184 42 U.S.C. § 12112. Although a covered entity may make pre-employment inquiries into the ability of an applicant to perform job-related functions, a covered entity may not conduct a medical examination or make inquiries of a job applicant as to whether the applicant is an individual with a disability or the nature or severity of the disability, unless the examination or inquiry is shown to be job-related and consistent with business necessity. See 42 U.S.C. § 12112(d). Section 12114(d) states that a test to determine the illegal use of drugs is not considered a medical examination for this purpose.

In Hoepfl v. Barlow, 906 F. Supp. 317 (E.D. Va. 1995), the court ruled a plaintiff did not have standing under the ADA to sue a physician who had refused to treat patients who were HIV positive.

In Murray v. Mayo Clinic, 934 F.3d 1101 (9th Cir. 2019) and 784 Fed. Appx. 995 (9th Cir. 2019), cert. denied, 206 L. Ed. 2d 855 (2020), the Court of Appeals for the Ninth Circuit ruled that an employee must show an adverse employment action would not have occurred "but for" a disability. The court overruled Head v. Glacier Northwest, Inc., 413 F3d 1053 (9th Cir. 2005), wherein it held that ADA discrimination claims are evaluated under a motivating factor causation standard. The court noted the decision of the Supreme Court in Gross v. FBS Financial Services, Inc., 557 U.S. 167 (2009), wherein the Supreme Court ruled that in bringing an age discrimination disparate treatment claim, a plaintiff must prove that age was the "but for" cause of a challenged adverse employment action. The court pointed out in Mayo Clinic that, following the Supreme Court decision in Gross, circuits had retreated from the motivating factor standard of causation in ADA cases and that it would join its sister circuits in holding that ADA discrimination claims under Title I must be evaluated under a "but for" causation standard.

In Colorado State Bd. of Medical Examiners v. Ogin, 56 P.3d 1233 (Colo. App. 2002), the court ruled the ADA does not prevent a professional licensing agency from imposing disciplinary sanctions against a "qualified individual with a disability." The court stated the act does not protect an individual with a disability who, by virtue of disability, is a direct threat to the public's safety. There was evidence in the case that the anesthesiologist plaintiff's disorder caused him to fall asleep during surgery.

185 42 U.S.C. § 12112(b)(5). A covered entity also discriminates against a disabled individual if the entity denies employment opportunities to a job applicant or employee who is an otherwise qualified individual with a disability because of the entity's need to make reasonable accommodation to the physical or mental impairments of the employee or applicant.

The term "reasonable accommodation" may include making existing facilities used by employees readily accessible to and usable by individuals with disabilities, and job restructuring, part-time or modified work schedules; reassignment to a vacant position; acquisition or modification of equipment, or devices; appropriate adjustment or modifications of examinations, training materials or policies; provision of qualified readers or interpreters; and other similar accommodations for individuals disabilities. See 42 U.S.C. § 12111(9).

Section 12111(10) defines an undue hardship as any action requiring significant difficulty or expense when considered in light of the following factors: (1) nature and cost of the accommodation; (2) overall financial resources of the facility or facilities involved in provision of the reasonable accommodation; (3) number of persons employed at the facility; (4) effect on expenses and resources, or impact otherwise of the accommodation upon operation of the facility; (5) overall size of the business of the covered entity with respect to number of its employees; (6) number, type, and location of facilities; (7) type of operation or operations of the covered entity, including composition, structure, and functions of the workforce of the entity; and

with a disability can be excluded from participation in, or be denied the benefits of, services, programs, or activities of a public entity.[186] Although the act exempted from its provision private clubs and religious organizations,[187] other nonprofit organizations are covered.[188]

The ADA incorporates by reference enforcement provisions of Title VII of the Civil Rights Act of 1964 discussed above, including injunctive relief and back pay.[189] The ADA provides an employer with a defense to a charge of

---

(8) geographic separateness and administrative or fiscal relationship of the facility or facilities in question to the covered entity.

In Kolling v. Blue Cross & Blue Shield of Michigan, 318 F.3d 715 (6th Cir. 2003), the Court of Appeals for the Sixth Circuit ruled that a "public accommodation," within the meaning of the ADA, is limited to a physical place. It held that the ADA cannot be applied to the contents of employer-furnished benefit plans and ruled that participants in such plans could not maintain an ADA action against the insurer based on the disparity of benefits provided for speech therapy.

186 42 U.S.C. §§ 12111(5)(B), 12113(c). The act does not prohibit a religious organization from giving preference in employment to individuals of a particular religion to perform work connected with the organization's activities. Additionally, a religious organization may require that all applicants and employees conform to the religious tenets of the organization.

In Board of Trustees of University of Alabama v. Garrett, 531 U.S. 356 (2001), the Supreme Court ruled the Eleventh Amendment bars suits against states by state employees for money damages for failure of a state to comply with provisions of Title I of the ADA, which addresses employment discrimination. The Court held that for Congress to authorize private individuals to recover money damages against a state, there must be a pattern of discrimination by the states that violates the Fourteenth Amendment. It stated the remedy imposed by Congress must be congruent and proportional to the targeted violation and decided that the ADA does not meet these requirements.

In Lovell v. Chandler, 303 F.3d 1039 (9th Cir. 2002), the Ninth Circuit Court of Appeals ruled the Eleventh Amendment does not bar claims against a state brought under Title II of the ADA, which prohibits any public entity from discriminating against "qualified" persons with disabilities in the provisions or operation of public services, programs, or activities. The act defines the term "public entity" to include state and local governments, as well as their agencies and instrumentalities. Plaintiffs sued the State of Hawaii because they were excluded from participation in a new state health care program. The program specifically excluded the aged, blind, and disabled. The Ninth Circuit noted that the Supreme Court in Board of Trustees of University of Alabama v. Garrett, 531 U.S. 356 (2001), expressly reserved the question of whether Title II is appropriate legislation under Section Five. Considering that reservation, the Ninth Circuit held that the Eleventh Amendment does not bar claims against the State brought under Title II of the ADA.

In Wessel v. Glendening, 306 F.3d 203 (4th Cir. 2002), the Court of Appeals for the Fourth Circuit also ruled the Eleventh Amendment does bar claims against a state under Title II of the ADA.

In Tennessee v. Lane, 541 U.S. 509 (2004), the Supreme Court agreed that the Eleventh Amendment does not bar suits against the state under Title II of the ADA, deciding that Title II does not exceed Congress' power under Section 5 of the Fourteenth Amendment.

187 42 U.S.C. § 12132.

188 The act designates day care centers; senior citizen centers; homeless shelters; food banks; museums; libraries; galleries; parks; zoos; amusement parks, or other places of recreation; schools including private schools; adoption agencies; or other social service center establishments, as being public accommodations that are covered by the act. See 42 U.S.C. § 12181.

189 42 U.S.C. § 12117. Section 12203 states that no person may discriminate against any individual because the individual opposed any act or practice made unlawful by the ADA or because the in-

discrimination if the employer can demonstrate that application of its qualification standards, tests, or selection criteria to screen out, or tend to screen out, or otherwise deny a job or benefit to an individual with a disability, is job-related and consistent with business necessity.[190]

A covered entity may prohibit the illegal use of drugs and the use of alcohol at the workplace by all employees.[191] It may also hold an employee, who engages in the illegal use of drugs or who is an alcoholic, to the same qualification standards for employment or job performance and behavior that it holds for other employees even if any unsatisfactory performance or behavior is related to the employee's drug use or alcoholism.[192]

---

dividual made a charge, testified, or participated in any manner in an investigation, proceeding, or hearing pursuant to the act.

In Barnes v. Gorman, 536 U.S. 181 (2002), the Supreme Court ruled punitive damages may not be awarded in suits brought under the ADA.

190 42 U.S.C. § 12113. The term "qualification standards" may include a requirement that an individual not pose a direct threat to the health or safety of other individuals in the workplace. For example, an employee may refuse to assign or continue to assign, to food handling, an individual who has an infectious or communicable disease that is transmitted to others, assuming the problem cannot be eliminated by reasonable accommodation.

191 42 U.S.C. § 12114(c)(1).

192 42 U.S.C. § 12114(c)(4).

In Raytheon Co. v. Hernandez, 540 U.S. 44 (2003), the Supreme Court ruled the Ninth Court of Appeals had improperly applied a disparate-impact analysis of a worker's claim for of disability discrimination under the ADA. The worker had tested positive for cocaine use and was forced to resign from his company for violating the company's workplace-conduct rules. Three years later, he applied to be rehired and attached letters from his pastor, who stated he was a faithful and active church member, and from an Alcoholics Anonymous counselor, who stated he was in recovery. Nevertheless, the company rejected the application. The worker sued under the ADA against the company on a disparate-treatment theory, that is, on an allegation that the company had rejected his application because of his record of drug addiction and/or because he was regarded as being a drug addict. The company contended its refusal to rehire the worker was based on its neutral policy of not rehiring employees who were terminated for violating the company's code of conduct. The Supreme Court determined that the employer's proffer of its neutral not-rehire policy plainly satisfied its obligation under McDonnell Douglas Corp. v. Green, 411 U.S (1973) to provide a legitimate, nondiscriminatory reason for refusing to rehire the worker. The Supreme Court concluded that, as a matter of law, the employer's policy was a legitimate, nondiscriminatory reason sufficient to defeat a prima facie case of discrimination.

CHAPTER VII. OBTAINING AND MAINTAINING TAX EXEMPT STATUS

A. INTRODUCTION

These last three chapters summarize the tax provisions relating to tax-exempt status for nonprofit hospitals and their affiliated organizations. This Chapter VII sets out the requirements, pursuant to Section 501(c)(3) of the Internal Revenue Code (I.R.C.), for a nonprofit hospital and its affiliated organizations to obtain and maintain tax-exempt status. Chapter VIII summarizes the provisions of I.R.C. § 509, and applicable provisions in I.R.C. § 170, to explain the two separate tax classifications of § 501(c)(3) organizations--the public charity and the private foundation--and to discuss the tax consequences of these two tax classifications. Chapter VIII additionally reviews applicative requirements of I.R.C. §§ 509 and 170 to support the further classification of a § 501(c)(3) hospital as a "public charity" for tax purposes and to summarize additional requirements for hospital affiliated and related organizations to be so classified. Chapter VIII further critiques the "private foundation" classification that may apply to the hospital affiliated and related organizations. It discusses how and when "public charity" status is more favorable than "private *nonoperating* foundation" classification with a consideration of the requirements for the more favorable "private *operating* foundation" categorization. Chapter IX sets out the provisions of I.R.C. §§ 511-514 regarding activities that are unrelated to a hospital's exempt purposes and will cause an otherwise tax-exempt hospital, and/or its affiliated and related organizations, to be subject to what is termed the unrelated business income tax. The requirements for nonprofit, tax-exempt hospitals summarized in Chapters VII, VIII, and IX dictate how the tax-exempt hospitals must operate. Accordingly, information provided in these chapters demonstrate that the structure of a nonprofit, tax-exempt hospital is determined and shaped by the tax law.

Additional introductory material follows and will provide parameters for tax-exempt status generally to assist in understanding the advantages and disadvantages of the special tax-exempt status for nonprofit hospitals and their affiliated and related organizations.[1]

As noted, hospitals and their affiliates qualify for tax exempt pursuant to I.R.C. 501(c)(3); that Code section also provides Section 501(c)(3) status to other

1 A coverage of all the law relating to tax-exempt organizations otherwise is beyond the scope of the three chapters as the chapters are limited to the tax law applicable to hospitals and their supporting organizations. A detailed discussion of the tax provisions applicable to nonprofit organizations generally is set out in Marilyn E. Phelan, Representing Nonprofit Organizations, Thomson Reuters, 2021, updated annually.

types of charitable organizations, such as educational, religious, and scientific organizations. Other provisions in I.R.C. § 501, and in I.R.C. §§ 521, 527, 528, and 529, grant tax-exempt status to several additional and differing types of nonprofit organizations. These include, among others, civic and social welfare organizations, labor and agricultural organizations, trade and professional organizations, social clubs, cemetery organizations, credit unions, war veterans' organizations, cooperatives, home-owners' associations, and political organizations.

Exempt organizations are referred to by their Internal Revenue Code classification. Charitable organizations, those required by I.R.C. § 501(c)(3) to be operated "exclusively for religious, charitable, scientific, public safety testing, literary, or educational purposes, fostering national or international amateur sports competition (if no part of activities involve provisions of athletic facilities or equipment), or for the prevention of cruelty to children or animals," are referred to as § 501(c)(3) organizations and are the most recognized tax-exempt organizations. Social welfare organizations, a category that would include civic associations and organizations, such as the Sierra Club, that, unlike § 501(c)(3) organizations, can also be involved in some political activity, can qualify for tax-exempt status under I.R.C. § 501(c)(4) and are referred to as § 501(c)(4) organizations. Labor and agricultural organizations, exempt pursuant to I.R.C. § 501(c)(5), are referred to as § 501(c)(5) organizations; professional organizations, qualified for exempt status under I.R.C. § 501(c)(6), are referred to as § 501(c)(6) organizations. Social clubs are called § 501(c)(7) organizations, while war veterans' organizations are referred to as § 501(c)(19) organizations. Political organization that can qualify for tax-exempt status pursuant to I.R.C. § 527, are called 527 organizations. Rules relating to the various tax classifications of nonprofit organizations differ for each classification. For example, donors may claim a charitable contribution deduction for contributions to a § 501(c)(3) organization, a § 501(c)(13) cemetery organizations and a §501 (c)(19) war veterans' organization but not to most other tax-exempt organizations. Section 501(c)(3) organizations cannot be involved in political activities whereas § 501(c)(4) organizations can so long as the majority of their activities relate to social welfare activities. Still, because of their ability to be involved in some political activities, there is no charitable contribution deduction for donations to the § 501(c)(4) organizations. For professional businesses, *dues* paid to a professional § 501(c)(6) organizations, such as the American Medical Association or the American Bar Association, may provide a taxpayer with a business deduction for tax purposes.

Except for public hospitals and other public healthcare institutions, a hospital, as well as any of its supporting organizations, are not automatically tax-exempt; they must apply for tax-exempt classification to qualify as charitable organizations under I.R.C. § 501(c)(3). A public hospital that is a governmental agency need not apply for exempt status, however, because governmental hospitals are automatically exempt from taxation. Additionally, governmental agencies related to hospitals are exempt from taxation under I.R.C. § 115, and thus also need not apply for exempt status. Further, donations to governmental entities made exclusively for public purposes provide donors with charitable contributions deductions pursuant to I.R.C. § 170(c)(1) without § 501(c)(3) classification. Qualification as a § 501(c)(3) organization then is not necessary for public hospitals and other public health care institutions.

As discussed in Chapter VIII, a hospital that qualifies as a § 501(c)(3) organization for tax purposes will also qualify under I.R.C. § 509 as a public charity. However, a hospital's affiliated organizations may be unable to qualify for the generally more favorable public charity status because, without sufficient public support, they are classified as private foundations for tax purposes. Nonetheless a supporting organization for a hospital that has few donors and, as a result, is classified as a private foundation for tax purposes, often can qualify for more beneficial tax treatment as a private "operating" foundation, also discussed in Chapter VIII.

B. SECTION 501(c)(3) STATUS

As noted previously, nonprofit hospitals and their supporting organizations seek tax-exempt classification under I.R.C. § 501(c)(3) as charitable organizations.[2] To obtain that status, both a hospital and its affiliated organizations would electronically file IRS Form 1023.[3] Until exempt status has been recognized by the

2 As noted previously, a public hospital need not apply for exempt status. Purely governmental entities are automatically tax exempt, and quasi-governmental organizations are exempt from taxation pursuant to I.R.C. § 115. Additionally, donations to governmental entities made exclusively for public purposes provide donors with charitable contributions deductions under I.R.C. § 170(c)(1).

3 A charitable organization must electronically file the IRS Form 1023 within twenty-seven months after the organization is established for the Internal Revenue Service to recognize exempt status from the organization's inception. If the organization does not file Form 1023 within the twenty-seven months, the IRS will recognize exempt status only from the date the IRS receives the application. Treas. Reg. § 1.508-1(a)(2). Smaller organizations may qualify to use the Form 1023EZ to apply

Internal Revenue Service (IRS), a hospital, or a supporting organization, files an information return, IRS Form 990, and indicates on the return that its application for exempt status is pending with the Internal Revenue Service.

A rehabilitation institution, outpatient clinic, community mental health or drug treatment center, or a skilled nursing facility may qualify as a hospital if the principal function of the institution is the providing of hospital or medical care.[4] Conversely, convalescent homes or homes for children or the elderly, or institutions training handicapped individuals to pursue some vocation do not qualify as hospitals.[5] Further, an organization that provides medical education or medical research is not a hospital unless it is also actively engaged in providing medical or hospital care to patients on its premises or in its facilities. This can be on an inpatient or outpatient basis, but it must be an integral part of its medical education or medical research functions.[6] To qualify as a medical research organization, an entity must have, or must have continuously available for its regular use, the appropriate equipment and professional personnel necessary to carry out its principal function.[7] Additionally, to be engaged primarily in medical research, an organization either must devote a substantial part of its assets to,

---

for tax exempt status under I.R.C. § 501(c)(3). A hospital completes Schedule C to the Form 1023 to answer numerous questions relating to its qualification as a hospital pursuant to § 501(c)(3) of the Code.

4 Treas. Reg. §1.170A-9(c)(1). The term "medical care" includes the treatment of any physical or mental disability or condition, whether on an inpatient or outpatient basis, provided the cost of the treatment is deductible as a medical expense under I.R.C. § 213. See Treas. Reg. §1.170A-9(c)(1).

5 Treas. Reg. § 1.170A-9(c)(1).

6 Treas. Reg. § 1.170A-9(c)(1)(i). Medical research is the conduct of investigations, experiments, and studies to discover, develop, or verify knowledge relating to the causes, diagnosis, treatment, prevention, or control of physical or mental diseases and impairments. See Treas. Reg. § 170A-9(c)(2)(iii). Medical research encompasses disciplines spanning the biological, social and behavioral sciences. Such disciplines include chemistry, behavioral sciences, biomedical engineering, virology, immunology, biophysics, cell biology, molecular biology, pharmacology, toxicology, genetics, pathology, physiology, microbiology, parasitology, endocrinology, bacteriology, and epidemiology. See Treas. Reg. § 170A-9(c)(2)(iii). A medical research organization must be engaged directly in the continuous active conduct of medical research in conjunction with a hospital and must have medical research as its primary function. See Treas. Reg. § 170A-9(c)(2)(ii). To qualify contributions to this organization for the less restrictive charitable contribution limitation (discussed in Chapter VIII), the organization must be committed to spend its contributions for the active conduct of medical research before January 1st of the fifth calendar year beginning after the date the contributions were made. This requirement is to assure that the organization is actively engaged in medical research and is not inactive or is primarily engaged in funding programs of other medical research organizations. See Treas. Reg. § 509(a)-2.

7 Treas. Reg. § 170A-9(c)(2)(iii).

or expend a significant percentage of its endowment for, these purposes.[8] While a medical organization need not be formally affiliated with a hospital to be considered primarily engaged directly in the continuous active conduct of medical research, there must be a joint effort on the part of the research organization and the hospital pursuant to an understanding that the two organizations will maintain continuing close cooperation in the active conduct of medical research.[9]

> Example: Healthcare Organization was created to promote human knowledge within the field of medical research and medical education. All of Healthcare's assets were donated by one individual and consist of stocks and bonds. Healthcare's endowment earns four percent annually which Healthcare expends in the conduct of various medical research programs in conjunction with Medical Hospital. Healthcare is located adjacent to Medical Hospital and makes substantial use of Medical Hospital's facilities. There is close cooperation between the staffs of Healthcare and Medical Hospital. Healthcare is directly engaged in the continuous active conduct of medical research in conjunction with a hospital and qualifies as a public charity for tax purposes.

Section 501(c)(3) organizations must be established and operated exclusively for charitable purposes. Thus, a hospital as a § 501(c)(3) organization must meet two tests--an organizational test and an operational test. The organizational test for qualification as a charitable organization requires that the articles of incorporation, certificate of formation, articles of association, or declaration of trust limit the organization to one or more charitable purposes.

A charitable organization may not be permitted to engage in activities not in furtherance of its exempt purposes (other than as an insubstantial part of its activities). The requirement that the articles of organization limit the organization's purpose and powers to charitable ones is not satisfied if the limitation

8 Treas. Reg. § 1.170A-9(c)(2)(v). An organization that devotes more than one-half of its assets to the continuous active conduct of medical research will meet this requirement. An organization that expends funds equaling three and one half percent or more of the fair market value of its endowment for the continuous active conduct of medical research also will have met the test. Treas. Reg. § 1.170A-9(c)(2)(v)(b). Engaging directly in the continuous active conduct of medical research does not include the disbursing of funds to other organizations for the conduct of research by them nor does it include the extending of grants or scholarships to others. Consequently, if an organization's primary purpose is to disburse funds to other organizations for the conduct of research or to extend grants or scholarships to others, it is not primarily engaged directly in the continuous active conduct of medical research. See Treas. Reg. § 1.170A-9(c)(2)(v)(c).

9 Treas. Reg. § 1.170A-9(c)(2)(vii).

is contained only in bylaws or other operating rules. It also is not satisfied by statements of officers that they intend to operate only for exempt purposes. A hospital (and any of its supporting organizations) must have its assets dedicated to the exempt purpose of health care in order to meet the organizational test. Upon dissolution, all assets of the organization must be distributed to a charitable entity for one or more exempt purposes, to the federal government, or to a state or local government, for a public purpose. Articles of organization for an organization seeking § 501(c)(3) status must contain provisions indicating that the above requirements have been met.

The operational test requires that a nonprofit organization be "operated exclusively"[10] for one or more exempt purposes. None of the earnings of a charitable organization may inure in whole or in part for benefit of private individuals or entities.[11] Additionally, if a substantial part of an organization's activities is attempting to influence legislation, the organization will be deemed an "action" organization, and unless it complies with certain Internal Revenue Code requirements noted below, will not meet the operational test.[12]

The term "charitable" is not specifically defined in the Internal Revenue Code. As one court early commented,[13] Congress and the courts originally conditioned a hospital's "charitable status on the level of free or below cost care that it provided for indigents." One court pointed out that "charitable 'status should not be "so limited" and stated that "the rendering of medical care is a charitable activity."[14] Still, a nonprofit hospital is required to show that it provides community benefits to obtain and maintain charitable tax exempt status.[15] The IRS has stated that a hospital or other health care organization does not

10 The Treasury has interpreted "exclusively" as "primarily." Treas. Reg. § 1.502(c)(3)-1(c)(1). The Regulation states that an organization must engage "primarily" in activities that accomplish one or more of its exempt activities.

11 See discussion of inurement below.

12 See requirements as set out in I.R.C. § 501(c)(3). Discussion below of lobbying activities of a § 501(c)(3) organization.

13 Sound Health Assoc. v. Comm., 71 T.C. 158 (1978). See also discussion in Korean-American Senior Mutual Assoc. v. Comm., T.C. Memo 2020-129, 120 T.C.M. 191 (2020).

14 Sound Health Assoc. v. Comm., 71 T.C. 158 (1978).

15 In FSA 200110030, the IRS concluded a hospital does not qualify for tax-exempt status under I.R.C. § 501(c)(3) unless it can demonstrate its stated policies to provide health care services to the indigent actually result in the delivery of significant health care services to the indigent.

(A FSA, or Field Service Advisory, provides tax advice from the IRS Chief Counsel. The date of the FSA appears immediately after "FSA." For example, the above FSA 200110030 was issued in 2001.)

automatically qualify for exemption under I.R.C. § 501(c)(3) merely because it promotes health.[16] A hospital or other health care organization must benefit primarily the community to qualify for § 501(c)(3) status.[17]

A determination of whether a hospital satisfies the community benefit is based on all the facts and circumstances. The IRS earlier set forth a series of

---

16 The IRS has pointed to the decisions in Redlands Surgical Services v. C.I.R., 113 T.C. 47 (1999), review denied, decision aff'd, 242 F.3d 904 (9th Cir. 2001), and Geisinger Health Plan v. C.I.R., 985 F.2d 1210 (3d Cir. 1993), wherein the courts made tax-exempt status for hospitals conditioned on hospitals being able to demonstrate that their charity care policies yielded significant health care services to the indigent.

In Priv. Ltr. Rul. 201615022, the Service ruled that a nonprofit corporation created to promote and support, directly or indirectly, the interests and purposes of a § 501(c)(3) healthcare corporation did not qualify for § 501(c)(3) status. The Service found that approximately half the organization's participating physicians were in independent practices or affiliated with other hospitals and regional health systems. The Service determined that because the organization did not engage in the direct delivery of medical care or provide health services to the general public, it was not performing a charitable purpose to qualify it for § 501(c)(3) status. It stated that negotiating with private health insurers on behalf of unrelated healthcare providers was not a charitable activity. Although the Service agreed that the corporation's electronic health records activities could further charitable purposes under § 501(c)(3), the fact that the corporation had some programs that furthered exempt purposes was immaterial because the presence of a substantial nonexempt purpose destroyed the exemption under § 501(c)(3) regardless of the number or importance of the organization's truly exempt purposes. The Service stated that the organization was not established pursuant to a statute, managed by government officials, or funded by government grants and that there was no government oversight of its activities.

(Priv. Ltr. Rul. refers to a private letter ruling from the Internal Revenue Service--a written instruction to a taxpayer that requests advice regarding the tax effect of a proposed event. The Service will apply the tax law to facts the taxpayer has provided. Assuming these facts do not change, a private letter ruling is effective as to the taxpayer requesting the advice but not as to other taxpayers. Still, these rulings do provide other taxpayers information regarding the IRS position on the issue or issues in the ruling. The first numbers of a private letter ruling provide the year the IRS issued the private letter ruling. For example, the private letter ruling above was issued in 2016.)

17 In Ltr. Rul. 201641027, the Service ruled that an organization whose purpose was to provide a centralized location to provide care to underserved populations in a rural area and to continue to advance and include more services at the needs of the populace did not qualify for § 501(c)(3) status because it was not formed by residents of the community. In addition, another organization was already located in the area so that medical care was already present. The Service noted that while the organization's goal was to increase healthcare services to those in need, the organization was not providing those services itself.

In Ltr. Rul. 201615018, the Service ruled that a corporation, whose mission was to provide a way for its members to cultivate and distribute, collectively and cooperatively, physician-recommended marijuana and that was formed to provide a courier service to qualified patients, who were members of the organization, did not qualify for § 501(c)(3) status. The Service stated that the organization's primary activity, the distribution of cannabis, was illegal because federal law does not recognize any health benefits of cannabis and classifies it as a controlled substance. The Service decided the organization's primary purpose of distributing cannabis not only violated federal law, it also furthered a substantial nonexempt purpose. The Service concluded the organization was operated for private purposes rather than for the public interest because the organization operated primarily for the benefit of its members and, thus, served the interests of a select group of individuals, rather than the community's or public's interest. As the Service ruled, a business or other activity that assists the community incidentally and only provides benefits to a limited number of members of the community more than incidentally is not charitable.

questions a hospital should address when developing the factual record on its charitable care policies and activities.[18] To request tax exempt status, a hospital must complete a Schedule C to IRS Form 1023. This schedule requires the hospital to respond to questions similar to those promulgated by the IRS. On an annual basis, a tax-exempt § 501(c)(3) hospital must file Form 990 and attach a Schedule H to report its indigent care and bad debts to show it provided a community benefit. The Patient Protection and Affordable Act[19] added Section 501(r) to the Internal Code to make nonprofit charitable hospitals more publicly oriented by requiring tax exempt hospitals to answer numerous required questions on the Schedule H a hospital must attach to its annual reporting form, the Form 990; answers to questions on the Schedule H must demonstrate the hospital's compliance with the voluminous requirements of I.R.C. § 501(r).[20]

---

18 The questions included the following:

1. Does the hospital have a specific, written plan or policy to provide free or low-cost health care services to the poor or indigent?

2. Under what circumstances may, or has, the hospital deviated from its stated policies on providing free or low-cost health care services to the poor or indigent?

3. Does the hospital broadcast the terms and conditions of its charity care policy to the public?

4. Does the hospital maintain and operate a full-time emergency room open to all persons regardless of their ability to pay?

5. What directives or instructions does the hospital provide to ambulance services about bringing poor or indigent patients to its emergency room?

6. What inpatient, outpatient, and diagnostic services does the hospital provide to the poor or indigent for free or for reduced charges?

7. Under what circumstances does the hospital deny health care services to the poor or indigent?

8. Does the hospital operate with the expectation of receiving full payment from all persons to whom it renders services?

9. How and when does the hospital ascertain whether a patient will be able to pay for the hospital's services?

10. What documents or agreements does the hospital require poor or indigent patients to sign before receiving care?

11. What is the hospital's policy on admitting poor or indigent patients as inpatients and outpatients?

12. Under what circumstances does the hospital refer poor or indigent individuals who require services to other hospitals in the area that do admit poor or indigent patients?

13. Does the hospital maintain separate and detailed records about the number of times, and circumstances under which, it provided free or reduced-cost care to the poor or indigent?

14. Does the hospital maintain a separate account on its books that segregates the costs of providing free or reduced-cost care to the poor or indigent? Does this account include any other items, such as write-offs for care to patients who were not poor or indigent?

19 Pub. L. 111-148, 124 Stat. 119 (2010).

20 The many requirements of § 501(r) have made tax-exempt status for hospitals much less favorable and definitely difficult to maintain. The Service has published Rev. Proc. 2015-21, discussed in more detail below, to provide correction and disclosure procedures under which the IRS will excuse cer-

To obtain and maintain tax-exempt status pursuant to I.R.C. § 501(c)(3), a hospital must not only meet the requirements of I.R.C. § 501(r), it also must continue to comply with mandates set out in I.R.C 501(c)(3) that it has no inurement nor does it provide any private benefit, that it is not involved in commercial activities in more than an insubstantial amount, that it is not involved in any political activities and only involved in insubstantial lobbying, if any. These Code section requirements are detailed below.

1. Section 501(r) Requirements.

The Patient Protection and Affordable Act[21] added Section 501(r) to the Internal Revenue Code to make nonprofit charitable hospitals more publicly oriented

---

tain failures to meet the requirements of § 501(r).

["Rev. Proc" is the abbreviation for "revenue procedure." A revenue procedure is an official statement from the IRS that provides the public with knowledge and/or awareness of the rights or duties of taxpayers or members of the public under federal statutes, particularly the Internal Revenue Code. Rev. Proc. 2015-21 was the twenty first revenue procedure issued in 2015.]

21 Pub. L. 111-148, 124 Stat. 119 (2010).

In Nat'l Federation of Ind. Business v. Sebelius, 567 U.S. 519 (2012), the Supreme Court declared the Affordable Care Act to be constitutional. A critical component of the act was an individual mandate, which provided that each "applicable" individual had to ensure the individual was covered under "minimum essential coverage." See 26 U. S.C. § 5000A(a). Individuals who were subject to the requirement but would not "obey the command" were liable for what was called a "shared responsibility payment" or "penalty pursuant to Section 5000A(b). The Supreme Court ruled the individual mandate in the act was within Congress' "taxing" power. Later, in King v. Burwell, 576 U.S 473 (2015), the Court ruled that the federal government was a "state" for purposes of another of the act's key provision. This provision granted subsidies to persons purchasing insurance through exchanges established by a "state." See 26 U.S.C. § 36B(b)-(c). When many states refused to establish such exchanges, the federal did so instead. The questioned provision was deemed constitutional by the Court finding the federal government to be a "state." In 2017, Congress reduced to zero the "shared responsibility payment" (penalty) imposed on persons who failed to abide by the individual mandate. Then, in Texas v. U.S., 945 F.3d 355 (5th Cir. 2019), the Court of Appeals for the Fifth Circuit declared that without the penalty tax, the Affordable Care Act was no longer a valid exercise of Congress' taxing power and declared the act's minimum essential coverage provision, codified at 26 US.C. § 5000A(a), to be unconstitutional. The plaintiffs contended the minimum essential coverage requirements were not severable from the rest of the act. The Supreme Court reversed and remanded the case in California v. Texas, Texas v. California, 104 S. Ct. 2104 (2021), ruling that the plaintiffs did not have standing to challenge Section 5000A(a)'s minimum essential coverage provision. The Court stated the plaintiffs had not shown a past or future injury fairly traceable to the defendant's conduct in enforcing the specific statutory provision they were attacking as unconstitutional.

In Little Sisters of the Poor Saints Peter and Paul Home v. Pennsylvania, 140 S. Ct. 2367 (2020), the Supreme Court previously recognized standing for two states in permitting them to contest a rule exempting the Little Sisters of the Poor and other religious employers from the Act's contraceptive mandate. The Supreme Court ruled the Departments of Health and Human Services and the Treasury had authority under the Affordable Care Act to promulgate religious and moral exemptions to the act. The Court referred to Burwell v. Hobby Lobby Stores, Inc. 573 U.S. 682 (2014), wherein the Court had ruled the contraceptive mandate in the act substantially burdened the free exercise of closely held corporations with sincerely held religious objections.

by requiring hospitals that are tax-exempt under Section 501(c)(3) to meet certain substantial additional requirements to retain their tax-exempt status.[22] Unfortunately, these requirements are much too comprehensive and not at all clear cut; they have made tax-exempt status for hospitals much less beneficial.

Pursuant to Section 501(r), a § 501(c)(3) hospital organization is required to meet four general requirements on a facility-by-facility basis:[23] (1) establish written financial assistance emergency medical care policies, (2) limit amounts charged for emergency or other medically necessary care to individuals eligible for assistance under the hospital's required financial assistance policy (FAP), discussed below,[24] (3) make reasonable efforts to determine whether an individual is eligible for assistance under the hospital's FAP before engaging in extraordinary collection actions against the individual, and (4) conduct a community health needs assessment (CHNA), discussed below, from which the hospital must adopt an implementation strategy at least once every three years to

22 Final Treasury regulations implemented under Section 501(r), Treas. Reg. § 1.501(r)-1 to 7, regarding additional requirements charitable hospital facilities must meet to be treated as tax exempt under I.R.C. § 501(c)(3), apply to a hospital's tax year that began after December 29, 2015. The regulations provide guidance on the requirements described in Section 501(r) these hospitals must meet, the reporting obligations relating to these requirements pursuant to I.R.C. § 6033(b), and the consequences for failing to satisfy the Section 501(r) requirements. A tax-exempt hospital that fails to meet the requirements of I.R.C. § 501(r) may have its Section 501(c)(3) status revoked and be subject to penalty taxes discussed below.

Pursuant to Treas. Reg. § 1.501(r)-2, in determining whether to revoke a hospital's Section 501(c)(3) status, the IRS will consider (1) whether the organization previously failed to meet the requirements of I.R.C. § 501(r) and, if so, whether the same type of failure previously occurred as well as the size, scope, nature and significance of the organization›s failure(s), (2) for those organizations that operate more than one hospital facility, the number, size, and significance of facilities that failed to meet Section 501(r) requirements, (3) the reason for the failure as well as whether the organization had established practices or procedure (formal or informal) reasonably designed to promote and facilitate overall compliance with § 501(r) and whether it routinely followed those procedures, with the failure(s) being an oversight or mistake in applying them, (4) whether the organization had implemented safeguards reasonably calculated to prevent similar failures, and (5) whether the organization corrected the failure(s) promptly after discovery.

23 Section 501(r) applies to hospital organizations on a facility-by-facility basis; thus, if a hospital organization operates more than one hospital facility, the organization is required to meet the additional requirements of Section 501(r) separately with respect to each facility. [The additional requirements apply to an organization that operates a facility required by a State to be licensed, registered, or similarly recognized as a hospital and any other organization the Secretary of the Treasury determines has the provision of hospital care as its principal function or purpose to constitute the basis of its exemption under I.R.C. § 501(c)(3).]

24 The FAP must include eligibility criteria for financial assistance and state whether the assistance includes free or discounted care, the basis for calculating amounts charged to patients, the method for applying for financial assistance, the actions the hospital may take in the event of nonpayment if the hospital does not have a separate billing and collections policy, and the measures to publicize widely the policy within the community served by the hospital.

meet the community health needs identified through the assessment.[25] A hospital must "establish" written policies and procedures to comply with § 501(r).[26]

a. Community Health Needs Assessment (CHNA)

A hospital that is tax exempt under Section 501(c)(3) must conduct a Community Health Needs Assessment (CHNA) at least once every three years. Section 501(c)(3) hospitals must have also adopted an implementation strategy to meet the community health needs identified in the CHNA. To conduct a CHNA, a § 501(c)(3) hospital must define the community it serves; must assess the health needs of that community; must consider input from persons who represent broad interests of the community the hospital serves, including those with special knowledge of, or expertise in, public health; must document the CHNA in a written report that an authorized body of the hospital facility adopts; and must make the report widely available to the public.[27]

---

25 The community health needs assessment must consider input from persons who represent the broad interests of the community served by the hospital including those with special knowledge of, or expertise in, public health. The assessment must be made widely known to the public.

26 Reg. § 1.501(r)-4(e) states that a policy adopted by an authorized body of a hospital, but not followed in any regular fashion, has not been "established."

A hospital sets out its compliance with I.R.C. § 501(r) by reporting on Schedule H to the Form 990, which is the form the hospital must file annually with the Internal Revenue Service. The Schedule H had added Part V, Section B, to assemble information on a hospital's compliance with the Affordable Care Act's requirements. The section that was added to the Schedule H requires separate reporting for each hospital facility. A filer will list the hospital facilities it operated during the tax year in Section A. The filer will report separately on Section B the activities, policies and practices of each of its hospital facilities listed in Section A. A filer will list its non-hospital healthcare facilities in Section C. A hospital must attach a copy of its most recent audited financial statements to its Schedule H. All hospitals also must address questions on Schedule H relating to community health needs assessments. [Because non-hospital healthcare facilities are not required to meet requirements of § 501(r), hospital organizations need not report on policies of non-hospital health care facilities.]

In Priv. Ltr. Rul. 201731014, the Service revoked the Section 501(c)(3) exempt status of a hospital because officials in charge of the hospital failed to meet the requirements of Section 1.501(r)-3 by not completing and adopting an Implementation Strategy as required by I.R.C. § 501(r)(3)(A)(ii) and by not making its CHNA report widely available to the public as required by I.R.C. § 501(r)(3)(B)(ii). Hospital administrators made it clear that they had neither the will, financial resources, nor the staff to follow through with the CHNA process required under I.R.C. § 1.501(r)-3 on a triannual basis. As a result, the IRS ruled its failure to meet the requirements of Section 1.501(r)-3 was considered willful and revoked its exempt status.

In Priv. Ltr. Rul. 201829017, the Service revoked the tax-exempt status of a hospital for its failure to comply with the requirements of I.R.C. § 501(r). Officials of the organization were unaware of the requirements and decided there was no tangible benefit from being a § 501(c)(3) organization. The organization was established as a governmental hospital and was operating as such. As such, the organization was also exempt under Section 501(c)(3). Hospital officials agreed to revocation of its exempt status because it would remain a governmental hospital.

27 A hospital facility's CHNA report is made widely available to the public only if the hospital makes

The CHNA process includes reviewing data on community health status, soliciting input from community members, selecting priority health needs, and implementing strategies to consider the priority needs.[28] In assessing community

it available on a web site and the facility has made widely available on a web site its two subsequent CHNA reports as well as making a paper copy of the report available for public inspection upon request and without charge at the hospital facility at least until the date the facility has made available for public inspection a paper copy of its two subsequent CHNA reports. See Treas. Reg. § 1.501(r)-3(b)(7)(i)(B). A hospital facility must make a paper copy of the CHNA report available for public inspection upon request and without charge. If a hospital conducts its CHNA in collaboration with other organizations and facilities, every hospital facility must document the information in a separate CHNA report unless it adopts a joint CHNA report. See Treas. Reg. § 1.501(r)-3(b)(6)(v). A joint report must be identified as applying to the hospital facility and all the collaborating hospital facilities and organizations included in the joint CHNA report must define their community to be the same.

The Affordable Care Act also added Section 4959 to the Code to impose an excise tax for failure to meet the CHNA requirements. Hospitals that are subject to Section 501(r)(3) requirements and that fail to meet the requirements are subject to a $50,000 excise tax pursuant to I.R.C. § 4959. A charitable hospital organization liable for the Section 4959 excise tax must file a return on IRS Form 4720 to report the excise tax liability. The hospital must file Form 4720 by the 15th day of the 5th month after the close of the hospital's tax year during which it incurred liability under § 4959.

Rev. Proc. 2015-21 states that the Service will pardon a hospital organization's failure to meet one or more of the requirements set out in I.R.C. § 501(r) if the failure is neither willful nor egregious and the hospital organization corrects the failure and makes disclosure in accordance with rules set forth in additional guidance the Treasury Department and the IRS would issue. Still, the hospital organization nonetheless may be subject to the excise tax under I.R.C. § 4959. A hospital must make its correction in accordance with principles that include (1) restoration of affected persons; (2) reasonable appropriate correction; (3) timing; and (4) implementation/modification of safeguards. The notice provides examples to illustrate the correction principles. A failure is disclosed for purposes of the revenue procedure if the hospital organization reports the following information on Schedule H with its Form 990: (1) a description of the failure, including the type of failure, the hospital facility or facilities where the failure occurred, the dates of the failure, the number of occurrences, the cause of the failure, the practices and procedures (if any) that were in place prior to the occurrence of the failure to detect or prevent the type of failure that occurred, and in the case of failures to meet the operational requirements in Section 1.501(r)-5 or (6), the number of persons affected and the dollar amounts involved, (2) a description of the discovery, including how it was made and the time of discovery, (3) a description of the correction made, including the method of correction, the date of correction, and whether all persons were restored to the position they would have been in had the failure not occurred and, if not, the reasons why, and (4) a description of the practices and procedures, if any, that were revised or newly established by the hospital organization for its hospital facility to minimize the likelihood of the type of failure recurring and to identify and correct promptly any future failure, or if no practices and procedures were revised or newly established, an explanation of why they were not.

28 In defining the community it serves, a hospital facility may consider all the relevant facts and circumstances, including the geographic area the hospital facility serves, the target population served, such as children, women, the aged, etc., and the principal functions, such as a specialty area or targeted disease. See Treas. Reg. § 1.501(r)-3(b)(v)(3). A hospital facility may not define its community to exclude medically underserved, low-income or minority populations who live in the geographic areas from which the hospital facility draws its patient (unless the populations are not part of the hospital facility's target patient population or affected by its principal functions). In addition, in determining the hospital's patient populations for purposes of defining its community, a hospital facility must consider all patients without regard to whether, or how much, they or their insurers pay for the care they receive or whether they are eligible for assistance under the hospital facility's FAP.

health needs of the community that a hospital serves, a hospital facility must identify significant health needs of the community, prioritize those health needs, and identify resources, to include organizations, facilities, and programs in the community as well as those of the hospital facility, that are potentially available to address those health needs.[29]

A hospital facility's implementation strategy to meet the community needs identified through the hospital facility's CHNA is a written plan that either describes how the hospital facility plans to address the health need or identified the health need as one the hospital facility does not intend to address and explains why the hospital facility does not intend to address the health need.[30] A hospital facility may develop an implementation strategy in collaboration with other hospital facilities or other organizations.[31] A hospital facility must solicit and consider input received from the following sources in identifying and prioritizing significant health needs and in identifying resources potentially available to address those health needs: (a) at least one state, local, tribal,

---

29 Treas. Reg. § 1.501(r)-3(b)(v)(4). For these purposes, the health needs of a community include requisites for the improvement or maintenance of health status both in the community at large and in parts of the community, such as particular neighborhoods or populations experiencing health disparities. These needs may include the need to address financial and other barriers to assessing care, to prevent illness, to ensure adequate nutrition, or to address social, behavioral, and environmental facts that influence health in the community. A hospital facility may determine whether a health need is significant based on all the facts and circumstances present in the community the hospital serves. In addition, a hospital facility may use any criteria to prioritize the significant health needs it identifies. These include, but are not limited to, the burden, scope, severity, or urgency of the health need; the estimated feasibility and effectiveness of possible interventions; the health disparities associated with the need; or the importance the community places on addressing the need.

30 To describe how the hospital facility plans to address a significant health need, the hospital facility's implementation strategy must describe actions the hospital facility intends to take to address the health need and the anticipated impact of these actions, identifies the resources the hospital facility plans to commit to address the health need, and describes any planned collaboration between the hospital facility and other facilities or organizations in addressing the health need. See Treas. Reg. § 1.501(r)-3(c)(2). To describe why a hospital facility is not addressing a significant health need, a brief explanation of the reason for not addressing the need is sufficient. The reasons may include resource constraints, other facilities or organizations in the community addressing the need, a relative lack of expertise or competency to address collectively the need, the need being a relatively low priority, and a lack of identified effective interventions to address the need.

31 Treas. Reg. § 1.501(r)-3(c)(4). A joint implementation strategy must clearly identify the hospital facility's role and responsibilities in taking the actions described in the implementation strategy and the resources the hospital facility plans to commit to the actions and include a summary or other tool that will help the reader easily locate portions of the joint implementation strategy that relate to the hospital facility. An authorized body of the hospital facility must adopt the implementation strategy on the fifteenth day of the fifth month after the end of the taxable year in which the hospital facility completes the final step for the CHNA regardless of whether the hospital facility began working on the CHNA in a prior taxable year.

or regional governmental public health department (or equivalent department or agency), (b) members of medically underserved, low-income, and minority populations in the community the hospital facility serves, and (c) written comments received on the hospital facility's most recently conduct CHNA and most recently adopted implementation strategy.[32]

b. Financial Assistance Policy (FAP)

A hospital facility meets the requirement that it must establish a written financial assistance policy (FAP) if it institutes a written FAP that includes the following: eligibility criteria for financial assistance and whether the assistance includes free or discounted care; the basis for calculating amounts charged to

32 Treas. Reg. § 1.501(r)-3(b)(v)(5). Medically underserved populations include populations experiencing health disparities or at risk of not receiving adequate medical care because of being uninsured or underinsured or due to geographic, language, financial, or other barriers. A hospital facility may also solicit and consider input received from a broad range of persons located in, or serving, its community, including, but not limited to, health care consumers and consumer advocates, nonprofit and community-based organizations, academic experts, local government officials, local school districts, health care providers and community health centers, health insurance and managed care organizations, private businesses, and labor and workforce representatives.

A hospital's CHNA report will adequately describe how the hospital facility considered input from persons who represent broad interest of the community it serves if the report summarizes, in general terms, any input provided by these persons and how and over what time period they provided the input (as examples, whether through meetings, focus groups, interviews, surveys, or written comments and between what approximate dates), provides the names of any organizations providing input and summarizes the nature and extent of the organizations' input; and describes the medically underserved, low-income, or minority populations represented by organizations or individuals that provided input. See Treas. Reg. § 1.501(r)-3(b)(6)(iii). A CHNA report does not need to name or otherwise identify any specific individual providing input. If a hospital facility solicits, but cannot obtain, input, the CHNA report must describe the hospital facility's efforts to solicit input from that source.

Documentation of a CHNA must include the following: (a) a definition of the community the hospital facility serves and a description of how the hospital determined the community, (b) a description of the process and methods the hospital used to conduct the CHNA, (c) a description of how the hospital solicited and considered input received from persons who represent the broad interest of the community the hospital serves, (d) a prioritized description of the significant health needs of the community identified through the CHNA, along with a description of the process and criteria used in identifying certain health needs as significant and prioritizing those significant health needs, (e) a description of the resources potentially available to address the significant health needs identified through the CHNA; and (f) an evaluation of the impact of any actions the hospital took since it finished conducting its immediately preceding CHNA, to address the significant health needs identified in the hospital's prior CHNA(s). See Treas. Reg. § 1.501(r)-3(b)(v)(6)(I).

A CHNA describes the process and methods used to conduct the CHNA if the CHNA report describes the data and other information used in the assessment, as well as the methods of collecting and analyzing the data and information and identifies any parties with whom the hospital facility collaborated, or with whom it contracted for assistance, in conducting the CHNA. See Treas. Reg. § 1.501(r)-3(b)(6)(ii). For data the hospital facility obtained from external source material, the CHNA report may cite the source material rather than describe the method of collecting the data.

patients; the method for applying financial assistance; in the case of an organization that does not have a separate billing and collections policy, the actions the organization may take in the event of nonpayment, including collections action and reporting to credit agencies.[33] With respect to a limitation on charges, the regulations provide for two methods to determine amounts generally billed (AGB): a lookback method and a prospective Medicare or Medicaid method.[34] For billing and collection, the regulations set out an eight-month period after the first post-discharge bill for a hospital to give a patient time to apply for financial assistance to meet the requirement that a hospital not engage in "extraordinary collection actions (ECAs)."[35] A hospital organization must establish a written policy for a hospital facility that requires the hospital facility to provide, without discrimination, care for emergency medical conditions to individuals regardless of whether they are FAP eligible.[36]

---

33 The written FAP must include, if applicable, any information obtained from sources other than an individual seeking financial assistance that the hospital facility uses and whether and under what circumstances it uses prior FAP eligibility determinations. See Treas. Reg. §§ 1.501(r)-4(a), (b). The FAP must determine presumptively whether an individual is FAP-eligible and include a list of any providers, other than the hospital facility itself, that deliver emergency or other medically necessary care in the hospital facility and that specifies which providers are covered by the hospital facility's FAP and which are not. Treasury regulations require translation of the FAP for limited English proficiency (LEP) populations that constitute the lesser of five percent or 1,000 persons. The regulation requires a hospital facility to make the FAP, FAP application form, and plain language summary of the FAP widely available on a website and make paper copies available upon request and without charge.

34 Treas. Reg. § 1.501(r)-5(b)(3), (b)(4). A hospital may use only one of these methods to determine AGB at any one time, but different hospital facilities operated by the same hospital organization may use different methods and a hospital facility may change the method it uses to determine AGB at any time.

35 Treas. Reg. § 1.501(r)-6(c). The Regulations, Treas. Reg. § 1.501(r)-6(b), further provide that ECAs include selling an individual's debt to another party; reporting adverse information about the individual to consumer credit reporting agencies; deferring, denying, or requiring a payment before providing medically necessary care because of an individual's nonpayment of bills for previously provided care covered under the hospital's FAP; and actions that require a legal or judicial process.

36 Treas. Reg. § 1.501(r)-4(c). A hospital facility's emergency care policy must prohibit the hospital facility from engaging in actions that discourage individuals from seeking emergency medical care. A hospital facility cannot demand that emergency department patients pay before receiving treatment for emergency medical conditions and cannot permit debt collection activities that interfere with the provision, without discrimination, of emergency medical care. A hospital organization has established a FAP, a billing and collections policy, or an emergency care policy for a hospital facility only if an authorized body of the hospital facility has adopted the policy for the hospital facility and the hospital facility has implemented the policy. See Treas. Reg. § 1.501(r)-4(d).

2. Inurement

Section 501(c)(3) of the Internal Revenue Code provides that "no part of the earnings of... [the charitable organization] inures to the benefit of any private shareholder of individual." This prohibition is similar to a private benefit limitation in that it prohibits the conferring of a benefit on private interest. The prohibition is absolute; it applies even if the inurement is insubstantial. The policy underpinnings of the non-inurement rule derive from the belief that charities should promote the public good rather than provide a private benefit. Additionally, to the extent that personnel or other private individuals, particularly a select few, materially benefit from a nonprofit organization's activities, the sincerity of the claimed nonprofit purposes may be called into question.[37]

The payment of excessive salaries or excessive rents and the use of a hospital's facilities to serve a private interest constitute inurement. Still, an organization's net earnings may inure to the benefit of private individuals in ways other than by actual distribution of profits or payment of excessive salaries.[38] If a second organization is created to serve to funnel income to an individual who controls a purportedly exempt organization and if the income exceeds a reasonable salary, income inures to the benefit of a private person.[39] If a particular individual or a limited number of individuals reap commercial benefits from the operation of a nonprofit organization, though they do not do so by direct acquisition or payment over to them of its earnings, the earnings nevertheless may inure to their benefit within the intendment of such phrasing so as to destroy the tax-exempt status of the organization.

---

37 Presbyterian & Reformed Pub. Co. v. Comm., 743 F.2d 148 (3rd Cir. 1984). In Bubbling Well Church of Universal Love, Inc. v. Comm., 670 F.2d 104 (9th Cir. 1981), the Court of Appeals for the Ninth Circuit commented that the potential for abuse is created by a person's control of a tax-exempt organization.

In Anclote Psychiatric Center, Inc. v. Comm., TC Memo 1998-273, the Tax Court agreed with the IRS that the tax-exempt status of a § 501(c)(3) organization should be revoked because sale of the organization's assets for less than the fair market value resulted in inurement to the purchaser's private shareholders who also were directors of the § 501(c)(3).

38 Presbyterian & Reformed Pub. Co. v. Comm., 743 F.2d 148 (3rd Cir. 1984). In Harding Hospital v. United States, 505 F.2d 1068 (6th Cir. 1974), the Court of Appeals for the Sixth Circuit ruled that if a particular individual or a limited number of individuals reap commercial benefits from the operation of an entity, though they do not do so by direct acquisition or payment over to them of the entity's earnings, the earnings nevertheless may inure to their benefit.

39 Hall v. Comm., 729 F.2d 632 (9th Cir. 1984).

3. Commercial Activities

The requirement that a tax-exempt organization be organized and operated "exclusively" for its specific exempt purpose presupposes that the organization will not engage in activities of a commercial nature that are unrelated to the tax-exempt purpose of the organization. However, a tax-exempt organization is regarded as being operated exclusively for its exempt purposes if its activities are primarily those which are carried on to accomplish one or more of its exempt purposes and if not more than an "insubstantial" part of its activities furthers a nonexempt purpose.[40] Thus, an "insubstantial" amount of nonexempt, or commercial, activity will not disqualify a hospital for tax-exempt status.[41]

There are no definitive guidelines as to how much commercial activity is "substantial" and, thus, could jeopardize the tax-exempt status of an organization.[42] Courts have established the following factors to be considered in determining whether an organization's nonexempt activities exceed the "benchmark of insubstantiality:" (a) the manner in which the organization's activities are conducted, (b) the commercial hue of the nonexempt activities, and (c) the existence and amount of profit from the activities.[43] Facts and circumstances of a particular activity determine whether tax-exempt status is in jeopardy.

a. Involvement in a Partnership

Charitable organizations have utilized the limited partnership arrangement to accomplish various commercial objectives.[44] Although the participation of a

40 The Regulations, Treas. Reg. § 1.502(c)(3)-1(c)(1), provide that an organization will not be operated exclusively for exempt purposes if more than an "insubstantial" part of its activities is not in furtherance of an exempt purpose.

41 Courts have focused on the manner in which activities of a tax-exempt organization are carried on, implicitly reasoning that an end can be inferred from the chosen means. See Presbyterian & Reformed Pub. Co. v. Comm., 743 F.2d 148 (3rd Cir. 1984). For example, should an organization's management decisions replicate those of a commercial enterprise, it can be inferred that at least one purpose of the organization is commercial and hence nonexempt. Should the nonexempt goal be substantial, tax-exempt status may be denied or revoked.

42 In Associated Master Barbers & Beauticians of America, Inc. v. Comm., 69 T.C. 53 (1977), the court revoked an organization's tax exemption where approximately thirty percent of its revenues were derived from nonexempt activity.

43 See American Institute for Economic Research v. United States, 302 F.2d 936 (Ct. Cl. 1962).

44 In Plumstead Theater Soc., Inc. v. Comm., 74 T.C. 1324 (1980), aff'd, 675 F.2d 244 (9th Cir. 1982), a nonprofit corporation established to promote the performing arts, created a limited partnership to

charitable organization in a partnership arrangement will not per se result in the denial of tax-exempt status, a partnership arrangement must be scrutinized closely to assure that any obligations imposed on the tax-exempt partner do not conflict with the exempt organization's ability to pursue its charitable goals. In all limited partnership arrangements, the initial focus is on whether the tax-exempt organization is serving a charitable purpose.

Once charitability has been established, the partnership arrangement must be examined to determine whether the arrangement permits the tax-exempt to function exclusively in furtherance of its tax-exempt purpose or purposes. The tax-exempt cannot operate for the benefit of the nonexempt partners. Because the tax-exempt organization must be in control of partnership projects so that the projects are administered for a nonprofit purpose, the tax-exempt must be the general partner. In addition, benefits received by the limited partners must be incidental to the public purpose served by the partnership.[45]

If a hospital is a partner in a commercial venture, it must be insulated sufficiently from serving the private interests of the partnership or the other, nonexempt, partners. If the limited partners are present, or were past, members of the hospital's board of directors, a conflict may arise between partnership obligations and tax-exempt objectives. As a result, involvement in the partnership could jeopardize the hospital's tax-exempt status.[46]

> Example. In Redlands Surgical Services v. Comm.,[47] the Tax Court ruled that a § 501(c)(3) surgical corporation, which was a general partner with a for-profit corporation in a partnership formed to acquire a majority interest in an outpatient surgical center, did not qualify for tax exempt status when it gave control to its for-profit partner.

Activities of a partnership are deemed to be the activities of the partners; a hospital as a partner in joint ventures with other partnerships, corporations, and

---

obtain financing for production of a play. The Court of Appeals for the Ninth Circuit ruled that the involvement of the tax exempt § 501(c)(3) organization as the general partner in a limited partnership was not indicative of private interest and was not a prohibitive activity.

45 GCM 39444 (1985). (A GCM is a memorandum opinion from the IRS General Counsel.)

46 One means to alleviate this problem is the establishment of an independent committee, composed of individuals who are not members of the hospital's board of directors and who are not limited partners, to monitor and oversee the hospital's activities as the general partner.

47 113 T.C. 47 (1999), aff'd, 242 F.3d 904 (9th Cir. 2001).

physician groups must retain control over the partnership to maintain its tax-exempt status.[48] A hospital should consider the ruling of the Internal Revenue Service in its Revenue Ruling 98-15 in seeking guidance regarding these reorganizations.[49] Instances in which the exempt status of a hospital was not adversely

48 INFO 2005-0051. The Service responded to a request for information concerning the tax consequences of a § 501(c)(3) hospital's involvement in a joint venture, wherein it would operate as a limited liability company with a physician group practice and with physicians of the hospital. The Service referred to Rev. Rul. 98-15, discussed below, and ruled that if the hospital retained effective control over the limited liability company and the limited liability company served charitable purposes, the manner in which the LLC conducted the activity would contribute importantly to the accomplishment of the hospitals charitable purpose of the promotion of health.

["Rev. Rul." is the abbreviation for "revenue ruling." It is a written instruction from the IRS to a taxpayer that requests advice regarding the tax effect of a proposed event. The IRS will apply the tax law to facts the taxpayer has provided. Unlike the private letter ruling, a "revenue ruling" will be effective to other taxpayers as well. Still the Service can revoke its revenue rulings. (The first numbers of a revenue ruling provide the year the IRS issued the ruling. For example, the revenue ruling above, Rev. Rul. 98-15, was issued in 1998.)]

In Priv. Ltr. Rul. 9709014, the IRS ruled that a § 501(c)(3) hospital would not lose tax-exempt status from a forty percent general partnership ownership in an ambulatory surgical center even though a for-profit corporation owned the remaining sixty percent interest. Private physicians were limited partners.

In Priv. Ltr. Rul. 200436022, the Service ruled that a proposed joint venture would not affect the tax-exempt status of a hospital. The hospital formed a limited liability company to serve as the general partner in a limited partnership. The hospital would be the sole member of the LLC. The limited partnership would consist of the LLC and the hospital. The LLC would hold one general partnership unit representing one percent of the partnership. The hospital would hold one limited partnership unit representing ninety-nine percent of the partnership. The partnership would sell limited partnership units to eligible physician investors and related physician groups. If the offering was fully subscribed, the LLC would continue to own one general partnership unit and the hospital would hold fifty-four limited partnership units. The investors would own forty limited partnership units and the manager of the partnership would own five limited partnership units. The partnership was formed to expand significantly the scope of available diagnostic imaging services in the local area by owning and operating a free-standing imagining center. The imaging services to be provided at the Center would include MRI, X-ray, CT, ultrasound, and mammography, most of which were not currently available in or around the local area. The Service noted, as provided in Rev. Rul. 98-15, that activities of a partnership are deemed to be the activities of the exempt organization, which owns the partnership interest, when evaluating whether the nonprofit organization is operated exclusively for exempt purposes. As the Service stated, based on Rev. Rul. 98-15, the question of whether a § 501(c)(3) organization whose principal activity is the participation in a partnership engaged in health care activities satisfies the community benefit standard depends on all the facts and circumstances. The Service referred to the fact that the LLC's board of managers would be representative of the community and the partnership agreement specifically provided that the duty of the partnership was to operate the partnership in a manner that furthered charitable purposes by promoting the health of a broad cross section of the community. The Service concluded this duty would override any duty to operate the partnership for the financial benefit of its members. It noted that the Center would have an open medical staff. The Service determined the facts and circumstances established the hospital's participation in the partnership would further its exempt purposes. Its participation would not constitute an unrelated trade of business and its distribute share of partnership profits would not be taxed.

49 In Rev. Rul. 98-15, 1998-1 C.B. 718, the IRS discussed whether a § 501(c)(3) organization would jeopardize its tax-exempt status by transferring its assets to a limited liability company (LLC) owned by the § 501(c)(3) and a for-profit corporation. The IRS considered two cases involving § 501(c)(3) organizations that operated acute care hospitals. Both proposed to transfer all their assets to the LLC. The governing documents of the LLCs provided that returns of capital and distributions of

affected by its engaging in commercial activities include the construction of a medical office building condominium by an exempt hospital and the transfer of a portion of the condominium to a partnership for a fair consideration, as well as the purchase by the hospital of convertible yield bonds in connection with the construction and transfer,[50] the provision of patient-related housing by an exempt organization to patients of several hospitals and to family members and

earnings made to owners of the LLCs would be proportional to ownership interests in the LLC. In the first case the LLC would have a five-member board, three members chosen by the § 501(c)(3) and two members chosen by the for-profit corporation. In the second situation, the board would have six members, three chosen by the nonprofit organization and three chosen by the for-profit. In the first case the governing instrument for the LLC would require the LLC to operate any hospital it owned in a manner that furthered charitable purposes by promoting health for a broad cross section of its community and that explicitly provided that the duty of members of the governing board to operate the LLC to further charitable purposes would override any duty they might have to operate the LLC for the financial benefit of its owners. In the event of a conflict between operation in accordance with the community benefit standard and any duty to maximize profits, members of the governing board would satisfy the community benefit standard without regard to consequences of maximizing profitability. Members of the governing board were not subject to such a requirement in the second situation. In both cases, the LLC would enter into a management agreement with a management company, but in the first situation, the management agreement was with a management company unrelated to either the nonprofit or the for-profit. However, in the second situation, the management contract was with a subsidiary of the for-profit organization. In the second situation, the management company could unilaterally renew the management agreement. The management company would have broad discretion over activities and assets of the LLC. It was permitted to enter all but "unusually large" contracts without board approval. In both cases the only activity of the § 501(c)(3) organizations after the transfer of their assets to the LLCs would be the funding of grants to support activities that promoted health in the community and that helped indigents obtain health care. Funding for the grants would come from distributions from the LLC. The IRS determined that in the first case the § 501(c)(3) organization would not jeopardize its tax-exempt status by forming the LLC and transferring its assets to the LLC. However, the IRS ruled that the nonprofit organization in the second situation would violate the requirements of I.R.C. § 501(c)(3) because it would not be operated exclusively for exempt purposes.

50 Priv. Ltr. Rul. 8632055. The hospitals wholly owned subsidiary corporation, a for-profit corporation, would be the sole general partner in a limited partnership organized to own and operate four floors of the medical office building condominium. The limited partnership interests would be sold to physicians on the staff of the hospital. Of the eight floors, the hospital would own four and lease them to physicians; the other four would be sold to the partnership. The IRS ruled construction of the medical office building was substantially related to its exempt purposes.

In Priv. Ltr. Ruls. 200325003 and 200325004, the Service ruled the involvement in a joint venture, an LLC, of a hospital that included a neonatal intensive care unit and a general acute care hospital, would not jeopardize the tax-exempt status of the hospitals. The LLC would operate the neonatal intensive care unit. The Service noted that Rev. Rul. 98-15 explicitly approved an exempt hospital forming a limited liability company. Both members of the LLC would be § 501(c)(3) organizations, and activities of the LLC would remain entirely in the control of the tax-exempt charities.

In Priv. Ltr. Ruls. 200327065 and 200327067, the IRS ruled a § 501(c)(3) organization that operated general acute care hospitals and other health services and facilities on and off a university campus, and a § 501(c)(3) organization, which owned and operated a general acute care hospital including a Level II neonatal nursery, would not jeopardize their tax-exempt status by forming an LLC to operate the existing nursery and a new Level III neonatal facility.

visitors of patients to the hospitals;[51] and a tax-exempt organization becoming a general partner in a partnership that would operate a day surgery center.[52]

---

51 Priv. Ltr. Rul. 8635078. In Ltr. Rul. 201744019, the Service referred to Rev. Rul. 98-15 in revoking tax-exempt status for a general acute care hospital, which was founded as a community hospital. Following financial difficulties, the hospital turned over control of all its operations to a for-profit entity that specialized in operating rural hospitals. The hospital was going to close prior to transferring control to the for-profit entity. Although the hospital attempted to ensure its exempt purposes were met by inserting a requirement in its transfer of management that the for-profit entity would provide charity care, the Service stated that there was no way for the hospital to guarantee this occurred. The hospital had no access to the books and records of the for-profit.

52 Priv. Ltr. Rul. 8638131. Most limited partners in the partnership would be physicians on the hospital staff. Because many physicians on the hospital staff would have an equity investment in the surgical center, they would be encouraged to keep their practice in the hospital. The IRS noted that in situations involving the joint acquisition and operation of facilities by exempt and nonexempt entities, the IRS will look to the protection of exempt assets against loss, the potential conflict between the interests of the exempt organization and the nonexempt entity, the advancement of charitable purposes, and the avoidance of undue benefit to private interests.

In Priv. Ltr. Rul. 8727080, the Service ruled a tax-exempt hospital would not jeopardize its tax-exempt status by entering into a general partnership agreement with a profit corporation (whose shareholders were obstetrical and gynecological physicians) to operate a profit organization providing specific services to women, prenatal and postnatal programs, breast mammography, ultrasound studies, and educational classes and seminars on various aspects of women's health. Persons using the services of the profit organization would be registered and treated as patients of that organization, thus, solving possible liability claims against the physicians and the hospital. The IRS concluded that income from the partnership and income from the lease of space and equipment, as well as loans to the organization, would not produce unrelated business taxable income to the hospital.

In Priv. Ltr. Rul. 9246004, the IRS ruled a § 501(c)(3) foundation that operated a hospital and a skilled nursing home would not have unrelated business taxable income from income it earned from a contract to provide health care to individuals enrolled in an Individual Practice Association (IPA). The IRS also ruled the foundation was not providing commercial-type insurance under I.R.C. § 501(m). No risk was being shifted to other organizations or individuals in the IPA.

In Priv. Ltr. Rul. 201925015, the Service ruled that an organization formed as a joint venture by two hospitals to serve consumers and outlying areas with medical equipment and supplies in homes and that leased and/or sold medical equipment, including walkers, wheelchairs, oxygen, etc., did not qualify for Section 501(c)(3) tax exempt status. The Service determined the organization had substantial non-exempt commercial activity. The organization stated that if a person qualified for financial assistance that person would pay at a reduced rate or obtain the item for free. The Service rejected the organization's position that the sale and rental of durable medical equipment to patients furthered the exempt purpose provision of health care services to patients and its argument that the organization should not be required to provide a substantial amount of charity care to operate as a § 501(c)(3) organization. The Service noted that the organization's financial assistance constituted less than a very small percent of the organization's activities, both in terms of revenue and based on the number of charity care patients served to total patients served. It ruled that providing health care services by selling and renting durable medical equipment was not a charitable activity. The Service also ruled that the organization would be liable for filing Form 990-T, discussed in Chapter IX, to report the unrelated business income tax due from durable medical equipment sales and rentals to the general public at commercial prices. The Service noted that the sale and rental of durable medical equipment at commercial market prices to the public was in direct competition with other for profit durable medical equipment providers. It assessed penalties under I.R.C. §§ 6651(a)(1) and (2) for failure to file and failure to pay.

b. Shareholder in a For-Profit Entity.

If a hospital's commercial activities become substantial, a separate for-profit entity, preferably a for-profit corporation, should be established. The assets used for commercial activities would be transferred to the for-profit corporation to prevent the hospital from jeopardizing its tax-exempt status. Activities of a separately incorporated subsidiary will not be attributed to the parent corporation unless there is clear and convincing evidence that the subsidiary is an arm, agent, or integral part of the parent corporation.[53] A parent corporation and its subsidiary are separate entities for tax purposes if the purposes for which the subsidiary was incorporated are the equivalent of business activities or the subsidiary subsequently carries on business activities. Thus, if a hospital organizes a subsidiary corporation with the intention that it will have some real and substantial business function, its existence generally would not be disregarded for tax purposes. However, the hospital should not so control the affairs of the subsidiary that the subsidiary is merely an instrumentality of the hospital parent.[54]

The exempt status of a hospital was not adversely affected by its engaging in commercial activities that included the acquisition by an exempt hospital of a twenty-five percent shareholder interest in a for-profit corporation that operated treatment facilities for various diseases;[55] the purchase of stock in a for-profit corporation formed to facilitate the participation of a for-profit professional corporation and an exempt hospital in joint commercial ventures for

53 See controlling opinion, Moline Properties, Inc. v. Comm., 319 U.S. 436 (1943).

54 If the subsidiary was so controlled, its corporate entity statute could be disregarded. See Priv. Ltr. Rul. 8706012.

55 Priv. Ltr. Rul. 8635045. In addition, any payments and dividends received by the hospital from the for-profit corporation did not result in unrelated business taxable income. The hospital entered into a research agreement with the for-profit corporation that would pay the hospital several million dollars. The for-profit organization received rights to any patentable technology developed through the research performed by a department in the hospital; however, the hospital retained control and broad direction over the research it performed pursuant to the agreement. The hospital retained full rights and unimpaired academic freedom to publish the results of the research. The IRS ruled the research was fundamental research because the results were freely available to the public; consequently, all income derived from research performed would not be unrelated business income. The IRS cited Rev. Rul. 76-296 that held commercially sponsored research otherwise qualifying as scientific research, the results of which, including all relevant information, are timely published in a form to be available to the interested public, constitutes scientific research carried on in the public interest.

the delivery of health care services;[56] and a reorganization of an exempt health care center.[57]

As noted previously, the fact that a tax-exempt organization maintains a controlling interest in a subsidiary for-profit corporation will not cause the commercial activities of the for-profit corporation to be attributed to the tax-exempt parent if the separate for-profit subsidiary is not an arm or an agent of the parent and provided the subsidiary is organized for some bona fide purpose of its own. The parent tax-exempt organization must not be so involved in, or in control of, the day-to-day operations of the subsidiary that the relationship between the parent and the subsidiary assumes the characteristics of a principal-agent relationship. Control through ownership of stock or power to appoint the board of directors of the subsidiary, of itself, will not cause attribution of the subsidiary's activities to the parent. The fact that board members of a subsidiary

---

56 In Priv. Ltr. Rul. 200102052, the IRS ruled two public charities, which were health care organizations, would not have unrelated business taxable income from distributions from an LLC of which the public charities were members. Two health care organizations established an LLC to operate rehabilitation services in the community. Board members of the LLC were composed of an equal number of representatives from each of the two charities. The charities shared ratably in profits from the LLC. The IRS noted the charities controlled the LLC; thus, it concluded that the LLC would be operated for charitable purposes. Further, the IRS determined operations of the LLC would further the exempt purposes of the charities so that income from the operations would not be income from an unrelated trade or business. The IRS decided the joint venture satisfied the requirements of Rev. Rul. 98-15.

57 See Priv. Ltr. Rul. 8632060. An exempt organization that operated a health center proposed to reorganize wherein one exempt organization would serve as parent corporation and the other tax-exempt organizations, including the tax-exempt in question, would be subsidiaries. Upon the corporate restructuring, the parent entity operated for the benefit of its tax-exempt subsidiaries by providing them with financial, management, and advisory support services. The IRS ruled that the reorganization would facilitate the realization of benefits by permitting more effective and efficient use of resources, as well as providing the ability to shift resources to meet the ever-changing community health needs. The corporate reorganization would enable the related and integrated health care providers to define operational responsibilities more clearly by separating management and planning, fund-raising, and taxable business activities from the operation of the hospital and the provision of health care services. The IRS ruled that sharing of assets and/or services among the exempt corporations would not result in unrelated business taxable income to any entity.

See also Priv. Ltr. Rul. 8639089, in which the IRS ruled ownership of stock in a corporate for-profit entity by a tax-exempt hospital did not constitute the carrying on of a trade or business and would not jeopardize the hospital's exempt status. The transfer of the profit corporation's profits to the hospital in the form of dividends would not be taxed.

In Priv. Ltr. Ruls. 8547047 and 8547048, the IRS ruled the transfer of assets pursuant to a reorganization of a hospital and a division of its functions among several new organizations would not constitute unrelated business taxable income. The new structure would include a parent organization and several new tax-exempt organizations. One of the new exempt organizations rented physical facilities to the others. The IRS stated that the rental payments from related entities would not constitute unrelated business taxable income.

for-profit corporation consist solely of directors or staff employees of the parent tax-exempt organization will not cause the subsidiary corporation to be viewed as an instrumentality of the parent as long as the subsidiary's board members are independent and self-governing, and the board members conduct all transactions between the parent and the subsidiary at arm's length. Problems will arise if the for-profit subsidiary is operated as another division of the tax-exempt parent. Should funds of the tax-exempt organization pass through the subsidiary organization to individuals so that funds of the tax-exempt organization inure to private individuals, the funds will be deemed to have originated from the tax-exempt organization and the parent may be disqualified for tax-exempt status.

Control of more than fifty percent of the stock, by vote or value, of a for-profit subsidiary will cause a portion of the interest, rents, royalties, and annuities distributed to the tax-exempt parent to be taxed.[58] However, dividends distributed to the tax-exempt parent are not taxed even though the parent has control of a 100 percent of the subsidiary stock.[59]

4. Lobbying and Political Activities.

Section 501(c)(3) prohibits § 501(c)(3) organizations from involvement in political activities. A § 501(c)(3) organization will be disqualified for tax-exempt status if it engages in *any* political activities involving the participation in, or intervention in, any political campaign on behalf of (or in opposition to) any candidate for public office.[60] Further, if a substantial part of the activities of a § 501(c)(3) organization consists of lobbying, the organization is deemed an "action" organization and cannot be exempt under Section 501(c)(3).[61]

58 Discussion in Chapter IX. If the subsidiary corporation is a nonstock corporation, the income will be taxed if representatives of the tax-exempt parent comprise more than fifty percent of the directors or trustees of the subsidiary. See Treas. Reg. § 1.512(b)-1(k)(4).

59 I.R.C. § 512(b)(3). Discussion in Chapter IX.

60 In Priv. Ltr. Rul. 202005020, the Service ruled that operation of a political action committee (PAC) by a subsidiary of a § 501(c)(3) healthcare system would constitute participation or intervention in a political campaign by the healthcare system.

61 In Ltr. Rul. 201932016, the Service deemed to be an "action" organization a corporation whose purposes were to educate the general public about the country's democracy and the continuing fight for equality, and to promote, through education and advocacy, democracy, voting rights and equality for all Americans. The Service ruled the organization did not qualify for § 501(c)(3) tax-exempt status.

A § 501(c)(3) organization will not meet the operational test (which requires the organization to operate exclusively for exempt purposes) if it engages in substantial lobbying activities, or, if it is a qualifying electing organization under I.R.C. § 501(h) (discussion below), and its lobbying expenditures exceed 150 percent of the permitted amounts as set out in I.R.C. § 4911 (also discussed below). Charitable entities, whether electing or nonelecting organizations, must report the amount of their lobbying expenditure amounts on the Schedule C that is then attached to their annual reporting form, the IRS Form 990.[62]

a. Definition of Lobbying

"Lobbying" is an attempt to influence legislation by propaganda or otherwise. An organization is regarded as attempting to influence legislation if the organization contacts, or urges the public to contact, members of a legislative body for the purpose of proposing or supporting legislation, or if it advocates the adoption or rejection of legislation.[63] "Direct" lobbying communication is any attempt to influence legislation through communication with: (a) any member or employee of a legislative body, or (b) any government official or employee, other than a member or employee of a legislative body, who may participate in the formulation of the legislation, but only if the principal purpose of the communication is to influence legislation.[64] "Grass roots" lobbying is the influencing

62 The Lobbying Disclosure Act, 2 U.S.C. § 1601 et. seq., requires tax-exempt organizations that engage in substantial lobbying (lobbying expenditures in excess of $20,000) to register with the Secretary of the Senate and the Clerk of the House of Representatives. The act requires an organization that has employees who are paid to lobby and who spend more than twenty percent of their time engaged in lobbying activities to register within forty-five days after an employee who is a lobbyist makes a "lobbying contact." The act applies only to federal lobbying activities. It does not include attempts to influence legislation by any state legislature or by any local governing body. An organization may use the federal tax definition of lobbying in determining whether an individual has made a "lobbying contact." Electing organizations under I.R.C. § 501(h) may attach that portion of Schedule C of Form 990 on which it reports lobbying expenditures to the IRS for reporting purposes under the Lobbying Disclosure Act. Failure to comply with requirements of the act will subject a tax-exempt organization of a fine up to $50,000. See 2 U.S.C. § 1606.

63 The term "legislation" is defined as any action by Congress, by any state legislature, by any local council or similar governing body, or by the public in a referendum, initiative, constitutional amendment, or similar procedure.

Lobbying for electing § 501(c)(3) organizations, discussed below, is divided into "direct" lobbying and "grass roots" lobbying communications.

64 Treas. Reg. § 56.4911-2(e). A communication with a legislator or government official will be "lobbying" only if the communication refers to specific legislation and reflects a view on such legislation. "Specific legislation" includes both legislation that already has been introduced in a legislative body

of legislation through any attempt to affect the opinions of the general public. Still, a communication will be treated as grass roots lobbying communication only if the communication (a) refers to specific legislation, (b) reflects a view on such legislation; and (c) encourages the recipient of the communication to take action with respect to such legislation.[65] An expenditure made for a communication that has both a lobbying and a bona fide nonlobbying purpose must be allocated between the lobbying and the nonlobbying purposes.[66]

---

and a specific legislative proposal that the organization either supports or opposes.

65 Treas. Reg. § 56.4911-3(b)(2). Communication encourages a recipient to take action with respect to legislation if the communication: (a) states that the recipient should contact a legislator or an employee of a legislative body, or should contact any other government official or employee who may participate in the formulation of legislation (but only if the principal purpose of urging contact with the government official or employee is to influence legislation); (b) states the address, telephone number, or similar information of a legislator or an employee of a legislative body; (c) provides a petition, tear-off postcard or similar material for the recipient to communicate his or her views to a legislator or an employee of a legislative body, or to any other government official or employee who may participate in the formulation of legislation (but only if the principal purpose of so facilitating contact with the government official or employee is to influence legislation; or (d) specifically identifies one or more legislators who will vote on the legislation as: opposing the communication's view with respect to the legislation; being undecided with respect to the legislation; being the recipient's representative in the legislature; or being a member of the legislative committee that will consider the legislation. See Treas. Reg. § 56.4911-3(b)(2).

The definition of grass roots lobbying is a three-part definition; it requires that communication contain a reference to specific legislation, that it reflects a view with respect to the legislation, and that it encourages the recipient to take action. Thus, grass roots communication may advocate or oppose legislation and still not be lobbying if it does not encourage the recipient to take action with respect to the legislation. Treas. Reg. § 56.4911-2(b). With one exception, the three-part grass roots lobbying definition is applicable to mass media communications. To be grass roots lobbying, mass media communication must contain a reference to the specific legislation, must reflect a view with respect to such legislation, and must encourage the recipient to take action. However, for a communication in the mass media that is made within two weeks before a vote by a legislative body, or by a legislative committee, on a highly publicized piece of legislation, the communication will be presumed to be grass roots lobbying if the communication reflects a view on the general subject of the legislation or encourages the public to communicate with legislators on the general subject of the legislation. Still, the organization can rebut the presumption by demonstrating that the communication is a type of communication regularly made by the organization in the mass media without regard to the timing of legislation or that timing of the communication was unrelated to the upcoming legislative action. See Treas. Reg. § 56.4911-2(b)(5).

A communication that is both a direct lobbying communication and a grass roots lobbying communication will be treated as grass roots lobbying communication except to the extent the organization can demonstrate the communication was made primarily for direct lobbying purposes. If the organization can demonstrate that the communication was made primarily for direct lobbying purposes, the organization then can make a reasonable allocation between the direct and the grass roots lobbying purpose served by the communication.

66 Treas. Reg. § 56.4911-3. The organization has not made a reasonable allocation if it includes as the lobbying expenditures only the amount expended for the specific sentence or sentences that encourage the recipient to take action with response to legislation.

b. Electing Organization

A hospital, or its supporting organizations, may elect under I.R.C. § 501(h) to engage in some specifically defined amount of lobbying.[67] For an electing organization, permissible lobbying expenditures are as follows:

(1) Twenty percent of exempt purpose expenditures up to $500,000;

(2) $100,000, plus fifteen percent of the excess of exempt purpose expenditures over $500,000 and up to $1,000,000;

(3) $175,000, plus ten percent of the excess exempt purpose expenditures over $1,000,000 up to $1,500,000; or

(4) $225,000, plus five percent of excess purpose expenditures over $1,500,000.

In no event may the permitted level exceed $1,000,000 for any one year.[68]

If an electing § 501(c)(3) organization exceeds the permissible amount, it is subject to a penalty tax of twenty-five percent of the excess amount.

Example. A hospital expends $400,000 expenditures in the current year to accomplish its exempt purposes. Its permissible lobbying expenditures for the year would be $80,000 (twenty percent of $400,000). Its permissible grass roots lobbying expenditures would be $20,000 (twenty-five percent of $80,000). Assume the hospital spends $100,000 for lobbying, $30,000 of which is grass roots lobbying. The hospital would be subject to a penalty of $5,000 [twenty-five percent x $20,000 ($100,000 - $80,000)]. The penalty for excess grass roots

67 Lobbying for electing organizations is defined as any attempt to influence legislation through communication with any member or employee of a legislative body, or with any government official or employee who may participate in the formulation of the legislation.

The election is made by filing Form 5768. The form must be signed and postmarked within the first day of the year to which it applies. The election, once made, is effective until revoked.

The amount of grass roots lobbying permissible expenditures is twenty-five percent of the lobbying permissible expenditures. An electing organization must keep a record of its lobbying and grass roots lobbying expenditures made during each year.

68 I.R.C. § 4911(c). Although the expenditure limitations for an electing organization may seem to permit excessive lobbying activities at first glance, the limitations are much more limited than initially assumed. The limitations are based on an organization's exempt "expenditures" rather than on the organization's revenues.

lobbying would be less [twenty-five percent of $10,000 ($30,000 - $20,000)]. The penalty tax would be the greater amount. Assume the hospital expends $130,000 for lobbying expenditures in the current year. The museum's lobbying expenditures would exceed 150 percent of the permissible amount; thus, the hospital possibly can lose its exempt status.

If two or more § 501(c)(3) organizations are members of an affiliated group of organizations and the organizations have elected under I.R.C. § 501(h), the organizations are treated as one for purposes of determining whether the organizations have made excess lobbying expenditures.[69]

c. Nonelecting Organization

A § 501(c)(3) organization that does not elect under I.R.C § 501(h) is subject to a subjective test. A nonelecting charitable organization will lose its tax-exempt status if it engages in "substantial" lobbying activities.[70] The term "substantial" is not defined. One court determined that if no more than five percent of the time and effort of an organization was devoted to lobbying, the lobbying was not "substantial."[71] Another court held that the lobbying activities of an organization must be balanced in the context of the objectives and circumstances of the organization to determine whether a substantial part of the activities are to influence, or to attempt to, influence legislation.[72] An election under I.R.C. §

69 I.R.C. § 4911(f)(1)(A). An organization is a member of an affiliated group if (a) the governing instrument of the organization requires it to be bound by decisions of another organization on legislative issues, or (b) the governing board of one organization includes persons who are designated specifically as representatives of another organization or are members of the governing board, officers, or paid executive staff members of the other organization and, if by aggregating their votes, the above noted persons have sufficient voting power to cause or prevent action on legislative issues by the first organization. Thus, two organizations are affiliated if one organization can control action on legislative issues by the other by reason of interlocking governing boards or by reason of provisions of the governing instruments of the controlled organization. The ability of one organization to control action on legislative matters of another organization is sufficient to cause the organizations to be affiliated. It is not necessary that control be exercised. See Treas. Reg. § 56.4911-7(a).

70 Section 501(c)(3) of the Internal Revenue Code states that to qualify for Section 501(c)(3) status, no substantial part of the organization's activities may constitute attempts to influence legislation or to carry on propaganda.

71 Seasongood v. Comm., 227 F.2d 907 (6th Cir. 1955).

72 Haswell v. United States, 500 F.2d 1133 (Ct. Cl. 1974). The court compared the lobbying activities of a § 501(c)(3) organization with its other activities and determined that the organization was engaged in substantial efforts to influence legislation and, thus, was disqualified for tax-exempt status. The

501(h) removes the uncertainty of judging whether an organization has met the subjective "substantial" test.

d. Exceptions to Lobbying

A communication is not a direct or grass roots lobbying communication if the communication falls within one of the following exceptions: (a) nonpartisan analysis, study, or research, including making the results available to the public, (b) examinations and discussions of broad social, economic, and similar problems, (c) requests for technical advice, and (d) communications pertaining to self-defense by the organization.[73] Lobbying does not include public discussion, or communication with members of legislative bodies or governmental employees, even if the general subject is legislation, should the discussion not address itself to the merits of a specific legislative proposal. Thus, expenditures for examinations and discussions of broad social, economic, and similar problems are not lobbying expenditures even though the problems are of the type with which the government would be expected to deal ultimately.

e. Penalty Taxes

A hospital can be liable for penalty taxes for involvement in lobbying and political campaign activities. Although I.R.C. § 501(c)(3) denies tax-exempt status for an organization that pays or incurs any amount for participating or intervening in any political campaign, a small and often unintentional political campaign expenditure may only subject the organization to a penalty tax.[74] If a §

lobbying expenditures were twenty percent of the organization's total expenditures for the year.

73 Treas. Reg. § 56.4911-2(b)(3). "Nonpartisan analysis, study, or research" is the independent and objective explanation of a particular subject matter, including any activity that is "educational." The term "educational" refers to the instruction or training of an individual in order to improve or develop his or her capabilities, or the instruction of the public on subjects useful to the individual and beneficial to the community. See Treas. Reg. § 53.4945-2(d).

"Nonpartisan analysis, study or research" may advocate a particular position or perspective so long as the presentation is a sufficiently complete and objective critique of the pertinent facts to permit an individual or the public to form an independent opinion or conclusion. The mere presentation of unsupported opinion does not qualify as nonpartisan analysis, study or research. See Treas. Reg. § 56.4911-2(c)(1).

74 Pursuant to I.R.C. § 4955, such an organization would be subject to an initial, first-tier, tax of ten percent of the amount involved. If the political expenditure is not corrected within a specified period set out in Section 4955, an additional tax of 100 percent of the expenditure. A political expenditure is corrected if all or a part of the expenditure, to the extent possible, is recovered and safeguards are established to prevent the organization from making future political expenditures. The correction

501(c)(3) organization loses its tax-exempt status because of substantial lobbying expenditures, it is also subject to a penalty tax under I.R.C. § 4912.[75]

C. PROPERTY TAX EXEMPTION

A nonprofit hospital that qualifies for federal tax exemption may have more difficulty in qualifying for exemption from state and local property taxes.[76] Most state statutes providing for exemptions from property taxes for nonprofit organizations utilize the language of I.R.C. § 501(c)(3) and, thus, require that tax-exempt nonprofit entities be organized exclusively to perform the charitable purposes set out in § 501(c)(3), i. e., religious, charitable, scientific, literary, or

---

period begins on the date the political expenditure is made and ends on the earlier of the date of mailing of a notice of deficiency for the first-tier tax or the date on which the first-tier tax is assessed. If the organization's manager agreed to the expenditure when the manager was aware the expenditure was a political expenditure, the manager may also be subject to a penalty tax—two and one half percent of the amount of the expenditure unless the agreement was not willful and was due to reasonable cause but an additional tax of fifty percent if the manager does not agree to a correction of the expenditure.

75 The tax is five percent of the amount of lobbying expenditures incurred during any year in which the organization has ceased to qualify for tax-exempt status. Section 4912 imposes a penalty tax of five percent of the amount of the lobbying expenditures on the organization's manager if the manager agreed to the making of the expenditures knowing that such expenditures would likely result in the organization losing its tax-exempt status.

76 In Pinnacle Health Hospitals v. Dauphin County Bd. of Assessment Appeals, 552 Pa. 199, 713 A.2d 1142 (1998), the Supreme Court of Pennsylvania indicated it would review a lower court ruling that a hospital was not entitled to a property tax exemption when the hospital transferred much of its income to a for-profit subsidiary. The lower court determined that the hospital was not free of a profit motive, which was a requirement for property tax exemption.

In Lamb County Appraisal Dist. v. South Plains Hospital-Clinic, Inc., 688 S.W.2d 896 (Tex. App. Amarillo 1985), writ refused n.r.e., (1986), the court looked not just to the nonprofit states of the hospital but also to the number of patients who were charity patients. Still, the court decided the fact the hospital did not have a stated admissions policy for determining charity status of patients did not mean it was not exclusively organized for charitable purposes.

educational purposes.[77] For hospitals, some states also require a hospital to provide medical care without regard to a patient's ability to pay.[78]

A nonprofit organization bears the burden of demonstrating that it falls within a state property tax exemption.[79] Courts have held that an exemption provision must be strictly construed against the organization and in favor of

---

77 See, e.g., Cal. Rev. & Tax. Code § 214 and Tex. Tax Code Ann. § 11.18.

In St. Joseph's Living Center, Inc. v. Town of Windham, 290 Conn. 695, 966 A.2d 188 (2009), a skilled nursing facility had appealed a decision of a town's board of assessment that denied its application for a property tax exemption. The Supreme Court of Connecticut ruled that the provision of long-term health care and spiritual support to the elderly in a nonprofit, nondiscriminatory manner and without regard to the individual's financial circumstances is a "charitable purpose." The court decided the facility relieved a burden that would otherwise be borne by the state. The facility was not using its property exclusively for its charitable purpose, but the court decided the restriction against a tax exemption for real property from which rents, profits, or income are derived is relevant only if the property is not being used for an exempt purpose because of the absence of suitable buildings and improvements. The court ruled that the property tax cannot be apportioned based on charitable and noncharitable uses of property and that a chapel at the facility was exempt from taxation as a house of religious worship owned by a religious organization.

78 See, e.g., Tex. Tax Code Ann. § 11.18(d)(1). See also Cal. Rev. & Tax. Code § 214, which provides that a hospital is not deemed to be organized or operated for a profit if its operating revenues, exclusive of gifts and grants, do not exceed ten percent of its operating expenses.

In Dialysis Clinic, Inc. v. Levin, 127 Ohio St. 3d 215, 938 N.E.2d 329 (2010), the court ruled a nonprofit provider of health care services did not qualify as a charitable institution that would entitle it to a charitable-purpose property tax exemption. The court determined that operation of a dialysis clinic, for which a tax exemption was sought, did not qualify as an exclusively charitable use of property. The court agreed with the Tax Commissioner that neither its acceptance of reimbursement from Medicare and Medicaid nor its write-off of bad debts constituted a charitable act. It also agreed that the organization's contributions to kidney research did not qualify the organization for charitable status vicariously based on the charitable nature of those to whom it contributed. The court noted that the record showed no unreimbursed free or charity care at the clinic. The court looked to the clinic's "bad-debt charity write-off" figure, which was 1.27 percent of its charges, but stated that case law does not require a threshold amount of unreimbursed care.

In Baruch SLS, Inc. v. Tittabawassee Township, 500 Mich. 345, 901 N.W.2d 843 (2017), the Supreme Court of Michigan ruled that a nonprofit corporation was not required to offer its services for free or to select its recipients using only arbitrary criteria to satisfy a charitable institution test for a real and personal property tax exemption. A § 501(c)(3) organization that was licensed as a specialized care unit with programs for the aged, developmentally disabled, physically handicapped, and mentally ill, operated an adult foster care facility. The court set out a definition of a "charity" as "a gift, to be applied consistently with existing laws, for the benefit of an indefinite number of persons, either by bringing their minds or hearts under the influence of education or religion, by relieving their bodies from disease, suffering or constraint, by assisting them to establish themselves for life, or by erecting or maintaining public buildings or works or otherwise lessening the burdens of government."

79 Sisters of Providence in Washington, Inc. v. Municipality of Anchorage, 672 P.2d 446 (Alaska 1983).

In Dialysis Ctrs. of Dayton, L.L.C. v. Testa, 150 Ohio St. 3d 208, 80 N.E.3d 477 (2017), the court ruled a center operated by a LLC did not qualify for a property tax exemption based on charitable use for a year during which private physicians, who were engaged in a profit-making venture, were co-owners of the LLC. The court ruled the centers were entitled to exemption during the year in which the LLC was owned by a nonprofit hospital except for those areas leased to private physicians. The court stated that for purposes of Ohio's charitable-use property tax exemption, the provision of medical or ancillary healthcare services qualifies as charitable if those services are provided on a nonprofit basis to those in need without regard to race, creed, or ability to pay. It further stated that case law "clearly provides that space leased by a charitable institution to private physicians for their practices does not qualify for the exemption."

the taxing authority.[80] Still, courts have also stated that these exemptions nonetheless must be construed with sufficient latitude to accomplish the intended purpose. The benefits conferred on the public by charities will be diminished if funds committed to the charity must be used to pay property taxes. Thus, a policy of construing too narrowly the property exemption for charities tends to deter charities from shouldering burdens that would otherwise be assumed by the state.[81]

The use of property for a physicians' office building wherein the physicians are engaged in profit-making practices has caused the property to be subject to property tax.[82] If a hospital provides special benefits to its staff doctors, some

---

80 In Community Health Care, Inc. v. Illinois Dept. of Revenue, 369 Ill. App. 3d 353, 859 N.E.2d 1196 (3d Dist. 2006), the court ruled a health care provider was not entitled to a charitable exemption from property taxes. The health care provider, a clinic, served medically underserved populations, residents of public housing, and the homeless. Its clients paid for services with private insurance, through Medicare and Medicaid, and grants. The court set out the qualifications for a clinic to be eligible for a property tax exemption as follows: (1) the clinic must be set up for the benefit of an indeterminate number of persons; (2) it must have no capital, capital stock or shareholders and cannot earn a profit or pay dividends; (3) it must derive its funds primarily from public and private charity and must hold those funds in trust for the objectives and purposes expressed in the charter; (4) it must dispense charity to all who need and apply for it and cannot provide a gain or profit in a private sense to any persons connected with it, and cannot appear to place obstacles of any character in the way of those who need and would avail themselves of the charitable benefits it dispenses; (5) the property must actually and factually be used exclusively for its charitable purpose regardless of any intent expressed in the organization's charter or bylaws; and (6) charity use must the primary purpose for which its property is used and not a secondary or incidental purpose. The court noted that clinic officials admitted the clinic used its property for charitable purposes only twenty-seven percent of the time. The remaining seventy-three percent of the time, it used its property as a not-for-profit medical clinic.

81 In Utah County by and Through County Bd. of Equalization of Utah County v. Intermountain Health Care, Inc., 725 P.2d 1357 (Utah 1986), the Supreme Court of Utah court determined that a hospital under construction was entitled to a charitable tax exemption from property taxes during the time of construction.

In AHS Hospital Corp. v. Town of Morristown, 28 N.J. Tax 456 (2015), the New Jersey Tax Court ruled a gift shop was not reasonably necessary for any hospital purpose, but rather it served as a form of competition to commercially owned facilities; thus, it was not exempt from the state's property tax. The court decided the gift shop did not qualify as a core hospital purpose as it did not provide any medical service that a hospital patient may require during pre-admission, during a hospital stay, or during post-admission." The court determined the gift shop was merely a convenience for hospital visitors who could otherwise purchase similar gift items at a variety of stores outside the hospital. The court also decided a day care area used by hospital employees, but not by patients, was not exempt from tax. It found the hospital cafeteria also failed to satisfy the profit test and, thus, was not exempt from tax.

82 In North Shore Medical Center, Inc. v. Bystrom, 461 So. 2d 167 (Fla. 3d DCA 1984), the court ruled the predominant use of a medical arts building was for the private, profit-making purposes of the physicians who rented the office space; thus, the court ruled the building was not exempt from state ad valorem taxes.

In Underhill v. Edwards, 400 So. 2d 129 (Fla. 5th DCA 1981), a property tax exemption was denied for the first floor of a hospital's new wing; the floor was rented to private medical doctors who used it for the

courts have ruled the hospital is not entitled to a property tax exemption as a charity.[83] Courts have ruled a hospital employee parking lot should not be taxed unless the parking lot also serves the needs of patients of physicians who have private practices nearby.[84] Property leased to a hospital generally has been subjected to taxation even in instances when the hospital was responsible for payment of the taxes.[85]

---

conduct of their private medical practice. The court stated that unless more than fifty percent of a building is being used for charitable, exempt purposes, a tax exemption for the building should be denied in toto.

See Matter of Tax Appeal of Queen's Medical Center, 6 Haw. App. 152, 715 P.2d 349 (1985), in which the court determined that use of property for a physicians' office building by physicians who were engaged in profit-making practices was not a hospital purpose within the meaning of the state property tax exemption.

In Evangelical Hosp. Ass'n v. Novak, 125 Ill. App. 3d 439, 80 Ill. Dec. 640, 465 N.E.2d 986 (2d Dist. 1984), the court ruled a hospital's corporate headquarters, from which it provided administrative and support services for its hospitals, schools of nursing, and senior citizens' residence units, was exclusively used for charitable purposes even though the property was separate from the hospital's premises.

83 See decision in Aransas Hospital, Inc. v. Aransas Pass Independent School Dist., 521 S.W.2d 685 (Tex. Civ. App. Corpus Christi 1975), writ refused n.r.e.

In AHS Hospital Corp. v. Town of Morristown, 28 N.J. Tax 456 (2015), the New Jersey Tax Court denied a hospital's claim for a property tax exemption based on the court's finding that hospital property was being used substantially for profit. The court referred to the case as one "of first impression" because, as the court stated, it was the first time a non-profit hospital's entire property tax exemption was called into question before the court. The court commented that non-profit hospitals have changed significantly "from their early origins as charitable alms houses providing free basic medical treatment to the infirm poor" to "sophisticated centers of medical care." It noted today's non-profit hospitals generate significant revenue and pay their professionals salaries that are competitive even by for-profit standards. The court found a profit-making purpose in employment agreements where revenues were divided between a hospital and its employed physicians. The court found that the hospital owned 100 percent of the stock in five for-profit private physician practices and that all the employee of these private practices, including the doctors, were employed by the hospital. The court found that the hospital loaned millions of dollars to these entities. The loans were termed "working capital" or just "capital" loans. There also were recruitment loans, which were given directly to private physicians to help them transition their practice into the local community. The loans were subject to forgiveness after a certain period of time, at which point the loan would become declared income of the physician. The court concluded that if all non-profit hospitals operated like the hospital in this case, "then for purposes of the property tax exemption, modern non-profit hospitals are essentially legal fictions." The tax court did decide that if the property tax exemption for modern non-profit hospitals was to exist at all in New Jersey, it was the function of the Legislature and not the courts to promulgate what the terms and conditions would be.

84 In Methodist Hospitals of Memphis v. Assessment Appeals Com'n, 669 S.W.2d 305 (Tenn. 1984), the Supreme Court of Tennessee decided there is no better way to ensure that needed hospital personnel are available on an around the-clock basis than to provide safe and convenient parking for the employees on hospital grounds. Thus, that court ruled that furnishing an employee parking lot was an integral part of the exempt purpose of the hospital.

But see Matter of Tax Appeal of Queen's Medical Center, 6 Haw. App. 152, 715 P.2d 349 (1985), in which the court ruled a parking lot that served not only the hospital needs but also the patients of physicians who were conducting their private practices in nearby buildings, could not be totally exempt from tax.

85 In Sisters of Providence in Washington, Inc. v. Municipality of Anchorage, 672 P.2d 446 (Alaska 1983), the Supreme Court of Alaska ruled equipment leased to a hospital was subject to the property tax. The court pointed to the fact that the lessor of the equipment was leasing the equipment to the

D. REORGANIZATIONS OF NONPROFIT HOSPITALS AND AFFILIATED ENTITIES

Because of the changing market in health care and the intensive competition for patients and physicians and because of increased requirements to maintain tax exempt status,[86] as well as the fact that too much involvement in activities that produce unrelated business taxable income[87] can cause a hospital to lose its exempt status, nonprofit hospital corporations have been engaged in extensive reorganizations to meet the growing demands of the health care industry.[88] Questions the hospital directors must address are the effect of these

hospital for a profit. The court stated that the lessor's use of the property should be considered.

In Healtheast v. County of Ramsey, 749 N.W.2d 15 (Minn. 2008), the Supreme Court of Minnesota ruled that the parent corporation of four public hospitals would be entitled to the property tax exemption if the lower court determined the parent corporation did not have a "purpose or existence apart from" the health care system. If the trial court so found, the court ruled the health care system should be considered the owner of the property. The court noted there was evidence the parent corporation might have performed services for entities outside the health care system. If so, that would be sufficient to make the parent an entity distinct and separate with an independent incorporation.

86 See discussion above, particularly the detailed and voluminous requirements of Section 501(r) that was added to the Internal Revenue Code in 2010 by the Affordable Care Act.

87 Some activities of hospitals that produce revenue from sources unrelated to the hospital's exempt purposes will produce income tax for the hospital despite its tax-exempt status. Discussion of unrelated business taxable income in Chapter IX.

88 In Priv. Ltr. Rul. 9402031, the IRS was asked to consider a reorganization in which one corporation would be the holding company for two § 501(c)(3) hospitals, a for-profit management company, a for-profit health maintenance organization (HMO), a for-profit insurance company, and a for-profit pharmacy. Bylaws for the pharmacy and the HMO would require that no more than fifty percent of the members of its board of directors could be persons who were directors, officers, or employees of the two hospitals. Employees of the HMO would not be employees of the hospital organizations. The for-profit management company, the HMO, and the insurance company would not lease space from the hospital. The hospital organizations' only source of income from the HMOs would be dividends paid through the chain of corporations. The IRS ruled that the creation and operation of the holding company and the for-profit organizations would not jeopardize the exempt status of the hospitals. It decided that the HMO was formed for bona business purposes and that the hospitals would not be involved in the HMO's daily activities. It further ruled that the dividend income would not constitute unrelated business taxable income. The IRS noted that activities of the for-profit subsidiaries were not attributable to the exempt parent corporations.

In TAM 200208027, the IRS ruled amounts advanced to a hospital's for-profit subsidiary would not be unrelated business taxable income to the hospital's tax-exempt parent. The IRS decided the parent, a public charity under § 509(a)(3), helped the hospital provide health care services to the community. It also noted the subsidiary's activities as a separate corporation could not be imputed to the parent.

(A TAM, or Technical Advice Memorandum, is a guidance memo or interpretation of tax law provided by the IRS Office of Chief Counsel upon a request from an IRS director regarding a technical or procedural question that arises during an IRS proceeding.)

In Priv. Ltr. Rul. 200134027 the IRS ruled an affiliation between two health care systems in different service areas would not affect the tax-exempt status of the health care systems nor result in unrelated taxable

reorganizations on their tax-exempt status and the possibility of tax penalties because of the reorganizations.[89]

The creation and operation of separate corporations related to a nonprofit hospital must center around a concern to retain public charity status for the nonprofit corporations within the controlled group.[90] In a review of the types

income. Although the integral part doctrine requires a parent-subsidiary relationship for exemption of an organization formed to provide corporate services to unrelated organizations, the Service concluded the substantial control one system would have over the other would bind the organizations into a relationship similar to that of a parent subsidiary.

In Priv. Ltr. Rul. 9438029, a § 501(c)(3) home health and hospice charity owned all the stock of a for-profit subsidiary established to operate a community based assisted-living facility. Through tax-exempt bond financing, the charity planned to construct new facilities to operate a hospice and an adult day care center. It would then no longer have a need for the for-profit subsidiary. The IRS ruled that liquidation of the subsidiary would not cause the charity to lose its tax-exempt, public charity status. It ruled any gain attributable to distribution of the subsidiary's assets to the charity would be excluded from unrelated business income under I.R.C. § 512(b)(5).

89 In Priv. Ltr. Rul. 20026058 the IRS ruled a § 501(c)(3) health care entity would not jeopardize its tax-exempt status by participating in a joint venture with local physicians and for-profit entities to increase the availability of a particular treatment to the community. The health care entity created a limited liability company to own and operate its treatment device and to provide the treatment. The health care organization contributed the device for a membership interest in the LLC. The physicians would contribute cash to the LLC in exchange for membership interests. The health care organization would have at least a sixty percent interest in the LLC. The LLC would be operated by a board of directors consisting of three directors appointed by the health care organization and two appointed by a majority of the physicians. The LLC's operating agreement provided that the LLC would further charitable purposes by promoting the health of the community and that the duty of the board to further charitable purposes would override any duty to operate the LLC for financial benefits. The IRS ruled that income the health care organization received from the LLC would not be unrelated business taxable income.

In Priv. Ltr. Rul. 201744019, the Service ruled a general acute care hospital that was founded as a community hospital but that turned over control of all hospital operations to a for-profit entity that specialized in operating rural hospitals after the hospital encountered financial problems, would no longer qualify for tax-exempt status. The Service noted an exempt hospital's entire focus must be on community welfare. It ruled the hospital failed to meet the operational test because it permitted an outsider for-profit entity to have complete control over its operations.

90 In Priv. Ltr. Rul. 202005020, the Service ruled that the operation of a political action committee (PAC) by a subsidiary of a § 501(c)(3) healthcare system would constitute participation or intervention in a political campaign by the healthcare system. The healthcare system was the sole, partial direct, or indirect member of several § 501(c)(3) organizations that owned and operated hospitals, nursing homes, and provided other healthcare services. It was the sole shareholder of a subsidiary that planned to establish and operate a PAC. The PAC would be a connected separate segregated fund of the subsidiary. The subsidiary would select the PAC's board of directors, which in turn would select the PAC's officers. The subsidiary and the PAC would solicit voluntary contributions to the PAC from employees of the subsidiary, the healthcare system, and other § 501(c)(3) organizations within the group. The healthcare system would also provide services and other resources to the subsidiary for which the subsidiary would reimburse the healthcare system for costs it incurred in providing the services and resources. The Service also ruled that the healthcare system's provisions of services and other resources to the subsidiary and the PAC constituted participation or intervention in a political campaign. The Service further ruled that providing the services and resources would cause

of organizations, particularly the different types of public charities with which a hospital can associate, the reader should first review the first part of Chapter VIII.

In a reorganization, a hospital board must consider the differing problems, discussed in Chapter VIII, relating to each type of public charity, i.e., the public charity subject to I.R.C. §§ 509(a)(1) and 170(b)(1)(A)(vi), which, as discussed in Chapter VIII, qualifies as a public charity by meeting a one-third support test;[91] the § 509(a)(2) organization, discussed in Chapter VIII, which qualifies as a public charity by its support from the general public; and one of the three types of § 509(a)(3) organizations that qualify for public charity status by their support of one or more public charities that qualify under I.R.C. § 509(a)(1) or (2). Because a § 509(a)(1) and 170(b)(1)(A)(vi) public charity must obtain more than one-third of its support from the general public, as discussed in Chapter VIII, gross receipts from the performance of services are not counted in the computation of the one-third support test. As a result, service organizations have difficulty maintaining public charity status under I.R.C. § 509(a)(1). Thus, the service organizations that provide a variety of health care services, such as a care facility for the aged,[92] an outpatient service and community health program,[93] nursing care,[94] or a home health agency[95] should be established as § 509(a)(2) organizations.[96] Because a § 509(a)(2) organization may not receive more than a third of its income from investment sources,[97] fund raising and investment of generated funds should be carried on by a separate corporation organized under I.R.C. §§ 509(a)(1) and 170(b)(1)(A)(vi) or as a supporting organization under I.R.C. § 509(a)(3). The §

the healthcare system to be operated for the benefit of private interests and would not further an exempt purpose.

91 One-third of its support must be from the general public. See discussion in Chapter VIII.

92 Priv. Ltr. Rul. 8715058.

93 Priv. Ltr. Rul. 8720048.

94 Priv. Ltr. Rul. 8718075.

95 Priv. Ltr. Rul. 8718074.

96 However, for § 509(a)(2) organizations, as noted in Chapter VIII, gross receipts derived from any one organization or person can be included in the numerator for purposes of applying the support test, only to the extent of the greater of $5,000 or one percent of the organization's total support for the year. The fact these organizations are for the most part serving other nonprofits within the controlled group, and thus, may have large gross receipts from one entity subject to the $5,000-one percent limitation, makes even a Section 509(a)(2) classification difficult.

97 Discussed in Chapter VIII.

509(a)(3) organizations need not meet a "general public support" test; thus, this classification became popular for the parent organization of a controlled group of nonprofit health care organizations.[98]

Reorganizations of nonprofit hospitals and health care organizations can take several forms.[99] To retain valued physicians, hospitals often have entered into partnership arrangements with members of the hospital staff and with profit organizations to manage and operate office buildings in which members of the hospital staff can lease offices.[100] Hospitals have also entered into incentive agreements with physicians whereby recruited physicians were offered advance compensation packages or loans with forgiveness provisions.[101]

---

98 The Type I § 509(a)(3) organization will be a subsidiary organization. The Type I § 509(a)(3) organization is described in Chapter VIII.

99 In Priv. Ltr. Rul. 200124021, the IRS ruled the merger of a tax-exempt parent organization and its tax-exempt subsidiary into the parent's wholly owned acute-care hospital would not result in unrelated business taxable income or affect the tax-exempt status of the organizations. Both the supporting organizations would transfer all their assets and liabilities to the hospital and would then terminate their existence. Amendments would be made to the hospital's articles of incorporation to include a name change. The IRS determined merger of the three organizations would not result in unrelated business taxable income because the transfers would be considered contributions to a § 501(c)(3) organization. The transfers would not affect the tax-exempt or public charity status of the organizations because the hospital would continue to operate as it had before the merger.

100 In Rev. Rul. 69-464, 1969-2 C.B. 132, the IRS ruled a hospital's efficiency is improved and the quality of patient care is enhanced by having doctors located nearby.

In Priv. Ltr. Rul. 8633036, a professional corporation, whose shareholders were staff physicians, and the hospital would have equal shares of stock in a for-profit corporation. The IRS determined the hospital's purpose in forming the for-profit corporation was to encourage a cooperative atmosphere between private physicians on its staff and the hospital, thereby assisting the hospital to recruit and retain qualified physicians necessary for the effective utilization of the hospital. While the hospital would benefit from the operations of the for-profit corporation, none of the income would inure to the benefit of individual physicians holding shares in the professional corporation or the newly formed for-profit corporation. The IRS ruled that while holding stock in the for-profit corporation would do nothing to further an exempt purpose, the holding of the stock would not, by itself, detract from the attainment of the hospital's exempt purpose. Any income the hospital received would be excluded from unrelated business income tax because dividends are specifically excluded under I.R.C. § 513(b)(1). (Discussion of the unrelated business income tax concept in Chapter IX.) Thus, the purchase of stock in the corporation would not jeopardize the exempt status of the hospital.

In Announcement 95-25, 1995-14 I.R.B. 11, the IRS described five situations involving physician recruitment which it would and would not approve. It ruled it will not approve hospital-physician joint ventures involving the sale of a hospital's net revenue stream. The IRS stated it will approve the payment of a bonus, guarantee of a mortgage on a residence, reimbursement of malpractice premiums for one year, subsidized office space, start-up financial assistance, moving expenses and the guarantee of a physician's private practice income for three years, as recruitment incentives.

101 In Rev. Rul. 97-21, 1997-1 C.B. 121, the IRS discusses the issue of whether a hospital jeopardizes its tax-exempt status when it provides incentives to recruit private physicians to join its medical staff or to provide medical services in a community. When a hospital recruits a physician for its medical staff who is to perform services for or on behalf of the hospital, the hospital must demonstrate that it is paying reasonable compensation for the physician's services. When a hospital recruits a physi-

Hospitals have entered into agreements with for-profit research corporations whereby the for-profit corporation receives rights to any patentable technology developed through research performed in the hospital and, in turn, remits a portion of the profits from marketing the results of the research, to the hospital.[102] Nonprofit hospitals have also engaged in reorganizations that are structured so that a parent nonprofit corporation, generally one that either is

---

cian for its medical staff to provide services to members of surrounding community but not necessarily for or on behalf of hospital, the hospital must comply with all of four requirements: (a) the hospital may not engage in substantial activities that do not further the hospital' s exempt purposes or that do not bear a reasonable relationship to the accomplishment of its exempt purposes, (b) the hospital must not engage in activities that result in the inurement of the hospital's net earnings to private individuals, (c) the hospital may not engage in substantial activities that cause the hospital to be operated for the benefit of private interest or for a substantial nonexempt purpose, and (d) the hospital may not engage in substantially unlawful activities. Rev. Rul. 97-21 considers five situations which involved hospitals providing incentives to recruit physicians.

In Priv. Ltr. Rul. 200211051, the IRS ruled the exempt status of a hospital would not be jeopardized by a restructuring whereby a nonprofit holding company would replace the hospital as the parent corporation of a health care system. The Service concluded that having a holding company replace the hospital as the parent would put proper emphasis on the component parts of the integrated delivery system rather than on the hospital. The holding company would be the sole member of the hospital's fundraising organization. The hospital would move its outpatient clinics, which were currently operated by its second and third-tier for-profit subsidiaries, into the hospital. It would transfer and operate directly its current outpatient physician practices, which then would function as departments of the hospital and be regarded as faculty physician practices. The IRS ruled that the restructuring would not affect the tax-exempt status of the hospital or the fundraising organization. Further, operation of the outpatient clinics would not be an unrelated business of the hospital.

102 In TAM 200151045, the Service concluded a § 501(c)(3) health care organization formed by a consortium of tax-exempt hospitals would not jeopardize its tax-exempt status by managing a limited partnership and receiving management fees. Because the state had limited the number of certificates of need it would issue to facilities seeking to operate lithotripters, several hospitals had created an organization to provide extra corporeal shock wave lithotripsy services to residents of a region. The organization then created a limited partnership to own and operate a lithotripsy center. The organization was the sole general partner, but member hospitals and member-hospital physicians owned seventy-five percent of the limited partnership interests. The Service ruled determined the limited partnership furthered the organization's exempt purposes and could act only in furtherance of those purposes. Thus, the Service concluded that activities of the partnership were substantially related to the exempt purposes of the organization.

In Priv. Ltr. Rul. 201814010, the Service ruled a non-profit corporation that developed, promoted, and supported software for physicians primarily benefitted the physicians and the medical practices and operations and, thus, served private rather than public purposes. The software was available to the general public although it targeted a specific audience—physicians operating a medical office or clinic. The Service concluded the physicians and their medical practices derived a commercial advantage from its open-source program because, in its absence, they would either need to develop their own software or would have to purchase commercial software. The Service noted that while the promotion of health is recognized as a charitable purpose, it stated not every activity that generally promotes health furthers charitable purposes under I.R.C. § 501(c)(3). The Service agreed that the software could benefit charitable medical facilities but that the benefits were also enjoyed by for-profit companies because any organization could use the software. The Service stated that because more than an insubstantial part of the corporation's activities was devoted to non-exempt purposes, the corporation was not operating exclusively for one or more exempt purposes and did not qualify for Section 501(c)(3) status.

involved in health education programs or that performs fund-raising activities, becomes a holding company for the non-profit hospital and for the various other nonprofit health-related organizations formed to engage in related exempt functions, such as outpatient services; care facilities for the aged; nursing homes; day care centers; rehabilitation programs, including speech therapy; and billing, data processing, collection, laundry and consulting services.[103] The parent nonprofit corporation may control a profit corporation established, as examples, to operate a pharmacy, a home health care organization, or a surgical center; to perform research for other entities; to operate a printing or graphics service; to sell laboratory services to physicians for use in their private practices; or to acquire and maintain a medical office building.[104] In addition, the parent organization may control a nonprofit fund-raising organization.

---

103 In Priv. Ltr. Rul. 200117043, the IRS ruled a public charity's participation in a joint venture to operate an ambulatory surgery center would not affect the charity's Section 501(c)(3) status. The charity joined in a partnership with another § 501(c)(3) organization to develop, construct, and operate an outpatient ambulatory surgery center. Each would contribute land and operating assets to the center. The center would provide medical services to all patients referred to it regardless of the patients' ability to pay and would provide free surgery services to indigent patients. The IRS also ruled that the charity's share of profits from the joint venture would not be subject be subject to the tax on unrelated business taxable income.

In Priv. Ltr. Rul. 200236049, the Service ruled the merger of one health care organization into another would not adversely affect the exempt status of the surviving entity. The organizations determined that a merger would permit a broader array of services, would better serve the geographic area, and would enhance efficiency and reduce costs.

In Priv. Ltr. Ruls. 200304041 and 200304042, the IRS ruled a hospital and a health care organization would not jeopardize their tax-exempt status by creating a LLC to operate a cardiac catheterization lab. The lab was set up to expand the hospital's existing services by segregating low-risk outpatients from hospital patients who receive cardiac services. The lab would provide outpatient services through a joint venture with cardiologists who had staff privileges at the hospital. The health care organization would have a fifty-two percent membership interest in the LLC with the physician group holding a forty-eight percent interest. The Service also ruled that payments the hospital received under a lease agreement it had with the LLC would not be unrelated business taxable income.

104 Priv. Ltr. Rul. 8716059 (pharmacy), Priv. Ltr. Ruls. 8715058, 8715040, 8715039 (home health care and surgical center), Priv. Ltr. Rul. 8718066 (medical office building).

In TAM 200218037, the IRS ruled a public charity would not jeopardize its exempt status by its interest, with for-profit partners, in a partnership that operated a magnetic resonance imaging (MRI) facility. The facility, which was formed by health care organizations to provide services to the public, qualified for Section 501(c)(3) status. It provided Medicare, Medicaid, and the same services to indigent patients that it provided all patients. No patients were denied treatment because of inability to pay. The facility had a broad-based community board that was representative of its member hospitals. The facility controlled the partnership's policies. Its interest in the partnership was equal in value to its contribution to the partnership, and its returns from the partnership were in proportion to its investment. The facility could ensure that partnership activities were used primarily to further exempt purposes so that any benefit to the for-profit limited partners was incidental to accomplishing exempt purposes. The partnership agreement also contained language that charitable interests would have priority over profit interests. The Service decided the facility qualified as a public charity under I.R.C. §§ 509(a)(1) and 170(b)(1)(A)(iii) or under I.R.C. §509(a)(2). (Discussion of these types of public charities in Chapter VIII.) It ruled that fees the facility received for

The Service has concluded a hospital association exempt under I.R.C § 501(c)(6)[105] can establish a subsidiary corporation to administer an insurance program to meet the rising cost of long-term care and the cutbacks in Medicare and Medicaid without jeopardizing its tax-exempt status.[106] The subsidiary

administrative and management services provided to the partnership would be unrelated business taxable income but that distributions to the facility from the partnership would not be taxed because partnership activities were substantially related to the facility›s exempt purposes.

105 A § 501(c)(6) hospital association provides services to its members, such as assisting in obtaining capital financing, providing counselling on business office problems, bidding for hospital supplies, and assisting in other aspects of hospital administration.

In Priv. Ltr. Rul. 200522022, the Service ruled a corporation organized to contract with hospitals and health care payors on behalf of participating physicians could not qualify for § 501(c)(6) status. The Service decided the corporation's activities were directed primarily to the performance of services for individual persons rather than for the improvement of business conditions of one or more lines of business. The organization described itself as a network of physicians in a specific county area, which contracted directly with local self-insured employers for their health benefits. The organization explained that keeping administrative costs to a minimum for the employer, the providers, and the patients was a major goal of its direct contracting. The Service concluded the organization provided member physicians with services by relieving them of having to conduct certain aspects of their businesses. It also concluded employers who participated in the organization's direct contracting arrangement were recipients of services that assisted them in the operation of their businesses. It noted the organization used its resources to negotiate competitive fees under the fee-for-services contract; made available a large and comprehensive provider panel; established a referral system for medical services; made available a local participating medical director to serve as an intermediary with the providers; and assisted them in developing a benefit design for their health plans. The Service also noted the organization engaged in activities that provided services to its malpractice insurer for which it was paid risk management fees.

106 Priv. Ltr. Rul. 8716004.

In Florida Hosp. Trust Fund v. C.I.R., 103 T.C. 140 (1994), decision aff'd, 71 F.3d 808 (11th Cir. 1996), the court ruled three organizations formed to provide insurance pools for its member hospitals did not qualify for Section 501(c)(3) status. The organizations were established as trust funds to provide centralized, cooperative insurance services to member hospitals. The member hospitals pooled their resources to provide self-insurance against medical malpractice and employment liability claims. The court noted I.R.C. § 501(m) prohibits Section 501(c)(3) or (4) status for organizations whose principal activities consist of providing insurance that can be purchased in the commercial market.

In Geisinger Health Plan v. C.I.R., 30 F.3d 494 (3d Cir. 1994), the Court of Appeals for the Third Circuit ruled a health maintenance organization that contracted with health care providers to offer prepaid health care to its subscribers, did not qualify for tax-exempt status under § 501(c)(3). The court ruled that the organization would not be tax exempt as an "integral part" of the hospital systems because its association with the health care organizations did nothing to increase the portion of the community which the health care organizations served.

In TAM 200245064, the IRS ruled a nonprofit corporation that contracted with employers, HMOs, insurance companies, and political subdivisions to provide services for the subscribers' employees or members, could no longer qualify as a social welfare organization under § 501(c)(4). The Service decided the organization's activities were not distinguishable significantly from those of a for-profit business. The corporation would arrange for the services through professionals with whom it contracted. The organization contended it operated its Medicare and Medicaid programs at a loss and, thus, was underwriting costs for governmental programs for the medically underserved. The IRS determined, however, that when the corporation's administrative expenses were added back, the programs brought in profits for the organization. The Service decided that, rather than underwriting unprofitable programs which supported governmental programs, the corporation's Medicare and Medicaid programs had economic and business purposes.

corporation can acquire all the stock of a corporation organized as an insurance agency that would market long-term care insurance to members of the hospital association.[107]

Dividends from profit corporations and earnings from services performed by nonprofit corporations within the group can be returned to the parent nonprofit organization without tax on the income. Rents and interest paid by profit corporations to a parent nonprofit organization are taxed if the proscription of § 512(b)(13), relating to income from a controlled organization, is not applicable.[108] Passive income (investment income) from a controlled organization (other than dividend income) is taxed only if the controlling organization owns at least fifty percent of all classes of stock or if at least fifty percent of the directors or trustees of a nonstock organization are either representatives of the parent or are directly or indirectly controlled by the parent nonprofit organization.[109]

E. CONVERSION FROM NONPROFIT STATUS TO FOR PROFIT STATUS

Some nonprofit hospitals have dissolved and have distributed their assets to for-profit entities.[110] Still, there have been concerns that there is a great potential for

107 Priv. Ltr. Rul. 8716004.

108 Discussion in Chapter IX. Dividends are not taxed even though derived from an organization controlled by an exempt organization. A part of passive income in the form of interest, annuities, royalties, or rents derived from a controlled organization will be taxed pursuant to I.R.C. § 512(b)(13).

109 I.R.C. § 512(b)(13) and Treas. Reg. § 1.512(b)-1(l)(4).

A director is a representative if the director is a director, agent, or employee of the parent nonprofit. A director is controlled if the parent nonprofit has the authority to remove the director. Reg. § 1.512(b)-1(k)(4).

The IRS ruled dividends would not be taxed to the nonprofit parent in Priv. Ltr. Ruls. 8803083 and 8803084 even though 100 percent of the common stock was owned by the parent. Control requires a fifty percent control of all classes of stock. If preferred stock is held by some other entity, the parent controlling the common stock would not have control under I.R.C. § 512(b)(13).

110 In Priv. Ltr. Rul. 9643039, the IRS ruled a § 501(c)(3) health care organization would not have adverse tax consequences from sale of its assets to an educational organization. It concluded the organization would continue to qualify as a public charity but as a school rather than as a hospital.

In Priv. Ltr. Rul. 200233024, the Service ruled a hospital that sold its general acute-care facility and earmarked the sale proceeds to an emergency medical services fund, would not jeopardize its tax-exempt status by using the fund to reimburse nonprofit and for-profit hospitals for uncompensated health care to indigents. None of the recipient hospitals were insiders. The Service decided the distributions would further the hospital's charitable purposes.

abuse in these transactions.[111] Although sales proceeds from a nonprofit health care organization's sale of its assets to a for-profit organization generally are distributed to other nonprofits, a problem arises when the nonprofit's assets are sold at less than fair market value and particularly when members of the board of directors of the dissolved nonprofit health care organization control, or are involved in, a for-profit successor.[112]

111 In State ex rel. Butterworth v. Anclote Manor Hosp., Inc., 566 So. 2d 296 (Fla. 2d DCA 1990), the attorney general of the state contended directors of a nonprofit corporation breached their fiduciary duty when they sold assets of the nonprofit for less than the fair market value to a for-profit corporation they owned. The court, however, ruled the attorney general had no standing to sue in a derivative capacity on behalf of the nonprofit corporation. The court also noted the IRS had not revoked the organization's tax-exempt status. Later, the IRS did revoke the corporation's tax-exempt status because the sale at less than fair market value constituted prohibited inurement. The Tax Court ruled in Anclote Psychiatric Center, Inc. v. Comm., T.C. Memo 1998-273 (1998) that sale of the organization's hospital for less than the fair market value resulted in inurement to the purchaser's private shareholders who also were directors of the § 501(c)(3) organization. There is a question whether the loss of tax-exempt status would have influenced the state court in ruling on the issue of breach of fiduciary duty.

The Attorney General for the State of New York issued a guidance document in 2018 that discusses the review that office will conduct regarding the sale to a for-profit entity of substantially all the assets of a nonprofit, specifically a nonprofit nursing home, to provide assistance for the board and management in the exercise of their fiduciary responsibilities to charitable beneficiaries regarding the sale of the charity's assets. The review requires a consideration and determination that a nonprofit nursing home has satisfied two factors or standards. The first standard involves a consideration of whether terms of the sale are fair and reasonable to the seller to assure the selling organization will receive optimal consideration for its property and the sale will not involve excessive risks to the selling organization. The second standard requires consideration of whether sale or transfer of assets, and the terms under which the assets are sold, will promote the mission and purposes of the charity. In considering the impact on a nursing home's charitable mission when a nursing home is sold, the guidance document noted that some nonprofit nursing homes are sole member corporations, effectively controlled by a related health care or fraternal organization that may have plans for proceeds of a sale only marginally related to the mission of the selling entity. It referred to some cases where, as a nursing home administrator approaches retirement, the directors decide to use proceeds of a sale to fund a grant making foundation and provide the administrator with a lucrative position overseeing a new grant making foundation. The guidance document lists as best practices in selling a nonprofit nursing a statement to the Charities Bureau that includes information, among several others, the following: fair value of the assets, debts, and liabilities of the selling entity; consideration to be received by the selling organization; use of proceeds of the sale; whether the selling organization will dissolve and, if so, how proceeds will be distributed under a plan of dissolution and distribution of assets; whether the transaction was recommended or authorized by vote of the directors, or if consent of members if required, how such consent was given; a five-year project of revenues and expenditures for the nursing home under current ownership; and whether and how the board evaluated the ability and willingness of the potential purchasers to a continuation of care. The statement should include a copy of the sales contract containing a clause the agreement is contingent upon approval by the Supreme Court or the Attorney General.

112 In Priv. Ltr. Rul. 200117043 the Service ruled a tax-exempt organization that sold its assets to a for-profit entity, must receive the fair market value of the assets, and the value must include going-concern value.

In Caracci v. C.I.R., 118 T.C. 379 (2002), the Tax Court agreed with the IRS that founders of tax-exempt health care organizations should be subject to the penalty tax set out in I.R.C. § 4958 for transferring assets of the exempt organizations to three for profit S corporations formed by the founders. (Discussion of I.R.C.

California had extensive statutes regulating the restructuring of nonprofit health care service plans.[113] A nonprofit health care service plan had to obtain prior approval from the Commissioner of Corporations to convert to for-profit status.[114] No profit from the sale of plan assets could inure to the benefit of any individual, and the sale or purchase of the nonprofit's assets had to be "consistent with and advance the public benefit, charitable, or mutual benefit purposes

---

§ 4958 penalty tax is in Chapter VIII under involvement in excess benefit transactions.) The Tax Court determined that assets of the tax-exempt organizations were worth much more than the consideration the organizations received for their assets. The penalty tax imposed on the founders was thirty-five percent of the net value of the assets, which the court determined to be more than $5M. The Tax Court decided revocation of tax-exempt status was not appropriate because the penalty tax was imposed on the successor S corporations and their creators. If tax exempt status was revoked, the court reflected that there would be no tax-exempt entities available to receive the assets. Although the Court of Appeals for the Fifth Circuit, 456 F.3d 444 (5th Cir. 2006), reversed the decision of the Tax Court, the decision of the Fifth Circuit was based on the Tax Court's acceptance of an appraiser's determination of the fair market value of the assets transferred to the for-profit entity and not on the Tax Court's interpretation of § 4958. The Fifth Circuit decided the transferred assets had no fair market value because it determined that liabilities of the transferor organization exceeded the value of its assets.

In St. David's Health Care System v. U.S., 349 F.3d 232 (5th Cir. 2003), the Court of Appeals for the Fifth Circuit overturned a district court's summary judgment ruling in favor of a nonprofit hospital that had its tax-exempt status revoked by the Internal Revenue Service because of a partnership it formed with a for-profit health care organization. The Fifth Circuit agreed with the IRS that St. David's would not be operated exclusively for charitable purposes if the for-profit organization had either formal or effective control over its activities. The court recognized that if a nonprofit enters into a partnership with a for-profit entity and retains control, the non-profit's activities via the partnership would primarily further exempt purposes; however, the court ruled that if the nonprofit ceded control to the for-profit, it could lose its tax-exempt status. The court decided there were genuine issues of material fact that had to be resolved before it could determine whether St. David's had ceded control to the for-profit entity. It vacated the district court's grant of summary judgment in favor of St. Davis's and remanded the case for further proceedings. The Fifth Circuit referred to the Tax Court's decision in Redlands Surgical Services v. C.I.R., 113 T.C. 47 (1999), aff'd, 242 F.3d 904 (9th Cir. 2001), in which the Tax Court rejected the taxpayer's argument that the central issue was not one of control but rather whether the partnership in fact performed charitable work. The documents creating the partnership must expressly state the partnership has a charitable purpose that will take priority over all other concerns; the partnership agreement must give the non-profit a majority vote in the partnership; and the partnership must be managed by an independent company that is not affiliated with the for-profit entity. The Fifth Circuit directed the district court to take evidence to determine whether St. David's had ceded control to the for-profit entity. If it had, the court ruled that it could not retain its tax-exempt status.

In Priv. Ltr. Rul. 9643039, the IRS ruled a § 501(c)(3) health care organization would not have adverse tax consequences from sale of its assets to an educational organization. It concluded the organization would continue to qualify as a public charity but as a school under I.R.C. §170(b)(1)(A)(ii), rather than as a hospital.

In Priv. Ltr. Rul. 200233024, the Service ruled a hospital that sold its general acute-care facility and earmarked the sale proceeds to an emergency medical services fund, would not jeopardize its tax-exempt status by using the fund to reimburse nonprofit and for-profit hospitals for uncompensated health care to indigents. None of the recipient hospitals were insiders. The Service decided the distributions would further the hospital's charitable purposes.

113 Cal. Health & Safety Code §§ 1399.70 to 1399.76.

114 Cal. Health & Safety Code § 1399.70.

of the plan."[115] No officer or director of the plan could have a financial interest in the sale or purchase.[116] One state, Minnesota, prohibited for-profit HMOs.[117]

F. STANDING (RIGHT) OF THE PUBLIC TO CHALLENGE TAX EXEMPT STATUS

Some members of the public have sought to invalidate the tax-exempt status of organizations that allegedly have failed to meet the requirements of tax-exempt status. There have been challenges to the tax-exempt status of many and various charities; some especially have questioned whether the hospital conglomerates should be tax-exempt. Still, it is difficult for members of the general public to dispute the actions of nonprofit organizations. Based upon decisions of the courts,[118] it is questionable whether a person whose own tax liability was not affected would ever have standing to litigate the federal tax liability of another. As one court[119] pointed out, the statutory scheme created by Congress is inconsistent with, if not preclusive of, third-party litigation of tax-exempt status.

> Example. In Abortion Rights Mobilization, Inc. v. Baker,[120] the Second Circuit Court of Appeals ruled that organizations and groups of individuals who were advocates of a woman's right to an abortion did not have standing to challenge

115 Cal. Health & Safety Code §1399.71(d)(2).

116 Id.

117 Minn. Stat. § 62D.02(4).

In Sarkis v. Heimburger, 933 F. Supp. 828 (E.D. Mo. 1996), a class action suit was filed on behalf of subscribers in health plans insured or administered by Blue Cross and Blue Shield against Blue Cross and others because of Blue Cross's creation of Right Choice, a for-profit health insurer and Blue Cross's subsequent transfer of approximately $434 million of its nonprofit assets to the new corporation. The petition alleged Blue Cross and other defendants purchased Healthlink, Inc., a health maintenance organization (HMO), for approximately three times its value of $30 million to minimize Blue Cross's assets and, thus, the amount it would be required to distribute to its nonprofit subscribers when it became a for-profit corporation. The petition alleged that Blue Cross and other defendants then encouraged Blue Cross subscribers to switch to Healthlink and its allegedly inferior HMO so that defendants could benefit from an illegal kickback scheme Healthlink engaged in, to its customers' detriment.

In Thompson v. Midwest Foundation Independent Physicians Ass'n, 124 F.R.D. 154 (S.D. Ohio 1988), plaintiffs prevented a for-profit conversion of a nonprofit HMO.

118 See, e. g., Simon v. Eastern Kentucky Welfare Rights Organization, 426 U.S. 26 (1976).

119 Fulani v. Brady, 955 F.2d 1324 (D.C. Cir. 1991).

120 885 F.2d 1020 (2nd Cir. 1989), cert. den., 495 U.S. 918 (1990).

the tax exempt status of the Catholic Church.[121] In a concurring opinion in Simon v. Eastern Kentucky Welfare Rights Organization,[122] Justice Stewart pointed out the special problems attendant upon the establishment of standing (right to sue) in tax cases when a litigant seeks to attack the tax status of a third party.

Additionally, while the public has an interest in the enforcement of a charity, the Attorney General of a state is the representative of the general public in compelling trustees and directors to perform their duties properly.[123]

121 The Catholic Church allegedly was involved in political campaigns on behalf of candidates who supported the church's views on abortions. The Second Circuit pointed to the decision of the Supreme in Allen v. Wright, 468 U.S. 737 (1984), in which the Court ruled that to have standing a person must show that the person has suffered an injury in fact that is both concrete in nature and particularized to that person. The court found no particularized injury in the Abortion Rights case.

122 426 U.S. 26 (1976).

123 The duties of nonprofit governing boards and the role of a state attorney general in representing the public are discussed in Chapter VI.

CHAPTER VIII. PUBLIC CHARITY AND PRIVATE FOUNDATION CLASSIFICATION FOR TAX PURPOSES

A. INTRODUCTION

The Internal Revenue Code (I.R.C.) divides charitable organizations described in I.R.C. § 501(c)(3) into two categories for federal tax purposes—public charities and private foundations.[1] Public charities generally are organizations that either

1 I.R.C. §§ 501(c)(3) and 509(a).

have broad public support or actively function in a supporting relationship to other charitable organizations having broad public support. To be a public charity, a § 501(c)(3) organization must be described in I.R.C. § 509. Every § 501(c)(3) organization will be a private foundation unless it falls into one of the categories specifically defined in I.R.C. §§ 509(a)(1) to (4). A charitable organization must give notice to the Service as to the provision of Section 509 that qualifies it as a public charity.[2] Private foundations are closely supervised by the Service and are subject to substantial penalties for engaging in certain prohibited acts.[3] In addition, contributions to private foundations receive less favorable tax treatment that do donations to public charities.[4] Consequently, it is important for an organization to classify itself correctly as a public charity if it can meet the provisions of I.R.C. § 509. Section 509 defines a private foundation by describing what it is not. Section 509 states that a private foundation is any § 501(c)(3) organization *other than* an organization described in I.R.C. §§ 509(a)(1) to (4). This language means that public charities are either § 509(a)(1), (2), (3) or (4) organizations.

A hospital is automatically classified as a public charity under I.R.C. § 509(a)(1) but also under I.R.C § 170(b)(1)(A)(iii)[5] and is referred to as a § 501(c)(3) organizations and a public charity under I.R.C. §§ 509(a)(1) and 170(b)(1)(A)(iii).[6] A hospital checks its Sections 509(a)(1) and 170(b)(1)(A)(iii) status on a Schedule A it must attach to the annual reporting Form 990.[7]

2 I.R.C. § 508(a).

3 These penalty taxes are set out in §§ 4941 to 4945 of the Internal Revenue Code and are discussed below.

4 The limitations are set out in I.R.C. § 170 and discussed below.

5 Section 170(b)(1)(A) of the Code becomes relevant with respect to a § 509(a)(1) public charity. The initial purpose of this Code section is to set out the charitable organizations with the most favorable treatment for purposes of the charitable contribution deduction. Section 509(a)(1) of the Code refers back to this Code section, Section 170(b)(1)(A), to classify these organizations for the favorable public charity status under I.R.C. § 509(a)(1). Accordingly, to understand the requirements for I.R.C. § 509(a)(1) status, consider the identity and qualifications of these public charities under I.R.C. § 170(b)(1)(A). The classifications pursuant to Section 170(b)(1)(A) for § 509(a)(1) organizations are: Section 170(b)(1)(A)(i)–churches; Section 170(b)(1)(A)(ii)–schools; Section 170(b)(1)(A)(iii)--hospital and medical research organizations; Section 170(b)(1)(A)(iv)–organizations for the benefit of state and municipal colleges and universities; Section 170(b)(1)(A)(v)–governmental units; and the publicly supported organizations identified in Section 170(b)(1)(A)(vi). A hospital then would be a § 501(c)(3) organization under §§ 509(a)(1) and 170(b)(1)(A)(iii). Its affiliated or supporting organizations would be § 501(c)(3) organizations under §§ 509(a)(1) and 170(b)(1)(A)(vi).

6 Public charity status is automatic for a hospital, which is classified under I.R.C. §170(b)(1)(A)(iii).

7 See annual reporting requirements discussed below.

Some organizations associated with hospitals that provide a variety of health care "services" to the general public can qualify for public charity status under I.R.C. § 509(a)(2). These would include, among others, childcare facilities for hospital employees, care facilities for the aged, nursing homes, and outpatient and community health programs. To qualify as a § 509(a)(2) organization, two tests must be met—a one-third support test and a not more than one-third gross investment test.[8]

An organization that receives little, if any, support from the general public can qualify as a public charity if it supports a qualified § 509(a)(1) or (2) public charity. Supporting organizations operated exclusively for the benefit of, and that are controlled by, § 509(a)(1) and (2) organizations, qualify for public charity status under I.R.C. § 509(a)(3). An advantage to Section 509(a)(3) status is that, unlike a § 509(a)(1) or (2) public charity, a § 509(a)(3) organization need not be concerned with annual fund drives, or providing services to the general public, to assure substantial public support.

Section 509(a)(4) excludes from private foundation status those § 501(c)(3) entities that are organized and operated for the purpose of testing products for public safety. These organizations test consumer products to determine their acceptability for use by the public and thus have no relevance with respect to tax classification of a hospital or its affiliated organizations.

As noted previously, a private foundation is a charitable organization that is supported, and often controlled, by one or a few donors. Because private foundations are controlled by a few individuals, they are supervised more closely by the IRS and are subject to substantial penalties for engaging in certain prohibited acts, discussed below. In addition, donations to private nonoperating foundations receive less favorable tax treatment than do contributions to public charities and private operating foundations. A § 501(c)(3) organization is presumed to be a private foundation unless it notifies and verifies to the IRS that it qualifies as a public charity.[9]

---

8 Treas. Reg. § 1.509(a)-3(a). These tests are described below. A § 501(c)(3) organization must attach a Schedule A to its annual reporting form, the IRS Form 990, to verify its public charity status. Except for churches, schools, and hospitals, which are automatically granted public charity status, the charitable organization must show on Schedule A the amount of their public support through a list of their donations from the public or their provision of public support for the public; thus, a charitable organization affiliated with a hospital would be required to show sufficient public support through its donations from the public or services rendered to the public to qualify for public charity status. See discussion below.

9 A charitable organization gives notice to the IRS that it qualifies for public charity status under one

B. DISQUALIFIED PERSON CHARACTERIZATION

A hospital director must be aware of the tax consequences attributed to individuals and entities that are "disqualified persons" to the organization. The amount of donations from "disqualified persons" is a determining factor in whether a hospital's affiliated or supporting organizations can qualify as tax-exempt charitable organizations and, in that context, as public charities for tax purposes. "Disqualified persons" include the following: (1) substantial contributors to a charitable organization--a person or entity that contributed an aggregate amount of more than $5,000 during a year if that amount is more than two percent of the total contributions and bequests received by the organization during that year; (2) managers of the nonprofit organization; (3) an owner of more than twenty percent of a corporation, partnership, or trust if the corporation, partnership, or trust contributed more than $5,000 to the organization, and provided that amount was more than two percent of total contributions received by the organization during the year; (4) a corporation, partnership, trust or estate, wherein any of the persons noted above has more than a thirty-five percent interest; and (5) the family of a substantial contributor but including only spouse, ancestors, lineal descendants and their spouses.

C. SECTION 509(A)(1) PUBLIC CHARITY

1. Hospital

A hospital or medical research organization must first qualify for Section 501(c)(3) status as discussed in Chapter VII. As noted above, a hospital then qualifies for public charity status under I.R.C. §§ 509(a)(1) and 170(b)(1)(A)(iii). Federal

of the provisions of I.R.C. § 509 at the same time it seeks tax exempt status, by filing Form 1023 electronically for both purposes--to obtain Section 501(c)(3) tax exempt status and to classify itself either as a private foundation or as a public charity. It must also indicate the provision under Section 509 that qualifies it for public charity status. The Form 1023 is available on the IRS website and is filed electronically.

As noted in Chapter VII, a charitable organization must file Form 1023 with the IRS within twenty-seven months after the organization is established for the IRS to recognize exempt status from the organization's inception. If the organization does not file Form 1023 within the twenty-seven months after its creation, the IRS will recognize exempt status only from the date the IRS receives the application. See Treas. Reg. § 1.508-1(a)(2).

hospitals and state, county, and municipal hospitals are included as qualifying for public charity status under I.R.C. §§ 509(a)(1) and 170(b)(1)(A)(iii) although these may qualify automatically because they are either governmental entities or public agencies exempt pursuant to I.R.C. § 115.[10]

2. Affiliated Organization–Public Support Test

An affiliated organization qualifies for public charity status if it obtains most of its funding from the general public or from donations from governmental units rather than from "disqualified persons."[11] A charitable organization is "publicly supported" if the total amount of support the organization normally receives, as an average over a five-year period, from governmental units or from the general public, is at least one third percent of total support. For these purposes, support does not include amounts received for services rendered, i. e., gross receipts.[12] Additionally, if support from services rendered is substantial, the organization cannot qualify as a § 509(a)(1) public charity. It must seek public charity status under I.R.C. § 509(a)(2).

a. Support Test.

Public support for a §509(a)(1) public charity, which is qualified under I.R.C. § 170(b)(1)(A)(vi), is measured by a fraction--the numerator of the fraction is the amount of support from governmental units and from the general public and the denominator is total support reduced by amounts received for services performed by the organization.The determination of public support is set out, and the support fraction determined, on the Schedule A to the Form 990.[13] The IRS reviews the information regarding public support provided on the Schedule A to determine on an annual basis if the organization continues to qualify as a public charity.

---

10 Discussion in Chapter VII.

11 The requirements to be "publicly supported" are set out in I.R.C. § 170(b)(1)(A)(vi) and in the Treasury Regulations pursuant to that Code section.

12 Amounts received for services rendered are excluded from both the numerator and the denominator of the support fraction. However, an organization that depends primarily on gross receipts for its support cannot qualify as a § 509(a)(1) public charity. This type organization should seek public charity status under I.R.C. § 509(a)(2).

13 Discussion of Form 990 and its Schedule A below.

Donations from "disqualified persons" are counted in full in the denominator of the one-third support fraction, but these donations are counted in the numerator of the fraction only to the extent of two percent of total support. In this manner, then, the support fraction requires the elimination of most of the support from substantial contributors in the numerator to determine whether a charitable organization is "publicly supported." This is to assure that support will be, in fact, from the general public rather than from a few substantial donors.

The one-third support test is computed for the five-year period including the current year and the four years immediately preceding the current year as described in the following example.

Example 1. A hospital auxiliary received support of $1,200,000 from the following sources in the current year and previous four years:

Contributions	$440,000
Governmental Unit (City)	80,000
United Fund	80,000
Investment Income	600,000
	$1,200,000

Of the $440,000 contributions, six contributors, who gave a total of $340,000, gave in excess of $24,000, or two percent of total support. To satisfy the support test, the numerator of the fraction must be $400,000, or one-third of total support of $1,200,000. The numerator for the fraction is $404,000, determined as follows:

Support from governmental units	$ 80,000
Indirect contributions from the general public (United Fund)	80,000
Contributions by various donors--no one in excess of two percent of total support) [$440,000 - $340,000 (contributions from disqualified persons)]	100,000
Six contributions (each in excess of $24,000 or two percent of total support), six times $24,000	144,000
	$404,000

The hospital auxiliary "normally" received in excess of one-third of its support from governmental units and from the general public, and it qualifies as a public charity under I.R.C. § 509(a)(1).

Example 2. Assume in year 5, an individual, gave $800,000 to the hospital auxiliary in Example 1 above. Total support would then be $2,000,000 ($1,200,000 set out in Example 1 plus $800,000 gift from the individual). To meet the one-third support test, $666,666 must be received from governmental units and the general public ($2,000,000 divided by one-third). Assume the six substantial contributors noted in Example 1 each gave in excess of $40,000, or two percent of total support of $2,000,000. As noted previously, contributions from disqualified persons count in the numerator only to the extent of two percent of total support; thus, each of the six contributions from the disqualified persons count in the numerator up to $40,000 (which is two percent of $2,000,000). For six contributors, $240,000 ($40,000 x 6) will be included in the numerator. In addition, $40,000 of the $800,000 gift can be counted in the numerator. Thus, $280,000 of the contributions from disqualified persons can be counted in the numerator of the one-third support fraction. The numerator of the one-third support fraction is computed as follows:

Support from governmental units	$ 80,000
Indirect contributions from the general public (United Fund)	80,000
Contributions by various donors (no one in excess of two percent of total support, or $40,000)	100,000
Seven contributions (each in excess of $40,000 or two percent of total support); $40,000 x seven	280,000
	$540,000

The $540,000 is less than one-third of total support of $2,000,000. [The organization needed $666,666 to meet the one-third support test ($2,000,000 divided by one-third). Thus, the hospital auxiliary will not meet the one-third support test.

Only $40,000 of the gift from the individual can be included in the numerator of the one-third support test. Because of the large gift from the individual, the hospital auxiliary then would not meet the one-third support. The above example illustrates the problem when a charity is given a large donation in one year.[14] Still, there is a possibility that the hospital auxiliary in Example 2 can qualify under another test for public charity status to avoid being classified as a private foundation. It may nonetheless be able to qualify as a publicly supported charity under Section 509(a)(1) if it can meet an alternative facts and circumstances test available under Section 509(a)(1), and discussed below, or can exclude the individual's large gift from both the numerator and the denominator of the support fraction as an unusual and unexpected donation, discussed below under "Unusual Grants." However, if the hospital auxiliary fails to meet the alternative facts and circumstances test and if it cannot exclude the gift as an unusual grant, it would not qualify as a public supported charity under I.R.C. § 509(a)(1).

The substantial contribution from the individual in Example 2 presented a dilemma for the hospital auxiliary. The charity would want to accept the contribution but would not want acceptance of the gift to cause it to lose its public charity status. Although the hospital auxiliary would attempt to qualify the gift as an unusual grant, if the auxiliary is organized and operated in a manner that would permit it to meet the facts and circumstances test, it would not encounter the problem of having to reject the large donation to sustain its public charity status.

b. Facts and Circumstances Test.

Even though an organization fails to meet the one-third support test, it still can qualify as a publicly supported charity status under I.R.C. §§ 509(a)(1) and 170(b)(1)(A)(vi) if it normally receives a substantial part of its support from governmental units and from direct or indirect contributions from the general public and if it meets certain other requirements.[15]

The percentage of support required for these purposes is at least ten percent of total support "normally" received.[16] "Facts and circumstances" to be considered in addition to the support requirement relate to the type of support received and the manner in which a nonprofit entity is organized. An entity

14 The hospital auxiliary could possibly qualify as a private "operating" foundation, which may be a more favorable tax status. See discussion below.

15 Treas. Reg. § 1.170A-9(e)(3).

16 Treas. Reg. § 1.170A-9(e). "Normally" is the average over the current year and a four-year period immediately preceding the current year.

must be organized and operated to attract new and additional public or governmental support on a continuous basis. This requirement is met if an organization maintains a continuous and bona fide program for solicitation of funds from the general public, community, or membership group involved, or if it carries on activities designed to attract support from governmental units or other charitable organizations. Consideration is given to the scope of an organization's fund-raising activities.

Five factors, in addition to the ten percent support test, are taken into consideration in determining an organization's public status under the "facts and circumstances" test. While an organization is not required to satisfy all of the five factors, the number required to satisfy the test and the weight accorded to each depends upon the nature and purpose of the organization. The factors are:

(1) Percentage of support received by an organization from public or governmental sources. The higher the percentage of support above the ten percent requirement, the lesser the burden of establishing the publicly supported nature of the organization through other factors, while the lower the percentage, the greater the burden. If the percentage is low, the source of endowment funds is noted. If such funds originally were contributed by a few individuals or by members of their families, the burden on the organization to establish compliance with other factors is increased.

(2) Sources of support. Consideration is given to whether support is from a representative number of persons or almost all from members of a single family.

(3) Representative governing body. The fact that an organization has a governing body that represents broad interests of the public, rather than personal or private interests of a limited number of donors, will be given weight in determining whether an organization is publicly supported. An organization has a "representative governing body" if its governing body is comprised of (a) public officials acting in their official capacities, (b) individuals selected by public officials, (c) persons having special knowledge or expertise in the particular field or discipline in which the organization is operating, (d) community leaders, or (e) for membership organizations, a broadly based membership.

(4) Availability of public facilities or services and public participation in programs or policies. The fact that an organization is of the type that generally

provides facilities or services directly for the benefit of the general public on a continuing basis is evidence that an organization is publicly supported. Other facts, such as members of the public participating in or sponsoring programs of the organization, an organization's use of a definitive program to accomplish its charitable work in the community, and an organization's receipt of a significant part of its funds from a public charity or governmental agency to which it is in some manner held accountable as a condition of the grant, also are considered evidence that an organization is publicly supported.

(5) Additional factors. Other facts to be considered include whether solicitation for dues paying members is designed to enroll a substantial number of persons in the community or area; whether membership dues for individual members have been fixed at rates designed to make membership available to a broad cross section of the interested public and whether activities of the organization likely will appeal to persons having some broad common interest or purpose.

c. Unusual Grants.

Unusual grants affect both § 509(a)(1) and § 509(a)(2) organizations in their attempts to meet the publicly supported tests. If a large gift or grant can qualify as an unusual grant, it can be excluded from both the numerator and the denominator of the fractions and, thus, lessen substantially the adverse effect of such a contribution on the publicly supported status of the organization.[17]

An unusual grant, which is excluded from an organization's support fraction, is a substantial contribution or bequest from a disinterested party that was attracted by reason of an organization's publicly supported nature, that is unusual or unexpected as to its amount, and that would, by reason of its size, adversely affect the status of an organization as a public charity. In determining whether a particular contribution can qualify as an unusual grant, all relevant facts and circumstances are considered. No single factor is determinative.[18]

A grant may be categorized as an unusual grant without a formal ruling from the IRS if the grant meets the requirements noted above and also the following conditions: (1) the grant or contribution was not made by a person (or related person) who created the organization or who was a substantial contributor prior

17 Treas. Reg. § 1.170A-9(e)(6).

18 Treas. Reg. § 1.509(a)-3(c)(4).

to the grant; (2) the grant was not made by a person in a position of authority such as a foundation manager, someone else who can exercise control over the organization, or a person who assumes a position of authority as a result of the grant; (3) the grant or contribution is in the form of cash, readily marketable securities, or assets that directly further the organization's exempt purpose; (4) the organization has met the required publicly supported test before the year of the grant; (5) the grantor has not imposed any material restrictions upon the organization in connection with the grant.[19]

D. SECTION § 509(A)(2) PUBLIC CHARITY.

A charitable organization that receives support from the general public in the form of receipts for services rendered or for other activities related to the organization's exempt functions may qualify as a public charity under I.R.C. § 509(a)(2). An affiliated or supporting organization to a hospital that obtains a substantial amount of its receipts from services rendered, such as a childcare facility associated with a hospital, would be in this category. As previously noted, a charitable organization that receives a substantial amount of its support from gross receipts (in performing its exempt function activities) cannot qualify as a public charity under I.R.C. §§ 509(a)(1) and 170(b)(1)(A)(vi). It, however, may qualify as a § 509(a)(2) public charity.

A § 509(a)(2) charity must meet two tests--a one-third support and a not more than one-third gross investment test. The one-third support test is similar to the one-third support test for § 509(a)(1) public charities except that gifts from disqualified persons cannot be included at all in the numerator of the support fraction although they are counted in full in the denominator, and gross receipts from the organization's exempt functions are included in both the numerator and the denominator. A § 509(a)(2) public charity cannot receive more than a third of its support from gross investment income. This is not a limitation for a

19 If an organization has doubt as to whether a grant or contribution may be excluded as an unusual grant, it should request a revenue ruling from the IRS. (See Rev. Proc. 2021-1 for procedures to be following in obtaining a revenue ruling. A same format is set out in its Appendix B.) Additional facts that the IRS may consider include: (1) whether the contribution was a bequest (a bequest is given more favorable consideration than a contribution made during the donor's life); (2) whether the organization was able to attract a significant amount of public support; (3) whether the organization may reasonably be expected to attract a significant amount of public support after the gift; and (4) whether the organization has a representative governing body.

§ 509(a)(1) charity; however, substantial investment income also is a problem for a § 509(a)(1) charity. The total amount of investment income is included in the denominator of the organization's one-third support test but is not included at all in the numerator. A substantial amount of investment income then can cause the organization difficulty in meeting the one-third publicly supported test.

1. Support Test.

An organization seeking public charity status under I.R.C. § 509(a)(2) will meet the one-third test if it «normally," as an average over a five-year period, receives more than one-third of its total support from any combination of gifts, grants, contributions, membership fees, and gross receipts from admissions, sales of merchandise, performance of services, or furnishing of facilities, unless any of these activities constitute an unrelated trade or business as discussed in Chapter IX. Funds from governmental units, from § 509(a)1) public charities, and from persons other than disqualified persons also are permitted sources for this test.

There are limitations on the amount of gross receipts from an individual or entity that can be included in the numerator of the support fraction to assure that receipts are derived, in fact, from the general public rather than from a few persons or entities. Gross receipts from related activities received from a person, or from a bureau or similar agency of a governmental unit, are included in the numerator of the one-third support test for any year only to the extent the gross receipts from the person or entity do not exceed the greater of $5,000 or one percent of the organization's support in that year.

Example 3. In the current year, a surgical center affiliated with a hospital received $200,000 support from the following sources:

Governmental bureau, for services rendered	$50,000
An individual, for services rendered	50,000
General public, for services rendered	40,000
Gross investment income	30,000
Contributions from individual substantial contributors (disqualified persons)	30,000
	$200,000

> Because the $50,000 received from the governmental bureau and from the individual is more than the greater of $5,000 or one percent of the surgical center's support for the year (one percent of $200,000, or $2,000), each amount is included in the numerator of the one-third support fraction only to the extent of $5,000. Contributions from disqualified persons cannot be included at all in the numerator of the fraction. The numerator of the support fraction, then, is $50,000, computed, as follows:
>
> | | |
> |---|---|
> | Governmental bureau | $ 5,000 |
> | Individual | 5,000 |
> | General public | 40,000 |
> | | $50,000 |
>
> Because the denominator of the fraction is $200,000, the one-third support test is not met for the year. Still, qualification is determined over a five-year period. While amount of gross receipts from any one individual or governmental unit is limited to the greater of $5,000 or one percent support on an annual basis, determination of whether an organization meets the support test to qualify as a § 509(a)(2) charity is made on a five-year basis. If the test is not met based on data for a five-year period, the organization will not qualify as § 509(a)(2) public charity. [The alternative facts and circumstances test is not available for a § 509(a)(2) organization.]

As set out in the above example, gross receipts from any individual or entity in excess of the greater of $5,000 or one percent of total support for a year are excluded from the numerator of the support fraction. This requirement limits § 509(a)(2) public charity status to those nonprofit organizations that provide services to the general public rather than to only a few individuals or entities. A § 509(a)(1) public charity, on the other hand, qualifies for public charity status because it receives "contributions" from the general public rather than from only a few donors.

2. Investment Income Test.

A § 509(a)(2) organization may not receive more than one-third of its support in any year from gross investment income and from the excess of its unrelated business taxable income over the tax imposed upon that income. Gross investment income is the gross amount of income from interest, dividends, rents, and royalties.

> Example 4. The gross investment test was met in Example 3 above. The surgical center did not receive more than one-third of its support from gross investment income. Its investment income was fifteen percent of its total support [$30,000 (gross investment income) divided by $200,000 (total support for the year)].

E. SECTION 509(A)(3) PUBLIC CHARITY.

An organization that receives little, if any, support from the general public can qualify as a public charity if it supports a qualified § 509(a)(1) or (2) public charity. Supporting organizations operated exclusively for the benefit of, and/or controlled by, § 509(a)(1) and (2) organizations, qualify for public charity status under I.R.C. § 509(a)(3). An advantage to Section 509(a)(3) status is that, unlike a § 509(a)(1) or (2) public charity, a § 509(a)(3) organization need not be concerned with annual fund drives, or providing services to the general public, to assure substantial public support. This type of public charity classification is discussed briefly below.

A publicly supported organization qualifies for public charity status under Section 509(a)(1) or (2), whereas a § 509(a)(3) organization is one that has established a specified relationship with, and in support of, a § 509(a)(1) or (2) public charity. Even though a single donor or only a few donors may fund such an organization, the organization nonetheless may qualify as a public charity if it has limited purposes and activities and if it relinquishes a substantial degree of independence. Private foundations that wish to obtain public charity status can obtain this status more easily by electing to qualify under I.R.C. § 509(a)(3).

An entity qualifies for § 509(a)(3) status by meeting three tests set out in Treasury regulations relating to the entity's organization and operation and its relationship with a § 509(a)(1) or (2) charity, or charities. A supporting entity under Section 509(a)(3) may not be controlled directly or indirectly by one or more disqualified persons other than foundation managers and other than one or more publicly supported organizations.[20]

---

20 Treas. Reg. § 1.509(a)-4(j). An organization is "controlled" if disqualified persons, by aggregating their votes or positions of authority, may require the organization to perform any act that significantly affects its operations, or may prevent the organization from performing these acts. A

1. Organizational Test.

A § 509(a)(3) organization must be organized exclusively for the benefit of, to perform functions of, or to carry out purposes of, one or more specified publicly supported charities.[21] The supporting organization's articles of incorporation must so limit its purposes and must not empower it expressly to engage in activities that are not in furtherance of those purposes. The articles must state the publicly supported organizations on whose behalf the supporting organization is operated and must not expressly empower the supporting organization to operate or benefit any other organization.

2. Operational Test.

A § 509(a)(3) organization must engage in activities that support or benefit its specified publicly supported charity, or charities. Its activities may include making payments for use of, or providing services or facilities for, members of the charitable class benefitted by its specified publicly supported charity, or charities.

3. Relationship with Publicly Supported Charities.

A supporting organization under Section 509(a)(3) must be responsive to the needs and demand of a public charity and must constitute an integral part of, or maintain a significant involvement in, operations of its supported charity, or charities. The relationship between the supporting organization and its supported charity, or charities, requires either the presence of a substantial degree of direction by the supported charity over conduct of the supporting organization, the presence of common supervision or control among governing bodies of all organizations involved, or a supporting organization responsive to, and significantly involved in, operation of the supported charity, or charities. To meet the relationship test, one of three types of relationships must exist between the supporting organization and its supported charity (or charities). A supporting

supporting organization will be controlled if voting power of disqualified persons is fifty percent or more of total voting power of the organization's governing body or if one or more of these persons has the right to exercise veto power over actions of the organization.

21 Treas. Reg. § 1.509(a)-4(a).

organization must either be (a) operated, supervised, or controlled by, (b) supervised or controlled in connection with, or (c) operated in connection with, one or more publicly supported charities.

a. Type I---Operated, Supervised, or Controlled By.

The distinguishing feature of this type of relationship is the existence of a substantial degree of direction by the publicly supported charity over conduct of the supporting organization. Each of the terms--operated by, supervised by, and controlled by--presupposes a substantial degree of direction over policies, programs, and activities of a supporting organization by a publicly supported charity. The relationship is comparable to that of a parent corporation and its subsidiary. The relationship is established by the fact that a majority of officers, directors, or trustees of the supporting organization are appointed or elected by members of the governing body, officers acting in their official capacity, or the membership of, the publicly supported charity.

b. Type II--Supervised or Controlled in Connection With.

The distinguishing feature of this relationship is the presence of common supervision or control among governing bodies of all organizations involved, such as the presence of common directors. There must be common supervision or control by persons supervising or controlling both the supporting organization and the publicly supported charity to ensure the supporting organization will be responsive to needs and requirements of the publicly supported charity. Thus, control or management of the supporting organization must be vested in the same persons who control or manage the publicly supported charity (or charities).

c. Type III--Operated in Connection With.

The distinguishing feature of this relationship is that the supporting organization is responsive to, and significantly involved in operations of, the publicly supported charity. A supporting organization is "operated in connection with" a public charity if it meets two tests--the responsiveness test and the integral part test.

The responsiveness test requires that a supporting organization be responsive to needs and demands of the designated publicly supported charity. To meet this test, at least one of the officers, directors, or trustees of the supporting organization must be elected or appointed by officers, directors, trustees, or members of the supported public charity. Additionally, at least one of the members of the governing body of the publicly supported charity must hold some important office in the supporting organization. Finally, there must be a close and continuous working relationship with officers, directors, or trustees of the supporting organization and the supported public charity. Officers and directors of the supported public charity must have a significant voice in affairs of the supporting organization. If the supporting organization is a charitable trust, each specified publicly supported charity must be a named beneficiary under the trust's governing instrument, and the beneficiary organization must have power to enforce the trust and compel an accounting under state law.

The integral part test requires that a supporting organization maintain a significant involvement in the operations of a publicly supported charity and that the designated publicly supported charity be dependent upon the supporting organization for the type of support it provides. This test requires that the supporting organization either be engaged in activities that the public charity would be required to undertake but for involvement of the supporting organization, or that the supporting organization make payments of substantially all its income in a sufficient amount to ensure that the public charity will be attentive to operations of the supporting organization.[22] The amount of support received by a publicly supported charity must represent a sufficient part of the charity's total support so as to insure attentiveness.

F. PROCEDURES TO OBTAIN PUBLIC CHARITY STATUS.

A charitable organization seeks to obtain public charity status at the same time it applies for tax exempt status--by filing the Form 1023 with the IRS. Form 1023 serves both as an application for exempt status and also as a notification to

22 Section 509(a)(3) supporting organizations are further classified into two categories: Type III supporting organizations that are functionally integrated (FI Type III) or Type III supporting organizations that are not functionally integrated (NFI Type III). A functionally integrated (FI) supporting organization is one that is not required to make payments to its supported organization because its activities are related to performing the functions of, or carrying out, the purposes of the supported organization(s). Additional discussion of the FI versus the NFI Type III is beyond this text.

the IRS that the organization is or is not a private foundation. A hospital designates itself on Form 1023 as a § 509(a)(1) organization, with its classification under I.R.C. § 170(b)(1)(A)(b)(iii).[23] For organizations affiliated with a hospital, the IRS will analyze information provided on the form to determine whether the organization meets the one-third support test and the not more than one-third investment income test for § 509(a)(2) organizations, and either the one-third or the ten percent support test for § 509(a)(1) organizations under I.R.C. §170(b)(1)(A)(vi). The charity would demonstrate its continuing public charity status by providing information regarding its support annually on a separate schedule to the annual reporting Form 990.

G. INVOLVEMENT IN EXCESS BENEFIT TRANSACTIONS

Certain "disqualified persons" are subject to a penalty tax on their involvement in "excess benefit transactions" with a public charity.[24] An "excess benefit transaction" is any transaction in which an economic benefit is provided by a public charity directly or indirectly to or for the use of a disqualified person if the value of the economic benefit provided exceeds the value of the consideration, including the performance of services, received by the charity for the benefit. The penalty tax on an "excess benefit transaction" is twenty-five percent of the excess benefit and is imposed on the disqualified person. If the excess benefit is not corrected within a "taxable period,"[25] a tax of 200 percent of the excess benefit is imposed on the disqualified person.[26]

---

23 As noted previously, for a hospital, the Code section would be Section 170(b)(1)(A)(iii); a hospital would be designated as a § 501(c)(3) organization with public charity status under I.R.C. §§ 509(a)(1) and 170(b)(1)(A)(iii).

24 I.R.C. § 4958. A disqualified person for this purpose is any person who was, at any time during a five-year period ending on the date of the transaction, in a position to exercise substantial influence over the affairs of the charity.

25 The "taxable period" is the period beginning with the date on which the transaction occurs and ending on the earliest of: (a) the date of the mailing of a notice of deficiency with respect to the initial tax or (b) the date on which the initial tax is imposed. See I.R.C. § 4958(f)(5). An excess benefit transaction is corrected by undoing the excess benefit to the extent possible and taking any additional measures necessary to place the organization in a financial position no worse than that in which it would have been had the disqualified person acted under the highest fiduciary standards. See I.R.C. § 4958(f)(6).

26 A penalty tax also is imposed on the organization's manager if the manager participated in the transaction, knowing the transaction was an excess benefit transaction unless the manager can show her participation was not willful and was due to reasonable cause. See I.R.C. § 4958(d)(2). Par-

1. Disqualified Persons under Section 4958.

A "disqualified person" under I.R.C. § 4958 is any person who has substantial influence over a charity during a five-year period ending on the date of a transaction with the charity. The definition of a "disqualified person" for purposes of Section 4958 is not the same as the definition for the "disqualified person" discussed above whose support for a public charity is limited in determining whether the organization meets the one-third support test. The following are included in the definition of a disqualified person for purposes of Section 4958: (1) members of the governing body who are entitled to vote; (2) presidents, chief executive officers, or chief operating officers;[27] and (3) treasurers and chief financial officers.[28] A person who has managerial control over a discrete segment of a charity may be in a position to exercise substantial influence over the entire charity and, thus, may be a disqualified person.[29] Some persons are deemed not to have substantial influence. They include employees who receive benefits from a public charity of less than a designated amount and are not substantial contributors to the charity.[30]

---

ticipation includes silence or inaction on the part of an organization manager where the manager is under a duty to speak or act. See Treas. Reg. § 53.4958-1(d)(3). If a manager relies on a "reasoned legal opinion" that a transaction is not an excess benefit transaction, the manager's participation in the transaction will be due to reasonable cause and not knowing or willful.

27 An individual serves as president, chief executive officer, or chief operating officer, regardless of title, if that individual has or shares ultimate responsibility for implementing decisions of the governing body or supervises management, administration, or operation of the charity.

28 An individual serves as treasurer or chief financial officer, regardless of title, if that individual has or shares ultimate responsibility for managing the charity's financial assets and has or shares authority to sign drafts or direct signing of drafts, or to authorize electronic transfer of funds, from a charity's bank accounts.

29 The facts and circumstances that tend to show a person has substantial influence over the affairs of a charity include, but are not limited to, the following:

(1) the person founded the charity;

(2) the person is a substantial contributor;

(3) the person's compensation is based on revenues derived from activities of the charity;

(4) the person has authority to control or determine a significant portion of the organization's capital expenditures, operating budget, or compensation for employees;

(5) the person has managerial authority or serves as a key advisor to a person with managerial authority;

(6) the person owns a controlling interest in a corporation, partnership, or trust that is a disqualified person. Treas. Reg. § 53.4958(e).

30 Treas. Reg. § 53.4958-3. The Regulations refers to I.R.C. § 414(q), which set out the amount of $80,000, but this amount has been adjusted for inflation.

2. Excess Benefit Transaction.

An "excess benefit transaction" is one in which a public charity provides a benefit to a "disqualified person" in excess of the consideration received for the benefit. It includes any financial and non-fair-market value transaction that benefits an individual. Excessive compensation paid to a director or employee of a public charity is an "excess benefit transaction." Compensation paid may not exceed what is reasonable under all circumstances. Compensation is reasonable if it is no more than an amount that ordinarily would be paid for like services by like enterprises under like circumstances.[31]

There is a rebuttable presumption that compensation is reasonable if a compensation arrangement was approved by a board or committee which: (1) was composed entirely of individuals who were unrelated to and not subject to control of the disqualified person involved in the arrangement; (2) obtained and relied upon appropriate data as to comparability;[32] and (3) documented adequately the basis for its determination.[33] If all three criteria are satisfied, penalty taxes are imposed only if the IRS develops sufficient contrary evidence to rebut the probative value of evidence established by the charity. For property sold or otherwise transferred by a public charity, there is a similar rebuttable presumption if the

31 A public charity must establish an intent to provide an economic benefit as compensation for services by reporting the benefit on a Form W-2 or a 1099. If the charity fails to provide evidence that it intended to provide an economic benefit as compensation for services when paid, any services provided by a disqualified person will not be treated as provided in consideration of the economic benefit. See Treas. Reg. § 53.4958-4(c)(ii).

32 Appropriate data include: compensation levels paid by similarly situated organizations, both taxable and tax-exempt, for functionally comparable positions, the location of the organizations, including the availability of similar specialties in the geographic area; independent compensation surveys by nationally recognized independent firms; or actual written offers from similar institutions competing for services of the disqualified person. See Treas. Reg. § 53.4958-6(d)(2).

33 Adequate documentation includes an evaluation of the individual whose compensation is being established and the basis of determining that the individual's compensation is reasonable in light of that evaluation and data.

In TAM 200244028, the IRS ruled that a health care organization did not meet the rebuttable presumption of reasonableness as to compensation paid its president and chief executive officer. The CEO and his spouse entered into a consulting agreement with the health care organizations. Compensation was split between the CEO and his spouse. The CEO would receive sixty percent of total compensation and his spouse would receive forty percent. The health organization's personnel committee relied on data provided by an executive compensation firm to establish that the compensation package for the CEO and his spouse was reasonable. The IRS concluded that both the CEO and his spouse were disqualified persons with respect to the health care organization. It concluded that the amended agreement was a new contract and that the health care organization did not satisfy all requirements for establishing a rebuttable presumption that compensation paid the CEO and his spouse was reasonable. It ruled that the wife would receive an excess benefit if the value of the total economic benefits she received exceeded the value of the services she performed.

sale or transfer was approved by an independent board that used appropriate comparability data and documented adequately its determination.[34]

A decision of a governing board is documented adequately if written or electronic records note: (1) the terms of the transaction that was approved and the date it was approved; (2) members of the governing body or committee who were present during the debate on the transaction or arrangement that was approved and those who voted for it; (3) the comparability data obtained and relied upon by the committee and how the data was obtained; and (4) actions taken with respect to consideration of the transaction by anyone who is otherwise a member of the governing body or committee but who had a conflict of interest with respect to the transaction or arrangement.

If a governing body or committee determines that reasonable compensation for a specific arrangement or fair market value in a specific transaction is higher or lower than the range of comparable data obtained, the governing body or committee must record the basis for its determination. For a decision to be documented concurrently, records must be prepared by the next meeting of the governing body or committee occurring after the final action or actions are taken. The records must be reviewed and approved by the governing body or committee as reasonable, accurate, and complete within a reasonable time thereafter.

> Example. The person employed as the president and director of a hospital board has been provided with a substantial salary increase plus a home and automobile. The home and automobile are part of the director's compensation package. As a result, the director is the highest paid hospital president and director in the state. It may be a problem for the director that he is the highest paid director. The board could not point to a higher paid director in its comparability data. If the IRS can contend successfully that the director's compensation package is excessive, the director will be subject to a twenty-five percent tax initially on the amount deemed excessive. Assume the Service proves the director's compensation is excessive in the amount of $100,000. The director would be subject to a penalty tax of $25,000 (twenty-five percent of $100,000). The director then would be required to repay the $100,000 to the hospital or be subjected to a penalty tax of $200,000 (200 percent of $100,000).[35]

---

34 Relevant information would include independent appraisals of the value of property a charity intends to purchase from, or sell or provide to, a disqualified person.

35 The Regulations, Treas. Reg. § 53.4958-4(a)(3)(i), pursuant to I.R.C. § 4958, exempt from the defini-

H. AFFILIATED ORGANIZATION WITH PRIVATE FOUNDATION STATUS FOR TAX PURPOSES

A §501(c)(3) organization that cannot meet the requirements of public charity status is a private foundation. A private foundation is subject to substantial restrictions and reporting requirements as well as to an excise tax on net investment income and penalty taxes for failure to comply with certain Code provisions. Private foundations receive most of their support from a small number of contributors and generally are controlled by their founders or substantial donors. Because these organizations may be more responsive to private individuals rather than to the general public, the IRS closely supervises their operations to make certain there are no abuses relating to their tax-exempt status and with respect to the tax benefits the donors received for donations to the organizations.

1. Classification as a Private Foundation.

As a § 501(c)(3) organization, a private foundation also applies for federal tax exempt status by filing Form 1023.[36] Classification as a private foundation continues until that status is terminated in accordance with I.R.C. § 507 discussed below.[37] The governing instrument of a private foundation must contain special

tion of an excess benefit transaction an "initial contract" that provides for a "fixed payment." An "initial contract" is defined as a binding written contract between a tax-exempt organization and a person who was not a disqualified person immediately prior to entering into the contract. A "fixed payment" is defined as "an amount of cash or other property specified in the contract or determined by a fixed formula specified in the contract, which is to be paid or transferred in exchange for the provision of specified services or property." The Regulations give as an example a tax-exempt organization entering into a contract to employ a chief financial officer at a salary of $200,000. Because the financial officer, as a new employee, would not be a disqualified person at the time of the contract, the contract would qualify as an "initial contract" subject to a fixed payment and § 4958 would not be applicable. However, if the financial officer is promoted subsequently to chief executive officer at a salary increase of $40,000, changes in the employment relationship would constitute material changes in the initial contract so that the board will have entered into a new contract with a then disqualified person and Section 4958 would be applicable. See Treas. Reg. § 53.4958-4(a)(3)(vii) Examples 1 and 4.

36 If a charitable organization does not attempt to qualify as a public charity because of its few donors, it would indicate on the Form 1023 that it is a private foundation. It should consider qualification as a private "operating" foundation described below. To do so, the charity would complete Schedule E of Form 1023.

37 Generally, notice of termination must be given the IRS. Failure to terminate a private foundation in the manner prescribed in I.R.C. § 507 will subject the foundation to substantial penalty taxes as noted below.

provisions that prohibit it from acting, or refraining from acting, in a manner that would make the foundation liable for penalty taxes unless state law has these provisions with respect to nonprofit entities organized in the state.

a. Charitable Contribution Deduction.

Gifts to private "nonoperating" foundations receive less favorable income tax treatment than do gifts to public charities and to private "operating" foundations. A donor may deduct gifts of appreciated long-term capital gain property to private nonoperating foundations only to the extent of the property's tax basis (which generally is the donor's cost less depreciation)[38] whereas gifts to public charities and to private operating foundations of appreciated property that would produce a long-term capital gain if sold are generally deductible in the amount of the property's fair market value. A private operating foundation is treated as a public charity for purposes of determining the charitable contributions deduction for donors.[39]

38 I. R. C. § 170(e)(1)(B). The Code states that the deduction is limited to the property's fair market value *less* the amount that would be a long-term capital gain if the property were sold at its fair market value. This means that a donor may deduct only the donor's tax basis in the property, generally cost lest depreciation.

There is an exception for some gifts of stock. A donor may deduct the fair market value of qualified appreciated stock, which is stock for which market quotations are readily available on an established securities market. A gift of the stock must be less than ten percent of the value of all outstanding stock in the corporation. The ten percent limitation applies to the aggregate amount of donations to all private nonoperating foundations by a donor, including spouse, siblings, ancestors, and lineal descendants. See I. R.C. § 170(e)(5).

Gifts to private nonoperating foundations are subject to a thirty percent of adjusted gross income annual limitation, twenty percent for gifts of capital gain property, whereas gifts to public charities and to private operating foundations were subject first to a fifty percent limitation with thirty percent for gifts of capital gain property. The fifty percent limitation was raised to sixty percent and then to 100 percent beginning in 2020. In addition, gifts to private nonoperating foundations are determined after all gifts to public charities have been computed. Gifts to private nonoperating foundations can be deducted only as to the excess of the current 100 percent limitation over total gifts to public charities.

39 A private nonoperating foundation that distributes a 100 percent of all contributions it received during the year by the fifteenth day of the third month after the close of the foundation's taxable year also is treated in the same manner as a public charity for purposes of determining the charitable contribution deduction for donors. See Treas. Reg. § 1.170A-9(g)(1). Private foundations maintaining a common fund wherein all contributions received are pooled also qualify donors for the same contribution deduction benefits available to public charities. See Treas. Reg. § 1.170A-9(h)(1).

b. Excise Tax.

A private foundation is subject to an excise tax of 1.39 percent of its net investment income.[40] Net investment income, which is subject to the excise tax, is the amount by which the sum of the organization's gross investment income exceeds ordinary and necessary expenses paid or incurred for production or collection of gross investment income or for the management, conservation, or maintenance of property held for production of investment income.[41] A private foundation may deduct only those expenses relating to its investment activities in computing its net investment income.[42]

Private foundations are subject to five two-tier excise taxes for engaging in certain prohibited acts or for failing to perform certain required acts. Some of the taxes are imposed on foundation managers and other disqualified persons, generally a charity's substantial contributors as discussed above, who engage in these acts rather than on the private foundation. The prohibited acts, or failures to act, are: (1) self-dealing, (2) failure to distribute income (to a public charity or to an "operating" foundation), (3) having excess business holdings, (4) making investments that jeopardize the charitable purpose of the foundation, and (5) making certain improper, taxable, expenditures.

There is an initial, first-tier, penalty tax for engaging in the above noted prohibited acts or failures to act, and an additional, second-tier, tax if the prohibited act or failure to act is not "corrected" within a designated time period.

40 I. R. C. § 4940. Prior to 2020, the tax was two percent but reduced to one percent for any year in which the private foundation's qualifying distributions equaled or exceeded the sum of the foundation's assets times the average percentage payout for a base period plus one percent of the foundation's net investment income for the year. See I. R. C. § 4940(e).

41 Treas. Reg. § 53.4940-1(e). Gross investment income is the gross amount of income from interest, dividends, rents, and royalties, excluding any amounts that were subject to the tax on unrelated business taxable income. Income of this category derived from assets devoted to charitable activities are included in gross investment income. See Treas. Reg. § 53.4940-1(d).

42 Treas. Reg. § 53.4940-1(e). A foundation could not include administrative expenses relating to grant making, for example. Expenses that are incurred for both investment and for exempt purposes are allocated between the two. Depreciation, which was computed using the straight-line method, is deductible in computing net investment income. Cost depletion is also deductible. Tax-exempt interest on governmental obligations and expenses incurred to produce this income are excluded from the computation. See Treas. Reg. § 53.4940-1(c)(2).

c. Self-Dealing.

Each act of self-dealing between a disqualified person and a private foundation is subject to an excise tax under I.R.C. § 4941. The tax is imposed upon the disqualified person who participated in the act, rather than on the private foundation, and applies regardless of whether the disqualified person was aware the act was one of self-dealing under I.R.C. § 4941. The penalty tax on self-dealing is ten percent of the "amount involved" for each year but is 200 percent of the amount involved if the act is not corrected.[43]

The term "self-dealing" refers to transactions, whether direct or indirect, between a private foundation and a disqualified person. It includes sales or exchanges of property, leases, and loans between a private foundation and a disqualified person; the provision of goods, services, or facilities by a private foundation to a disqualified person, unless the goods were made available to the general public on at least as favorable a basis as they were made available to the disqualified person; a disqualified person's use of a private foundation's income or assets; a private foundation's payment of compensation to a disqualified person, unless the payment is a reasonable amount for the performance of personal services that are reasonable and necessary to perform the foundation's exempt purposes; and payment of money or property to a government official.[44] Self-dealing can occur even though the disqualified person who participated in a prohibited act received nonpecuniary benefits.

43 The foundation manager has been subject to an initial tax of two and one-half percent of the amount involved, maximum of $10,000, if the foundation manager knew the act was self-dealing and the manager willfully participated. An additional tax of fifty percent of the amount involved, maximum of $10,000, has been imposed on the manager if the manager refused to agree to a part or all of the correction of the self-dealing act.

"Amount involved" is the greater of the amount of money and the fair market value of other property given or the amount of money and the fair market value of other property received. See Treas. Reg. § 53.4941(e)-1(b). In the case of payment of compensation, "amount involved" is the excess compensation (amount above a reasonable compensation) paid by the private foundation.

The correction period begins on the date of the self-dealing act and ends on the earliest of: (1) the date when the act is corrected, (2) the date the IRS mails a deficiency notice of tax on the self-dealing act, or (3) the date when the initial tax is assessed. See I.R.C. § 4941(e)(1). Should the self-dealing act not be corrected within this period, the additional penalty tax of 200 percent of the amount involved is imposed.

44 I. R.C. § 4941(d). For purposes of § 4941 only, a disqualified person includes government officials.

Example. In Estate of Reis v. Comm.,[45] Reis, who was the executor of the Mark Rothko estate and also a director of the Mark Rothko Foundation (a private foundation), was found liable for self-dealing penalty taxes under I.R.C. § 4941 in excess of $18 million dollars. Executors of the Mark Rothko estate entered into contracts on behalf of the estate with a gallery in which Reis was a director and an employee. The contracts provided that the paintings of Mark Rothko could be sold only by the gallery for a period of twelve years and at a commission to the gallery of fifty percent of proceeds from the sales. Surviving members of Mark Rothko's family filed a lawsuit in New York state courts to set aside the twelve-year exclusive sales contract and to remove Reis as executor of the estate. Most of the relief sought by the family was granted. The IRS audited the foundation and determined that Reis was involved in self-dealing. Reis contended that assets of the estate were separate and distinct from assets of the foundation and that assets of the foundation were not used for his benefit or transferred to him. The court agreed with the IRS that because the foundation was a beneficiary under Mark Rothko's will, the foundation had a vested beneficial interest in property of the estate. Thus, property of the estate was treated as an asset of the private foundation. The court did rule that a disqualified person who receives only tenuous benefits from his use of an asset of a private foundation will not be subject to self-dealing taxes. It granted Reis the opportunity to demonstrate in a trial on the merits that he had no substantial benefit from the transaction. In Stamos v. Comm.,[46] the court held Stamos, another of the executors of the Mark Rothko estate, liable for self-dealing excise taxes in excess of $19 million because of the exclusive contract the executors entered into on behalf of the estate. Stamos also served as a director of the Mark Rothko private foundation.

A disqualified person's use of a private foundation's income or assets ordinarily is self-dealing.[47]

---

45 87 T. C. 1016 (1986).

46 87 T. C. 1451 (1987).

47 The transfer of real or personal property by a disqualified person to a private foundation is treated as a sale or exchange if the property is subject to a mortgage or similar lien which the foundation assumes or if it is subject to a mortgage or similar lien which a disqualified person placed on the property within the ten-year period ending on the date of the transfer. A disqualified person can lend money to a private foundation only if the loan is without interest or other charge and only if the proceeds of the loan are used exclusively for the organization's exempt purposes.

d. Failure to Distribute Income.

A private nonoperating foundation must distribute its income to public charities or to private operating foundations. Section 4942 of the Internal Revenue Code subjects a private nonoperating foundation that does not distribute the net income it received during a year, by the end of the following year, to a penalty tax of thirty percent of any "undistributed income." There is an additional tax of a 100 percent of any undistributed income remaining at the end of a correction period.[48] As a result, as noted below, the annual IRS tax form for private foundations, the Form 990-PF, which must be filed with a state's attorney general's office, is a good source of funding for hospitals and affiliated charitable organizations.

"Undistributed income" subject to the penalty tax is a "distributable amount" reduced by "qualifying distributions," the net investment income excise tax, and any regular taxes paid by the foundation.[49] "Distributable amount" is an amount equal to the "minimum investment return" of the foundation, discussed below, reduced by the sum of any regular taxes imposed on the foundation and the net investment income excise tax. "Qualifying distributions" are expenditures for charitable purposes, for reasonable administrative expenses, and for amounts "set aside" for charitable projects.[50]

There are limited exceptions to the rule that transactions between a private foundation and a disqualified person are acts of self-dealing. A transaction between a private foundation and a corporation, which is a disqualified person, pursuant to a liquidation, merger, redemption or other corporate adjustment, is not an act of self-dealing if all securities received that are of the same class as those held by the foundation prior to the transaction are subject to the same terms, and the terms provide for receipt by the foundation of no less than fair market value. A person can lease property to a private foundation but only if the lease is without charge. Performing trust functions and general banking services by a bank or trust company that is a disqualified person is not an act of self-dealing if services are reasonable and necessary in performing the exempt purposes of the foundation and compensation paid the bank or trust company is not excessive.

48 The correction period is the earlier of the date of mailing of a notice of a tax deficiency regarding the initial tax or the date on which the initial tax was assessed.

49 Treas. Reg. §53.4942(a)-2. The amount is not reduced by the penalty taxes imposed pursuant to I.R.C. §§ 4942-4945.

50 Qualifying distributions include amounts paid for charitable purposes, contributions to public charities and to private "operating" foundations to be used by the recipient charity for charitable purposes, amounts paid to acquire assets to be used directly to carry out a charitable or other public purpose, and any qualifying amounts "set aside" for charitable purposes. Program-related investments and reasonable and necessary administrative expenses are qualifying distributions. Conversion of an asset previously not used for charitable purposes to a charitable use is a qualifying distribution. Amount of the qualifying distribution is the fair market value of the converted asset on the conversion date. See Treas. Reg. § 53.4942(a)-3(a)(5).

A private nonoperating foundation can "set aside" amounts for a specific charitable project and have the

A foundation's minimum investment return is five per cent of the fair market value of all the foundation assets not used for charitable purposes less any acquisition indebtedness on the property. Assets used by a foundation for its exempt purposes and any assets used in a functionally related business are not included in the computation."[51]

> Example. A trust classified as a private nonoperating foundation for tax purposes was established to provide operating funds for a hospital. The trust acquired by bequest a ranch worth $5,000,000. There were no liabilities on the ranch. The trust received $100,000 as net rental income from the ranch during the current year. Pursuant to I.R.C. § 4942, the trust is required to distribute to the hospital at least $250,000 (five percent of $5,000,000) by the end of the next year.[52] If the trust does not distribute this amount by the end of the next year, it will be subject to the excise tax, initially thirty percent, of the undistributed amount. If the undistributed amount is not distributed by the end of the correction period, the penalty tax will be a 100 percent of the undistributed amount. Considering that the amount of rental income the trust received from the ranch is less that the required amount the trust must distribute to the hospital each year, the trust may be forced to sell the ranch. Retention of the ranch could cause the ranch to pay tax penalties of as much as $150,000. [Five percent of $5,000,000 is $250,000. This amount must be distributed but because the

---

amounts treated as qualifying distributions if the charity engaged in the project will complete the proposed project in five years and the private foundation can better accomplish needs of the project by set-aside funds than by an immediate payment of funds. See I.R.C. § 4942(g)(2). Generally, the IRS must approve set-asides in advance.

51 Treas. Reg. § 53.4942(a)-2(c). Any pledge of money or property to the foundation also is not included. A functionally related business is a trade or business that is related to the foundation's exempt purposes.

Assets used for exempt purposes include administrative assets, such as office equipment and supplies; real estate, physical facilities on public display, such as paintings and works of art; interest in a functionally related business; reasonable cash balances; and program-related investments. A reasonable cash balance is determined on an annual basis of one and one-half percent of the combined fair market value of all foundation assets used in determining minimum investment return. Any amount of cash in excess of the one and one-half percent figure that is treated as exempt purpose property must be explained on the foundation's annual return (Form 990PF).

Property that is used both for exempt and nonexempt purposes is considered as being used entirely for exempt purposes if at least ninety-five percent of total use is for exempt purposes. If less than ninety-five percent is used for exempt purposes, a reasonable allocation must be made between exempt and nonexempt uses.

52 This is the trust's minimum investment return. Because the ranch was not used for charitable purposes, the minimum investment return is five percent of its net value.

trust had income of $100,000, the undistributed amount will be $150,000.] The $150,000 will be subject to a penalty initially of thirty percent of this amount. If not corrected, the penalty is 100 percent. Problems discussed in this example should cause an organization classified as a private nonoperating foundation for tax purposes to reconsider accepting a donation of property that is not bringing in annual net income at least five percent of the value of the property unless the foundation intends to sell the property immediately.

As noted previously, because a private nonoperating foundation must distribute its income to public charities or private nonoperating foundations to avoid the hundred percent penalty, a hospital or other charitable organization official should consider applying for grants from these foundations. A private foundation must file the Form 990PF discussed below annually to report its activities for the year. A private nonoperating foundation must provide information about its grant program on the Form 990PF. It must indicate how a charity applies for a grant– the form it must use, how a proposal must be submitted, any deadlines for proposals, the person to whom a grant proposal must be submitted and that person's address. A copy of the Form 990PF must be filed with the state's Office of the Attorney General at the same time it is filed with the IRS, by the fifteenth day of the fifth month following the close of the foundation's tax year; thus, these forms are easily accessible.

e. Excess Business Holdings.

The combined holdings of a private foundation and all its disqualified persons may not exceed twenty percent of the voting stock (or profits interest in a partnership or joint venture) of a business enterprise.[53] If control of a business enterprise is in persons other than disqualified persons, permitted holdings can be as much as thirty-five percent.

If a private foundation's business holdings exceed the permissible amount, the foundation will be subject to an initial penalty tax of ten percent of the value of the foundation's excess holdings. Should a foundation continue to have

53 I. R. C. § 4943. Section 4943 does not apply to a foundation's holdings in a functionally related business or to a trade or business in which at least 95 percent of the gross income is derived from passive sources. Gross income from passive sources includes dividends, interest, rents from real property (and from personal property leased with real property if rents from the personal property are an incidental amount), royalties and gains from sales of property and goods other than inventory items. See Treas. Reg. § 53.4943-10(b).

excess holdings after the end of a correction period,[54] the foundation is subject to a second-tier penalty tax of 200 percent of the excess holdings. The amount of excess holdings is determined as of the day during the year when the foundations' holdings in any business are the greatest.

f. Jeopardizing Investments.

A private foundation is subject to an excise tax on investments that could jeopardize performance of its exempt purposes. Section 4944 of the Internal Revenue Code imposes an initial tax of ten percent of an amount invested in a jeopardizing investment. If the foundation does not remove its investment from jeopardy,[55] an additional penalty tax of twenty-five percent of the amount of the investment is imposed.[56]

The jeopardizing effect of each investment is determined on an individual basis, considering the foundation's portfolio as a whole. No category of investment is treated as per se jeopardizing.[57] Although program-related investments are not jeopardizing investments, investments will not qualify as program-related if the primary purpose for making the investment is the production of

54 The correction period is the earlier of the IRS's mailing of a notice of deficiency for the initial tax or the date on which the IRS assesses the initial tax.

A private foundation that acquires excess business holdings other than by purchase can avoid the excise tax by disposing of the excess holding within ninety days from the date the foundation knows, or has reason to know, of the event that caused the foundation to have excess holdings. The ninety-day period is extended to include the period during which the foundation is prevented by federal or state securities laws from disposing of the holdings. If a private foundation acquires excess holding because of a gift or bequest, it has five years to dispose of the holdings before it has liability for the penalty tax. See Treas. Reg. §§ 53.4943-2; 53.4943-6.

55 A date after the earlier of the mailing of a tax deficiency notice for the ten percent penalty, or the date on which the IRS assesses the ten percent penalty.

56 I.R.C. § 4944(b)(1). A foundation manager also may be liable for a tax on jeopardy investments. A manager's participation must be willful and not due to reasonable cause. A manager's action is due to reasonable cause if the manager relied on advice of counsel expressed in a reasoned written legal opinion. In addition, the manager may rely on advice of a qualified investment counselor, given in writing in accordance with generally accepted practices, that a particular investment would provide for long- or short-term financial needs of the foundation.

57 Certain investments are scrutinized closely. Trading in securities on margin, trading in commodity futures, investments in working interests in oil and gas wells, purchase of "puts" and "calls," purchase of warrants, and selling short are considered speculative investments. See Treas. Reg. § 53.4944-1(a)(2). The determination of whether an investment is speculative is made at the time of the investment and not subsequently on the basis of hindsight.

income or for appreciation of the property rather to accomplish a foundation's exempt purposes.

g. Taxable Expenditures.

A private foundation is subject to a two-tier penalty tax on any "taxable expenditures." Section 4945 of the Internal Revenue Code imposes an initial penalty tax of twenty percent of the amount involved in a "taxable expenditure."[58] Taxable expenditures include amounts expended for the following purposes: (1) to carry on propaganda or to attempt to influence legislation;[59] (2) to influence the outcome of any specific public election or to carry on any voter registration drive; (3) to make a grant to an individual for travel, study, or other similar purposes unless certain requirements are satisfied;[60] (4) to make a grant to an organization other than a public charity unless expenditures responsibility is exercised; and (5) to carry out any purpose other than a charitable one, as defined in § 501(c)(3) of the Internal Revenue Code. If expenditures are not

58 A taxable expenditure includes any amount paid or incurred by a private foundation for a purpose other than a charitable one. Expenditures for unreasonable administrative expenses, including compensation, consultant fees, and other fees for services rendered, will be taxable expenditures unless the foundation can demonstrate the expenses were paid or incurred in the good faith belief they were reasonable and payment was consistent with ordinary business care and prudence.

59 Attempts to "influence legislation" relate to communications with a member or employee of a legislative body, or with an official of the executive department of a government, or efforts to affect the opinion of the general public with respect to legislation being considered by a legislative body. Amounts paid to provide technical advice or assistance to a governmental body, a governmental committee, or a subdivision of either, in response to a written request by that body of committee, is not a taxable expenditure. Further, engaging in nonpartisan analysis, study, or research and making result of the work available to the public is not an attempt to influence legislation. Amounts paid to appear before, or to communicate with, any legislative body with respect to a possible decision of that body which affects the existence of a private foundation, its powers and duties, its tax-exempt status, or deductibility of contributions to the foundation, is not a taxable expenditure.

60 A grant, scholarship, fellowship, internship, prize or award, to an individual for travel, study, or some other similar purpose will be a taxable expenditure unless the following requirements are met: (1) the foundation awards grants on an objective and nondiscriminatory basis and pursuant to a procedure the IRS approved in advance and (2) the foundation demonstrates to the IRS that the grant qualifies as a scholarship and will be used at an educational institution, or the purpose of the grant was to achieve a specific exempt charitable purpose.

The requirement of advance approval of a private foundation's scholarship procedures is strictly enforced. If approval is obtained later, it will not be made retroactive. Expenditures made prior to IRS approval will be taxable expenditures. An application for tax exempt status on Form 1023, which details the scholarship grant program of a private foundation, will serve as a request for approval of the program. If the IRS has not notified an organization that its grant procedures have been approved or disapproved within forty-five days after the organization has submitted properly a request for approval, the organization may consider its procedures approved until it receives actual notice from the IRS that its procedures are not acceptable.

corrected within the taxable period,[61] a second-tier tax of 100 percent of the amount of expenditures is imposed. A foundation corrects a taxable expenditure by recovering part or all of the expenditure to the extent possible.

A private foundation must exercise "expenditure responsibility" for grants to organizations unless a recipient organization is a public charity [or is a private operating foundation that is exempt from the excise tax on net investment income (discussion below)].[62] In exercising expenditure responsibility, a private foundation must exert all reasonable efforts, and establish adequate procedures, to make certain all grants are spent solely for purposes for which they were made.[63]

2. Private Operating Foundation.

A charitable organization affiliated with a hospital that provides some healthcare but that is a private foundation because it was organized and is funded by only a few donors should seek private operating foundation status. Donations to private operating foundations receive identical tax treatment as donations to public charities. Additionally, a private operating foundation may be the recipient of qualifying distributions from a private nonoperating foundation if the donor foundation does not control the operating foundation.

Private operating foundations are subject to the same restrictions and penalty taxes as are nonoperating foundation except for the tax on failure to distribute income. Except for "exempt operating foundations," a private operating foundation must pay the excise tax on net investment income.

---

61 The earlier of date of mailing of a notice of deficiency as to the initial ten percent penalty tax or date on which the ten percent tax is assessed.

62 The foundation exercises expenditure responsibility by obtaining a full and complete report from each grantee on how funds were spent. It must make a full, detailed report with respect to the expenditures to the IRS.

A grantee's failure to make grant reports will cause a grant to be a taxable expenditure unless the grantor (1) awarded the grant according to expenditure responsibility requirements, (2) complied with all reporting requirements, (3) made a reasonable effort to obtain required reports, and (4) withheld any future payments on any grant until the grantee organization provided the report. Required reports are submitted with the foundation's annual return, the Form 990PF.

63 Each grant to a nonpublic organization must be subject to a written commitment, signed by an appropriate officer, director or trustee of the grantee organization, that the grantee will repay any portion of the grant not used for grant purposes, will submit full and complete annual reports on the manner in which funds were spent, will make its books available to the grantor, and will not use funds for lobbying, to influence outcome of any public election or any voter education drive, and will not undertake any activity other than a charitable one. See Treas. Reg. § 53.4945-5(b).

An "exempt operating foundation" is not required to pay the excise tax on net investment income.[64] An exempt operating foundation is one that has been supported publicly for at least ten years, has a governing body that at all times during the year consisted of individuals at least seventy-five percent of whom were not disqualified individuals, and is broadly representative of the general public. None of the foundation officers can be a disqualified person.

To be classified as a private operating foundation, an entity must meet an income test and must satisfy either an assets test, an endowment test, or a support test.

a. Income Test.

The income test requires a foundation to make "qualifying distributions" *directly* for the active conduct of activities constituting its exempt purposes equal in value to substantially all of the lesser of its "adjusted net income" or its "minimum investment return."[65] "Adjusted net income" is the excess of a foundation's gross income for the year over its deductions. Gross income does not include gifts, grants, or contributions but does include income from a functionally related business.[66] "Minimum investment return" is five percent of the foundation's total assets not used for charitable purposes less the acquisition indebtedness on those assets. "Qualifying distributions" are those expenditures used by a foundation "directly" in furtherance of its exempt purposes.[67]

Amounts paid to acquire or maintain assets that are used directly in the conduct of a foundation's exempt activities, such as operating assets of an organization affiliated with a hospital, are considered to be direct expenditures for the

64 I.R.C. § 4940(d). An exempt operating foundation must obtain a ruling letter from the IRS recognizing its status and must attach a copy of the ruling letter to its annual return, the Form 990PF discussed below.

65 "Substantially all" is eighty-five percent or more. Because private operating foundations must make qualifying distributions for the active conduct of their exempt activities in this amount, they are not subject to the penalty tax for failure to distribute income.

66 Treas Reg. § 53.4942(a)-2(d). Net short-term capital gains are included, but long-terms gains are not. Gross income also includes certain items called income modifications. Income modifications include tax-exempt interest and amounts received that previously were treated as qualifying distributions, such as amounts previously set aside for a specific project but not necessary for the purposes for which they were set aside.

67 Treas. Reg. § 53.4942(b)-1. Grants made to other organizations to assist those organizations in conducting activities that help accomplish their exempt purposes are "indirect" expenditures and cannot be counted in determining whether the organization had sufficient qualifying distributions.

active conduct of the foundation's exempt activities. Administrative expenses and other operating costs necessary to conduct the foundation's exempt activities also are treated as qualifying distributions "directly" expended for the active conduct of the foundation's exempt activities so long as the amounts are reasonable.[68]

Because a private operating foundation need only make qualifying distributions equal in value to eighty-five percent of the lesser of its adjusted net income or its minimum investment return, a foundation that would have only a few assets used for nonexempt purposes can qualify easily as an operating foundation. A charitable foundation with only a few assets that it does not use for exempt purposes generally would have no difficulty in meeting the income test and either the assets or the endowment test.

b. Assets Test.

A private foundation will meet the assets test if sixty-five percent or more of its assets are devoted directly to the active conduct of activities constituting the foundation's exempt purposes, to functionally related businesses, or to any combination thereof. Assets must be actually used directly in the active conduct of exempt activities. Assets held for the production of income or for investment are not devoted directly to the active conduct of a foundation's exempt activities even though income from the assets is used to perform exempt activities.

c. Endowment Test.

A private foundation will meet the endowment test if it makes qualifying distributions directly for the active conduct of activities constituting its exempt purpose in an amount that is not less than two-thirds of its minimum investment return.

68 Payments to individuals in the form of grants, scholarships, or other such payments are qualifying distributions made directly for the active conduct of the organization's exempt activities only if the foundation maintains some significant involvement in active programs in support of which it made the grants or scholarships. Significant involvement requires more active participation than just selecting, screening, and investigating applicants for grants.

d. Support Test.

A foundation will meet the support test if eighty-five percent of its support other than gross investment income is received normally from the general public and from five or more exempt organizations. A foundation cannot receive more than twenty-five percent of its support from any one exempt organization and cannot receive more than half its support from gross investment income.[69]

> Example. A charitable organization affiliated with a hospital that provides some healthcare services for the hospital was established by one donor. It receives no support from the general public; thus, it cannot qualify as a public charity. It should attempt to be classified as an operating foundation because it is involved in health care in some respect. Assume its income for the year was $1,000,000. Its expenses relating to the production of its income were $250,000. Reasonable expenses of managing the organization were $300,000. It purchased needed equipment costing $400,000 during the year. The organization's building and its contents, along with other assets used in activities directly to perform the organization's exempt purposes, are valued at $10,000,000. The organization has other assets not related to its exempt purposes valued at $3,000,000. The organization would qualify as an operating foundation. Its adjusted net income is $750,000 ($1,000,000 - $250,000) and its minimum investment return is $150,000 ($3,000,000 x five percent). Qualifying distributions total $700,000 ($300,000 + $400,000). The qualifying distributions were more than, but definitely at least eighty-five percent, of the lesser of adjusted net income or minimum investment return; thus, the income test is satisfied. In addition, the assets test is satisfied in that almost seventy-seven percent of the organization's assets [$10,000,000 (assets used for exempt purposes) divided by $13,000,000 (total assets)] are devoted directly to the active conduct of the organization's exempt purposes.

69 Support from any one exempt organization is counted only if the foundation receives support from no fewer than five exempt organizations. Support from the general public can be counted only to the extent that total amount of support received from any one individual, trust, or corporation does not exceed one percent of the foundation's total support for the period.

3. Termination of Private Foundation Status.

Unless and until a private foundation affirmatively performs functions required to terminate voluntarily its private foundation status, it will remain subject to the penalty tax provisions discussed above--§§ 4940-4945 of the Internal Revenue Code. A private foundation can terminate its status either by transferring all its net assets to one or more public charities organized under I.R.C. § 509(a)(1) or by itself converting to public charity status. The IRS of its own volition can terminate the existence of a private foundation if the foundation has engaged in willful and repeated acts (or failures to act) that are subject to the penalty taxes.[70]

a. Termination Tax.

A private foundation is subjected to a substantial penalty tax if it is terminated involuntarily. The termination tax is the lesser of (1) the total amount of all tax benefits (income, estate, and gift) derived by all substantial contributors since the foundation's inception plus the increase in taxes imposed on the foundation had it been a taxable organization, or (2) the value of the net assets of the foundation. The termination tax, then, generally will cause a foundation to transfer all its assets to the federal government. There is no termination penalty tax imposed on a voluntary termination if the termination follows procedures set out in I.R.C. § 507.

b. Voluntary Termination.

Section 507 of the Internal Revenue Code provides that a private foundation may terminate voluntarily its status as a private foundation in one of the two following methods: (1) transfer all its net assets to one or more public charities that have qualified under I.R.C. § 509(a)(1) for at least sixty months immediately preceding the transfer or (2) qualify itself as a public charity under either I.R.C. § 509(a)(1), (2), or (3) for a continuous sixty-month period after it has given the IRS notice of intent to terminate.

If a private foundation chooses to terminate voluntarily by transferring its assets to a public charity, it must make certain the public charity is one described

70 I.R.C. § 507(a)(2). One willful and flagrant act or failure to act that is voluntary, conscious, and knowingly committed and that is deemed to be a gross violation of the penalty tax provisions will permit the IRS to terminate a foundation.

in I.R.C. § 509(a)(1) and that it has qualified under Section 509(a)(1) for at least sixty months immediately preceding the distribution. Section 509(a)(2) and (3) public charities may not be transferee organizations for this purpose.

A private foundation may terminate its status by itself meeting the requirements of either I.R.C. § 509(a)(1), (2), or (3) for a continuous sixty-month period. The foundation must notify the Internal Revenue Service before commencement of the period that it is terminating its private foundation status.[71] It can seek qualification under I.R.C. § 509(a)(3) as a supporting organization of a § 509(a)(1) or (2) public charity. As noted previously, a charitable private hospital is a § 509(a)(1) public charity; thus, an affiliated organization can terminate its private foundation status by qualifying under I.R.C. § 509(a)(3) as a public charity supporting a named hospital.

I. ANNUAL REPORTING REQUIREMENTS

A charitable organization qualifying as a public charity must file an annual information return on the IRS Form 990 specifying receipts and expenditures and indicating current financial status as well as providing the IRS with considerable additional information about the organization.[72] A hospital must attach to its Form 990, Schedules A and H. For Schedule A, it simply checks a block on the Schedule A[73] that it is a hospital. It must attach a completed Schedule H to demonstrate that it meets the requirements of I.R.C. § 501(r) regarding its CHNA

71 I.R.C. § 507(b)(1)(B). A private foundation giving notice to the IRS is treated as if it were a new organization with its first tax year beginning on the date of commencement of the sixty-month period. The notice must state the Section 509 Code section under which the organization seeks classification.

72 The Form 990 with copies of its sixteen schedules are available on the IRS website. An organization that fails to file a return or that fails to include the required information on the return is subject to a penalty computed on a daily basis. See I.R.C. § 6652.

The annual return forms for public charities must be made available for public inspection for a period of three years after the date the returns are filed. See I.R.C. § 6104. There is a substantial penalty for willful failure to permit public inspection of the returns. See I.R.C. § 6685. A public charity must make its annual returns available for public inspection during its regular business hours at its principal office or, if the organization regularly maintains one or more regional or district offices having three or more employees, at each of its regional or district offices. An individual may make a request to inspect the organization's annual return in person or in writing. The organization must provide the individual a copy without charge other than a reasonable fee for any reproduction and mailing costs.

73 Part I of Schedule A on line 3. A hospital is not required to include any other parts of the Schedule A. A medical research organization operated in conjunction with a hospital checks a block on line 4 of Part I of the Schedule A.

and FAP discussed in Chapter VII. Hospital affiliated organizations check their Section 509(a)(1), (2), or (3) public charity status on the Schedule A and complete additional required information to demonstrate support over a five year period or its support of § 509(a)(1) or (2) organizations if it is a § 509(a)(3) public charity.

If the charity has elected to be subject to lobbying expenditure limitations,[74] it must provide information on a separate schedule, currently the Schedule C, which the IRS reviews to determine whether the organization exceeded the limitations. Even though a public charity does not elect to be subject to the limitations, it still must list lobbying expenditures it paid or incurred during the year on the separate Schedule C.

All nonprofit organizations must complete and file a Schedule J with the Form 990 if they provide the following benefits to employees or directors: first-class travel, housing allowance or residence for personal use, payments for business use of personal residence, health or social club dues, other personal services, such as maid or chauffeur services, or salaries in excess of $100,000, to include compensation of more than $10,000 for former directors and more than $150,000 from the organization and related organizations.

With respect to highly paid employees and except for compensation paid to a licensed medical professional that is for the professional's performance of medical or veterinary services, tax-exempt organizations, which pay either compensation of $1 million or more to any of their five highest-paid employees or that pay parachute payments to any of its five highest paid employees which are contingent on these person's separation from the organization, are now subject to a twenty-one percent tax on "excess" compensation.[75] The excise tax is reported on IRS Form 4720. For this purpose, while compensation paid for the "direct" performance of medical services is excluded from the excise tax, compensation for administration, research, and teaching is not exempt.[76] These services are subject to the tax. A health organization must determine the amount paid for direct medical services versus compensation for other duties

74 Discussion of lobbying activities in Chapter VII.

75 The excise tax is imposed pursuant to I.R.C. § 4960, which was added to the Internal Revenue Code in 2017 by the Tax Cuts and Jobs Act of 2017, Pub. No. 115-97, 131 Stat. 2054.

76 Although compensation for "direct" medical services is excluded from the tax, the medical services exclusion is complicated.

from various documents, including billing records and timesheets; thus, computation of the medical services exclusion can become complicated.[77]

Remuneration for medical services is disregarded for purposes of determining whether an individual is a covered employee and for purposes of determining whether a payment is a parachute payment.[78] The excise tax on a parachute payment can apply to a parachute payment that is less than $1 million. It applies to a payment made to one of the organization's five highest compensated employees that is contingent on that person's separation from the organization and that equals or exceeds three times a base amount. The base amount is the average of employee's annual salary for the most recent five years. For example, if a highly paid employee of a hospital's affiliated organization, who had an average salary of $200,000 for the past five years, is paid $900,000 contingent upon that person's separation from the organization, the employer organization must pay an excise tax of $63,000, computed as follows: $900,000 - $600,000 (three times the base amount) = $300,000 × twenty-one percent = $63,000. Assume a hospital affiliated organization has paid an assistant, who is one of the organization's five highest paid employees, an average salary of $900,000 for the past five years. Upon her separation from the organization, she is paid a separation payment in the amount of $5,000,000. The organization will be subject to an excise tax of $483,000 [$5,000,000 - $2,700,000 ($900,000 × three) = $2,300,000 × twenty-one percent = $483,000]. The determination of who is a covered employee for purposes of assessing the penalty excise tax is made based on an employee's compensation from the tax-exempt employer but also compensation for services performed for a related organization, using a more than fifty percent control test.[79] The IRS provides the following examples.

77 Compensation does not include amounts paid to a designated Roth contribution as defined in I.R.C. § 402A(c).

78 Additionally, compensation paid to a member of a nonprofit organization's board of directors for serving in that capacity is not remuneration because fees received by the director for performing services constitute self-employment income, rather than wages. See I.R.C. § 3401(a).

79 The IRS has provided ten keys on how to apply Section 4960 in Notice 2019-9 and in proposed Treasury regulations, Sections 53.4960-0 to 53.4970-5. They provide that an employee is not one of a covered nonprofit organization's five highest-compensated employees if, during the calendar year ending with or within the taxable year, the organization paid less than ten percent of the employee's total remuneration for services performed as an employee of the organization and all its related organizations.

Example 1. X and Y, two nonprofit organizations affiliated with a hospital both employed A during the current calendar year—X paid fifty percent and Y paid fifty percent. A is a covered employee of both X and Y for the current calendar year and all future taxable years.

Example 2. X in Example 1 paid ninety-five percent and Y paid five percent of A's remuneration for services performed for the two organizations. A is a covered employee of X for the current calendar year and all future taxable years but is not a covered employee of Y for the current calendar year.

Example 3. A is employed sixty percent by X organization with compensation of $1,200,000 and forty percent by Y organization with compensation of $800,000. X and Y are related hospital affiliated nonprofit organizations; thus, A is considered to have been paid $2 million for purposes of I.R.C. § 4960 ($1,200,000 plus $800,000). The total excise tax is $210,000 (twenty-one percent of the $1,000,000 excess remuneration]. Because X paid sixty percent of the compensation, it is liable for $126,000 of the excise tax. Y paid forty percent of A's compensation and is liable for $84,000 of the excise tax.

As noted previously, a private foundation files Form 990PF annually with the IRS to set out its activities during the preceding year and to demonstrate it continues to qualify for § 501(c)(3) status. Both private nonoperating foundations and private operating foundations file the Form 990PF. A private foundation must file a copy of the Form 990PF with the Attorney General of the state in which it has residence at the same time it files the form with the IRS.[80]

---

80 A private foundation also must make the form available for a three-year period to anyone requesting a copy. See I.R.C. § 6104(d). Returns for the three most recent tax years and the foundation's Form 1023 must be made available to the public during regular business hours at the foundation's principal offices. Failure to comply with a public inspection or copying request will subject the foundation to penalty provisions of I.R.C § 6652(c)(1)(C), (D) of $20 per day, maximum of $10,000. See Reg § 301.6104-3(e).

A foundation may have an employee present during an inspection of the return, but it must permit the individual conducting the inspection to take notes freely. See Reg § 301.6104-3(e). If the individual provides photocopying equipment at the place of inspection, the foundation must permit the individual to photocopy any return at no charge. The foundation may charge a reasonable fee for providing copies.

If the district director determines that a foundation is the subject of a harassment campaign and that, as a result, requests would not be in the public interest, the foundation need not fulfill a request for copies. See Reg. § 301.6104-5.

Those charitable organizations having unrelated business taxable income[81] in excess of $1,000 must also file a Form 990-T by the 15th day of the fifth month following the close of their taxable year and pay tax on the net income from unrelated activities or sources. As discussed in Chapter IX, tax liability on unrelated business income is computed in the same manner as for the corresponding taxable entity; a tax-exempt corporation would be subject to corporate rates, whereas a tax-exempt trust would be taxed in the same manner as a taxable trust.[82]

81 Discussion in Chapter IX.

82 I.R.C. § 511(a), (b); Reg. § 1.511-3(a).

CHAPTER IX.
UNRELATED BUSINESS TAXABLE INCOME

Nonprofit organizations have had to seek additional sources of revenues in recent years because of the dwindling of governmental grants and charitable contributions.[1] There is the additional problem that restrictions attached to many donations prevent the nonprofit organization from using a substantial amount of its donations for operational purposes. Because of the need to obtain a more dependable long-term method of obtaining revenue, many exempt organizations have become involved in income producing activities. Some exempt organizations are conducting these businesses through partnerships and through related subsidiaries. Because of the increased use of income producing activities by exempt organizations, the Internal Revenue Service has become more active in auditing these activities.

A hospital and its affiliated or supported tax-exempt organizations will be taxed on activities that are unrelated to the organizations' exempt purposes.[2] Additionally, while any unrelated business activities will cause these otherwise tax-exempt organization to incur income tax liability, these activities can also cause a loss of their tax-exempt status should the organization become too heavily involved in unrelated activities.[3] In such instances, an inquiry may be made of the purpose for which the increased business activity is directed. Still, success in certain business activities does not, in and of itself, jeopardize the tax-exempt status of an organization if that organization remains true to its stated exempt purpose goals.[4] Limited commercial activity is permitted, but if that activity produces what is termed "unrelated business taxable income," the charitable organization is taxed on that income in the same context as a for-profit organization.[5]

1 The continuing increase in the amount of the standard deduction, and thus the lesser importance of a charitable contribution deduction that is available only if a taxpayer itemizes deductions, has provided less incentive for charitable giving.

2 The taxation of unrelated business taxable income is set out in I.R.C. §§ 511-514.

3 Presbyterian & Reformed Pub. Co. v. Comm., 743 F.2d 148 (3rd Cir. 1984).

In Orange County Agr. Soc., Inc. v. Comm., 893 F.2d 529 (2nd Cir. 1990), the Court of Appeals for the Second Circuit stated that a nonprofit organization which has substantial nonexempt activities cannot avoid revocation of its tax-exempt status simply by paying unrelated business income tax on the unrelated activities.

4 In Presbyterian & Reformed Pub. Co. v. Comm., 743 F.2d 148 (3rd Cir. 1984), the Court of Appeals for the Third Circuit commented that an organization may be forced to choose between expanding its commercial activities and influence on the one hand and maintaining its tax-exempt status on the other.

5 The organization must file IRS Form 990-T to report and pay tax on that income. See discussion of

The theory for subjecting otherwise tax exempt organizations on these activities is that an unrelated business activity distorts the exempt purposes of the organization and is a form of unfair competition to taxable organizations.[6] The fact that profits from an unrelated business are used by the exempt organization to perform its charitable functions has no bearing upon whether the business is taxed.[7]

Taxable income is determined by computing the organization's net income from any unrelated trade or business, its income from some net rentals from personal property a part of its net investment income from controlled organizations, and a percentage of its net income from debt-financed properties.[8]

B. INCOME FROM AN UNRELATED TRADE OR BUSINESS

A hospital and its related tax-exempt organizations will be taxed on any income the organization derives from an "unrelated trade or business." "Unrelated business taxable income" is defined as gross income derived from any unrelated trade or business, regularly carried on, less deductions directly connected with carrying on the trade or business. An "unrelated trade or business" is one in which conduct of business transactions is not related substantially to the exercise or performance of an organization's charitable purposes.[9]

---

reporting requirements below.

6 See H.R. 2319, 81st Cong., 2d. Sess. 36 (1950), cited in 1950 C.B. 483. The source, and not the destination, of funds is considered in determining whether activities are unrelated to an organization's exempt purposes and, thus, subject to tax.

7 Discussion in University Hill Foundation v. C. I. R., 446 F.2d 701 (9th Cir. 1971). Still, although it is the source of funds that determines taxability, the ultimate use or destination of the funds, as well as the extent of involvement in an unrelated commercial activity, has relevance in judging whether involvement in the unrelated business jeopardizes the organization's tax-exempt status.

In Church by Mail, Inc. v. Comm., 765 F.2d 1387 (9th Cir. 1985), the Court of Appeals for the Ninth Circuit commented that the objective or purpose to which the income of a charity is devoted is the ultimate test in determining whether the organization is operated exclusively for an exempt purpose.

Courts have held that even though substantial profits were made from certain activities, an organization could nonetheless remain tax exempt if all the profits realized were used exclusively for its exempt purposes.

8 See I.R.C. §§ 512, 514 and discussion below.

9 I.R.C. § 513(a). The term "trade or business" includes an activity performed for production of income from the sale of goods or the performance of services.

1. Not Substantially Related to a Hospital's Charitable Purpose

Determining whether activities of a hospital are "substantially" related to a hospital's charitable purposes necessitates an examination of the relationship between any of the hospital's income-generating activities and the accomplishment of the hospital's exempt purposes. A trade or business is related to a nonprofit organization's exempt purposes only where conduct of the business has a causal relationship to the achievement of the organization's exempt purposes. The causal relationship must be substantial.[10]

Some activities of nonprofit hospitals are specifically stated to generate unrelated business taxable income. Sales not directly related to the exempt functions of the hospital, such as sales by a hospital pharmacy to the public, the sale of laboratory services, and other supplies that are bought as an incident of patients' visits to private physicians, but not because of the patients' use of hospital facilities, produce taxable income to a nonprofit hospital.[11] Income from the furnishing of services, listed in I.R.C. § 501(e)(1)(A) and discussed below, such as data processing, purchasing, warehousing, billing and collection, food, clinical, industrial engineering, laboratory, printing, communications, and personnel, by a nonprofit hospital to other hospitals is tax exempt only if the recipient

10 Treas. Reg. § 1.513-1(d). Production or distribution of goods or performance of services must contribute importantly to the accomplishment of a hospital's charitable purposes. In determining whether an organization's activities contribute importantly to the accomplishment of its exempt purposes, size and extent of activities must be considered in relationship to the nature and extent of the exempt function they purport to serve. These rules apply equally to a hospital's affiliated organizations' unrelated activities.

11 Even though the majority of a hospital's sales are to patients, those sales to nonpatients will nonetheless be taxed. The fragmentation rule permits an activity to be broken into its component parts. Activities of producing or distributing goods or performing services from which an amount of gross income is derived do not lose identity as trades or businesses merely because they are carried on within a larger aggregate of similar activities or within a larger complex of other endeavors which may be related to the exempt purposes of the organization. See Reg. § 1.513-1(b). Thus, as an example, the regular sale of pharmaceutical supplies to the public by a hospital pharmacy does not lose identity as a trade or business merely because the pharmacy also furnishes supplies to the hospital and patients of the hospital in accordance with its exempt purposes. See Treas. Reg. § 1.513-1(b).

Income from sales to patients is related income. The IRS has defined a patient as: (1) a person admitted to the hospital as an inpatient; (2) a person receiving general or emergency, diagnostic, therapeutic or preventive health services from outpatient facilities of a hospital; (3) a person directly referred to the hospital's outpatient facilities by a private physician; (4) a person refilling a prescription written during the course of his treatment as a patient in the hospital; (5) a person receiving medical services as part of a hospital administered home health-care program; and (6) a person receiving medical care and services in a hospital affiliated extended-care facility. See Rev. Rul. 68-376, 1968-2 C.B. 246.

hospitals also are tax exempt and have facilities that do not serve more than 100 inpatients.[12]

Medical research will be taxed if it is carried on for the primary purpose of commercial or industrial application. However, research performed for the United States, its agencies, or instrumentalities or for a state or its political subdivisions is specifically excluded from the definition of unrelated business taxable income.[13] In addition, research performed by a medical school or hospital is excluded.[14]

Although income from a service performed by a hospital for a nonpatient of the hospital is generally treated as unrelated business taxable income, a service performed for a nonpatient can, under certain circumstances, contribute to the advancement of the exempt purpose of the hospital and thus, not be taxed.[15] This service generally will be deemed to relate to the exempt purposes of the hospital if:

1. the activity contributes to the training and education of medical students, interns, nurses, or physicians in the hospital;

---

12 I.R.C. § 513(e). Laundry services are not included in the list of exempt services; therefore, income from the provision of this service would be taxed. To be tax exempt, the services must be provided at a fee or charge that does not exceed the actual cost to the hospital providing the service. The cost can include straight-line depreciation and a reasonable amount for return on capital goods used to provide these services. For these purposes, a rate of return on capital goods will be considered "reasonable" if it does not exceed, on an annual basis, one and one-half times the average of the rates of interest on public debt obligations issued to the Federal Hospital Insurance Trust Fund. See Treas. Reg. § 1.513-6.

13 I.R.C. § 512(b)(7). The research in this case is not taxed even if it is "unrelated."

14 I.R.C. § 512(b)(8). A hospital can exclude all income from research whether the research is fundamental or applied. However, research does not include ordinary testing or inspection. See Reg. § 1.512(b)-1(f)(4).

15 In Priv. Ltr. Rul. 9617045, the IRS ruled a health organization would not have unrelated business income from the operation of a placement service. The placement service, a computerized database of information regarding the state's health care practice needs and related topics, matched providers to health care needs in the state. It could be accessed without charge by medical students, residents, interns, and practicing physicians who wished to establish a medical practice in the state. It had no advertisements or logos of health care providers. Subscribers to the database were § 501(c)(3) organizations. Candidates who obtained a position with a subscriber paid no compensation to the database. The IRS decided that operation of the database served the exempt purpose of improving access to medical care. It decided that the absence of fees distinguished the database from a commercial employment agency.

2. the hospital possesses technologically advanced facilities that enable it to perform tests that could not be performed at other medical laboratories in the area, or, in an emergency, the tests or services could be performed by the hospital faster than at other medical laboratories in the area; or

3. the activity or service is provided in an isolated area not adequately served by other exempt or commercial laboratories.[16]

Hospitals engage in activities involving both the sale of goods and providing of services to other health care organizations and private physicians that can cause a hospital to have income from an unrelated trade or business. The legislative history of I.R.C. § 513 reveals the concern shared by both the House and the Senate that certain business income from collateral functions was being shielded from taxation by its relation to other exempt activities. One activity specifically mentioned was the sales by a hospital pharmacy to the general public.[17] The courts have treated income from hospital sales as taxable income unless the sales are for the convenience of hospital patients, are in furtherance of the exempt functions of the hospital, or are incidental to the use of

---

16 Priv. Ltr. Rul. 8131063.

In Priv. Ltr. Rul. 200309031, the IRS ruled a hospital would not have unrelated business taxable income from revenue it received from its operation of a provider-based clinic that would offer a broad range of physician services. The services would be provided by physicians currently employed by a taxable subsidiary. The hospital would pay the subsidiary an arm's length fee for their services. The IRS concluded that revenue the hospital received for services the physicians provided would be income from an activity substantially related to the hospital's exempt purpose of promoting health care.

17 See S. Rep. No. 552, 91st Cong., 1st Sess., 1969 U.S.C.C.A.N. 2027, 2104.

In Hi-Plains Hospital v. U.S., 670 F.2d 528 (5th Cir. 1982), the Court of Appeals for the Fifth Circuit early ruled that pharmacy sales by a hospital to private patients of the doctors in the area were substantially related to the provisions of hospital services and, therefore, not taxable income. The court did state sales to the public, as distinguished from sales to private patients of the doctors, would be taxed unless the sales involved only a small amount of money and were made only occasionally.

In Priv. Ltr. Rul. 200203070, the Service ruled a tax-exempt hospital would not be taxed on sales from a pharmacy the hospital operated both for its inpatients and for other patients who were not inpatients. The hospital was located in a rural area where there was a shortage of physicians. The pharmacy was formed to help residents who had difficulty obtaining prescriptions. The hospital also performed services for a laboratory, seventy percent of which was owned by the hospital's subsidiary. The laboratory provided services to the hospital, its patients, and residents. The Service ruled that only the percentage of income for performing the services that equaled the percentage of income generated by performing tests for hospitals, which were not small rural hospitals, or for residents of counties, that were not served by small rural hospitals, would be taxed. The hospital also extended income guarantees and other incentives to recruit physicians. The Service ruled this extension of income guarantees would not jeopardize the hospital's tax-exempt status.

hospital facilities.[18] The providing of services by one hospital to another health care organization will be taxed unless the conditions of I.R.C. § 513(e), discussed below, are met.

The Internal Revenue Service has ruled that the sale of hearing aids to hospital patients by an exempt hospital whose primary activity is rehabilitating the handicapped, including those with hearing deficiencies, would not constitute an unrelated trade or business.[19] It also much earlier ruled that the sale of pharmaceutical supplies to private patients of physicians who have offices in a hospital-owned medical building would not constitute an unrelated business.[20] Prescription sales to hospital patients would not be an unrelated business; however, prescription sales to private patients or to the public would be taxed unless they are only occasional sales.[21]

Income from sales not directly related to the exempt functions of a hospital nor provided for the convenience of patients or hospital employees will be taxed

---

18 Discussion in Carle Foundation v. U.S., 611 F.2d 1192 (7th Cir. 1979).

In Priv. Ltr. Rul. 8707041, the IRS ruled the operation of activities that consist of the designing, manufacturing, furnishing and fitting of orthopedic and prosthetic devices by an exempt organization, which operated health programs and facilities, would not constitute an unrelated trade or business.

In Priv. Ltr. Rul. 9517029, the IRS ruled a tax-exempt medical school would not have unrelated business income from its distributive share of profits from a limited liability company (LLC) formed to own and operate two hospitals used to train its students and residents. The IRS cited St. Luke's Hospital of Kansas City v. U.S., 494 F. Supp. 85 (W.D. Mo. 1980).

In Priv. Ltr. Ruls. 9739036, 9730937, 9739038, and 9739039, the IRS ruled that tax-exempt hospitals would not lose their tax-exempt status by contributing property and cash to, and becoming a member of, LLCs. The parents of two for-profit subsidiaries were also members of the LLCs. The LLCs were established to operate diagnostic laboratory facilities that would service the hospitals' patients and the public. Income from laboratory services would be allocated to the hospitals. The IRS also ruled profits from the LLCs would not be taxed except for those derived from the provision of services to persons who were not patients of the hospitals.

In Priv. Ltr. Rul. 9739001, the IRS ruled a hospital would not have unrelated business taxable income from its share of ordinary income from a partnership that provided purchasing services for its limited partners. The hospital was a limited partner and received about two percent of the partnership income from purchasing services. The IRS stated that to the extent purchasing activities of the partnership were directed to organizations other than the hospital corporations that were limited partners, the income would be unrelated and would be taxed.

19 Rev. Rul. 78-435, 1978-2 C.B. 181.

20 Rev. Rul. 68-375, 1968-2 C.B. 245.

21 Discussion in Carle Foundation v. U.S., 611 F.2d 1192 (7th Cir. 1979), and Hi-Plains Hospital v. U.S., 670 F.2d 528 (5th Cir. 1982). In Hi-Plains Hospital, the Court of Appeals for the Fifth Circuit ruled that pharmacy sales to private patients of doctors are substantially related to the provision of hospital service and, thus, are not taxable where the hospital is in a rural community and the availability of the hospital's pharmacy for use by the doctors' private patients is causally related to inducing doctors to practice there.

to the hospital.[22] For example, a hospital with laundry facilities that sells laundry services to other hospitals is carrying on an unrelated trade or business.[23] Additionally, the Service has ruled a hospital that performs Pap smear tests for nonpatients is engaged in an unrelated trade or business. The Service ruled such an activity would not be an integral part of a hospital's operations even if it were performed for efficient medical service if it is for the convenience of private practitioners who are neither students, officers, nor employees of the hospital.[24]

Income from the sale of laboratory services, pharmaceuticals, and other supplies that are bought as an incident of patients' visits to private physicians, but not because of their use of hospital facilities, would be taxed.[25] Sales of this type are made to produce income and are not for the convenience of patients or hospital employees. However, the IRS has ruled that a hospital's operation of a laboratory for patients of local physicians was not an unrelated trade or

---

22 Rev. Rul. 69-633, 1969-2 C.B. 121. Sales made for the convenience of patients or hospital employees are discussed below.

In Priv. Ltr. Rul. 9204033, the IRS ruled a tax-exempt organization that operated a regional hospital system to promote the general health of the public in its service area would not have unrelated business taxable income from providing needed management skills to a small for-profit hospital in the organization's service area. The for-profit hospital, whose shareholders were local doctors and pharmacists, needed a more sophisticated and expert manager to maintain beneficial health care in the community. The IRS decided the organization's provision of services would benefit public rather than private interests. It determined that the agreement enabled the organization to further its purpose of providing quality health care to the community.

23 This type of service is not covered by the exemption under I.R.C. § 513(e), discussed below.

In HCSC-Laundry v. U. S., 450 U.S. 1 (1981), the Supreme Court denied tax-exempt status to a nonprofit corporation that provided laundry and linen services to fifteen nonprofit hospitals. The court stated that because laundry service was omitted from the types of hospital service organizations could practice, the organization was not entitled to tax-exempt status.

In IRS Priv. Ltr. Rul. 9841049, the IRS ruled an acute care hospital would not have unrelated business taxable income from providing mobile services to other hospitals. The hospital provided diagnostic and therapeutic health care services on an inpatient and outpatient basis and had designed vans to transport medical equipment, supplies, and employees to contracting hospitals.

24 See Priv. Ltr. Rul. 8131063.

25 Rev. Rul. 68-375, 1968-2 C.B. 245.

In Priv. Ltr. Rul. 9739043, the IRS ruled income from laboratory testing would be income from a related trade or business and would not be taxed. The tax-exempt organization was formed to improve the diagnosis and treatment of periodontal disease and was affiliated with a dental school. The organization taught students the proper interpretation of laboratory results in the management of dental patients.

In Priv. Ltr. Rul. 9851052, the IRS ruled a sale of medical literature and equipment would not be unrelated business income. The charity planned to sell medical literature and evaluation equipment developed by a past president to determine the degree of developmental disorders in children. The organization would pay royalties to charities designated by the past president but would not pay the past president. The IRS decided the sale was related to the charity's educational purpose and that any benefit to the past president was incidental.

business where the hospital's exempt purpose was to provide health care to the community and the nearest commercial laboratory was several miles away.[26] A teaching hospital was not taxed on income produced from permitting staff members to use the pathology department for tests on private patients. Because tests produced the volume needed to operate a teaching program, the Service ruled the services were related to the hospital's exempt purposes.[27]

2. Business Regularly Carried On

A trade or business from which income is derived is taxed only if it is "regularly carried on."[28] In determining whether a business is regularly carried on, the

26 See Priv. Ltr. Rul. 8121098.

In Priv. Ltr. Ruls. 8124006 and 8124076, the IRS ruled lab services provided to private patients of local physicians would be tax exempt as the providing of health care for a community if the hospital did not compete with commercial labs either because they were not equipped to provide the services or they were not available in the area.

In Priv. Ltr. Rul. 9851054, the IRS ruled a hospital service organization would not have unrelated business income from a joint laboratory created to provide lab services for five nonprofit hospitals.

27 See St. Luke's Hospital of Kansas City v. U.S., 494 F. Supp. 85 (W.D. Mo. 1980).

The IRS has agreed with the court in St. Luke's Hospital of Kansas City v. U.S., 494 F. Supp. 85 (W.D. Mo. 1980), that a teaching hospital, which conducted nonpatient laboratory testing on specimens needed for the conduct of its teaching activities, was not engaged in an unrelated trade or business where the outside testing services contributed importantly and substantially to the hospital's teaching program. However, the IRS has announced it will not follow that part of the decision in St. Luke's Hospital case that held the hospital's testing upon specimens obtained from private office patients of the hospital's staff physicians who were not patients of the hospital was not an unrelated trade or business. It is the position of the IRS that a hospital's staff physicians are neither "members" nor "employees" of the hospital in their capacities as private practitioners. Consequently, the providing of laboratory testing services on specimens referred by staff physicians in their private capacities would not be the carrying of an activity primarily for the convenience of its members, officers, or employees within the meaning of I.R.C. § 513(a)(2). See Rev. Rul. 85-109, 1985-2 C.B. 165 and discussion below of activities carried on primarily for the convenience of a hospital's members, officers, or employees.

In Rev. Rul. 85-110, 1985-2 C.B. 166, the IRS noted that while the general rule is that the providing of diagnostic laboratory testing services to nonpatients constitutes an unrelated trade or business for a tax-exempt hospital, there are unique circumstances wherein the services may further the exempt function of the hospital. The IRS listed, as an example, the emergency laboratory diagnosis of blood samples from nonpatient drug overdose or poisoning victims to identify specific toxic agents. The IRS stated that if referral of these specimens to other locations would be detrimental to the health of hospital nonpatients, a hospital could provide the emergency services in furtherance of its exempt function of promoting community health. In addition, if other laboratories are not available within a reasonable distance from the area served by the hospital or are clearly inadequate to conduct tests needed by hospital nonpatients, a hospital's testing services may further its exempt function of promoting community health. Whether the unique circumstances exist will be decided by the IRS on a case-by-case basis. A tax-exempt hospital performing diagnostic laboratory services on specimens of nonpatients of the hospital is required to keep records by patient and nonpatient classification to establish the portion of income subject to the unrelated trade or business income tax under I.R.C. § 511.

28 I.R.C. § 512(a)(1).

frequency and continuity with which activities for the production of income are conducted and the manner in which they are pursued are considered. Activities will be conducted regularly if they manifest a sequence and continuity and are pursued in a manner similar to comparable commercial activities of taxable organizations. Activities normally conducted on a year-round basis will not be regularly carried on if an exempt organization engages in these activities for only a few weeks. But where activities are undertaken generally by a commercial business only on a seasonable basis, conduct of such activities by an exempt organization during a significant portion of the season would constitute regular conduct of the trade or business.[29]

Example. A hospital's operation of a sandwich stand for three weeks at a state fair would not be the regular conduct of a trade or business. However, operation of a year-round business activity for one day each week, such as its operation of a commercial parking lot on Saturday of each week, would constitute the regular carrying on of a trade or business.

3. Exploitation of Hospital's Exempt Function

A tax-exempt organization may use an asset or facility necessary for the conduct of its exempt functions in a commercial context. Income from the added use of the assets or facility would be income from an unrelated trade or business.[30]

Example. A hospital has a theater auditorium specially designed and equipped for showing of educational films in connection with its healthcare programs. The theater is used in the evenings as an ordinary motion picture theater for public entertainment. Income from operation of the theater in the evenings would be income from an unrelated trade or business.

---

29 Treas. Reg. § 1.513-1(c). Business activities that are intermittent are compared with the manner in which commercial activities of the same type are generally pursued by taxable organizations to determine whether they are "regularly carried on" by an exempt organization. Income producing or fund-raising activities conducted for only a short period of time ordinarily will not be treated as regularly carried on if the activities occur only sporadically. Further, the fact that activities are conducted on an annual recurring basis will not cause them to be regularly conducted.

30 Treas. Reg. § 1.513-1(d). The fact that the asset or facility is needed to perform the organization's exempt functions is not material.

When a tax-exempt organization uses its facilities for both tax-exempt purposes and for production of unrelated business taxable income, its expenses are allocated between the two activities on some reasonable basis.

An exempt organization may generate goodwill or a reputation that would be capable of being exploited in commercial endeavors. Unless commercial activities generated by exploiting the organization's exempt purposes contribute importantly to the accomplishment of an exempt purpose, any income from such activities is income from an unrelated trade or business.

> Example. A hospital exploits its reputation by selling endorsements of various drugs. The endorsements do not contribute importantly to the hospital's accomplishment of its exempt purpose; thus, income from such endorsements would be income from an unrelated business.

4. Specific Exclusions from Unrelated Trade or Business

The IRS has determined that certain otherwise commercial activities of a hospital will not be taxed if all sales are through volunteers, or the sales are performed for the convenience of patients and hospital employees.[31] Certain activities are specifically excluded from the definition of an unrelated trade or business so that income from these ventures is not subject to tax. Excluded activities are:

(1) Any trade or business in which substantially all work in carrying on the business is performed for the organization without compensation, i. e., by volunteers.

(2) Any trade or business carried on by a charitable organization primarily for convenience of its members, patients, guests, officers, or employees.

(3) Any trade or business that consists of selling donated merchandise.[32]

a. Gift Shops

Operation of a gift shop can cause unrelated business taxable income. Sales of items in a gift shop must have a causal relationship to an organization's exempt

31 See Rev. Rul. 69-267, 1969-1 C.B. 160.

32 These activities are specifically excluded from unrelated business designation under I.R.C. § 513(a).

purposes to be considered a related activity. Determination is made on an item-by-item basis. Sales of items that relate to the organization's exempt purposes would not be taxed. Sales of other items, that do not contribute importantly to the organization's exempt purposes, would be taxed. Still, as noted below, if a gift shop is managed and operated by volunteers, none of the sales will be taxed. A hospital's operation of a gift shop, patronized by patients and visitors making purchases for patients and employees, is a specific exclusion from an unrelated trade or business.[33]

b. Snack Bar and Cafeteria

A hospital's operation of a cafeteria and coffee shop primarily for employees, medical staff, and visitors would not be an unrelated trade or business.[34] The IRS has ruled that operation of a snack bar, cafeteria, or coffee shop will not be an unrelated business activity if the operation is for the convenience of a charitable organization's members, employees, staff, and visitors.[35]

c. Parking Lot.

A hospital's operation of a parking lot for the convenience of patients and employees would also not constitute an unrelated trade or business.[36] However,

33 Rev. Rul. 69-267, 1969-1 C.B. 160. In GCM 39762, Chief Counsel for the IRS concluded that an organization operating a gift shop on the premises of a for-profit hospital could qualify for tax-exempt status under I.R.C. § 501(c)(3). Because the operation of the gift shop and gift cart improved the comfort and well-being of the hospital patients, the organization could qualify for tax-exempt status even though it also provided a benefit to the for-profit hospital. The Chief Counsel concluded that the benefit to the hospital was incidental.

In AHS Hospital Corp. v. Town of Morristown, 28 N.J. Tax 456 (2015), the court ruled a gift shop was not reasonably necessary for any hospital purpose, but rather it served as form of competition to commercially owned facilities; thus, it was not exempt from the state's property tax. (See discussion of exemption from property taxes in Chapter VII.) The court determined the gift shop was merely a convenience for hospital visitors who could otherwise purchase similar gift items at a variety of stores outside the hospital. The court also decided a day care area used by hospital employees but not by patients was not exempt from tax. It found the hospital cafeteria also failed to satisfy the profit test and, thus, was not exempt from tax.

34 Rev. Rul. 69-268, 1969-1 C.B. 160.

Still, in Priv. Ltr. Rul. 9720002, with respect to a restaurant in a museum, the IRS ruled the museum would be taxed on its proceeds from restaurant sales to customers who did not pay a museum admission fee. The museum had advertised the restaurant monthly in a local magazine and had provided public access to the restaurant.

35 See Rev. Rul. 69-268, 1969-1 C. B. 160; Rev. Rul. 74-399, 1974-2 C. B. 172.

36 Rev. Rul. 69-269, 1969-1 C.B. 161.

if a parking lot is operated for the general public, income from its operation would be taxed.[37]

d. Fund Raising Activities.

Fund raising activities generally are excepted from unrelated business status because these activities normally are not regularly carried on, are usually conducted by volunteers, and often involve the sale of donated merchandise.

5. Income from Advertising.

Generally, proceeds from an exempt organization's sale of advertising in a periodical or other publication will constitute income from an unrelated trade or business activity involving exploitation of the organization's exempt activities. The amount of unrelated business taxable income is the sum of the net advertising income less any circulation loss.[38]

> Example. A hospital conducts an intensive advertising solicitation campaign for several months. The advertising would be "regularly carried on" and the proceeds would be taxed.

The fact that the organization is selective as to the advertising it carries does not cause the advertising to be substantially related to the organization's exempt purposes.[39] However, while the publication of ordinary commercial advertising

---

37 Priv. Ltr. Rul. 8735004.

38 Circulation income or loss is attributable to the production, distribution or circulation of a publication including amounts realized from the sale or distribution of the readership content of a periodical. See Treas. Reg. § 1.512(a)-1(f). Circulation income is not taxed, but a circulation loss can offset advertising income.

39 See Rev. Rul. 82-139, 1982-2 C.B. 108.

In U.S. v. American College of Physicians, 475 U.S. 834 (1986), the Supreme Court reversed a decision of the Federal Circuit Court of Appeals, American College of Physicians v. U.S., 743 F.2d 1570 (Fed. Cir. 1984), wherein the Court of Appeals for the Federal Circuit had ruled advertising in a professional journal published by a tax-exempt organization that was related to the exempt purpose or function of the organization, would not be taxed. The publication of the tax-exempt organization contained commercial advertising related to medical products; the organization demonstrated advertising relating to drugs served an essential function to disseminate information on recent developments with respect to drugs to member physicians. The organization accepted advertisements only of products and services related to the practice of internal medicine and regulated the accuracy of the information provided in the advertisements. The Federal Circuit had ruled the advertisements served to fulfill an important educational function and, even though the

for products and services used by members of an exempt organization is considered an unrelated business, the sale of listings in a magazine, which merely identify the purchaser and contain no advertising message, or which just inform the general public about significant events and which are not designed to stimulate demand for a product or a service of the advertiser, would not be taxable.[40]

The amount of unrelated business taxable income attributable to the sale of advertising in exempt organization periodicals is the sum of net gross advertising income less any circulation loss.[41] Readership costs reduce the circulation income; if there is net gain from circulation, the gain is not taxed. A loss, however, will offset gross advertising income. Gross advertising income is all amounts derived from the unrelated advertising activities of an exempt organization periodical; circulation income is income attributable to the production, distribution or circulation of a periodical including amounts realized from the sale or distribution of the readership content of the periodical.[42]

Where the right to receive an exempt organization periodical is associated with membership or similar status in the organization for which dues, fees or other charges are received, circulation income includes that portion of membership receipts allocable to the periodical.[43] Allocable membership receipts are the amount that would have been charged if the periodical was that of a taxable organization and was published for profit.[44]

Deductions attributable to exempt organization periodicals include the total periodical costs or the total deductions attributable to the periodical.[45] Total periodical costs are the sum of the direct advertising costs of the periodical and the readership costs of the periodical. An allocation can be made of costs attributable both to an exempt organization periodical and to other activities

---

educational function may have been secondary to a purpose of raising revenue, the sales were substantially related to the exempt purpose of educating internists. However, the Supreme Court decided the principal motive in accepting the advertising was to obtain revenue and ruled the revenue would be taxed. The Supreme Court did reject the position of the IRS that published advertising is per se taxable. The Court decided if American College of Physicians controlled its advertisements and accepted only advertisements relating to new developments in pharmaceuticals or coordinated advertisements with editorial comment, the revenue could possibly be tax-exempt.

40 See Rev. Rul. 82-139, 1982-2 C.B. 108; Rev. Rul. 76-93, 1976-1 C.B. 170.

41 Treas. Reg. §1.512(a)-1(f)(3).

42 Treas. Reg. § 1.512(a)-1(f)(3).

43 Treas. Reg. § 1.512(a)-1(f)(3)(iii).

44 Id.

45 Treas. Reg. § 1.512(a)-1(f)(6).

of the organization.[46] Direct advertising costs of an exempt organization periodical include all expenses, depreciation and other exempt items directly connected with the sale and publication of advertising.[47] Readership costs are those expenses directly connected with the production and distribution of the readership content of the periodical.[48]

6. Income from Sponsorships.

Income from sponsorships is taxed as income from advertising unless amounts received from the sponsorships constitute "qualified" sponsorship payments.[49] A "qualified sponsorship payment" is a payment received by a tax-exempt organization from a person engaged in a trade or business when there is no substantial return benefit to the payor other than the use or "acknowledgment" of the name or logo of the payor's business. To qualify as a "qualified sponsorship payment," there can be no arrangement or expectation that the payor will receive any substantial return benefit other than the use or "acknowledgment" of the name or logo (or product lines) of the payor's trade or business in connection with the activities of the payee charity. This use or acknowledgment does not include advertising the payor's products or services (including messages containing qualitative or comparative language, price information, or other indications of savings or value; an endorsement; or an inducement to purchase, sell, or use such products or services). Additionally, a "qualified" payment cannot be contingent upon the level of attendance at certain events, broadcast ratings, or other factors indicating the degree of public exposure to one or more events. The payment cannot include entitlement of the payor to the use or acknowledgment of the payor's name or logo in regularly scheduled and printed material published by or on behalf of the payee charity that is not related to and primarily distributed in connection with a specific event conducted by the payee charity.

> Example. A hospital organizes an exhibition and receives a large payment from a corporation to help fund the exhibition. The hospital recognizes the corporation's support by using the corporate name and established logo in materials

---

46 Id.

47 Treas. Reg. § 1.512(a)-1(f)(6)(ii).

48 Treas. Reg. § 1.512(a)-1(f)(6)(iii).

49 I.R.C. § 513(i).

publicizing the exhibition, including banners, posters, brochures, and public service announcements. The hospital also hosts a dinner for the corporation's executives. The Treasury stated, in an example with similar facts, that use of the corporate name and logo in connection with the exhibition constituted acknowledgment of the sponsorship and, thus, was not a substantial return benefit.[50] However, the Treasury also stated that the dinner for corporate executives was a substantial return benefit because the value of the dinner exceeded two percent of the total payment; only that portion, if any, of the payment that exceeded the fair market value of the dinner could be a qualified sponsorship payment.

7. Trade Shows

Conventions or trade show and public entertainment activities are not treated as unrelated trades or businesses for § 501(c)(3) organizations.[51]

8. Furnishing of Services

Under I.R.C. § 513(e), income from the furnishing of services, such as data processing, purchasing, warehousing, billing and collection, clinical, industrial engineering, laboratory, printing, and personnel, by one hospital to other hospitals will be tax exempt if the recipient hospitals are tax-exempt hospitals or government hospitals and have facilities that do not serve more than a 100 inpatients.[52] The services performed must be related to the exempt purposes or function of the recipient hospital, and the services must be provided at cost.[53] Cost is defined as actual cost plus straight line depreciation and a reasonable return for capital goods used to provide the services.[54]

---

50 Treas. Reg. § 1.513-4(f).

51 I.R.C. § 513(d)(3).

52 I.R.C. § 513(e).

53 Id.

54 See I.R.C. § 513(e). A rate of return on capital goods will be considered reasonable if it does not exceed, on an annual basis, a percentage equal to one and one-half times the average of the rates of interest of special issues of public debt obligations issued to the Federal Hospital Insurance Trust Fund for each of the months during which capital goods are used in providing the service.

See Treas. Reg. § 1.513-6(a)(3). For a determination of the cost of services and the applicable rate of return, see 42 U.S.C. § 1395x(v)(1)(A), (B) and the regulations thereunder.

Example. A large hospital provides various services to other tax-exempt hospitals. It furnishes a billing and collection service to hospitals A and B, a data processing service to hospitals C and D, and a purchasing service to hospitals E and F. All the hospitals have facilities to serve no more than 100 inpatients except hospital B. The services are furnished at cost to all hospitals except that hospital D is charged a fee of more than the cost for the data processing service. The billing and collection service will be taxed as income from an unrelated trade or business because they were not provided solely to tax-exempt hospitals having facilities to serve not more than 100 inpatients. The data processing services will also be taxed as income from an unrelated trade or business because the services were provided at a fee of more than cost. The purchasing service will not be an unrelated trade or business because it satisfies all three requirements of I.R.C. § 513(e).

Hospital service organizations, exempt from taxation under I.R.C. § 501(e), are often formed to provide services excluded from the unrelated business income tax under Section 513(e) on a cooperative basis to other nonprofit hospitals. Hospital associations exempt as business leagues under I.R.C. § 501(c)(6) provide services to members of the association, such as assisting in obtaining capital financing, providing counselling on business office problems, bidding for hospital supplies, and assisting in other aspects of hospital administration. If these activities are provided for a fee rather than based on a membership dues charge, the activities of these associations will be an unrelated trade or business.[55] Further, should these activities become substantial, tax-exempt status of the hospital association can be jeopardized.

---

55 See Priv. Ltr. Rul. 8022016.

In Priv. Ltr. Rul. 200307094, the Service ruled a health care organization would not jeopardize its tax-exempt status by operating a Web-based health care provider information and job opportunity database. The Web-based service matched physicians, nurses, and other medical personnel with employment opportunities. Potential job candidates could get free access to the service and were not charged a fee when they secured a job through the service. The Web-based service also would be used to help tax-exempt hospitals in rural areas recruit physicians. The Service ruled that any income the health care organization received from operating the service would not be unrelated business income.

In Priv. Ltr. Rul. 9841049, the IRS ruled an acute care hospital would not have unrelated business taxable income from providing mobile services to other hospitals. The hospital provided diagnostic and therapeutic services on an inpatient and outpatient basis. It had designed specially vans to transport medical equipment, supplies and employees to contracting hospitals.

Generally, income from investments is passive income and thus not unrelated business taxable income. Dividends, interest, annuities, royalties, as well as gains from the sale, exchange, or other disposition of investment property, normally are not taxed.

1. Rental Income

Except for rents from debt-financed property or from property rented to controlled organizations (see discussion below), rents from real property are not taxed.[56] Rents from personal property generally are taxed. Additionally, rents from real property will not be excluded from unrelated business income if more than fifty percent of total rents received are attributable to personal property, determined at the time the personal property is first placed in service.

If an exempt organization renders special services to lessees, payments for occupancy do not constitute rent from real property and will be taxed. Services are rendered to a lessee if they are primarily for the lessee's convenience and are other than those normally rendered in connection with the rental of property for occupancy only.[57]

Rents from personal property are taxed unless the personal property is leased with real property and the rents attributable to the personal property are an incidental amount of the total rents received.[58]

> Example. A hospital leases a large room in its building for catered parties, meetings, wedding receptions and other such events. The hospital provides bartending and other personal services at these events. Although the rent is from real property, the income generated from leasing the room would be taxed because special services are rendered.

56 Treas. Reg. § 1.512(b)-1(c)(2). If the amount of rent from real property depends in whole or in part on income or profits derived from leased property, other than an amount based on a fixed percentage of gross receipts or sales, rents will not be excluded from unrelated business income.

57 The supplying of maid service would be this type of special service, but the furnishing of utilities or the cleaning of public entrances, stairways, and lobbies would not be.

58 Treas. Reg. § 1.512(b)-1(c)(2)(ii)(b). Rents attributable to personal property are an incidental amount if rents are ten percent or less of total rents from leased property. The percentage is determined at the time the lessee first places personal property in service.

2. Royalty Income

Royalty income is excluded from the unrelated business tax. Courts have ruled that income from renting a member list is royalty income and, thus, is not taxed.[59]

> Example. A hospital has a joint venture for an affinity card arrangement with a credit card company wherein the hospital will receive income from the credit card company from credit cards depicting the hospital's name and logo. Courts have ruled that affinity card income is royalty income and, thus, is not taxed.[60]

D. INCOME FROM A CONTROLLED ORGANIZATION

Although investment income generally is not taxed, a portion of interest, annuities, royalties, or rents derived from an organization controlled by a tax-exempt organization will be included in unrelated business taxable income.[61] Dividends received from a controlled organization are not taxed, however.

"Control" of an organization is stock ownership of more than fifty percent, in vote or value, and ownership of more than fifty percent of the profits or capital interests of a partnership or more than fifty percent ownership of any beneficial interest in any other entities. In a nonstock organization, control means that

59 Sierra Club, Inc. v. Comm., 86 F.3d 1526 (9th Cir. 1996). The Court of Appeals for the Ninth Circuit decided that income from rental of member lists was "passive" and did not constitute compensation for services rendered.

In Common Cause v. Comm., 112 T.C. 332 (1999) and Planned Parenthood Federation of America v. Comm., T.C. Memo 1999-206, the court decided that an organization's master and rental lists were intangibles in which the organization had ownership rights. If an organization does not engage directly in any significant activities with regard to rental list transactions, the court stated the income from the sale of its mailing list is royalty income.

60 Oregon State Univ. Alumni Ass'n v. Comm., 193 F.3d 1098 (9th Cir. 1999); Sierra Club, Inc. v. Comm., T.C. Memo 1999-86.

61 If amounts are included as unrelated business taxable income under other Code provisions, they are not treated also as unrelated business income from a controlled organization. Treas. Reg. § 1.512(b)-1(l)(5). However, for rent derived from a controlling organization's lease of debt-financed property to a controlled organization, the amount of rent included in unrelated business taxable income of the controlling organization first is determined under rules relating to income from a controlled organization. Only that portion of rents not taxed as income from a controlled organization will be subject to rules relating to income from debt-financed property.

more than fifty percent of the directors or trustees are either representatives of, or are directly or indirectly controlled by, the tax-exempt organization.[62]

The amount of income that is unrelated business taxable income to the controlling organization depends on whether the controlled organization also is tax-exempt or is a for-profit organization. If the controlled organization is tax-exempt, the amount of business taxable income is the amount a payment to a controlling organization reduces the unrelated business taxable income of the controlled organization. If the controlled organization is a for-profit entity, the amount of taxable income is the portion of the controlled organization's taxable income that would reduce its unrelated business taxable income if it were tax-exempt.

E. INCOME FROM UNRELATED DEBT-FINANCED PROPERTY

To prevent a for-profit organization from using the exempt status of a nonprofit organization to shield income from taxation, (by buying a business through debt financing, leasing it and paying off the debt with nontaxable rent income), income from a tax-exempt organization's debt-financed property is taxed in proportion to the amount of acquisition debt on the property.[63] Debt-financed

62 Treas. Reg. § 1.512(b)-1(l)(4). A trustee or director is controlled if the tax-exempt organization has power to remove the trustee or director and can designate a new trustee or director.

63 In Mayo Clinic v. United States, 124 A.F.T.R. 2d 2019-5448, 2019-2 U.S.T.C. P 50,246 (D. Minn. 2019), a nonprofit corporation and tax-exempt organization that was the parent organization of several hospitals, clinics, and a college of medicine and science comprised of five distinct medical schools, brought a tax refund suit to obtain $11,501,621 in tax refunds, alleging that it was qualified as an educational organization and thus was entitled to a tax exemption for certain passive income. Although passive income is excluded from unrelated business income for a tax-exempt organization, if the passive income comes from debt-financed real property, the amount excluded from taxable income is reduced. Still, there also is an exception to this exception. If the recipient organization is a "qualified organization" under I.R.C. § 514(c)(9)(C), all the passive income can be excluded even if it came from debt-financed real property. An educational organization described in I.R.C. § 170(b)(1)(A)(ii) is a "qualified organization." The government asserted that the clinic's primary function was health care, not education, even though the government agreed that Mayo had a faculty, curriculum, students, and a place where educational activities were regularly carried on. The government contended the clinic was not an educational organization because a Treasury regulation, Secion 1.170A-9(c)(1), provides that an organization cannot qualify as an "educational organization" under I.R.C. § 170(b)(1)(A)(ii) unless education is the organization›s "primary function" and any noneducational activities are "merely incidental" to its educational activities. These requirements do not appear explicitly in the statute. The court ruled that the Treasury Department exceeded the bounds of its statutory authority when it promulgated the primary-function requirement and merely incidental test in the Treasury regulations. The court decided that nothing precluded the organization from qualifying both as an educational organization and an academic health center. The court ruled the

property is property that is not used to perform a tax-exempt organization's exempt purposes and that is subject to acquisition indebtedness.[64] The portion of income from such property that is subject to tax is called unrelated debt-financed income. Gain on the sale of debt-financed property is taxed. The amount of the taxable income is determined by multiplying net income from the property by a percentage, computed by dividing "average acquisition indebtedness" on the property by "average adjusted basis" of the property. The percentage is called the debt/basis percentage.

Acquisition indebtedness is the unpaid amount of any indebtedness incurred by an exempt organization in acquiring or improving debt-financed property.[65] Average acquisition indebtedness is the average amount of acquisition indebtedness on unrelated property for a specific year, except that for purposes of computing gain or loss on the sale of the property, it is the highest amount of acquisition indebtedness during the twelve-month period ending on the date of the sale or other disposition.

Average acquisition indebtedness is computed by determining the amount of the outstanding principal indebtedness on the first day in each calendar month during a year in which the organization has such property, adding these

---

medical clinic qualified as an educational organization and was entitled to a tax refund for taxes paid on that passive income.

64 Treas. Reg. §1.514(b)-1(b)(1). To the extent property is used to carry out a tax-exempt organization's exempt purposes, the property is not treated as debt-financed property. Property is used for an exempt purpose if eighty-five percent or more of its use is devoted to an organization's exempt purposes. Property used for research activities and property used in a related trade or business would not be debt-financed property.

In IRS Priv. Ltr. Rul. 9814040, an exempt cooperative service organization, which was formed to purchase accounts receivable from member hospitals, received $500 million from the sale of industrial development bonds. The IRS ruled a tax-exempt hospital would not have debt-financed income from the sale of its accounts receivable to the exempt cooperative hospital service organization. It concluded that the hospital's sale of its receivables would not cause adverse tax consequences to the hospital. The IRS ruled the cooperative's debt could not be attributed to the hospital. The IRS also ruled the hospital would not have unrelated business income from the investment of proceeds from the sale of its receivables.

65 Any indebtedness incurred before acquisition or improvement of the property will be acquisition indebtedness if the indebtedness would not have been incurred but for acquisition or improvement of the property. See I.R.C. § 514(c. Should an exempt organization acquire debt-financed property for an indeterminate price, initial acquisition indebtedness is the fair market value of the property on the date of acquisition less any down payment. See Treas. Reg. § 1.514(a)-1(a)(4).

If property acquired is subject to a mortgage, the outstanding principal indebtedness secured by the mortgage is treated as acquisition indebtedness even though the organization does not assume or agree to pay the indebtedness. For property acquired by gift or bequest, any outstanding mortgage will not be treated as acquisition indebtedness for the ten-year period following the date of acquisition. See Treas. Reg. §1.514(c)-1(b). For property acquired by gift, this is the case if the mortgage was placed on the property more than five years before date of the gift and the donor held the property for more than five years prior to the gift.

amounts together, and dividing the sum by the total number of months the organization held the property during the year.

Example 1. A hospital purchased a building on July 1 that was not used to perform its exempt purposes.The building cost $510,000. A portion of the purchase price, $300,000, was paid with borrowed funds. The hospital makes payments of $21,000 per month--$20,000 attributable to principal and $1,000 to interest--on its purchase money loan. The average acquisition indebtedness for the year is $250,000, computed as follows:

Month	Indebtedness on first day of each calendar month the property is held
July	$300,000
August	280,000
September	260,000
October	240,000
November	220,000
December	200,000
	$1,500,000

Average acquisition indebtedness: $1,500,000 divided by six months = $250,000

Average adjusted basis of debt-financed property is the average amount of the adjusted basis (generally cost less depreciation) of the property during the portion of the year the property is held by the tax-exempt organization.[66] It is the average of the adjusted basis of the property as of the first day during the taxable year the organization holds the property and the adjusted basis on the last day during a year that the organization holds the property.

Example 2. The hospital in example 1 claimed depreciation on the building of $20,000 for the year. The average adjusted basis of the building is $500,000, computed as follows: Beginning basis, cost, of $510,000 plus ending basis of

66 Treas. Reg. § 1.514(a)-1(a)(2). The organization must adjust the property for depreciation for the entire time the organization has held the property regardless of whether it was exempt from taxation during any of that time period.

$490,000, which would be basis of cost, $510,000, less depreciation of $20,000, divided by two.

Example 3. Average acquisition indebtedness on the building the hospital purchased, as noted in the example 1, was $250,000. Average adjusted basis, as computed in the example 2 was $500,000. The debt/basis percentage would be fifty percent--average acquisition indebtedness/average adjusted basis = $250,000/$500,000. If the hospital receives net rental income of $30,000 from the building, $15,000 will be debt-financed income. Additionally, fifty percent of expenses directly connected with the building would be deductible in computing net debt-financed income.

F. REPORTING REQUIREMENTS

Those organizations having unrelated business taxable income in excess of $1,000 must file IRS Form 990-T by the 15th day of the fifth month following the close of their taxable year and pay tax on the net income from unrelated activities or sources.[67] Tax liability on unrelated business income is computed in the same manner as for the corresponding taxable entity; a tax-exempt corporation would be subject to corporate rates, whereas a tax exempt trust would be taxed in the same manner as a taxable trust.[68] Tax-exempt organizations must make quarterly payments of estimated tax for the unrelated business income tax.[69] The estimated quarterly payments are made under the same rules applicable to corporations. Thus, the taxes must be paid by making a deposit of the taxes through the Federal Tax Deposit (FTD) system by the due dates for paying estimated taxes.

67 Treas. Reg. § 301.6033-2(i).

68 I.R.C. § 511(a), (b); Treas. Reg. § 1.511-3(a).

69 See I.R.C. § 6655(g)(3).

www.ingramcontent.com/pod-product-compliance
Lightning Source LLC
LaVergne TN
LVHW052243200926
848481LV00002B/259